ABSTRACTS OF EARLY DEEDS
of
NASH COUNTY NORTH CAROLINA

BOOKS 1-6

BY

Joseph W. Watson

Southern Historical Press, Inc.
Greenville, South Carolina

This volume was reproduced
from a personal copy located in
the Publishers private library

Please direct all correspondence and book orders to:
SOUTHERN HISTORICAL PRESS, Inc.
PO Box 1267
Greenville, SC   29602-1267

Originally printed: Fort Worth, TX 1966
Copyright by: Arrow Printing
ISBN #978-1-63914-127-2
Printed in the United States of America

AUTHOR'S FOREWORD

This work was undertaken primarily as the result of a visit to the State Archives in Raleigh. A well-known genealogist asked why the Nash County deeds were so mixed up and why were so many missing. After abstracting the first twenty deed books, 1777-1854, I shall try to explain what has happened.

The original deed books were numbered Book A, B, C, etc. through probably Book N. Book A is still in existence and references were made to these other books. The present books are numbered Book 1, 2, 3, etc. Book 0 was the entry book for lands surveyed and taken up in Nash County. It was begun on April 20. 1778 by Edward Moore, entry taker for the county, and the last entry was made in 1799. Book A began with April Ct. 1778. Micajah Thomas was C. C. and Wm. S. Mearns was P. Regr. It concluded with April Ct. 1780, with Wm. Hall as C. C. This book includes many land grants which were omitted when the book was recopied, mostly as part of Book 1. Book A was examined throughout and approved by commissioners appointed by the Court of Nash County, May Term, 1809.

Deed Book 1 was recopied from several books and is not in chronological order. It contains a loose grantor-grantee index, in those days called an "Alphabet." On page 10 there is a footnote "Error in transcribing - the above transcribed in the Book M, page 129 from Book A. page 13." On page 13, July Ct. 1778, through the end of the book, all entries were footnoted with "This is a true copy from record" by Ld. F. Ellen, P.R., with W. S. Mearns, F.R. This probably meant the "present register" and the "former register." Pages 1-108 were copied from Book A, pages 1-192. Pages 109-320 were copied from Book B, pages 1-320. Pages 321-380 were copied from Book E, pages 1-61. Pages 381-408 were copied from Book F, pages 1-45.

Deed Book 2 has the letter J in the preface and a loose index with the words "Alphabet to Book J." It contains only land grants, both from Earl Granville and from the State of N. C., until 1804. In the back of the book is the statement "These indices have been revised twice and found to be correct," by B. H. Sorsby, J. P., Register, Feby. 1868. This is the original book.

There is a notice in the front of Book 3 "This book is divided into two parts - each commencing page 1, hence, in looking for a deed, if the index points to a page and you don't find it in the first part, it can be found by looking to that page in the last part, Book 3, 1782-1787." There is a loose index in the front of the book on the back of which reads "This Alphabet for the book B & A grants, February, 1808. The other part of the index is for the other part of the book indexed separately with Deeds of Sales for the book AB." Book 3, page 1, was taken from Book A, page 18, a Granville grant. Page 2 was a State of N. C. grant from Book B, page 342, registered in 1781 by W. S. Mearns, P.R., and copied later by Ld. F. Ellen, P.R. Book 3 continues with Book B, pages 342-433. On page 93 it skips back from B-433 to B-232 and proceeds to B-341. Book 3, pages 162-279, were copied from Book A, pages 125-268. Book 3, page 280, was the beginning of Book C, page 1. Book C was made up of deeds beginning Feb. Term 1785, and only had 78 pages. Book D then began in Book 3, page 364. Book D was composed of deeds and contained 96 pages. This completed Deed Book 3, which was examined and approved by S. Westray, Arch. Griffin, and Jas. Williams. These same three men were commissioners

iii

appointed by the Nash County Court, May Term 1809, who also examined Book A, as stated in the back of Book A. The entire book was "a true copy by L. F. Ellen, P. R."

Deed Book 4 has a loose index in the front of the book, autographed by Benja. H. Sorsby, March 31, 1868. The book appears to be the original.

Deed Book 5 has an index in the front of the book inscribed No. M. It begins with a State of N. C. grant on page O, and Bills of Sale beginning in 1805 fill pages 1-41. Book F, pages 47-142, were copied in Book 5, pages 42-100, "copied from record by L. F. Ellen, P. R." Book G, pages 1-36, were copied in Book 5, pages 100-A through 125. In Book 5, page 127, is the deed from Book B-315. On page 129 is the deed from Book A-14. Book 5 resumed on page 130 with May Term 1809, L. F. Ellen, P. R. Book 5 was examined and approved by S. Westray, Archd. Griffin, and Jas. Williams, Aug. 1, 1809.

Deed Book 6 is inscribed in the back and on the flyleaf as Book K. A loose index is in the book inscribed "For Book K, 1794 until 1801, Alphabet for same." A reverse index is in the book, made on blue paper, this paper having been used in the courthouse around and after 1850. It was probably made by B. H. Sorsby about 1868. Book 6 is original throughout.

The first Register of Deeds in Nash County was William Skip with Mearns, who served in this capacity from the formation of the county in 1777 (1778 when the first court met) until his death in 1804. His successor, Lodrick F. Ellen (Flewellen), who served from 1805 until 1823, probably recopied most of the earlier deed books for some reason during his tenure of office. Other deed books will be discussed as they appear.

The first twenty-four deed books are, or were, indexed in the front of the books through Nov. 15, 1870. These indexes include land grants, bills of sale, power of attorney, and all transactions of every kind that were recorded. The present grant or-grantee index only includes transactions of real estate. Therefore, it can easily be seen that the present index is inadequate for genealogical purposes. This index has been recently made, during the tenure of those who work in the office at the present time. In abstracting these books page by page, I noticed that some of my page numbers were not identical with those in the index. This I cannot explain. Some of the page numbers were duplicated and often there was an ommission of several pages.

In the early days of the county, deeds were oftentimes recorded in groups. There would be several deeds from one particular section of the county in series and then several from another section. Quite often county officials would be witnesses. The most usual witnesses were related to the grantor or grantee. In some cases, people were witnesses to several deeds in sequence, many written years apart and held before recording. Many witnesses lived on the opposite side of the county from the principals and were probably at the courthouse on official business of their own.

A large percentage of deeds were probably never recorded. Some people saved deeds for years and recorded several at one time. Many deeds were put on record after the land had been resold, probably because the grantee desired the previous deed on record for the sake of security. In very many cases, one of the witnesses to a deed purchased the property involved shortly thereafter from the new owner. Some deeds were recorded twice, probably through error, and other deeds were begun and not finished. Justices of the Peace were frequent witnesses, especially in cases where the wife also signed the deed. The wives were questioned separately from their husbands concerning their voluntary signing of the deeds, relinquishing their right of dower or thirds, according to an Act of Assembly about 1803. Only one lady in the county served as a J. P., and this was Ellen Mecom. She was also a preacher and served about 1825-1850.

In reading these deed books, one can place almost any family in the county, with the exception of some large land-owners who bought scattered tracts. Some people living on opposite sides of the county were closely related, often having the same given names. Nicknames were seldom used in legal work, especially among the men. Quite often in deeds involving wives, however, the lawyers used Ann for Nancy, Polly for Mary, Sally for Sarah, Patsey for Martha, and other nicknames. Probably they were unaware of the correct given name. Several alterations of names took place, such as McDaniel, McEatman, McBatchelor, and McWilliams. These were originally Daniel, Eatman, Batchelor, and Williams. Other changes in names were Flewellen, which became F. Ellen and finally Ellen; also, Longbottoms which became L. Bottoms and finally Bottoms. There were several other changes in family names over the years and many of the names included here are no longer heard.

In conclusion, there were many duplications in the names of creeks and branches by the earliest settlers. As they lived miles apart with little or no transportation facilities and little visiting, this was not uncommon. We have two Turkey Creeks, two Cabin Branches, one Beaver Dam Swamp and two Beaver Branches, and other duplications. Nearly all property was located on a stream of some kind and this made the descriptions of property confusing. And so they used Tar River for a dividing line. In nearly every case, one of the identical streams would be on the north side of the river and the other on the south side. Keeping this in mind, unless a deed stated that the property was on the bank of Tar River, it could be five or ten miles away from the river, on the north side or south side..

JOSEPH W. WATSON

406 Piedmont Avenue
Rocky Mount, N. C.

NOTE: In the event that a certified copy is desired of any of the deeds contained herein, a typed copy may be obtained by writing to the Register of Deeds, Nashville, N. C. or a photostatic copy may be obtained by writing to the N. C. State Dept. of Archives and History, Raleigh, N. C.

REGISTER OF DEEDS FOR NASH COUNTY

William S. Mearns	1778 - 1804
Loderick F. Ellen	1805 - 1823
W. G. Whitfield	1823 - 1827
Jesse H. Drake	1828 - 1831
John G. Blount	1831 - 1837
Samuel W. W. Vick	1837 - 1840
John W. W. Drake	1840 - 1840
J. J. Q. Taylor	1841 - 1845
German W. Ward	1845 - 1851
Will G. Freeman	1852 - 1853
Wm. H. Joyner	1853 - 1857
J. I. Harris	1857 - 1860
N. C. Harrison	1861 - 1867
B. H. Sorsby	1867 - 1868
William T. Griffin	1868 - 1874
A. W. Bridgers	1874 - 1878
John J. Drake	1878 - 1882
J. G. Sills	1882 - 1888
R. F. Drake	1888 - 1890
J. H. Exum	1890 - 1894
J. H. T. Baker	1894 - 1898
J. A. Whitaker	1898 - 1906
J. R. Whitaker	1906 - 1908
J. B. Boddie	1908 - 1935
Empress Boddie	1935 - 1936
Wm. S. Bunn	1936 - 1956
Catherine F. Griffin	1956 -

TABLE OF CONTENTS

INDEX TO NASH COUNTY DEED BOOK 1

—A—

Adams 265, Lackfield 90, Robt. 229

Adkins, Thos. 93

Adkinson, Jas. 17

Alford, Lodwick 233

Allen, Arthur 145, 407 (2), Thos. 407 (2)

Anderson, Francis 174, Peter 229 (2), 265, 349, 378, 395

Andrews, John 16, 25, 334. Wm. 16, 25, 99, 164, 168, 176, 305 (2), 313 (2), 314, 334 (3), 370

Annes, Jas. 9

Armstrong, Thos. 378

Arnett, S. W. 323

Arrington 50, Arthur 41, 59, 103. 111, 157, 178 (2), 272, 281, 322, 354, 361, 362, 363, 392, 400, Benj. 171, 406. Eliz. 59, Jas. 393, John 322, 361, 362, 363. Jos. 152. 153. 272, 354, 356, 362, 363, 393, 401, 404, (2), Martha 59, Wm. 272, 392

Atkins, Henry 1. 32, 196, 221, Thos. 231 (2)

Atkinson 300, Benj. 47. Burwell 240, 342, Ephraim 340, 342, 358, Martha Cooper 300, Michael 261. 262. 274, 298, 299 (2), 300. Jas. 340, 358, Nathan 153, Newit 19. 24, Thos. 37, 47, 88 (2), 316, 317

Avent, Rebecka 5, Thos. 5, Wm. 5, 6, 20, 30, 60, 210, 265, 349, 371, 378 (3)

—B—

Baggett, Nicholas 308, 321

Bailey (Bailie. Baley), Eliz. 232, John 27, Rich. 82, 197, Wm. 27, 232

Baker, Allen 383. Jas. 190, Wm. 315 (2), 383

Ballard, Chris. 190, 221. 248, 353, 370, 383, David 129, 155, Edw. 156, Fred. 223, 224, 225, John 383, Peter 151, 156, Wm. 383, 402, Wm. Midleton 326

Banes, Benj. 353, Henry 25, 164, 334, 342, 370

Barker, Jessey 8

Barlow, Henry 32, 156 346

Barnes 93, Dempsey 389, Jacob 42, 88 (3). 353 (2), Jas. 187, 366, John 353, Wm. 42, 88, 94, 181, 187, 365

Barrendene, Wm. 108, 293

Barrot (t), John 364, Nathan 364

Bass, Abraham 4, 76, 121 (3) 124 (2), 125, 189, 246, 336, Ann 308, Charity 247, Isaac 76, 117, 120 (2), 123 (2), 133, 308. 398 (2), Jesse 308, Jethro 120, John 4, 121, 247 (2), 257 (2), Mary 189, Sion 121, 149 (2), 189, 280, 375 (2)

Ba(t)chelor 209, Jos. 175, Marg. 126, Sam. 34, Sarah 34, Solomon 34, Stephen 126, Wm. 179, 181 (2), 222, 271 (2)

Battle, Elisha 165, Jacob 165, Jas. 30, 56. 60, 61, 190, 257, 265, 328, Wm. 6, 30, 61, 188, 229 (2), 247, 256, 265, 349, 378 (2)

356 (2), 371, 404, Jesse 74, 322, John 165, 284, Susannah 322,
Beckwith, Henry 9 (2)
Bell 50, 91, 349, 393, Arthur 90, 174, Elias 174, Elisha 371 (2), Eliz.
361, Green 67, 68, Jas. 174, Simon 360, Thos. 178, 281, Wm. 256
Biggs, John 9, 288, 296
Bird, Jas. 329
Blackburn, George 217
Blackwell, George 389
Blu, John 22
Blunt, Wm. 115 (2)
Boddie 342, Bennet(t) 17, 76, 123, 201, 308, Elijah 139, 140, 201,
250, George 358, Nathan 17 (2), 23, 24, 76, 103, 111, 119, 123,
143, 170, 201, 340, 358, Wm. 7, 131, 170, 398
Bonds, Crese 382, John 179, 181, 231 (2), 307 (2), 350, 355, 382,
405
Bone, John 402
Boon, Benj. 43,64, 149, 177, 254, 375, 379, Susanah 177
Boothe, Andrew 393, Benj. 264, 292, Martha 292
Bottoms (Longbottoms), Sam. 190, 248, 289, 353
Boutin, John 15, 68
Boyet(t), Jacob 114, Wm. 269 (2)
Boykin, Benj. 283 (2)
Bradbury, George 278
Bradl(e)y, Denis 48, Jas. 346
Branch, Edmund 327 (2)
Brantl(e)y, Britten 75, John 93, 156, Matthews 93, 192, 193, 221,
250
Braswell, Arthur 48, 69, 71, 101, 134, 287, 345, 360, Benj. 295, 302,
Henry 48 (2) 76, 79, 93, 117, 123, 133, 134, 203, 280, 287, Jacob
69 (2), 71, 327, 383, Martha 134, Sam. 7, Wm. 9, 10, 51, 71, 266,
268, 302 (2), 311
Bridgers, Benj. 44, 45 (2), 180 (2), 256 (2), Eliz. 4, 61, Harty 336,
Micajah 336, Samson 5, Sam. 4, 45, 56 (4), 61 (2), 121, 246, 256,
Wm. 4, 121, 125, 247, 336
Brinkley, Wm. 378
Brotton, Jesse 379
Brown, Chas. 123, Zachariah 216
Bruce, Walter 25
Bryant (Briant), Benj. 319, Gale 244, Jas. 9, 123 (2), Sam. 145, 163,
199, 295,342 (2), Wm. 8, 116, 235, 319
Bunn, Benj. 29, 39, 171 (2), 253 (2), 275, 276, 347 (2), David 39,
136, 193, 261, 275, 347, Joel 353, 406, John 21, 39, Josiah 215, 223,
224, 225, 253, 303, R. 347, Redmun 39
Buntin, Jeremiah 176, Wm. 142
Burge, Eliz. Buckner 379, Jeremiah 307, 316, 317, Rich. 209, 221
Burne, Henry 206, 222, 227, 228
Butt (s), Jacob 396, 397, Joshua 174
Buttenton, 66
Button, John 302

John 152, 404, Lewis 115, Miles 136, O. 31, Sam. 148 (2), 212, 384, 392, 404, Thos. 297, Wm. 115, 212, Young 343

Dawson, Dempsey 150, 251, 269, 389

Deans (Deens), Daniel 35, 135, 137, 157, 191, 216, 296, Eliz. 191, Henry 168, 176, 305 (2), 313 (2), 314, 334, Jeremiah 314, John 115, Rich. 134, Thos. 216

Defnal, Wm. 175 (2)

Denson 96, Benj. 223 (2), 224, 225, Jethro 97, 172, 281, 338, John 225, Jos. 207, 223

Denton, Wm. 26

De(a) venport, Delly 334, John 81, 194, 277, 292, 298

Devaughan, Sam. 87

Dew, Duncan 150, 251, John 28, 150 (2), 379, Wm. 387

Dickeson 167

Dickinson (Dickenson) 235, Jacob 138, 179 (2), 181, 184, 195, 222, 227, 228, 233, 304, 401 (2), Mourning 138, 179, 184, 227

Dison, Hosea 87 (2), Mary 382

Doimar, John 315

Dormin, Michael 381

Dortch, Ann 109, 162 (2), Lewis 109, 162 (2), 308, Wm. 162

Douglas, Dorcas 91, Jas. 90 (2), 91 (2), 97 (2), 404

Drake 4, 45, Albrittain 44, 202, 256 (2), Ann 168, Edmund 332, Edwin 332, Jas. 44, 256 (2), Matthew 11, 97, 111, 168, 176, 307, 310 (2), 345, 360, Nath. 310, Wm. 6, 280

Duck, Jacob 153, Sarah 153

—E—

Eason 214, Sam. 175, Wm. 145, 175

Eastwood, Jas. 304

Eayts, Badue 209

Edmondson, Ambrose 345, 360

Edwards, Arthur 107, John 248, 289, Sam. 197, Solomon 88, 237, Thos. 357

Ellen (Ellin, Flewellen), Howell 51, 76, 140, 261, 262, 339, 364, Wm. 10, 51

Erwin, Walter 249

Etheridge (Ethridge), Jeremiah 146, Lott 174, 234, 371, Peter 119, Wm. 174

Evans, Chas. 297 (2), David 81, Eliz. 333, 386, Ferbrey 297, John 107, 131, 238 (2), 307, 333, 386, 395, Sherrod 386

Exum 130, 274, John 78 (2), 128, 186. Jos. 36, 37, 78, 88 (2), 105, 128, 166, 186, 200, 231, 237, 275, 276, 303, (2), 304, 307, 316 (2), 317, 337, Priscilla 166, 186, 237, Thos. 37, 63, 78

—F—

Falk, John 153

Fargurson, John 402

Finch , Hen. 1

Flowers, Benj. 330 (2), Eliz. 96, 360, **Hardy** 225, 315, **Henry** 389,

Hilliard 98, 188, Eleas 198, Isaac 172, 198 (2), 218, 257, 278, 281, 282, 322, 345, 354, 360, Jeremiah 41, 217, 292, 324, Robt. 41
Hines, Isham (Isom) 60, 128 (2), 187, 284, 321 Kinchen 63, Lewis 36, 37, 50, 63, 83, 109, 111 (2), 112 130, 186, 274

Hinn(i)ant, Jas. 209, John 142, 160, 209, 335 (2)
Hinton, Chris. 345, 360, Sarah 345
Hodge, Thos. 120
Hogg, Jas. 90 (2)
Hokaway, Thos. 315
Holland 105, 386, 395, Daniel 327, Rich. 327
Hooks, Dorcas 310, Wm. 101, 185, 310 (2)
Horn(e) 98, 188, H. 42, 261, 262, 275, 276, Henry 36 (3), 53, 63 (2), 99, 111 (3), 192, 292 (2),299 (2), 300 (2), 351, Isaac 109, 130, Jacob 63, Joel 109, 130, 194, 241, Josiah 194, 241, Michael 28 (2), 114, 150, 251, 269 (2), 351, Melbry 241, Milbrey 184, Patience 351, Piety 300, Sarah 186, Thos. 28, 36, 160, 249, 251 (3), 283, 292, 331, 351, Wm. 42, 63, 181 (3), 194, 196, 241, 298, Wilson 251 (2)
House, Jacob 304
Hunt, Daniel 328. David 327, Jesse 275 (2), 279, 339, John 328, 356 (2), 361, 362, 363 (2), 404 (4), Micajah Braswell 339, Thos. 328 (2), 362, 363
Hunter 365, Eliz. 204, 231, Priscilla 231, Thos. 53, 79, 99, 140, 143, 179, 181, 187, 194, 204, 223, 224, 225 (2), 231, 261, 262 (2), 266, 270, 275, 279, 299, 337, 339
Hutchens (Hutchins), Lewis 376, Thos. 358

—J—

Jackson, George 357
Jameson, Jas. 99, 181, 192, 193, 277
Jenkins (Jinkins), Fanney 50, Francis 36, 111 (2), Jesse 153, John 166, Rogers 50, 60, 128
Johnson, Benj. 96, Cornelius 96, Edw. 171, Gabriel 9, Jas. 171, Josiah 148, 392, Sampson 96, Sarah 96, Wm. 29, 171
Johnston, Josiah 6, 257
Jolley, Peter 39
Jones, Ann 219, Jas. 107, 230, John 14, 68, 97, 98 (2), 162 (2), 198, 200, 219 (3), 299, Jos. 98, 188, 198 (2), 219 (2), Newsome 168, 219, Robt. 219, Sam. 182
Jordan (Jorden), Cornelius 311, Jos. 38, Joshua 311 (2), Sarah 38
Joyner (Joiner) 225, Burrell 145, Burwell 407, Hardy 292, Jacob 145, 292, 353, Jesse 353, Jiles 158, John 190, 353 (2), Jos. 370, Milly 145, Nathan 85, 357, Wm. 72 (2), 85, 224

—K—

Keff (Kiff), Jas. 174, 385
Kent 395, Jesse 232 (2), 329, 373 (2)
Kersey, Thos. 190, 353
King, Julian 287. 323 (2), 374, 376, 396
Kirby (Kerby) 264, 292, John 332, Wm. 233, 332

Knight, Anne 331 (2), Eliah 285, John 331, Kinsman 331 (2), Spier 153

—L—

Lake 268

Lamkin, Lewis Ablewis 381

Lamon, Arch. 21, 72, 85, 86, 96, D. 145, Duncan 3, 23, 27, 28, 32, 72, 85, 86, 96 (2), 111, 208, 301, 315, 391, John 391 (2)

Lancaster, A. 202, 210, Abs. 11, 12, Jean 226, 305, 313, Wm. 164, 202, 226 (2), 305, 311, 313, 342

Landingham 242, Jas. 315

Lane, Benj. 312, John 312, Newit 146, 312, 319 (2)

Langley 293, Oswell (Ozwell) 107, 157

Larence, Jas, 8

. Laseter (Lasiter), Hansel 159 (2), 328, John 234 (2), Lemuel 328, 395, Sam. 159 (3), 234 (2), Sion 395, Tobias 234, 395 (2), Wm. 26

Lee, Jesse 38, Jonn 38

Lewis 214, 391, George 335, Lydia 240, Thos. 2 (2), 68, 125, 180, 213, 240, 254, Wm. 2, 55, 98, 178, 356, 404

Linch, Brian 286

Lin (d) sey, John 25, 182, Jos. 129, Wm. 26, 129 (2), 155 (3), 182

Lineham, Denis 120

Lockhart, Jas. 82. 89, Joel 211

Locus, Francis 174 (2)

Long, Rich, 47

Longbottoms, see Bottoms

Lott, John 232

—M—

Mabins, Chas. 397

Mann, Augs. 60, David 9 (2), 196, Denton 210, 256, John 5, 30, 66, 67, Thos. 38, 44, 210 (2), 310, Wm. 5, 60

Manning (Maning, Mannen), Benj. 155, Jesse 252, John 35, 137, 175 (2), 271, Matthias 18, 33, 34, 35, 119, 126, 135, 137, 258 (2), 288, 296, Sala 137, Willibe 23, 24, 76, 131, 134, 255

Maple, Thos. 134, 153, Wm. 134

Marshall, David 115 (2)

Mason, Foster 368, 369, Henry 308. 338, Mark 15, 59, 172, 338, 368 (2), 369 (2), Ralph 218, 278, 308, Widow 15, Wm. 368 (2)

Massee, P. Raynian 218

Massingale (Massingill), Amey 48, Ann 185, Eliz. 48, 177, 185, George 48, 257, James 48 (3), 79 (2), 101, 123, 133 (2), 177, 185, 203, Mark 185, Matthew 101, Walker 48, 79, 123, 133, 203, 280 (2)

Matthews 278, Benj. 200, 218, Jacob 115, Jas. 202, Jos. 218, Wm. 218, 235

Matthis, Jas. 19

McNeil 5, 6

Mearns, W. S. 14, 31, 97, 145, 188, 198, 219, 238 (2), 245, 246, 310,

328, 356, 393, 404, Wm. Skipwith 13

Mecain, Patrick 36, 130
Mecom, Thos. 329
Megee, Wm. 16, 314
Melton 199, 235, John 335
Menoshan, Wm. 334
Merriman, Francis 277, Thos. 274
Merritt (Merit), Jas. 57, Wm. 68, 162 (2), 217 (2)
Miller, John 343, Lewis 297, Sam. 297, 343 (2)
Mills, George 90
Minton, John 321, Jos. 278, 308 (2), 321 (2)
Mishan, Mathew 117
Mitchell, 404
Montfort, Jos. 50
Mooneyham 22, 27
Moore 83, Bathsheba 54, David 384, Edw. 1, 2, 16, 19, 29 (2), 32, 81,
    87, 111, 118, 171, 202 (2), 211, 215, 221, 235, Elisha 53 (2), 54,
    99, Jas. 16. 26 (2), 155, 202, John 53 (3), 54 (2), 83 (2), 88, 99
    (2), 112 (3), 321 (2), Lewis 54, 111, Wm. 250

Morgan, Henry 3, Jas. 240, John 391
Morphis, Jas. 232, 301, John 301, Mary 3, 301 (2), Patience 232
Morris (s) 17, Bathsheba 360, Chloe 360, Mitchel 99, Preston 117,
    Thos. 23, 24, 99, 117, 131, 143, 255, 318, 340 (2), 342, 345, 360

Mountree, Francis 153
Murray, Wm. 389

—N—

Nelson, Jas. 162, Wm. 208
Newsom (e), Isaac 162, 322
Nichols, Jeremiah 160, 269, 373
Nicholson 272, 344, 374, David 68, Edw. 2, 81, 163, 230, Thos. 68, 73
Norris, Jas. 209

—O—

Odom, Aaron 271
O'Neal, Arthur (Arter) 18, 135, 137, 140, 293, Benj. 181
Oliver, Jas. 366
Owens, Daniel 288

—P—

Pace, Eliz. 45, Thos. 45
Parker, Francis 13, 246, 332, Jos. 245
Parks, Jimima 344, Wm. 213, 344
Parrish, Edw. 287
Parrott, Jos. 18
Pas(s)more, John 101, 149, 375, Jos. 174
Peed, Henry 117 (2), 398
Perry, Wm. 295
Pettiway 295
Phillips, Ephraim 360, Jos. 389, Wm. 330

Pit(t)man, Jesse 244, 389, Joel 181, 187, Wm. 175 (2), 181
Pitts, Lewis 91
Poland (Poulan, Pouland), John 252, 326, 357, 383, Wm. 225, 326
(2), 402
Pollock 395
Pope, Hardyman 153 (2), Lazarus 394 (3), Solomon 86 (2)
Porter, George 212
Portis, George 384, 392, Jeremiah 384, John 148, 212 (2), 384, 392,
404
Powell, Chas. 278 (2), Elijah 79, 101, 149, 201 (2), Eliz. 101, Jesse
327, John 242, 282, Jos. 174, 252, Nath. 57, 272, Sampson 10, 76,
123 (2), 133, 134, 143, 170, 201, 255 (2), 287, 342, Willoughby
272, 325
Price, Thos. 82, 89
Pridgen, David 21, 75, 102, 214, 248, 267, 289, 291, 383, 400, 407,
Drury 214, Jesse 34, 75, 96, 291
Pritchett, Chris, 165, Priscilla 165
Pumphrey, Sylvanus 358
Purs(s)ell, Edw. 146, 311
Pusly, Edw. 302
Pyland, Caroline 178, 281, Robt. 30, 178, 281

—R—

Rackley, John 15, Parson 293
Raines, John 316, 317
Ransome, Rich. 404
Rawls, John 338
Ray, Wm. 295 (2)
Reasons, Wm. 144
Reese, Randolph 324
Revel 192, 275, 339, Elijah 53, 99, 284, Micajah 54, 81, 83, 112, 276,
298, 321
Rice, John 145, 385
Richardson, Jas. 189, 255, 340, Thos. 119, 318, Wm. 48, 123, 133
(2), 185, 280
Ricks 223, 224, 355, Abraham 138, 206, 207, Benj. 86 (2), Isaac 36,
Jacob 138, 206, 222, 228, Joel 206 (2), 207 (2), 227, Lewis 9,
228, Patience 207 (2), Rhody 396, Thos. 206, 207, Wm. 9 (2),
222, 227, 271
Roberss, Matthew 171
Robertson, John 321, Peter 115, 239, 308, 321, Wm. 379
Rogers, Jacob 338, John 220, 233, Mary 79, Peleg 220 (2), 385,
Robt. 48, 338, 346
Rose, Burwell 335, Francis 50, 68, 245, 259, 260, 282, 317, 374, 379,
Sarah 137, Wm. 338
Ross 262 (2), Andrew 81, 187, 192, 194, 337, Ann 192, Williamson
226, 305
Rowe, John 52, Wm. 52, 283
Ruffin, Robt. 8 (2), Sarah 8, Wm. 8 (3), 157

—S—

Sandeford, Pheraby 50, Tomkins 50, 68, Wm. 15, 50, 68, 109, 354

Sanders 360, John 311, Nath. 291, Thos. 311 (3), Wm. 338

Saul, Abram 260, Abraham 282, Absolom 162 (2), 259

Savage, Drewry 155, Kinchen 155

Scott, John 129, 315, Marg. 129

Screws, Henry 45, 315 (2)

Sealy (Selah), Jos. 357 (4), 387, 402, 406, Thos. 47

Seath, Arthur 370

Shelly 4

Shepherd, John 2

Sheppard, John 289

Sherrod, Edmond 387, Jenny 387, Jordan 244, 387

Sikes, Sam (p) son 17, 310

Slatter, Wm. 349

Skinner 152, Emmanuel (Manuel) 53, 54, 112, 365, 366, 403, Nicholas 42, 81, 94, 181, 186, 187, 192, 193, 194 (2), 261 (2), 262, 274, 277 (2), 284, 298, 299, Sam. 53 (2), 99, 298, 366 (2), 403 (2), Sarah 187, 284 (2), Wm. 63, 81, 181, 365

Smelly 22, John 27

Smith 91, Barbary 79, Benj. 47, 93, 156, 190, 215, 353, 370, Brittain 145, Jas. 90, 91, 273, Nath. 22, Nehemiah 365, Simon 370

Sorsby, Alex. 379, Sam. 316, 317, 379

Spight, John 63, 303, Josiah 298, Mary 300, Sarah 186, Wm. 88 (2), 186 (3), 231 (2), 303 (2)

Springer, Mildred 405

Stainback, Thos. 292

Stallings (Stallions) 81, Jacob 18, 136, 192, 261, 275, 347, Moses 211, 350 (2)

Stevens (Stephens) 52, Frances 282, Henry 282, Joshua 311

Strickland 301, 366, 403, David 79, 140, 275, 339, Dinah 232, Eliz. 275, Hardy 163, 342, Jacob 1, 163, 303, 304, 342, John 1, Lazarus 374, 379, 382, Mark 211, Sam. 373, Simon 87, 118, 232, Solomon 145 (2), 163, 342 (2), Wm. 1

Sumner, Jos. 199

Sutton, George 191, 288, 296, 344, Lucy 344, Thos. 344

—T—

Tablet 74

Talbert (Tolbert, Tolbot), Isaac 60, 129, 325, 354

Tanner, John 42

Tarlington, John 228

Taylor, Arthur 244, Benj. 3 (2), 208, 301, Cornelius 164, 334, Daniel 146, Disey 118, 232, Drewry (Drury) 357, 394 (3), Fred 208, Harry 235, 338, 398, Jas. 232, 344, John 3, 87 (2), 208, 211 (2), 232, 251, 391, 394, Mary 232, Micajah 401, Mills 128, Reuben (Rubin) 50, 153, 166, 186, Rich. 208, Sam. 232 (5), 373, Wm. 60, 128, Wilson 19, 326, 351, 373, 394 (2), 400, 402

Telfair, Alex. 31, Hugh 31

Thomas 123, 131, 203, Anne 111, Jethro 167, 235, Jos. 376 Micajah

Whiddon (Whidon, Whitton) 195, John 23, 102, 107, Lott 230, Mary 151, 293, Noah 333, 395, 397, Wm. 23, 93, 103 (2), 105 (2), 106 (2), 107 (2), 108, 131 151, 230 (2), 250, 293, 333, 386 (2), 395 (5)

Whitaker, Robt. 45

White, John 191, 216, 288, 296, Jos. 331, Judeth 216

Whitehead 24, 76, 356, 374, 404, Arthur 200, Benj. 66, 67, 68, Bennett 200, Henry 66, 67, 68, Isaac 325, Jacob 20, 36, 111 (2), 166, 217, 322, Lazarus 74 (2), 217, 242 (2), 325, Mary 74, 325, Nathan 66, 68, Thos. 68, Wm. 14, 166 (4), 200 (2), 325, 370

Whitehouse, John 102 (2), 139, 195, 222

Whitfield Benj. 14, 98, 212, 384, 393, Israel 405, John 116, 199, Reuben 195, 333, 397, 405, Solomon 195, Thos. 102 (2), 105, 167, 195, 396

Whitl(e)y, Arthur 253, Brittain 267, 289, Ferriby 21, Jonas Barnes 253, Nathan 21

Wiggins, John 242, 273

Wilder, Job 23

Williams 59, 245 393, Arthur 240, 312, Benj. 286, Billy 196, Cooper 11, 12. 372, Drury 330, 351, Elias 6, Howell 50, Jas. 332, 355, Joel 252, 350, John 31, 61, 91, 246, 247, 364, 371 (2), Jonas 57, 174, 196, 252, 269. 330, 350, 351 (2). 379, Mary 98 188, 198, Matthew 176, Nathan 232, Philander 196, 248, 267 (2). 291, 381. Pilgrim 251, 351, Reuben 3, Roland 196, 252, Sam. 85. Simon 233, 235, 286, Thos. 83, 94, 101, 165, 181, 274, 277, 284, 292, 300, 321, 324, Wm. 188, 331

Williamson, Ann 52, 134, Hardy 52, 134, Jos. 22, 52, 134, Sarah 134

Willis, Thos. 140, 266, 270 339

Wilson, Edw. 204, 266, 270, 279 (3), 321, 337, John 204, 279, 321, 339, Thos. 218, 278

Wimberly, George 184, 227, 241, 376 (2)

Winstead, Rich. 381

Womble Joshua 143

Wombwell, Jos. 28

Wood, Aaron 404, Bennet 404

Woodard. Jas. 69, 71, Jesse 153, Luke 134, 153, Thos. 134, 153

Worrell, Wm. 101, 108, 181

Wright, Elisha 158, John 259 260. Jos. 114, 360. Lemuel 114 (2), 249, 360, Patience 73, Sarah 158, Susannah 59, Wm. 172, 259, 260, 374 Win'd 73

Wyatt, Jas. 66, 68, 73 (2), 369, Jesse 374, Sarah 374

—Y—

Youell, Henry 293

Young, 268, Robt. 20, 76, 79, 285, 311, 364, 376, 396, Stephen 117 (2), 120, 342, Wm. 264

DB 1-1 EDWARD MOORE of Edgecombe Co. to his son-in-law, EDWARD CLINCH, May 25, 1774, for 10 pds. and love and affection a tract of 285 acres on the south side of Tar River adjoining William Strickland and Jacob Strickland, whereon said Clinch then lived. Wit: Hen. Finch, John Strickland, and Henry Atkins.

DB 1-2 THOMAS LEWIS of Edgecombe Co. to JOHN SHEPHERD of same, Sept. 19, 1775, for 55 pds. proc. money 150 acres on the south side of Sapony Swamp at the mouth of Spring Branch, it being part of the tract that William Lewis bought of Thomas Lewis. Wit: Edward Moore, Edward Nicholson, and Ethelred Dance.

DB 1-3 BENJAMIN TAYLOR of Nash Co. to MARY MORPHES of same, April 7, 1778, for 30 pds. proc. money a tract of 200 acres, it being part of a larger tract granted to Duncan Lamon by Earl Granville on July 23, 1761 and transferred to Benja. Taylor. Wit: Reuben Williams, Henry Morgan, and John Taylor.

DB 1-4 SAMUEL BRIDGERS and wife, ELIZABETH BRIDGERS, of Nash Co. to WILLIAM BRIDGERS of same, Jan. 17, 1778, for 400 pds. proc. money a tract of 327 acres on the south side of of Swift Creek adjoining Shelly, Watson, and Drake. Wit: Abraham Bass, Trimagan Thompson, and John Bass.

DB 1-5 THOMAS AVENT and REBECKA AVENT of Edgecombe Co. to WILLIAM AVENT of same, Nov. 25, 1777, for 60 pds. proc. money a tract of 140 acres on the north side of Swift Creek adjoining Crawman and McNeil. Wit: Samson Bridgers, John Mann, and William Mann.

DB 1-6 WILLIAM AVENT of Edgecombe Co. to JOSIAH JOHNSTON of same, Dec. 3, 1777, for 186 pds. 13 sh. 4 p. proc. money a tract of 140 acres on the north side of Swift Creek adjoining Crawman and McNeil. Wit: William Drake, Elias Williams, and William Battle.

DB 1-7 MICAJAH THOMAS of Nash Co. to BENJAMIN HEDGEPETH of same, Jan. 31, 1778, for 50 pds. proc. money 100 acres on the north side of Tucker's Swamp adjoining Chapman, it being part of a tract granted by Earl Granville to Peter Hedgepeth on July 23, 1761 and sold by him to said Thomas. Wit: William Boddie, Peter Hedgepeth, and Samuel Braswell.

DB 1-8 WILLIAM RUFFIN and SARAH RUFFIN of Northampton Co. to WILLIAM CHAPMAN of Nash Co., Jan. 11, 1778, for 80 pds. proc. money two tracts of land on the south side of Tar River, one of 202 acres granted by Earl Granville to Robert Ruffin, father of said William Ruffin, on Nov. 9. 1754 on the north side of Turkey Creek and on the south side of Tar River; the other tract by deed from James Larence to said William Ruffin, Feb. 28, 1761, containing 160 acres on the south side of Tar River adjoining William Bryant and the Rocky Branch. Wit: Jessey Barker and Robert Ruffin.

DB 1-9 MICAJAH THOMAS of Nash Co. to LEWIS RICKS of same, March 7, 1778, for 70 pds. proc. money two tracts of land, one of 200 acres being part of a tract granted to William Braswell by Gov. Gabriel Johnson on March 21, 1742, conveyed by him to Henry Beckwith, and by Henry Beckwith to David Mann on Feb. 24, 1750. The other tract of 75 acres was part of a grant by James Annes and Francis Corbin, agents of Earl Granville, on March 25, 1752 to William Ricks and conveyed from William Ricks to David Mann on May 25, 1752. The first tract was on the south side of Founteen's Branch and the second tract was on Maple Branch. Wit: John Biggs, Christopher Vann, and James Briant.

DB 1-10 SAMPSON POWELL of Nash Co. to WILLIAM FLEWELLIN, JR. of same, April 6, 1778, for 213 pds. proc. money a tract of 206 acres adjoining William Braswell. Wit: Britain Gandy and Richard Thomas.

DB 1-11 ISHAM WHELESS and wife, AMEY WHELESS. of Edgecombe Co. to COOPER WILLIAMS of same, Nov. 21, 1777, for 200 pds. proc. money a tract of 200 acres on the south side of Swift Creek adjoining Benjamin Wheless, Sr. Wit: Micajah Thomas, Matthew Drake, and Abs. Lancaster.

DB 1-12 WILLIAM HILL of Nash Co. to SION HILL and LEWIS HILL of same, March 23, 1778, for 200 pds. Virginia money a tract of 516 acres on the south side of Swift Creek adjoining Cooper Williams and was all the land he owned in the county. Wit: Abs. Lancaster and William Clanton Hill.

DB 1-13 THOMAS GILCHRIST of Halifax Co. to WILLIAM SKIPWITH MEARNS of Edgecombe Co., Oct. 3, 1777, for 40 pds. proc. money 100 acres on the south side of Swift Creek at the mouth of Spring Branch, it being a parcel of land conveyed by Francis Parker to John Watson and Alexander Cairns on Feb. 21, 1753. Wit: James Churchill and Davis Connell.

DB 1-14 WILLIAM WHITEHEAD of Edgecombe Co. to BENJAMIN WHITFIELD of same, Feb. 7, 1777, for one farthing per year a lease on a tract of 100 acres on the north side of Mill Swamp, the mill and one acre excepted, for 15 years. Wit: John Jones and W. S. Mearns.

DB 1-15 JOHN RACKLEY of Nash Co. to MARK MASON of same, Feb. 21, 1778, for 100 pds. Virginia money, a tract of 100 acres adjoining Widow Culpepper and Widow Mason on the creek. Wit: John Boutin, William Sandeford, and James Churchill.

DB 1-16 WILLIAM HARRISS of Edgecombe Co. to JAMES MOORE of same, Oct. 25, 1777, for 65 pds. 6 sh. 8 p. proc. money 49 acres on Little Peachtree Creek, it being part of a tract granted by Earl Granville to William Megee on Dec. 30, 1760. Wit: Wm. Andrews, Edward Moore, and John Andrews.

DB 1-17 DEAL COLLINS of Nash Co. to NOAH CHADWICK of same, May 21, 1778, for 20 pds. proc. money a tract of 50 acres, it being part of the tract granted by Earl Granville to James Adkinson on Oct. 15, 1761, adjoining Morris, the Medow Branch, and

Nathan Boddie. Wit: Nathan Boddie, Samson Sikes, and Bennett Boddie.

DB 1-18 JOSEPH PARROTT of Edgecombe Co. to ARTAR O'NEAL, Nov. 6, 1777, for 33 pds. 6 sh. 8 p. a tract of 100 acres on Little Sapony Creek and Sikes Branch. Wit: Matthians Maning and Jacob Stallings.

DB 1-19 NEWIT ATKINSON of Edgecombe Co. to EDWARD MOORE of same, Oct. 26, 1775, for 100 pds. proc. money 150 acres on Spring Branch and the creek, it being part of a tract granted to Abner Hill and conveyed by him to James Matthis on May 23, 1761. Wit: Wilson Taylor and Mark Cooper.

DB 1-20 MICAJAH THOMAS of Nash Co. to JAMES DANIEL of same, April 14, 1777, for 170 pds. proc. money 422 acres on the north side of Pig Basket Creek or Braswell's Creek, it being a tract granted by Earl Granville to Robert Young on Nov. 8, 1755 and conveyed by him to Jacob Whitehead on June 15, 1764. Wit: Wilson Vick and William Avent.

DB 1-21 NATHAN WHITLEY and wife, FERRIBY WHITLEY, of Bute Co., N.C. to DAVID PRIDGEN of Nash Co., May 30, 1778, for 200 pds. proc. money a tract of 175 acres on the north side of Tar River. Wit: Archibald Lamon and John Bunn.

DB 1-22 ELIJAH WELCH of Edgecombe Co. to NATHANIEL SMITH of same, Dec. 17, 1772, for 50 pds. proc. money a tract of 250 acres on the north side of Turkey Creek adjoining Smelly. Mooneyham, and Contentnea Creek, it being part of a larger tract granted to John Blu by Earl Granville. Wit: Jos. Williamson, Edward Collins, and William Colwell.

DB 1-23 WILLIAM VESTER of Edgecombe Co. to WILLIBE MANNING of same. Feb. 6, 1777, for 40 pds. proc. money 60 acres on the south side of Peachtree Creek, it being part of a tract granted by Earl Granville to Job Wilder on April 21, 1745. Wit: Nathan Boddie, Thomas Morris, and Elesebeth Turner.

DB 1-23 WILLIAM WHIDDON of Edgecombe Co. to JOHN WHIDDON of same, Jan. 30, 1776, for 30 pds. proc. money a tract of 200 acres on the north side of Sapony Swamp. Wit: Dun. Lamon and Marcom Cooper.

DB 1-24 WILLIAM VESTER of Edgecombe Co. to NATHAN BODDIE of same, Feb. 6, 1777. for 30 pds. proc. money 95 acres on the north side of Peachtree Creek adjoining Whitehead, it being part of a tract sold by Newit Atkinson to William Vester. Wit: Thomas Morris, Willibe Manning, and Elizabeth Turner.

DB 1-25 WILLIAM ANDREWS of Edgecombe Co. to JOHN LINSEY of same, Jan. 2, 1776, for 12 pds. proc. money 100 acres adjoining Tucker. it being part of a tract granted to Abner Hill on Aug. 1, 1762. Wit: Walter Bruce, Henry Banes, and John Andrews.

DB 1-26 THOMAS TUCKER to BENJAMIN TUCKER, Dec. 4, 1777, for 70 pds. 13 sh. 4 p. proc. money 100 acres on Little Peachtree Creek adjoining William Lassiter. the road and James More, it being a tract of land granted to Abner Hill. Wit: William

Linsey, James More, and William Denton.

DB 1-27 WILLIAM BAILIE of Johnston Co. to ELIJAH WELCH of Edgecombe Co.. Aug. 15, 1772, for 50 pds. proc. money a tract of 250 acres on the north side of Turkey Creek adjoining John Smelly, Mooneyham, and Contentnea Creek, it being part of a larger tract granted to John Bailie by Earl Granville. Wit: Dun. Lamon and Jacob Flowers.

DB 1-28 JOHN DEW of Edgecombe Co. to MICHAEL HORN of same, Dec. 18, 1777, for 100 pds. proc. money a tract of 95 acres on the north side of Toisnot Swamp adjoining Michael Horne and Thomas Horne. Wit: Dun. Lamon and Jos. Wombwell.

DB 1-29 EDWARD MOORE of Nash Co. to FULGUM VES-TER of same, Jan. 19, 1778, for 30 pds. proc. money 108 acres on Maple Creek adjoining William Johnson and Benjamin Bunn, it being part of a tract of 474 acres granted to Edward Moore by Earl Granville on May 1, 1752. Wit: Arthur Vester and George Green.

DB 1-30 JOHN MANN of Nash Co. to WILLIAM BATTLE of same, Feb. 2, 1778, for 714 pds. 13 sh. 4 p. proc. money a tract of 536 acres on the north side of Swift Creek adjoining the Gideon Swamp.   Wit: William Avent, James Battle, and Robert Pyland.

DB 1-31 THOMAS GILCHRIST and wife, MARTHA GIL-CHRIST, to JOHN WILLIAMS, April 1, 1777, for 45 pds. proc. money a tract of 150 acres on the south side of Swift Creek, which land was sold by William Mearns to John Watson and Alexander Cairnes on March 8, 1748. Wit: Alexander Telfair, Hugh Telfair, and O. Davis.

DB 1-32 HENRY BARLOW of Edgecombe Co. to HENRY ATKINS of same, April 2, 1774, for 25 pds. proc. money a tract of 120 acres on Sapony Swamp, Holland's Branch, and Sapony Creek. Wit: Dun. Lamon and Edward Moore.

DB 1-33 THOMAS WARRAN and wife, SARAH WARRAN, of Nash Co. to JOSEPH TUCKER of same, April 6, 1778, for 50 pds. proc. money a tract of 70 acres on the south side of Great Sapony Swamp. Wit: Matthias Manning, Jr. and Lewis Tucker.

DB 1-34 SOLOMON BACHELOR and wife. SARAH BACHE-LOR, of Bute Co., N.C. to SAMUEL BACHELOR of Nash Co., Jan. 5, 1778, for 20 pds. proc. money a tract of 120 acres on the south side of Hendrick's Branch. Wit: Matthias Manning, Jr. and Jesse Pridᵍen.

DB 1-35 JAMES TUCKER, SR. and wife, PRISCILLA TUCK-ER, of Nash Co. to ROBERT TUCKER of same, Jan. 9, 1778. for 20 pds. proc. money a tract of 100 acres on the south side of Little Sapony Creek adjoining Daniel Deens. Wit: Matthias Manning, Jr. and John Manning.

DB 1-36 HENRY HORN of Edgecombe Co. to LEWIS HINES of Nash Co.. Feb. 20, 1778, for 170 pds. proc. money two tracts of land containing 422 acres, they being the two tracts granted to Patrick Mecain and Jacob Whitehead by deeds dated 1760 and 1752 and from them to Isaac Ricks and Francis Jenkins, deeds bearing date 1753 and 1762, and from them to George Harrell and Henry

Horn, deeds bearing date 1759 and 1768, and from George Harrell to Henry Horn in 1770, the land lying on Compass Creek adjoining George Harrell and Joseph Exum. Wit: Wilson Curl and Thomas Horn.

DB 1-37 JOSEPH EXUM of Nash Co. to LEWIS HINES of same, Sept. 9, 1778, for 30 pds. current money 100 acres on the north side of Compass Creek, it being part of a tract taken up by Thomas Exum, deceased, and a deed granted him by Earl Granville. Wit: Wilson Curl and Thomas Atkinson.

DB 1-38 JESSE LEE of Dinwiddie Co., Va. to JOHN LEE of Halifax Co., N.C., March 25, 1778, for 42 pds. current money a tract of 250 acres near Swift Creek on Shelley's Swamp adjoining Thomas Mann and the Short Swamp. Wit: Joseph Jorden and Sarah Jorden.

DB 1-39 DAVID BUNN, SR. of Edgecombe Co. to REDMUN BUNN of same, Sept. 26, 1777. for 50 pds. proc. money a tract of 150 acres on the south side of Tar River adjoining the Jumping Run and Peter Jollev. Wit: Benjamin Bunn and John Bunn.

DB 1-41 EDWARD CLINCH of Nash Co. to JOSEPH JOHN CLINCH of same, April 30, 1778, for 350 pds. a tract of 350 acres on the south side of Swift Creek adjoining Joseph Clinch and Jeremiah Hilliard, it being land granted to Robert Hilliard on March 6, 1740. Wit: Arthur Arrington and William Hall.

DB 1-42 WILLIAM BARNS of Nash Co. to NICHOLAS SKINNER of same, Sept. 30, 1778. for 125 pds. proc. money land on both sides of Stony Creek where John Tanner built a sawmill. He bought his right of Jacob Barns. Wit: William Horn and H. Horn.

DB 1-43 JESSE UNDERWOOD of Edgecombe Co. to BENJAMIN BOON of Bute Co. N.C., Oct. 30, 1776, for 50 pds. Virginia money a tract of 130 acres adjoining Michael Council and the Collins Road. it being land purchased from Peter Hedgepeth; also, another tract of 100 acres adjoining Michael Council and the Tumbling Run, it being land purchased from M'chael Council. Wit: Thomas H. Hall, John Webb, and Benjamin Westray.

DB 1-44 BENJAMIN BRIDGERS. SR. of Nash Co. to JOHN CLYBERN and wife, MARY. Oct. 8, 1778, out of love and affection for his daughter, Mary Clybern, and her husband, John Clybern, all his estate, money, goods, and chattels and all right to and use of the plantation of 100 acres whereon he then lived. Wit: Thomas Mann, Albrittain Drake, and James Drake, Sr.

DB 1-45 THOMAS PACE and wife, ELIZABETH PACE, of Nash Co. to HENRY SCREWS of same, Oct. 12, 1778, for 100 pds. proc. money a tract of 150 acres on the south side of Beaver Dam Swamp. Wit: James Wall and Manuel Underwood.

DB 1-45 SAMUEL BRIDGERS of Edgecombe Co. to BENJAMIN BRIDGERS, SR. of same, Aug. 10, 1757, for 10 sh. proc. money a tract of 100 acres on the north side of Swift Creek adjoining Drake. Wit: Robert Whitaker and Benjamin Bridgers.

DB 1-47 THOMAS ATKINSON of Edgecombe Co. to BENJAMIN ATKINSON of same, Oct. 4, 1777, for 10 pds. proc. money a tract of 200 acres on the north side of Sapony Creek adjoining Benjamin Smith. Wit: Richard Long and Thomas Sealey.

DB 1-48 ROBERT ROGERS of Nash Co. to HENRY BRAS-WELL of same, Oct. 31, 1778, for 50 pds. proc. money 100 acres adjoining Denis Bradly, Chapman, and Wiliba Tucker, it being part of a tract deeded in 1762. Wit: James Masingil, William Ritchason, and Arthur Braswell.

DB 1-48 GEORGE MASSINGIL and wife, AMEY MASSIN-GIL, of Nash Co. to HENRY BRASWELL of same, Oct. 1, 1778, for 40 pds. proc. money 70 acres on the west side of Back Swamp. it being part of a tract deeded to James Massingil by Earl Granville on March 16, 1761. Wit: James Massingil, Walker Massingil, and Elizabeth Massingil.

DB 1-50 WILLIAM SANDEFORD and wife, PHERABY SANDEFORD, of Nash Co. to TOMKINS SANDEFORD of same, Feb. 19, 1779, for 129 pds. proc. money 86 acres adjoining Davis Connell, Bell. the Parker's Branch, and Arrington, it being part of a tract bought from Jos. Montfort on Oct. 11. 1768. Wit: Francis Rose, Howell Williams, and Mathew Griffin.

DB 1-50 ROGERS JENKINS and wife, FANNEY JENKINS, of Nash Co. to ISAM HYNES of same, April 5, 1779, for 200 pds. current money 300 acres on the south side of Beach Run. it being part of a tract he bought from James Cain on Oct. 10, 1778. Wit: Lewis Hines and Rubin Taylor.

DB 1-51 WILLIAM FLEWELLEN of Nash Co. to WILLIAM WALKER of Halifax Co., Nov. 13, 1778, for 700 pds. proc. money a tract of 206 acres adjoining William Braswell. Wit: Howell Ellin and Fedrick Daniel.

DB 1-52 JOHN ROWE of Nash Co. to STEPHEN COBB of Dobbs Co., N. C., April 4, 1779, for 100 pds. current money the seventh part of a tract of 291 acres on the north side of Contentnea Creek adjoining Stevens, it being land granted to William Rowe on Feb. 23. 1761. Wit: Joseph Williamson, Ann Williamson, and Harry Williamson.

DB 1-53 ELISHA MOORE of Nash Co. to SAMUEL SKIN-NER, SR. of same, Jan. 21, 1779, for 290 pds. 5 sh. current money 256 acres on the north side of Stony Creek adjoining Elijah Revel, Henry Horn, and Thomas Hunter, it being part of a tract of 692 acres granted by Earl Granville to John Moore. Sr. on June 1. 1762, conveyed by him to John Moore. Jr., on June 3, 1773, and to Elisha Moore on May 3, 1777. Wit: John Moore, Emmanuel Skinner, and Samuel Skinner. Jr.

DB 1-54 JOHN MOORE of Nash Co. to MANUEL SKINNER of same, Jan. 19, 1779, for 50 pds. current money 100 acres on the north side of Stony Creek adjoining Micajah Revel and the Thomas' Road, it being part of a tract of 700 acres granted to John Moore by Earl Granville on June 1, 1762. Wit: Elisha Moore, Lewis Moore, and Bathsheba Moore.

DB 1-55 REDMUND WELLS of Craven Co. to STEPHEN WELLS of Edgecombe Co., Oct. 31, 1775, for 45 pds. proc. money a tract of 100 acres on the north side of Tar River adjoining the Wildcat Branch and Frederick Wells, it being part of a grant to Stephen Wells, Sr. from Earl Granville. Wit: Joseph Crowell and William Lewis.

DB 1-56 SAMUEL BRIDGERS of Nash Co. to TRIMMAKIN THOMPSON of same, his son-in-law, Oct. 21, 1778, for love and affection 100 acres adjoining said Samuel Bridgers, is being part of a tract granted to Samuel Bridgers on Oct. 15, 1761. Wit: James Battle and Samuel Bridgers.

DB 1-57 JAMES CAIN of Nash Co. to JAMES WALL of same, April 6, 1779, for 160 pds. Virginia money a tract of 160 acres on the south side of Fishing Creek at the mouth of Beaver Dam Swamp adjoining Nathaniel Powell, including the mill. Wit: Jonas Williams and James Merritt.

DB 1-59 SUSANNAH WRIGHT of Nash Co. to MARK MASON of same, March 31, 1779, according to agreement, a tract of 30 acres adjoining Williams and the Gum Branch, lying on both sides of the road. Wit: Arthur Arrington, Jr., Martha Arrington, and Elizabeth Arrington.

DB 1-60 JAMES CAIN and wife, MARGET CAIN, of Nash Co. to ROGERS JINKENS of same, Oct. 10, 1778, for 400 pds. proc. money land on the north side of Beach Run adjoining William Taylor. Wit: Isom Hines, Isaac Tolbot, and James Thompson.

DB 1-60 WILLIAM CROWMAN and ANN CROWMAN, his mother, of Nash Co. to WILLIAM AVENT of same, Nov. 8, 1778, for 300 pds. proc. money a tract of 100 acres on the north side of Swift Creek, conveyed to him by deed on Aug. 14, 1751. Wit: James Battle, William Mann, and Augs. Mann.

DB 1-61 SAMUEL BRIDGERS and wife, ELIZABETH BRIDGERS, of Nash Co. to WILLIAM BATTLE of same, Oct. 21, 1778, for 700 pds. proc. money 430 acres adjoining Trimakin Thompson and John Williams, it being part of a tract granted to him by Earl Granville on Oct. 14, 1761. Wit: James Battle, Trimagin Thompson, and Samuel Bridgers.

DB 1-63 WILLIAM HAMLIN, son and heir of Stephen Hamlin, decd. of Sussex Co., Va. to WILSON CURL of Nash Co., Feb. 11, 1779, for 40 pds. Virginia money a tract of 440 acres adjoining Henry Horn and the Compass Creek, the deed bearing date March 10, 1761. Wit: Lewis Hines and Kinchen Hines.

DB 1-63 HENRY HORN of Edgecombe Co. to THOMAS THORP of same, Jan. 28, 1778, for 200 pds. proc. money a tract of 652 acres granted to him by Earl Granville on Nov. 3, 1761, adjoining Thomas Exum and John Spight. Wit: William Horn, Jacob Horn, and William Skinner.

DB 1-64 PETER HEDGEPETH of Nash Co. to BENJAMIN BOON of same, Oct. 30, 1778, for 14 pds. Virginia money 130 acres on his own line, Cotton's Crost, and the main road, it being part of a tract granted to Peter Hedgepeth by Earl Granville. Wit: Michael Council.

DB 1-66 BENJAMIN WHITEHEAD of Nash Co. to his brother, HENRY WHITEHEAD. July 5, 1779, for love and affection a tract of 345 acres on the south side of Pollock's Beaver Dam Swamp adjoining James Wyatt, Nathan Whitehead, and Buttenton. Wit: Wm. Hall and John Mann.

DB 1-67 BENJAMIN WHITEHEAD of Nash Co. to his brother, HENRY WHITEHEAD, July 5, 1779, for love and affection a tract of 200 acres on the south side of Pollock's Beaver Dam Swamp. Wit: Green Bell and John Mann.

DB 1-68 BENJAMIN WHITEHEAD, THOMAS WHITEHEAD, DAVID NICHOLSON, Wm. SANDEFORD, ERASMUS CULPEPPER, GREEN BELL, and TOMKINS SANDEFORD to HENRY WHITEHEAD, son of Nathan Whitehead, decd., for love and affection three negroes by name, April 5, 1779. Wit: John Boutin and Francis Rose.

DB 1-68 EDWARD COOPER of Edgecombe Co. to THOMAS NICHOLSON of Halifax Co., May 20, 1777, for 5 pds. proc. money a parcel of 12 acres on the south side of Round Stone Swamp adjoining James Wyatt and the road, it being part of a tract granted to John Jones, Sr. Wit: Thomas Lewis, William Merit, and James Grant.

DB 1-69 JACOB BRASWELL of Nash Co. to his son, JACOB BRASWELL, of same, July 6, 1779, for love and good will a tract of 236 acres adjoining his own line and the road. Wit: Arthur Braswell and James Woodard.

DB 1-71 JACOB BRASWELL of Nash Co. to his son, WILLIAM BRASWELL, of same, July 6, 1779, for love and good will a tract of 291 acres adjoining Jesse Powell and the road. Wit: Arthur Braswell and James Woodard.

DB 1-72 WILLIAM JOINER, SR. of Nash Co. to WILLIAM JOINER, JR. of same, May 13, 1779, for 10 pds. proc. money a tract of 300 acres on the south side of Polecat Branch. Wit: Dun. Lamon and Archd. Lamon.

DB 1-73 JAMES WYATT of Halifax Co. to THOMAS NICHOLSON of same, Jan. 3, 1775, for 80 pds. proc. money a tract of 200 acres on the Round Stone Branch adjoining said Wyatt. Wit: Win'd. Wright, Stephen Weaver, and Patience Wright.

DB 1-74 LAZARUS WHITEHEAD and wife, MARY WHITEHEAD, of Nash Co. to JAMES TURNER of same, Dec. 26, 1778, for 40 pds. proc. money a tract of 313 acres on the north side of Lane's Swamp adjoining Henry and Tablet. Wit: Jesse Battle and Lazarus Whitehead, Jr.

DB 1-75 DAVID PRIDGEN of Nash Co. to BRITTEN BRANTLE of same, May 15, 1778, for 16 pds. proc. money 350 acres on the north side of Tar River at the Great Meadow, the tract bearing date July 23, 1761. Wit: Jesse Pridgen.

DB 1-76 JAMES DANIEL of Nash Co. to FEDRICK DANIEL of same, March 3, 1779, for 56 pds. 13 sh. 4 p. current money 140 acres on the north side of Pig Basket Creek, or Braswell's Creek, adjoining James Daniel's back line, it being part of a tract granted to Robert Young by Earl Granville on Nov. 8, 1755 and sold to

Whitehead on June 1, 1764. Wit: Howell Flewellin and David Daniel.

DB 1-76 WILLIBE MANNING of Nash Co. to SAMPSON POWELL of same, March 17, 1779, for 20 pds. proc. money 300 acres on the north side of Back Swamp adjoining Isaac Bass, it being part of a tract granted to Abraham Bass by Earl Granville on March 16, 1761. Wit: Nathan Boddie, Bennett Boddie, and Henry Braswell.

DB 1-78 JOSEPH EXUM of Nash Co. to JOHN EXUM of same, Oct. 30, 1778, for 100 pds. current money 155 acres on the south side of Compass Creek. it being part of a tract granted to Thomas Exum, deceased, on March 2, 1761 and was the land whereon John Exum then lived. Wit: Wilson Curl and Benja. Watkins.

DB 1-79 JAMES MASINGALE of Nash Co. to WALKER MASINGALE of same, July 1, 1779, for 10 pds. proc. money 90 acres on the north side of Back Swamp, it being part of a tract granted to said James Masingale by Earl Granville on March 16, 1761. Wit: Henry Braswell, Elijah Powell, and Mary Rogers.

DB 1-79 THOMAS HART and wife, PATIENCE HART, of Nash Co. to HARTWELL HART of same, July 1, 1779, for 20 sh. current money 150 acres on Beaver Dam Branch and the Thomas Hart line, it being part of a tract granted to Robert Young by Earl Granville on Nov. 11, 1756 and sold by him to Thomas Hart. Wit: Thomas Hunter, David Strickland, and Barbary Smith.

DB 1-81 EDWARD CLINCH of Nash Co. to EDWARD NICHOLSON of same, July 31, 1778, for 100 pds.. a parcel of 12 acres on Tar River adjoining said Clinch. Wit: Edward Moore, David Evans. and Ethelred Dance.

DB 1-81 MICAJAH REVEL of Edgecombe Co. to NICHOLAS SKINNER of same, Aug. 1, 1777, for 2 pds. Virginia money 2 acres on the south side of Stony Creek adjoining Stallings, it being part of a tract taken up by Andrew Ross dated Feb. 28, 1761. Wit: John Deavenport and William Skinner.

DB 1-82 JAMES LOCKHART of Johnson Co. to SOLOMON CARTER of Nash Co.. March 19, 1778, for 100 pds. proc. money 100 acres on the south side of Tar River at the mouth of Horse Pen Branch it being part of a tract granted to Richard Baley on April 20, 1745. Wit: Thomas Carter and Thomas Price.

DB 1-83 JOHN MOORE of Nash Co. to WILSON CURL of same, Aug. 26. 1779. for 2000 pds. current money 300 acres on both sides of Kirby's Creek adjoining Thomas Williams. Micajah Revel, the Thomas' Road. and Moore, it being part of a tract of 700 acres granted to John Moore by Earl Granville on June 1, 1762. Wit: Lewis Hines and Moses Harrell.

DB 1-85 WILLIAM JOINER of Nash Co. to NATHAN JOINER of same. May 13, 1779. for 10 pds. current money a 300 acre plantation on the north side of Tar River adjoining the Great Branch and Samuel Williams. Wit: Dun. Lamon and Arch'd. Lamon.

DB 1-86 BENJAMIN RICKS of Edgecombe Co. to ARTHUR WESTER of same, May 5, 1774, for 10 pds. proc. money 100 acres on the north side of Tar River and on Maple Creek, it being part of a tract granted to Solomon Pope by Earl Granville on March 3, 1761 and conveyed by Pope to Benjamin Ricks. Wit: Dun. Lamon, Jacob Flowers, and Arch'd. Lamon.

DB 1-87 SIMON STRICKLAND of Nash Co. to HOSEA DISON of same, Oct. 1, 1779, for 200 pds. current money a tract of 70 acres on Toisnot Swamp whereon said Dison then lived adjoining John Taylor and the Crooked Branch. Wit: Edward Moore, John Taylor, and Sam'l Devaughan.

DB 1-88 JACOB BARNES, JR. of Nash Co. to WILLIAM BARNES of same, Jan. 13, 1779, for 60 pds. current money 15 acres on the south side of Stony Creek, it being part of a tract of 363 acres granted to Jacob Barnes, Sr. by Earl Granville on Nov. 10, 1757 and conveyed by him to Jacob Barnes, Jr. Wit: John Moore and Moses Harrell.

DB 1-88 THOMAS ATKINSON of Nash Co. to JOSEPH CURL of Edgecombe Co., Feb. 11, 1779, for 440 pds. current money the 150 acre tract and plantation whereon he then lived on the north side of Compass Creek adjoining Joseph Exum and William Spight, it being part of a tract taken up by Wm. Spight, conveyed to Jacob Underwood, and by him conveyed to Thomas Atkinson. Wit: Joseph Exum, Wilson Kurl, and Solomon Edwards.

DB 1-89 JAMES LOCKHART of Johnston Co. to SOLOMON CARTER of Nash Co., March 19, 1778, for 100 pds. proc. money a tract of 100 acres on the south side of Tar River at the mouth of Horse Pen Branch adjoining William West. Wit: Thomas Carter and Thomas Price.

DB 1-90 JAMES SMITH, SR. of Edgecombe Co. to JAMES DOUGLAS of same, Aug. 10, 1775, for 10 pds. Virginia money 50 acres adjoining James Hogg, James Douglas, Robert Clark, and Arthur Bell, it being part of a tract granted to him by Lackfield Adams. Wit: James Hogg and George Mills.

DB 1-91 JAMES DOUGLAS and wife, DORCAS DOUGLAS, of Edgecombe Co. to JOHN WILLIAMS of Halifax Co., Dec. 19, 1777, for 55 pds. Virginia money a tract of 150 acres adjoining Smith, Davis, Bell, and Robert Clark, which land was conveyed to said Douglas by two deeds from James Smith, Sr. Wit: Joseph Ward and Lewis Pitts.

DB 1-93 THOMAS HERSEY of Edgecombe Co. to BENJAMIN SMITH of same, Dec. 23, 1771, for 13 pds. 6 sh. 8 p. proc. money a tract of 100 acres on the north side of Sapony Creek adjoining Barnes, which land was formerly conveyed by Moses Atkinson to Thomas Hersey. Wit: Thomas Adkins and William Gyner.

DB 1-93 JOHN BRANTLY of Nash Co. to MATTHEW BRANTLY of same, March 10, 1779. for 200 pds. current money a tract of 112½ acres on the south side of Great Sapony Swamp. Wit: Marcom Cooper, William Whitton, and Henry Braswell.

DB 1-94 STEPHEN WATKINS of Edgecombe Co. to MOSES HARRELL of Nash Co., Feb. 7, 1779, for 50 pds. proc. money 150 acres on both sides of Kirby's Creek adjoining the Folsom Road and Thomas' Road, it being part of a tract granted to Thomas Williams on March 2, 1761. Wit: Nicholas Skinner and William Barnes.

DB 1-96 JACOB FLOWERS and wife, ELIZABETH FLOWERS, of Edgecombe Co. to DUNCAN LAMON of same, March 6, 1775, for 200 pds. proc. money a 200 acre plantation on the south side of Tar River adjoining Lamon and Dorman's Branch; also, for 100 pds. another tract of 85 acres on the north side of Tar River and, for 40 pds., a tract of 205 acres on Maple Creek and Polecat Branch adjoining Denson and the road leading to the Lamon's Ferry Crossing. Wit: John Cohoon, Jesse Pridgen, and Arch'd Lamon.

DB 1-96 CORNELIUS JOHNSON of Nash Co. to STEPHEN COBB of Dobbs Co., N.C., March 6, 1779, for 200 pds. current money 371 acres on both sides of Contentnea Creek, it being a tract granted to Benjamin Johnson on Aug. 1, 1762. Wit: Sampson Johnson, Sarah Johnson, and Ben Cobb.

DB 1-97 JAMES DOUGLAS of Edgecombe Co. to EDWARD COOPER of same, April 22, 1775, for 50 pds. a tract of 60 acres on Beaver Dam Swamp adjoining the Dawset Wall line and the Round Stone Swamp, it being part of a tract conveyed to James Douglas, Sr. by John Jones on Feb. 14, 1771. Wit: W. S. Mearns, Matthew Drake, and Jethro Denson.

DB 1-98 JOSEPH JONES of Nash Co. to LILAH GRIFFEN of same, Dec. 31, 1778, for 50 pds. proc. money 50 acres adjoining Horn, Hilliard, and John Jones, it being part of a tract conveyed to Mary Williams by Ebenezer Folsome on July 24, 1764. Wit: John Jones, William Lewis, and Benjamin Whitfield.

DB 1-99 SAMUEL SKINNER, SR. of Nash Co. to MITCHEL MORRISS of same, Jan. 4, 1780, for 580 pds. 10 sh. current money a 256 acre plantation on the north side of Stony Creek adjoining Elijah Revel, Henry Horn, and Thomas Hunter, it being part of a grant for 692 acres by Earl Granville to John Moore, Sr. on June 1, 1762, conveyed by deed to John Moore, Jr. on June 3, 1773. and conveyed by him to Elisha Moore on May 3, 1777. Wit: Thomas Morriss, James Jameson, and Wm. Andrews.

DB 1-101 MOSES HARRELL of Nash Co. to WILLIAM WORRELL of same, Nov. 3, 1779, for 600 pds. current money 150 acres on both sides of Kirby's Creek and Folsom's Road, it being part of a tract granted to Thomas Williams on March 2, 1761. Wit: Edward Gandy and Micajah Thomas.

DB 1-101 MATTHEW MASSINGALE of Nash Co. to WILLIAM HOOKS of same, Nov. 18, 1779, for 800 pds. a tract of 240 acres adjoining James Massingale, Jr. and John Passmore. it being part of a grant to David Chapman by Earl Granville on March 16, 1761. Wit: Eliiah Powell, Arthur Braswell, and Elizabeth Powell.

DB 1-102 THOMAS WHITFIELD of Nash Co. to JOHN

WHITEHOUSE of same, April 4, 1780, for 50 pds. current money 100 acres adjoining Whitfield, Whitehouse, and John Whiddon, it being part of a tract granted to him by the State of N.C. on Nov. 10, 1779. Wit: Wm. Hall and David Pridgen

DB 1-103 ISHAM GANDY of Nash Co. to WILLIAM WHITTON of same, March 10, 1780, for 400 pds. current money a tract of 100 acres on the north side of Little Sapony Creek at the bridge adjoining Whitton. Wit: Nathan Boddie, Wm. Hall, and A. Arrington.

DB 1-105 THOMAS WHITFIELD, SR. of Nash Co. to WILLIAM WHIDON of same, April 1, 1780, for 100 pds. current money a 300 plantation on the south side of Ready Branch adjoining Whidon and Holland, it being part of a tract granted to him by the State of N.C. on Nov. 10, 1779. Wit: Wm. Hall and Jos. Exum.

DB 1-106 WILLIAM WHIDDON, SR. of Nash Co. to WILLIAM WHIDON, JR. of same, Oct. 14, 1779, for 100 pds. current money a tract of 100 acres on the northwest side of Sapony Swamp. Wit: Marcom Cooper and Sarah Cooper.

DB 1-107 OSWELL LANGLEY of Nash Co. to WILLIAM WHIDDON, JR. of same, Aug. 24, 1770 (?), for 100 pds. current money a tract of 212 acres on the north side of Sapony Swamp adjoining William Whiddon and James Jones.   Wit: John Evans, John Whiddon, and Arthur Edwards.

DB 1-108 WILLIAM WORRELL of Nash Co. to WILLIAM WHIDDON of same, 1780, for 1600 pds. a tract of 360 acres in the fork of Sapony Creek adjoining William Barrendene. Wit: Wm. Hall.

DB 1-109 ANN DORTCH of Nash Co. to her son, LEWIS DORTCH, of same, Jan. 26, 1779, one negro, one horse, and furniture, after her death Wit: Wm. Sandeford and Thomas Hanis.

DB 1-109 WILSON CURL of Nash Co. to ISAAC HORN of same, Sept. 27, 1780, for 1000 pds. 100 acres on the north side of Compass Creek adjoining his own line, it being part of two tracts granted to Stephen Hamlin and Wilson Curll. Wit: Lewis Hines and Joel Horn.

DB 1-111 HENRY WATKINS of Nash Co. to LEWIS HINES of same, Aug. 30, 1779, for 500 pds. current money a 100 acre plantation on Compass Creek adjoining Henry Horn, Lewis Hines, and Wilson Curl, it being part of a tract granted to Jacob Whitehead by Earl Granville on March 16, 1761 containing 650 acres. It was conveyed by Whitehead to Francis Jinkins on Feb. 11, 1762, by Jinkins to Henry Horn on Aug. 4, 1768, and by Henry Horn to said Henry Watkins. Wit: Wilson Curl and Lewis Moore.

DB 1-111 MICAJAH THOMAS and wife, ANNE THOMAS, of Nash Co. to DUNCAN LAMON, EDWARD MOORE, MATTHEW DRAKE, NATHAN BODDIE, and ARTHUR ARRINGTON, Commissioners for letting the public building for the county, April 4, 1780, for 10 pds. current money 3 acres on the south side of Peachtree Creek. Wit: Edward Gandy and James Cain.

DB 1-112 JOHN MOORE of Nash Co. to HENRY WATKINS

of same, Aug. 30, 1779, for 500 pds. 200 acres on both sides of Kirby's Creek adjoining Moore, Wilson Curl, Micajah Revel, and Emmanuel Skinner, it being part of a 700 acre tract granted to John Moore by Earl Granville on June 1, 1762. Wit: Wilson Curl and Lewis Hines.

DB 1-114 LEMUEL WRIGHT of Nash Co. to JOSEPH WRIGHT of same, March 30, 1780, for 8 pds. proc. money a tract of 300 acres on both sides of the Great Swamp adjoining Lemuel Wright. Wit: Mikel Horn and Jacob Boyett.

DB 1-115 WILLIAM BLUNT of Halifax Co. to ARTHUR DAVIS of same, Jan. 4, 1780, for 400 pds. a tract of 183 acres in Nash and Halifax counties on the south side of Fishing Creek adjoining Blunt and Gainer. Wit: William Davis, Peter Robertson, and David Marshall.

DB 1-115 WILLIAM HADLEY of Halifax Co. to DIOCLESION DAVIS of Edgecombe Co., March 25, 1777, for 22 pds. proc. money 150 acres in Edgecombe Co. on the south side of Fishing Creek adjoining John Deens and Lewis Davis, which land was purchased by said Hadley from Jacob Matthews on Sept. 27, 1762. Wit: Arthur Davis, David Marshall, and James Ward.

DB 1-116 WILLIAM HENDRICK of Nash Co. to WILLIAM BRIANT of Edgecombe Co., Oct. 17, 1779, for 600 pds. current money a tract of 201 acres. Wit: Matthew Carter and John Whitfield.

DB 1-117 STEPHEN YOUNG of Nash Co. to HENRY PEED of same, April 3, 1780, for 100 pds. a tract of 164 acres on the north side of Peachtree Creek adjoining Henry Peed, Henry Braswell, and Isaac Bass, which land was granted to Stephen Young on Nov. 10, 1779. Wit: Thomas Morris, Mathew Mishan, and Preston Morris.

DB 1-118 BENJAMIN CRUMPLER and wife, FERUBISE CRUMPLER, of Nash Co. to DISEY TAYLOR of same, Dec. 21, 1779, for 150 pds. a 1-6 part of the 196 acre tract on which she then lived, the 96 acres conveyed by deed from Earl Granville on Feb. 12, 1762 and the other 100 acres by deed from John Scott dated Nov. 29, 1752. Wit: Edward Moore, Simon Strickland, and West Crumpler.

DB 1-119 SOLOMON VESTER of Nash Co. to PETER ETHERIDGE of same, March 31, 1780, for 500 pds. a tract of 250 acres on the north side of Sapony Creek on the Bare Branch adjoining Thomas Richardson and Nathan Boddie. Wit: Matthias Manning, Jr. and William Vester.

DB 1-120 ISAAC BASS of Nash Co. to JETHRO ,BASS of same, Jan. 25, 1780, for 5 pds. proc. money a tract of 200 acres adjoining Isaac Bass and Little Peachtree Creek. Wit: Denis Lineham, Thomas Hodge, and Stephen Young.

DB 1-121 ABRAHAM BASS of Nash Co. to SION BASS of same, Jan. 20, 1779, for 10 pds. proc. money 120 acres on both sides of Tumbling Run adjoining Abraham Bass and Samuel Bridgers, it being a tract conveyed to Abraham Bass by James West. Wit: John Bass and William Bridgers.

DB 1-123 JAMES BRYANT to ISAAC BASS, March 29, 1780, for 1000 pds. a tract of 225 acres on the north side of Peachtree Creek adjoining Isaac Bass, Charles Brown, and Thomas, which land was granted to James Bryant by the State of N.C. on Sept. 10, 1779. Wit: Nathan Boddie, Bennett Boddie, and Samson Powell.

DB 1-123 WILLIAM RICHARDSON of Nash Co. to JAMES MASSINGALE of same, March 17, 1780, for 10 pds. a tract of 100 acres on the Back Swamp. Wit: Henry Braswell, Samson Powell, and Walker Massingale.

DB 1-124 WILLIAM HILL of Chatham Co. to ABRAHAM BASS, Dec. 30, 1779, for 10 pds. current money 300 acres adjoining Abraham Bass, it being part of a tract granted since the fourth year of independence. Wit: Lewis Hill and Peter Hedgepeth.

DB 1-125 WILLIAM HILL of Chatham Co. to THOMAS LEWIS, Dec. 31, 1779, for 5 pds. current money 160 acres adjoining Sion Hill, Lewis Hill, Abraham Bass, and William Bridgers, it being part of a tract granted since the fourth year of independence. Wit: Lewis Hill and Joel Walker.

DB 1-126 STEPHEN BACHELOR and wife, MARGARET BACHELOR, of Nash Co. to JOHN WARREN of same, July 1, 1779, for 50 pds. a tract of 40 acres on the south side of Great Sapony Swamp. Wit: Matthias Manning, Jr.

DB 1-128 ISHAM HINES of Nash Co. to MILLS TAYLOR of same, Dec. 28, 1779, for 1000 pds. 319 acres on the south side of Beach Run adjoining William Taylor, it being part of a tract Isham Hines bought of Roger Jenkins. Wit: Joseph Exum and John Exum.

DB 1-129 JAMES CAIN of Nash Co. to ISAAC TALBERT of same, April 20, 1779, for (?) a tract of 234 acres on the south side of Lane's Swamp. Wit: John Scott and Margaret Scott.

DB 1-129 JOSEPH LINSEY to DAVID BALLARD, Jan. 22, 1780, for 1500 pds. current money 100 acres on Little Peachtree Creek adjoining William Linsey. it being part of a tract granted to Abner Hill on Dec. 30, 1760. Wit: William Linsey and Benjamin Tucker.

DB 1-130 WILSON CURL of Nash Co. to LEWIS HINES of same, Sept. 27, 1780. for 10,000 pds. proc. money 300 acres on Compass Creek adjoining Wilson Curl and Exum, it being parts of three tracts of land granted to Patrick Mecain, Stephen Hamlin, and Wilson Curl. Wit: Isaac Horn and Joel Horn.

DB 1-131 JOHN TURNER of Nash Co. to THOMAS MORRIS of same, July 4, 1780, for 800 pds. current money a tract of 143 acres on the Back Swamp adjoining Willaby Manning, William Boddie, and Thomas, which land was granted to John Turner on Nov. 10, 1779. Wit: William Wheddon and John Evans.

DB 1-133 WILLIAM RICHARDSON of Nash Co. to HENRY BRASWELL of same, March 17, 1780, for 10 pds. a tract of 295 acres on the Back Swamp adjoining James Massingale, Richardson, and Isaac Bass. Wit: James Massingale, Samson Powell, and Walker Massingale.

DB 1-134 SAMPSON POWELL of Nash Co. to WILLABE MANNING of same, June 8, 1780, for 1000 pds. a tract of 640 acres on both sides of Little Peachtree Creek adjoining William Harris and Richard Deans. Wit: Henry Braswell, Arthur Braswell, and Martha Braswell.

DB 1-134 JOSEPH WILLIAMSON and wife, ANN WILLIAMSON, to THOMAS WOODARD, April 3, 1780, for 250 pds. current money 225 acres on both sides of Contentnea Creek, part in Johnston Co. and part in Edgecombe or Nash Co. adjoining William Maple and the Reedy Branch, it being part of a tract granted to Thomas Maple on March 25, 1752. Wit: Luke Woodard, Hardy Williamson. and Sarah Williamson.

DB 1-135 JAMES TUCKER of Nash Co. to DANIEL DEENS of same, Nov. 22, 1780, for 3000 pds. current money a tract of 275 acres on the south side of Little Sapony Creek adjoining Green Hill. Wit: Matthias Manning, Jr., James Tucker, and Arthur O'Neal.

DB 1-136 JACOB STALLIONS of Nash Co. to BRITTAIN GANDY of same, Dec. 18, 1780, for 10.000 pds. current money a tract of 200 acres on the north side of Tar River adjoining David Bunn. Wit: Wm. Hall and Miles Davis.

DB 1-137 MARK WALL, of Nash Co. and wife, MARY WALL, to JAMES TUCKER, SR. of same, Sept. 28, 1779, for 500 pds. a tract of 225 acres on the south side of Little Sapony Creek adjoining Daniel Deens, the Tarkill Branch, Arthur O'Neal. and John Manning. Wit: Matthias Manning, Jr.. Sala Manning, and Sarah Rose.

DB 1-138 ABRAHAM RICKS of Nash Co. to JACOB RICKS of same, Aug. 19, 1780, for 50 pds. proc. money a 400 acre plantation adjoining his own line. Wit: Jacob Dickinson and Mourning Dickinson.

DB 1-139 UZZELL GOODSON of Nash Co. to SAMUEL WESTRAY of same. Dec. 16. 1784, for 16 pds. 150 acres adjoining Whitehouse, it being part of a tract granted to George Goodson by Earl Granville on Oct. 15, 1754. Wit: Micajah Thomas and Elijah Boddie.

DB 1-140 ISRAEL WEST of Halifax Co. to THOMAS HUNTER of Nash Co., June 18, 1784, for 20 pds. Virginia money a tract of 150 acres on the north side of Stony Creek at Laseter's Branch adjoining David Strickling's former line and Thomas Willis, which land fell to the said Israel West by the death of his father. Wit: James Daniel, Howell Ellen. and Richard Thomas.

DB 1-140 JAMES TUCKER, SR. to ARTHUR O'NEAL, both of Nash Co., Feb. 16, 1785, for 5 pds. specie a tract of 40 acres on Sapony Swamp adjoining said Tucker. Wit: Wilson Vick and Elijah Boddie.

DB 1-142 SAMUEL CARTER of Nash Co. to his son, MATHEW CARTER, Oct. 4, 1784, for 10 sh. specie and love and affection, all of his natural and temporal living, namely: eight negroes, household furniture, livestock, and crops. He also gave him power of attorney. Wit: John Hinniant, William Buntin, and Charles Carter.

DB 1-143 SAMPSON POWELL of Nash Co. to NATHAN BODDIE of same, Feb. 17, 1785, for 50 pds. 350 acres adjoining Thomas Morris and the Parrish Branch, it being part of a tract granted to Joshua Womble by Earl Granville and conveyed by him to Micajah Thomas. Wit: Thomas Hunter and Samuel Westray.

DB 1-144 PRISCILLA WELLS of Nash Co. to JOSHUA WELLS of same, Feb. 14, 1785, for 10 pds. specie all that which her husband, Steph Wells, gave and bequeathed to her in his will including land, furniture, and livestock. Wit: Joseph Crowell, William Reasons, and Thomas Wells.

DB 1-145 SAMUEL BRYANT of Nash Co. to SOLOMON STRICKLAND of same, April 5, 1784, for 40 pds. specie a tract of 300 acres on the south side of Turkey Creek at the mouth of Solomon Strickland's spring branch. Wit: Wm. S. Mearns and John Rice.

DB 1-145 JACOB JOYNER and wife, MILLY JOYNER, to BURRELL JOYNER of Nash Co., March 23, 1784, for 20 pds. specie a tract of 100 acres on the east side of Sapony Creek adjoining the March Branch, William Eason, and Arthur Allen. Wit: D. Lamon and Brittain Smith.

DB 1-146 EDWARD PURSSELL of Nash Co. to JEREMIAH ETHRIDGE of same, Feb. 11, 1785, for 50 pds. specie 230 acres on the north side of Little Sapony Swamp, it being part of a tract granted to Newet Lane on Sept. 17, 1744. Wit: Daniel Taylor and Jacob Carter.

DB 1-148 DELILAH GRIFFIN of Nash Co. to JOSIAH JOHNSON of same, Dec. 4. 1784. for 69 pds. 4 sh. 60 acres on the south side of Fishing Creek adjoining Samuel Davis, which tract was purchased by Delilah Griffin from John Portris. Wit: Hardy Griffin, Dioclesan Davis, and Samuel Davis.

DB 1-149 SION BASS of Nash Co. to JOHN GAY of same, March 15, 1784, for 25 pds. Virginia money 100 acres adjoining John Pasmore and John Gay, it being part of a tract granted to Sion Bass by Gov. Richard Caswell in 1779. Wit: Benjamin Boon, Elijah Powell, and Michael Collins.

DB 1-150 MICHAEL HORN of Nash Co. to JOHN DEW of same, Feb. 3, 1785, for 40 sh. specie a parcel of 2½ acres on the north side of Toisnot Swamp at Dew's Ford, it being intended for use by John Dew to build a mill. Wit: Dempsey Dawson and Duncan Dew.

DB 1-151 WILLIAM WHIDDON and wife, MARY WHIDDON, of Nash Co. to PETER BALLARD of same, Jan. 4, 1785, for 77 pds. 10 sh. Virginia money a tract of 112 acres on the south side of Great Sapony Swamp. Wit: Marcom Cooper and Isom Gandy.

DB 1-152 RICHARD VICK of Nash Co. to HENRY VICK of same, April 6, 1784, for 5 sh. specie a tract of 400 acres on the south side of Stony Creek adjoining Watkins, Skinner, and Wester. Wit: Joseph Arrington and John Davis.

DB 1-153 JESSE JINKINS to HARDYMAN POPE, June 1, 1784, for 55 pds. a tract of 250 acres adjoining Reuben Taylor, Nathan Atkinson, Joseph J. Clinch, Spier Knight, and said Pope. Wit: Joseph J. Clinch and Joseph Arrington.

DB 1-153 JACOB DUCK and wife, SARAH DUCK, of Nash Co. to THOMAS WOODARD, SR. of same, June 7, 1784, for 90 pds. specie 125 acres of land. The 100 acres was granted to Francis Mountree by patent, on Contentnea Creek at the mouth of Mill Creek, and the 25 acres was part of a tract granted to Thomas Maples on Contentnea Creek. Wit: John Falk, Luke Woodard, and Jesse Woodard.

DB 1-155 WILLIAM LINSEY of Nash Co. to DREWRY SAVAGE of same, Jan. 7, 1784, for 50 pds. a 150 acre plantation on the north side of Little Peachtree Creek adjoining Linsey, Micajah Thomas, and James Moore, it being part of a 300 acre tract granted to said Linsey on Nov. 10, 1779. Wit: David Ballard, Benjamin Mannin, and Kinchen Savage.

DB 1-156 HENRY BARLOW of Nash Co. to PETER BALLARD of same, Feb. 17, 1785, for 60 pds. specie a tract of 90 acres on the south side of Sapony Creek adjoining John Brantley. Edward Ballard, and Benjamin Smith. Wit: Wilson Vick and Amos Gandy.

DB 1-157 JOHN GRIFFIN and wife, SARAH GRIFFIN, of Nash Co. to their four children, WILLIE, ALLEN, LEWIS, and MARY GRIFFIN, Aug. 16, 1784, for love and affection two negroes and their increase. Wit: Arthur Arrington and Hardy Griffin.

DB 1-157 WILLIAM RUFFIN of Northampton Co. to DANIEL DEENS of Edgecombe Co., Dec. 4, 1775, for 30 pds. Virginia money a tract of 200 acres on the north side of Sapony Swamp. Wit: Demps. Watts and Ozwell Langly.

DB 1-158 ELISHA WRIGHT and wife, SARAH WRIGHT, of Nash Co. to JOHN CHITTY of Southampton Co., Va., Feb. 18, 1784, for 86 pds. 13 sh. 4 p. a tract of 100 acres on the east side of Pig Basket Creek. Wit: John Vick and Jiles Joyner.

DB 1-159 SAMUEL LASETER of Nash Co. to HANSEL LASETER of same, March 28, 1781, for 1000 pds. and paternal love and affection for his son, Hansel Laseter, a tract of 160 acres on the south side of Fishing Creek adjoining Samuel Laseter, the Jonas Branch, and Joseph Hayes, it being part of a tract granted to Samuel Laseter by Earl Granville on Oct. 15, 1761. Wit: R. Clark and William Cooper.

DB 1-160 JAMES GRICE of Johnston Co. to THEOPHILUS GRICE of Nash Co., July 24, 1784, for 10 sh. pro. money a tract of 150 acres on the north side of Contentnea Creek, it being a grant to John Hinnient on April 20, 1745 which descended from him to James Grice by deed of gift to his daughter, Elizabeth Grice, wife of James Grice. Wit: Thomas Horn, Jeremiah Nichols, and Lewis Grice.

DB 1-162 LEWIS DORTCH and wife, ANN DORTCH, of Nash Co. to ISAAC NEWSOM of same, July 23, 1784, for 300 pds. a tract of 200 acres on the north side of Swift Creek adjoining Wm. Dortch, James Nelson, and Thomas Hart. Wit: Wm. Merritt, John Jones, and Absolom Sauls.

DB 1-162 LEWIS DORTCH and wife, ANN DORTCH, of Nash Co. to ISAAC NEWSOM of same, July 23, 1784, for 100 pds. a tract of 150 acres on the north side of Swift Creek. Wit: Wm. Merritt, John Jones, and Absolom Sauls.

DB 1-163 HARDY STRICKLAND of Nash Co. to SOLOMON STRICKLAND of same, April 6, 1784, for 40 pds. specie a tract of 400 acres on Turkey Creek adjoining Jacob Strickland and Samuel Bryant. Wit: Edward Nicholson and Thos. Viverett.

DB 1-164 WILLIAM ANDREWS of Franklin Co. to HENRY BANES of Nash Co., Sept. 6, 1784, for 30 pds. a tract of 200 acres on both sides of Little Turkey Creek adjoining Benjamin Tucker, Cornelius Taylor's spring branch, and Banes' Branch. Wit: Wm. Lancaster, John Harris, and John Townson.

DB 1-165 CHRISTOPHER PRITCHETT and wife, PRISCILLA PRITCHETT, of Halifax Co. to JOHN BATTLE of Edgecombe Co., Oct. 5, 1784, for 5 pds. in gold and silver 100 acres on or near Compass Creek adjoining Thomas Thorp and Wilson Curl, it being part of a tract granted to Thomas Williams on Nov. 10, 1779. Wit: Elisha Battle and Jacob Battle.

DB 1-166 ALEXANDER THOMPSON of Nash Co. to REUBEN TAYLOR of same, Dec. 12, 1783, for 130 pds. specie a 180 acre plantation on the north side of Beach Run, it being part of two tracts, one conveyed by William Whitehead to Jacob Whitehead on June 6, 1750 and back to William Whitehead on Sept. 26, 1759; the other being part of a tract granted to John Jinkins on May 1, 1762 and conveyed by him to said Whitehead on March 2, 1764; then the two said tracts were conveyed from Wm. Whitehead to Alexander Thompson on Sept. 24, 1771. Wit: Joseph Exum and Priscilla Exum.

DB 1-167 RICHARD THOMAS of Nash Co. to MOURNING THOMAS of same, Nov. 23, 1784, for 5 sh., a tract of 100 acres on the north side of Stony Creek adjoining Dickeson, Richard Thomas, and Thomas Whitfield. Wit: Wilson Vick and Jethro Thomas.

DB 1-168 HENRY DEENS of Nash Co. to JAMES GRIFFIN of same, March 15. 1783, for 50 pds. a 200 acre plantation on the north side of Turkey Creek adjoining Wm. Harris and William Andrews. Wit: Ann Drake, Newsome Jones, and Matthew Drake.

DB 1-170 SAMPSON POWELL to WILLIAM BODDIE, Feb. 4, 1785, for 80 pds. current money a tract of 350 acres, it being part of a Granville grant. Wit: Nathan Boddie and Micaiah Thomas.

DB 1-171 EDWARD JOHNSON of Orangeburg District, S C. to BENJAMIN BUNN of Nash Co., April 30, 1784, for 20 pds. specie a 40 acre plantation on the north side of Maple Creek adjoining Edward Moore's old line and Benja. Bunn, where William Johnson formerly lived. Wit: Matthew Roberss (?), James Johnson, and Benjamin Arrington.

DB 1-172 JETHRO DENSON of Nash Co. to EDMOND COOPER of same, Jan. 26, 1785, for 34 pds. 16 sh. specie a tract of 200 acres on the south side of Beaver Dam Swamp adjoining William Wright, Isaac Hilliard, and William Hackney. Wit: Mark Mason, Jr. and Henry Freeman.

DB 1-174 FRANCIS LOCUS of Nash Co. to FRANCIS ANDERSON of same, Feb. 11, 1785, for 40 pds. specie a tract of 300 acres on the north side of Turkey Creek and south side of Tar River adjoining Locus and Chapman. Wit: William Chapman, Joseph Powell, and James Keff.

DB 1-174 JAMES BELL of Nash Co. to JOSHUA BUTT of Halifax Co., Oct. 25, 1783, for 66 pds. 13 sh. 4 p. a tract of 200 acres adjoining Arthur Bell, Jonas Williams, John Cooper, Lot Etheridge, and Elias Bell, it being part of a tract granted to Joseph Passmore on Oct. 15, 1761. Wit: William Etheridge and James Grant.

DB 1-175 JOHN MANNING of Edgecombe Co. to JOSEPH BATCHELOR of Nash Co., Oct. 9, 1784, for 30 pds. 13 sh. 4 p. a 200 acre tract adjoining Thomas Harbert and the Sike's Branch, it being the upper part of a tract granted by Earl Granville to William Defnal on March 2, 1761, conveyed from Defnal to Wm. Pittman, and from Pittman to said Manning. Wit: Samuel Eason and William Eason.

DB 1-176 JAMES GRIFFIN of Nash Co. to MATTHEW DRAKE of same, April 12, 1785, for 68 pds. specie a tract of 200 acres on the north side of Turkey Creek adjoining Wm. Harris and Wm. Andrews. conveyed to said Griffin by Henry Deans on March 15, 1783. Wit: Matthew Williams and Jeremiah Buntin.

DB 1-177 JAMES MASSENGILL and wife, ELIZABETH MASSENGILL, of Nash Co. to JOHN GAY of Franklin Co., Mar. 16, 1781, for 1000 pds. current money a tract of 200 acres at the mouth of the Quarter Branch and on the Back Swamp. Wit: Matthew Counsel. Benjamin Boon, and Susanah (?) Boon.

DB 1-178 ROBERT PYLAND and wife, CAROLINE PYLAND, of Nash Co. to ARTHUR ARRINGTON. JR. of same, Sept. 26, 1778, for 20 pds. proc. money 45 acres on the north side of Swift Creek adjoining Arthur Arrington and the Parker Branch, it being part of a tract granted to Thomas Bell by Earl Granville on June 20, 1749. Wit: Hardy Griffin and Wm. Lewis.

DB 1-179 JACOB DICKENSON and wife, MOURNING DICKENSON, of Nash Co. to WILLIAM BATCHELOR of same, Jan. 3, 1782, for 90 pds. hard money a tract of 200 acres on the north side of the Crooked Branch and on the Jacob Dickenson line. Wit: John Bonds and Thomas Hunter.

DB 1-180 BENJAMIN BRIDGERS of Nash Co. to his son, BENJAMIN BRIDGERS, of same, Nov. 23, 1780, for love and affection a certain amount of livestock and furniture. Wit: Thomas Lewis and Dioclesian Davis.

DB 1-181 WILLIAM WORRELL of Nash Co. to JOSEPH CURL of Edgecombe Co., Oct. 16, 1781, for 43 pds. Virginia money 150 acres on both sides of Kirby's Creek adjoining the Folsom Road and Thomas Road, it being part of a tract granted to Thomas Williams on March 2, 1761. Wit: Nicholas Skinner and James Jamison.

DB 1-181 WILLIAM BATCHELOR of Nash Co. to THOMAS HUNTER of same, Jan. 1, 1782, for 150 pds. 200 acres on the north side of Stony Creek on O'Neal's Branch adjoining William Barnes and Joel Pittman, it being part of a tract said Batchelor bought of Wm. Horn, which said Horn bought of Benja. O'Neal, and part of another tract that said Horn bought of William Pittman. Wit: Jacob Dickenson, John Bonds, and William Skinner.

DB 1-182 JOHN LINDSEY of Nash Co. to SAMUEL JONES of Franklin Co., April 4, 1780, for 1000 pds. current money a 100 acre plantation adjoining Thomas Tucker, it being part of a tract granted to Abner Hill on Aug. 1, 1762. Wit: Benjamin Tucker and William Linsey.

DB 1-184 JACOB DICKENSON and wife, MOURNING DICKENSON, of Edgecombe Co. to GEORGE WIMBERLY, June 29, 1782, for 30 pds. specie a tract of 100 acres of land. Wit: Elias Fort and Milbrey Horn.

DB 1-185 JAMES MASSINGILL and wife, ANN MASSINGILL, of Nash Co. to MARK MASSINGILL of same, Sept. 29, 1780, for 100 pds. a tract of 100 acres on the Back Swamp adjoining William Hooks. Wit: John Gay, William Richardson, and Elizabeth Massingill.

DB 1-186 WILLIAM SPIGHT and wife, SARAH SPIGHT, of Nash Co. to LEWIS TREVATHAN of Edgecombe Co., Feb. 15, 1783, for 39 pds. Virginia money 263 acres on the north side of Compass Creek adjoining John Exum, Lewis Hines, Reuben Taylor, and Wm. Spight, it being part of a tract granted to said Wm. Spight by deed in 1761. Wit: Joseph Exum, Priscilla Exum, Sarah Horn, and Nicholas Skinner.

DB 1-187 JOEL PITMAN of Nash Co. to ISOME HINES of same, March 30, 1782, for 110 pds. Virginia money 110 acres on Stony Creek adjoining Thomas Hunter, William Barnes, and James Barnes, it being part of a tract taken up by Andrew Ross on Feb. 28, 1761. Wit: Nicholas Skinner and Sarah Skinner.

DB 1-188 MARY WILLIAMS of Nash Co. to JOSEPH JONES of same, Feb. 4, 1778, for 8 pds. proc. money 50 acres adjoining Horn and Hilliard, it being part of a tract conveyed to her from Ebenezer Folsome by deed on July 24, 1764. Wit: W. S. Mearns, Wm. Williams, and Wm. Battle.

DB 1-189 ABRAHAM BASS and wife, MARY BASS, of Nash Co. to STEPHEN WEBB, Feb. 26, 1781, for 500 pds. Virginia money a tract of 100 acres of land. Wit: John Gay, James Richardson, and Sion Bass.

DB 1-190 JAMES BAKER of Nash Co. to CHRISTOPHER BALLARD of same, April 2, 1782, for 100 pds. current money a tract of 223 acres on the south side of Sapony Creek adjoining Ben Smith, John Joyner, Thomas Kersey, and Samuel Bottoms. Wit: Wm. Hall and James Battle.

DB 1-191 DANIEL DEANS and ELIZABETH DEANS to GEORGE SUTTON, 1780, for 37 pds. 10 sh. Virginia money a 275 acre plantation on Little Sapony Swamp adjoining Green Hill. Wit: John White and John Watts.

DB 1-192 JACOB STALLINGS of Nash Co. to NICHOLAS SKINNER of same, Jan. 25, 1781, for 9000 pds. a 100 acre plantation on the south side of Stony Creek, it being the land that Andrew Ross gave to his daughter, Ann, bearing date 1749, adjoining Henry Horn and Revel. Wit: James Jameson and Matthew Brantley.

DB 1-193 BRITTAIN GANDY of Nash Co. to NICHOLAS SKINNER of same, Jan. 25, 1781, for 9000 pds. a tract of 500 acres on south side of Stony Creek adjoining David Bunn and the river. Wit: James Jameson and Matthew Brantley.

DB 1-194 WILLIAM HORN of Bertie Co. to NICHOLAS SKINNER of Nash Co., Jan. 4, 1782, for 30 pds. 10 sh. in silver or gold 37 acres on Stony Creek adjoining Thomas Hunter and Nicholas Skinner, it being part of the land taken up by Andrew Ross on March 25, 1749. Wit: John Devanport, Joel Horn, and Josiah Horn.

DB 1-195 THOMAS WHITFIELD of Nash Co. to REUBEN WHITFIELD of same, Sept. 27, 1781, for 100 pds. a 300 acre plantation adjoining Whiddon, the Ready Branch, and John Whitehouse. Wit: Jacob Dickenson and Solomon Whitfield.

DB 1-196 JONAS WILLIAMS of Edgecombe Co. to BILLY WILLIAMS of same, Sept. 25, 1775, for 66 pds. 13 sh. 4 p. proc. money a tract of 200 acres on the south side of Toisnot Swamp adjoining William Horn, David Mann, and the Beaver Dam Branch. Wit: Roland Williams. Henry Atkins, and Philander Williams.

DB 1-197 SOLOMON CARTER and wife, ELIZABETH CARTER, of Nash Co. to THOMAS CARTER, April 2, 1780, for 300 pds. 100 acres on the south side of Tar River, it being land that Samuel Edwards sold to Solomon Carter and part of a patent granted to Richard Baley. Wit: Samuel Carter and Susannah Carter.

DB 1-198 DELILAH GRIFFIN of Nash Co. to ISAAC HILLIARD of same, Feb. 9, 1780, for 1000 pds. current money, 50 acres adjoining Hilliard and John Jones, it being part of a tract conveyed from Mary Williams to Joseph Jones on Feb. 4, 1778 and from Joseph Jones to Delilah Griffin by the name of Lilah Griffin on Dec. 31, 1779. Wit: Wm. S. Mearns and Eleas Hilliard.

DB 1-199 MATTHEW CARTER of Johnston Co. to JOHN WHITFIELD, March 22, 1781, for 40 pds. a tract of 380 acres on the north side of Tar River adjoining Micajah Thomas, Joseph Sumner, and Melton. Wit: Samuel Bryant and Brittain Gandy.

DB 1-200 WILLIAM WHITEHEAD of Nash Co. to BENNETT WHITEHEAD of same, March 30, 1782, for 100 pds. a 457 acre plantation, excepting one grist mill and two acres of land, adjoining William Whitehead's mill swamp, Arthur Whitehead, and John Jones. Wit: Jos. Exum and Benja. Matthews.

DB 1-201 ELIJAH POWELL of Nash Co. to WILLIAM HARRIS of same, Jan. 30, 1782, for 15 pds. a tract of 250 acres on Little Peachtree adjoining Sampson Powell, which land was granted by the State to said Elijah Powell. Wit: Nathan Boddie, Bennett Boddie, and Elijah Boddie.

DB 1-202 EDWARD MOORE of Nash Co. to JAMES MOORE of same, April 2, 1782, for 100 pds. proc. money a tract of 150 acres, it being part of a tract granted to Abner Hill and conveyed by him to James Matthews, bearing date May 23, 1761. Wit: William Lancaster, and Albritain Drake.

DB 1-203 JOHN TURNER of Granville Co. to JAMES MASSINGIL of Nash Co., Feb. 14, 1782, for 10 pds. a tract of 50 acres on the Charles Branch and Thomas' line, it being part of a deed bearing date 1779. Wit: Henry Braswell and Walker Massingil.

DB 1-204 THOMAS HUNTER of Nash Co. to EDWARD WILSON of same, Feb. 25, 1782, for 60 pds. 233 acres on the north side of Stony Creek, it being part of a 700 acre tract granted by Gov. Caswell on Nov. 10, 1779. Wit: Elizabeth Hunter, Henry Vick, and John Wilson.

DB 1-206 ABRAHAM RICKS of Nash Co. to JOEL RICKS of same, Oct. 7, 1782, the 200 acre tract of land where Joel Ricks then lived adjoining Jacob Ricks. Wit: Henry Burne and Thos. Ricks.

DB 1-207 PATIENCE RICKS of Nash Co. to her son, THOMAS RICKS, Oct. 2, 1782, a tract of 80 acres on Little Polecat adjoining Patience Ricks, Joseph Denson, and Joel Ricks. Wit: Joel Ricks and Abraham Ricks.

1-208 JOHN TAYLOR to SOLOMON CARTER of Nash Co., Aug. 15, 1780, for 20 pds. Virginia money a tract of 50 acres on the south side of Tar River adjoining Thomas Carter, Richard Taylor, and Duncan Lamon. Wit: Benjamin Taylor, William Nelson, and Frederick Taylor.

DB 1-209 THOMAS WARRING of Nash Co. to RICHARD BURGE of same, Nov. 28, 1782, for 130 pds. in gold or silver a tract of 265 acres on Hendrick's Branch adjoining Batchelor. Wit: Thomas Carter and Solomon Carter.

DB 1-209 JAMES NORRIS of Johnston Co. to BENJAMIN COBB of Nash Co., Feb. 15, 1780, for 600 pds. proc. money 100 acres on the north side of Contentnea Creek, it being part of a tract granted to John Hinnant on Feb. 23, 1761. Wit: James Hinnant and Badue Eayts.

DB 1-210 WILLIAM AVENT of Nash Co. to THOMAS MANN of same, May 9, 1782, for 3 pds. a parcel of 4 acres on the south side of the Short Swamp adjoining Thomas Mann. Wit: A. Lancaster and Denton Mann.

DB 1-211 JOHN TAYLOR of Nash Co. to MARK STRICKLAND of same, Oct. 7, 1782, for 20 pds. specie a tract of 200 acres on the north side of Turkey Creek adjoining Taylor. Wit: Edward Moore, Joel Lockhart, and Moses Stallings.

DB 1-212 JOHN PORTIS of Nash Co. to DELILAH GRIFF-IN of same, Oct. 5, 1782, for 400 silver dollars 60 acres on the south side of Fishing Creek adjoining Samuel Davis, it being part of a tract which John Portis purchased of George Porter. Wit: Amos Wheless, Wm. Davis, and Benjamin Whitfield.

DB 1-213 SION HILL and wife, DREWSILLA HILL, of Nash Co. to THOMAS LEWIS of same, Oct. 4, 1780, for 1000 pds. current money 250 acres on the south side of Swift Creek, it being part of a tract conveyed from William Hill to his sons, Sion Hill and Lewis Hill, and from Lewis Hill to Sion Hill. Wit: William Hendrick and Wm. Parks.

DB 1-214 DAVID PRIDGEN of Nash Co. to DRURY PRIDGEN of same, July 20, 1782, for 60 pds. Virginia money 150 acres on the south side of Sapony Swamp in two tracts, the latter adjoining Lewis and Eason and was part of a Granville grant on March 25, 1752. Wit: Thomas Viverett and Daniel Wills.

DB 1-215 MICAJAH THOMAS of Nash Co. to WILLIAM HALL of same, Jan. 9, 1783, for 100 pds. in gold or silver three tracts of land: (1) 130 acres on the north side of Sapony Swamp adjoining Benjamin Smith; (2) 320 acres on Bounce's Branch and Little Polecat; (3) 150 acres on the north side of Sapony Swamp. Wit: Edward Moore and Josiah Bunn.

DB 1-216 DANIEL DEANS of Veiss Co. (?) to THOMAS DEANS of Nash Co., Sept. 13, 1782, for 50 pds. proc. money 225 acres on Sapony Swamp, it being part of a tract granted to Zachariah Brown. Wit: John White and Judeth White.

DB 1-217 JACOB WHITEHEAD of Nash Co. to LAZARUS WHITEHEAD of same, Jan. 2, 1783, for 275 pds. 16 sh. 4 p. a tract of 160 acres on the south side of Swift Creek adjoining Joseph John Clinch and Jeremiah Hilliard. Wit: George Blackburn, Wm. Merritt, and Wm. Merritt.

DB 1-218 THOMAS WILSON to ISAAC HILLIARD of Nash Co., Jan. 3, 1783, for 30 pds. specie 75 acres on the north side of Swift Creek adjoining Joseph Matthews, Davis Council, and Benjamin Matthews, it being part of a tract conveyed to William Matthews bv Ebenezer Folsome on Sept. 8, 1762. Wit: Ralph Mason and P. Raynian Massee.

DB 1-219 JOHN JONES of Nash Co. to his ward and nephew, ROBERT JONES, son of Joseph Jones, June 18, 1781, for love and affection 80 acres on the south side of Swift Creek, it being a tract conveyed from Joseph Jones to John Jones on Aug. 20, 1780. Wit: W. S. Mearns, Thomas Griffin, and Newsome Jones, Ann Jones, wife of John Jones, surrendered her right of dower.

DB 1-220 PELEG ROGERS of Wake Co. to WILLIAM CHAPMAN, JR. of Nash Co., Feb. 24, 1782, for 30 pds. specie, a tract of 337 acres on both sides of Turkey Creek, it being a grant from Earl Granville to Peleg Rogers on Oct. 30, 1754. Wit: Burrel Henry, Bartholomew Cornady, and John Rogers.

DB 1-221 HENRY ATKINS of Nash Co. to CHRISTOPHER BALLARD of same, June 29, 1782, for 100 pds. specie a tract of

120 acres on Sapony Swamp at Holland's Branch. Wit: Richard Burge, Edward Moore, and Matthew Brantley.

DB 1-222 RICHARD THOMAS of Nash Co. to WILLIAM RICKS of same, July 1, 1782, for 30 pds. specie a 200 acre plantation on the south side of Long Branch adjoining William Batchelor, John Whitehouse, Goodson, and Jacob Ricks. Wit: Henry Burne and Jacob Dickenson.

DB 1-223 THOMAS HUNTER of Nash Co. to JOSEPH DENSON of same, July 2, 1782, for 20 pds. specie a 200 acre plantation on Maple Creek adjoining Benja. Denson and Ricks. Wit: Frederick Ballard, Josiah Bunn, and Benjamin Denson.

DB 1-224 THOMAS HUNTER of Nash Co. to BENJAMIN DENSON of same, July 2, 1782, for 5 sh. specie a tract of 200 acres adjoining William Joyner, Ricks and the Polecat Branch. Wit: Frederick Ballard, Josiah Bunn, and Amos Gandy.

DB 1-225 THOMAS HUNTER of Nash Co. to JOHN DENSON of same, July 2, 1782, for 5 sh. current money a tract of 240 acres on Maple Creek adjoining William Pouland, Hardy Flowers, and Joiner. it being part of a new survey entered by said Thomas Hunter. Wit: Frederick Ballard, Josiah Bunn, and Benjamin Denson.

DB 1-226 WILLIAMSON ROSS of Nash Co. to JAMES CULPEPPER of same, Feb. 26, 1782, for 50 pds. a tract of 266 acres on the west side of Turkey Creek. Wit: William Lancaster, Sr., William Lancaster, Jr., and Jean Lancaster.

DB 1-227 JACOB DICKINSON and wife, MOURNING DICKINSON, of Nash Co. to HENRY BURNE of same, April 2, 1782, for 200 pds. Virginia money two tracts of land: (1) 199 acres on both sides of Peachtree Creek and Long Branch; (2) 151 acres on Peachtree Creek. Wit: William Ricks, George Wimberly, and Joel Ricks.

DB 1-228 RICHARD THOMAS of Nash Co. to JOHN TARLINGTON of same, July 1, 1782, for 20 pds. specie a 100 acre plantation on the north side of Long Branch adjoining Jacob Ricks, Lewis Ricks, and the public road. Wit: Jacob Dickenson and Henry Burne.

DB 1-229 JAMES COCKS of Nash Co. to his son, JOHN COCKS. Feb. 10. 1781, for paternal love and affection a tract of 100 acres adjoining William Battle, Peter Anderson, and Robert Adams. Wit: William Battle and Peter Anderson.

DB 1-230 WILLIAM WHIDDON of Nash Co. to BRINKLEY GANDY of same, June 16, 1782, for 80 pds. specie a tract of 212 acres on the south side of Sapony Swamp adjoining William Whiddon and James Jones. Wit: Edward Nicholson and Lott Whiddon.

DB 1-231 JOSEPH CURL of Edgecombe Co. to JOHN BONDS of Nash Co., Feb. 1, 1782, for 20 pds. in gold or silver the 150 acre plantation whereon said Bonds then lived, on the north side of Compass Creek adjoining Joseph Exum and William Spight, it being part of a tract that Wm. Spight took up and conveyed to Jacob Underwood, from Underwood to Thomas Atkins, and from Atkins to Joseph Curl. Wit: Thomas Hunter, Priscilla Hunter, and Elizabeth Hunter.

DB 1-232 JAMES TAYLOR and wife, MARY TAYLOR; WILLIAM BAILEY and wife, ELIZABETH BAILEY; SIMON STRICKLAND and wife, DINAH STRICKLAND; JAMES MORPHIS and wife, PATIENCE MORPHIS; DICEY TAYLOR; BENJAMIN CRUMPLER and wife, FEREBESE CRUMPLER, all of Nash Co., to JESSE KENT of same, Feb. 22, 1783, for 80 pds. specie 196 acres on Turkey Creek adjoining Samuel Taylor and Jesse Kent, it being a tract of 96 acres granted to Samuel Taylor on Feb. 12, 1761 and part of a tract granted to John Lott on April 20, 1745 and conveyed to Samuel Taylor on Nov. 29, 1752. Samuel Taylor died intestate and the land became vested in the sisters of said Samuel Taylor as co-heiresses. Wit: Nathan Williams, Richard Four, and John Taylor.

DB 1-233 JOHN ROGERS to LODWICK ALFORD, July 4, 1780, for 4000 pds. current money a tract of 300 acres on the north side of Moccasin Creek. Wit: William Chapman, Simon Williams, Wm. Kerby, and Jacob Dickenson.

DB 1-234 SAMUEL LASITER of Nash Co. to JOHN LASITER of same, March 28, 1781, for 2000 pds. and paternal love and affection for his son, John Lasiter, a tract of 300 acres on the south side of Fishing Creek adjoining Tobias Lasiter, Lott Etheridge, and Cooper, it being part of a tract granted to Samuel Lasiter by Earl Granville on Oct. 15, 1761. Wit: R. Clark and William Cooper.

DB 1-235 WILLIAM CHAPMAN of Nash Co. to JOHN CHAPMAN of same, July 3, 1780, for 2000 pds. a tract of 160 acres on the south side of Tar River adjoining William Bryant and the Rocky Branch. Wit: Edward Moore, Harry Taylor, and Simon Williams.

DB 1-235 RICHARD THOMAS of Nash Co. to WILLIAM MATTHEWS of same, Jan. 31, 1783, for 12 pds. 85 acres on the south side of Stony Creek adjoining Dickenson, the Long Branch, and Melton, it being part of a grant to said Thomas on March 30, 1780. Wit: Wilson Vick and Jethro Thomas.

DB 1-237 JACOB UNDERWOOD of Nash Co. to SOLOMON EDWARDS of same, Sept. 29, 1780, for 50 pds. 53 acres on the south side of Compass Creek adjoining Thomas Thorp, it being part of a tract granted to said Underwood by Gov. Caswell. Wit: Joseph Exum and Priscilla Exum.

DB 1-238 BRITTAIN GANDY of Nash Co. to his son, BRITTAIN GANDY, for paternal love and affection, Oct. 3, 1780, the one-half of his estate, lands, goods, etc. Wit: W. S. Mearns and John Evans.

DB 1-238 BRITTAIN GANDY of Nash Co. to his son, JOHN GANDY, for paternal love and affection, Oct. 3, 1780, the remaining half of his estate not given to his son, Brittain Gandy. Wit: W. S. Mearns and John Evans.

DB 1-239 WILLIAM HACKNEY and wife, MILLY HACKNEY, of Nash Co. to PETER ROBERTSON, April 4, 1783, for 20 pds. specie a tract of 200 acres adjoining Hackney. Wit: Thomas Coleman and Sarah Coleman.

DB 1-240 THOMAS LEWIS and wife, LYDIA LEWIS, of Nash Co. to SION HILL of same, April 22, 1779, for 800 pds. current money a tract of 300 acres on the south side of Tar River at the mouth of Southwell's Creek adjoining Arthur Williams. Wit: James Morgan and Burwell Atkinson.

DB 1-241 WILLIAM HORN of Bertie Co. to GEORGE WIMBERLY of Edgecombe Co., Dec. 26, 1780, for 33 pds. a tract of 100 acres on Pig Basket Creek. Wit: Joel Horn, Melbry Horn, and Josiah Horn.

DB 1-242 LAZARUS WHITEHEAD of Nash Co. to JOHN POWELL, Jan. 16, 1783, for 400 pds. a tract of 400 acres on the south side of Fishing Creek adjoining John Wiggins, the county line, his own line, James Cain, and Landingham. Wit: Emmanuel Underwood, Thomas Colman, and Lazarus Whitehead, Jr.

DB 1-244 GALE BRYANT of Nash Co. to THOMAS VIVERETT of same, Feb. 21, 1782, for 120 pds. specie a 150 acre plantation on Tar River below Pastor Ford adjoining Jordan Sherrod, it being part of a tract granted to Arthur Taylor by Earl Granville on Oct. 26, 1753. Wit: Jas. Cobb, Jesse Pitman, and Nath'l Hickman.

DB 1-245 JOHN COOPER of Nash Co. to his son, JAMES COOPER, of same, April 8, 1783, for 10 pds. and paternal love and affection, 100 acres on the north side of Swift Creek adjoining Williams, it being part of a tract conveyed to John Cooper by Joseph Parker. Wit: W. S. Mearns and Francis Rose.

DB 1-246 SION WEST of Nash Co. to JOHN WILLIAM of Halifax Co., Oct. 22, 1782, for 100 pds. specie 385 acres on Tumbling Run adjoining Abraham Bass and Samuel Bridgers, it being part of a tract granted by Earl Granville to Jacob West on June 1, 1762. Wit: W. S. Mearns, Francis Parker, and William Cooper.

DB 1-247 JOHN BASS and CHARITY BASS of Nash Co. to WILLIAM BRIDGERS of same, July 21, 1780, for 10 pds. a tract of 320 acres on the south side of Swift Creek adjoining William Battle, West, and John Bass. Wit: John Williams and Stephen Webb.

DB 1-248 SAMUEL LONG BOTTOMS of Nash Co. to DAVID PRIDGEN of same, Jan. 26, 1782, for 31 pds. 19 sh. gold or silver 120 acres at the mouth of Holland's Branch on Sapony Creek adjoining Samuel Cannady, it being part of a 240 acre grant to John Edwards by Earl Granville on April 30, 1750. Wit: Phillander Williams and Christopher Ballard.

DB 1-249 THOMAS HORN, JR. of Nash Co. to the BLOOMERY COMPANY, erected on a swamp known as the Great Swamp, the privilege to dig and to make use of all the iron ore on his land for 2 sh. 6 p. hard money or iron at 6 p. per pound for every hundred weight that the said Bloomery made out of the ore, March 1, 1779. Wit: Jas. Cobb, Lem'l Wright, and Walter Erwin.

DB 1-250 MATTHEW BRANTLEY of Nash Co. to WILLIAM WHIDDON of same, June 3, 1782, for 75 pds. specie a tract of

112 acres on the south side of Sapony Creek. Wit: Elijah Boddie and William Moore.

DB 1-251 THOMAS HORN of Nash Co. to his brother, WILSON HORN, with love, good will, and affection, July 3, 1783, a tract of land on the southwest side of Toisnot Swamp adjoining Pine Log Branch and the road, it being part of 150 acres granted to John Taylor on Feb. 14, 1754; also, part of a tract granted to Thomas Horn, father of said Thomas Horn and Wilson Horn, by Pilgrim Williams on Jan. 20, 1763. Wit: Michael Horn, Duncan Dew, and Dempsey Dawson.

DB 1-252 JOSEPH POWELL of Nash Co. to ROLAND WILLIAMS of same, Dec. 29, 1782, for 250 silver dollars 332 acres adjoining Joel Williams and the Little Swamp, it being part of a tract granted to Jesse Mannen by Earl Granville for 432 acres on Nov. 3, 1761. Wit: Jonas Williams and John Poulan.

DB 1-253 JONAS BARNES WHITLY of Nash Co. to BENJAMIN BUNN, SR. of same June 19, 1783, for 13 pds. Virginia money 100 acres on the north side of Maple Creek adjoining Benjamin Bunn and the Rooty Branch, it being part of a tract granted to his father, Arthur Whitly, on March 16, 1761. Wit: Wm. Hall and Josiah Bunn.

DB 1-254 WILLIAM HILL of Chatham Co. to JOEL WALKER, Dec. 31, 1779, for 30 pds. 200 acres adjoining Ben Boon, John Webb, the main road, and Council, it being part of a tract granted since the independance. Wit: Thomas Lewis and Lewis Hill.

DB 1-255 SAMPSON POWELL of Nash Co. to JAMES RICHARDSON of same, Aug. 10, 1782, for 15 pds. a tract of 100 acres on the east side of the Back Swamp adjoining said Powell and Micajah Thomas, formerly the property of Willabe Manning. Wit: Thomas Morris, Francis Hamilton, and Francis Chadwick.

DB 1-256 JOHN CLYBURN of Nash Co. to BENJAMIN BRIDGERS. SR., Oct. 1, 1779, all that which Bridgers had given to him by deed of gift on Oct. 8, 1778, except 50 acres that was given to him in a former deed of gift registered in Edgecombe Co. Wiit: James Drake, Sr., Wm. Bell, and Albrittain Drake.

DB 1-256 TRIMAGIN THOMPSON of Bladen Co. to JAMES DRAKE. SR., Jan. 22, 1780, for 800 pds. 100 acres adjoining Wm. Battle. Sr., it being part of a tract granted to Samuel Bridgers by Earl Granville on Oct. 15, 1761. Wit: Abr. Lanst., Denton Mann, and Albrittain Drake.

DB 1-257 JOHN BASS of Nash Co. to GEORGE MASSENGILL of same, June 8, 1780, for 40 pds. proc. money a tract of 200 acres adjoining Isaac Hilliard and John Bass. Wit: James Battle, Josiah Johnston, and Henry Thompson.

DB 1-258 THOMAS TUCKER and VINCY TUCKER of Nash Co. to JOHN HEFLIN of Vain (?) Co., Feb. 23, 1780, for 500 pds. a tract of 150 acres on the north side of Great Sapony Creek adjoining Christopher Vaughan and Matthias Manning. Wit: Matthias Manning, Jr. and Robert Tucker.

DB 1-259 ABSALOM SAUL of Nash Co. to WILLIAM

WRIGHT, June 12, 1783, for 160 pds. a tract of 208½ acres on the south side of Beaver Dam Swamp. Wit: Francis Rose and John Wright.

DB 1-260 ABRAM SAUL to WILLIAM WRIGHT, June 12, 1783, for 160 pds. specie a tract of 208½ acres on the south side of Beaver Dam Swamp. Wit: Francis Rose and John Wright.

DB 1-261 NICHOLAS SKINNER of Nash Co. to WILSON CURL of same, Nov. 24, 1783, for 100 pds. Virginia money 200 acres on the north side of Tar River adjoining David Bunn, it being a tract bought by said Skinner from Jacob Stallings. Wit: H. Horn, Thomas Hunter, Howell Ellen, and Michael Atkinson.

DB 1-262 NICHOLAS SKINNER of Nash Co. to WILSON CURL of same, Nov. 24, 1783, for 110 pds. Virginia money 250 acres on both sides of Stony Creek adjoining Thomas Hunter, Micajah Thomas, and Ross' patent line, it being part of a grant to said Ross on March 25, 1749. Wit: H. Horn, Thomas Hunter, Howell Ellen, and Michael Atkinson.

DB 1-264 WILLIAM HILL of Chatham Co. to BENJAMIN BOOTHE of Edgecombe Co., April 9, 1783, for 90 pds. specie a tract of 340 acres on the north side of the road adjoining John Webb and Kerby. Wit: Sion Hill and William Young.

DB 1-265 JOHN COCKS and ELIZABETH COCKS of Nash Co. to SWAN TROUGHTON of same. Dec. 24, 1783, for 50 pds. specie a tract of 100 acres adjoining William Battle, Peter Anderson, and Adams. Wit: James Battle and Wm. Avent.

DB 1-266 THOMAS HUNTER of Nash Co. to JOHN VICK of same, Jan. 6, 1784, for 5 sh. a tract on the north side of Stony Creek adjoining David Daniel, William Braswell, Thomas Willis, and Edward Wilson, Jr. Wit: Wilson Vick and Benjamin Vick.

DB 1-267 JOSEPH CROWELL of Nash Co. to PHILLANDER WILLIAMS of same, Jan. 7, 1784, for 16 pds. specie a tract of 40 acres on the south side of Tar River adjoining said Williams and Joseph Crowell. Wit: David Pridgen and Brittain Whitly.

DB 1-268 DAVID DANIEL and wife. MAGDALANE DANIEL, of Nash Co. to LEWIS VICK of Southampton Co., Va., Feb. 24, 1784, for 80 pds specie 100 acres adjoining Young and Lake, it being part of a tract granted to Wm. Braswell by Earl Granville on July 24, 1761. Wit: Benjamin Vick and John Vick.

DB 1-269 WILLIAM BOYET of Nash Co. to MICHAEL HORN of same, Jan. 5, 1784. for 5 pds. specie a tract of 100 acres on the east side of Lott's Branch, a branch of Toisnot, adjoining said Boyet. the county line, and said Horn. Wit: Dempsey Dawson, Jonas Williams, and Jeremiah Nichols.

DB 1-270 JOHN VICK of Nash Co. to BENJAMIN VICK of same, Jan. 6. 1784, for 5 sh. specie a track of 133 acres on the north side of Stony Creek adjoining Benjamin Vick's old line, Edward Wilson, Jr., and Thomas Willis. Wit: Thomas Hunter and John Vick.

DB 1-271 JOHN MANNING of Edgecombe Co. to WILLIAM BATCHELOR of Nash Co., Feb. 7, 1784, for 20 pds. hard money a tract of 192 acres on the north side of Sapony Swamp at the Great Branch adjoining said Batchelor. Wit: Wm. Ricks and Aaron Odom.

DB 1-272 WILLOUGHBY POWELL of Nash Co. to NATHANIEL POWELL of same, Jan. 6, 1782, for 100 pds. a tract of 650 acres on the south side of Beaver Dam Swamp adjoining Cain's Mill Swamp, Cain, Davis Connel, and Nicholson. Wit: Arthur Arrington, Joseph Arrington, and William Arrington.

DB 1-273 JAMES SMITH of Franklin Co. to JOHN HARRISON of Nash Co., Aug. 27, 1779, for 240 pds. a tract of 100 acres on the south side of Fishing Creek. Wit: Francis Ward and John Wiggins.

DB 1-274 THOMAS WILLIAMS of Edgecombe Co. to MICHAEL ATKINSON of Nash Co, May 3, 1782, for 5 pds. Virginia money a tract of 50 acres on Compass Creek adjoining Thomas Thorp, Exum, Lewis Hines, and Wilson Curl. Wit: Nicholas Skinner and Thomas Merriman.

DB 1-275 JESSE HUNT of Nash Co. to ELIZABETH STRICKLAND of same, Dec. 9, 1782, for 30 pds. specie 200 acres on the east side of Lasiter's Branch adjoining Revel and David Strickland, it being part of a tract granted to Jesse Hunt. Wit: Thomas Hunter, Richard Thomas, and Hartwell Hart.

DB 1-275 WILSON CURL and wife, MOURNING CURL, of Nash Co. to JOHN WATKINS of Edgecombe Co., March 26, 1784, for 75 pds. 200 acres on the north side of Tar River adjoining Benja. Bunn and David Bunn, it being a tract of land taken up by Jacob Stallings in 1769. Wit: Joseph Exum and H. Horn.

DB 1-276 WILSON CURL and wife, MOURNING CURL, of Nash Co. to JOHN WATKINS of Edgecombe Co., March 26, 1784, for 65 pds. a tract of 102 acres on the south side of Stoney Creek adjoining Benjamin Bunn and Micajah Revel. Wit: Joseph Exum and H. Horn.

DB 1-277 THOMAS WILLIAMS of Nash Co. to NICHOLAS SKINNER of same, Dec. 15, 1781, for 5 pds. Virginia money a tract of 50 acres adjoining John Devanport and said Skinner. Wit: James Jameson and Francis Merriman.

DB 1-278 THOMAS WILSON of Wayne Co. to CHARLES POWELL, Jan. 2, 1784. for 100 pds. a tract of 200 acres on Swift Creek adjoining Ralph Mason, Charles Powell, Matthews, and Isaac Hilliard. Wit: George Bradbury and Joseph Minton.

DB 1-279 JOHN VICK of Nash Co. to EDWARD WILSON of same. April 5, 1784, for 20 pds. specie 100 acres on both sides of Lasiter's Branch adjoining Edward Wilson, Jesse Hunt, and Vick, it being part of a tract granted to Thomas Hunter. Wit: Edward Wilson, Jr., Benjamin Vick, and John Wilson.

DB 1-280 STON BASS of Nash Co. to WALKER MASSENGILL, of same Feb. 22, 1783, for 20 pds. specie 100 acres adjoining said Massengill, it being part of a grant made by Gov. Caswell. Wit: Henry Braswell, Wm. Drake, and Wm. Richardson.

DB 1-281 ROBERT PYLAND and wife, CAROLINE PY-

NASH COUNTY NORTH CAROLINA DEEDS

LAND, of Nash Co. to ISAAC HILLIARD of same, Nov. 22, 1783, for 300 pds. specie 176 acres on the north side of Swift Creek adjoining Harcy Griffin, Arthur Arrington, and the Parker's Branch, it being part of a tract of 443 acres granted to Thomas Bell by Earl Granville in 1749. Wit: Hardy Griffin, Jethro Denson, and Archibald Griffin.

DB 1-282 HENRY STEVENS and Wife, FRANCES STEVENS, of Nash Co. to ISAAC HILLIARD of same, Nov. 1, 1783, for 100 pds. Virginia money a tract of 639 acres on both sides of the head of Pine Log Swamp adjoining Abraham Saul. Wit: Hardy Griffin, Francis Rose, and John Powell.

DB 1-283 BENJAMIN BOYKIN of Wayne Co. to WILLIAM ROWE of Nash Co., June 3, 1783, for 66 2/3 silver dollars 100 acres on the north side of Contentnea Creek, it being part of a tract granted to said Boykin on March 4, 1761. Wit: Thomas Horn, Elijah Coleman, and John Flowers.

DB 1-284 NICHOLAS SKINNER and wife, SARAH SKINNER, of Nash Co. to JOHN BATTLE of Edgecombe Co., Dec. 16, 1783, for 3 pds. 6 sh. 8 p. 100 acres on Compass Creek adjoining Henry Watkins, Elijah Revel, Thomas Thorp, and Wilson Curl, it being part of a tract granted to Thomas Williams on Nov. 10, 1779. Wit: Isham Hines and Sarah Skinner, Jr.

DB 1-285 HARTWELL HART and wife, SARAH HART, of Nash Co. to LEWIS VICK of Southampton Co., Va., Oct. 29, 1783, for 160 pds. 13 sh. 4 p. specie 150 acres on Beaver Dam Branch adjoining Thomas Hart, it being part of a tract granted to Robert Young by Earl Granville on Nov. 11, 1756, conveyed by deed to Thomas Hart, and by him conveyed to Hartwell Hart on July 1, 1779. Wit: Wilson Vick, John Vick, and Eliah Knight.

DB 1-286 BRIAN LINCH of Franklin Co. to SIMON WILLIAMS of Nash Co., July 25, 1781, for 33 pds. 13 sh. hard money 100 acres on the river, part in Nash Co. and part in Franklin Co. Wit: Jacob Carter and Benjamin Williams.

DB 1-287 MICAJAH THOMAS of Nash Co. to SAMPSON POWELL of same, Jan. 5, 1782, for 120 pds. a tract of 700 acres adjoining Edward Parrish, it being a grant from Earl Granville on Nov. 3, 1762. Wit: Henry Braswell, Arthur Braswell, and Julian King.

DB 1-288 JOHN BIGGS, JR. of Nash Co. to DEMPSEY VANN of same, Jan. 14, 1783, for 20 pds. proc. money a tract of 125 acres on the north side of Great Sapony Creek adjoining Thomas Tucker, Matthias Manning, and Daniel Owens. Wit: George Sutton and John White.

DB 1-289 DAVID PRIDGEN of Nash Co. to SAMUEL LONGBOTTOMS of same, May 8, 1783, for 30 pds. specie 120 acres at the mouth of Holland's Branch adjoining Sapony Creek and the Samuel Cannady line, it being part of a 240 acre grant from Earl Granville to John Edwards on April 30, 1750. Wit: John Sheppard and Brittain Whitly.

DB 1-291 JOSEPH CROWELL of Nash Co. to PHILLAN-

DER WILLIAMS of same, Aug. 11, 1783, for 200 pds. specie 300 acres on the south side of Tar River at his own corner, it being part of a tract granted to Nathaniel Sanders on Sept. 25,1741. Wit: David Pridgen and Jesse Pridgen.

DB 1-292 BENJAMIN BOOTH and MARTHA BOOTH of Edgecombe Co. to JACOB JOINER of Nash Co., May 19, 1783, for 90 pds. specie 3 and 40 acres on the north side of the road adjoining John Webb and Kirby. Wit: Thos. Stainback and Hardy Joiner.

DB 1-292 JOHN DEVANPORT of Nash Co. to HENRY HORN of same, Dec. 19, 1782, for 70 pds. Virginia money a tract of 150 acres on the south side of Compass Creek adjoining Thomas Williams and Henry Horn. Wit: Jeremiah Hilliard, Wilson Curl, and Thomas Horn.

DB 1-293 WILLIAM WHIDDON and MARY WHIDDON of Nash Co. to PARSON RACKLEY of same, Oct. 2, 1783, for 100 pds. specie a tract of 360 acres in the fork of Sapony adjoining William Barrendene and Langley. Wit: Arthur O'Neal and Henry Youell.

DB 1-295 WILLIAM RAY of Wake Co. to JACOB HARTS-FIELD of Franklin Co., Oct. 7, 1783, for 4 pds. specie 100 acres on the side of Turkey Creek adjoining Wm. Perry, Pettiway, and the Ready Branch, near the county line, it being part of a tract granted to William Ray by the governor on Oct. 25, 1782. Wit: Samuel Bryant and Benjamin Braswell.

DB 1-296 JOHN BIGGS, JR. of Nash Co. to DEMPSEY VANN of same, Jan. 14, 1783, for 20 pds. proc. money a tract of 175 acres on the north side of Great Sapony Creek adjoining Thomas Tucker, Matthias Manning, and Daniel Deans. Wit: George Sutton and John White.

DB 1-297 CHARLES EVANS and FERBREY EVANS of Nash Co. to SAMUEL MILLER of same, Feb. 5, 1783, for 20 pds. proc. money 300 acres adjoining Thomas Davis, it being a tract granted to said Evans. Wit: James Ward and Lewis Miller.

DB 1-298 NICHOLAS SKINNER of Nash Co. to MICHAEL ATKINSON of same, May 3, 1782, for 125 pds. Virginia money 365 acres of land, it being parts of three deeds, adjoining John Devanport, Joseph Curl. Micajah Revel, and William Horn. Wit: Josiah Spight and Samuel Skinner.

DB 1-299 MICHAEL ATKINSON of Nash Co. to HENRY HORN of Edgecombe Co., Jan. 25, 1783, for 20 pds. Virginia money 50 acres on the north side of the Tarboro Road. it being part of a tract bought of Nicholas Skinner adjoining Atkinson and Henry Horn. Wit: John Jones, Thomas Hunter. and Wilson Curl.

DB 1-300 THOMAS WILLIAMS of Edgecombe Co. to HENRY HORN, Jan. 27, 1782, for 5 pds. Virginia money a tract of 50 acres adjoining Atkinson, Horn, Randolph Harris. and the Compass Creek. Wit: Michael Atkinson, Mary Spight, Martha Cooper Atkinson, and Piety Horn.

DB 1-301 MARY MORPHIS of Wake Co. to JOHN MORPHIS of Nash Co., Sept. 12. 1783, for 70 pds. specie 200 acres of land.

it being part of a larger tract granted to Duncan Lamon by Earl Granville on July 23, 1761 and conveyed by him to Benjamin Taylor, who sold the same to Mary Morphis.   Wit: James Morphis and———Strickland.

DB 1-302 JACOB CARTER of Nash Co. to WILLIAM BRASWELL of same, Sept. 10, 1783, for 50 pds. specie 340 acres on Turkey Creek adjoining his own line, Edward Pusly, and said William Braswell, with one acre at his mill excepted, this being part of the land taken up by said Carter.   Wit: Benjamin Braswell and John Button.

DB 1-303 WILLIAM SPIGHT of Nash Co. to JOSEPH GRANT of Edgecombe Co., Jan. 20, 1783, for 56 pds. 10 sh. Virginia money 140 acres on the north side of Compass Creek adjoining Joseph Exum, it being part of a tract that Wm. Spight bought of John Spight.   Wit: Jos. Exum, Josiah Bunn, and Jacob Strickland.

DB 1-304 JOSEPH GRANT of Edgecombe Co. to JACOB HOUSE of same, Oct. 6, 1783, for 42 pds. 10 sh. specie a tract of 140 acres on the north side of Compass Creek adjoining Joseph Exum, it being the same tract described in the preceding deed. Wit: James Eastwood, Jacob Strickland, and Jacob Dickenson.

DB 1-305 HENRY DEANS of Nash Co. to WILLIAM ANDREWS of Franklin Co., Jan. 30, 1783, for 50 pds. specie 110 acres on the north side of Turkey Creek adjoining Andrews, Williamson Ross, the road, and Benjamin Tucker, it being part of a tract granted to said Henry Deans on Oct. 25, 1782,.   Wit: Wm. Lancaster, Jean Lancaster and James Griffin.

DB 1-307 JOHN BONDS of Nash Co. to JEREMIAH BURGE of same, Oct. 7, 1783, for 60 pds. specie a 150 acre plantation on the north side of Compass Creek adjoining Joseph Exum and Lewis Trevathan, it being a tract that John Bonds bought of Joseph Curl. Wit: John Evans and Matthew Drake.

DB 1-308 ISAAC BASS and wife, ANN BASS, of Nash Co. to JESSE BASS of same, Oct. 6, 1783, for 60 pds. a tract of 350 acres on Peachtree Creek and Green's Branch.   Wit: John Gay, Bennett Boddie, and Stephen Webb.

DB 1-308 WILLIAM HACKNEY and wife, MILLY HACKNEY, of Nash Co. to JOSEPH MINTON of same, July 7, 1783, for 100 pds. current money a tract of 100 acres adjoining Nicholas Baggett, Hackney, Minton, Peter Robertson, and Lewis Dortch. Wit: Henry Mason and Ralph Mason.

DB 1-310 WILLIAM HOOKS and wife, DORCAS HOOKS, of Nash Co. to MATTHEW DRAKE of same, April 6, 1784. for 100 pds. specie 640 acres adjoining Matthew Drake, Nathaniel Drake, and Thomas Mann, it being a tract granted to William Hooks by Gov. Alexander Martin.   Wit: W. S. Mearns and Sampson Sikes.

DB 1-311 THOMAS SANDERS of Edgecombe Co. to JOSHUA JORDAN, Oct. 7, 1783, for 20 pds. 210 acres on the north side of Contentnea Creek adjoining Sanders, Jordan, and Hedgepeth, it being part of a tract granted to Thomas Sanders on Nov.

10, 1779. Wit: Cornelius Jordan, Jr., John Hedgepeth, and John Sanders.

DB 1-311 JACOB CARTER of Nash Co. to JOSHUA STEP-HENS of same, July 1, 1783, for 40 pds. specie, 300 acres on the north side of Tar River adjoining Robert Young, Edward Pursell, the Turkey Creek, and William Braswell, it being part of a tract granted to said Carter on Oct. 25, 1782. Wit: William Lancaster and George Foreman.

DB 1-312 SION HILL and wife, DREWSILLA HILL, of Nash Co. to NEWIT LANE of same, Oct. 2, 1783, for 30 pds. hard money the 100 acre plantation whereon Sion Hill then lived on the north side of Tar River adjoining Arthur Williams. Wit: John Lane, William Hendrick, and Benjamin Lane.

DB 1-313 HENRY DEANS of Nash Co. to WILLIAM AN-DREWS of Franklin Co., Jan. 30, 1783, for 40 pds. specie 50 acres on Brittain's Branch and Andrews' line, it being part of a tract granted to Henry Deans on Oct. 25, 1782. Wit: William Lancaster, Jean Lancaster, and James Griffin.

DB 1-314 JEREMIAH DEANS of Nash Co. to WILLIAM ANDREWS of Franklin Co., April 5, 1784, in the behalf of the Society of the Regular Baptists, for 50 pds. a parcel of 2 acres, it being part of a tract granted to William Megee in 1761. Wit: Henry Deans, James Culpepper, and Christopher Culpepper.

DB 1-315 JOHN SCOTT of Nash Co. to HENRY SCREWS, March 18, 1784, for 50 pds. a tract of 40 acres on the north side of Cabin Branch adjoining Screws and James Cain. Wit: James Landingham and Thomas Hokaway.

DB 1-315 HARDY FLOWERS of Edgecombe Co. to WILL-IAM BAKER, JR. of Nash Co., Aug. 9, 1782, for 30 pds. current money a tract of 500 acres on the north side of Tar River adjoining Joiner, the road leading from Duncan Lamon's to Stony Creek, Polecat, and the Meadow Branch. Wit: William Baker and John Doimar.

DB 1-316 THOMAS ATKINSON of Wilks Co., Georgia to JEREMIAH BURGE of Nash Co., Oct. 21, 1783, for 200 pds. a tract of 310 acres between the head of Beach Run and Compass Creek adjoining Jacob Underwood, Joseph Exum, and his own line. Wit: Joseph Exum, Samuel Sorsby, and John Raines.

DB 1-317 JEREMIAH BURGE of Nash Co. to JACOB UN-DERWOOD of same, April 17, 1784, for 3 pds. 4 sh. 20 acres adjoining Joseph Exum and the Long Branch, it being part of a tract that Thomas Atkinson took up on Nov. 10, 1779. Wit: Samuel Sorsby, Francis Rose, and John Raines.

DB 1-318 SOLOMON VESTER of Nash Co. to WILLIAM VESTER of same, Dec. 26. 1783, for 40 pds. specie a tract of 250 acres on the north side of Sapony Creek and on Bear Branch adjoining Wm. Vester and Thomas Richardson, it being a former grant to Solomon Vester on Jan. 18, 1779. Wit: Thomas Morris and Hannah Harrison.

DB 1-319 WILLIAM WARBURTON and ALICE WARBUR-

TON of Nash Co. to NEWIT LANE of same, Jan. 31, 1784, for 6 pds. hard money a tract of 50 acres on Sapony Creek and Brushy Pond adjoining Newit Lane. Wit: William Hendrick, Benjamin Bryant, and William Bryant.

DB 1-321 WILSON CURL of Nash Co. to EDWARD WILSON of same, Sept. 14, 1786, for 150 pds. a 300 acre plantation on both sides of Kirby's Creek adjoining Thomas Williams, Micajah Revel, the Thomas' Road, and Moore, it being part of a 700 acre tract granted to John Moore by Earl Granville on June 1, 1762. Wit: Isham Hines and John Wilson.

DB 1-321 PETER ROBERTSON of Nash Co. to JOHN MINTON of same, Nov. 9, 1786, for 25 pds. a tract of 50 acres on the south side of Pine Log Swamp adjoining Nicholas Baggett and Joseph Minton. Wit: Joseph Minton and John Robertson.

DB 1-322 JESSE BATTLE and wife, SUSANNAH BATTLE, of Nash Co. to ISAAC HILLIARD of same, Oct. 25, 1786, for 500 pds. Virginia money a tract of 500 acres on the north side of Swift Creek on Lane's Swamp and the Thomas Hart line, it being part of a 563 acre grant by Earl Granville to Jacob Whitehead on May 14, 1756. Wit: Arthur Arrington, John Arrington, and Isaac Newsome.

DB 1-323 JOSEPH VICK of Nash Co. to JULIAN KING of same, Nov. 13, 1786, for 10 pds. specie 100 acres on Turkey Creek adjoining Julian King. it being a tract granted to Joseph Vick on Nov. 1, 1784. Wit: Micajah Thomas and S. W. Arnett.

DB 1-324 JOSEPH CURL of Nash Co. to RANDOLPH REESE of Edgecombe Co., June 3, 1786. for 100 pds. specie 150 acres on both sides of Kirby's Creek adjoining Folsom's Road and Thomas' Road. it being part of a tract granted to Thomas Williams on March 2, 1761. Wit: Randolph Harriss and Jeremiah Hilliard.

DB 1-325 LAZARUS WHITEHEAD and wife, MARY WHITEHEAD, of Nash Co. to ROBERT THOMPSON, Aug. 11, 1786, for 50 pds. a tract of 307 acres on the south side of Long Swamp adjoining the county line, the Watery Branch, Isaac Tolbert, James Turner, and Thompson. Wit: Willoughby Powell, William Whitehead, and Isaac Whitehead.

DB 1-326 WILLIAM MIDLETON BALLARD of Nash Co. to WILLIAM POULAN of same, Sept. 11, 1786, for 20 pds. specie a tract of 175 acres on Jacob's Swamp adjoining William Poulan and the Rooty Branch. Wit: Wilson Taylor and John Poulan.

DB 1-327 EDMUND BRANCH of Nash Co. to DAVID HUNT of same, Oct. 26, 1786, for 25 pds. 50 acres adjoining Jesse Powell, William Walker, and Jacob Braswell, it being part of a tract granted to Edmund Branch on Oct. 25, 1782. Wit: Richard Holland and Daniel Holland.

DB 1-328 THOMAS HUNT of Nash Co. to JAMES BATTLE of same, Feb. 1, 1787, for 150 pds. specie 160 acres adjoining Lemuel Laseter, the Jonas Branch, and Joseph Hayes, it being part of a tract conveyed from Hansel Laseter to Ambros Hadly and from said Hadly to Thomas Hunt. Wit: W. S. Mearns, John Hunt, and Daniel Hunt.

DB 1-329 RICHARD FORE of Nash Co. to JESSE KENT of same, Aug. 26, 1786, for 50 pds. specie a tract of 434 acres on Turkey Creek at the mouth of Rocky Branch above the improvement he purchased of James Bird. Wit: Thomas Mecom and William Conner.

DB 1-330 JACOB FLOWERS of Johnston Co. to BENJAMIN FLOWERS of Nash Co., March 2, 1786, for 12 pds. specie a tract of 350 acres adjoining Benjamin Flowers and William Phillips. Wit: Jonas Williams and Drury Williams.

DB 1-331 KINSMAN KNIGHT and ANNE KNIGHT, of Nash Co. to JOSEPH WHITE, JR. of same, Feb. 10, 1787, for 12 pds. 10 sh. Virginia money 100 acres on Pig Basket Creek adjoining Thomas Horn, it being part of a grant to John Knight by Gov. Caswell, demised by him to his wife, Ann, for her natural life and, at her death, bequeathed to his son, Kinsman. Wit: John Chitty and Wm. Williams.

DB 1-332 JOHN KIRBY of Southampton Co., Virginia to WILLIAM KIRBY of Nash Co., Feb. 26, 1785, for 51 pds. 10 sh. proc. money 250 acres in the upper part of Nash Co. and lying partly in Franklin Co., on the south side of Red Bud Creek, it being land formerly granted to Francis Parker. Wit: James Williams, Edmund Drake, and Edwin Drake.

DB 1-333 WILLIAM WHIDDON of Nash Co. to NOAH WHIDDON of same, Jan. 13, 1787, for 10 pds. current money a tract of 80 acres on the south side of Ready Branch adjoining Marcum Cooper's path, the road, and Reuben Whitfield. Wit: John Evans and Elizabeth Evans.

DB 1-334 WILLIAM ANDREWS of Franklin Co. to WILLIAM ANDREWS of Bertie Co., Dec. 1, 1786, for 400 pds. specie 465 acres on the north side of Turkey Creek adjoining William Hammons, the road, Thomas Tucker, Henry Banes, Little Turkey Creek, and Cornelius Taylor, it consisting of three tracts, two sold by Abner Hill to William Andrews of Franklin Co. and one by Henry Deans. Wit: John Andrews, William Menoshan, and Delly Devanport.

DB 1-335 JOHN HINNANT of Nash Co. to GEORGE LEWIS of same, Dec. 6, 1786, for 70 pds. specie a tract of 500 acres on the north side of Tar River at the mouth of Deep Branch adjoining Solomon Carter and the Walnut Branch; also, another tract John Hinnant bought of Burwell Rose adjoining Matthew Carter, Thomas Warring, and John Melton. Wit: Solomon Carter and Thomas Carter.

DB 1-336 ABRAHAM BASS of Nash Co. to his granddaughter, HARTY BRIDGERS, of same, July 7, 1785, for love and affection one negro girl. Wit: William Bridgers and Micaiah Bridgers.

DB 1-337 WILSON CURL of Nash Co. to JOSEPH CURL of same, Jan. 17, 1787, for 110 pds. Virginia money a 150 acre plantation on the north side of Stony Creek adjoining Andrew Ross and

Thomas Hunter. Wit: Joseph Exum and Edward Wilson.

DB 1-338 WILLIAM ROSE of Franklin Co. to his son-in-law, JACOB ROGERS, of Nash Co., Sept. 19, 1786, for love and affection one negro girl. Wit: Robert Rogers and Harrey Taylor.

DB 1-338 MARK MASON of Nash Co. to HENRY MASON of same, Feb. 12, 1787, for 5 sh. specie a tract of 350 acres on the south side of Beaver Dam Swamp. Wit: Jethro Denson, William Sanders, and John Rawls.

DB 1-339 JESSE HUNT of Nash Co. to MICAJAH BRAS-WELL HUNT of same, Dec. 22, 1785, for 80 pds. specie a tract of 340 acres adjoining Thomas Willis, Thomas Hunter, Revel, John Wilson, and David Strickland. Wit: John Chitty and Howell Ellen.

DB 1-340 MARTHA CHADWICK of Nash Co. to EPHRAIM ATKINSON of same, June 30, 1783, for 10 pds. 50 acres adjoining Morris, the Meadow Branch, and Nathan Boddie, it being part of a tract granted by Earl Granville to James Atkinson on Oct. 15, 1761. Wit: Thomas Morris, James Richardson, and Hannah Harrison.

DB 1-341 BURWELL ATKINSON of Nash Co. to EPHRAIM ATKINSON of same, April 12, 1783, for 16 pds. current money a tract of 75 acres on the north side of Peachtree Creek adjoining Culpepper, the Meadow Branch, and Boddie. Wit: Sampson Powell and Thomas Morris.

DB 1-342 SOLOMON STRICKLAND of Nash Co. to STEPHEN YOUNG of Johnston Co., Nov. 4, 1786, for 100 pds. gold and silver two tracts of land whereon said Strickland then lived which he purchased of Hardy Strickland and Samuel Bryant: (1) 400 acres adjoining Jacob Strickland and Samuel Bryant; (2) 300 acres on the south side of Turkey Creek adjoining the first tract. Wit: Henry Banes and William Lancaster.

DB 1-343 ARCHIBALD DAVIS of Halifax Co. to his cousin, SAMUEL MILLER, of Nash Co., Dec. 15, 1786, for love and affection the 146 acre plantation whereon Samuel Miller then lived on the south side of Fishing Creek. Wit: Young Davis and John Miller.

DB 1-344 WILLIAM PARKS and JIMIMA PARKS of Nash Co. to THOMAS SUTTON of same, Feb. 12, 1787, for 60 pds. Virginia money a tract of 250 acres on Tar River at the mouth of Deep Bottom Branch and on Arthur Williams' Branch adjoining Nicholson and James Taylor. Wit: George Sutton and Lucy Sutton.

DB 1-345 THOMAS MORRISS of Nash Co. to AMBROSE EDMONDSON of same, Feb. 12, 1787, for 125 pds. 640 acres on Pig Basket Creek adjoining Arthur Braswell, Matthew Drake, and Isaac Hilliard, it being a tract granted to Charles Watson on Jan. 13, 1779. Wit: Christopher Hinton and Sarah Hinton.

DB 1-346 HENRY BARLOW of Nash Co. to JAMES BRADLEY of same, Nov. 4, 1786, for 60 pds. a tract of 100 acres on the north side of Little Peachtree Creek. Wit: William Webb and Robert Rogers.

DB 1-347 JOHN WATKINS of Nash Co. to BENJAMIN BUNN of same, Oct. 30, 1786, for 200 pds. 200 acres on the north side of Tar River adjoining Benjamin Bunn and David Bunn, it being a tract taken up by Jacob Stallings in 1769. Wit: R. Bunn, Wilson Vick, and Wm. Fort.

DB 1-349 WILLIAM AVENT of Nash Co. to JOHN HAR-RISON of same, Jan. 19, 1785, for 40 pds. specie a tract of 100 acres adjoining James Cocks, William Battle, and Bell. Wit: Peter Anderson and William Slatter.

DB 1-350 MOSES STALLINGS of Nash Co. to JOEL WILL-IAMS of same, Sept. 7, 1786, for 20 pds. 150 acres on the south side of an entry of 300 acres made by said Stallings on Nov. 1, 1784. Wit: John Bond and Jonas Williams.

DB 1-351 MICHAEL HORN and wife, PATIENCE HORN, of Nash Co. to JONAS WILLIAMS of same. May 24, 1786, for 53 pds. 6 sh. 8 p. a tract of 70 acres on the north side of Toisnot Swamp adjoining Jonas Williams (formerly Pilgrim Williams), it being the upper part of a 300 acre tract granted to Thomas Horn on June 25, 1749. Wit: Wilson Taylor, Drury Williams, and Henry Horn.

DB 1-353 CHRISTOPHER BALLARD of Nash Co. to JACOB JOINER of same, Sept. 16, 1786, for 100 pds. a tract of 223 acres on the south side of Sapony Creek adjoining Ben Smith, John Joiner, Thomas Kersey, and Samuel Bottoms. Wit: Jesse Joiner and John Joiner.

DB 1-353 JACOB BARNES of Nash Co. to JOHN BARNES of same, Jan. 19, 1787, for 20 pds. 164 acres on both sides of Stony Creek, near the falls and crossing said falls, it being part of a tract granted to Jacob Barnes by Earl Granville on Nov. 10, 1757. Wit: Benjamin Banes and Joel Bunn.

DB 1-354 ISAAC TALBOOT of Nash Co. to ISAAC HILL-IARD of same, May 7, 1787, for 39 pds. 3 sh. 3 p. a tract of 234 acres on the south side of Lane's Swamp. Wit: Arthur Arring-ton, Joseph Arrington, and Wm. Sandeford.

DB 1-355 WILSON VICK of Nash Co. to SAMUEL WEST-RAY of same, May 15, 1787, for 70 pds. specie a tract of 150 acres on Maple Creek adjoining Laine's Road, the Long Branch, and Ricks' line. Wit: James Williams and John Bonds.

DB 1-356 JOHN HUNT of Nash Co. to JAMES BATTLE of same, April 2, 1787, for 23 pds. 10 sh. Virginia money 50 acres on the north side of Beaver Dam Swamp adjoining Cooper, White-head, and Battle (formerly Laseter), it being part of a tract gran-ted to John Hunt by Earl Granville on Aug. 1, 1762. Wit: W. S. Mearns, Wm. Lewis, and Joseph Arrington.

DB 1-357 JOSEPH SEALY of Nash Co. to NATHAN JOIN-ER of same. Sept. 10, 1786, for 16 pds. specie a tract of 150 acres on Sapony Creek adjoining George Jackson, Thomas Edwards, Joseph Sealy, Jr., and John Poulan, it being part of a grant from the State to Joseph Sealy on Sept. 24, 1785. Wit: Joseph Sealy, Jr. and Drury Taylor.

DB 1-358 SYLVANUS PUMPHREY of Nash Co. to NATH-

AN BODDIE of same, April 18, 1787, for 200 silver dollars 125 acres adjoining Culpepper, it being part of a tract granted to James Atkinson by Earl Granville on Oct. 15, 1761; also, another tract of 8 acres on both sides of Peachtree Creek where Ephraim Atkinson built a mill. Wit: George Boddie and Thomas Hutchins.

DB 1-360 JOHN FLOWERS and ELIZABETH FLOWERS of Nash Co. to JOSEPH WRIGHT of same, Nov. 6, 1786, for 20 pds. a tract of 250 acres on Contentnea Creek and Sheppard's Branch adjoining Ephraim Phillips and Sanders. Wit: James Cobb, Lemuel Wright, and Simon Bell.

DB 1-360 AMBROSE EDMONDSON of Nash Co. to CHRISTOPHER HINTON of same, March 20, 1787, for 90 pds. specie 320 acres on Pig Basket Creek adjoining Arthur Braswell, Matthew Drake, and Isaac Hilliard, it being part of a tract granted by the State to Charles Watson on Nov. 10, 1779. Wit: Thomas Morriss, Chloe Morriss, and Bathsheba Morriss.

DB 1-361 CANNON COOPER of Nash Co. to JOHN ARRINGTON of same, Jan. 2, 1786, for 60 pds. current money a tract of 100 acres on the north side of Swift Creek adjoining John Hunt and Elizabeth Bell, it being land bequeathed to said Cannon Cooper by his father, John Cooper. Wit: Arthur Arrington and Hardy Griffin.

DB 1-362 REUBEN COOPER of Nash Co. to JOHN ARRINGTON of same, Nov. 29, 1785. for 50 pds Virginia money a tract of 100 acres adjoining Hardy Griffin, John Hunt, and Joseph Arrington, it being a tract bequeathed to him by his father, John Cooper. Wit: Thomas Hunt and Arthur Arrington.

DB 1-363 JOHN HUNT of Nash Co. to JOHN ARRINGTON of same, Nov. 29, 1785, for 1 pd. 6 sh. 8 p. a parcel 4 acres adjoining Joseph Arrington, the Haw Branch, and Cooper's old line, it having been conveyed by John Cooper to said Hunt. Wit: Thomas Hunt and Arthur Arrington.

DB 1-364 JAMES DANIEL of Nash Co. to JOHN BARROT of Southampton Co., Virginia, May 2, 1786, for 150 pds. 282 acres on the north side of Pig Basket Creek or Braswell's Creek adjoining James Daniel and Federick Daniel, it being a tract granted to Robert Young by Earl Granville on Nov. 8, 1755. Wit: John Chitty, Howell Ellen, Nathan Barrott, and John Williams.

DB 1-365 NEHEMIAH SMITH of Johnston Co. to WILLIAM SKINNER of Nash Co., Dec. 21, 1786, for 50 pds. Virginia money 2 and 65 acres on the north side of Stony Creek adjoining Hunter and Wm. Barnes. Wit: E. Skinner, John Harrell and Tesey Thomas.

DB 1-366 SAMUEL SKINNER of Edgecombe Co. to EMMANUEL SKINNER of Nash Co., Oct. 30, 1786, for 45 pds. 100 acres on the south side of Stony Creek adjoining Strickland and the road it being part of a grant of 665 acres to James Oliver by Earl Granville in 1761. Wit: Samuel Skinner and James Barnes.

DB 1-368 MARK MASON of Nash Co. to WILLIAM MASON of same. Aug. 13, 1787, for 370 pds. specie a tract of 206 acres on Beaver Dam Swamp and the Meadow Branch adjoining Foster

Beaver Dam Swamp and the Meadow Branch adjoining Foster Mason and William Mason. Wit: Mark Mason and James Conway.

DB 1-369 MARK MASON of Nash Co. to FOSTER MASON of same, Aug. 13, 1787, for 380 pds. specie a tract of 236 acres on the Round Stone Swamp adjoining the road and James Wyatt. Wit: Mark Mason and James Conway.

DB1-370 ARTHUR SEATH of Dinwiddie Co., Virginia to WILLIAM ANDREWS of Nash Co., June 19, 1787, for 100 pds. current money one negro girl. Wit: Allen Haddon and Henry Banes.

DB 1-370 CHRISTOPHER BALLARD of Nash Co. to JOSEPH JOINER of same, Feb. 3, 1787, for 18 pds. 12 sh. a tract of 62 acres on the south side of Sapony Creek adjoining Ben Smith and Holland's Branch. Wit: Simon Smith and William Whitehead.

DB 1-371 ELISHA BELL of Nash Co. to JOHN HARRISON of same, Feb. 17, 1787, for 190 pds. specie 246 acres on Beaver Dam Swamp adjoining Robert Clark, it being a tract of land conveyed from John Williams to Elisha Bell and from Lott Etheridge to John Williams. Wit: Wm. Avent, James Battle, and Ben Ward.

DB 1-372 WILLIAM HILL of Chatham Co. to LEWIS HILL of Nash Co., April 14, 1782, for 50 pds. a tract of 160 acres adjoining Lewis Hill and Cooper Williams. Wit: Richard Hill and Lydia Hill.

DB 1-373 SAMUEL STRICKLAND of Nash Co. to JESSE KENT of same, Nov. 8, 1787, for 20 pds. a tract of 196 acres on Turkey Creek adjoining Samuel Taylor and Jesse Kent. Wit: Wilson Taylor and Jeremiah Nichols.

DB 1-374 JAMES CAIN of Nash Co. to JAMES DANIEL of same, Nov. 13, 1787, for 43 pds. a tract of 200 acres on Toisnot Swamp adjoining Lazarus Strickland and Johnson's Branch. Wit: Wilson Vick and Julian King.

DB 1-374 JESSE WYATT and wife, SARAH WYATT, of Halifax Co. to WILLIAM WRIGHT of Nash Co., Aug. 4, 1787, for 200 pds. specie a tract of 178 acres on the north side of Beaver Dam Swamp adjoining Francis Rose, Whitehead, and Nicholson. Wit: Davis Connell and Thomas Connell.

DB 1-375 SION BASS to STEPHEN WEBB, Feb. 5, 1787, for 50 pds. a tract of 140 acres on the south side of the Tarborough Road adjoining Webb, John Passmore, and Sion Bass. Wit: James Connell and Benjamin Boon.

DB 1-376 GEORGE WIMBERLY of Edgecombe Co. to MICAJAH THOMAS of Nash Co., Nov. 22, 1786, for 400 pds. specie two tracts of land, one granted by Earl Granville on Dec. 12, 1760 to Mourning Thomas and conveyed by deed from her to said Wimberly; the other tract granted by Earl Granville to one Watson and from Watson to Joseph Thomas, both tracts containing 600 acres, on the south side of Pig Basket Creek adjoining Robert Young and Micajah Thomas. Wit: Lewis Hutchens and Julian King.

DB 1-378 WILLIAM AVENT of Nash Co. to THOMAS ARM-
STRONG of same, Sept. 1, 1786, for 220 pds. in state certificates
granted to officers and soldiers of the Continental Line of the
State, 100 acres adjoining William Battle, Peter Anderson, and
William Avent, it being the plantation and land that formerly belonged to Mr. John Cox. Wit: William Battle and William Brinkley.

DB 1-379 SAMUEL SORSBY of Nash Co. to his daughter,
ELIZABETH BUCKNER BURGE, of same, Jan. 5, 1788, one negro
girl for the remainder of her natural life and then to her heirs.
Wit: William Robertson and Alexander Sorsby.

DB 1-379 SAMUEL WESTRAY, Sheriff of Nash Co., to
JAMES COBB of Wayne Co., Nov. 11, 1788, at public auction for
31 pds. a tract of land on Toisnot Swamp containing 300 acres, it
being a grant from the State to Lazarus Strickland on Oct. 25,
1782. It was sold as the property of JESSE BROTTON to satisfy
three executions obtained by Jonas Williams, John Dew, and Benjamin & James Cobb & Co. Wit: Francis Rose and Benjamin
Boon.

DB 1-381 JOSEPH CROWELL and wife, M A R T H A
CROWELL. of Nash Co. to LEWIS ABLEWIS LAMKIN of same,
Aug. 17, 1787, for 300 pds. Virginia money a tract of 612 acres on
the south side of Tar River adjoining Michael Dormin. Wit: Phillander Williams, Peter Hatten, and Richard Winstead.

DB 1-382 MARY DISON of Nash Co. to WILLIAM WEST
and LAZARUS STRICKLAND, May 11, 1787, for 70 pds. certain
livestock and furniture. Wit: John Bonds, and Crese Bonds.

DB 1-382 MATTHEW CARTER of Johnston Co. to SOLO-
MON CARTER of Nash Co., April 2, 1782, for 200 pds. silver
money a tract of 347 acres on the north side of Tar River adjoining Samuel Carter and the Walnut Branch. Wit: Samuel Carter
and Susannah Carter.

DB 1-383 WILLIAM BALLARD of Nash Co. to ALLEN
BAKER of same Feb. 6, 1787, for 40 pds. Virginia money 100 acres
on the east side of Jacobs Swamp adjoining Christopher Ballard,
the Rooty Branch, John Ballard, and John Poland, it being part of
a tract granted to Jacob Braswell on Dec. 6, 1760. Wit: David
Pridgen and William Baker.

DB 1-384 DELILAH GRIFFIN and BENJAMIN WHIT-
FIELD of Nash Co. to NATHAN GREEN of same, Oct. 15, 1787,
for 200 pds. 60 acres on the south side of Fishing Creek adjoining
the Muddy Branch and Samuel Davis, it being part of a tract purchased by John Portis from George Portis. Wit: David Moore
and Jeremiah Portis.

DB 1-385 WILLIAM CHAPMAN, JR. of Nash Co. to JOHN
RICE of same, March 16, 1787, for 40 pds. specie 200 acres on the
west side of Turkey Creek, it being part of a tract granted to Peleg
Rogers by Earl Granville on Oct. 30, 1754 for 337 acres. Wit:
Richard Fore and James Kiff.

DB 1-386 WILLIAM WHIDDON of Nash Co. to JOHN

EVANS of same, Feb. 3, 1787, for 150 pds. a tract of 300 acres on the south side of Ready Branch adjoining the road, Whiddon, and Holland. Wit: Elizabeth Evans and Sherrod Evans.

DB 1-387 JORDAN SHERROD and wife, JENNY SHERROD, of Nash Co. to THOMAS VIVERETT of same, Sept. 27, 1787, for 200 pds. 125 acres adjoining the road, the river, and Viverett, it being part of a tract granted to Edmond Sherrod for 335 acres on the north side of Tar River in 1753. Wit: William Dew, Joseph Selah, and Henry Viverett.

DB 1-389 THOMAS VIVERETT of Nash Co. to DEMPSEY DAWSON of same, April 19, 1787, for 45 pds. specie 74 acres adjoining Henry Flowers, Dempsey Barnes, George Blackwell, and Joseph Phillips, it being part of a 300 acre tract granted to said Thomas Viverett on Aug. 11, 1786. Wit: Jesse Pitman and William Murray.

DB 1-391 DUNCAN LAMON of Nash Co. to JOHN CHAPMAN of same, Oct. 15, 1787, for 10 pds. specie a tract of 440 acres on the south side of Tar River adjoining John Lamon, John Taylor, John Morgan, and Lewis. Wit: William Chapman and John Lamon.

DB 1-392 JOSIAH JOHNSON of Nash Co. to DELILAH GRIFFIN of same, Dec. 21, 1785, for 150 pds. 60 acres on the south side of Fishing Creek adjoining the Muddy Branch and Samuel Davis, it being part of a tract purchased by John Portis from George Portis. Wit: Arthur Arrington and William Arrington.

DB 1-393 JOSEPH ARRINGTON, JR. of Nash Co. to ANDREW BOOTHE of same, Aug. 23, 1785, for 100 pds. specie 100 acres on the north side of Swift Creek adjoining Bell and Williams, it being a tract formerly conveyed from John Cooper to James Cooper. Wit: James Arrington, W. S. Mearns, and Benja. Whitfield.

DB 1-394 LAZARUS POPE of Nash Co. to DREWRY TAYLOR of same, Sept. 28, 1786, for 50 pds. specie 320 acres on Dickenson's Branch adjoining Lazarus Pope, Drewry Taylor and Wilson Taylor. It being half of a tract granted to said Lazarus Pope by the State on Oct. 7, 1782. Wit: Wilson Taylor, Drewry Taylor, and John Taylor.

DB 1-395 LEMUEL LASETER of Nash Co. to PETER ANDERSON of same, Feb. 20, 1787, for 500 pds. specie a tract of 243 acres on the south side of Fishing Creek adjoining Tobias Laseter and Pollock. Wit: J. Harrison, Tobias Laseter, and Sion Laseter.

DB 1-395 WILLIAM WHIDDON of Nash Co. to MICAJAH THOMAS of same, Jan. 8, 1788, for 600 pds. a tract of 100 acres on the northwest side of Sapony Creek conveyed from Lewis Perret to Wm. Whiddon, Sr., and conveyed by him to Wm. Whiddon, Jr. on Oct. 14, 1779; also, another tract of 690 acres granted to Wm. Whiddon, Jr. by the State of N.C.; a third tract of 287 acres granted to Isham Gandy by the State and conveyed by him to Wm. Whiddon, Jr. in two separate deeds, one dated March 10, 1780 and the other Dec. 28, 1784, the three tracts being on Little

Sapony Creek adjoining Noah Whiddon, Marcum Cooper's path, John Evans, Kent (then Holland), and Cotise. Wit: Marcum Cooper, S. Westray, and Solomon Cotten.

DB 1-396 MICAJAH THOMAS of Nash Co. to JULIAN KING of same, July 18, 1787, for 200 pds. a tract of 300 acres on the south side of Pig Basket Creek adjoining Thomas Whitfield and Robert Young (then James Daniel). Wit: Rhody Ricks and Jacob Butts.

DB 1-397 NOAH WHIDDON of Nash Co. to MICAJAH THOMAS of same, Jan. 8, 1788, for 30 pds. a tract of 77 acres on the south side of the Ready Branch adjoining Marcum Cooper's path and Reuben Whitfield. Wit: Charles Mabins, Solomon Cotten, and Jacob Butts.

DB 1-398 JOHN PETTY COBB of Nash Co. to ISAAC BASS of same, Oct. 20, 1787, for 160 pds. a tract of 200 acres adjoining Tucker. Isaac Bass, and Henry Peed. Wit: J. Gay, Harry Taylor, and William Boddie.

DB 1-400 ARTHUR ARRINGTON, Sheriff of Nash Co. to SOLOMON WELLS of same, May 14, 1787, for 10 pds. 16 sh. at public sale a tract of 75 acres adjoining David Pridgen and Solomon Wells, sold as the property of ABSALOM WELLS, heir at law of Daniel Wells. Wit: Wilson Vick and Wilson Taylor.

DB 1-401 JACOB DICKINSON of Edgecombe Co. to MICAJAH THOMAS of Nash Co., Feb. 13, 1788, for 30 pds. 30 acres in the fork of the Meadow Branch, it being part of a tract granted to said Dickinson by the State. Wit: Joseph Arrington and John Tillery.

DB 1-402 WILLIAM POULAN of Nash Co. to JOHN BONE of same, Aug. 24, 1787, for 35 pds. specie a tract of 175 acres adjoining William Ballard and John Fargurson's former corner. Wit: Wilson Taylor and Joseph Selah. Jr.

DB 1-403 SAMUEL SKINNER, JR. of Edgecombe Co. to JOHN HARRELL of Nash Co., March 23, 1787, for 40 pds. specie a tract of 90 acres on the south side of Stony Creek adjoining Lamon's Road and Strickland. Wit: Emmanuel Skinner and Samuel Skinner.

DB 1-404 RICHARD RANSOME of Franklin Co. to BENNET WOOD of Halifax Co., Sept. 29, 1787, for 46 pds. a tract of 444 acres adjoining Archibald Davis, Mitchel, Samuel Davis, and John Portis. Wit: John Davis and Aaron Wood.

DB 1-404 JOHN HUNT of Nash Co. to JOSEPH ARRINGTON, JR. of same. April 2, 1787, for 155 pds. 10 sh. 96 acres on both sides of Haw Branch adjoining James Douglas' former line and Harris Branch, it being part of a tract conveyed by John Cooper to John Hunt on Aug. 5, 1752; also, another tract of 290 acres on the south side of Beaver Dam Swamp adjoining Cooper, Hunt, Arrington, and Whitehead, it being part of a tract granted to said John Hunt by Earl Granville on Aug. 1, 1762. Wit: W. S. Mearns, William Lewis, and James Battle.

DB 1-405 ISRAEL WHITFIELD of Nash Co. to MILDRED

SPRINGER of same, July 16, 1785, for 40 pds. specie a tract on the north side of Peachtree Creek adjoining his old line, Pig Basket Creek, and Richard Thomas. Wit: John Bonds and Reuben Whitfield.

DB 1-406 JOSEPH SEALY of Nash Co. to LEWIS CURL of same, Jan. 10, 1788, for 100 pds. specie a tract of 150 acres on the south side of Maple Creek adjoining Benjamin Arrington and William Cain. Wit: Joel Bunn and James Watkins.

DB 1-407 THOMAS ALLEN of Nash Co. to ARTHUR ALLEN of same, Feb. 4, 1788, for 20 pds. current money a parcel of 3 acres on the north side of Sapony Creek, it being the land and orchard that Arthur Allen, deceased, willed to Thomas Allen. Wit: David Pridgen and Burwell Joiner.

—A—

Alford 12, John 206
Allen, Arthur 41, 172
Andrews, Wm. 133
Arrington 77, Arthur 102, Peter 140, Jos. 38, 39, 40, 203, 204, 230, 231, 260
Atkins, 172
Atkinson, Jas. 122, Newet 104

—B—

Backar, John 172
Baggett, Barnabe 100
Bailey, Henry 194, Rich. 51, Wm. 240
Baker 13, John 41
Ball, 67
Barnes 43, Dempsey 126, 127, Jas. 172
Barrow 261, Barnebe 201, 202
Bass 64, 198, Abraham 165, Isaac 59
Batchelor 197, 200, Stephen 46, 47, 73
Battle, Jas. 216, John 111, Wm. 140
Beckwith, Sion 212
Bell, Green 124, Thos. 77
Bennett 69, 71, Wm. 62, 67, 137
Bisset(t), David 255, 275
Blackwell, Jesse 126, 127
Boddie 141, Nathan 59, 62, 65, 125, 138, Wm. 138
Boon, Benj. 173
Bowers, 224
Boyakin 233, 264, Benj. 72
Braswell, Arthur 69, 79, 80, Jacob 139, 156, Robt. 139, Sam. 167, Wm. 91, 205, 250
Bridgers 204, Benj. 1, Sam. 81, Wm. 38
Brown 205, Jas. 120, 174, 209, 238, Jeremiah 36, 104, 114, 122, Zachariah 88
Bryant 188, Sam. 128, Wm. 197, 200
Bunn, Benj. 42, 90, David 42, 90, John 89
Bunten, Jeremiah 112

—C—

Cain (Cane) 134, Hardy 70, Jas. 14, 70 (2), 90, 99, 131, 135
Canady, Sam 13, 172
Carpenter, Thos. 116, 117
Carsey, Thos. 13
Carter 205, Chas. 94, 95, 96, Micajah 168, Sam. 51, Solomon 112, Thos. 209
Chapman 50, David 165
Clinch, Edw. 143, 182, Jos. John 111, 142

Coats, John 31
Cobb 174, 233, B. 106, Benj. 193, 264
Cockrell 268, 269, 270, 273, Jacob 220, Joel 272, John 129
Coleson 218, 269, Chester 271, 274
Collins, Jesse 192, 194, Solomon 125
Cone, Jas. 119, 121, 230, 256, Joshua 231
Cooper, John 49, 102, Carcom 136
Counsel 198, Michel 173
Cox, John 87
Crickman (Creekman, Crickmore) 171, Robt. 53, 115
Crowell 226, 258, Martha 253
Crowman, 1
Crumpler, West 274
Culpepper 64, 248, Benj. 28, Widow 86
Curl, Wilson 108

—D—

Dafnel, Wm. 47
Dance 107, 262, Ethelred 196, Ezekiel 255
Daniel, David 167
Davis 65, Baldy 38, Sam. 40, Solzy 40
Dawson, Joshua 76
Deans 251, Jeremiah 133, Rich. 17
Denson, Benj. 134
Devanport, 59
Devaughan, Sam. 95, 174, 175, 177, 208, 209
Dew, Arthur 127, Duncan 260, John 127
Dickinson (Dickerson) 251, Wm. 171, 184
Dixon 97, 211
Dortch 100, Lewis 147, Wm. 147
Dozier, Wm. 180
Drake 81, Jas. 1, Martha 21, Matthew 19 (2), 212, 228, Nath. 21,
     Wm. 228 (2)
Driver 95, 144, 263, Thos. 215, Wm. 215

—E—

Eason 224, Sam. 172, Wm. 41, 172
Eatman, John 129, 210, 218, 220, 223, 233, 234, 264, 273, Urban 234
Etheridge, Jeremiah 128, Lot 49

—F—

Ferrell, Hansel 262
Finch 209, Claiborne 251
Flood, Enoch 211
Flowers, Benj. 41, 45, 207, Hardy 134, Henry 127
Folk, John 57
Fore, Rich. 95
Foreman, Benj. 27
Fulsom, Nath. 103

—G—

Gandy, Edw. 92, 93, 113
Glover, John 200
Goodson, 89
Green, George 184, 274, Jas. 178, Nathan 38, 203, 204
Grice, Alex. 58
Griffin, Arch. 101, Hardy 20, Lewis 77, John 77
Grizzel (1) 168, Harwood 208, Herod 94, Wm. 94, 95, 96, 208

—H—

Hackney, Wm. 100
Hamilton, Thos. 224
Hammons, Jesse 231, John 186
Harrington, 50
Harris 146. Wm. 65
Harrison, Jethro 207
Harrod, 185
Hartford, 230, 231
Hatley, John 15
Hedgepeth, Peter 165
Hendrick, 159
Henry, Joshua 25
Hersey, Thos. 76
Hickman, Theophilus 122
Hill, Abner 10, 30, Green 11, 31, Wm. 173
Hilliard 221, Jeremiah 227
Hogg 275, Chas. 255
Holland, Antony 69, Rich. 139
Honey, Thos. 67
Horn, Edw. 211, 257, Henry 43, 60, 120, Isaac 60, Thos. 174, 209, 244, 246, 247, 272, Wm. 249
Hunt 118, John 102
Hunter, Thos. 134, 167, 190

—J—

Johnson, Matthew, 198
Johnston, Jacob 199
Jones, Fred 116, 121
Jordan, Wm. 256
Joyner (Joiner), Jordan 252, 253, 258, Wm. 76, 134

—K—

Kent, John 145
Kersey, Thos. 41
Kirby, 173

—L—

Lamkin (Lampkin, Lambkin) 211, 252, 265, Lewis Ablewis 226, 258
Lamon 96, 257, 265, Duncan 217
Lancaster 171, Robt. 257, Wm. 53
Lane, Newit 16, 128, 150, Wm. 159

Langley, Ausil 136, Ozal 22
Laseter, Lemuel 15, 49, 102, Tobias 15, 49, Wm. 30
Lavingston, Jos. 91
Ledbetter, John 145, Rowland 145
Lee, Jas. 54, 55
Lewis 191, Henry 194, Nath. 144
Linsey, Wm. 183
Locus, Francis 146, 162

—M—

Macon, Thos. 219
Mann, Allen 140, David 13, 26, 63, Thos. 1
Manning, Matthias 16, 46, 47, 48, 74, 136, 189, Rich. 142, Willough-
    by 59
Marshall, Dixon 217
Mason 185, Abner 124, 216, Mark 248, Ralph 100, Widow 86
Mathis, Benj. 44
McGee, Wm. 10
McNeil, Fanny 122
Mitchell, Sam. 39
Moone(y)ham 94, 208
Moore, Edmund 99, Edw. 13, 22, 23, 55, 56, 93, 195, 236, 238, 249,
    Jas. 178, 183, 186, John 43
Morgan 255, John 98, Wm. 230, Wm. S. 179
Moyes, 226

—N—

Nairn, John 191
Newton, Benj. 111
Nichols 207, 223, Jacob 233, Jeremiah 57, 58
Nicholson, Edw. 182, Josiah 122, Lemuel 248
Norriss, Wm. 60

—O—

Odom, 50
Oliver 42, Jas. 78
O'Nail, Amos 170
Owens, Daniel 110, 179, John 110

—P—

Pace, Jas. 109
Parker, Francis 21, Gab'l 246, Solomon Dorson 222
Par(r)ish 64, Edw. 66, John 114
Perry, Benj. 206, Wm. 118
Petticob, John 145
Phillips, Jos. 52, Wm. 224
Pierce, Joshua 136
Pitman 43, Wm. 43
Pollard, Thos. 92
Pollock, 180
Pope, Hardy 111, Sampson 78, Solomon 78
Powell 124, Nath. 248, Wm. 162

Pridgen 211, 219, Hardy 217, 263
Pursell, Edw. 128

—R—

Rackley 188, Francis 189, Matthew 189
Ransom 39, Rich. 40
Redman, Barth. 82
Revell, Edmund 42
Richardson, Thos. 64
Ricks 134, Benj. 26, Isaac 82, 89, Wm. 78
Robbins, John 179
Robertson, Peter 100
Rogers 33, 255, John 18, 54, 170, Thos. 201
Ross 43, 108, Andrew 47, Daniel 73, Wm. 12, 58
Rosser, 50
Russell (Pussell), Edw. 133

—S—

Savedge, Drewry 183, 186
Sa(u)nders, John 210, 234
Sealy, Jos. 172
Shelley, 81
Sikes, John 17
Skinner 42, Nicholas 227
Smell(e)y, Moses 106, Wm. 52
Smith 63, Benj. 13
Sorsby, Alex. 212, Benj. 203
Stallions, Moses 99
Strickland 99, 112, 193, Elisha 119, Hardy 256, 267, Henry 34, 107,
    256, Jacob 122, 153, 182, 249, John 104, 148, Lazarus 131, 132,
    135, 163, Mark 55, 195, 196, 261, 262, 275, Simon 164, 169, Solo-
    mon 109, 118, 119, 121, 146, 148, 149

—T—

Taylor 142, Arthur 153, 156, Daniel 133, John 35, 37 (2), 99, 143,
    179, Reuben 227, Sam. 24
Thomas, Jethro 101, Joseph 5, Micajah 68, 71, 137, 138, 139, 199,
    Mourning 68
Thorn, 233
Tisdale 209, Henry 191
Tucker 200, Benj. 221, Jas. 31, Job 59, 188, 189, 197, Thos. 32, 275,
    Willabe 50

—V—

Vestra, Wm. 16
Vick 233, Jos. 35, 36, 37, Robt. 33, 34, 35, 36, 37, 98, 114, 256

—W—

Ward, Francis 203, 225, Jos. 225
Warren 188, John 128
Waters, Thos. 107
Watkins 43

Watson, 81
Wells 258, John 253, Stephen 45
West, John 130, 131, 132, 175, Wm. 37, 78, 163
Wester, Wm. 36
Wheatley, Arthur 42
Whiddon 113
Whitten 22
Whitehead 122, 147, Arthur 29, Henry 180, Nathan 102, 141
Whitehouse, John 113
Whitfield, Thomas 62, 67
Whitley 45, 78, 223, Arthur 56, George 234
Whittington (Whittenton), Rich. 44, 75
Wilder, Wm. 86, 248
Wilhite, Wm. 199
Williams 203, 204, 206, 251, 265, Benj. 205, Billy 268, 269, 270, 271,
    272, Drewry 208, Jas. 185, 190, Joel 266, John 212, Jonas 53, 120,
    209, 222, 236, 237, 238, 272, 273, Nathan 272, Phillander 226, Pil-
    grim 240, 244, 246, 250, 266, 267, Roland 107, 266, 267, Sam. 13,
    209, 223, Thos. 43, 60
Williamson, Hardy 193, 264, Jos. 193
Willis 190, 211
Wilson, Thos. 100
Wimberly, George 139
Winbourn (e) (Winborn) 194, 263, Abraham 169, 219, David 192,
    John 213, 219, Josiah 166, 213, 214
Winstead 211, David 265, Peter 97, Sam. 265
Wombell, Johua 66
Womwell, 64
Wood (w) ard 69, 264, Jas. 61, Jos. 209
Woodel, Jos. 177
Worrell, Rich. 18

—Y—

Yeats 264
Young, Robt. 68, 103

ABSTRACTS OF NASH COUNTY DEEDS—BOOK 2

DB 2-1 EARL GRANVILLE grant to THOMAS MANN of Edgecombe Co., April 1, 17-3, a tract of 518 acres adjoining the Short Swamp, Crowman, his own line, James Drake, Swift Creek, and Benjamin Bridgers.

DB 2-5 EARL GRANVILLE grant to JOSEPH THOMAS of Edgecombe Co., March 25, 1749, a tract of 151 acres adjoining his own line.

DB 2-10 EARL GRANVILLE grant to WILLIAM McGEE of Edgecombe Co., Dec. 30, 1760. a tract of 377 acres adjoining Abner Hill.

DB 2-11 EARL GRANVILLE grant to GREEN HILL of Halifax Co., Dec. 8, 1760, a tract of 304 acres on the south side of Sapony Creek at the mouth of Ben's Meadow Branch.

DB 2-12 EARL GRANVILLE grant to WILLIAM ROSS of Granville Co. March 1, 1762, a tract of 487 acres in Granville Co. on both sides of Turkey Creek adjoining Alford.

DB 2-13 EARL GRANVILLE grant to SAMUEL WILLIAMS of Edgecombe Co., July 23, 1761, a tract of 690 acres on the north side of Baker's Branch adjoining Samuel Canady, Baker, Thomas Carsey, Edward Moore, David Mann, and Benjamin Smith.

DB 2-14 EARL GRANVILLE grant to JAMES CANE of Edgecombe Co., July 3, 1760, a tract of 375 acres on both sides of Beaver Dam Swamp.

DB 2-15 EARL GRANVILLE grant to TOBIAS LASETER of Edgecombe Co., March 4, 1761, a tract of 418 acres on the south side of Fishing Creek adjoining John Hatley and Lemuel Laseter.

DB 2-16 EARL GRANVILLE grant to WILLIAM VESTRA of Edgecombe Co., Aug. 10, 1762, a tract of 618 acres adjoining Newit Lane and Matthias Manning.

DB 2-17 EARL GRANVILLE grant to RICHARD DEANS of Edgecombe Co., June 1, 1762, a tract of 700 acres adjoining John Sikes at the mouth of Little Swamp on Little Peachtree Creek.

DB 2-18 EARL GRANVILLE grant to JOHN ROGERS of Edgecombe Co., Feb. 3, 1761, a tract of 308 acres on the north side of Peachtree Creek adjoining Richard Worrell.

DB 2-19 EARL GRANVILLE grant to MATTHEW DRAKE of Edgecombe Co., Sept. 19, 1760, a tract of 400 acres adjoining said Drake.

DB 2-20 EARL GRANVILLE grant to HARDY GRIFFIN of Edgecombe Co., Nov. 3, 1761, a tract of 700 acres on the east side of Reedv Branch.

DB 2-21 EARL GRANVILLE grant to NATHANIEL DRAKE of Edgecombe Co., Aug. 4, 1761, a tract of 510 acres on the south prong of Wolf Pit Branch adjoining Martha Drake, his own line, and Francis Parker.

DB 2-22 EARL GRANVILLE grant to EDWARD MOORE of Edgecombe Co., Nov. 6, 1761, a tract of 617 acres on Sapony Swamp adjoining Ozal Langley and Whitten.

DB 2-23 EARL GRANVILLE grant to EDWARD MOORE of Edgecombe Co., March 16, 1761, a tract of 600 acres on the south side of Polecat Branch.

DB 2-24 EARL GRANVILLE grant to SAMUEL TAYLOR of Edgecombe Co., Feb. 12, 1761, a tract of 275 acres on both sides of Contentnea Creek.

DB 2-25 EARL GRANVILLE grant to JOSHUA HENRY of Edgecombe Co., Feb. 19, 1761, a tract of 160 acres on the north side of Tar River and on both sides of Turkey Creek.

DB 2-26 EARL GRANVILLE grant to BENJAMIN RICKS of Edgecombe Co., Aug. 4, 1761, a tract of 700 acres adjoining David Mann and his own line.

DB 2-27 EARL GRANVILLE grant to BENJAMIN FORE-MAN of Edgecombe Co., July 7, 1760, a tract of 129 acres on both sides of Beaver Dam Swamp.

DB 2-28 EARL GRANVILLE grant to BENJAMIN CULPEP-PER of Edgecombe Co., July 3, 1760, a tract of 312 acres on the north side of Moccasin Creek adjoining his plantation.

DB 2-29 EARL GRANVILLE grant to ARTHUR WHITE-HEAD of Edgecombe Co., March 16, 1761, a tract of 457 acres adjoining his own line and Whitehead's Mill Swamp.

DB 2-30 EARL GRANVILLE grant to ABNER HILL of Edge-combe Co., Aug. 1. 1762. a tract of 555 acres adjoining the tract where he then lived and William Laseter.

DB 2-31 EARL GRANVILLE grant to JAMES TUCKER of Edgecombe Co., Aug. 10. 1760, a tract of 700 acres adjoining John Coats and Green Hill.

DB 2-32 EARL GRANVILLE grant to THOMAS TUCKER of Edgecombe Co., Feb. 26, 1761, a tract of 225 acres on the south side of Sapony Creek.

DB 2-33 STATE of N.C. grant to ROBERT VICK by Gov. Alex. Martin, Nov. 1, 1784, a tract of 91 acres on the north side of Turkey Creek adjoining his own corner and Rogers.

DB 2-34 STATE of N.C. grant to ROBERT VICK by Gov. Alex. Martin, Nov. 1, 1784, a tract of 100 acres on the north side of Tur-key Creek adjoining Henry Strickland.

DB 2-35 STATE of N.C. grant to ROBERT VICK. JR. by Gov. Alex. Martin, Nov. 1, 1784, a tract of 200 acres on Toisnot Swamp adjoining his father's line, John Taylor, and Joseph Vick.

DB 2-36 STATE of N. C. grant to JOSEPH VICK by Gov. Alex. Martin, Nov. 1. 1784, a tract of 200 acres on Toisnot Swamp adjoining Robert Vick, William Wester, and Jeremiah Brown.

DB 2-37 STATE of N. C. grant to ROBERT VICK by Gov. Alex. Martin, Nov. 1, 1784, a tract of 400 acres on Toisnot Swamp adjoining John Taylor, William West, and Joseph Vick.

DB 2-38 STATE of N. C. grant to NATHAN GREEN by Gov. Sam. Johnston. Nov. 26, 1789, a tract of 200 acres on the south side of Great White Oak Swamp adjoining Joseph Arrington, Will-iam Bridgers, and Baldy Davis.

DB 2-39 STATE of N. C. grant to JOSEPH ARRINGTON by Gov. Sam. Johnston, Nov. 26, 1789, a tract of 321 acres on the north side of the Great White Oak Swamp adjoining his own line, Ransom, and Samuel Mitchell.

DB 2-40 STATE of N. C. grant to JOSEPH ARRINGTON by Gov. Sam. Johnston, Nov. 26, 1789, a tract of 162½ acres on the south side of Great Fishing Creek adjoining his own line, Solzy Davis, Samuel Davis, and Richard Ransom.

DB 2-41 EARL GRANVILLE grant to ARTHUR ALLEN of Edgecombe Co., Feb. 17, 1761, a tract of 280 acres on the north side of Sapony Creek adjoining Benjamin Flowers, the Tar River, Thomas Kersey, John Baker, and Wm. Eason.

DB 2-42 EARL GRANVILLE grant to EDMUND REVELL of Egecombe Co., April 1, 1763, a tract of 700 acres adjoining Skinner, Oliver, Arthur Wheatley, Benjamin Bunn, and David Bunn.

DB 2-43 EARL GRANVILLE grant to WILLIAM PITMAN of Edgecombe Co., April 1, 1763, a tract of 305 acres adjoining Ross, Thomas Williams, John Moore, Henry Horn, Watkins, Barnes, and Pitman.

DB 2-44 EARL GRANVILLE grant to BENJAMIN MATHIS of Edgecombe Co., July 7, 1760, a tract of 170 acres on the north side of Swift Creek adjoining Richard Whittenton.

DB 2-45 EARL GRANVILLE grant to STEPHEN WELLS of Edgecombe Co., Nov. 26, 1761, a tract of 595 acres at his own corner on Tar River adjoining the Wildcat Branch, Benjamin Flowers, and Whitley.

DB 2-46 EARL GRANVILLE grant to MATTHIAS MANNING of Edgecombe Co., Feb. 26, 1761, a tract of 385 acres at his own corner on the north side of Sapony Creek adjoining Stephen Batchelor.

DB 2-47 EARL GRANVILLE grant to MATTHIAS MANNING of Edgecombe Co., Aug. 10, 1762, a tract of 611 acres on Sapony Creek adjoining Stephen Batchelor, Andrew Ross, and William Dafrel.

DB 2-48 EARL GRANVILLE grant to MATTHIAS MANNING of Edgecombe Co., Feb. 26, 1761, a tract of 240 acres on the north side of Reedy Branch.

2-49 EARL GRANVILLE grant to LEMUEL LASETER of Edgecombe Co., Oct. 15, 1761, a tract of 560 acres adjoining his own line, Tobias Laseter, Lot Etheridge, John Cooper, and the Fishing Creek.

DB 2-50 EARL GRANVILLE grant to WILLABE TUCKER of Edgecombe Co., June 1, 1762, a tract of 700 acres adjoining his own line, Chapman, Odom, the Bare Branch, Harrington, Rosser, and Great Peachtree Creek.

DB 2-51 EARL GRANVILLE grant to SAMUEL CARTER of Edgecombe Co., Feb. 12, 1761, a tract of 515 acres on the north side of Tar River adjoining Richard Bailey.

DB 2-52 EARL GRANVILLE grant to WILLIAM SMELLEY

of Edgecombe Co., Feb. 12, 1761, a tract of 280 acres adjoining Joseph Phillips.

DB 2-53 STATE of N.C. grant to WILLIAM LANCASTER by Gov. Alex. Martin, Dec. 20, 1791, a tract of 500 acres on both sides of the Beaver Dam adjoining Robert Crickman and Jonas Williams.

DB 2-54 STATE of N.C. grant to JAMES LEE by Gov. Alex. Martin, Oct. 9, 1783, a tract of 280 acres on Moccasin Creek adjoining John Rogers.

DB 2-55 STATE of N.C. grant to JAMES LEE by Gov. Alex. Martin, Nov. 1, 1784, a tract of 300 acres on Toisnot Swamp adjoining Edward Moore and Mark Strickland.

DB 2-56 EARL GRANVILLE grant to ARTHUR WHITLEY of Edgecombe Co., March 16, 1761, a tract of 500 acres on the north side of the Great Branch adjoining Edward Moore.

DB 2-57 EARL GRANVILLE grant to JEREMIAH NICHOLS of Edgecombe Co., Aug. 1, 1762, a tract of 320 acres adjoining John Folk and the Mash Swamp.

DB 2-58 STATE of N.C. grant to JEREMIAH NICHOLS by Gov. Alex. Martin, Dec. 20, 1791, a tract of 275 acres on the north side of Contentnea Creek adjoining Alexander Grice and William Ross.

DB 2-59 STATE of N.C. grant to JOB TUCKER by Gov. Richard Caswell, March 30, 1780, a tract of 183 acres on Peachtree Creek adjoining Nathan Boddie, Devanport, Willoughby Manning, and Isaac Bass.

DB 2-60 EARL GRANVILLE grant to ISAAC HORN of Edgecombe Co., June 1, 1762, a tract of 550 acres adjoining Henry Horn, William Norriss, his own line, Thomas Williams, and the Compass Creek.

DB 2-61 EARL GRANVILLE grant to JAMES WOODWARD of Edgecombe Co., Feb. 24, 1761 a tract of 312 acres on the south side of Pig Basket Creek.

DB 2-62 EARL GRANVILLE grant to NATHAN BODDIE of Edgecombe Co., May 1, 1762, a tract of 479 acres adjoining Thomas Whitfield and William Bennett.

DB 2-63 EARL GRANVILLE to DAVID MANN of Edgecombe Co., March 16, 1761, a tract of 643 acres on the south side of Bounse's Branch adjoining Smith.

DB 2-64 EARL GRANVILLE grant to THOMAS RICHARDSON of Edgecombe Co., June 1, 1762, a tract of 596 acres on the north side of the Back Swamp adjoining Bass, Wombwell, Parrish, and Culpepper.

DB 2-65 EARL GRANVILLE grant to NATHAN BODDIE of Edgecombe Co., Aug. 10, 1762, a tract of 675 acres adjoining William Harris, Davis, and the Turkey Branch.

DB 2-66 EARL GRANVILLE grant to JOSHUA WOMBELL of Edgecombe Co., Nov. 3, 1761, a tract of 700 acres adjoining Edward Parish.

DB 2-67 EARL GRANVILLE grant to THOMAS WHITFIELD of Edgecombe Co., June 30, 1760, a tract of 490 acres on both sides of Peachtree Creek adjoining Wm. Bennett, Thomas Honey, and Ball.

DB 2-68   EARL GRANVILLE grant to MOURNING THOMAS of Edgecombe Co., Dec. 12, 1760. a tract of 400 acres adjoining Robert Young, her own line, and Micajah Thomas.

DB 2-69 EARL GRANVILLE grant to ANTONY HOLLAND of Edgecombe Co., Nov. 3, 1761, a tract of 684 acres adjoining Arthur Braswell, Bennett, and Woodward.

DB 2-70 EARL GRANVILLE grant to JAMES CANE of Edgecombe Co., Dec. 10, 1760, a tract of 435 acres on the south side of Fishing Creek adjoining Hardy Cane, James Cane, and Cane's Mill Swamp.

DB 2-71 EARL GRANVILLE grant to MICAJAH THOMAS of Edgecombe Co., Nov. 3, 1761, a tract of 570 acres adjoining his own line, Bennett, the Lewis' Branch, the Reedy Branch, and the creek.

DB 2-72 EARL GRANVILLE grant to BENJAMIN BOYKIN of Edgecombe Co., March 4, 1761, a tract of 320 acres on the north side of Contentnea Creek.

DB 2-73 EARL GRANVILLE grant to DANIEL ROSS of Edgecombe Co., March 16, 1761, a tract of 160 acres on both sides of Sapony Creek adjoining Stephen Batchelor.

DB 2-74 EARL GRANVILLE grant to MATTHIAS MANNING of Edgecombe Co., Feb. 26. 1761, a tract of 600 acres on the east side of the Great Bare Branch.

DB 2-75 EARL GRANVILLE grant to RICHARD WHITTINGTON of Edgecombe Co., 1760. a tract of 123 acres on Swift Creek.

DB 2-76 EARL GRANVILLE grant to WILLIAM JOYNER of Edgecombe Co., Feb. 17, 1761, a tract of 180 acres on the north side of Tar River adjoining Thomas Hersey and Joshua Dawson.

DB 2-77 EARL GRANVILLE grant to JOHN GRIFFIN of Edgecombe Co., April 1, 1762, a tract of 95 acres on the north side of Swift Creek adjoining Thomas Bell, Lewis Griffin, and Arrington.

DB 2-78 EARL GRANVILLE grant to SOLOMON POPE of Edgecombe Co., Nov. 3, 1761, a tract of 700 acres on the south side of Stony Creek adjoining James Oliver, William West, Whitley, William Ricks, and Sampson Pope.

DB 2-79   EARL GRANVILLE grant to ARTHUR BRASWELL of Edgecombe Co., Feb. 26, 1761, a tract of 250 acres on both sides of Pig Basket Creek.

DB 2-80   EARL GRANVILLE grant to ARTHUR BRASWELL of Edgecombe Co., Nov. 3, 1761, a tract of 627 acres on both sides of Pig Basket Creek near Anthony's Branch.

DB 2-81 EARL GRANVILLE grant to SAMUEL BRIDGERS of Edgecombe Co., May 7. 1756, a tract of 427 acres on both sides of Swift Creek between Shelley's and Watson's, adjoining both of them and Drake.

DB 2-82 EARL GRANVILLE grant to ISAAC RICKS of Edgecombe Co., March 25. 1752, a tract of 128 acres adjoining his own line, Bartholomew Redman, and the river.

DB 2-86 EARL GRANVILLE grant to WILLIAM WILDER of Edgecombe Co., May 2, 1752, a tract of 100 acres on the south side of Fishing Creek adjoining the Widow Culpepper and the Widow Mason.

DB 2-87 EARL GRANVILLE grant to JOHN COX of Edgecombe Co., March 25, 1752, a tract of 315 acres on Beaver Dam Swamp.

DB 2-88 EARL GRANVILLE grant to ZACHARIAH BROWN of Edgecombe Co., 1754, a tract of 450 acres on the south side of the south prong of Sapony Creek.

DB 2-89 EARL GRANVILLE grant to ISAAC RICKS of Edgecombe Co., April 27, 1754, a tract of 73 acres on the south side of Tar River adjoining his own line, Goodson, and John Bunn.

DB 2-90 EARL GRANVILLE grant to DAVID BUNN of Edgecombe Co., March 25, 1752, a tract of 445 acres on the north side of Tar River adjoining James Cain, Benjamin Bunn, and his own line.

DB 2-91 EARL GRANVILLE grant to JOSEPH LAVINGSTON of Edgecombe Co., Oct. 24, 1754, a tract of 206 acres adjoining William Braswell.

DB 2-92 EARL GRANVILLE grant to THOMAS POLLARD of Edgecombe Co., March 25, 1752, a tract of 360 acres on the north side of Sapony Creek adjoining Edward Gandy.

DB 2-93 EARL GRANVILLE grant to EDWARD GANDY of Edgecombe Co., May 1, 1752, a tract of 380 acres on the north side of Sapony Creek adjoining Edward Moore.

DB 2-94 STATE of N.C. grant to HEROD GRIZELL by Gov. Alex. Martin, Dec. 20, 1791, a tract of 400 acres on Mooneham's Mill Branch adjoining William Grizell, Charles Carter, and Mooneham.

DB 2-95 STATE of N.C. grant to WILLIAM GRIZELL by Gov. Alex. Martin, Dec. 20, 1791, a tract of 386 acres adjoining Driver's spring branch, Richard Fore, the road, Samuel Devaughan, and Charles Carter.

DB 2-96 STATE of N.C. grant to WILLIAM GRIZELL by Gov. Alex. Martin, Dec. 20, 1791, a tract of 640 acres adjoining Lamon's old line and Charles Carter.

DB 2-97 STATE of N.C. grant to PETER WINSTEAD by Gov. Alex. Martin, Dec. 20, 1791, a tract of 410 acres on the south side of Tar River adjoining Dixon.

DB 2-98 STATE of N.C. grant to JOHN MORGAN by Gov. Alex. Martin, Nov. 1, 1784, a tract of 160 acres on Turkey Creek adjoining Robert Vick.

DB 2-99 STATE of N.C. grant to MOSES STALLIONS by Gov. Alex. Martin, Nov. 1, 1784, a tract of 300 acres on Toisnot Swamp adjoining John Taylor, Edmund Moore, James Cain, and Strickland.

DB 2-100 STATE of N.C. grant to BARNABE BAGGET by Gov. Alex. Martin, Nov. 1, 1784, a tract of 500 acres on the north side of Swift Creek adjoining Thomas Wilson, Ralph Mason, Peter

Robertson, Dortch, and William Hackney..

DB 2-101 STATE of N.C. grant to ARCHIBALD GRIFFIN by Gov. Alex. Martin, Dec. 20, 1791, a tract of 18 acres in the fork of Stony Creek adjoining his own corner and the south side of Pig Basket Creek near the ford, Jethro Thomas, and Peachtree Creek.

DB 2-102 EARL GRANVILLE grant to JOHN HUNT of Edgecombe Co., Aug. 1, 1762, a tract of 340 acres adjoining his own line, John Cooper, Arthur Arrington, Nathan Whitehead, and Lemuel Laseter.

DB 2-103 EARL GRANVILLE grant to NATHANIEL FULSOM of Edgecombe Co., June 13, 1760, a tract of 600 acres adjoining Robert Young and Whitehead's Mill Swamp.

DB 2-104 STATE of N.C. grant to NEWET ATKINSON by Gov. Alex. Martin, Dec. 20, 1791, a tract of 183 acres on Turkey Creek adjoining Jeremiah Brown and John Strickland.

DB 2-106 STATE of N.C. grant to MOSES SMELLY by Gov. Alex. Martin, Dec. 20, 1791, a tract of 200 acres on the Mash Swamp adjoining B. Cobb.

DB 2-107 STATE of N.C. grant to HENRY STRICKLAND by Gov. Alex. Martin, Dec. 20, 1791, a tract of 34 acres on the south side of Tar River adjoining Roland Williams, Dance, Thomas Waters, and his own line.

DB 2-108 STATE of N.C. grant to WILSON CURL by Gov. Alex. Martin, Dec. 20, 1791, a tract of 17 acres on the east side of Stony Creek adjoining Ross and his own line.

DB 2-109 STATE of N.C. grant to JAMES PACE by Gov. Sam. Johnston, Nov. 26, 1789, a tract of 95 acres on the south side of Turkey Creek adjoining Solomon Strickland.

DB 2-110 STATE of N.C. grant to JOHN OWENS by Gov. Alex. Martin, Dec. 20, 1791, a tract of 100 acres on the south side of Tar River adjoining Daniel Owens.

DB 2-111 STATE of N.C. grant to BENJAMIN NEWTON by Gov. Alex. Martin, Dec. 20, 1791, a tract of 66 acres adjoining John Battle, his own line, Hardy Pope, and Joseph John Clinch.

DB 2-112 STATE of N.C. grant JEREMIAH BUNTEN by Gov. Alex. Martin, Dec. 20, 1791, a tract of 50 acres on the north side of Tar River adjoining his own line, Strickland, and Solomon Carter.

DB 2-113 STATE of N.C. grant to EDWARD GANDY by Gov. Alex. Martin, Dec. 20, 1791, a tract of 130 acres on the north side of Sapony Creek adjoining John Whitehouse and Whiddon.

DB 2-114 STATE of N.C. grant to JOHN PARISH by Gov. Alex. Martin, Dec. 20, 1791, a tract of 400 acres on Turkey Creek adjoining Jeremiah Brown and Robert Vick.

DB 2-115 STATE of N.C. grant to ROBERT CRICKMORE by Gov. Sam. Johnston, Nov. 26, 1789, a tract of 300 acres on both sides of Beaver Dam Swamp above the Juniper Prong.

DB 2-116 STATE of N.C. grant to FREDERICK JONES by Gov. Alex. Martin, Nov. 1, 1784, a tract of 200 acres on Turkey Creek adjoining Thomas Carpenter and the county line.

DB 2-117 STATE of N.C. grant to THOMAS CARPENTER by

Gov. Sam. Johnston, Nov. 26, 1789, a tract of 300 acres on both sides of Little Creek adjoining his own line.

DB 2-118 STATE of N.C. grant to WILLIAM PERRY by Gov. Sam. Johnston, Nov. 26, 1789, a tract of 280 acres on the branches of Turkey Creek adjoining his own corner, Solomon Strickland, and Hunt.

DB 2-119 STATE of N. C. grant to JAMES CONE by Gov. Alex. Martin, Nov. 1, 1784, a tract of 400 acres on both sides of Turkey Creek adjoining Solomon Strickland and Elisha Strickland, near the county line.

DB 2-120 STATE of N.C. grant to HENRY HORN by Gov. Alex. Martin, Dec. 20, 1791, a tract of 190 acres on Wilder's Mill Branch adjoining Jonas Williams and James Brown.

DB 2-121 STATE of N.C. grant to JAMES CONE by Gov. Alex. Martin, Nov. 1, 1780 (?), a tract of 200 acres on the south side of Turkey Creek adjoining Solomon Strickland, his own line, and Frederick Jones.

DB 2-122 STATE of N.C. grant to JAMES ATKINSON by Gov. Alex. Martin, Dec. 20, 1791, a tract of 153 acres on Turkey Creek adjoining Theophilus Hickman, Jacob Strickland, and Jeremiah Brown.

DB 2-122 STATE of N. C. grant to FANNY McNEIL by Gov. R. Caswell, March 14, 1786, a tract of 208 acres on the south side of Beaver Dam Swamp adjoining Josiah Nicholson and Capt. Whitehead.

DB 2-124 STATE of N.C. grant to GREEN BELL by Gov. Alex. Martin, Dec. 20, 1791, a tract of 127 acres on the south side of Fishing Creek and on Beaver Dam Swamp adjoining Powell and Abner Mason.

DB 2-125 STATE of N.C. grant to SOLOMON COLLINS by Gov. Alex. Martin, Dec. 20, 1791, a tract of 47 acres on the north side of Little Sapony Creek adjoining his own line and Nathan Boddie.

DB 2-126 STATE of N.C. grant to DEMPSEY BARNES by Gov. Rd. Caswell, Aug. 11, 1786, a tract of 400 acres on the south side of the Little Swamp adjoining his own line and Jesse Blackwell.

DB 2-127 STATE of N.C. grant to DEMPSEY BARNES by Gov. Rd. Caswell, Aug. 11, 1786, a tract of 640 acres on both sides of the Little Swamp adjoining Jesse Blackwell, John Dew, Arthur Dew, and Henry Flowers.

DB 2-128 STATE of N.C. grant to JEREMIAH ETHERIDGE by Gov. Rd. Caswell, Nov. 1, 1784, a tract of 221 acres on Sapony Creek adjoining Edward Pursell, his own line, John Warren, Jr., Newit Lane, and Samuel Bryant.

DB 2-129 STATE of N.C. grant to JOHN COCKRELL by Gov. Rd. Caswell, Oct. 9, 1783, a tract of 640 acres on Bloomery Swamp adjoining John Eatman.

DB 2-130 STATE of N. C. grant to JOHN WEST by Gov. Rd. Caswell, Sept. 24, 1785, a tract of 300 acres on Turkey Creek.

DB 2-131 STATE of N.C. grant to JOHN WEST by Gov. Rd. Caswell, Sept. 24, 1785, a tract of 200 acres adjoining his own line, Lazarus Strickland, and James Cain.

DB 2-132 STATE of N.C. grant to JOHN WEST by Gov. Rd. Caswell, Sept. 24, 1785, a tract of 300 acres on the east side of Toisnot Swamp adjoining Lazarus Strickland.

DB 2-133 STATE of N.C. grant to DANIEL TAYLOR by Gov. Rd. Caswell, Aug. 11, 1786, a tract of 100 acres on the east side of Turkey Creek adjoining Edward Russell, William Andrews, Jeremiah Deans, and his own line.

DB 2-134 STATE of N.C. grant to THOMAS HUNTER by Gov. Rd. Caswell, March 30, 1780, a tract of 640 acres on Maple Creek adjoining Benjamin Denson, Cain, Hardy Flowers, William Joiner. and Ricks.

DB 2-135 STATE of N.C. grant to JAMES CAIN by Gov. Alex. Martin, Nov. 1, 1784, a tract of 200 acres on Toisnot Swamp adjoining Lazarus Strickland.

DB 2-136 STATE of N.C. grant to MATTHIAS MANNING, SR. by Gov. Alex. Martin, Nov. 1, 1784, a tract of 587 acres on the north side of Sapony Creek adjoining Ausil Langley, Joshua Pierce, and Marcom Cooper.

DB 2-137 STATE of N.C. grant to MICAJAH THOMAS by Gov. Rd. Caswell, March 14, 1786. a tract of 249 acres on the north side of Sapony Creek adjoining William Bennett.

DB 2-138 STATE of N.C. grant to MICAJAH THOMAS by Gov. Rd. Caswell, Sept. 24, 1785, a tract of 150 acres adjoining his own line, Nathan Boddie, and William Boddie.

DB 2-139 STATE of N.C. grant to MICAJAH THOMAS by Gov. Rd. Caswell, Sept. 24, 1785, a tract of 393 acres on both sides of Pig Basket Creek adjoining his own line, Richard Holland, George Wimberly. Jacob Braswell, and Robert Braswell.

DB 2-140 STATE of N.C. grant to PETER ARRINGTON by Gov. Sam. Johnston, Nov. 30, 1795. a tract of 342 acres on the north side of Swift Creek adjoining William Battle and Allen Mann.

DB 2-141 STATE of N.C grant to NATHAN WHITEHEAD by Gov. Rd. Dobbs Spaight, July 9, 1794, a tract of 26 acres on the north side of Peachtree Creek adjoining his own line and Boddie.

DB 2-142 STATE of N.C. grant to JOSEPH JOHN CLINCH by Gov. Alex. Martin, Dec. 20, 1791, a tract of 36 acres on the south side of Swift Creek adjoining Richard Manning and Taylor.

DB 2-143 STATE of N.C. grant to EDWARD CLINCH by Gov. Alex. Martin, Dec. 20, 1791, a tract of 272 acres on both sides of Turkey Creek adjoining Clinch and John Taylor.

DB 2-144 STATE of N.C. grant to NATHANIEL LEWIS by Gov. R. D. Spaight, July 16, 1795. a tract of 300 acres in the fork of Turkey Creek and Moccasin Creek adjoining Driver.

DB 2-145 STATE of N.C. grant to ROWLAND LEDBETTER by Gov. Sam. Johnston, Nov. 26, 1789, a tract of 150 acres on both sides of Clark's Branch adjoining John Petticob, John Ledbetter. and John Kent.

DB 2-146 STATE of N.C. grant to FRANCIS LOCUS by Gov. Alex. Martin, Nov. 1, 1784, a tract of 150 acres on the south side of Turkey Creek adjoining Solomon Strickland and Harris.

DB 2-147 STATE of N.C. grant to LEWIS DORTCH by Gov. Alex. Martin, Dec. 20, 1791, a tract of 61 acres on the north side of Swift Creek adjoining his own line, Whitehead, and William Dortch.

DB 2-148 STATE of N.C. grant to JOHN STRICKLAND by Gov. Alex. Martin, Nov. 1, 1784, a tract of 200 acres on Turkey Creek including his own improvements, adjoining Solomon Strickland.

DB 2-149 STATE of N.C. grant to SOLOMON STRICKLAND by Gov. Alex. Martin. Nov. 1, 1784, a tract of 250 acres on Turkey Creek and the Great Branch.

DB 2-150 EARL GRANVILLE grant to NEWIT LANE of Edgecombe Co., Feb. 6, 1762, a tract of 460 acres on Sapony Swamp adjoining his own line.

DB 2-153 EARL GRANVILLE grant to ARTHUR TAYLOR of Edgecombe Co., Aug. 1, 1761, a tract of 700 acres on both sides of Tar River adjoining his own line and Jacob Strickland.

DB 2-156 EARL GRANVILLE grant to ARTHUR TAYLOR of Edgecombe Co., Aug. 1, 1761, a tract of 700 acres on both sides of Tar River adjoining Jacob Braswell and his own line.

DB 2-159 EARL GRANVILLE grant to WILLIAM LANE of Edgecombe Co., Dec. 6, 1760, a tract of 402 acres near Hendrick's old path on the south side of Lane's Mill Branch.

DB 2-162 STATE of N.C. grant to WILLIAM POWELL by Gov. Alex. Martin, Nov. 16, 1790, a tract of 400 acres on Turkey Creek adioining Francis Locus.

DB 2-163 STATE of N.C. grant to WILLIAM WEST by Gov. Alex. Martin, Nov. 1, 1784, a tract of 177 acres on the west side of Toisnot Swamp adioining his own line and Lazarus Strickland.

DB 2-164 STATE of N.C. grant to SIMON STRICKLAND by Gov. Alex. Martin, Oct. 25, 1780, a tract of 200 acres on Toisnot Swamp adioining his own line.

DB 2-165 EARL GRANVILLE grant to PETER HEDGE-PETH of Edgecombe Co., July 23, 1762, a tract of 700 acres adjoining David Chapman, Tucker's Swamp, and Abraham Bass.

DB 2-166 STATE of N.C. grant to JOSIAH WINBORNE by Gov. Alex. Martin, Dec. 20, 1791, a tract of 150 acres on the south side of Beaver Dam Branch adjoining his own line.

DB 2-167 STATE of N.C. grant to SAMUEL BRASWELL by Gov. Alex. Martin, Nov. 1, 1784, a tract of 200 acres on the north side of Stony Creek adjoining David Daniel, Thomas Hunter, and his own line.

DB 2-168 STATE of N.C. grant to MICAJAH CARTER by Gov. Richd. Dobbs Spaight, July 16, 1795, a tract of 132 acres on Mooneham's Mill Branch adjoining Grizzel.

DB 2-169 STATE of N.C. grant to ABRAHAM WINBORN by Gov. Alex. Martin, Dec. 20, 1791, a tract of 33 acres on the north side of Moccasin Creek adjoining Simon Strickland.

DB 2-170 STATE of N.C. grant to AMOS O'NAIL by Gov. Alex. Martin, Nov. 1, 1784, a tract of 200 acres on the north side of Moccasin Creek adjoining John Rogers and his own improvement.

DB 2-171 STATE of N.C. grant to WILLIAM DICKERSON by Gov. Rich'd. Dobbs Spaight, July 16, 1795, a tract of 300 acres on the Beaver Dam adjoining Creekman and Lancaster.

DB 2-172 EARL GRANVILLE grant to SAMUEL EASON of Edgecombe Co., March 16, 1761, a tract of 440 acres adjoining John Backar, Samuel Canady, Atkins, James Barnes, Joseph Sealy, William Eason, and Arthur Allen.

DB 2-173 STATE of N.C. grant to WILLIAM HILL by Gov. Rd. Caswell, Nov. 10, 1779, a tract of 640 acres on the south side of Redbud Creek adjoining Benjamin Boon, Kirby, and Michel Counsel.

DB 2-174 STATE of N.C. grant to JAMES BROWN by Gov. Wm. R. Davie, Dec. 13, 1798, a tract of 125 acres adjoining his own line, Thomas Horn, Cobb, and Samuel Devaughan.

DB 2-175 STATE of N.C. grant to SAMUEL DEVAUGHAN by Gov. Alex. Martin, Dec. 20, 1791, a tract of 300 acres on Turkey Creek at his own corner adjoining John West.

DB 2-177 STATE of N.C. grant to SAMUEL DEVAUGHAN by Gov. Alex. Martin, Nov. 1, 1784, a tract of 300 acres on Turkey Creek adjoining Joseph Woodel.

DB 2-178 STATE of N.C. grant to JAMES GREEN by Gov. Benj. Williams, Feb. 18, 1800, a tract of 200 acres on the north side of Peachtree Creek adjoining James Moore.

DB 2-179 STATE of N.C. grant to WILLIAM S. MORGAN by Gov. B. Williams, Nov. 26, 1799, a tract of 200 acres adjoining John Taylor, John Robbins, and Daniel Owens.

DB 2-180 STATE of N.C. grant to WILLIAM DOZIER by Gov. B. Williams, Dec. 28, 1799, a tract of 91 acres on the south side of Fishing Creek adjoining Pollock and Henry Whitehead.

DB 2-182 STATE of N.C. grant to EDWARD CLINCH by Gov. Rd. Caswell, Sept. 24, 1785, a tract of 100 acres on the south side of Tar River adjoining his old line, Edward Nicholson, and Jacob Strickland.

DB 2-183 STATE of N.C. grant to JAMES MOORE by Gov. W. R. Davie. June 10, 1799, a tract of 45 acres adjoining Drewry Savedge and William Linsey.

DB 2-184 STATE of N.C. grant to GEORGE GREEN by Gov. B. Williams, March 14, 1800, a tract of 150 acres on the south side of Juniper Swamp adjoining his own line, and William Dickinson.

DB 2-185 STATE of N.C. grant to JAMES WILLIAMS by Gov. B. Williams, Dec. 6, 1799, a tract of 51 acres on the south side of Stony Creek adjoining Harrod and Mason.

DB 2-186 STATE of N. C. grant to JAMES MOORE by Gov. B. Williams. Dec. 16, 1799, a tract of 200 acres on both sides of Little Peachtree Creek adjoining John Hammons and Drewry Savidge.

DB 2-188 STATE of N.C. grant to JOAB TUCKER by Gov. W. R. Davie, June 10, 1799, a tract of 100 acres on the south side of Great Sapony Creek adjoining Rackley, Warren, Bryant, and his own line.

DB 2-189 STATE of N.C. grant to JOAB TUCKER by Gov. W. R. Davie, June 10, 1799, a tract of 100 acres on both sides of Great Sapony Creek adjoining his own line, Matthias Manning, Matthew Rackley, and Francis Rackley.

DB 2-190 STATE of N.C. grant to JAMES WILLIAMS by Gov. B. Williams, Nov. 14, 1800, a tract of 14 acres on the north side of Stony Creek adjoining Willis and Thomas Hunter.

DB 2-191 STATE of N.C. grant to HENRY TISDALE by Gov. B. Williams, March 12, 1800, a tract of 100 acres on the north side of Moccasin Creek adjoining John Nairn, Lewis, and his own line.

DB 2-192 STATE of N.C. grant to JESSE COLLINS by Gov. B. Williams, March 12, 1800, a tract of 245 acres on both sides of Beaver Dam Branch adjoining David Winborn and his own line.

DB 2-193 STATE of N.C. grant to HARDY WILLIAMSON by Gov. B. Williams, March 12, 1800, a tract of 50 acres on the north side of Contentnea Creek adjoining Benjamin Cobb, Strickland, and Joseph Williamson.

DB 2-194 STATE of N.C. grant to JESSE COLLINS by Gov. B. Williams, March 12, 1800, a tract of 336 acres adjoining Winbourne, Henry Bailey, and Henry Lewis.

DB 2-195 STATE of N.C. grant to MARK STRICKLAND by Gov. Alex. Martin, Nov. 1, 1784, a tract of 200 acres on Toisnot Swamp adjoining Edward Moore and his own line.

DB 2-196 STATE of N.C. grant to MARK STRICKLAND by Gov. Alex. Martin, Nov. 1, 1784, a tract of 100 acres on Toisnot Swamp adjoining his own line and Ethelred Dance.

DB2-197 STATE of N.C. grant to JOAB TUCKER by Gov. B. Williams, Dec. 6, 1799, a tract of 100 acres on the south side of Great Sapony Creek adjoining William Bryant, Batchelor, and his own line.

DB 2-198 STATE of N.C. grant to MATTHEW JOHNSON by Gov. B. Williams, Dec. 28, 1799, a tract of 100 acres on Tumbling Run Creek adjoining Counsel and Bass.

DB 2-199 STATE of N.C. grant to JACOB JOHNSTON by Gov. B. Williams, Dec. 28, 1799, a tract of 75 acres adjoining Micajah Thomas and William Wilhite.

DB 2-200 STATE of N.C. grant to JOHN GLOVER by Gov. W. R. Davie, June 10, 1799, a tract of 20 acres on Sapony Creek adjoining William Bryant, Batchelor, and Tucker.

DB 2-201 STATE of N.C. grant to BARNEBE BARROW Gov. Alex. Martin. Oct. 25, 1782, a tract of 200 acres on Turkey Creek adjoining Thomas Rogers and his own line.

DB 2-202 STATE of N.C. grant to BARNEBE BARROW by Gov. Alex. Martin. Oct. 25, 1782, a tract of 100 acres on Turkey Creek and on the Forked Branch below the schoolhouse.

DB 2-203 STATE of N.C. grant to JOSEPH ARRINGTON by Gov. B. Williams, Sept. 29, 1800, a tract of 182 acres adjoining Nathan Green, Benjamin Sorsby, Francis Ward, Williams, and his own line.

DB 2-204 STATE of N.C. grant to JOSEPH ARRINGTON by Gov. B. Williams, Sept. 29, 1800, a tract of 180 acres adjoining Williams, Bridgers, and Nathan Green.

DB 2-205 STATE of N.C. grant to BENJAMIN WILLIAMS by Gov. B. Williams, Dec. 20, 1800, a tract of 25 acres adjoining William Braswell, Carter, the county line, and Brown.

DB 2-206 STATE of N.C. grant to JOHN ALFORD by Gov. B. Williams, Dec. 20, 1800, a tract of 400 acres on Turkey Creek adjoining Benjamin Perry, the county line, Williams, and his own line.

DB 2-207 STATE of N.C. grant to JETHRO HARRISON by Gov. B. Williams, Nov. 14, 1800, a tract of 100 acres adjoining Benjamin Flowers, Nichols, and his own line.

DB 2-208 STATE of N.C. grant to SAMUEL DEVAUGHAN by Gov. B. Williams, Nov. 18, 1800, a tract of 96 acres on Mooneyham's Mill Branch adjoining Harwood Grizzle, Mooneyham, Drewry Williams, and William Grizzle.

DB 2-209 STATE of N.C. grant to SAMUEL DEVAUGHAN by Gov. B. Williams March 12, 1800, a tract of 442 acres adjoining Thomas Horn, Joseph Woodward, Thomas Carter, James Brown, Jonas Williams, Finch, Tisdale, and Samuel Williams.

DB 2-210 STATE of N.C. grant to JOHN SAUNDERS, JR. by Gov. B. Williams, May 6, 1801, a tract of 30 acers on the south side of Mill Stone Swamp at his own corner adjoining John Eatman.

DB 2-211 STATE of N.C. grant to ENOCH FLOOD by Gov. B. Williams, Oct. 4, 1800, a tract of 200 acres on Town Creek adjoining Winstead, Dixon, Willis, Lampkin, Edward Horn, and Pridgen.

DB 2-212 STATE of N.C. grant to ALEXANDER SORSBY by Gov. B. Williams, Nov. 30, 1801, a tract of 16 acres on Tar River Branch adjoining John Williams. Matthew Drake, and Sion Beckwith.

DB 2-213 STATE of N. C. grant to JOHN WINBORN by Gov. B. Williams, Nov. 14, 1800, a tract of 200 acres on the north side of Beaver Branch adjoining Josiah Winborn.

DB 2-214 STATE of N.C. grant to JOSIAH WINBORN by Gov. B. Williams, March 12, 1800, a tract of 300 acres on his own line and Mooneyham's Meadow.

DB 2-215 STATE of N.C. grant to WILLIAM DRIVER by Gov. B. Williams, March 12, 1800, a tract of 100 acres adjoining Thomas Driver.

DB 2-216 STATE of N.C. grant to ABNER MASON by Gov. W. R. Davie, June 10, 1799, a tract of 50 acres adjoining James Battle and his own line.

DB 2-217 STATE of N.C. grant to HARDY PRIDGEN by Gov. B. Williams, Dec. 27, 1799, a tract of 200 acres on the south side of

Tar River adjoining the county line, Duncan Lamon, and Dixon Marshall.

DB 2-218 STATE of N.C. grant to JOHN EATMAN by Gov. B. Williams, June 10, 1800, a tract of 200 acres on Woolden Swamp adjoining Coleson and his own line.

DB 2-219 STATE of N.C. grant to JOHN WINBOURN by Gov. B. Williams, Nov. 14. 1800, a tract of 200 acres on the south side of Beaver Dam Branch adjoining Thomas Macon, Abraham Winbourn, and Pridgen.

DB 2-220 STATE of N.C. grant to EATMAN by Gov. B. Williams, March 12, 1800, a tract of 100 acres on the Great Swamp adjoining Jacob Cockrell and his own line.

DB 2-221 STATE of N.C. grant to BENJAMIN TUCKER by Gov. B. Williams, March 12, 1800, a tract of 32 acres on Little Peachtree Creek adjoining Hilliard and his own line.

DB 2-222 STATE of N.C. grant to SOLOMON DORSON PARKER by Gov. W. R. Davie, June 10, 1799, a tract of 50 acres on the south side of Tar River adjoining the county line, Jonas Williams, and his own line.

DB 2-223 STATE of N.C. grant to JOHN EATMAN by Gov. B. Williams, June 10, 1800, a tract of 100 acres on the north side of the Marsh Swamp adjoining Samuel Williams, Whitley. Nichols, and his own line.

DB 2-224 STATE of N.C. grant to THOMAS HAMILTON by Gov. B. Williams, June 16, 1800, a tract of 300 acres on both sides of White Oak adjoining Bowers, William Phillips, Eason, and the Juniper Branch.

DB 2-225 STATE of N.C. grant to JOSEPH WARD by Gov. B. Williams, Dec. 20, 1799, a tract of 34 acres on the south side of Fishing Creek at his own corner adjoining Francis Ward.

DB 2-226 STATE of N.C. grant to LEWIS ABLEWIS LAMBKIN by Gov. B. Williams, Dec. 10, 1801, a tract of 105 acres adjoining Phillander Williams, Moyes, Crowell, and his own line.

DB 2-227 STATE of N.C. grant to NICHOLAS SKINNER by Gov. Alex. Martin, Oct. 25, 1782, a tract of 100 acres on Beach Run adjoining his own line, Jeremiah Hilliard, and Reuben Taylor.

2-228 STATE of N.C. grant to MATTHEW DRAKE. son of William, by Gov. James Turner, Dec. 18, 1802, a tract of 35 acres on the south side of Swift Creek adjoining William Drake.

DB 2-230 STATE of N.C. grant to JOSEPH ARRINGTON, JR. by Gov. B. Williams, Nov. 16, 1801, a tract of 182 acres adjoining Hartford, the county line, James Cone, and William Morgan.

DB 2-231 STATE of N.C. grant to JOSEPH ARRINGTON, JR. by Gov. B. Williams, Nov. 16, 1801, a tract of 300 acres on Turkey Creek adjoining Jesse Hammons, Joshua Cone, and Hartford.

DB 2-223 STATE of N.C. grant to JACOB NICHOLS by Gov. B. Williams, April 18, 1800, a tract of 180 acres on Marsh Swamp adjoining his own line, Boyakin, Thorn, Vick, Cobb, and John Eatman.

DB 2-234 STATE of N.C. grant to URBAN EATMAN by Gov.

B. Williams, July 29, 1800, a tract of 16 acres on Rocky Branch adjoining John Sanders, John Eatman, and   George Whitley.

DB 2-236 STATE of N.C. grant to JONAS WILLIAMS by Gov. Alex. Martin, Nov. 1, 1784, a tract of 96 acres on Beaver Dam Swamp adjoining Edward Moore and his own line.

DB 2-237 STATE of N.C. grant to JONAS WILLIAMS by Gov. Alex. Martin, Nov. 1, 1784, a tract of 250 acres on Beaver Dam Swamp.

DB 2-238 STATE of N.C. grant to JONAS WILLIAMS by Gov. Rd. Caswell, Aug. 11, 1786, a tract of 480 acres on Turkey Creek and Toisnot adjoining Edward Moore and James Brown.

DB 2-240 EARL GRANVILLE grant to WILLIAM BAILEY of Edgecombe Co., March 11, 1761, a tract of 110 acres on the north side of Toisnot Swamp adjoining Pilgrim Williams and his own line.

DB 2-244 EARL GRANVILLE grant to PILGRIM WILLIAMS of Edgecombe Co., June 1, 1762, a tract of 287 acres on the south side of Toisnot Swamp adjoining Thomas Horn.

DB 2-246 EARL GRANVILLE grant to THOMAS HORN of Edgecombe Co., June 25, 1749, a tract of 360 acres on the north side of Toisnot Swamp adjoining Gab'l Parker and Pilgrim Williams.

DB 2-247 EARL GRANVILLE grant to THOMAS HORN of Edgecombe Co., Nov. 26, 1761, a tract of 487 acres adjoining his own line.

DB 2-248 EARL GRANVILLE grant to LEMUEL NICHOLSON of Edgecombe Co., Nov. 26, 1761, a tract of 670 acres adjoining Mark Mason, Nathaniel Powell, Culpepper, and Wm. Wilder, Jr.

DB 2-249 EARL GRANVILLE grant to WILLIAM HORN of Edgecombe Co., July 23, 1761, a tract of 700 acres on the north side of Toisnot Swamp adjoining Edward Moore, on the south side of Toisnot, and on the south side of Beaver Dam Branch adjoining Jacob Strickland.

DB 2-250 EARL GRANVILLE grant to WILLIAM BRASWELL of Edgecombe Co., March 2, 1761, a tract of 240 acres on the north side of Toisnot Swamp adjoining Pilgrim Williams.

DB 2-251 STATE of N.C. grant to CLAIBORNE FINCH by Gov. B. Williams, Oct. 5, 1802, a tract of 150 acres on both sides of Juniper Swamp adjoining his own line, Deans, Dickerson, and Williams.

DB 2-252 STATE of N.C. grant to JORDAN JOYNER by Gov. B. Williams, Dec. 6, 1799, a tract of 150 acres on Town Creek adjoining Lambkin.

DB 2-253 STATE of N.C. grant to MARTHA CROWELL by Gov. B. Williams, Nov. 14, 1800, a tract of 100 acres on Town Creek adjoining John Wells, Jordan Joyner, and the county line.

DB 2-255 STATE of N.C. grant to EZEKIEL DANCE by Gov. B. Williams, Nov. 19, 1802, a tract of 300 acres on the north side of Turkey Creek adjoining David Bisset, Charles Hogg, Morgan, and Rogers.

DB 2-256 STATE of N.C. grant to JAMES CONE by Gov. B. Williams, Jan. 30, 1802, a tract of 200 acres on the south side of

Turkey Creek adjoining Hardy Strickland, Henry Strickland, Robert Vick, and William Jordan.

DB 2-257 STATE of N.C. grant to ROBERT LANCASTER by Gov. B. Williams, Nov. 16, 1801, a tract of 100 acres adjoining Lamon and Edward Horn.

DB 2-258 STATE of N.C. grant to LEWIS ABLEWIS LAMBKIN by Gov. James Turner, Dec. 15, 1802, a tract of 424 acres near Town Creek adjoining Jordan Joyner, Wells, Crowell, and his own line.

DB 2-260 STATE of N.C. grant to JOSEPH ARRINGTON by Gov. B. Williams, Nov. 26, 1802, a tract of 24 acres on the south side of Toisnot Creek adjoining Duncan Dew.

DB 2-261 STATE of N.C. grant to MARK STRICKLAND by Gov. James Turner, Nov. 23, 1803, a tract of 20 acres on Turkey Creek adjoining Barrow and his own line.

DB 2-262 STATE of N.C. grant to MARK STRICKLAND by Gov. James Turner, Aug. 24, 1803, a tract of 300 acres on Turkey Creek adjoining Dance and Hansel Ferrell.

DB 2-263 STATE of N.C. grant to HARDY PRIDGEN by Gov. B. Williams, Aug. 13, 1802, a tract of 28 acres on the north side of Moccasin Creek adjoining Driver, Winborn, and his own line.

DB 2-264 STATE of N.C. grant to HARDY WILLIAMSON by Gov. James Turner, Nov. 19, 1803, a tract of 134 acres on the north side of Contentnea Creek adjoining John Eatman, Yeats, Benjamin Cobb, Woodard, and Boyakin.

DB 2-265 STATE of N.C. grant to DAVID WINSTEAD by Gov. James Turner, Nov. 23, 1803, a tract of 52 acres on Town Creek adjoining Samuel Winstead, Lamon, Williams, and Lambkin.

DB 2-266 STATE of N.C. grant to PILGRIM WILLIAMS by Gov. James Turner, Dec. 15, 15. 1802, a tract of 70 acres on Toisnot Swamp adjoining Rowland Williams and Joel Williams.

DB 2-267 STATE of N.C. grant to PILGRIM WILLIAMS by Gov. James Turner, Dec. 15, 1802, a tract of 100 acres adjoining Rowland Williams and Hardy Strickland.

DB 2-268 STATE of N. C. grant to BILLY WILLIAMS by Gov. James Turner, Dec. 9, 1802, a tract of 100 acres on the south side of Beaver Dam Swamp adjoining Cockrell and his own line.

DB 2-269 STATE of N.C. grant to BILLY WILLIAMS by Gov. James Turner, Dec. 9, 1802, a tract of 300 acres on the south side of Beaver Dam Swamp adjoining Coleson Cockrell, and his own line.

DB 2-270 STATE of N.C. grant to BILLY WILLIAMS by Gov. James Turner, Dec. 9, 1802, a tract of 100 acres on north side of the Great Swamp adjoining Cockrell and his own line.

DB 2-271 STATE of N.C. grant to BILLY WILLIAMS by Gov. Rd. Caswell, Aug. 11, 1786, a tract of 200 acres on the Great Swamp adjoining Chester Coleson.

DB 2-272 STATE of N.C. grant to JONAS WILLIAMS by Gov. Alex. Martin, Nov. 1, 1784, a tract of 400 acres on the south side of Toisnot Swamp adjoining Nathan Williams, Thomas Horn, Joel Cockrell, and Billy Williams.

DB 2-273 STATE of N.C. grant to JONAS WILLIAMS by Gov. Alex. Martin, Nov. 1, 1784, a tract of 640 acres on Toisnot and the Great Swamp adjoining Cockrell, John Eatman, and his own line.

DB 2-274 STATE of N.C. grant to CHESTER COLESON by Gov. Rd. Caswell, Sept. 24, 1785, a tract of 400 acres on Contentnea and the Great Swamp adjoining West Crumpler, George Green, and the Wolf Den Branch.

DB 2-275 STATE of N.C. grant to DAVID BISSETT by Gov. James Turner, Oct. 11, 1804, a tract of 200 acres adjoining Mark Strickland, Hogg, Thomas Tucker, and his own line.

—A—

Adams 98, Robt. 32, 128, 286, 311

Alford, Drewry 133, 442, Isaac 442, Lodwick 364, 365, 366

Allen, Arthur 33

Anderson, Chas. 286, Peter 181, 196, 405, Wm. 389

Andrews 396, Wm. 13, 39, 133, 157, 219, 300

Arrendell, Bridgers 368, Eliz. 368

Arrington, Arthur 2, 164, 354, 416, 434, Jas. 354, 390, Jos. 287, 329, 334, 354, 390, 416

Atkins, Benj. 379

Atkinson, Benj. 43, 56, 57, 58, 59, 362, Ephraim 381, 383, Henry 134, 258, Jas. 381 (2), 383, John 340, Martha 443, Michael 460, Nathan 4, 197, 443, Thos. 171, 200, 237, 270, 339, Wm. 286, 349

Avent, Wm. 405

—B—

Bagget(t) 173, Nicholas 292

Bailey, John 281

Baker, Jas. 158, 183, Penelope 282, Thos. 282

Ballard, Chris. 134, 316, David 156, 444, Edw. 187, 201, 249, 378, Peter 316 (3), Wm. 305

Banes, Henry 89

Barber, Sam. 148, 156

Barlow (Barler) 134, Henry 201, 444, John 444, Sam. 158

Barnes, Burwell 281, Henry 396, Jacob 153, Jas. 344, John 153, 386, Wm. 344

Barron, Barnaby 262

Bass 8, 98, 192, 349, 392, Abraham 44, 78, 266, 340, 452, Augustin 456, Isaac 34, 35, 130, 182, 194, 207, 234, 256, 355, 362, 369, 375, 411, 436, 456, Jethro 436, 450, John 97, 179, 202, 266, Sion 44, 78, 174

Batchelor, Wm. 160

Battle D. 282, Jacob 282, Jas. 329, Jesse 172, John 282, Martha 329, Wm. 7, 8, 32, 45, 128, 179, 181, 196, 198, 202, 286, 311

Beckwith (Beckworth), Boling 16, 195, 243, 414, Thos. 6, 18, 458 (2),

Bell 128, 286, 328, 329, Benj. 311, Elias 196, 293, Elisha 306, 397 (2), Green 32, 293 (2), 311 (2), Isabel 311, Jas. 32, Wm. 306, 311

Betts, Jos. 164

Bennett 168, 210

Biggs, John 84, 96, 132, 133, 265, 322, 375 (2)

Bishop, Asea 450

Blackburn, George 401

Blackwell, George 461 (2)

Blunt 426, Benj. 424, 426, John 424, 426, Mary 424, 426

Boddie, E. 299, Elijah 298, 333, 355, 422, 452, 453, 459, George 451,

Nathan 36, 40, 59, 67, 70, 84, 150, 180, 194, 245, 255, 383, 436, 453. Temperance 453, Wm. 56, 59, 67, 97, 192, 223, 451, 454
Bond(s), John 129, 316, 346, 446
Boothe 147, 280, Andrew 390 (2), Jesse 276, 277
Bottoms 183, Sam. 158, 338, Wm. L. 336
Boyet(t), Wm. 20, 131
Boykin 29, 126, 428, Drewry 14, 55, 111, 116, 343 (2), Hardy 55, 111, 116, 142, 144, 445
Branch, Edmund 18, 414, 458
Brantley 33, 58, 88, Jacob 249, 318, John 201, 318, Lewis 336
Braswell 192, 361, Arthur 16, 56, 65, 67, 169, 195, 243, 414 (3), 454 (2), 456, 459, Henry 182, 369, Jacob 5, 16, 18, 65, 195, 414, 459, Sam. 226, 382, Wm. 5, 6, 16, 18, 41, 90, 166, 357, 450, 458
Bridgers, Benj. 7, 152, 244, Sam. 1, Wm. 78, 179, 244, 325, 340, 349
Brittain, Chas. 13, 219, 300
Britton 164
Brown, Chas. 34, 35, 130, 234, 256, 355, 409, 436, Jas. 108, 110, 118, 161, 343 (2), 414, Jeremiah 203, Thos. 387
Bryant 58, Benj. 307, 448 (2), Jas. 34, 35, 234, Sam. 81, 82, 185, 215, 218, 222, 333, 380, 448, Wm. 47, 297 (2), 298, 307, 330 (2)
Bunn 73, Benj. 19, 22, 38, 63, 91, 120, 124, 125, 153, 160, 259, 303 313 (2), 325 (3), 345, 395 (2), Burwell 403, David 22, 153, 224, 303 (2), Henry 312, 450, Joel 395, John 303, Josiah 313, 395, R. 460, Redmun 303, 345, 346, 437
Buntin(g), Jeremiah 334, 411, Wm. 11, 38, 64, 85, 268, 411
Burge, Henry 446, Jeremiah 443
Butt, Joshua 293

—C—

Cain (Cane) 416, Jacob 172, 379, Jas. 141, 171, 177, 299 (2), 379, 393
Carlile, Jas. 408, 453
Carpenter, Thos. 28, 101
Carstarphen, Jas. 451
Carter 85, 140, 411, Jacob 41, 184, 302, Solomon 297, 321, 322, 327, 330, 421, Thos. 129
Chapman 98, David 174, 394, John 166, 298, 407, 417, 418, Wm. 30, 119, 191, 211, 242, 275, 366, 407 (2), 417 (2), 418, 421
Chitty, John 382, 458
Chrester, Jesse 369
Clark, John 387, Robt. 306 (2), Wm. 397
Clinch 12, Edw. 154, 209, 248, Jos. 4, Jos. John 197, 225, 283, 309
Cobb, Benj. 14, 108, 109, 319, 323, 343, David 109, 137, Jas. 19, 323, 325, John 375, John Pitty 362, Stephen 110, 111, 116, 142, 144, 250, 323, 325, 391
Cocker 32
Cockrell, 352, Jacob 351, John 145
Coleman, Elijah 428
Collins, Behen 423, Jesse 423, Solomon 70, 356
Colson, Chester 77
Cooper, Jas. 328 (2), 329, John 328, 329, 434, Marcum 11, 190, 358,

359 (2), 370 (2), Mark 409, Reuben 354, 434, 438, 441, Wm. 434 (2)

Cotten, Solomon 422

Cox (Cockes) 311, Jas. 128, 196, 286

Crawman 181, 198

Crowell 75, 151, 321, 334, Jos. 315 (2), 420 (2), Martha 420

Crumpler 125, 325

Culpepper 381, 416, 452, Benj. 408, 453, Jas. 300

Curl, Jos. 17, 79, 421, 460, Lewis 345, Wilson 2, 246, 429

—D—

Dance, Ethelred 154

Daniel(s) 6, David 344, Fred. 5

Davis 31, 129, 280, Arch. 398, 399, 424, 425, 426, Arthur 399, 405, 424, 426, Dioclesian 236, John 399, John 424, 426, Lewis 236, 390, Miles 404, Thos. 7, 181, 196, 236

Deans (Deens), Daniel 245, 265, Henry 39, 157, 300, 364, 409, Jas. 107, Jeremiah 41, 157, 184, John 269, Rich. 40, 84, 130, 186, Thos. 38, 85, 259, 268, 409, 411

Denson, Jesse 345

Devaughan, Sam. 343, 414

Devanport, John 2, 460

Dew, Duncan 325, John 461

Dickinson (Dickerson) 127, Jacob 99, 228, 229

Dison, Hosea 95

Dortch, Lewis 292, Wm. 173

Douglas, Jas. 162, 164

Dozier 299, John 387

Drake, Hines 377, 458, Jas. 179, Matthew 8, 18, 35, 65, 83, 130, 167, 169, 193, 195, 240, 256, 299, 321, 334, 414, 436, 456, 458, 459, Nath. 45, 83, Wm. 45

Driver 365

Duck, Jacob 27, 111, 142, 143, 144, 431

—E—

Eason, Sam. 339 (2), Wm. 33

Eatman, John 86, 87, 121, 145, 323, 351, 352 (2)

Eddens, John 365

Edge, John 345

Edwards, Jacob 289, 403, 440, Solomon 237, Thos. 378

Ellin (Flewellin), Howell 6, 344, 355, 433

Esell, Eliz. 329, Thos. 328, 329

Etheridge, Jeremiah 132, 216, 302, 375, 442, Lot 306, Peter 356 (2), 371

Evans, Chas. 7, John 134, 404

Exum, John 2. 246, 389, 435, Jos. 4, 171, 200, 241, 270, 283, 284, 295, 344, 413, 433, 440, Thos. 437

—F—

Flowers 124, 325, Benj. 61, 73. 91, 114, 120. 121, 125, 144, 319, 323, 325, 391, Henry 117, Jacob 94, 120, 391, John 19, 146

Folsome. Ebenezer 346 (3), Israel 346, Nath. 346
Fort, Wm. 460
Fowler, Batt 364, Jos. 365, 366(2)

—G—

Gainer, Jos. 390
Gandy 168, 188, 210, Brinkley 190, 304, 358, 359, 370 (2), Edw. 57,
    321, Isham (Isom) 189, 322, 338, 341
Gardner, George 399, 447, (2), Pryor 398 (2), 399, 447
Gay, John 367, 369, 377, 392, 394, 401, 432, 449, Patience 401
Glover, Thos. 385
Gooding (Gooden), Jas. 31, 152, 269
Goodson 57, 228
Goodwin, Eliz. 455, Jas. 48, 455 (3), John 455, P. 408, Robt. 455
Grant, Jas. 293, Jos. 389, 413
Green, Mary 374, Nathan 280
Grice, Alex. 430, 431, Jas. 26, 27, 430, 431, Lewis 430, 431, Theophi-
    lus 26, 27, 430, 431, 445
Griffin, Hardy 2, 354, Jas. 300, John 164, Jos. 162
Gross, Francis 330, 442

—H—

Hackney 141, 173, 292, Rachel 379
Hadley, Ambrus 438, 441 (2)
Hall, Wm. 300, 313, 341, 450, 451
Hamlin, Stephen 2, 246
Hammons, Wm. 375
Hardy, Thos. 53, 75, 321, 334
Harrington, Arthur 162
Harris(s) 122. Hardy 437, Jacob 381, 383, Wm. 39, 89, 186, 219,
    240, 396, 442, 444
Harrison 71, Jethro 257, 271, 461, John 9, 397, 405
Hart 6, 54, Hartwell 226
Hatten (Hatton), Peter 159, 321
Hawkins, Phil. 452
Hayes, Jos. 199, 441
H(e)artsfield, Andrew 368, 372, Jacob 368 (2), 372
H(e)gepeth 98, 267. Benj. 401, 414, John 428, Peter 44, 174, 392
Henderson, Jacob 450
Hendrick(s), Ethelred 330, Wm. 47, 176, 218, 252, 297 (2), 307, 330
    (2)
Hill, Abner 444, Lewis 152, 349, Thos. 204, Wm. 78
Hilliard 8, Isaac 62, 149, 169, 192, 202. 230, 231, 232, 266, 346, 456,
    Jeremiah 68, 225, 284 (2). 403, 440 (2)
Hines, Isam 344 (2), Lewis 389, 406, 435, 437
Hinnant (Hinat) 27, 431
Holliman, Jas. 374
Hooks, Dorcas 394. 432. Wm. 8, 83, 394, 432 (2)
Holland 80. 99, 189. 341, John 387
Horn 220. 232, Edw. 386 (2), H. 291, Henry 346 (2), Isaac 246,
    Jacob 437, Joel 296, Michael 20, 135, 391, Patience 391, Thos. 110,

—M—

Mainer (Mainor), Aaron 389, 435 (3)
Mann, Allen 349, Denton 349, Thos. 1, 7, 8, 45, 48, 83, 152, 179, 198, 208, 349, 360, 455, Wm. 31, 208
Manning 70, 299, John 96, 138 (2),160, 265, 322, 336, Matthias 113, 138, 206 245, 265, 322, 327, 336, 356, 371, 409 (2), Rich. 4, Willaby 174, 223, Wm. 138, 336
Marshall, Dixon 151, 153, 412 (2), 427 (2)
Mason, Mark 23, 102, Ralph 62, 292
Massingale (Massingill), Jas. 174, 182, 392, 449, Mark 394, Walker 449
Matthews 62, Wm. 312, 376
Mearns, W. S. 390
Melton 228, 307, Eliz. 297, John 47, 54, 60, 176, 220, 297, 330, 376, 385, Mary 312
Merritt (Merret) 263, 309, Benj. 200, 221, 241, Wm. 283
Miller 426, Sam. 399
Mitchell, Mial 432, Sam. 280, Wm. 432
Montford 98
Moone(y)ham 103, 281, Enoch 343
Moore 72, Bathsheba 288, 335, Edw. 24, 25, 64, 121, 140, 250, 258, 261, 319 (2), 323(2), Elisha 2, Jas. 89, 240, 396 (2), John 2, Reuben 360
Morphis(s), Bashford 377, Jas. 272, 274
Morris(s). Chloe 371, John 77, Thos. 356, 371, 381, 383, 408, 414, 454 (2), 456

—N—

Nairn, John 374, Wm. 374
Newton, Benj. 295, 439
Nichols. Jacob 116, 144, 264, Jeremiah 110, 111, 114 (2), 144, 217, 238, 430, 431
Nicholson 164, Edw. 154, 209, 212, 235, 321 (2), George 141, 177, 204, 205, Josiah 401, Lemuel 102, Malachi 401, Wright 401
Nofler 422
Norris, Jas. 227

—O—

Oliver, Jas. 288
O'Neal (O'Nails), Arthur 96, 322
Owens, Daniel 30, 37, 52

—P—

Pace 401
Pall, Wm. 115
Parker, Aaron 135, Eliz. 131, 135, 159, Gabriel 21, 135, Wm. 253
Par(r)ish 452, Edw. 408, 453
Parrot 442
Passmore 392, John 401, 432
Paterson, Young 298
Peed (Pede), Henry 207, 362, 377
Pegg 442

19, 29 247, 267, 391 (2), 428

Savage (Savedge), Benj. 392, Drewry 148, Kinchen 305, Michael 348, Moses 348

Scott, John 299

Segraves, Jacob 372

Selah (Sealy, Seley), Jos. 24, 187, 249, 318 (2), 378 (2)

Sellers 24, 25, Arthur 268, John 11, 64, 65, 409, 459, Jos. 88, Wm. 64, 88

Sesmore, Rich. 293

Shephard 257

Sherrod 58

Sikes, Jacob 355, John 40, 130, 194, 255, 256, 355 (3), 356, 409, 436 (2), Matthew 355, 409, Phillip 364

Skinner 22, Emmanuel 288, 335, Nicholas 2, 178, 284 (3), Sam. 335 (2), 433, Wm. 433

Slatter, John 311

Smelley 281

Smith, Abraham 288 (3), Benj. 43. 134, 158, 183, 187, 201, 316, 339, Brittain 315, 427, Jas. 397, Jos. 288 (2), Nath. 281, Nehemiah 288

Sorsby, Sam. 4, 79, 136, 200, 221, 263, 309

Southall, Holmon 399

Sp(eight 233, John 437, Wm. 171. 406

Stallings (Stallions), Jacob 22, 224, Jas. 289, 435

Stephens, Robt. 429

Strickland 3, 115, 129, David 10, 237, 279, 296, 382, 387, Eliz. 387, Hardy 82. Henry 12, 85, 211, 242, 296, 411, 417, Jacob 82, 104, 235, 239, Lazarus 49, 50, 407, 417, 418, 446 (2), Simon 95, 407, 417, 418, Solomon 81, 122, 372, 421, Wm. 277

Sturdivant, Chas. 360

Sumner, Jos. 47, 176. 218. 252, 297, 385

Sutton George 96, 310, 322

—T—

Talbert, Isaac 172, 204

Tallington 312

Taylor 261, 274, Benj. 262. Daniel 41, 214. 297, 302, Harry 340, 367, Jas. 448, John 30, 46, 95, 140, 147, 253, 254, 262, 276, 277, 446, Mills 68, 289, 403, 440, Reuben 233, 283, 284 (3), 295, 403 (2), 406, 440 (3), 443, Wm. 291, 393, Wilson 53, 74, 305, 351, 352

Thomas 16, 36, 43, 44, 192, 223, 234, 252. 266, Amos 454. Mary 290, Micajah 30. 35, 52. 56, 57, 59, 67, 90, 92, 97, 98. 99, 127, 148, 150, 166, 167, 168, 210, 229, 240, 243, 298, 318, 333, 341, 369, 370, 380, 385, 401. 419, 422 (2), 450 (2), 451 (2), 452, 459. Jesse 127, 376, Jethro 290. 312. Jos. 99, 376, Rebeckah 312, Rich. 57, 228, 287, 290, 312 (2), 376

Thom(p)son 168, 202, 205. 210, 443, Alex. 406, Widow 346

Thorp, Thos. 2, 10, 237, 437

Tisdale, Henry 107

Tomlinson, Isaac 54

Trevathan, Lewis 389 (2), 406 (2), 435. Willis 435

Tucker 362, Benj. 89, 396 (2), Jas. 96, Jos. 76, 113, 327, Marg.

348 Robt. 310, Sarah 332 (2), Thos. 70, 207, 245, 265, 348, 396, Viney 348, Willaby 98, 322, 332

Turner, John 44, 97, 223, 449 (2), Wm. 449

—U—

Underwood 416, Jacob 10, 17, 237, 270

—V—

Vaden, Wm. 366

Vanlandingham, Francis 75, 135, 334, Thos. 177, 205, 260

Vaughan 113, Chris. 245, 332, Ephraim 327 (2), 332, Stephen 332, Thos. 383

Vester 70, Solomon 84, 180, Wm. 84, 180, 206, 302, 371, 375

Vick, Benj. 357, Henry 433, John 361, Jos. 46, 95, Lewis 382, Rich. 226, 287, 312, 357, 361, Wilson 287, 290, 299, 357, 361, 378, 419, 460

Viverett, Thos. 304

—W—

Walker, Thos. 392, Wm. 5, 18, 458

Warburton, Alice 307, Wm. 60, 307

Ward 426, Francis 9, 398, 399, 447, Jos. 9, Willis 85, 411

Warren, John 222, 442, Thos. 259, 380

Watkins, Henry 246, Jas. 414, John 460, Littleberry 433

Watson, Chas. 169, 192, 375, 456 (2)

Webb, Ann 377, John 403, Stephen 348, 377, 392, 401

Wells, Daniel 340, Joshua 338, 340, Solomon 338 (2), 339, 340, Stephen 316

West, Jacob 164, Sion 179, 202, 266, Wm. 387

Wester, Arthur 395 (2), Fulgham 313, Wm. 132

Westray, Sam. 315, 419

Wheatley 395

Wheless 31, 48, 455

Whiddon (Whitton, Whittin) 189, 304, John 80, 316, Lott 407, 417, 418, Wm. 80, 138, 188, 304, 322, 336 (2), 341 (2), 358 (2), 359

White, John 310, Jos. 346 (2)

Whitehead 164, Arthur 162, 220, 231, Benj. 199, Jacob 225, 443 (2), Lazarus 172, 177, 204, 205, 287, 299, 379, 401, Thos. 354 (2), Wm. 17, 79, 136, 200, 220, 237, 283, 443 (2)

Whitehouse, John 80, 229

Whitfield 127, 168, 188, 210, 228, 229, 312, Benj. 390, 425, John 385, Reuben 404 (2), Solomon 69, Thos. 69, 80, Wm. 64

Whittington 424

Wiggins, Joel 4, 263, 309, John 405

Williams 9, 53, 328, 329, 434, Arter 448, Benj. 385, Billy 351 (2), 352, Cesley 316 (3), Cooper 208, John 7, 8, 32, 152, 306 (2), Jonas 305, 321, 351, 352 (2), Jos. 227, Nathan 145, 351, Phillander 315 (2), 340, 412 (2), Reuben 52, 90, 92, 253, Rowland 74, 154, 212, 414, Sam. 43, 75, 316, 321, 334, Simon 41, 184, Thos. 2, 10, 282, Wm. 193

Williamson, Hardy 445, Jas. 445, Jos. 111, 238

Willis 357, Stephen 58, Thos. 226, 279
Wilson, Edw. 429, John 296, Robt. 429, Thos. 62
Wimberly 16, 127
Winbourn, Josiah 100, 103, 423
Winstead, Jos. 58, Rich. 159
Womble 452
Wood, Aaron 280
Woodard Dempsey 389, 413, Thos. 238
Woodel, Jos. 155, 161, 414 (2)
Wright 77, Jas. 19. Jos. 93, 94, Lemuel 72, 93, 94
Wyatt, Henry 203, Jas. 102, 164

—Y—

Y(e)ates, Charity 137, Wm. 227
Youell, Henry 420
Young, Dinah 362, Robt. 213, 346, 419   (2), Stephen 207, 362,
    380, 419 (2)

DB 3-1 EARL GRAINVILLE grant to THOMAS MANN of Edgecombe Co., Aug. 10, 1762, a tract of 690 acres adjoining Samuel Bridgers and his own line.

DB 3-2 STATE of N. C. grant to THOMAS WILLIAMS by Gov. Rd. Caswell, Nov. 10, 1779, a tract of 550 acres on Compass Creek adjoining Nicholas Skinner, John Davenport, John Moore, Elisha Moore, Elijah Revel, Thomas Thorp, John Exum, Wilson Curl and Stephen Hamlin.

3-2 STATE of N. C. grant to ARTHUR ARRINGTON by Gov. Rd. Caswell, March 30, 1780, a tract of 13 acres on the north side of Swift Creek adjoining Hardy Griffin, Robert Pyland, and his own line.

DB 3-3 STATE of N. C. grant to SAMPSON POWELL by Gov. Rd. Caswell, March 30, 1780, a tract of 640 acres on Turkey Creek adjoining Strickland.

DB 3-4 STATE of N. C. grant to RICHARD MANNING by Gov. Rd. Caswell, Nov. 10, 1779, a tract of 570 acres on the north side of Beach Run adjoining Joseph Exum, Samuel Sorsby, Joel Wiggins, Jelks, Joseph Clinch, and Nathan Atkinson.

DB 3-5 STATE of N. C. grant to WILLIAM BRASWELL, Jr. bv Gov. Rd. Caswell, March 30. 1780, a tract of 640 acres on Pig Basket Creek adjoining Jacob Braswell, William Walker, Frederick Daniels, and his own line.

DB 3-6 STATE of N. C. grant to WILLIAM BRASWELL, JR. by Gov. Rd. Caswell, March 30, 1780, a tract of 640 acres on Pig Basket Creek adjoining Daniels, Howell Flewellin, Hart, Knight, Thomas Beckwith, and his own line.

DB 3-7 STATE of N. C. grant to JOHN WILLIAMS by Gov. Rd. Caswell, March 30, 1780, a tract of 640 acres on Gideon Swamp adjoining Charles Evans, Thomas Davis, William Battle, Thomas Mann, and Benjamin Bridgers.

DB 3-8 STATE of N. C. grant to JOHN WILLIAMS of Halifax Co. by Gov. Rd. Caswell, March 30, 1780, a tract of 995 acres on the south side of Swift Creek and on Pig Basket Creek adjoining Thomas Mann, William Battle, Bass. Hillard, Matthew Drake, Jesse Powell. and William Hooks.

DB 3-9 STATE of N. C. grant to JOSEPH WARD by Gov. Rd. Caswell. March 30, 1780, a tract of 222 acres on the south side of Fishing Creek adjoining John Harrison, Williams, and Francis Ward.

DB 3-10 STATE of N. C. grant to ELLJAH REVEL by Gov. Rd. Caswell, March 30, 1780, a tract of 287 acres on the north side of Stony Creek adjoining David Strickland, Jesse Hunt, Thomas Wiliams, Thomas Thorp, Jacob Underwood, and his own line.

DB 3-11 STATE of N. C. grant to JOHN SELLARS by Gov. Rd. Caswell, March 30, 1780, a tract of 440 acres on the north side of Sapony Creek adjoining Marcum Cooper, Joshua Pierce ,and Wiliams Buntin.

DB 3-12 STATE of N. C. grant to HENRY STRICKLAND by Gov. Rd. Caswell, March 30, 1780, a tract of 176 acres on the south side of Tar River near the main road adjoining Clinch, the Horse Pen Branch, and his own line.

DB 3-13 STATE of N. C. grant to WILLIAM ANDREWS by Gov. Rd. Caswel. March 30, 1780, a tract of 640 acres on the north side of Tar River and on Turkey Creek adjoining Sampson Powell. Edward Pursell. and Charles Brittain's Branch.

DB 3-14 STATE of N. C. grant to BENJAMIN COBB by Gov. Rd. Caswel, March 30, 1780, a tract of 640 acres on the Mash Swamp adjoining Drewry Boykin.

DB 3-15 STATE of N. C. grant to LEWIS JOYNER by Gov. Rd. Caswell, March 30, 1780, a tract of 300 acres on Tar River adjoining his father, Duncan Lamon, and Laslie.

DB 3-16 STATE of N. C. grant to JACOB BRASWELL by Gov. Rd. Caswell, March 30, 1780, a tract of 474 acres on Pig Basket Creek adjoining William Braswell, Arthur Braswell, Boling Beckwith, Thomas, Wimberly, and his own line.

DB 3-17 STATE of N. C. grant to JACOB UNDERWOOD by Gov. Alex. Martin, Oct. 25, 1782, a tract of 60 acres on Swift Creek adjoining Joseph Curl, Wililam Whitehead, and his own line.

DB 3-18 STATE of N. C. grant to EDMUND BRANCH by Gov. Alex. Martin. Oct. 25, 1782, a tract of 397 acres on Pig Baskte Creek adjoining Matthew Drake. Jesse Powell, Jacob Braswell, William Walker, William Braswell. Thomas Beckwith, and Cooper Jones.

DB 3-19 STATE of N. C. grant to JAMES COBB by Gov. Alex. Martin, Oct. 25, 1782, a tract of 250 acres on Contentnea Creek adjoining Thomas Sanders, John Flowers, James Wright, Benja. Bunn, and his own line.

DB 3-20 STATE of N. C. grant to WILLIAM BOYETT by Gov. Alex Martin , Oct. 25, 1782, a tract of 214 acres on the north side of Tar River and on Lott's Branch adjoining Michael Horn and the county line.

DB 3-21 STATE of N. C. grant to GABRIEL PARKER by Gov. Alex Martin, Oct. 25, 1782, a tract of 100 acres on Lott's Branch.

DB 3-22 STATE of N. C. grant to BENJAMIN BUNN by Gov. Alex. Martin. Oct. 25, 1782, a tract of 30 acres on Stony Creek adjoining the road, David Bunn, Jacob Stallings, and Skinner.

DB 3-23 STATE of N. C. grant to MARK MASON by Gov. Alex. Martin, Oct. 25, 1782, a tract of 50 acres on Beaver Dam Swamp adjoining his own line.

DB 3-24 STATE of N. C. grant to EDWARD MOORE   by Gov. Alex. Martin, Oct. 25, 1782, a tract of 190 acres on Tar River adjoining Joseph Seley, John Poland, Sellers, and his own line.

DB 3-25 STATE of N. C. grant to EDWARD MOORE by Gov.

Alex Martin, Oct. 25, 1782, a tract of 298 acres on Tar River adjoining Sellers and his own line.

DB 3-26 STATE of N. C. grant to THEOPHILUS GRICE by Gov. Alex Martin, Oct. 25, 1782, a tract of 250 acres on Contentnea Creek adjoining James Grice.

DB 3-27 STATE of N. C. grant to THEOPHILUS GRICE by Gov. Alex Martin, Oct. 25, 1782, a tract of 50 acres on Contentnea Creek adjoining Jacob Duck, James Grice, and Hinat.

DB 3-28 STATE of N. C. grant to THOMAS CARPENTER by Gov. Alex Martin, Oct. 25, 1782, a tract of 314 acres on Moccasin Creek and Raccoon Branch.

DB 3-29 STATE of N. C. grant to THOMAS SANDERS by Gov. Alex. Martin, Oct. 25, 1782, a tract of 290 acres on Contentnea Creek adjoining Ephraim Phililps, John Sanders, Boykin, and Rowe.

DB 3-30 STATE of N. C. grant to   WILLIAM CHAPMAN by Gov. Alex . Martin, Oct. 25, 1782, a tract of 300 acres on Tar River adjoining John Taylor, Bryant's Creek, Micajah Thomas, and Daniel Owens.

DB 3-31 STATE of N. C. grant to WILLIAM MANN by Gov. Alex. Martin, Oct. 25, 1782. a tract of 497 acres on the north side of Swift Creek adjoining James Gooden, Wheless, and Davis.

DB 3-32 STATE of N. C. grant to GREEN BELL by Gov. Alex. Martin, Oct. 25, 1782, a tract of 620 acres on Swift Creek and Fishing Creek adjoining Robert Adams, Wililam Battle, James Bell. John Williams. and Cocker.

DB 3-33 STATE of N. C. grant to ARTHUR ALLEN by Gov. Alex. Martin, Oct. 25, 1782, a tract of 700 acres on Sapony Creek adjoining David Pridgen. Wililam Eason, Jackson, and Brantley.

DB 3-34 STATE of N. C. grant to ISAAC BASS by Gov. Alex. Martin. Oct. 25. 1782, a tract of 169 acres on Peachtree Creek adioining Charles Brown, James Bryant, and his own line.

DB 3-35 STATE of N. C. grant to ISSAC BASS by Gov. Alex. Martin, Oct. 25, 1782, a tract of 188 acres on Peachtree Creek adjoining Matthew Drake, Charles Brown, James Bryant, and Micaiah Thomas.

DB 3-36 STATE of N. C. grant to NATHAN BODDIE by Gov. Rd. Caswell, March 30, 1780, a tract of 81 acres on Peachtre Creek adjoining Thomas and his own line.

DB 3-37 STATE of N. C. grant to DANIEL OWENS by Gov. Alex. Martin, Oct. 25, 1782, a tract of 500 acres on Tar River and Chapman's Road.

DB 3-38 STATE of N. C. grant to THOMAS DEENS by Gov. Alex. Martin. Oct. 25, 1782, a tract of 400 acres on Sapony Creek adjoining Ben Bunn, Wililam Buntin, and his own line.

DB 3-39 STATE of N. C. grant to HENRY DEENS by Gov. Alex. Martin, Oct. 25, 1782. a tract of 640 acres on Turkey Creek adjoining Wm. Harris, Wililam Andrews, and Ross.

DB 3-40 STATE of N. C. grant to RICHARD DEENS by

Gov. Alex. Martin, Oct. 25, 1782, a tract of 142 acres on Little Peachtree Creek adjoining John Sikes, Nathan Boddie, and Powell.

DB 3-41 STATE of N. C. grant to JEREMIAH DEENS by Gov. Alex. Martin, Oct. 25, 1782, a tract of 242 acres on Little Turkey Creek adjoining Wm. Braswell, Jacob Carter, Simon Williams, Daniel Taylor, and Edward Pursell.

DB 3-42 STATE of N. C. grant to THOMAS ROGERS by Gov. Rd. Caswell, March 30, 1780, a tract of 400 acres on Turkey Creek adjoining his own line.

DB 3-43 STATE of N. C. grant to WILLIAM JOYNER, JR. by Gov. Alex. Martin, Oct. 25, 1782, a tract of 159 acres on Polecat adjoining Ricks, Ben Atkinson, Thomas, Ben Smith, Samuel Williams, and his own line.

DB 3-44 STATE of N. C. grant to SION BASS by Gov. Alex. Martin, Oct. 25, 1782, a tract of 458 acres on Pig Basket Creek adjoining Sampson Powell, Peter Hedgepeth, Abraham Bass Thomas, John Turner, and his own line.

DB 3-45   STATE of N. C. grant to WILLIAM DRAKE by Gov. Rd. Caswell, March 30, 1780, a tract of 640 acres on the south side of Swift Creek adjoining Nathaniel Drake, Wililam Battle, Nicholas Lewis , and Thomas Mann.

DB 3-46 STATE of N. C. grant to JOSEPH VICK by Gov. Alex. Martin, Oct. 25, 1782, a tract of 281 acres on Toisnot Swamp adjoining Duncan Lamon and John Taylor.

DB 3-47 STATE of N. C. grant to WILLIAM HENDRICK by Gov. Alex. Martin, Oct. 25, 1782, a tract of 62 acres on Tar River adjoining William Bryant, John Melton, and Joseph Sumner.

DB 3-48 STATE of N. C. grant to JAMES GOODWIN by Gov. Alex. Martin, Oct. 25, 1782, a tract of 400 acres on the north side of Swift Creek adjoining Wheless, Thomas Mann, and his own line.

DB 3-49 STATE of N. C. grant to LAZARUS STRICKLAND by Gov. Alex. Martin, Oct. 25, 1782, a tract of 300 acres on Toisnot Swamp and the Great Branch.

DB 3-50 STATE of N. C. grant to LAZARUS STRICKLAND by Gov. Alex. Martin, Oct. 25, 1782, a tract of 297 acres on Toisnot Swamp adjoining his own line.

DB 3-51 STATE of N. C. grant to WILLIAM RAY by Gov. Alex. Martin, Oct. 25, 1782, a tract of 216 acres on Turkey Creek adjoining Nathaniel Hunt, the county line, and his own line.

DB 3-52 STATE of N. C. grant to JULIAN KING by Gov. Alex. Martin, Oct. 25, 1782, A tract of 640 acres adjoining Daniel Owens, Rollings, Reuben Wililams and Micajah Thomas

DB 3-53 STATE of N. C. grant to LAZARUS POPE, by Gov. Alex. Martin Oct. 25, 1782, a tract of 640 acres on the south side of Tar River adjoining Wilson Taylor, Thomas Hardy, Wililams, and his own line.

DB 3-54 STATE of N. C. grant to ISAAC TOMLINSON by Gov. Alex. Martin, Oct. 25, 1782, a tract of 300 acres on Whitehead's Mill Swamp adjoining John Melton and Hart.

DB 3-55 STATE of N. C. grant to DREWRY BOYKIN by Gov. Alex. Martin, Oct. 25, 1782, a tract of 440 acres on Marsh Swamp adjoining Hardy Boykin .

DB 3-56 STATE of N. C. grant to BENJAMIN ATKINSON by Gov. Alex. Martin, Oct. 25, 1782, a tract of 120 acres on Pig Basket Creek adjoining Arthur Braswell, Wililam Boddie, and Micajah Thomas.

DB 3-57 STATE of N. C. grant to BENJAMIN ATKINSON by Gov. Alex Martin. Oct. 25, 1782, a tract of 150 acres on Sapony Creek adjoining Edward Gandy, Micjah Thomas, Ricks. Richard Thomas, and Goodson.

DB 3-58 STATE of N. C. grant to BENJAMIN ATKINSON by Gov. Alex. Martin, Oct. 25, 1782, a tract of 350 acres on the north side of Tar River adjoining Jos. Winstead, Stephen Willis, Sherrod, Bryant, Pouland, and Brantley.

DB 3-59 STATE of N. C. grant to BENJAMIN ATKINSON by Gov. Alex. Martin, Oct. 25, 1782, a tract of 133 acres on Pig Basket Creek adjoining William Boddie, Nathan Boddie, and Micajah Thomas.

DB 3-60 STATE of N. C. grant to WILLIAM WARBURTON by Gov. Alex. Martin, Oct. 25, 1782, a tract of 200 acres on Sapony Creek adjoining Newit Lane and John Melton.

DB 3-61 STATE of N. C. grant to BENJAMIN FLOWERS by Gov. Rd. Caswell, Nov. 10, 1779, a tract of 640 acres on Little Swamp adjoining his own improvement.

DB 3-62 STATE of N. C. grant to THOMAS WILSON by Gov. Rd. Caswell, March 13, 1780, a tract of 200 acres on Swift Creek adjoining Ralph Mason, Charles Powell, Matthews, and Isaac Hilliard.

DB 3-63 STATE of N. C. grant to WILLIAM PHILLIPS by Gov. Alex. Martin, Oct. 29, 1782, a tract of 150 acres on Contentnea Creek adjoining Benjamin Bunn and Jethro Phililps.

DB 3-64 STATE of N. C. grant to WILLIAM WHITFIELD by Gov. Alex. Martin, Oct. 25, 1782, a tract of 300 acres on Sapony Creek adjoining John Sellers, William Bunting, William Sellers, and Edward Moore.

DB 3-65 STATE of N. C. grant to JOHN SELLERS by Gov. Alex Martin, Oct. 25, 1782, a tract of 640 acres on Pig Basket Creek adjoining Arthur Braswell, Matthew Drake, Jesse Powell, and Jacob Braswell.

DB 3-66 STATE of N. C. grant to EPHRAIM PHILLIPS by Gov. Alex. Martin, Oct. 29, 1782, a tract of 101 acres on Contentnea Creek and Sheppard's Branch adjoining Sanders and his own line.

DB 3-67 STATE of N. C. grant to WILLIAM BODDIE by Gov. Alex. Martin, Oct. 9, 1783, a tract of 640 acres on Pig Basket Creek adjoining Arthur Braswell, Nathan Boddie, Micajah Thomas, and his own line.

DB 3-68 STATE of N. C. grant to MILLS TAYLOR by Gov.

Alex. Martin, Oct. 25, 1782, a tract of 200 acres on Beach Run adjoining Jeremiah Hilliard, the county line, and his own line.

DB 3-69 STATE of N. C. grant to SOLOMON WHITFIELD by Gov. Alex. Martin, Oct. 25, 1782, a tract of 94 acres on Pig Basket Creek adjoining Thomas Whitfield and his own line.

DB 3-70 STATE of N. C. grant to SOLOMON COLLINS by Gov. Alex. Martin, Oct. 25, 1782, a tract of 386 acres on Sapony Creek adjoining Nathan Boddie, Thomas Tucker, Manning, Thomas Richardson, and Vester.

DB 3-71 STATE of N. C. grant to John Sanders by Gov. Alex. Martin, Oct. 25, 1782, a tract of 306 acres on Contentnea Creek adjoining Phillips and Harrison.

DB 3-72 STATE of N. C. grant to JOSEPH PHILLIPS by Gov. Alex. Martin, Oct. 9, 1783, a tract of 640 acres on the north side of the Great Swamp adjoining Lemuel Wright, Moore, and his own line.

DB 3-73 STATE of N. C. grant to BENJAMIN FLOWERS by Gov. Alex. Martin, Oct. 9, 1783, a tract of 640 acres on Sheppard's Branch adjoining Bunn and John Sanders.

DB 3-74 STATE of N. C. grant to WILSON TAYLOR by Gov. Alex Martin, Oct. 9, 1783, a tract of 500 acres on the south side of Tar River adjoining Rowland Williams and his own line.

DB 3-75 STATE of N. C. grant to FRANCIS VANLAND-INGHAM by Gov. Alex. Martin, Oct. 25, 1782, a tract of 640 acres on the south side of Tar River adjoining Thomas Hardy, Lazarus Pope, Crowell, and Samuel Wililams.

DB 3-76 STATE of N. C. grant to JOSEPH TUCKER by Gov. Alex. Martin, Oct. 25, 1782, a tract of 200 acres on Sapony Creek adjoining Lane and his own line.

DB 3-77 STATE of N. C. grant to JOHN MORRIS by Gov. Alex Martin, Oct. 9, 1783, a tract of 300 acres on the north side of the Great Swamp adjoining the county line, Joseph Phillips, Wright, Chester Colson and his own line.

DB 3-78 STATE of N.C. grant to WILLIAM BRIDGERS by Gov. Alex. Martin, Oct. 25, 1782. a tract of 290 acres on Swift Creek adjoining William Hill, Abraham Bass, Sion Bass, and his own line.

DB 3-79 STATE of N. C. grant to SAMUEL SORSBY by Gov. Alex. Martin, Oct. 25, 1782, a tract of 105 acres on Swift Creek adjoining Joseph Curl, William Whitehead, the road, and his own line.

DB 3-80 STATE of N. C. grant to THOMAS WHITFIELD by Gov. Rd. Caswell, Nov. 10, 1779, a tract of 700 acres on the north side of Sapony Creek adjoining John Whitehehouse, Holland, William Whiddon, and John Whiddon.

DB 3-81 STATE of N. C. grant to SAMUEL BRYANT by Gov. Alex. Martin, Oct. 9, 1783. a tract of 300 acres on the south side of Turkey Creek adjoining Solomon Strickland.

DB 3-82 STATE of N. C. grant to HARDY STRICKLAND by Gov. Alex. Martin, Oct. 9, 1783, a tract of 400 acres on Turkey

Creek adjoining Jacob Strickland and Samuel Bryant.

DB 3-83 STATE of N. C. grant to WILLIAM HOOKS by Gov. Alex. Martin, Oct. 9, 1783, a tract of 640 acres on Swift Creek adjoining Matthew Drake, Nathaniel Drake, Thomas Mann, and Jesse Powell.

DB 3-84 STATE of N. C. grant to WILLIAM VESTER by Gov. Alex. Martin, Oct. 25, 1782, a tract of 640 acres on Sapony Creek adjoining Solomon Vester, John Biggs, Elijah Powell, Richard Deans, Nathan Boddie, and his own line.

DB 3-85 STATE of N. C. grant to WILLIS WARD by Gov. Alex Martin, Oct. 25, 1782, a tract of 199 acres on Tar River adjoining Thomas Deans, William Buntin, Henry Strickland, and Carter.

DB 3-86 STATE of N. C. grant to John EATMAN by Gov. Rd. Caswell, March 30, 1780, a tract of 500 acres on the Great Swamp and Juniper Swamp.

DB 3-87 STATE of N. C. grant to JOHN EATMAN by Gov. Rd. Caswell, March 30, 1789, a tract of 300 acres on the Great Swamp adjoining his own line.

DB 3-88 STATE of N. C. grant to WILLIAM SELLERS by Gov. Rd. Caswell, March 30, 1780, a tract of 370 acres on Sapony Creek adjoining Brantley and Joseph Sellers.

DB 3-89 STATE of N. C. grant to BENJAMIN TUCKER by Gov. Rd. Caswel, March 30, 1780, a tract of 100 acres on Peachtree Creek adjoining James Moore, Henry Banes, and William Harris.

DB 3-90 STATE of N. C. grant to REUBEN WILLIAMS by Gov. Alex. Martin, Oct. 25, 1782, a tract of 581 acres on the south side of Tar River adjoining William Braswell, Micajah Thomas, and Bryant Linch.

DB 3-91 STATE of N. C. grant to JETHRO PHILLIPS by Gov. Alex. Martin. Oct. 29, 1782, a tract of 250 acres on Contentnea Creek and Sheppard's Branch adjoining Ben Flowers, William Phillips, and Benja. Bunn.

DB 3-92 STATE of N. C. grant to REUBEN WILLIAMS by Gov. Alex. Martin, Oct. 25, 1782, a tract of 300 acres on the south side of Tar River adjoining Micajah Thomas, Charles Rollings, and his own line.

DB 3-93 STATE of N. C. grant to JOSEPH WRIGHT by Gov. Alex Martin, Oct. 25, 1782, a tract of 50 acres on Bloomery Swamp adjoining Joshua Jordan, Sanders, Lemuel Wright, and the county line.

DB 3-94 STATE of N. C. grant to LEMUEL WRIGHT by Gov. Alex Martin, Oct. 25, 1782, a tract of 150 acres on Bloomery Swamp adjoining Joseph Phillips, Jacob Flowers, Joseph Wright, and his own line.

DB 3-95 STATE of N. C. grant to HOSEA DISON by Gov. Alex. Martin, Oct. 25, 1782, a tract of 156 acres on Toisnot Swamp adjoining John Taylor, Joseph Vick, and Simon Strickland.

DB 3-96 STATE of N. C. grant to ARTHUR O'NAILS by

Gov. Alex. Martin, Oct. 25, 1782, a tract of 38 acres on Sapony Creek adjoining John Biggs, John Manning, James Tucker, and George Sutton.

DB 3-97 STATE of N. C. grant to MICAJAH THOMAS by Gov. Alex Martin, Oct. 9, 1783, a tract of 640 acres on Pig Basket Creek adjoining John Bass, Wililam Boddie, and John Turner.

DB 3-98 STATE of N. C. grant to MICAJAH THOMAS by Gov. Alex. Martin, Oct. 9, 1783, a tract of 633 acres on the Back Swamp adjoining Bass, Hedgepeth, Chapman, Willaby Tucker, Adams, and Montford.

DB 3-99 STATE of N. C. grant to MICAJAH THOMAS by Gov. Alex. Martin, Oct. 9, 1783, a tract of 1000 acres on Peach tree Creek adjoining Jacob Dickinson, Jos. Thomas, Holland, James Woodard, the Pig Basket Creek, and his own line.

3-100 STATE of N. C. grant to JOSIAH WINBOURN by Gov. Alex. Martin, Oct. 25, 1782. a tract of 300 acres on the north side of Beaver Dam Swamp adjoining John Kent.

DB 3-101 STATE of N. C. grant to THOMAS CARPENTER by Gov. Alex. Martin, Oct. 9, 1783, a tract of 300 acres on Mocasin Creek.

DB 3-102 STATE of N. C. grant to MARK MASON by Gov. Alex. Martin, Oct. 9, 1783, a tract of 700 acres on Fishing Creek and Round Stone Swamp adjoining Lemuel Nicholson, James Wyatt, John Jones, and his own line.

DB 3-103 STATE of N. C. grant to JOSIAH WINBOURN by Gov. Alex. Martin, Oct. 25, 1782, a tract of 345 acres on Beaver Dam Swamp adjoining Mooneyham's meadow.

DB 3-104 STATE of N. C. grant to JACOB STRICKLAND by Gov. Rd. Caswel, March 30, 1780, a tract of 640 acres on Haw Branch near his own improvement.

DB 3-105 STATE of N. C. grant to THOMAS ROGERS by Gov. Alex. Martin, Nov. 1, 1784, a tract of 150 acres on Turkey Creek adjoining Sampson Powell, Peleg Rogers, and the Jumping Branch.

DB 3-106 STATE of N. C. grant to THOMAS ROGERS by Gov. Alex Martin, Nov. 1, 1784, a tract of 100 acres on Turkey Creek and the Jumping Branch.

DB 3-107 STATE of N. C. grant to HENRY TISDALE by Gov. Alex. Martin, Nov. 1, 1784, a tract of 300 acres on the Millstone adjoining James Deans.

DB 3-108 STATE of N. C. grant to BENJAMIN COBB by Gov. Alex Martin, Nov. 1, 1784, a tract of 50 acres on Contentnea Creek and the Marsh Swamp adjoining James Brown and his own line.

DB 3-109 STATE of N. C. grant to DAVID COBB by Gov. Alex. Martin, Nov. 1, 1784, a tract of 200 acres on Contentnea Creek and Allen's Branch adjoining Benjamin Cobb.

DB 3-110 STATE of N. C. grant to STEPHEN COBB by Gov. Alex. Martin, Nov. 1, 1784, a tract of 200 acres on Mash Swamp adjoining James Brown and Thomas Horn, including a small mash where Jeremiah Nichols found iron ore.

DB 3-111 STATE of N. C. grant to STEPHEN COBB by Gov. Alex Martin, Nov. 1, 1784, a tract of 640 acres on the north side of Contentnea Creek and on Marsh Smawp adjoining Joseph Williamson, Jeremiah Nichols, Jacob Duck, Hardy Boykin, and Drewry Boykin.

DB 3-112 STATE of N. C. grant to JOHN RICE by Gov. Alex. Martin, Oct. 9, 1783, a tract of 400 acres on Lee's Creek.

DB 3-113 STATE of N. C. grant to LUCY PERRY by Gov. Rd. Caswell, Nov. 10, 1779, a tract of 103 acres on the north side of Sapony Creek adjoining Matthias Manning, Vaughan, and Joseph Tucker.

DB 3-114 STATE of N. C. grant to JEREMIAH NICHOLS, JR. by Gov. Alex. Martin, Nov. 1, 1784, a tract of 250 acres on Little Swamp adjoining Jeremiah Nichols, Sr. and Benjamin Flowers.

DB 3-115 STATE of N. C. grant to WILLIAM PALL by Gov. Alex. Martin, Oct. 9, 1783, a tract of 140 acres on Turkey Creek adjoining Strickland.

DB 3-116 STATE of N. C. grant to HARDY BOYKIN by Gov. Alex. Martin, Nov. 1, 1784, a tract of 400 acres on Marsh Swamp adjoining Stephen Cobb, Jacob Nichols, Drewry Boykin, and his own line.

DB 3-117 STATE of N. C. grant to THOMAS HORN, JR. by Gov. Alex. Martin, Nov. 1, 1784, a tract of 320 acres on Toisnot Swamp adjoining Henry Flowers and his father's line.

DB 3-118 STATE of N. C. grant to THOMAS HORN, JR. by Gov. Alex. Martin, Nov. 1, 1784, a tract of 500 acres on the Marsh Swamp adjoining James Brown.

DB 3-119 STATE of N. C. grant to FRANCIS LOCUS by Gov. Alex. Martin, Oct. 9, 1783, a tract of 525 acres on Turkey Creek adjoining William Chapman.

DB 3-120 STATE of N. C. grant to JACOB FLOWERS by Gov. Alex. Martin, Oct. 9, 1783, a tract of 320 acres on the Great Swamp adjoining Benjamin Bunn near Benjamin Flowers' corner and Joseph Phillips.

DB 3-121 STATE of N. C. grant to EDWARD MOORE by Gov. Alex. Martin, Oct. 9. 1783, a tract of 640 acres on the Great Swamp, including the Bloomery adjoining Benjamin Flowers, Joseph Phillips, and John Eatman.

DB 3-122 STATE of N. C. grant to WILLIAM PERRY by Gov. Alex. Martin, Nov. 1, 1784, a tract of 300 acres in the fork of Turkey Creek adjoining Solomon Strickland, Harris, and Willim Ray.

DB 3-123 STATE of N. C. grant to JOHN SANDERS by Gov. Rd. Caswell, March 30, 1780, a tract of 300 acres on Millstone Swamp.

DB 3-124 STATE of N. C. grant to BENJAMIN BUNN by Gov. Alex. Martin. Oct. 9, 1783, a tract of 640 acres on Sheppard's Branch adjoining Flowers and his own line.

DB 3-125 STATE of N. C. grant to BENJAMIN BUNN by Gov. Alex. Martin, Oct. 9, 1783, a tract of 640 acres on the Great Swamp and Horse Pen Branch adjoining Crumpler, Benjamin Flowers, and his own line.

DB 3-126 STATE of N. C. grant to WILLIAM ROW by Gov. Alex. Martin, Nov. 1, 1784, a tract of 200 acres on Contentnea Creek adjoining Boykin and John Sanders.

DB 3-127 STATE of N. C. grant to JULIAN KING by Gov. Alex. Martin, Oct. 25, 1782, a tract of 300 acres on the north side of Stony Creek adjoining Micajah Thomas, Jesse Thomas, Dickerson, Whitfield, and Wimberly.

DB 3-128 STATE of N. C. grant to ROBERT ADAMS by Gov. Alex. Martin, Oct. 25, 1782, a tract of 74 acres on the north side of Swift Creek adjoining James Cox, William Battle, and Bell.

DB 3-129 STATE of N. C. grant to THOMAS CARTER by Gov. Alex. Martin, Nov. 1, 1784, a tract of 250 acres on Tar River adjoining Strickland, Davies. John Bonds, and his own line.

DB 3-130 STATE of N. C. grant to JOHN SIKES by Gov. Alex. Martin, Nov. 1, 1784, a tract of 500 acres on Little Peachtree Creek adjoining Isaac Bass, Charles Brown, Matthew Drake and Richard Deens.

DB 3-131 STATE of N. C. grant to ELIZABETH PARKER by Gov. Alex. Martin, Nov. 1, 1784, a tract of 100 acres on Toisnot Swamp adjoining William Boyet.

DB 3-132 STATE of N. C. grant to JOHN BIGGS by Gov. Alex. Martin, Nov. 1, 1784, a tract of 300 acres on Sapony Creek adjoining William Wester and Jeremiah Etheridge.

DB 3-133 STATE of N. C. grant to WILLIAM ANDREWS by Gov. Alex. Martin, Nov. 1, 1784, a tract of 200 acres on the north side of Tar River and on Sapony Creek adjoining John Biggs, Drewry Alford, Edward Pursell, and his own line.

DB 3-134 STATE of N. C. grant to CHRISTOPHER BALLARD by Gov. Alex. Martin, Nov. 1, 1784, a tract of 221 acres on Sapony Creek adjoining Henry Atkinson, Barlow, Benjamin Smith, and John Evans.

DB 3-135 STATE of N. C. grant to ELIZABETH PARKER by Gov. Alex. Martin, 1784, a tract of 300 acres on the north side of Toisnot Swamp adjoining Michael Horn, Francis Vanlindingham, Gabriel Parker, and Aaron Parker.

DB 3-136 STATE of N. C. grant to WILLIAM WHITEHEAD by Gov. Alex. Martin, Oct. 9, 1783, a tract of 700 acres on Swift Creek adjoining Samuel Sorsby and his own line.

DB 3-137 STATE of N. C. grant to CHARITY YEATES by Gov. Alex. Martin, Nov. 1, 1784, a tract of 300 acres on the north side of Contentnea Creek adjoining David Cobb.

DB 3-138 STATE of N. C. grant to WILLIAM MANNING by Gov. Alex. Martin, Oct. 25, 1782, a tract of 484 acres on Sapony Creek adjoining Matt Manning, John Manning, William Whiddon, and John Manning, Jr.

DB 3-139 STATE of N. C. grant to DUNCAN LAMON by

Gov. Rd. Caswell, March 30, 1780, a tract of 570 acres on Tar River adjoining his own line and the county line.

DB 3-140 STATE of N. C. grant to DUNCAN LAMON on behalf of JOHN LAMON, a minor. by Gov. Alex. Martin, Nov. 1, 1784, a tract of 1000 acres on the south side of Tar River adjoining Carter, Duncan Lamon, Edward Moore, and John Taylor.

DB 3-141 STATE of N. C. grant to JAMES CAIN by Gov. Rd. Caswell, March 30, 1780, a tract of 700 acres on Fishing Creek adjoining John Powell, George Nicholson, Hackney, and his own lone.

DB 3-142 STATE of N. C. grant to JACOB DUCK by Gov. Alex. Martin, Nov. 1, 1784, a tract of 250 acres on the Mash Swamp adjoining Hardy Boykin and Stephen Cobb.

DB 3-143 STATE of N. C. grant to JACOB DUCK by Gov. Alex. Martin, Nov. 1, 1784 , a tract of 21 acres on Contentnea Creek adjoining his own line.

DB 3-144 STATE of N. C. grant to JACOB DUCK by Gov. Alex. Martin, Nov. 1, 1784, a tract of 300 acres on the north side of Contentnea Creek and on Marsh Swamp adjoining Jeremiah Nichols, Stephen Cobb, Hardy Boykin Jacob Nichols, Benjamin Flowers, and his own line.

DB 3-145 STATE of N. C. grant to THOMAS HORN by Gov. Alex. Martin. Nov. 1, 1784, a tract of 350 acres on Toisnot Swamp adjoining Nathan Williams, John Eatman, John Cockrell, Thomas Horn, Jr.. and his own line.

DB 3-146 STATE of N. C. grant to JOHN FLOWERS by Gov. Alex. Martin, Oct. 25, 1782, a tract of 250 acres on Contnea Creek and Sheppard's Branch adjoining Ephraim Phillips and Sanders.

DB 3-147 STATE of N. C. grant to DUNCAN LAMON by Gov. Rd. Caswell. Sept. 24, 1785, a tract of 840 acres on Tar River adjoining John Taylor. Boothe, Jacob Lewis. and his own line.

DB 3--148 STATE of N. C. grant to JOHN JONES by Gov. Rd. Caswell, Sept. 24. 1785, a tract of 200 acres betwen Great and Little Peachtree Creeks adjoining Drewry Savage, Micajah Thomas, Samuel Barber. William Linsey, and the county line.

DB 3-149 STATE of N. C. grant to ISAAC HILLIARD by Gov. Rd. Caswell. Sept. 24, 1785, a tract of 400 acres on the south side of Swift Creek adjoining his own line.

DB 3-150 STATE of N. C. grant to NATHAN BODDIE by Gov. Rd. Caswell. Sept. 24, 1785. a tract of 450 acres on the north side of Sapony Crek adjoining Micajah Thomas and his own line.

DB 3-151 STATE of N. C. grant to DIXON MARSHALL by Gov. Rd. Caswell, March 14, 1786, a tract of 673 acres on the south side of Tar River adjoining Duncan Lamon and Crowell.

DB 3-152 STATE of N. C. grant to BENJAMIN BRIDGERS by Gov. Rd. Caswell. Aug. 11, 1786, a tract of 400 acres on both sides of Swift Creek adjoining Thomas Mann, Lewis Hill, John Lee, John Williams. James Gooding, and his own line.

DB 3-153 STATE of N. C. grant to DIXON MARSHALL by

Gov. Rd. Caswell, March 14, 1786, a tract of 720 acres on the north side of Tar River adjoining Benjamin Bunn, David Bunn, Duncan Lamon, Lewis Joiner, John Barnes, and Jacob Barnes.

DB 3-154 STATE of N. C. grant to ROWLAND WILLIAMS by Gov. Rd. Caswell, Sept. 24, 1785, a tract of 300 acres on the north side of Little Swamp adjoining Ethelred Dance, Edward Clinch, and Edward Nicholson.

DB 3-155 STATE of N.C. grant to JOSEPH WOODEL by Gov. Alex. Martin, Nov. 1, 1784, a tract of 300 acres on Mash Swamp including the improvements whereon Thomas Jarvis did live.

DB 3-156 STATE of N. C. grant to SAMUEL BARBER by Gov. Rd. Caswell. Sept. 24, 1785, a tract of 100 acres on the north side of Little Peachtree Creek adjoining David Ballard, William Lindsey, and the county line.

DB 3-157 STATE of N. C. grant to WILLIAM ANDREWS by Gov. Rd. Caswell, Sept. 24, 1785, a tract of 300 acres on the north side of Turkey Creek adjoining Jeremiah Deans, Henry Deans, and his own line.

DB 3-158 STATE of N. C. grant to SAMUEL BARLOW, JR. by Gov. Rd. Caswell, March 30, 1780, a tract of 146 acres on Sapony Creek adjoining Benjamin Smith, James Baker, and Samuel Bottoms.

DB 3-159 STATE of N. C. grant to RICHARD WINSTEAD by Gov. Rd. Caswell, Aug. 11, 1786, a tract of 300 acres on Town Creek adjoining Peter Hatton, Elizabeth Parker, Duncan Lamon, the county line, and his own line.

DB 3-160 STATE of N. C. grant to WILLIAM BATCHELOR by Gov. Rd. Caswell, Sept. 24, 1785, a tract of 110 acres on both sides of Sapony Creek adjoining Benja. Bunn, John Manning, and his own line.

DB 3-161 STATE of N. C. grant of JAMES BROWN by Gov. Rd. Caswell, Sept. 24, 1785, a tract of 640 acres on both sides of Wilder's Mill Branch adjoining Joseph Woodel.

DB 3-162 STATE of N. C. grant to JOHN ROGERS by Gov. Rd. Caswell, Nov. 10, 1779, a tract of 300 acres on the north side of Moccasin Creek adjoining Lee.

DB 3-162 EARL GRANVILLE grant to ARTHUR HAR-RINGTON of Edgecombe Co., March 2, 1761, a tract of 365 acres adjoining Joseph Griffin, James Douglas, and Arthur Whitehead.

DB 3-164 STATE of N. C. grant to JOHN JONES by Gov. Rd. Caswell, Nov. 10, 1779, a tract of 227 acres on the south side of Fishing Creek adjoining Pollock, James Wyatt, Nicholson, Whitehead, and his own line.

DB 3-164 EARL GRANVILLE grant to ARTHUR AR-RINGTON of Edgecombe Co., July 24, 1761, a tract of 420 acres adjoining Jacob West, Joseph Griffin, James Douglas, John Griffin, Jos. Betts. and Britton.

DB 3-166 STATE of N. C. grant to MICAJAH THOMAS by Gov. Rd. Caswell, Nov. 10, 1779, a tract of 640 acres on the south side of Tar River adjoining John Chapman, William Braswell, and his own line.

DB 3-167 STATE of N. C. grant to MICAJAH THOMAS by Gov. Rd. Caswell, Nov. 10, 1779, a tract of 640 acres on Little Swamp adjoining Matthew Drake and his own line.

DB 3-168 STATE of N. C. grant to MICAJAH THOMAS by Gov. Rd. Caswell, Nov. 10, 1779, a tract of 985 acres on the south side of Peachtree Creek adjoining Gandy, Hunt, Thomson, Bennett, Whitfield, and his own line.

DB 3-169 STATE of N. C. grant to CHARLES WATSON by Gov. Rd. Caswell, Nov. 10,1779, a tract of 640 acres on Pig Basket Creek adjoining Arthur Braswell, Matthew Drake, and Isaac Hilliard.

DB 3-170 STATE of N. C. grant to WILLIAM HORN by Gov. Rd. Caswell, Nov. 10, 1779, a tract of 5 acres on Tar River adjoining the county line.

DB 3-171 STATE of N.C. grant to JOSEPH EXUM by Gov. Rd. Caswell, Nov. 10, 1779, a tract of 200 acres on both sides of Beach Run adjoining Thomas Atkinson, William Speight. and James Cane.

DB 3-172 STATE of N. C. grant to LAZARUS WHITEHEAD by Gov. Rd. Caswell, Nov. 10, 1779, a tract of 640 acres on the north side of Swift Creek adjoining George Lane's Swamp, Jesse Battle, Powell, Jacob Cain, Isaac Talbert and his own line.

DB 3-173 STATE of N. C. grant to WILLIAM DORTCH by Gov. Rd. Caswell, Nov. 10, 1779, a tract of 500 acres on the north side of Swift Creek adjoining George Powell, Baggett, Hackney, and his own line.

DB 3-174 STATE of N. C. grant to SION BASS by Gov. Rd. Caswell, Nov. 10, 1779, a tract of 640 acres on Back Swamp adjoining David Chapman, James Massingale, Willaby Manning, and Peter Hedgepeth.

DB 3-175 STATE of N.C. grant to JOHN KNIGHT by Gov. Rd. Caswell, Nov. 10,1779, a tract of 100 acres on Pig Basket Creek adjoining Thomas Horn.

DB 3-176 STATE of N. C. grant to JOHN MELTON by Gov. Rd. Caswell, Nov. 10 1779, a tract of 300 acres on the north side of Tar River adjoining Joseph Sumner and Wililam Hendricks.

DB 3-177 STATE of N.C. grant to LAZARUS WHITEHEAD by Gov. Rd Caswell, Nov. 10, 1779, a tract of 500 acres on the south side of Fishing Creek adjoining James Cain, George Nicholson, Thomas Vanlandingham, and his own line.

DB 3-178 STATE of N.C. grant to WILLIAM HORN by Gov. Rd. Caswell, Nov. 10, 1779, a tract of 96 acres on the north side of Stony Creek adjoining Nicholas Skinner and his own line.

DB 3-179 STATE of N.C. grant to JAMES DRAKE by Gov. Rd. Caswell, Nov. 10, 1779, a tract of 218 acres on the south side of Swift Creek adjoining William Bridgers, Sion West, John Bass, William Battle, Thomas Mann, and his own line.

DB 3-180 STATE of N. C. grant to SOLOMON VESTER by Gov. Rd. Caswell, Nov. 10, 1779, a tract of 500 acres on the north side of Sapony Creek and on Bear Branch adjoining William Vester, Thomas Richardson, and Nathan Boddie.

DB 3-181 STATE of N.C. grant to WILLIAM BATTLE by Gov. Rd. Caswell, Nov. 10, 1779, a tract of 640 acres on the north side of Swift Creek adjoining Crawman, Peter Anderson, Thomas Davis, the Gideon Swamp, and his own line.

DB 3-182 STATE of N. C. grant to WILLIAM RICHARDSON by Gov. Rd. Caswell, Nov. 10, 1779, a tract of 400 acres on the Back Swamp adjoining James Massingale, Henry Braswell, Isaac Bass, and his own line.

DB 3-183 STATE of N C. grant to JAMES BAKER by Gov. Rd. Caswell, 1779, a tract of 200 acres on the south side of Sapony Creek adjoining Ben Smith, John Joyner, Thomas Kersey, and Bottoms.

DB 3-184 STATE of N. C. grant to SIMON WILLIAMS by Gov. Rd. Caswell, Nov. 10, 1779, a tract of 250 acres on the west side of Turkey Creek adjoining Jacob Carter, William Ross, Jeremiah Deans, and the county line.

DB 3-185 STATE of N. C. grant to SAMUEL BRYANT by Gov. Rd. Caswell, Nov. 10, 1779, a tract of 200 acres on the north side of Tar River adjoining Newit Lane and his own line.

DB 3-186 STATE of N. C. grant to SAMPSON POWELL by Gov Rd. Caswell, Nov. 10, 1779, a tract of 640 acres on Little Peachtree Creek adjoining William Harris and Richard Deans.

DB 3-187 STATE of N. C. grant to JOHN JOINER by Gov. Rd. Caswell, Nov. 10, 1779. a tract of 300 acres on the south side of Sapony Creek adjoining Thomas Kersey, Benja. Smith, Edward Ballard, and Joseph Sealy.

DB 3-188 STATE of N. C. grant to WILLIAM WHIDDON by Gov. Rd. Caswell, Nov. 10, 1779, a tract of 690 acres on the north side of Sapony Creek adjoining Gandy, Kent, Whitfield, his own line, and the Little Sapony Creek.

DB 3-189 STATE of N. C. grant to ISHAM GANDY by Gov Rd. Caswell, Nov. 10, 1779, a tract of 287 acres on the north side of Little Sapony Creek adjoining Whittin and Holland.

DB 3-190 STATE of N. C. grant to BRINTLEY GANDY by Gov. Rd. Caswell, Nov. 10, 1779. a tract of 238 acres on the south side of Sapony Creek adjoining Ozwell Langley and Marcum Cooper.

DB 3-191 STATE of N. C. grant to WILLIAM CHAPMAN, SR by Gov. Rd. Caswell, Nov. 10, 1779, a tract of 100 acres on the north side of Turkey Creek adjoining his own line and the Wolf Pit Branch.

DB 3-192 STATE of N. C. grant to WILLIAM BODDIE by Gov. Rd. Caswell, Nov. 10. 1779, a tract of 640 acres on Bettey's Branch adjoining Isaac Hilliard, Charles Watson, Bass, Thomas, and Braswell.

DB 3-193 STATE of N. C. grant to MATTHEW DRAKE by Gov. Rd. Caswell, Nov. 10. 1779, a tract of 444 acres on the north side of Tar River Branch adjoining Jesse Powell, Cooper Jones, William Williams, John Jones, and his own line.

DB 3-194 STATE of N. C. grant to NATHAN BODDIE by Gov. Rd Caswell, Nov. 10, 1779, a tract of 800 acres on Sapony Creek adjoining Isaac Bass, John Sikes, and his own line.

DB 3-195 STATE of N. C. grant to ARTHUR BRASWELL by Gov. Rd. Caswell, Nov. 10, 1779, a tract of 538 acres on the north side of Pig Basket Creek adjoining Boling Beckwith, Matthew Drake, Jacob Braswell, and his own line.

DB 3-196 STATE of N. C. grant to JAMES COCKS by Gov. Rd. Caswell, Nov. 10, 1779, a tract of 200 acres on the north side of Gideon's Swamp adjoining Peter Anderson, Thomas Davis, Elias Bell, and William Battle.

DB 3-197 STATE of N. C. grant to JOSEPH JOHN CLINCH by Gov. Rd. Caswell, Nov 10, 1779, a tract of 200 acres on the south side of Swift Creek adjoining Jesse Jinkins, Nathan Atkinson, and his own line.

DB 3-198 STATE of N. C. grant to THOMAS MANN by Gov. Rd. Caswell, Nov. 10, 1779, a tract of 300 acres on the north side of Swift Creek adjoining Crawman, William Battle, and his own line.

DB 3-199 STATE of N. C. grant to ARTHUR LASSITER by Gov. Rd. Caswell. Nov. 10, 1779, a tract of 68 acres on the south side of Fishing Creek adjoining Jos. Hayes, Lemuel Lassiter, Hunt, Benjamin Whitehead. and Pollock.

DB 3-200 STATE of N. C grant to SAMUEL SORSBY by Gov. Rd. Caswell, Nov. 10, 1779, a tract of 506 acres on Jarrel's Branch adjoining Benjamin Merritt, Joseph Exum, Thomas Atkinson, William Whitehead, and his own line.

DB 3-201 STATE of N. C. grant to HENRY BARLOW by Gov. Rd. Caswell, Nov. 10, 1779, a tract of 90 acres on the north side of Sapony Creek adjoining John Brantley, Edward Ballard, and Benjamin Simth.

DB 3-202 STATE of N. C. grant to JOHN BASS by Gov. Rd. Caswell, Nov. 10, 1779, a tract of 640 acres on Pig Basket Creek adjoining Isaac Hilliard, Sion West, William Battle, and Thomson.

DB 3-203 STATE of N. C grant to JEREMIAH BROWN by Gov. Rd. Caswell, Nov. 10, 1779, a tract of 640 acres on the north side of Turkey Creek including his own improvement and adjoining Henry Wyatt's improvements.

DB 3-204 STATE of N. C. grant to LAZARUS WHITEHEAD by Gov. Rd. Caswell, Nov. 10, 1779, a tract of 240 acres on the north side of Beaver Dam Swamp adjoining Isaac Talbert, George Nicholson, Thomas Hill, and his own line.

DB 3-205 STATE of N. C. grant to LAZARUS WHITEHEAD by Gov. Rd. Caswell, Nov. 10, 1779, a tract of 1000 acres on the north side of Swift Creek adjoining Thompson, the county line, the Long Swamp, Thomas Vanlandingham, George Nicholson, and his own line.

DB 3-206 STATE of N. C grant to THOMAS RICHARDSON by Gov. Rd. Caswell, Nov. 10, 1779, a tract of 100 acres on the north side of Bare Branch adjoining Matthias Manning and William Vester.

DB 3-207   STATE of N. C. grant to STEPHEN YOUNG by Gov. Rd. Caswell, Nov. 10, 1779, a tract of 329 acres on the north side of Peachtree Creek adjoining Thomas Tucker, Isaac Bass, William Richardson, Henry Pede, and his own line.

DB 3-208   STATE of N. C. grant to WILLIAM MANN by Gov. Rd. Caswell, Nov. 10, 1779, a tract of 36 acres on the south side of Swift Creek adjoining Thomas Mann and Cooper Williams.

DB 3-209   STATE of N. C grant to EDWARD NICHOLSON by Gov. Rd. Caswell, Nov. 10, 1779, a grant of 70 acres on the south side of Tar River adjoining Edward Clinch and his own line.

DB 3-210   STATE of N. C. grant to MICAJAH THOMAS by Gov. Rd. Caswell, Nov. 10, 1779, a tract of 985 acres on the south side of Peachtree Creek adjoining Gandy, Thomson, Bennett, Whitfield, Kent, and his own line.

DB 3-211   STATE of N. C. grant to WILLIAM CHAPMAN, JR. by Gov. Rd. Caswell, Nov. 10, 1779, a tract of 200 acres on both sides of Turkey Creek adjoining Henry Strickland and his father's line

DB 3-212   STATE of N. C. grant to EDWARD NICHOLSON by Gov. Rd. Caswell, Nov. 10. 1779, a tract of 100 acres on the north side of Little Swamp adjoining Rowland Williams.

DB 3-213   STATE of N. C. grant to EDWARD PURSELL by Gov. Rd. Caswell, Nov. 10, 1779, a tract of 300 acres on Little Creek adjoining Robert Young and his own line.

DB 3-214   STATE of N. C. grant to EDWARD PURSELL by Gov. Rd. Caswell, Nov. 10, 1779, a tract of 640 acres on both sides of Turkey Creek adjoining his own line on Little Creek and Daniel Taylor

DB 3-215   STATE of N. C. grant to EDWARD PURSELL by Gov. Rd. Caswell, Nov. 10, 1779, a tract of 200 acres on the north side of Tar River adjoining Samuel Bryant.

DB 3-216   STATE of N. C. grant to JEREMIAH ETHERIDGE by Gov. Rd. Caswell, Nov. 10, 1779, a tract of 200 acres on Sapony Creek adjoining Edward Pursell.

DB 3-217   STATE of N. C. grant to JEREMIAH NICHOLS by Gov. Rd. Caswell, Nov. 10, 1779, a tract of 300 acres on the north side of Contentnea Creek adjoining his own line

DB 3-218   STATE of N. C. grant to NEWIT LANE by Gov. Rd. Caswell. Nov. 10, 1779, a tract of 318 acres on the north side of Tar River adjoining William Hendricks, Samuel Bryant, Joseph Sumner, and his own line.

DB 3-219   STATE of N. C. grant to WILLIAM ANDREWS by Gov. Rd. Caswell, Nov. 10, 1779, a tract of 80 acres on the south side of Little Peachtree Creek adjoining William Harris, Sampson Powell, and Charles Brittain.

DB 3-220   STATE of N. C. grant to JOHN MELTON by Gov. Rd. Caswell, Nov 10, 1779, a tract of 640 acres in the fork of Whitehead's Mill Swamp adjoining Arthur Whitehead, Horn, and William Whitehead.

DB 3-221 STATE of N. C. grant to BENJAMIN MERRITT by Gov. Rd. Caswell, Nov. 10, 1779. a tract of 364 acres on the south side of Swift Creek adjoining Samuel Sorsby.

DB 3-222 STATE of N. C. grant to JOHN WARREN, SR. by Gov. Rd. Caswell, Nov. 10, 1779, a tract of 200 acres on Little Turkey Creek adjoining Samuel Bryant.

DB 3-223 STATE of N. C. grant to JOHN TURNER by Gov Rd. Caswell, Nov. 10, 1779, a tract of 287 acres on the Back Swamp adjoining Willaby Manning, William Boddie, and Thomas.

DB 3-224 STATE of N. C. grant to JACOB STALLIONS by Gov. Rd. Caswell, Nov. 10, 1779, a tract of 200 acres on the north side of Tar River adjoining David Bunn.

DB 3-225 STATE of N. C. grant to JACOB WHITEHEAD by Gov. Rd. Caswell, Nov. 10, 1779, a tract of 320 acres on the south side of Swift Creek adjoining Joseph Clinch, Jeremiah Hilliard, and Hardy Pope.

DB 3-226 STATE of N. C. grant to THOMAS HUNTER by Gov. Rd. Caswell. Nov. 10, 1779, a tract of 700 acres on the north side of Stony Creek adjoining William Hunt, Samuel Braswell, Richard Vick, Thomas Willis, Hartwell Hart, and his own line.

DB 3-227 STATE of N. C. grant to WILLIAM YATES by Gov. Rd. Caswell, Nov. 10, 1779, a tract of 500 acres on the north side of Contentnea Creek adjoining James Norris and Joseph Williams.

DB 3-228 STATE of N. C. grant to RICHARD THOMAS by Gov. Rd. Caswell, Nov. 10, 1779, a tract of 640 acres on both sides of Stony Creek adjoining Jacob Dickerson, Goodson, Ricks, Melton, Whitfield, the Maple Creek, and his own line.

DB 3-229 STATE of N. C. grant to JACOB DICKERSON by Gov. Rd. Caswell, March 30, 1780, a tract of 400 acres on the south side of Stony Creek adjoining Micajah Thomas, Whitfield, John Whitehouse, and his own line.

DB 3-230 STATE of N. C. grant to ISAAC HILLIARD by Gov. Rd. Caswell, March 30, 1780, a tract of 53 acres on the north side of Swift Creek adjoining Sandeford and his own line.

DB 3-231 STATE of N. C. grant to ISAAC HILLIARD by Gov. Rd. Caswell, March 30, 1780, a tract of 348 acres on Swift Creek adjoining John Jones, Arthur Whitehead, the mill swamp, Thomas Horn, and John Knight.

DB 3-232 STATE of N. C. grant to ISAAC HILLIARD by Gov. Rd. Caswell, March 30, 1780, a tract of 627 acres on Swift Creek adjoining John Jones, Horn, and his own line.

DB 3-233 STATE of N. C. grant to REUBEN TAYLOR by Gov. Rd. Caswell. Nov. 10, 1779, a tract of 150 acres on the south side of Beach Run adjoining Speight and his own line.

DB 3-234 STATE of N. C. grant to JAMES BRYAN by Gov. Rd. Caswell. Nov. 10, 1779, a tract of 225 acres on the north side of Peachtree Creek adjoining Isaac Bass, Charles Brown, and Thomas.

DB 3-235 STATE of N. C. grant to JACOB STRICKLAND by

Gov. Rd. Caswell, Nov. 10, 1779, a tract of 13 acres on the south side of Tar River adjoining Edward Nicholson and his own line.

DB 3-236 STATE of N. C. grant to DIOCLESIAN DAVIS by Gov. Rd. Caswell, Nov. 10, 1779, a tract of 287 acres adjoining Thomas Davis and Lewis Davis.

DB 3-237 STATE of N. C. grant to JACOB UNDERWOOD by Gov. Rd. Caswell, Nov. 10, 1779, a tract of 466 acres on both sides of Compass Creek adjoining David Strickland, Thomas Thorp, Solomon Edwards. Thomas Atkinson, and William Whitehead.

DB 3-238 STATE of N. C. grant to JOSEPH WILLIAMSON by Gov. Rd. Caswell, Nov. 10, 1779, a tract of 640 acres on the north side of Contentnea Creek adjoining Jeremiah Nichols, Thomas Woodward, and the Marsh Swamp.

DB 3-239 STATE of N. C. grant to JACOB STRICKLAND by Gov. Rd. Caswell, Nov. 10, 1779, a tract of 200 acres on the south side of Tar River adjoining his own line.

DB 3-240 STATE of N. C. grant to WILLIAM LINSEY by Gov. Rd. Caswell, Nov. 10,1779, a tract of 300 acres on the north side of Little Peachtree Creek adjoining James Moore, William Harris, Sampson Powell, Matthew Drake, Micajah Thomas, and his own line.

DB 3-241 STATE of N. C. grant to BENJAMIN MERRET by Gov. Rd. Caswell, Nov. 10, 1779, a tract of 110 acres on the south side of Beach Run adjoining Joseph Exum.

DB 3-242 STATE of N. C. grant to HENRY STRICKLAND by Gov. Rd. Caswell, Nov. 10, 1779, a tract of 585 acres on both sides of Turkey Creek adjoining William Chapman.

DB 3-243 STATE of N. C. grant to BOLING BECKWORTH by Gov. Rd. Caswell. Nov. 10, 1779, a tract of 400 acres on the north side of Pig Basket Creek adjoining Micajah Thomas and Arthur Braswell.

DB 3-244 STATE of N. C. grant to WILLIAM BRIDGERS by Gov. Rd. Caswell, Nov. 10, 1779, a tract of 75 acres on the north side of Swift Creek adjoining Benjamin Bridgers and his own line.

DB 3-245 STATE of N. C. grant to THOMAS TUCKER by Gov. Rd. Caswell, Nov. 10, 1779, a tract of 550 acres on the north side of Sapony Creek adjoining Matthias Manning. Jr., Christopher Vaughan. Daniel Deans, Nathan Boddie and his own line.

DB 3-246 STATE of N. C. grant to WILSON CURL, by Gov. Rd. Caswell Nov. 10. 1779, a tract of 150 acres on the south side of Compass Creek adjoining Stephen Hamlin, Isaac Horn, Henry Watkins, John Exum, and his own line.

DB 3-247 STATE of N. C. grant to EPHRAIM PHILLIPS by Gov. Rd. Caswell, Nov. 10, 1779. a tract of 300 acres on both sides of Sheppard's Branch adjoining Widow Row and Thomas Sanders.

DB 3-248 STATE of N. C. grant to EDWARD CLINCH by Gov. Rd. Caswell, Nov. 10, 1779, a tract of 540 acres on the south side of Tar River adjoining his own line and the Horse Pen Branch.

DB 3-249 STATE of N. C. grant to JOSEPH SELEY by Gov.

Rd. Caswell, Nov. 10, 1779, a tract of 640 acres on Jacobs Swamp adjoining John Poland, Edward Ballard, and Jacob Brantley.

DB 3-250 STATE of N. C. grant to STEPHEN COBB by Gov. Rd. Caswell, Nov. 10, 1779, a tract of 640 acres on Contentnea Creek adjoining Edward Moore and his own line.

DB 3-251 STATE of N. C. grant to ELIJAH POWELL by Gov. Rd. Caswell, Nov. 10, 1779, a tract of 250 acres on the south side of Little Peachtree Creek adjoining Sampson Powell.

DB 3-252 STATE of N. C. grant to JOSEPH SUMNER by Gov. Rd. Caswell, Nov. 10, 1779, a tract of 356 acres on the north side of Tar River adjoining adjoining Newit Lane, William Hendricks, Thomas, and his own line.

DB 3-253 STATE of N. C. grant to JOHN TAYLOR by Gov. Rd. Caswell, Nov. 10, 1779, a tract of 700 acres on the south side of Tar River at the head of Bryant's Creek adjoining William Parker and including the improvements of Reuben Williams.

DB 3-254 STATE of N. C. grant to JOHN TAYLOR by Gov. Rd. Caswell, Nov., 1779, a tract of 475 acres on the north side of Turkey Creek adjoining Lamon.

DB 3-255 STATE of N. C. grant to NATHAN BODDIE by Rd. Caswell, Nov. 10, 1779, a tract of 400 acres adjoining John Sikes.

DB 3-256 STATE of N. C. grant to CHARLES BROWN by Gov. Rd. Caswell, Nov. 10, 1779, a tract of 300 acres on the north side of Peachtree Creek adjoining John Sikes, Isaac Bass, and Matthew Drake.

DB 3-257 STATE of N. C. grant to JETHRO HARRISON by Gov. Rd. Caswell, Nov. 10, 1779, a tract of 530 acres on Shephard's spring branch adjoining William Phillips.

DB 3-258 STATE of N. C. grant to HENRY ATKINSON by Gov. Rd. Caswell, Nov. 10, 1779, a tract of 200 acres on the north side of Tar River adjoining Edward Moore and his own line.

DB 3-259 STATE of N. C. grant to BENJAMIN BUNN by Gov. Rd. Caswell, Nov. 10, 1779, a tract of 640 acres on the south side of Sapony Creek adjoining Thomas Deans and Thomas Warren.

DB 3-260 STATE of N. C. grant to THOMAS VANLAND- INGHAM by Gov. Rd. Caswell, Nov. 10 1779, a tract of 150 acres on the north side of the long swamp adjoining the county line.

DB 3-261 STATE of N. C. grant to EDWARD MOORE by Gov. Rd. Caswell, Nov. 10. 1779, a tract of 300 acres on the north side of Tar River andjoining Taylor and his own line.

DB 3-262 STATE of N. C. grant to JOHN TAYLOR by Gov. Rd. Caswell, Nov. 10, 1779, a tract of 260 acres on the north side of Turkey Creek adjoining Barnaby Barron and including the improvements of Benjamin Taylor.

DB 3-263 STATE of N. C. grant to JOEL WIGGINS by Gov. Rd. Caswell, Nov. 10, 1779, a tract of 121 acres on the south side of Swift Creek adjoining Jelks, Merret, and Samuel Sorsby.

DB 3-264 STATE of N. C. grant to JACOB NICHOLS by

Gov. Rd. Caswell, Nov. 10, 1779, a tract of 200 acres on the north side of Conetntnea Creek and both sides of Rooty Branch

DB 3-265 STATE of N. C. grant to JOHN BIGGS by Gov. Rd. Caswell, Nov. 10, 1779, a tract of 350 acres on the north side of Sapony Creek adjoining Thomas Tucker, Daniel Deans, Matthias Manning, and John Manning.

DB 3-266 STATE of N. C. grant to JOHN BASS by Gov. Rd. Caswell, Nov. 10, 1779, a tract of 640 acres on Pig Basket Creek adjoining Isaac Hilliard, Sion West, Abraham Bass, Thomas, and his own line.

DB 3-267 STATE of N. C. grant to THOMAS SANDERS by Gov. Rd. Caswell, Nov. 10, 1779, a tract of 640 acres on the north side of Contentnea Creek adjoining Widow Row, Ephriam Phillips, Jordan, the county line, and Hedgpeth.

DB 3-268 STATE of N. C. grant to WILLIAM BUNTING by Gov. Rd. Caswell, Nov. 10, 1779, a tract of 640 acres on the south side of Sapony Creek adjoining Joshua Pierce, Arthur Sellers, and Thomas Deans.

DB 3-269 STATE of N. C. grant to JAMES GOODEN by Gov. Rd. Caswell, Nov. 10, 1779, a tract of 640 acres on the south side of White Oak Run adjoining John Deans.

DB 3-270 STATE of N. C. grant to THOMAS ATKINSON by Gov. Rd. Caswell, Nov. 10, 1779, a tract of 302 acres between the heads of Compass Creek and Beach Run adjoining Jacob Underwood, Joseph Exum, and his own line.

DB 3-271 STATE of N. C. grant to WILLIAM PHILLIPS by Gov. Rd. Caswell, Nov. 10, 1779, a tract of 350 acres on Sheppard's Branch adjoining Ephraim Phililps, Jethro Harrison, and his own line.

DB 3-272 STATE of N. C. grant to JOHN KENT by Gov. Rd. Caswell, March 30, 1780, a tract of 570 acres on Turkey Creek adjoining Jesse Kent and James Morphis.

DB 3-273 STATE of N. C. grant to JOHN KENT by Gov. Rd. Caswell, March 30, 1780, a tract of 100 acres on Turkey Creek adjoining his own line.

DB 3-274 STATE of N. C. grant to JAMES MORPHIAS by Gov. Rd. Caswell, March 30, 1780, a tract of 250 acres on Turkey Creek adjoining Jesse Kent and Taylor.

DB 3-275 STATE of N. C. grant to WILLIAM CHAPMAN, Jr. by Gov. Rd. Caswell, March 30, 1780, a tract of 85 acres on Turkey Creek adjoining his father's line and his own line.

DB 3-276 STATE of N. C. grant to JESSE BOOTHE by Gov. Rd. Caswell, March 30, 1780, a tract of 300 acres on Cooper's Creek adjoining Thomas Lewis, John Taylor, and Lemmon.

DB 3-277 STATE of N. C. grant to JESSE BOOTHE by Gov. Rd. Caswell, March 30, 1780, a tract of 137 acres on the south side of Tar River adjoining Duncan Lamon, William Strickland, John Taylor, and his own line.

DB 3-278 STATE of N. C. grant to JOHN ROGERS by Gov. Rd. Caswell, March 30, 1780, a tract of 180 acres on the north side of Moccasin Creek.

DB 3-279 STATE of N. C. grant to JESSE HUNT by Gov. Rd. Caswell, March 30, 1780, a tract of 640 acres on the north side of Stony Creek adjoining Thomas Willis, Hunter, Revel, and David Strickland.

DB 3-280 YOUNG DAVIS of Nash Co. to NATHAN GREEN of Halifax Co., Nov. 20, 1784, for 54 pds. a tract of 200 acres on the south side of White Oak Swamp adjoining Davis and Boothe. Wit: Samuel Mitchell and Aaron Wood.

DB 3-281 NATHANIEL SMITH of Edgecombe Co. to DUN-CAN LAMON of same, April 5, 1773, for 50 pds. proc. money 250 acres on the north side of Turkey Creek adjoining John Smelley, Mooneyham, and Contentnea Creek it being part of a tract granted to John Bailey by Earl Granville. Wit: Burwell Barnes and Robert Lancaster.

DB 3-282 THOMAS BAKER and wife PENELOPE BAKER, of Ninety-Six District in South Carolina to JOHN BATTLE of Edgecombe Co., Feb. 1, 1785, for 13 pds., 6 sh., 8 p. in gold and silver 100 acres of land, it being part of a tract granted to Thomas Williams on Nov. 10, 1779 and lying in the south part of this tract which remained unsold. Wit: Jacob Battle, Christopher Prichett, and D. Battle.

DB 3-283 WILLIAM MERRITT of Nash Co. to REUBIN TAYLOR of same, April 28, 1784, for 100 pds. a tract of 110 acres on the north side of Beach Run adjoining Joseph Exum. Wit: William Whitehead and Joseph J. Clinch.

DB 3-284 NICHOLAS SKINNER of Nash Co. to REUBIN TAYLOR of same, July 7, 1783, for 13 pds. specie two adjoining tracts of land on Beach Run: (1) 200 acres adjoining Jeremiah Hilliard and Reubin Taylor; (2) 100 acres adjoining Nicholas Skinner, Jeremiah Hililard, and Reubin Taylor, both tracts having been granted to Nicholas Skinner on Oct. 25, 1782. Wit: Joseph Exum and Elisha Pope.

DB 3-286 ROBERT ADDAMS of Nash Co. to WILLIAM AVENT of same, Aug. 17, 1783, for 50 pds. a tract of 100 acres adjoining James Cocks, William Battle, and Bell. Wit: Lancaster and Charles Anderson.

DB 3-287 RICHARD VICK of Nash Co. to WILSON VICK, Feb. 15, 1785, for 5 pds. specie a tract of 400 acres on the south side of Stony Creek adjoining Lane's Road, Ricks, Lewis Ricks, Richard Thomas, and Maple Creek. Wit: Joseph Arrington and Lazarus Whitehead.

DB 3-288 ABRAHAM SMITH of Johnston Co. to NEHE-MIAH SMITH of same, Dec. 22, 1785 for 20 pds. specie a plantation on the north side of Stony Creek, it being a one-third part of a tract purchased by Joseph Smith, father of said Abraham Smith in 1764; 100 acres of said land was purchased of William Horn and the other part containing 165 acres was purchased of

James Oliver and given by Joseph Smith to said Abraham Smith in his will. Wit: Emmanuel Skinner and Bathsheba Moore.

DB 3-289 MILLS TAYLOR of Nash Co. to JACOB ED-WARDS of Edgecombe Co., Aug., 17, 1784, for 18 pds. specie a tract of 100 acres on the north side of Tar River adjoining the Edgecombe Co. line and Eli Jones. Wit: James Stallings.

DB 3-290 RICHARD THOMAS of Nash Co. to MARY THO-MAS of same Nov. 23, 1784, for 5 sh. a tract of 170 acres on the south side of Maple Creek. Wit: Wilson Vick and Jethro Thomas.

DB 3-291 ROGER JENKINS and wife, FRANCIS JENKINS, of Nash Co. to HARDYMAN POPE of same, Dec. 16, 1782, for 200 pds. specie a tract of 398 acres on Beach Run adjoining William Taylor. Wit: Jesse Johnson, H. Horn, and Elisha Pope.

DB 3-292 NICHOLAS BAGGET of Nash Co. to PETER ROB-ERTSON of same, Feb. 3, 1785. for 12 pds. specie a tract of 200 acres adjoining Lewis Dortch, Hackney, Ralph Mason, and Peter Robertson. Wit: John Powell and Allinson Powell.

DB 3-293 GREEN BELL of Nash Co. to JOSHUA BUTT of Halifax Co., Oct. 27, 1783, for 66 pds. 13 sh. 4 p. specie 140 acres on Pollock's Beaver Dam Swamp adjoining Elias Bell, it being part of a tract on which Green Bell then lived. Wit: James Grant and Richard Sesmore.

DB 3-295 SPEAR KNIGHT of Nash Co. to BENJAMIN NEWTON of same, July 29, 1784 for 30 pds. specie 100 acres on Beach Run adjoining Hardy Pope it being part of a tract which said Knight bought of John Jenkins, Jr. Wit: Joseph Exum, Elisha Pope, and Reuben Taylor.

DB 3-296 THOMAS HUNTER of Nash Co. to ELIJAH REVEL of same, Jan. 30, 1785, for 15 pds. Virginia money 45 acres on both sides of Lasiter's Branch adjoining said Hunter and the old road, it being part of a tract said Thomas Hunter bought of David Strickland. Wit: Joel Horn, Henry Strickland, and John Wilson.

DB 3-297 JOHN MELTON and wife, ELIZABETH MEL-TON of Nash Co. to WILLIAM HENDRICK of same, Oct. 2, 1784, for 25 pds. hard money a tract of 200 acres on the north side of Tar River adjoining Joseph Sumner, William Bryant, and William Henddricks. Wit: Solomon Carter, Wm. Bryant, and Daniel Taylor.

DB 3-298 JOHN CHAPMAN of Nash Co. to MICAJAH THOMAS of same, Oct. 11, 1784, for 85 pds. current money a tract of 160 acres on the south side of Tar River adjoining William Bryant. Wit: Elijah Boddie and Young Patterson.

DB 3-299 MATTHEW DRAKE, Sheriff of Nash Co., to JAMES CAIN of same, Oct. 6, 1784, at public auction for 25 pds. specie a tract of 200 acres adjoining James Cain, Lazarus White-head, and John Powell, sold as the property of JOHN SCOTT to satisfy two executions, one obtained by the admrx. of Manning and the other by the exrs. of Dozier. Wit: Wilson Vick and E. Boddie.

DB 3--300 HENRY DEAN of Nash Co. to CHARLES BRIT-
TAIN of same, Oct. 6, 1784, for 5 pds. specie a tract of 270 acres
adjoining James Culpepper, William Andrews, and James Griffin.
Wit: Wm. Hall.

DB 3-302 EDWARD PURSELL of Nash Co. to JEREMIAH
ETHERIDGE of same, Feb. 11, 1785, for 50 pds. specie 218 acres
adjoining Pursell, Sapony Creek, and the Bear Branch, it being
part of a tract granted to William Vester on Aug. 10, 1762. Wit:
Daniel Taylor and Jacob Carter.

DB 3-303 DAVID BUNN, SR. of Edgecombe Co. to BEN-
JAMIN BUNN, JR. of same Sept. 26, 1777, for 50 pds. proc.
money a 100 acre plantation on the north side of Tar River and
on Stony Creek, it being part of a tract granted to said Bunn on
April 20, 1745. Wit: John Bunn and Redmun Bunn.

DB 3-304 BRINKLEY GANDY of Nash Co. to PARSON
RACKLEY of same, Feb. 17, 1783, for 10 pds. specie a parcel of
6 acres on the south side of Sapony Swamp adjoining Whiddon,
the Schoolhouse Branch, and Jones' former line. Wit: Thomas
Viverett and Wm. Whiddon.

DB 3-305 WILLIAM BALLARD of Nash Co. to WILLIAM
POULAN of same, Feb. 10, 1785, for 13 pds. 17 sh. specie a tract
of 100 acres on Jacobs Swamp adjoining Kinchen Savage, William
Poulan, and the Rooty Branch. Wit: Jonas Williams and Wilson
Taylor.

DB 3-306 JOHN WILLIAMS of Halifax Co. to ELISHA
BELL of Nash Co., April 10, 1784 for 120 pds. specie 246 acres
on Beaver Dam Swamp adjoining Robert Clark, it being a tract
conveyed to John Williams by Lot Etheridge. Wit: William Bell
and Robert Clark.

DB 3-307 WILLIAM WARBURTON and wife, ALICE WAR-
BURTIN, of Nash Co. to WILLIAM BRYANT of same, Jan. 31,
1784, for 18 pds. hard money a tract of 150 acres on Sapony Creek
adjoining Melton. Wit: William Hendrick and Benjamin Bryant.

DB 3-309 JOEL WIGGINS of Nash Co. to ETHELRED
JELKS of same, Dec. 15. 1783, for 60 pds. a tract of 121 acres
on the south side of Swift Creek adjoining Jelks, Merret, Samuel
Sorsby, and the Stony Branch. Wit: Joseph J. Clinch and John
Rains.

DB 3-310 ROBERT TUCKER of Wein (Wayne) Co. to
JAMES TUCKER, July 30, 1782, for 30 pds. proc. money a tract
of 100 acres on Little Sapony Creek adjoining George Sutton. Wit:
James Tucker, Sr. and John White.

DB 3-311 GREEN BELL and wife ISABEL BELL, of Nash
Co. to JOHN SLATTER of same, Jan. 29, 1784, for 100 pds. specie
310 acres on Fishing Creek adjoining Robert Adams, William
Battle, and Cockes. it being part of a tract granted to said Bell
on Oct. 25. 1782. Wit: W. S. Mearnes, Benja. Bell. and Wm. Bell.

DB 3-312 RICHARD THOMAS and wife REBECKAH THO-
MAS. of Nash Co. to JETHRO THOMAS of same, Nov. 23, 1784,
for 60 pds. a tract of 400 acres on both sides of Peachtree Creek

at Young's Ford adjoining Richard Thomas, the road Tallington, Maple Creek, Richard Vick, and Whitfield. Wit: Henry Bunn, William Matthews, and Mary Melton.

DB 3-313 FULGHAM WESTER of Nash Co. to BENJAMIN BUNN, SR. of same, March 3, 1785, for 100 pds. specie a tract of 108 acres on Maple Creek adjoining William Johnson and Benjamin Bunn. Wit: William Hall and Josiah Bunn.

DB 3-315 JOSEPH CROWELL of Nash Co. to PHILLANDER WILLIAMS of same, May 9, 1784 for 100 pds. proc. money a tract of 275 acres on the south side of Tar River adjoining Phillander Williams, Brittain Smith Jesse Pridgen, and Joseph Crowell, it being part of a patent granted to Nathaniel Sanders. Wit: James Lee and Samuel Westray.

DB 3-316 PETER BALLARD, BENJAMIN SMITH, CHRISTOPHER BALLARD, STEPHEN WELLS, and JOHN WIDDON, all of Nash Co., to PHILLANDER WILLIAMS of same, guardian to Cesely Williams, daughter of Samuel Williams, deceased, Oct. 8, 1783 a bond in the sum of 2000 pds. for the following purpose: Peter Ballard had married said Cesely Williams and requested Phillander Williams to deliver to him the property of his wife, consisting of negroes, cattle, outstanding accounts, and other things bequeathed to Cesely by her father. Wit: D. Lamon and John Bond.
Peter Ballard signed a receipt for 3 negroes, 600 silver dollars, 23 cattle and other listed property, with Hardy Joyner as witness.

DB 3-318 JOSEPH SEALY, Jr. of Nash Co. to JOHN BRANTLEY, JR. of same, May 6, 1785, for 20 pds. specie 160 acres on the south side of Jacobs Swamp adjoining Jacob Brantley and John Poland, it being part of a tract granted to said Sealy on Nov. 10, 1779. Wit: Micajah Thomas and Mourning Ricks.

DB 3-319 EDWARD MOORE of Nash Co. to JETHRO PHILLIPS of same, March 10, 1785, for 100 pds. specie 4 and 34 acres (?) on the Great Swamp adjoining Joseph Phillips and Benjamin Flowers, it being part of a 640 acre tract granted to said Edward Moore on Oct. 9, 1783. Wit: Benja. Cobb and Joseph Phillips.

DB 3-321 EDWARD NICHOLSON of Nash Co. to PETER HATTEN of same, May 10, 1785 for 50 pds. specie two tracts of land: (1) 640 acres adjoining Thomas Hardy, Lazarus Pope, Crowell, and Samuel Wililams; (2) 360 acres adjoining the other tract, it being described in a deed from Matthew Drake, Sheriff, to Edward Nicholson on Feb. 14. 1785.
Wit: Solomon Carter Edward Gandy, and Jonas Williams.

DB 3-322 ISOM GANDY of Nash Co. to BURWELL ROSE of same, Feb. 12, 1785, for 50 pds. specie 175 acres on the north side of Little Sapony Creek adjoining Williba Tucker, Matthias Manning, George Sutton, Arthur O'Neal and John Manning, it being part of a tract granted to John Biggs on Nov. 10, 1779. Wit Solomon Carter and Wm. Whiddon.

DB 3-323 EDWARD MOORE of Nash Co. to STEPHEN

COBB of Wayne Co., March 10, 1785, for 500 pds. specie 206 acres on the Great Swamp adjoining John Eatman, Benjamin Flowers, Jethro Phillips, and the Bloomery Swamp, it being part of a tract granted to said Edward Moore on Oct. 9, 1783 for 640 acres. Wit: Benja. Cobb, Joseph Phillips, and Jas. Cobb.

DB 3-325 BENJAMIN BUNN of Nash Co. to STEPHEN COBB, merchant of Wayne Co., Feb. 27, 1784, for 200 pds. specie two tracts on the Great Swamp and Sheppard's Branch: (1) 640 acres adjoining Flowers which was granted to said Bunn on Oct. 9, 1783; (2) 640 acres on Horse Pen Branch adjoining Crumpler, Benjamin Flowers, and Moore, which was granted to said Bunn on Oct. 9, 1783. Wit: Jas Cobb, Wm. Bridgers, and Duncan Dew.

DB 3-327 LUCY PERRY of Nash Co. to EPHRIAM VAUGHAN of same, Jan. 31, 1785, for 40 pds. a tract of 103 acres on the north side of Sapony Creek adjoining Matthias Manning, Vaughan, and Joseph Tucker. Wit: Solomon Carter and Parsons Rackley.

DB 3-328 JAMES COOPER and wife MARGARET COOPER, Nash Co. to THOMAS ESELL of same, Dec. 18, 1784, for 80 pds. specie 100 acres on the north side of Swift Creek adjoining Bell and Williams, it being a tract of land conveyed to James Cooper by John Cooper. Wit: W. S. Mearns and John Hunt.

DB 3-329 THOMAS ESELL and wife, ELIZABETH ESELL of Nash Co. to JOSEPH ARRINGTON of same, March 17, 1785, for 80 pds. specie 100 acres on the north side of Swift Creek adjoining Bell and Williams, it being a tract conveyed from John Cooper to James Cooper. Wit: James Battle and Martha Battle.

DB 3-330 JOHN MELTON of Nash Co. to WILLIAM BRYANT of same, Oct. 1, 1784, for 10 pds. specie 100 acres adjoining William Bryant and William Hendricks. it being part of a tract whereon Ethelred Hendrick formerly lived. Wit: Solomon Carter, William Hendrick, and Francis Gross.

DB 3-332 CHRISTOPHER VAUGHAN of Nash Co. to STEPHEN VAUGHAN of same, March 1, 1785, for 50 pds. specie a tract of 200 acres which was granted by Earl Granville to Andrew Ross on March 25, 1749, given by said Andrew Ross in his will to his daughter, Sarah Tucker and sold by said Sarah Tucker and Williby Tucker to Wm. Pitman. Wit: Burwell Rose and Ephraim Vaughan.

DB 3-333 MICAJAH THOMAS of Nash Co. to PARSON RACKLEY of same, March 3, 1785 for 40 pds. 200 acres on the north side of Tar River adjoining Samuel Bryant, it being part of a tract granted to Edward Pursell on Nov. 10, 1779. Wit: Elijah Boddie and Mourning Ricks.

DB 3-334 Matthew Drake, Sheriff of Nash Co. to EDWARD NICHOLSON of same, Feb. 14, 1785, at public auction for 30 pds. specie two tracts of land sold as the property of FRANCIS VANLANDINGHAM at the instance of said Edward Nicholson: (1) 640 acres adjoining Thomas Hardy, Lazarus Pope, Crowell, and Samuel Williams; (2) 360 acres adjoining the other tract. Wit: Joseph Arrington and Jeremiah Buntin.

DB 3 335 SAMUEL SKINNER, SR. of Nash Co. to SAMUEL SKINNER, JR. of Edgecombe Co., May 5, 1785, for love and affection for his son a tract of 200 acres on the south side of Stony Creek near the mouth of Poplar Branch. Wit: Emanuel Skinner and Bathsheba Moore.

DB 3-336 WILLIAM MANNING of Edgecombe Co. to WILLIAM L. BOTTOM of Nash Co., May 7, 1785, for 46 pds. 13 sh. 4 p. a tract of 484 acres on Sapony Swamp adjoining Matthias Manning, John Manning, and William Whiddon. Wit: Wm. Whiddon and Lewis Brantley.

DB 3-338 DAVID PRIDGEN of Nash Co. to SOLOMON WELLS of same, May 4, 1785, for 20 pds. specie a tract of 100 acres lying between Solomon Wells and David Pridgen adjoining Joshua Wells. Wit: Samuel Bottoms and Isom Gandy.

DB 3-339 SAMUEL EASON, SR. of Nash Co., to his son, SAMUEL EASON JR., of same, March 26, 1785 a tract of 100 acres on Mash Branch adjoining Thomas Atkinson and Ben Smith. Wit: David Pridgen and Solomon Wells.

DB 3-340 ABRAHAM BASS of Nash Co. to his wife's granddaughter, ELIZABETH ROGERS, daughter of Robert Rogers of Nash Co., April 8, 1785. for love and affection a negro girl Wit: Harry Taylor and William Bridgers.

DB 3-340 DANIEL WELLS of Nash Co. to DAVID PRIDGEN of same, Dec. 4, 1784, for 20 pds. specie a tract of 100 acres lying between Solomon Wells and David Pridgen adjoining Joshua Wells. Wit: Phillander Williams and John Atkinson.

DB 3-341 ISHAM GANDY of Nash Co. to WILLIAM WHIDDON of same, Dec. 28, 1784, for 40 pds. specie 187 acres on Sapony Creek at the road adjoining William Whiddon and Holland, it being the remaining part of a grant to said Gandy on Nov. 10, 1779. Wit: Wm. Hall and Micajah Thomas.

DB 3-343 JAMES BROWN of Nash Co. to DREWRY BOYKIN of same, March 5. 1785. for 20 pds. specie 200 acres on Mash Swamp adjoining Benjamin Cobb and Drewry Boykin, it being part of a grant of 300 acres to James Brown on March 30, 1780. Wit: Samuel Devaughan and Enoch Mooneham.

DB 3-344 ISAM HINES of Nash Co. to DAVID DANIEL of same, April 30, 1785, for 150 pds. specie 110 acres on the north side of Stony Creek adjoining Thomas Hunter William Barnes, and James Barnes, it being part of a tract granted to Andrew Ross by Earl Granville on Feb. 28, 1761 and conveyed by Joel Pitman to said Hines on March 30, 1782. Wit: Joseph Exum and Howell Ellin.

DB 3-345 JESSE DENSON of Nash Co. to LEWIS CURL of Edgecombe Co., Dec. 11, 1784. for 133 pds. 6 sh. 8 p. a tract of 150 acres on the south side of Maple Creek on Polecat Branch. Wit: Redmun Bunn. Benjamin Bunn, and John Edge.

DB 3-346 HENRY HORN of Wayne Co. to JOSEPH WHITE,

SR. of Nash Co., March 25, 1785, for 400 silver dollars two tracts of land: (1) 550 acres adjoining Robert Young, Joseph White, Widow Thompson, Whitehead's Mill Swamp, and Ready Branch; (2) 450 acres adjoining the aforesaid tract, Isaac Hilliard, and Little Pig Basket Creek. The first tract was granted to Nathaniel Folsome by Earl Granville on June 30, 1760, came by descent to Israel Folsome and was conveyed by him to Ebenezer Folsome on June 11, 1762. The second tract was granted to Ebenezer Folsome by Earl Granville on Aug. 8, 1761 and both tracts were conveyed to Henry Horn by Ebenezer Folsome on Nov. 24, 1772. Wit: John Bond, David Pridgen, and Redmun Bunn.

DB 3-348   THOMAS TUCKER and wife, VINEY TUCKER, and his mother, MARGARET TUCKER, of Nash Co. to STEPHEN WEBB of same. Feb. 6, 1782, for 25 pds. Virginia money a tract of 25 acres. Wit: Elijah Powell, Michael Savage, and Moses Savage.

DB 3-349   THOMAS LEWIS and wife, LYDIA LEWIS, of Nash Co. to DENTON MANN of same, Feb. 24, 1785, for 140 pds. Virginia money two tracts of land on the south side of Swift Creek and on Red Bud Creek: (1) 250 acres with the manor house and plantation whereon said Thomas Lewis then lived; (2) 160 acres adjoining the first tract on the south side, also, Lewis Hill, Bass, and William Bridgers. Wit: William Avent, Allen Mann, and Thomas Mann.

DB 3-351   JONAS WILLIAMS of Nash Co. to BILLY WILLIAMS of same, March 10, 1785, for 50 pds. specie a tract of 400 acres adjoining Nathan Williams, Thomas Horn, Jacob Cockrell, Billy Williams, and Toisnot Swamp. Wit: Wilson Taylor and John Eatman.

DB 3-352 JONAS WILLIAMS of Nash Co. to BILLY WILLIAMS of same, March 10, 1785, for 100 pds. specie a tract of 640 acres on the Great Swamp adjoining Jonas Williams, John Eatman, Cockrell, and his own line. Wit: Wilson Taylor and John Eatman.

DB 3-354   JAMES ARRINGTON of Nash Co. to JOSEPH ARRINGTON of same, July 30, 1785, for 150 pds. a tract of 185 acres adjoining Thomas Whitehead, Reuben Cooper, Arthur Arrington, and William Sandeford. Wit: Hardy Griffin and Thomas Whitehead.

DB 3-355 JOHN SIKES, SR. of Nash Co. to JOHN SIKES, JR. of Edgecombe Co., Aug. 10, 1785, for 50 pds. a tract of 100 acres on Little Peachtree Creek adjoining Isaac Bass, Charles Brown, and Matthew Sikes but, if John Sikes Jr. should die without an heir, the land would pass to Jacob Sikes, his brother. Wit: Elijah Boddie and Howell Ellin.

DB 3-356   SOLOMON COLLINS of Nash Co. to PETER ETHERIDGE of same, Jan. 7, 1785, for 10 pds. specie a tract of 50 acres at the head of Little Bear Branch adjoining Thomas Richardson, Peter Etheridge, and Matthias Manning. Wit: Thomas Morris and John Sikes.

DB 3-357 RICHARD VICK of Nash Co. to BENJAMIN VICK of same, Aug. 10, 1785, for 5 sh. a tract of 200 acres on the north

side of Stony Crek adjoining Willis and Wm. Braswell.
Wit: Thomas Horn and Wilson Vick.

DB 3-358 BRINKLEY GANDY of Nash Co. to MARCOM COOPER of same, May 19, 1785 for 40 pds. Virginia money a tract of 206 acres on the south side of Sapony Swamp adjoining William Whiddon and James Jones. Wit: David Pridgen and Wm. Whiddon.

DB 3-359 BRINKLEY GANDY of Nash Co. to MARCOM COOPER of same, May 19, 1758, for 60 pds. Virginia money a tract of 163 acres on the south side of Sapony Swamp adjoining Ozwell Langley's former line and Marcom Cooper.
Wit: David Pridgen and Wm. Whiddon.

DB 3-360 JOHN LEE of Halifax Co. to REUBEN MOORE, May 29, 1785, for 90 pds. a tract of 250 acres near Swift Creek on Shelly's Swamp adjoining Thomas Mann.
Wit: Charles Sturdivant and Wililam Jordan.

DB 3-361 RICHARD VICK of Nash Co. to JOHN VICK of same Aug. 10, 1785, for 5 sh. a tract of 200 acres on the north side of Stony Creek adjoining Braswell.
Wit: Thomas Horn and Wilson Vick.

DB 3-362 STEPHEN YOUNG and wife, DINAH YOUNG, of Nash Co. to JOHN PITTY COBB of same, April 5, 1783, for 80 pds. a tract of 200 acres adjoining Tucker, Isaac Bass and Henry Peed.
Wit: Ben Atkinson and David Pridgen.

DB 3-364 JAMES BUD LEE of Wake Co. to LODWICK ALFORD, April 6, 1785, for 100 pds. specie a tract of 300 acres on both sides of Moccasin Creek on the dividing line between James B. Lee and Robert Lee, which property was given to them by their father, James Lee, deceased, together with a one-half interest in a mill on Moccasin Creek that was willed to him by his father.
Wit: Phillip Sikes, Henry Deens, and Batt Fowler.

DB 3-365 JOHN ROGERS of Nash Co. to LODWICK ALFORD of Wake Co., Dec. 19, 1784, for 80 pds. a tract of 82 acres on Moccasin Creek adjoining James Lee and Driver.
Wit: James B. Lee. John Eddens. and Joseph Fowler.

DB 3-366 JOHN ROGERS of Wake Co. to LODWICK ALFORD of same, June 8, 1783, for 40 pds. specie a tract of 188 acres on the north side of Moccasin Creek.
Wit: Joseph Fowler, William Chapman Jr., Joseph Fowler (repeat) and Wililam Vaden.

DB 3-367 WILLIAM RICHARDSON of Nash Co. to ROBERT ROGERS of same, May 3, 1785, for 10 pds. a parcel of 10 acres of land.
Wit: John Gay and Harry Taylor.

DB 3-368 WILLIAM RAY of Wake Co. to JACOB HEARTSFIELD of Franklin Co., Dec. 20, 1784, for 26 pds. 13 sh. 4 p. 116 acres on the south side of Turkey Creek adjoining Hunt (then Petwav), the county line, and Jacob Heartsfield. it being the remaining part of a tract granted to William Ray by the State.

Wit: Bridgers Arrendell, Andrew Heartsfield. and Elizabeth Arrendell.

DB 3-369 SAMPSON POWELL of Nash Co. to JESSE CHRESTER of Halifax Co., Feb. 28, 1784 for 40 pds. specie a tract of 200 acres on the Back Swamp adjoining Isaace and Micajah Thomas.
Wit: Henry Braswell and John Gay.

DB 3-370 BRINKLEY GANDY of Nash Co. to MARCOM COOPER of same, Feb. 19, 1785, for 50 pds. 75 acres on the south side of Sapony Creek adjoining Marcum Cooper, it being part of a tract granted to said Gandy on Nov. 10, 1779.
Wit: Micajah Thomas and Mourning Ricks.

DB 3-371 THOMAS RICHARDSON of Nash Co. to PETER ETHERIDGE of same, March 9, 1785, for 20 pds. specie a tract of 100 acres adjoining Matthias Manning and Wililam Vester, which land was granted to said Richardson on Nov. 10, 1779.
Wit: Thomas Morriss and Chloe Morriss.

DB 3-372 WILIAM PERRY of Nash Co. to JACOB HEARTSFIELD of Franklin Co. April 1, 1785, for 30 pds. 270 acres in the fork of Turkey Creek adjoining Solomon Strickland, William Ray, and William Perry, it being the place where he then lived and part of a grant dated Nov. 1. 1784.
Wit: Thomas Ray, Baker Ray, Jacob Segraves, and Andrew Hartsfield.

DB 3-374 JAMES HOLLIMAN of Johnson Co. to JOHN NAIRN of Nash Co., Feb. 11, 1778, for 45 pds. proc. money a tract of 114 acres on the north side of Moccasin Swamp and Moccasin Creek, it bein gland granted to James Permenter by Earl Granville.
Wit: William Nairn and Mary Green.

DB 3-375 JOHN BIGGS of Nash Co. to WILLIAM HAMMONS of same, April 7, 1785, for 45 pds. a tract of 300 acres on Sapony Creek adjoining William Vester and Jeremiah Etheridge, it being land granted to John Biggs on Nov. 1, 1784.
Wit: John Cobb, Isaac Bass, and Charles Watson.

DB 3-376 RICHARD THOMAS of Nash Co. to JESSE THOMAS, Nov. 15, 1784, for 60 pds, specie a 193 acre plantation on both sides of Peachtre Creek adjoining Joseph Thomas.
Wit: Wm. Matthews and John Melton.

DB 3-377 STEPHEN WEBB and wife, ANN WEBB, of Nash Co. to HENRY PEED, Feb. 4, 1783, for 25 pds. Virginia money a tract of 25 acres of land.
Wit: John Gay, Hines Drake, and Bashford Morphiss.

DB 3-378 JOSEPH SELAH of Nash Co. to THOMAS EDWARDS of same, Aug. 8, 1785, for 40 pds. specie a tract of 100 acres on Ready Branch adjoining Joseph Selah, Jr. and Edward Ballard.
Wit: Wilson Vick and Wm. Ricks.

DB 3-379 JAMES CAIN of Nash Co. to BENJAMIN ATKINS of same, July 11, 1785, for 43 pds. specie a tract of 50 acres

on the south side of Beaver Dam Swamp adjoining Rachel Hackney.
Wit: Lazarus Whitehead and Jacob Cain.

DB 3-380 EDWARD PURSELL of Nash Co. to MICAJAH THOMAS of same. Dec. 13, 1784, for 50 pds. specie 200 acres on the north side of Tar River adjoining Samuel Bryant, it being all of a tract granted to said Edward Pursell on Nov. 10, 1779.
Wit: Stephen Young and Thomas Warren.

DB 3-381 EPHRAIM ATKINSON of Pitt Co. to SYLVANUS PUMPHREY of Nash Co., Feb. 24, 1785, for 50 pds. 125 acres on Stony Branch adjoining Culpepper, it being part of a tract granted to James Atkinson by Earl Grainville on Oct. 15, 1761.
Wit: Thomas Morriss, James Atkinson, and Jacob Harriss.

DB 3-382 JESSE HUNT and wife, ELIZABETH HUNT, of Nash Co. to JOHN CHITTY, SR. of same, June 10, 1785, for 15 pds. a tract of 100 acres adjoining David Strickland and Hunt.
Wit: Lewis Vick Samuel Braswell, and Drew Hunter.

DB 3-383 EPHRAIM ATKINSON of Pitt Co. to SILVANUS PUMPHREY of Nash Co., Feb. 24, 1785, for 10 pds. 80 acres on both sides of Peachtree Creek, it being part of a tract granted by Thomas Vaughan to Nathan Boddie.
Wit: Thomas Morriss, James Atkinson, and Jacob Harriss.

DB 3-385 JOHN WHITFIEID of Nash Co. to THOMAS GLOVER, May 7, 1785, for 80 pds. a tract of 380 acres on the north side of Tar River adjoining Micajah Thomas, Joseph Sumner, John Melton, and Burwell Rose.
Wit: Hardy Hunt and Benjamin Williams.

DB 3-386 JAMES JOLLY of Nash Co. to EDWARD HORN of same, April 11, 1785, a tract of land on the south side of Tar River adjoining Jolly, to be rented to Horn for a period of 12 years with an annual rent of 5 shililngs.
Wit: Archd. Lamon, John Lamon. and John Barnes.

DB 3-387 DAVID STRICKLAND and wife, ELIZABETH STRICKLAND, of Edgecombe Co. to THOMAS HUNTER, Jan. 4, 1777. for 65 pds. proc. money a tract of 246 acres adjoining Thomas Brown, William West, and the Laseter's Branch.
Wit: John Dozier, John Holland. and John Clark.

DB 3-389 LEWIS TREVATHAN of Nash Co. to AARON MAINOR of Edgecombe Co., Sept. 15, 1785, for 80 pds. a tract of 180 acres on the north side of Compass Creek adjoining John Exum, Lewis Hines, Lewis Trevathan, and Joseph Grant.
Wit: John House, William Anderson. and Dempsey Woodard.

DB 3-390 ANDREW BOOTHE of Nash Co. to JOSEPH ARRINGTON, JR. of same, Aug. 23, 1785. for 200 pds. specie a tract of 200 acres on the south side of Fishing Creek and on the White Oak Swamp adjoining Lewis Davis, it having been conveyed to Andrew Boothe by Joseph Gainer by deed dated Oct. 7, 1754.
Wit: James Arrington, Benja. Whitfield, and W. S. Mearns.

DB 3-391 JACOB FLOWERS of Johnston Co. to THOMAS SANDERS of Nash Co., Oct. 18, 1785, for 40 pds. specie a 320 acre

plantation and woodland on the Great Swamp adjoining Stephen Cobb, Joseph Phillips, and Benjamin Flowers.
Wit: Michael Horn, Patience Horn, and Thomas Sanders Sr.

DB 3-392 PETER HEDGEPETH of Nash Co. to STEPHEN WEBB of same, Feb. 26, 1785, for 50 pds. a tract of 200 acres adjoining Bass, Thomas Walker, and Passmore.
Wit: John Gay, James Massingale, and Benja. Savedge.

DB 3-393 WILLIAM LASETER of Edgecombe Co. to JAMES CAIN of same, Oct. 28, 1776, for 200 pds. proc. money a tract of 638 acres on both sides of Beach Run adjoining Wm. Taylor.
Wit. Thomas Hunter, Priscilla Hunter, and Treacey Powell.

DB 3-394 WILLIAM HOOKS and wife, DORCAS HOOKS, of Nash Co. to ROBERT ROGERS of same, Aug. 13. 1785, for 100 pds. a tract of 160 acres adjoining Mark Massingill the swamp, and the Quarter Branch, it being part of a grant to David Chapman by Earl Granville on March 16, 1761. Wit: John Gay, Jacob Rogers, and Sampson Powell.

DB 3-395 BENJAMIN BUNN of Nash Co. to ARTHUR WESTER of same, Aug. 13, 1785, for 40 sh. 50 acres on the north side of Maple Creek adjoining Wester and Wheatley, it being part of a tract granted to said Bunn on Oct. 9, 1783.
Wit: Joel Bunn and Josiah Bunn.

DB 3-396 BENJAMIN TUCKER of Nash Co. to THOMAS TUCKER of same, Aug. 8, 1785, for 20 pds. specie 100 acres on the south side of Peachtree Creek adjoining James Moore, Henry Barnes, Andrews, and William Harris, it being a tract granted to said Tucker on March 13, 1784.
Wit: James Moore and William Linsey.

DB 3-397 JAMES SMITH of Franklin Co. to JOHN HARRISON of Nash Co., Jan. 13, 1786. for 40 pds. a tract of 85 acres on Beaver Dam Swamp adjoining Elisha Bell.
Wit: Elisha Bell and William Clark.

DB 3-398 ARCHIBALD DAVIS of the Town of Halifax to FRANCIS WARD of Nash Co., Feb. 9, 1785. for 75 silver dollars a tract of 150 acres on the south side of Fishing Creek adjoining Gardner.
Wit: Pryor Gardner.

DB 3-399 ARCHIBALD DAVIS of the Town and County of Halifax to GEORGE GARDNER of Halifax Co., Nov. 19. 1785, for 791 dollars three tracts of land on the south side of Fishing Creek containing 1582 acres: (1) 394½ acres adjoining Arthur Davis and Francis Ward; (2) 619½ acres adjoining the foresaid tract; (3) 568 acres adjoining the second tract. Samuel Miller, John Davis, and Fishing Creek.
Wit: Holmon Southall and Pryor Gardner.

DB 3-401 BENJAMIN HEDGEPETH of Nash Co. to JOSIAH JOHNSON of Franklin Co., Jan. 4, 1786, for 100 pds. a tract of

130 acres adjoining John Passmore, Stephen Webb, and Micajah Thomas.
Wit: John Gay and Patience Gay.

DB 3-401 WRIGHT NISHOLSON of Bartley Co., South Carolina to JOSHIAH NICHOLSON of Nash Co., Jan. 6, 1783, for 200 pds. a tract of 410 acres on the south side of Cain's Mill Swamp adjoining Pace.
Wit: Lazarus Whitehead, George Blackburn, and Malachi Nicholson.

DB 3-403 JACOB JOYNER and MILLY JOYNER of Nash Co. to WILLIAM KIRBY of same, Jan. 19, 1786, for 90 pds. spe cie a tract of 340 acres on the north side of the road adjoining John Webb and Kirby.
Wit: Jacob Ricks and William Joyner.

DB 3-403 JEREMIAH HILLIARD of Edgecombe Co. to REUBEN TAYLOR of Nash Co., May 25, 1785. for 20 pds. a tract of 130 acers on the south side of Beach Run adjoining said Taylor, Elisha Pope, Mills Taylor, and Jacob Edwards.
Wit: Burwell Bunn.

DB 3-404 REUBEN WHITFIELD, SR. of Nash Co. to his son REUBEN WHITFIELD, JR. of same, Nov. 17, 1785, for love and affection a tract of 150 acres at the mouth of Roger's Branch.
Wit: John Evans and Miles Davis.

DB 3-405 PETER ANDERSON of Nash Co. to JOHN HARRISON of same, Nov. 10, 1784, for 170 pds. specie a tract of 207 acres on the north side of Gideon's Branch. Wit: Wm. Avent, Arthur Davis, and John Wiggins.

DB 3-406 LEWIS TREVATHAN of Edgecombe Co. to ALEXANDER THOMPSON of Nash Co., Aug. 31, 1785, for 20 pds. specie 100 acres on the north side of Compass Creek adjoining Lewis Hines. Reuben Taylor, the Watery Branch, and Martin's Poccosin, it being part of a tract that said Lewis Trevathan bought of William Spight on Feb. 15, 1783. Wit: Micajah Pope, John Jinkins, and Jesse Jinkins.

DB 3-407 WILLIAM CHAPMAN. SR. of Nash Co. to SIMON STRICKLAND of Johnston Co.. Nov. 23. 1785, for 30 pds. specie a track of 100 acres on the north side of Turkey Creek and on the south side of Tar River adjoining Chapman's old line and the Wolf Pit Branch. Wit: Lazarus Strickland, John Chapman, and Lott Whitton.

DB 3-408 THOMAS MORRISS of Nash Co. to JAMES CARLILE of Franklin Co., Oct. 22. 1785, for 120 pds. Virginia money a tract of 202 acres adjoining Benjamin Culpepper which land was granted to Edward Parish on March 2, 1761. Wit: P. Goodwin and Samuel Jones.

DB 3-409 JOHN SELLERS of Nash Co. to MATTHIAS MANNING of same, Dec. 16. 1785, for 9 pds. Virginia money a tract of 200 acres on the north side of Sapony Creek adjoining Mark Cooper and Matthias Manning. Wit: David Pridgen and Thomas Deans.

DB 3-409 JOHN SIKES to his grandson MATTHEW SIKES,

Aug. 17, 1785, for love and affection a tract of 250 acres on the south side of Little Peachtree Creek. Wit: Charles Brown and Henry Deans.

DB 3-411 WILLIS WARD of Norfolk Co., Virginia to JEREMIAH BUNTIN of Nash Co., Nov. 22, 1785, for 24 pds. specie a tract of 199 acres adjoining Thomas Deans, William Buntin, Henry Strickland. and Carter. Wit: John Rice and Isaac Bass.

DB 3-412 DIXON MARSHALL of Warren Co. to PHILLANDER WILLIAMS of Nash Co., Jan. 14, 1786, for 39 pds. Virginia money 78 acres on the south side of Tar River adjoining Williams' old line and Lamon, it being part of a track of land and being confiscated property which said Marshall had purchased. Wit: William Lancaster and John Lamon.

DB 3-413 JACOB HOUSE of Edgecombe Co. to MICAJAH POPE of Nash Co., Sept. 5, 1785. for 50 pds. Virginia money a 150 acre plantation on the north side of Compass Creek adjoining Joseph Exum, it being the same tract that Jacob House bought of Joseph Grant on Oct. 6, 1783. Wit: Hardyman Pope and Dempsey Woodard.

DB 3-414 JOSEPH WOODEL of Nash Co. to JAMES BROWN of same, Feb. 25, 1785, for 10 pds. specie 100 acres on the Mash Swamp adjoining Rowland Williams. it being part of a grant to Joseph Woodel on Nov. 1, 1784. Wit: Samuel Devaughan and Thomas Horn.

DB 3-414 ARTHUR BRASWELL of Bladen Co. to THOMAS MORRISS of Nash Co., Nov. 25, 1758, for 250 pds. Virginia money three tracts of land on both sides of Pig Basket Creek: (1) 250 acres on the north side of the creek granted to said Braswell by Earl Granville on Feb. 26, 1761; (2) 627 acres on the south side of the creek near Anthony's Branch; (3) 538 acres adjoining Boling Beckwith, Matthew Drake, and Jacob Braswell. a tract granted to said Arthur Braswell by the State on Nov. 10. 1779. Wit: Edmund Branch, Benjamin Hedgpeth. and James Watkins.

DB 3-416 NATHANIEL POWELL of Nash Co. to NATHAN POWELL of same, Feb. 3, 1782, for 100 pds. 106 acres on Beaver Dam Swamp adjoining Cain, Underwood, Culpepper, and Fishing Creek, it being half of a 212 acre tract which was bequeathed by Nathaniel Powell, deceased, to the said Nathaniel and Nathan above mentioned. Wit: Arthur Arrington, Willoughby Powell, and Joseph Arrington.

DB 3-417 WILLIAM CHAPMAN, JR. of Nash Co. to SIMON STRICKLAND of Johnston Co., Nov. 23, 1785, for 90 pds. specie two tracts of land on both sides of Turkey Creek and on the south side of Tar River: (1) a 200 acre grant adjoining Henry Strickland, and William Chapman, Sr.; (2) an 85 acre grant adjoining his father's line, his own line, and Turkey Creek. Wit: Lazarus Strickland, Lott Whitton, and John Chapman.

DB 3-418 WILLIAM CHAPMAN, SR. of Nash Co. to SIMON STRICKLAND of Johnston Co., Nov. 23, 1785, for 80 pds. specie 202 acres on the north side of Turkey Creek and south side of Tar

River, it being a grant from Earl Granville to Robert Ruffin on Nov. 9, 1754. Wit: Lazarus Strickland, John Chapman, and Lott Whitton.

DB 3-419   STEPHEN YOUNG of Nash Co. to MICAJAH THOMAS of same. Jan. 23, 1786, for 250 pds. specie 383 acres on the north side of Tar River and on Wolf Branch, it being part of a tract granted by Earl Granville to William Lane on July 3, 1760, conveyed by him to Robert Young by deed, and conveyed by the said Robert Young by will to his son, the said Stephen Young. Wit: Wilson Vick and Samuel Westray.

DB 3-420   JOSEPH CROWELL and wife, MARTHA CROWELL, of Nash Co. to LEWIS ABLEWIS LAMKIN of same, Feb. 23, 1786, for 200 pds. specie a tract of 284 acres on the south side of Tar River adjoining Crowell. Wit: D. Lamon, Archd. Lamon, and Henry Youell.

DB 3-421   SOLMON STRICKLAND of Nash Co. to JOSEPH CURL of same, Feb. 17, 1786, for 120 pds. Virginia money three negroes by name. Wit: Solomon Carter and William Chapman, Jr.

DB 3-422   MICAJAH THOMAS of Nash Co. to THOMAS LEWIS of same, Feb. 20. 1786, for 200 pds. specie 200 acres on the north side of Tar River in two tracks: (1) on Tar River adjoining Nofler and Laseter; (2) on the north side of Tar River, it being part of a tract granted by Earl Granville to John Lawrence and conveyed to said Thomas in two deeds, the first on Feb. 16, 1746 and the second deed on Feb. 13, 1757. Wit: Elijah Boddie and Solomon Cotten.

DB 3-423   JOSIAH WINBOURN of Nash Co. to JESSE COLLINS of same, Oct. 22, 1785, for 186 pds. 8 sh. a tract of 150 acres on Beaver Dam Swamp and the Cabbin Branch. Wit: John Kent and Behen Collins.

DB 3-424   ARCHIBALD DAVIS of Halifax Co. to JOHN DAVIS of Nash Co., Sept. 28, 1785, for 60 pds. specie a tract of 150 acres on the south side of Fishing Creek adjoining Whittington. Wit: Arthur Davis, John Blunt. Mary Blunt. and Benjamin Blunt.

DB 3-425   RICHARD RANSOM of Franklin Co. to JOHN PORTIS of Nash Co.. March 16. 1786. for 97 silver dollars 220 acres lying partly in Franklin Co. and partly in Nash Co. adjoining Richard Ransom. Archibald Davis. John Portis, and the Jumping Branch. Wit: Benjamin Whitfield and Gace Portis.

DB 3-426   ARCHIBALD DAVIS of Halifax Co. to ARTHUR DAVIS of same, Sept. 28. 1785. for 40 pds. specie a tract of 150 acres on the south side of Fishing Creek adjoining Blunt, Ward, and Miller. Wit: John Davis, John Blunt, Mary Blunt, and Benjamin Blunt.

DB 3-427   DIXON MARSHALL of Warren Co. to BRITTAIN SMITH of Nash Co., Jan. 14. 1786, for 50 pds. 125 acres on the south side of Tar River adjoining Lamon and the road, it being part of a tract of confiscated land purchased by said Marshall. Wit: William Lancaster and John Lamon.

DB 3-428   THOMAS SANDERS of Edgecombe Co. to JOHN

HEDGEPETH, Feb. 23, 1786, for 10 pds. a tract of 240 acres on the north side of Contentnea Creek adjoining Boykin, Row, Ephraim Phillips. and John Sanders. Wit: Thomas Horn and Elijah Coleman.

DB 3-429   EDWARD   WILSON of   Nash Co. to ROBERT STEPHENS of same, April 29, 1786, for 67 pds. 10 sh. 233 acres on the north side of Stony Creek adjoining Thomas Hunter, it being part of a 700 acre grant by the State of N. C. on Nov. 10, 1779. Wit: Wilson Curl and Robert Wilson.

DB 3-430   THEOPHILUS GRICE of Nash Co. to ALEXANDER GRICE of same, July 24, 1784, for 10 sh. a tract of 125 acres on the north side of Contentnea Creek adjoining James Grice. Wit: Thomas Horn, Jeremiah Nichols, and Lewis Grice.

DB 3-431   THEOPHILUS GRICE of Nash Co. to ALEXANDER GRICE of same, July 24, 1784, for 10 sh. a tract of 50 acres on the north side of Contentnea Creek adjoining Jacob Duck, James Grice, and Hinnant. Wit: Thomas Horn, Jeremiah Nichols, and Lewis Grice.

DB 3-432 WILLIAM HOOKS and DORCAS HOOKS of Nash Co. to MIAL MITCHELL of same. March 3, 1783, for 20 pds. a tract of 80 acres on the Quarter Branch adjoining John Passmore and Hooks.   Wit: John Gay,   William Mitchell,   and Sampson Powell.

DB 3-433   LITTLEBERRY WATKINS of Nash Co. to WILLIAM SKINNER of same, Aug. 14, 1786, for 60 pds. Virginia money a tract of 100 acres on the south side of Stony Creek adjoining Henry Vick and Samuel Skinner. Wit: Joseph Exum and Howell Ellin.

DB 3-434   WILLIAM COOPER of Nash Co. to REUBEN COOPER of same, Nov. 28, 1785, for 106 pds. 13 sh. 4 p. the 200 acre plantation whereon he then lived on Beaver Dam Swamp and Ready Branch adjoining Williams, it being the land conveyed by John Cooper to said William Cooper by deed of gift on March 14, 1772. Wit: Arthur Arrington and Thomas Hunt.

DB 3-435   AARON MAINER of Edgecombe Co. to WILLIS TREVATHAN of same, May 3, 1786, for 86 pds. 13 sh. 4 p. specia a 180 acre plantation on the north side of Compass Creek adjoining John Exum, Lewis Hines, said Mainer. Micajah Pope, and the Watery Branch, it being part of a tract that the said Mainer bought of Lewis Trevathan. Wit: Jesse Johnson and James Stallings.

DB 3-436 CHARLES BROWN of Nash Co. to JETHRO BASS of same. March 15. 1786, for 50 pds. a tract of 300 acres on the north side of Little Peachtree Creek adjoining John Sikes, Isaac Bass. and Matthew Drake. Wit: Nathan Boddie and John Sikes.

DB 3-437   THOMAS THORP of Nash Co. to HARDY HARRIS of Edgecombe Co., Aug. 12, 1786, for 125 pds. Virginia money a tract of 652 acres adjoining Thomas Exum and John Spight. Wit: Redmun Bunn, Lewis Hines. and Jacob Horn.

DB 3-438   HANSEL LASTER of Nash Co. to AMBRUS HADLEY of Halifax Co., Jan. 16, 1786, for 50 pds. 160 acres on the south side of Fishing Creek adjoining Lemuel Laseter, Joseph House, and the Jonas' Branch, it being a tract of land conveyed by Lemuel Laseter to his son, Hansel Laseter, by deed dated March 28, 1781. Wit: Thomas Hunt and Reuben Cooper.

DB 3-439 SPIER KNIGHT of Nash Co. to REBECKAH POPE of same, June 2, 1786, for 30 pds. 75 acres lying between the Great Branch and Beach Run and adjoining Benjamin Newton, the county line, and Hardyman Pope, it being part of a tract of land granted to John Jinkins, Sr. by Earl Granville. Wit: Christopher Ing.

DB 3-440 REUBEN TAYLOR of Nash Co. to JOHN POPE of same. Sept. 19, 1785, for 20 pds. specie 130 acres on the south side of Beach Run adjoining Jeremiah Hilliard, Reuben Taylor, Elisha Pope, Mills Taylor, and Jacob Edwards, it being part of a tract which Reuben Taylor bought of Jeremiah Hilliard. Wit: Joseph Exum and Micajah Pope.

DB 3-441 AMBRUS HADLEY of Halifax Co. to THOMAS HUNT of Nash Co., June 20, 1786, for 150 pds. current money 160 acres on the south side of Fishing Creek adjoining Lemuel Laseter, Joseph Hayes, and the Jonas' Branch, it being a tract conveyed from Hansel Laseter to Abrus Hadley on Jan. 16, 1786. Wit: Reuben Cooper and Daniel Hunt.

DB 3-442 DREWRY ALFORD of Franklin Co. to FRANCIS GROSS of Nash Co., Aug. 11, 1786. for 50 pds. specie a tract of 500 acres on the north side of Tar River adjoining John Warren, Jeremiah Etheridge, Pegg. Parrot, and Pursell. Wit: William Harris and Isaac Alford.

DB 3-443 NATHAN ATKINSON and MARTHA ATKINSON of Nash Co. to REUBEN TAYLOR of same. Oct. 12. 1785, for 100 pds. a tract of 220 acres on Beach Run adjoining Thompson and Jenkins. Part of the said land was conveyed by William Whitehead to Jacob Whitehead by deed dated June 6, 1750, part was conveyed by Jacob Whitehead to William Whitehead by deed dated May 5, 1761, and part was granted to John Jenkins on May 1, 1762. Wit: Elisha Pope and Jeremiah Burge.

DB 3-444 DAVID BALLARD to HENRY BARLER. Feb. 17, 1785, for 40 pds. 100 acres on Little Peachtree Creek it being part of a tract granted to Abner Hill on Dec. 30, 1760. Wit: William Lindsey, John Barlow, and William Harris.

DB 3-445 HARDY BOYKIN of Nash Co. to THEOPHILUS GRICE of same, March 2, 1786, for 31 pds. specie a tract of 75 acres on the north side of Contentnea Creek adjoining Wm. Row. Wit: Jas. Williamson and Hardy Williamson.

DB 3-446 LAZARUS STRICKLAND, SR. of Nash Co. to LAZARUS STRICKLAND, JR. of same, Aug. 4, 1786. for 10 pds. a tract of 100 acres on Toisnot Swamp adjoining John Taylor. Wit: John Bonds and Henry Burge.

DB 3-447 GEORGE GARDNER of Nash Co. to PRYOR GARDNER of Halifax Co., March 14, 1786, for 71 pds. 5 sh. Virginia money a tract of 475 acres adjoining George Gardner. Wit: Mark Pitts and Francis Ward.

DB 3-448 NEWIT LANE and ELIZABETH LANE of Nash Co. to SAMUEL BRYANT of same, Sept. 14, 1784, for 80 pds. a tract of 100 acres on the south side of Tar River adjoining Benjamin Bryant and Arter Wililams' Branch. Wit: James Taylor and Benjamin Bryant.

DB 3-449 JOHN TURNER of Nash Co. to WILLIAM TURNER of same, Dec. 26, 1785, for 20 pds. 90 acres on the east side of Charles Branch, being part of a tract granted to John Turner on Nov. 10, 1779. Wit: John Gay, Walker Massingill. and James Massingill.

DB 3-450 JACOB HENDERSON of Nansemond Co., Virginia to WILLIAM BRASWELL of Nash Co.. Oct. 13, 1786, for 15 pds. Virginia money one negro boy. Wit: Micajah Thomas and Wm. Hall.

DB 3-450 ASEA BISHOP of Norfolk Co., Virginia to MICAJAH THOMAS of Nash Co., Oct. 16, 1786, for 110 pds. Virginia money two negroes by name. Wit: Henry Bunn and Jethro Bass.

DB 3-451 JAMES CARSTARPHEN of Halifax Co. to JULIAN KING of Nash Co., Sept. 25, 1786, for 100 pds. specie one negro girl. Wit. Micajah Thomas and William Hall.

DB 3-451 ROBERT PEOPLES of Northampton Co. to WILLIAM BODDIE of Nash Co., Feb. 16, 1786, for 100 pds. one negro girl. Wit: Michjah Thomas and George Boddie.

DB 3-452 MICAJAH THOMAS of Nash Co. to ELIJAH BODDIE of same, Oct. 5, 1786, for 10 pds. 596 acres on the north side of the Back Swamp adjoining Abraham Bass, Womble, Parrish, and Culpepper, it being a tract granted by Earl Grainville to Thomas Richardson on June 1 1762. Wit: Phil. Hawkins, Jr. and Julian King.

DB 3-453 JAMES CARLILE of Nash Co. to ELIJAH BODDIE of same, Oct. 24, 1786, for 200 pds. a tract of 202 acres adjoining Benjamin Culpepper, which land was granted by Earl Granville to Edward Parrish on March 2, 1761. Wit: Nathan Boddie, John Kilby. and Temperance Boddie.

DB 3-454 THOMAS MORRISS of Nash Co. to WILLIAM BODDIE of same, Aug. 14, 1786. for 30 pds. specie 100 acres on west side of Pig Basket Creek, it being part of a tract granted by Earl Granville to Arthur Braswell and conveved by said Braswell to Thomas Morriss. Wit: Amos Thomas and Elizabeth Jones.

DB 3-455 JAMES GOODWIN of Nash Co. to JOHN GOODWIN of same. June 30. 1786, for 100 pds. specie 108 acres adjoining Thomas Mann, Wheless, and James Goodwin, it being part of a tract whereon the said James Goodwin then lived. Wit: Robert Goodwin and Elizabeth Goodwin.

DB 3-456 CHARLES WATSON of Nash Co. to THOMAS MORRISS of same. June 30, 1785. for 100 pds. a tract of 640 acres on both sides of Pig Basket Creek adjoining Arthur Braswell,

Matthew Drake, and Isaac Hilliard, it being a grant to said Watson by the State of N. C. on Nov. 10, 1779. Wit: Isaac Bass and Augus-Bass.

DB 3-458 EDMOND BRANCH of Nash Co. to THOMAS BECKWITH of same, Oct. 26, 1786, for 101 pds. 2 sh. Virginia money a tract of 337 acres adjoining Matthew Drake, Cooper Jones, Jesse Powell, William Walker, William Braswell, and Thomas Beckwith. Wit: John Chitty and Hines Drake.

DB 3-459 JOHN SELLERS of Nash   Co. to JESSE POW-ELL of same, March 31, 1786, for 71 pds. a tract of 640 acres on Pig Basket Creek adjoining Arthur Braswell, Matthew Drake, Jesse Powell, and Jacob Braswell, Wit: Micajah Thomas and Elijah Boddie.

DB 3-460 MICHAEL ATKINSON of Nash Co. to JOHN WATKINS of same, Oct. 30, 1786, for 200 pds. a tract of 315 acres on Kirby's Creek adjoining John Devenport, Joseph Curl, Micajah Revel, and William Horn, it being parts of three deeds. Wit: R. Bunn, Wilson Vick, and Wm. Fort.

DB 3-461 GEORGE BLACKWELL of Edgecombe Co. to Joseph Phillips of Nash Co., Feb. 21, 1786. for 10 pds. specie a tract of 100 acres on the south side of Mill Branch in Edgecombe Co. adjoining John Dew and George Blackwell. Wit: Jethro Harrison and Jethro Phillips.

—A—

Adams, Robt. 269
Adkins, Benj. 55
Alford 69, Drewry 15, 16, Sam. 109, 113
Allen 164, 178, Arthur 191, Eliz. 32, 136, 171, Thos. 32, 246
Alston, Phil. 55
Anderson, George 34, Howel 105, Peter 256
Andress, Jos. 112
Andrews, Lilia 70, Wm. 70 (2)
Arrington, Arthur 39, 157, 199, John 39, 131, 157, 199, 230, 243, 283, Jos. 133 (2), 157 (2), 158, 202, 211 (2), Cover* (2), Mourning, cover* (2), Peter 101, Wm. 101, 119, 148, 149, 157 (2), 158, 199, 211 (2), 230, 232
Atkinson (Adkinson), Benj. 22, 32, 164, 173 (2), 232, Henry 51, John 12, 183, 246, Michael 227, Moses 183, Newett 180, Thos. 12, 164, 173
Avent, Sarah 199, Wm. 63 (2), 199 (3), 223, 241, 256, 260 (2)

—B—

Baggett, Granbery 191, Nicholas 46, 168, 191 (2)
Ba(i)ley, David 76, Henry 83 (2), John 71
Baker, Wm. 109
Ballard, Chris. 51, Edw. 33, 114, 153 (2) 271, Peter 51, 143 (2), 153 (2), 189, 271, Wm. 51, 128
Barkesdale, Wm. 202
Barlow 51
Barnes 183, Benj. 5, 111 (2), David 111, Dempsey 221, Jas. 106, 124, Jesse 111, Jos. 75, 213, 214, 221, T. 135, 148, Wm. 106, 162, 172, 193
Barrett, John 137
Bass, Augustin 238, Isaac 15, 16, 113, 142 (3), 217, 238, 252, Jesse 16, 142, John 142
Batchelor 265, Jos. 251, Stephen 102, 256 (2), Wm. 125, 179 (2), 181 (3), 189 (2)
Battle, cover* Jas. 19, 147, 158, 200 (3), 217, 223, 241, John 9, 19, 20, 63, 99, 147, 200 (3), 269, Martha cover*, Mary 200, 223, Wm. 20, 63 (2), 147 (3), 223 (3), 269
Beckwith, Amos 211, 259, Bolen 51 (2), 195 (2), Burrell 259
Bell 211, Burrell 160, Elias 256, Green 95, 99 (3), 217, 269, Robt. 183, Wm. 20, 97, Zadek 160
Bennett Wm. 24, 140
Benton 66, Aggea 65
Bevan, Ann 134, Thos. 134 (2)
Bird, Jas. 3
Bishop, Benj. 162

Blackwell, Jesse 221
Blunt, Benj. 238, Rich. 238
Boddie, George 24, 240, Nathan 12, 24, 55, 96, 173, 240, Wm. 24, 55 (3), 142, 145 (2) 156, 173 (2)
Bond(s), J. 17, 50, 140, 235, 273, 274, John 59, 76, 228
Bone, John 33
Boon, B. 223, Benj. 15, 16, 131, 166, 265
Booth(e), Andrew 157, 211 (2)
Bottom, Sam. L. 270
Bout, Wm. 162
Bowers, John 251
Boykin, Drewry (Drury) 11 (3), 222 (3), Hardy 11
Brantl(e)y 164, 178, 246, Jacob 114, 153 (4), 270, 271, John 153, Lewis 232, Matthew 114, 153 (2)
Braswell 113, 249, Arthur 55, 173, 195, Britain 277, Colley 134, Demey 195. Henry 16, 217 (3), Jacob 249, 250, 275, 277, Jesse 249, Micajah 243, Nathan 275, Robt. 128, 250, Robin 82, 128, Wm. 275
Brewer, Allen 23, Hardy 23, 62
Brickell (Brickle), Thos. 109, 113
Bridgers, Benj. 64, 74, 204, Hearty 166, Josiah 204, Micajah 166, Sam. 77 (3), Wm. 131, 166
Broughton, Jesse 180
Brown, Arthur 101 (2), 119, 135, 148, Chas. 142, Jas. 11 (2), 99 (3), 186, 222 (2)
Brvant (Bryan, Brian) 164, Evin 192, 198, Jas. 89, Jones 142 (2), Sam. 92, 93, 94, 271 (2), Sharad 178, Wm. 43, 62, 75, 197, 198, 213, 214, 266
Bunn 102, 233, Benj. 5 (2), 25, 31, 106, 111, 123, 139, 181, 184, 190, 264, Burwell (Burrel) 31, 245, Henry 44, 73, 79, 81, 82, 137, 170, 266, Joel 162, 172, 193, 284, Redmun 5, 48, 119, 130 (2), Willie 31, 115
Buntin (Bunten), Jeremiah 233, Wm. 12
Burge, Rich. 284
Burn(e), Henry 36 (2), 38, 179, 181
Butts 99

—C—

Cain, Jas. 9 (2), 13, 21, 22, 47 (2), 75 (2), 84, 86, 186, 213 (2), 214 (2), 217, 254, Wm. 40, 49
Carney, Thos. 256
Carter 65, 66, Chas. 27 (2), Eliz. 274, Matthew 228, Sam. 44, 59, Solomon 44, 233, 274, Thos. 274
Chapman. John 50, Wm. 42, 50, 279
Chitty, John 105
Clark, Robt. 19
Clinch, Hannah 13. Jos. J. 13
Cobb, Benj. 11, 222, Jas. 180 (2), 184 (3), 264 (2), Nathan 17, 27, Stephen 27, 184
Cockrell (Crockril), Jacob 1, 2, 25, John 273

—D—

—E—

Ellen, Howell 84, 104, 128
Etheridge, Jeremiah 144, Lot 19, 20, Peter 12, 265
Evans David 55, 173 (2), 249, 250, John 51, 57, 128, Wm. 260
Exum, John 203, 208, Jos. 48, 123, 195, 258 (2)
Ezell, Thos. 211

—F—

Fall, George 165
Ferrell, Bird 6, 98 (2)
Finch, Allen 175, Isham 86
Flowers, Benj. 25, 117, 190, Hardy 230, 232, Henry 221, John 99, 177, 184, 258, 264, Wm. 117
Floyd, Penuel 230, 259, Shadrack 109, 113
Folsom, Ebenezer 86
Ford, Jos. 24
Fore, Rich. 3, 75, 86
Foreman, Benj. 47 (2), 87

—G—

Gandy, Amos 153, 157, Edw. 178, 226, 232 (2)
Ganer, Wm. 68
Gardner 234, George 95, 99, Pryor 95, 99 (2), 234, 269
Gay, John 108
Gilchrist, Thos. 262
Glover, Sam. 126
Goodman, John 197
Goodson, George 226
Goodwin, Jas. 236, John 132, Martin 132
Green, George 175, Jas. 20, John 97, 158
Griffin, Arch. 36, 37, 38, 39, 40, 82 (2), 137, 170, 224 (2), 266, 278, 282 (2), Delilah 38, 40, 49, 103, 138, 243 (2), George 46, Hardy 37, 39, 101, 104, 158, Jos. 39 (3), Micajah 39, Pierce 8, 39, 205, Thos. 209, 211
Grissel, Thos. 17

—H—

Hackney 254, Rachel 22
Hadley, Ambroise 34, Jos. 34
Hall, Wm. 23, 135, 136, 191, 283, Wm. Henry cover*
Hamilton, Francis 138, Thos. 55
Hammon(d)s, Jessey 69, Wm. 69, 144, 240, 284
Harrell, John 75, 121, 124, 272, Orpa 284, Reuben 272
Harris(s), Anselm 53, 203, Daniel 230, Hardy 53, Jethro 286, Marget 112, Randolph 227, Wm. 112 (3)
Harrison, Charlotte 192, 197, 198, Henry 192, 197 (2), 198 (2), Jethro 177, 179, 258, 264, John 19, 28, 241
Hart, Thos. 130, 211
Hatten Peter 62
Hays 238, John 266
Hearn 234

Heawood, Wm. 164
Hefler, John 12
Hendrick, Isaac 256, Wm. 197
Hill 69, Abner 6, Drusilla 228, Lewis 64 (5), 74 (2), Rebeckah 64,
  Sion 64 (2), 228 (2), Wm. 64
Hilliard 265, 276, Elias 101, 119, 148, Isaac 145, 168, Jas. 47, 80, 86,
  205 (2), Jeremiah 203, 208
Hines 276, Fred. 70, 168, 203, 208, 242, 276, 278, Hartwell 276, 280,
  Lewis 203, 208 (2), 227
Hinton 265, Chris 145, H. 265, Robt. 70, 168, 276
Holland 249, 250, Anthony 24, Daniel 45, 51, 57 (2), Rich. 45 (2)
Hood, Edw. 27
Hooks, Wm. 217
Horn(e), Edw. 115, H. 227, Henry 106, Jacob 203, 258, 264, Jere-
  miah 190, Joel 135, 148, 227, Josiah 65, 119, 135, 139, 148. 188,
  190, 203, Michael (Mikel) 16 (4), Patience 16, Thos. 2, 16 (2),
  32, 190, 258, 264, Wm. 1, 65, 101 (2), 106, 119 (2), 148
Hunt, Jesse 138, Wm. 211
Hunter 105, Arch. 89, 104, Thos. 55 (2), 232

—I—

Irwin, Henry 55

—J—

Jackson, Elliz. 98, 157 (2), 158 (2), Jubl. 133, Wm. 98, 157, 158 (2)
Jelks 80
Johnston, Josiah 199
Jolley, Jas. 115 (2)
Jones 276, Allen 278, Brittain 8, 209, 278, Ely 60 (2), Fedrick 109,
  113, Francis A. 205, John 8, 28, 60, 70 (2), 86 (2), 154 (2), 205
  (4), 278, Lazarus 205, 278, Sam. 6, 98, Willie 55
Jordan, Cornelius 227
Joyner (Joiner) 230, 232, Burrel 191, Cornelius 128, 143, 190, Curtis
  190, Jacob 190, Jesse 51, 128, 143. John 128, 190, Jordan 35, Jos.
  51, 190, Nathan 143, Wm. 23, 41 (2), 109
Judge, Jas. 202
Judkins, J. 173 (2)

—K—

Keen, Currell 71
Kent. Burrel 247, Jesse 244, 246, 247, John 244, 247, Marmeduke
  247, Stephen 246. 247
King, Julian 128, 142
Kirby 101, Wm. 183
Kirk, Isaac 208
Kitchen, Jesse 168, 191
Knight, Ann 259, Jas. 6. 21, Kinsman 259, Spear 21
Knox, John 101, 119, 148

—L—

Lamkin, Lewis Ablewis 62, 89
Lamon 109, Archchlus 162, Duncan 5, 42, 111, 149, 162, John 42

—P—

Pace, Thos. 254

Parker, Eliz. 16 (2), Francis 13, 206, Solomon Dawson 16, Unity 13, Wm. 8

Parrott, Jos. 66

Passmore, Wm. 69

Peed, Henry 16 (5), 109, 113 (5)

Perry, Anne 218, Benj. 218, Ephraim 160, Jas. 160, 218

Phillips, Ephraim 177 (2), 179 (3), 184, 227, 258 (2), 264, 286, Ethelred 13, Gabreal 227, Jethro 4, Jos. 4, 117, 190, 227, Sharood 177, 179, 227, Wm. 184

Pitts, John 145

Pointer, Daniel 55

Poland 164, 178, Wm. 230, 232

Pollock 154

Pope, Elisha 267, John 258, 267, Josiah 13, Sarah 13, Simon 164

Porch, Wm. 65

Portis, George 68, 83, Jeremiah 10, 236, 262, John 68, 83 (3), 236, 262 (2)

Powell 217, 275, Alanson 9, 21, 22, Chas. 168, Daniel 124 (2), Elijah 112 (2), John 9, 21, 22, Nathan 6, 254, Nath. 29 (2), 205, 253, 254, Sampson 160, 217, Willoughby 6, 29, 205, 254

Pridgen, Abijah 183, 265, David 30, 32, 35, 122, 135 (2), 136 (2), 171, 178, 183, 246 (2), 265, Drewry 32, 136, 246 (2), 256, Hardy 30, 32, 122, 135 (2), Jesse 35

Pritchett, John 144, 192, Wm. 144

Puckitt (Pockett), Abraham 50, 165

Pumphrey, Sylvanious 204

Pursell 93, Edw. 92

—R—

Rackley, Francis 251, Matthew 43, Parsons 251

Ransom(e), Amy 10, 83, Jas. 83, Rich. 10, 83 (2)

Reese, Randolph 31, 53

Revel 138, 280, Elias 129, Elijah 106, Henry 106, Micajah 48, 106, 119, 188 (2), 281, Selah 106

Reynolds, John 165

Richard, Wm. 217

Richardson (Richeson), Sarah 171, Thos. 12, 171, Wm. 16, 108, 113, 217 (3), 219 (2)

Ricks 23, 79, 170, 272, Abra. 131, Benj. 171, Jacob 106, 130, 232, Jas. 130, John 130 (4), Jonathan 147 (3), Lewis 147, Mourning 194, Wm. 232

Ridley (Ridle), Ann 147, Thos. 147 (3), 152

Robertson, Peter 269

Rogers 183, Jacob 134, Jesse 134, 238, Peleg 50, 165, Robartes 134, Robt. 16, 108 (2), 113, Thos. 160

Rollings, Chas. 218, 220 (2)

Rose, Burrel 43, 116, 187, Jack 66

Ross 65, Andrew 106, Wm. 65, 69, Williamson 69, 176 (2)

Rowlet, Wm. 9

Ruffin, Lod. 119
Rutherford, Robt. 160

—S—

Sandeford, Benj. 206. 252, 269
Sanders 177, Cornelius 190, 221, John 179, Rachael 190, Thos. 184, 190 (2), 264
Screws, Henry 9
Sedgley, John 212
Selah (Seley), Jos. 33, 114, 136, 153, 164, 178
Sellers, Arthur 270, Jas. 270, Wm. 114, 143, 153, 270
Sheppard, John 12, 183
Sherod, Jordan 33
Sikes, John 240
Simmons, Dunkin 235, H. 183
Skinner, Emmanuel 48, 75, 124, 152, 168, 216, 243, 281, Josiah 281, Judey 75, Marey 75, Wiley 272, 281, Wm. 75, 168, 216
Slatter, Eliz. 269, John 260, 269
Smelley, John 71, 76
Smith 226, Batson118, 147, 230, Benj. 128, 190, Brittain 149, Moses 265 (2), Sam. 208
Sorsby, Alex. 280
Springer, Mildred 49
Stallings, Jas. 60
Stark, Reuben 44
Stevens, Jeremiah 6, 61, 274, John 6, Jos. 61
Strickland 118, 272, David 105 (2), 126, 138, 243, Eliz. 138, Hardy 271, Harmun 235, Henry 59, 168, 235 (2), 243, 273, Jacob 84, 105, 214, 271, Jos. 170, 232, Lazarus 180, 208, Mark 84, 235, Mary 170, 232, Noah 59, Solomon 271
Strother, Jas. 220
Sulevant, Cornelius 274
Sumner 192
Sutton, George 116

—T—

Talbert, Isaac 23
Tallington, Eliz. 170, 272
Tann, Benj. 42
Taylor, Benj. 175, Daniel 61, 66, 176, Demey 62, 258, Eliz. 258, 267, Harry 108, John 84, 186, 214, 279, Kinchen 267, Mills 60, 267, Reuben 208, 258, 267 (2), Wilson 59, 175
Tennyson, Mathew 284
Thomas 142. 173. 283, Jacob 191, Jesse 125 (2), 189 (2), Jethro 37, 44, 152. 153, 157, 170, 272. John 40, 49, 76, Micajah 55 (2), 125, 173, 183, 189, 194 (2), 195, 279. Rich. 40, 49, 90, Sam. 75, 118, 121. Susannah 272, Tisey 124, 245
Thompson, Alex. 208, Eliz. 140, Robt. 23, 86, Trimakin 77
Tillery, J. 51, 57, John 62
Tisdal(e), Henry 122, Wm. 30, 178
Tomlinson, Isaac 211

Trevathan, Willis 258
Tucker, Jas. 116 (2), 187 (2), Jos. 43, Thos. 6, 15, 58, 98, 180, 265,
    Willaby 16 (3), 113 (3), Wm. 58
Turner, Jas. 23, John 51, 57, 156, Wm. 156

—U—

Underwood 276, Emmanuel 6, 46, 205, Howel 168, Jacob 242, 280,
    Malichi 280, Zacheriah 242

—V—

Vaughan, Chris. 12, Demps. 58, Stephen 12, Steven 58
Vester, Mary 12, Solomon 12 (2), Wm. 12 (2), 144
Vick 276, Benj. 54, Henry 36, 75, 118, John 25, 54, 99, 125, 153, 157,
    189, 222, Jos. 161 (2), Joshua 126, Jurden 161, Lewis 126, 211,
    Mary 232, Rich. 54, 126, Robt. 161, 164, 235, Sophia 73, Wilson 36,
    37, 38, 40, 41, 54, 73, 79, 81, 83, 86, 109, 115, 125, 131, 139, 153,
    157, 189, 212, 216, 226, 230, 232
Viverett Henry 33, Thos. 4, 33

—W—

Walker, Patrick 149 (2)
Wall, Mark 233
Wallace, George 55
Walrond, Masag 132
Warburton (Warbinton) 73, John 103
Ward 238, Benj. 234, Francis 234, Jos. 95, 99
Warren, Daniel 256, John 91, 92, 93, 94, Thos. 31, 102
Watkins, Henry 129, 281, 284, Jas. 41, 109 (2), John 51, 65 (2),
    101, 119 (2), 188 (2), Rachel 245
Watson, Chas. 145
Watts, Demsy 21
Weaver, Stephen 199
Webb, Rice 176, Stephen 15 (2), 16
Wells 136, Lewis 31, Solomon 135, Stephen 164, 178
West, John 75, 86, Nathan 244, Wm. 161
Westray 162, Sam. 15, 16, 62, 75, 84, 89, 125, 147, 153 (2), 157 (2),
    194, 213, 214, 226, 232
Wheeler, Jos. 165
Wheless, Sally 103, Wm. 183
Whiddon, John 30
White 211, A. 243, Armeger 219, Jos. 131, 209, 259 (2)
Whitehead 86, 154, Bennett 86, Eliz. 252, Henry 122, 154, Isaac 46,
    124, Jonathan 154, Lazarus 9, 23, 124 (2), Nathan 252, Thos.
    252 (3), 253, Wm. 23, 70 (2), 276, 278 (2)
Whitehouse, John 125, 189
Whitfield 125, Abraham 224, 282, Benj. 38, 40, 49, 70, 103, 137,
    168, 203, 266, Hardy 40, 49, Isaac 224, 282, Jacob 224, 282, John
    176, Mary 15, Rhoda 32, Solomon 38, 73, 81, 90, 224 (2), 282,
    Thos. 38, 40 (3), 49 (4), 73 (2), 79, 81 (2), 90 (2), 119, Wm.
    270, Willis 32, 82, 125, 137, 189 (2), Young 49, 138
Whitley, Arthur 193, Drury 179, 286, George 286, Jonas Barnes

162 (2), 172, 193 (2), Josiah 162, 172, 193 (2), Micajah 179, 286 (2)

Whittington, Rich. 278

Williams 97, 99, 158, 211, 259, 265, Benj. 65, 70, Burrell 74, Cooper 10, 64, Drewry (Rrury) 71, 76, 83, 89, 117, 221, 244, 247, Eliz. 70, Henry 70, Jas. 104, 128 (2), Joel 84, 186, John 95, 99, 166, 262 (2), Jonas 16, 20, 83, 99, 117, Mary 39, N. 262, Philander 71, 191, Reuben 218, 220, Rich. 70, Rowland (Roling) 17, 71, Samson 70, Simon 65 (2), 66 (2), 70, Wm. 86, 218, 220

Williamson, Absalom 246, David 246, Jos. 180

Willis, Wm. 138

Wilson 281, Edw. 106, 281, Eliz. 129, 138, John 103, 118, 129, 138, 152, 216, 227, 243

Winslow, W. 211, Wm. 104

Winstead, David 162, Griffin 162, Jos. 164, 178, Peter 35, Rich. 162, Thos. 162

Wood(w)ard 250, Aaron 51, David 195, 249, Jas. 24, 45, 57, 194, Jesse 247, Thos. 59

Worley, Robt. 142

Wright, Archelus 238, Jos. 177, 184, 264, Wm. 253, Winfield 21

Wyatt, Demsey 175

Young, Stephen 16, 89, 93, 113, 271 (3)

* See section at end of Deed DB 4-286.

4-1 STATE of N.C. grant to JACOB COCKRIL by Gov. Alex. Martin, Nov. 1, 1784, a tract of 100 acres on the east side of Beaver Dam Swamp adjoining William Horn.

DB 4-2 STATE of N. C. grant to JACOB COCKRIL by Gov. Alex Martin, Nov. 1, 1784, a tract of 250 acres on Toisnot Swamp adjoining Thomas Horn and John Eatman.

DB 4-3 STATE of N. C. grant to RICHARD FORE by Gov. Alex Martin, Oct. 25, 1782, a tract of 434 acres on Turkey Creek and Rocky Branch above the improvements he purchased of James Bird.

DB 4-4 STATE of N. C. grant to JETHRO PHILLIPS by Gov. Rd. Caswell, Aug. 11, 1786, a tract of 320 acres on both sides of Cabbin Branch adjoining Thomas Viverett, Joseph Phillips, and his own line.

DB 4-5 DIXON MARSHALL of Warren Co. to BENJAMIN BUNN, SR. of Nash Co.. June 22, 1789, for 20 pds. specie 120 acres between Cattail Marsh and the Great Branch adjoining Duncan Lamon, Benjamin Bunn, and new road, it being part of a tract granted to Capt. Dixon Marshall by State. Wit: Redmun Bunn and Benjamin Barnes.

DB 4-6 JAMES KNIGHT of Edgecombe Co. to WILLOUGHBY POWELL of Nash Co., Dec. 1, 1788, for 154 pds. specie four negroes, three horses, furniture, etc. Wit: Emanuel Underwood and Nathan Powell.

DB 4-6 SAMUEL JONES of Granville Co. to BIRD FERRELL of Franklin Co., Sept. 10, 1787, for 60 pds. specie 100 acres on Turkey Creek adjoining Thomas Tucker, it being part of a tract granted to Abner Hill on Jan. 1, 1762. Wit: Jeremiah Stevens and John Stevens.

DB 4-8 PIERCE GRIFFIN of Nash Co. to JOHN JONES of same. Sept. 15, 1789, for 3 pds. specie a parcel of 5 acres of land. Wit: W. S. Means, Brittain Jones, and William Parker.

DB 4-9 JAMES CAIN of Nash Co. to WILLIAM ROWLET of Chesterfield Co., Virginia, Nov. 7, 1789, for 25 pds. specie a tract of 300 acres on the south side of Cabin Branch adjoining Henry Screws, James Cain, John Powell, Landingham, and Lazarus Whitehead. Wit: John Battle and Alanson Powell.

DB 4-10 AMY RANSOM and RICHARD RANSOM of Franklin Co. to COOPER WILLIAMS of Nash Co., Nov. 9, 1789, for 35 pds. specie one still with all the appurtenances. Wit: Denton Mann and Jeremiah Portis.

DB 4-11 DREWRY BOYKIN of Nash Co. to RICHARD DEAN of same, May 9, 1789. for 20 pds. specie 200 acres on Marsh Swamp adjoining Benja. Cobb and Drewry Boykin, it being land that said Boykin purchased of James Brown and part of a tract of 300 acres granted to James Brown by the State on March 30, 1780. Wit: J. Nichols and Hardy Boykin.

DB 4-12 JOHN HEFLER of Nansemond Vo., Virginia to STE-

PHEN VAUGHN of, Nash Co., Nov. 23, 1788, for 500 pds. specie a tract of 150 acres on the north side of Great Sapony Creek adjoining Christopher Vaughan and Matthias Manning. Wit: William Buntin and John Atkinson.

DB 4-12 WILLIAM VESTER, SR. and wife, MARY VESTER, of Nash Co. to SOLOMON VESTER of same, Nov. 10, 1789, for 60 pds. specie 250 acres on the north side of Sapony Creek and on Bear Branch adjoining William Vester, Thomas Richardson, Peter Etheridge. and Nathan Boddie, it being part of a grant of 500 acres to the said Solomon Vester on Nov. 9, 1779. Wit: John Sheppard, Thomas Atkinson and William Linsey.

DB 4-13 JOSIAH POPE and wife, SARAH POPE; NORS WORTHY MIALS and wife, PURITY MIALS; FRANCIS PARKER and wife, UNITY PARKER, all of Edgecombe Co. to JAMES CAIN of Nash Co., Jan. 24 1789, for 155 pds. specie a tract of 150 acres on the south side of Beaver Dam Swamp. Wit: Ethelred Phillips Joseph J. Clinch, and Hannah Clinch.

DB 4-15 SAM WESTRAY, Sheriff of Nash Co., to ISAAC BASS of same, Feb. 11 1789, for 5 pds. 10 sh. specie at public auction a tract of 25 acres sold as the property of DREWRY ALFORD to satisfy an execution obtained by Mary Whitfield and being the same land conveyed from Thomas Tucker to Stephen Webb. Wit Stephen Webb, Benja. Boon, and W. S. Mearns.

DB 4-16 SAM WESTRAY, Sheriff of Nash Co., to JESSE BASS of same, Feb. 11, 1789, for 19 pds. 1 sh. at public auction three tracts of land sold as the property of DREWRY ALFORD: (1) 164 acres on the north side of Peachtree Creek adjoining Henry Peed Henry Braswell, and Isaac Bass, it being a tract conveyed from Stephen Young to Henry Peed; (2) 40 acres adjoining Robert Rogers, William Richardson, and the Peachtree Creek, it being a tract sold by Willaby Tucker to Henry Peed; (3) 10 acres adjoining Willaby Tucker, Henry Peed, and the Peachtree Creek, it being a parcel sold by Willaby Tucker to Henry Peed. Wit: Stephen Webb. Benja. Boon, and W. S. Mearns.

DB 4-16 MICHAEL HORN and wife, PATIENCE HORN, of Nash Co. to JONAS WILLIAMS, Sept. 30, 1789, for 283 pds. 17 sh 6 p. Virginia money all their plantations and woodland in Nash Co. 757 acres on the north side of Toisnot Swamp: (1) 360 acres or Cattail Branch adjoining Elizabeth Parker and Toisnot Swamp formerly granted to Thomas Horn on June 25, 1749; (2) part of a tract of 487 acres granted to Thomas Horn on Nov. 26, 1761; (3) part of a tract of 300 acres granted to Elizabeth Parker on Nov. 1 1784; (4) part of a tract of 300 acres said Michael Horn purchased of Dempsey Dawson on Dec. 30. 1772; (5) 95 acres said Michael Horn purchased of John Dew on Dec. 18. 1777. Wit: Dempsey Dawson, Solomon Dawson Parker. and Mikel Horn, Jr.

DB 4-17 NATHAN COBB of Wayne Co. to ROLING WILLIAMS of Nash Co., March 9, 1790. for 100 pds. a tract of 150 acres on both sides of Mooneham's Mill Branch adjoining Thomas

Grissel and Thomas Mooneham. Wit: J. Bonds and Edward Nicholson.

DB 4-19 ROBERT CLARK of Nash Co. to JOHN HARRISON
of same, Oct. 5, 1789, for 70 pds. Virginia money 150 acres on the
south side of Beaver Dam Swamp, it being part of a tract of 396
acres granted to Lot Etheridge on Feb. 27, 1761. Wit: John Battle
James Battle, and Tobias Lasseter.

DB 4-20 WILLIAM BELL of Nash Co. to ARTHUR LASE-
TER of same, Dec. 12, 1789, for 155 pds. 200 acres adjoining Lot
Etheridge and Jonas Williams, it being part of a grant to John
Cooper for 530 acres on March 7, 1761. Wit: John Battle, James
Green and Wm. Battle.

DB 4-21 JAMES KNIGHT of Edgecombe Co. to JAMES CAIN
of Nash Co., March 30, 1789, for 150 pds. specie a negro slave sup-
posed to be in employ of Demsy Watts of Norfolk Co., Virginia and
who formerly belonged to the estate of Winfield Wright. Wit: Alanson Powell, Spear Knight, and John Powell.

DB 4-22 BENJAMIN ATKINSON of Nash Co. to JAMES
CAIN of same, March 3, 1789, for 40 pds. specie a tract of 50 acres
on the south side of Beaver Dam Swamp adjoining Rachel Hackney.
Wit: Alanson Powell and John Powell.

DB 4-23 ROBERT THOMPSON of Edgecombe Co. to CHAR-
LES LEE of Nash Co., Feb. 6, 1790, for 30 pds. Virginia money a
tract of 100 acres on the south side of Long Swamp adjoining
Isaac Talbert. James Turner, and the Wattery Branch. Wit: Lazarus Whitehead and William Whitehead.

DB 4-23 BENJAMIN DENSON of Nash Co. to HARDY
BREWER of same. Dec. 7. 1789, for 35 pds. Virginia money a tract
of 200 acres adjoining William Joyner and Ricks. Wit: Wm. Hall
and Allen Brewer.

DB 4-24 JOHN COLLINS of Washington Co. to WILLIAM
BODDIE of Nash Co., Dec. 8, 1789, for 15 pds. specie 100 acres on
Long Branch adjoining William Bennett and James Woodard, it
being part of a tract granted to Anthony Holland by Earl Gran-
ville on Nov. 3, 1761. Wit: Nathan Boddie, George Boddie, and
Joseph Ford.

DB 4-25 WEST CRUMPLER and wife, BEDY CRUMPLER
of Nash Co. to JOHN EATMAN of same, Feb. 4. 1790, for 40 pds.
specie 150 acres of land in two tracts: (1) 100 acres adjoining Benjamin Bunn and Benjamin Flowers; (2) 50 acres on Juniper Swamp
and his own line, it being part of a tract granted to said Crumpler
on Nov. 1, 1784. Wit: Jacob Cockrell and John Vick.

DB 4-27 CHARLES CARTER of Nash Co. to NATHAN
COBB of Wayne Co.. Nov. 19, 1789. for 100 pds. specie a tract of
150 acres on both sides of Mooneham's Mill Branch on the north
side of Contentnea Creek whereon said Carter then lived. Wit: Edward Hood and Stephen Cobb.

DB 4-28 MARK MASON. SR. of Nash Co. to MARK MASON
JR. of same. March 3. 1790, for 5 pds. specie a tract of 110 acres
adjoining Widow Culpepper, Widow Mason, and the creek. Wit

Jethro Denson, John Jones, Jr. and John Harrison.

DB 4-29 NATHANIEL POWELL of Halifax Co. to BENJAMIN COOPER of Nash Co., Jan. 5, 1790, for 60 pds. 12 sh. specie 101 acres at the mouth of Ralph's Prong, it being a parcel of land conveyed from Willoughby Powell to Nathaniel Powell. Wit: W S. Mearns, Jethro Denson, and Edmund Cooper.

DB 4-30 JOHN WHIDDON of Nash Co. to WILLIAM TISDALE of same, Sept. 25, 1790, for 90 pds. Virginia money a tract of 200 acres on the north side of Sapony Swamp. Wit: David Pridgen, Hardy Pridgen, and Marcum Cooper.

DB 4-31 BENJAMIN BUNN, SR. of Nash Co. to his son WILLIE BUNN, Sept. 11, 1790, for love and affection a tract of 640 acres on the south side of Sapony Creek adjoining Thomas Deans and Thomas Warren. Wit: Randolph Reese, Lewis Wells and Burwell Bunn.

DB 4-32 WILLIS WHITFIELD and wife, RHODA WHITFIELD, of Nash Co. to DAVID PRIDGEN of same, Jan. 5, 1790, for 30 pds. a tract of 150 acres adjoining Drewry Pridgen, Thomas Allen, Benjamin Atkinson, and Elizabeth Allen. Wit. Thomas Horn and Hardy Pridgen.

DB 4-33 JOSEPH SELAH, JR. of Nash Co. to JORDAN SHEROD of same, Sept. 27, 1787, for 200 pds. specie a tract of 480 acres on Jacobs Swamp adjoining John Bone and Edward Ballard. Wit: Wm. Dene, Thos. Viverett, and Henry Viverett.

DB 4-34 ARTHUR DAVIS of Halifax Co. to JOSEPH HADLEY of same, Feb. 13, 1790, for 15 sh. specie one acre of land on the south side of Great Fishing Creek. Wit: George Anderson and Ambroise Hadley.

DB 4-35 PETER WINSTEAD of Nash Co. to JORDAN JOYNER of same, April 6, 1790, for 60 pds. a tract of 200 acres on the south side of Tar River at the head of Town Creek adjoining Thomas Dixon. Wit: David Pridgen and Jesse Pridgen.

DB 4-36 HENRY BURN of Nash Co. to ARCHIBALD GRIFFIN of same, Oct. 14, 1790, for 100 pds. two tracts of land on both sides of Peachtree Creek: (2) 141 acres on the creek on the old line. Wit: Wilson Vick and Henry Vick.

DB 4-37 JETHRO THOMAS of Nash Co. to ARCHIBALD GRIFFIN of same, Oct. 14, 1790, for 30 pds. a tract of 100 acres on the north side of Peachtree Creek. Wit Wilson Vick and Hardy Griffin.

DB 4-38 THOMAS WHITFIELD of Nash Co. to ARCHBALD GRIFFIN of same, Feb. 22. 1790, for 130 pds a tract of 65 acres adjoining Delilah Griffin, Solomon Whitfield, and Henry Burns Wit: Wilson Vick and Benja. Whitfield.

DB 4-39 MICAJAH GRIFFIN and PIERCE GRIFFIN of Nash Co. to HARDY GRIFFIN of same, Dec. 28. 1789, for 256 pds. 16 sh. a tract of 271 acres adjoining Matthew Drake, it being the tract that Joseph Griffin, Sr. purchesed from Mary Williams on Aug. 14, 1771, and was given by Joseph Griffin, Sr. to his son, Joseph, in his will. Wit: Arthur Arrington, John Arrington, and

Archd. Griffin.

DB 4-40 DELILAH GRIFFIN of Nash Co. to ARCHIBALD GRIFFIN of same, Feb. 22, 1790, for 130 pds. two tracts of land on the north side of Stony Creek: (1) 150 acres on the north side of Peachtree Creek along the old line to Pig Basket Creek, adjoining Richard Thomas; (2) all the land that was bequeathed to Hardy Whitfield in the will of Thomas Whitfield, Sr. deceased, the bonds being ascertained in two deeds, one from William Cain to Thomas Whitfield and the other from John Thomas to Thomas Whitfield, containing by estimation 150 acres. Wit: Wilson Vick and Benja. Whitfield.

DB 4-41 JAMES WATKINS of Nash Co. to WADE MOORE of same, Dec. 11, 1789, for 60 pds. specie a tract of 150 acres on the north side of Tar River adjoining Lewis Curl and William Joyner. Wit: Wilson Vick and William Joyner.

DB 4-42 DUNCAN LAMON of Nash Co. to BENJAMIN TANN of same, Oct. 15, 1787, for 10 pds. specie a tract of 200 acres on the south side of Tar River and on Cooper's Creek. Wit: William Chapman and John Lamon.

DB 4-43 JOSEPH TUCKER of Nash Co. to MATTHEW RACKLEY of same, Jan. 31, 1791, for 50 pds. specie a tract of 100 acres on the swamp. Wit: Burrel Rose and Wm. Bryant.

DB 4-44 REUBEN STARK of Nash Co. to SAMUEL CARTER of same, July 27, 1784, for 92 pds. specie one negro boy. Wit: Solomon Carter.

DB 4-44 HENRY BUNN of Nash Co. to JETHRO THOMAS of same, Jan. 27, 1789, for 25 pds. Virginia money one negro girl. Wit. John Melton and Josiah Melton.

DB 4-45 RICHARD HOLLAND of Nash Co. to DANIEL HOLLAND of same, Sept. 16, 1788, for 500 dollars a tract of 25 acres on the northeast side of Pig Basket Creek which tract was granted to said Richard Holland,by Earl Granville on July 13, 1745. Wit: Solomon Cotton and James Woodard.

DB 4-46 GEORGE GRIFFIN of Nash Co. to ISAAC NEWSOM of same, Nov. 8, 1788, for 22 pds. specie a tract of 50 acres on the south side of Pine Log Swamp adjoining Nicholas Baggett and Joseph Minton. Wit: Emanuel Underwood and Isaac Whitehead.

DB 4-47 BENJAMIN FOREMAN of Nash Co. to ISAAC NEWSOME of same, April 7, 1789, for 150 pds. specie 200 acres on the south side of Beaver Dam Swamp, it being a tract of land bequeathed by James Cain to his son, James Cain, and conveyed by him to said Benjamin Foreman. Wit: Matthew Drake, W. S. Mearns, and James Hilliard.

DB 4-48 EMANUEL SKINNER of Nash Co. to DAVID DANIEL of same, March 6, 1790, for 5 pds. a tract of 50 acres on the north side of Stony Creek adjoining Micajah Revel and Thomas' Road. Wit: Redmun Bunn and Jos. Exum.

DB 4-49 MILDRED SPRINGER of New Bern district of N C. to DELILAH GRIFFIN of Nash Co., July 19, 1787, for 80 pds.

specie two tracts of land on the north side of Stony Creek: (1) 150 acres on the north side of Peachtree Creek along the old line to Pig Basket Creek, adjoining Richard Thomas; (2) all the land that was willed by Thomas Whitfield to his son, Hardy Whitfield, being 150 acres in two deeds, one from William Cain to Thomas Whitfield and the other from John Thomas to Thomas Whitfield. Wit. Benja. Whitfield, Thos. Whitfield, and Young Whitfield.

DB 4-50 JOHN CHAPMAN of Nash Co. to ABRAHAM PUC-KITT of same. March 13, 1790, for 20 pds. 170 acres on the north side of Turkey Creek, it being all the land on the north side of Turkey Creek in the tract which Peleg Rogers obtained by patent from Earl Granville. Wit: J. Bonds and William Chapman.

DB 4-51 BOLEN BECKWITH of Nash Co. to DANIEL HOL-LAND of same. Feb. 28, 1789, for 60 pds. specie 200 acres on the north side of Pig Basket Creek adjoining Holland's Branch and Aaron Woodward it being part of a tract granted to said Bolen Beckwith by the State of N. C. on Nov. 10, 1779. Wit: John Turner, J. Tillery, and John Watkins.

DB 4-51 CHRISTOPHER BALLARD of Nash Co. to WIL-LIAM BALLARDof same, Jan. 28, 1790, for 500 pds. a tract of 120 acres on Sapony Swamp adjoining Holland's Branch; also, a tract of 220 acres on Sapony Creek ajoining Henry Atkinson, Barlow, John Evans, and Hollands Branch. The 120 acres was received by deed and the 220 acres by grant, excepting 62 acres sold out of the grant to Joseph Joyner. Wit: Peter Ballard and Jesse Joiner.

DB 4-53 RANDOLPH REESE of Edgecombe Co. to JOSEPH KURL of Nash Co., Dec. 10, 1789, for 150 pds. specie a tract of 241 acres on both sides of Kirby's Creek adjoining Thomas' Road and Folsom's Road. Wit: Hardy Harris and Anselm Harris.

DB 4-54 RICHARD VICK of Nash Co. to JOHN VICK of same, Nov. 9, 1790, for 10 pds. a tract of 100 acres on the north side of Stony Creek adjoining John and Benjamin Vick's line. Wit: Wilson Vick and Joseph Denson.

DB 4-55 DAVID EVANS of Nash Co. to WILLIAM BODDIE of same, Jan. 26, 1793, for 40 pds. two tracts of land granted by the State of N. C. to Benjamin Adkins on Oct. 25, 1782: (1) adjoining William Boddie, Nathan Boddie, and Micajah Thomas; (2) adjoining Arthur Braswell, William Boddie, and Micajah Thomas, containing in the two tracts about 260 acres. Wit: Thos. Hamilton and Willie Jones.

DB 4-55 GEORGE WALLACE of Halifax Co. to THOMAS HUNTER of Edgecombe Co., March 20, 1776, for 33 pds. 6 sh. 8 p. proc. money a tract of 116 acres on Stony Creek adjoining said Thomas Hunter. Wit: Henry Irwin, Daniel Pointer, and Phil. Alston.

DB 4-57 DANIEL HOLLAND of Nash Co. to JOHN EVANS of same, March 3, 1789, for 100 Spanish milled dollars a tract of 100 acres adjoining Daniel Holland, the Miry Branch, and Lewis' Branch. Wit: J. Tillery John Turner, and James Woodard.

DB 4-58 THOMAS TUCKER of Nash Co. to ROBERT COCK-RUM of same, Sept. 16, 1785, for 35 pds. a tract of 150 acres on the south side of Little Sapony Swamp adjoining Daniel Deens, Demps. Vaughan, and Steven Vaughan. Wit: William Manning and William Tucker.

DB 4-59 HENRY STRICKLAND of Nash Co. to NOAH STRICKLAND of same, Aug. 10, 1789, for 100 pds. a tract of 200 acres on the north side of Tar River adjoining Samuel Carter and Thomas Woodard. Wit: John Bonds and Wilson Taylor.

DB 4-60 JACOB EDWARDS of Edgecombe Co. to ELY JONES of same, Sept. 17, 1785 for 25 pds. specie a tract of 100 acres on the north side of Tar River adjoining Ely Jones and the Edgecombe Co. line, which said land was granted to Mills Taylor. Wit: James Stallings and John Jones.

4-61 DANIEL TAYLOR of Nash Co. to JEREMIAH STEVENS of Franklin Co., June 21, 1787, for 50 pds. specie a tract of 57 acres on the west side of Turkey Creek. Wit: Jeremiah Deens and Joseph Stevens.

DB 4-62 SAMUEL WESTRAY, Sheriff of Nash Co., to LEWIS ABLEWIS LAMKIN of same, May 13, 1789, for 2 pds. 3 sh. specie at public auction a tract of 360 acres on the south side of Tar River, sold as the property of PETER HATTEN on Aug. 11, 1788 to satisfy executions obtained by John Dew, John Tillery and Hardy Brewer. Wit: William Bryant and Demey Taylor.

DB 4-63 WILLIAM BATTLE of Nash Co. to THOMAS MANN of same Dec. 23 ,1790 for 9 pds. cash, a tract of 51 acres on the north side of Swift Creek adjoining William Battle, Thomas Mann, and William Avent. Wit: John Battle, Wm. Avent. and Allen Mann.

DB 4-64 LEWIS HILL and wife, REBECKAH HILL of Nash Co. to DENTON MANN of same, Nov. 6, 1789, for 135 pds. Virginia money a tract of 270 acres on the south side of Swift Creek by certificate of survey made by John H. Drake, surveyor for Nash Co., adjoining said Denton Mann, said Lewis Hill, Cooper Williams, Benjamin Bridgers, and Red Bud Creek. It was the land whereon said Lewis Hill then lived and was conveyed from William Hill to Sion and Lewis Hill and from Sion Hill to Lewis Hill. Wit: Silas Drake and Allen Mann.

DB 4-65 WILLIAM HORN of Bertie Co. to JOSHIAH HORN of Nash Co., Jan. 28, 1791, for 200 pds. Virginia money a tract of 200 acres lying in both Nash and Edgecombe counties. beginning at the mouth of Kirby's Creek and adjoining John Watkins, Ross. and the river. Wit: John Watkins and Joseph Curl.

DB 4-65 SIMON WILLIAMS of Nash Co. to AGGEA BENTON of same, Aug. 11, 1787, for 20 pds. a tract of 100 acres adjoining Carter, William Ross, and the county line, which land was granted to Simon Williams by the State of N. C. on Nov. 10, 1779. Wit: Benjamin Williams. Wm. Porch and Mary Mullins.

DB 4-66 SIMON WILLIAMS of Franklin Co. to JAMES CULPEPPER of Nash Co., Jan. 15, 1791, for 30 pds. a tract of 150 acres on the west side of Turkey Creek adjoining Jack Rose,

Benton, Jeremiah Deens, and Carter, which land was granted to Simon Wililams by the State of N. C. on Nov. 10, 1779. Wit: Daniel Taylor, Joseph Parrott, and Thomas Morriss.

DB 4-68 ARCHIBALD DAVIS of Franklin Co. to JOHN PORTIS of Nash Co., March 27, 1789, for 50 pds. a tract of 334 acres in Nash and Franklin counties on the north side of White Oak Swamp. Wit: George Portis and Wililam Ganer.

DB 4-69 WILLIAMSON ROSS of Franklin Co. to WILLIAM HAMMONDS of Nash Co., March 2, 1786, for 80 pds. specie 350 acres in Nash and Franklin counties on both sides of Turkey Creek adjoining Alford and Hill, it being a tract granted to William Ross by Earl Granville on March 1 1762. Wit: Wm. Passmore and Jessey Hammon.

DB 4-70 WILLIAM WHITEHEAD of   Nash Co. to JOHN JONES of same, Feb. 10, 1780, for 100 pds. Virginia money a 100 acre plantation whereon Benjamin Whitfield formerly lived on the north side of Whitehead's Mill Swamp between said Whitehead and said Jones. Wit: Benjamin Mathis, Frederick Hines, and Robert Hinton.

DB 4-70 SIMON WILLIAMS and ELIZABETH WILLIAMS of Franklin Co. to BENJAMIN WILLIAMS of Nash Co., Feb. 9, 1791, for 1000 pds. specie 302 acres in Nash and Franklin counties on both sides of Tar River adjoining Wililam Andrews and the road, it being parts of two tracts, one granted to Samson Williams by patent bearing date Dec. 1, 1744; the other granted to Richard Williams. Wit: Wm. Andrews, Henry Williams, and Lidia Andrews.

DB 4-71 CURRELL KEEN of Chesterfield Co., Virginia to DRURY WILLIAMS of Nash Co., Feb. 28, 1791, for 90 pds. a tract of 250 acres on the north side of Turkey Creek adjoining John Smelley, Mooneham and Contentnea Creek, it being part of a deed granted to John Baley and Earl Granville. Wit: Philander Williams and Rowland Williams.

DB 4-73 THOMAS WHITFIELD of Nash Co. to HENRY BUNN of same, March 16, 1791, for 400 dollars two tracts of land: (1) 130 acres on the south side of Pig Basket Creek above Warburton's house; 265 acres adjoining said Thomas Whitfield and Solomon Whitfield. Wit: Sophia Vick and Wilson Vick.

DB 4-74 LEWIS HILL of Franklin Co. to DENTON MANN of Nash Co., Feb. 23, 1791, for 3 pds. Virginia money a parcel of 6 acres on the south side of Swift Creek adjoining said Mann and Thomas Mann, it being the land conveyed from Benjamin Bridgers to said Lewis Hill. Wit: Burrell Williams and Allen Mann.

DB 4-75 WILLIAM SKINNER and JUDEY SKINNER of Nash Co. to JOHN HARRELL of same, Aug. 17, 1790, for 60 pds. Virginia money a tract of 100 acres on the south side of Stony Creek adjoining Henry Vick and Samuel Thomas. Wit: Marey Skinner and Emmanuel Skinner.

DB 4-75 SAM WESTRAY, Sheriff of Nash Co., to JAMES CAIN of same, May 13 1790, for 45 pds. at public auction a tract of 300 acres belonging to the estate of EDWARD MOORE, deceased, sold to satisfy a judgment obtained by James Cain. It lay on the east side of Turkey Creek adjoining Richard Fore and John West. Wit: Joseph Barnes, Jr. and Wm. Bryan.

DB 4-76 BENGEMUN CRUMPLER of Nash Co. to DRURY WILLIAMS of same, April 9, 1788, for 40 pds. 100 acres on the west side of Turkey Creek, it being part of a tract bought by John Thomas from John Smelley. Wit: John Bond and David Bailey.

DB 4-77 JAMES DRAKE of Nash Co. to JOHN DRAKE of same, April 10, 1790, for paternal love and affection for son, John Drake, 100 acres of land adjoining Samuel Bridgers, it being a tract granted by deed of gift to Trimakin Thompson from Samuel Bridgers and to said Bridgers by a deed from Earl Granville bearing date Oct. 15, 1761. Wit: Benjamin Drake.

DB 4-79 JOSEPH DENSON of Nash Co. to THOMAS WHITFIELD of same, March 18, 1791, for 250 dollars a tract of 200 acres on the south side of Maple Creek adjoining Benjamin Denson and Ricks. Wit: Wilson Vick and Henry Bunn.

DB 4-80 WILLIAM MERRITT and wife, NANCY MERRITT, Nash Co. to ISAAC DORTCH of Northampton Co., Dec. 27, 1790, for 210 pds. Virginia money a tract of 280 acres on the south side of Swift Creek adjoining Jelks, William Merritt, Benjamin Merritt, and the road. Wit: James Hilliard and Isaac Newsom.

DB 4-81 THOMAS WHITFIELD of Nash Co. to SOLOMON WHITFIELD of same, May 10, 1791, for 5 pds. 65 acres on the north side of Peachtree Creek adjoining both parties, it being part of a tract granted by the State of N. C. to Thomas Whitfield, Sr. Wit: Wilson Vick and Henry Bunn.

DB 4-82 HENRY BUNN of Nash Co. to WILLIS WHITFIELD of same, Oct. 1790, for 60 pds. Virginia money a tract of 190 acres on the south side of Peachtree Creek adjoining Archibald Griffin's acre at the mill. Wit: Archd. Griffin and Robin Braswell.

DB 4-83 RICHARD RANSOME and mother, AMY RANSOME, of Franklin Co. to JOHN PORTIS of Nash Co., March 23, 1790, for 13 pds. 10 sh. specie 22½ acres lying in both Nash and Franklin counties adjoining Portis and Ransome Davis, it being part of a tract of land that devolved to the said Richrad Ransome by the death of his father, James Ransome, who died intestate. Wit: George Portis and John Portis.

DB 4-83 HENRY BAILEY of Nash Co. to DRURY WILLIAMS of same, May 12, 1789 for 40 pds. specie a tract of 150 acres on the east side of Turkey Creek adjoining Henry Bailey and John Driver. Wit: Wilson Vick and Jonas Williams.

DB 4-84 SAMUEL WESTRAY, Sheriff of Nash Co., to MARK STRICKLAND of same, May 12, 1790, for 310 pds. at public auction a tract of 620 acres belonging to the estate of EDWARD MOORE, deceased, sold to satisfy a judgment obtained by James Cain. It was located on the north side of Toisnot Swamp adjoining Jacob Strickland, according to a survey of Aug. 8, 1761. Wit:

Howell Ellen, John Taylor, and Joel Wililams.

DB 4-86 JAMES CAIN of Nash Co. to ISHAM FINCH of same, May 11, 1791, for 25 pds. specie a tract of 150 acres on Turkey Creek adjoining Richard Fore and John West. Wit: Wilson Vick and Edward Nicholson.

DB 4-86 JOHN JONES of Nash Co. to JAMES HILLIARD of same, Jan. 26, 1791 for 416 pds. specie 400 acres on the south side of Swift Creek adjoining Robert Thompson's former line and Whitehead; also, one acre on the north side of Swift Creek adjoining the old mill seat. This was a tract of land granted by Earl Granville to Ebenezer Folsom, conveyed by him to William Matthews, and from said Matthews to John Jones in two deeds. Wit: W. S. Mearns, William Williams, and Bennett Whitehead.

DB 4-87 MARK MASON of Nash Co. to ABNER MASON of same, Jan. 24, 1791, for 5 pds. specie 287 acres adjoining William Mason, Abner Mason, Nicholson, and the Beaver Dam Swamp, it being part of a tract granted bv Earl Granville to Benjamin Foreman. Wit: Jethro Denson and Mark Mason, Jr.

DB 4-89 SAM WESTRAY, Sheriff of Nash Co., to DRURY WILLIAMS of same, May 10 1790, for 13 pds. at public auction a tract of 200 acres adjoining John Naron. It was sold as the property of JAMES BRYANT to satisfy a judgment obtained by Stephen Young. Wit: Lewis Ablewis Lamkin and Archd. Hunter.

DB 4-90 STATE of N. C. grant to THOMAS WHITFIELD SR. by Gov. Alex. Martin, Oct. 9, 1783, a tract of 195 acres on the south side of Pig Basket Creek adjoining Solomon Whitfield, Thomas Whitfield, Jr., Richard Thomas, Jacob Dickerson, and his own line.

DB 4-91 STATE of N. C. grant to JOHN WARREN, SR. by Gov. Alex Martin, Oct. 25, 1782, a tract of 100 acres on Little Turkey Creek adjoining his own line.

DB 4-92-STATE of N. C. grant to JOHN WARREN, SR. by Gov. Alex. Martin, Oct. 25, 1782, a tract of 77 acres on Sapony Creek adjoining Samuel Bryant, Edward Pursell, and his own line.

DB 4-93 STATE of N. C. grant to JOHN WARREN, SR, by Gov. Alex. Martin, Oct. 25, 1782. a tract of 146 acres on Turkey Creek adjoining Samuel Bryant, Stephen Young, Pursell, and his own line.

DB 4-94 STATE of N. C. grant to JOHN WARREN, SR. by Gov. Rd. Caswell, March 30, 1780, a tract of 200 acres on Little Turkey Creek adjoining Samuel Bryant.

DB 4-95 STATE of N. C. grant to GREEN BELL by Gov Sam Johnston Nov. 27, 1789, a tract of 112 acres on the south side of Great Fishing Creek and on both sides of Green's Branch adjoining John Williams, Joseph Ward, George Gardner, Prior Gardner, and his own line.

DB 4-96 STATE of N. C. grant to SOLOMON COLLINS by Gov. Rd. Caswell, Sept. 24, 1785, a tract of 75 acres on the north side of Sapony Creek adjoining Nathan Boddie.

DB 4-97 REUBEN COOPER of Nash Co. to JOHN GREEN

of Halifax Co., Nov. 29, 1787, for 200 pds. 200 acres on the west side of Reedy Branch adjoining Williams and Beaver Dam Swamp. it being a tract of land conveyed from William Cooper to Reuben Coopei. Wit: William Lewis and William Bell.

DB 4-98 BIRD FERRELL of Nash Co. to ELIZABETH JACKSON of same, Dec. 17, 1790, for 150 silver dollars 100 acres on Turkey Creek adjoining Thomas Tucker it being a tract of land conveyed by Samuel Jones to Bird Ferrell by deed on Sept. 10, 1787. Wit: W. S. Mearns and Wm. Jackson.

DB 4-99 GREEN BELL of Nash Co. to EDMUND DRAKE of same, Jan. 15, 1790, for 150 pds. specie 170 acres adjoining Williams, Pryor Gardner, John Battle, Butts, and Pollock's Beaver Dam Swamp, it being a tract granted to Green Bell by the State of N. C.; also, another tract of 112 acres adjoining Green Bell, John Williams, Joseph Ward, George Gardner, Pryor Gardner, and the preceding tract, this also granted to Green Bell by the State of N. C. Wit: W. S. Mearns and Augustin Drake.

DB 4-99 JAMES BROWN of Nash Co. to JOHN FLOWERS of same, Feb. 26, 1791, for 45 pds. Virginia money a tract of 250 acres on the north side of Wilder's Mill Branch adjoining said Brown and the Rooty Branch, it being part of a grant of 640 acres by the State to James Brown on Sept. 24, 1785. Wit: Jonas Williams and John Vick.

DB 4-101 WILLIAM ARRINGTON, Sheriff of Nash Co., to ARTHUR BROWN of Bertie Co., Aug. 10, 1791 for 15 pds. at public auction a tract of 185 acres on the north side of Tar River at the county line between Nash and Edgecombe counties adjoining Kirby and John Watkins. This property belonging to WILLIAM HORN, was sold to satisfy a judgment against William Horn and Arthur Brown obtained in Northampton Co. court by John Knox, admr. of Elias Hilliard, deceased. Wit: Hardy Griffin and Peter Arrington.

DB 4-102 STATE of N. C. grant to STEPHEN BATCHELOR by Gov. Alex. Martin, Nov. 1, 1784, a tract of 100 acres on the north side of Tar River and on Sapony Creek adjoining Thomas Warren and Bunn.

DB 4-103 DELILAH GRIFFIN of Nash Co. to JOHN WILSON of same, Sept. 15, 1790, for 120 pds. specie one negro woman and one negro girl. Wit: John Warbinton, Sally Wheless, and Benja. Whitfield.

DB 4-104 WILLIAM WINSLOW and HARDY GRIFFIN of Nash Co. to HOWELL ELLEN of same, April 23, 1791, for 45 pds. Virginia money one negro woman. Wit: James Williams and Arch Hunter.

DB 4-105 JOHN CHITTY of Nash Co. to HOWEL ANDERSON of same, Jan. 15, 1790, for 60 pds. specie a tract of 100 acres adjoining David Strickland and Hunter. Wit: David Strickland and Jacob Strickland.

DB4-106 WILLIAM HORN of Nash Co. to WILSON CURI of same, Aug. 10, 1786, for 185 pds. Virginia money a tract of 225 acres on the river adjoining Andrew Ross, the meeting house, and Stony Creek. Wit: Jacob Ricks and Henry Horn.

DB 4-106 ELIJAH REVEL of Nash Co. to MICAJAH REVEL of same, Aug. 25, 1785, for 25 pds. Virginia money a tract of 100 acres adjoining James Barnes, Bn. Bunn, and William Barnes. Wit: Henry Revel, Selah Revel, and Edward Wilson.

DB 4-108 ROBERT RODGERS of Nash Co. to WILLIAM RICHARDSON of same, May 3, 1785, for 10 pds. a parcel of 10 acres adjoining said Robert Rodgers. Wit: John Gay and Harry Taylor.

DB 4-109 JAMES WATKINS of Nash Co. to WILSON CURL of same, Nov. 15, 1791, for 40 pds. 250 acres on the north side of Tar River adjoining Lewis Curl, Wade Moore, William Joiner, Lamon's Road, and Lamon's line, it being part of a tract that James Watkins bought of Wililam Baker. Wit: Wilson Vick and Joseph Denson.

DB 4-109 HENRY PEED of Beaufort Co. to THOMAS BRIC-KLE of Franklin Co., Sept. 13, 1790, for 25 pds. a tract of 25 acres in Nash Co. Wit: Shadrack Floyd, Federick Jones, and Sam'l Alford.

DB 4-111 DIXON MARSHALL of Warren Co. to BENJAMIN BARNES of Nash Co., May 14, 1791, for 26 pds. a tract of 80 acres on the north side of Tar River adjoining Benjamin Bunn, Sr., the new road, Duncan Lamon, and Benjamin Barnes. Wit: David Barnes and Jesse Barnes.

DB 4-112 WILLIAM HARRISS and MARGET HARRISS of Nash Co. to JOSEPH ANDRESS, March 12, 1790, for 40 pds. 250 acres on the south side of Little Peachtree Creek adjoining Willoughby Manning, it being a tract granted by the State to Elijah Powell and conveyed by said Powell to said Harriss. Wit: Benja. Manning and William Harriss.

DB 4-113 HENRY PEED of Beaufort Co. to THOMAS BRIC-KELL of Franklin Co., Sept. 13, 1790, for 200 pds. three tracts of land. (1) 40 acres on Peachtree Creek adjoining Robert Rogers and William Richardson, it being part of a grant by Earl Granville to Willobe Tucker in 1762 and sold by said Tucker to Henry Peed; (2) 10 acres on Peachtree Creek adjoining Willobe Tucker and Henry Peed, secured in the same manner as the first tract; (3) 164 acres on the north side of Peachtree Creek adjoining Henry Peed, Braswell, and Isaac Bass, which tract Henry Peed purchased of Stephen Young. Wit: Sam'l Alford, Fedrick Jones, and Shadrack Floyd.

DB 4-114 STATE of N. C. grant to JACOB BRANTLY by Gov. Alex. Martin, Oct. 25, 1782, a tract of 240 acres on Sapony Creek adjoining Edward Ballard, Matthew Brantley, Joseph Seley, and Wm. Sellers.

DB 4-115 JAMES JOLLEY of Nash Co. to his son-in-law WILLIE BUNN, of same, Aug. 16, 1791, for love and affection a tract of 100 acres on the south side of Tar River on Jolley's back line. Wit: Wilson Vick and Edward Horn.

DB 4-116 JAMES TUCKER, SR. of Nash Co. to JAMES TUCKER, JR. of same, Jan. 30, 1792, "doth freely grant" to his son 35 acres of land in Nash Co. Wit: Burrel Rose and George Sutton.

DB 4-117 WILLIAM FLOWERS of Nash Co. to BENJAMIN FLOWERS of same. Oct. 7, 1791, for 100 pds. Virginia money a tract of 280 acres adjoining Joseph Phillips. Wit: Jonas Williams and Drury Williams.

DB 4-118 SAMUEL THOMAS of Nash Co. to MARMADUKE MASON of same Feb. 13, 1792, for 49 pds. a tract of 100 acres on the south side of Stony Creek adjoining Henry Vick, Lamon's Road, and Strickland. Wit: John Wilson and Batson Smith.

DB 4-119 THOMAS WHITFIELD of Nash Co. to JACOB DICKENSON of Edgecombe Co., Feb. 15, 1792, for 120 pds. specie one negro man. Wit: Redmun Bunn and Lod. Ruffin.

DB 4-119 WILLIAM ARRINGTON, Sheriff of Nash Co., to JOHN WATKINS of same, Sept. 28, 1791, for 50 pds. 1 sh. at publim auction a tract of 200 acres on the north side of Tar River adjoining John Watkins, Micajah Revel, and Joseph Curl. This property, belonging to WILLIAM HORN, was sold to help satisfy a judgment against William Horn and Arthur Brown obtained in Northampton Co. court by John Knox, admr. of Elias Hilliard, deceased. Wit: Josiah Horn.

DB 4-121 JOHN HARRELL of Nash Co. to HINES DRAKE of same. May 11, 1791, for $42.50 one negro girl. Wit: Samuel Thomas.

DB 4-122 HENRY WHITEHEAD of Nash Co. to HENRY TISDAL of same, Feb. 1792, for 150 pds. a tract of 312 acres on Moccasin Creek, according to a deed dated July 3, 1760. Wit: David Pridgen and Hardy Pridgen.

DB 4-123 JOSEPH EXUM of Nash Co. to SOLOMON EDWARDS of same, Feb. 14, 1792, for 50 pds. one negro boy. Wit: Benja. Bunn and Hines Drake.

DB 4-124 EMANUEL SKINNER of Nash Co. to JAMES BARNES of same, Feb. 27, 1790, for 30 pds. specie a tract of 50 acres on the north side of Stoney Creek adjoining Thomas' Road. Wit: John Harrell and Tisev Thomas.

DB 4-124 DANIEL POWELL of Nash Co. to LEWIS DORTCH of same, Jan. 13, 1792, for 100 pds. Virginia money a 100 acre plantation on the north side of Swift Creek; also, another tract of 20 acres adjoining the aforesaid tract. granted to the said Powell by deed of sale dated Jan. 1, 1767. Wit: Lazarus Whitehead, Isaac Whitehead, and Lazarous Whitehead.

DB 4-125 JACOB DICKINSON of Edgecombe Co. to JOHN VICK of Nash Co., Jan. 11, 1792. for 400 dollars two tracts on the south side of Peachtree Creek: (1) 200 acres adjoining Jesse Thomas, Michajah Thomas, Whitfield, and John Whitehouse; (2) 200 acres on the road adjoining William Batchelor. Willis Whitfield, and Jesse Thomas. Wit: Wilson Vick and Sam Westray.

DB 4-126 DAVID STRICKLAND of Nash Co. to JOSHUA VICK of Southampton Co.. Virginia, March 18, 1781, for 135 pds. Virginia money a tract of 400 acres on Compass Creek. Wit: Richard Vick, Lewis Vick, and Samuel Glover.

DB 4-128 ROBERT (ROBIN) BRASWELL of Nash Co. to JAMES WILLIAMS of same, Dec. 20, 1791, for 58 dollars a tract of 100 acres adjoining Julian King and Daniels. Wit: Howell Ellen and James Wililams.

DB 4-128 WILLIAM BALLARD of Nash Co. to CORNELIUS JOINER of same, Feb. 3, 1792, for 60 pds. parts of two tracts containing 297 acres on the south side of Sapony Creek adjoining Benjamin Smith and John Evans. Wit: Jesse Joiner and John Joiner.

DB 4-129 HENRY WATKINS of Nash Co. to ELIAS REVEL of same, June 5, 1786, for 10 pds. specie a tract of 75 acres on the north side of Kirby's Creek. Wit: John Wilson and Elizabeth Wilson.

DB 4-130 JOHN RICKS of Nash Co. to REDMUN BUNN of same, Feb. 1, 1791, for 260 pds. a 200 acre plantation on the south side of Tar River in Nash and Edgecombe counties adjoining Redmun Bunn and "the north corner of the late dwelling house of John Ricks, deceased", it being the land left to said John Ricks in the last will of his father, John Ricks, deceased. Wit: Jacob Ricks, Thomas Hart, and James Ricks.

DB 4-131 JOSEPH WHITE of Nash Co. to WILLIAM BRIDGER and BENJAMIN BOON of same, May 11, 1791, for 261 pds. specie his goods, chattels, lands, and tenements of all kinds whatsoever. Wit: Wilson Vick, John Arrington, and Abra. Ricks.

DB 4-132 JOHN MOSS, admr. of Capt. JOHN GOODWIN, deceased, of the county of York to JAMES DRAKE, Feb. 9, 1791, for 50 pds. Virginia money one negro girl. Wit: Martin Goodwin, Masag Walrond, and John H. Drake.

DB 4-133 SOLZAY DAVIS of Franklin Co. to JOSEPH ARRINGTON, JR. of Nash Co., March 1, 1792, for 160 silver dollars 160 acres on the south side of Fishing Creek adjoining Arrington, it being a tract of land given to Solzay Davis by her father in his will. Wit: William Lancaster and Jubl. Jackson.

DB 4-134 THOMAS BEVAN of Nash Co. to JACOB ROGERS of same, Feb. 10, 1792, for 100 pds. Virginia money livestock and furniture that Thomas Bevan bought at the sale of Robartes Rogers, deceased. Wit: Jesse Rogers, Ann Bevan, and Colley Braswell.

DB 4-135 ARTHUR BROWN of BERTIE CO. to JOSIAH HORNE of Nash Co., April 25, 1792, for 36 pds. one negro man. Wit: Joel Horn and T. Barnes.

DB 4-135 DAVID PRIDGEN of Nash Co. to HARDY PRIDGEN of same, May 6, 1792, for 10 pds. specie a tract of 125 acres on the north side of Tar River adjoining Solomon Wells and David Pridgen, it being the land whereon Hardy Pridgen then lived. Wit: Wm. Hall.

DB 4-136 ELISABETH ALLEN of Nash Co. to DAVID PRIDGEN of same, May 6, 1792, for 18 pds. Virginia money a tract of 150 acres adjoining Drewry Pridgen, Joseph Seley, Wells, David

Pridgen, and William Eason. Wit: Wm. Hall.

DB 4-137 WILLIS WHITFIELD of Nash Co. to BENJA-
MIN WHITFIELD of same, April 9, 1792, for 60 pds. Virginia
money a tract of 190 acres on the south side of Peachtree Creek
adjoining Archibald Griffin's acre at the mill. Wit: Henry Bunn
and John Barrett.

DB 4-138 JOHN WILSON, and wife. ELIZABETH WILSON,
of Nash Co. to DELILAH GRIFFIN of same, Aug. 10, 1791, for
150 pds. specie 200 acres adjoining Revel and David Strickland,
it being part of a tract granted to Jesse Hunt and conveyed by
him to the said Elizabeth. then Strickland. by deed on Dec. 9, 1782.
Wit: Young Whitfield, William Willis, and Francis Hamilton.

DB 4-139 WILSON CURL of Nash Co. to JOSEPH CURL of
same, Feb. 28, 1792, for 100 pds. Virginia money a tract of 125
acres on the north side of Tar River and east side of Stoney Creek
adjoining Joseph Curl, Josiah Horn, and the meeting house. Wit:
Benjamin Bunn and Wilson Vick.

DB 4-140 ELIZABETH THOMPSON of Edgcombe Co. to
WILLIAM MATHEWS of Nash Co., March 8, 1792, for 100 dollars
a tract of 350 acres on Little Sapony Creek adjoining Wm. Bennett. Wit: J. Bonds and Briant O'Neal.

DB 4-142 REUBEN MOORE of Nash Co. to ROBERT WOR-
LEY of Halifax Co., June 4, 1788, for 60 pds. a tract of 250 acres
near Swift Creek on Shelley's Swamp adjoining Thomas Mann.
Wit: J. Matthews and Richard Matthews.

DB 4-142 ISAAC BASS of Nash Co. to JOHN BASS of same
May 14. 1792, for 20 pds. specie two tracts of land: (1) 225 acres
on the south side of Peachtree Creek adjoining Isaac Bass, Charles Brown, and Thomas, it being a tract granted to Jones Bryant
by the State on Sept. 10, 1779; (2) 150 acres on the south side of
Peachtree Creek adjoining Bryant and Jesse Bass. it being part of
a tract granted by Earl Granville to Isaac Bass in 1772. Wit: William Boddie and Julian King.
JOINER wf- cmw ycmfwvf

DB 4-143 PETER BALLARD of Nash Co. to NATH-
AN JOINER, April 21, 1792. for 60 pds. Virginia money a tract
of 200 acres on the south side of Sapony Creek adjoining Peter
Ballard and William Sellers. Wit: Jesse Joiner and Cornelius Joyner.

DB 4-144 WILLIAM HAMMONDS of Nash Co. to WILLIAM
PRITCHETT of Edgecombe Co.. Nov. 11 1791, for 50 pds. a tract
of 300 acres on Sapony Creek adjoining William Vester and Jeremiah Etheridge. Wit: John Pritchett, Lemuel L.—and Sherod
Deens.

DB 4-145 AMBROSE EDMONDSON of Nash Co. to JOHN
PITTS of same. March 28, 1792, for 90 pds. Virginia money a tract
of 320 acres adjoining Christopher Hinton, Thomas Morris, Wm.
Boddie, and Isaac Hilliard, it being part of a grant to Charles Watson by the State on Nov. 10, 1779. Wit: Thomas Morris and William Boddie.

DB 4-147 Division of the estate of WILLIAM BATTLE, deceased, among his heirs at law by commissioners, May 15, 1792: (1) to JAMES BATTLE, 450 acres on the south side of Swift Creek; (2) to WILLIAM BATTLE, 364 acres on the north side of Swift Creek and a tract of 640 acres granted by the State of N. C. to said William Battle, deceased, on Nov. 10, 1779; (3) to JOHN BATTLE, 422 acres on the north side of Swift Creek. The valuations and differences in value were given. May Ct. 1792.

DB 4-147 THOMAS RIDLEY of Nash Co. to JONATHAN RICKS of same. May 9, 1792, in return for Jonathan Ricks paying all the just debts of said Thomas Ridley (Riddle), a tract of 280 acres, it being all his right in his wife's third in the land of her late husband, Lewis Ricks, deceased. Also, Jonathan Ricks should give to his wife. Ann Ridley, a sufficient maintenance for and during her life. Wit: Sam Westray and Batson Smith.

DB 4-148 ARTHUR BROWN of Bertie Co. to JOSIAH HORNE of Nash Co., April 25, 1792, for 120 pds. Carolina currency a tract of 185 acres sold by Wm. Arrington, Sheriff, on Aug. 10, 1791,, by virtue of an execution obtained by John Knox, admr. of Elias Hilliard, against William Horne. Wit: Joel Horn and T. Barnes.

DB 4-149 WILLIAM ARRINGTON, Sheriff of Nash Co., to PATRICK WALKER of Warren Co., Aug. 15, 1792, for 100 pds. at public auction a tract of land adjoining Duncan Lamon. Crowell, Brittain Smith, Marshall, and Lamon's Road, sold as the property of DIXON MARSHALL to satisfy a judgment obtained by Patrick Walker against said Marshall in Granville Co. Wit: None.

DB 4-152 JOHN WILSON of Nash Co. to JETHRO THOMAS of same, March 12, 1792, for 39 pds. one negro girl. Wit: Emmanuel Skinner and Thomas Ridle.

DB 4-153 WILSON VICK of Nash Co. to JOHN VICK of same, May 10. 1792, for 660 dollars a tract of 250 acres on the south side of Stony Creek adjoining Jethro Thomas, Samuel Wester, and the Maple Creek. Wit: Samuel Westray and Amos Gandy.

DB 4-153 JACOB BRANTLY of Nash Co. to PETER BALLARD of same, Aug. 27. 1791, for 200 pds. two tracts of land: (1) 112½ acres on the south side of Sapony Creek along a dividing line made by John Brantly between his sons, Jacob and Matthew Brantly, it being a tract bequeathed to the said Jacob Brantly by his father; (2) 240 acres adjoining Edward Ballard, Matthew Brantly, Joseph Seley, Wm. Sellers, and Peter Ballard, it being a tract granted to said Jacob Brantly by the State on Oct. 25, 1782. Wit: William Linsev and Edward Ballard.

DB 4-154 JOHN JONES of Halifax Co. to HENRY WHITEHEAD of Nash Co., Aug. 1, 1792, for 12 pds. 120 acres on the south side of Fishing Creek and east side of Pollock's Beaver Dam Swamp adjoining Pollock. Nicholson, and Whitehead. it being part of a tract granted to said John Jones by the State. Wit: Jonathan Whitehead.

DB 4-156 THOMAS MORRISS of Nash Co. to JOHN TUR-

NER of same, Aug. 28, 1787, for 50 pds. a tract of 136 acres on Charles Branch adjoining Manning. Wit: Wm. Boddie and Wm. Turner.

DB 4-157 WILSON VICK of Nash Co. to JOHN VICK of same, May 10, 1792, for 660 dollars a tract of 250 acres on the south side of Stony Creek adjoining Jethro Thomas, Samuel Wester, the Maple Creek, and Lane's Road, near the old race paths. Wit: Samuel Westray and Amos Gandy.

DB 4-157 ELIZABETH JACKSON of Nash Co. to WILLIAM ARRINGTON of same, Oct. 6, 1790 for 75 pds. Virginia money 147½ acres on the north side of Swift Creek adjoining Andrew Booth, William Arrington, Joseph Arrington, and John Arrington, it being a tract of land conveyed by deed from William Jackson to said Elizabeth Jackson. Wit: Arthur Arrington, Jos Arrington, and Wm. Lewis.

DB 4-158 WILLIAM JACKSON of Nash Co. to WILLIAM ARRINGTON of same, Oct. 18, 1788, for 95 pds. 5 sh. a tract of 147 acres adjoining Elizabeth Jackson, Joseph Arrington, Elizabeth Jackson's other corner (formerly James Cooper), Williams, and John Green (formerly William Cooper), it being part of a tract conveyed from Hardy Griffin to William Jackson. Wit: James Battle and W. S. Mearns.

DB 4-160 BURREL BELL of Wake Co. to EPHRAIM PERRY of Franklin Co., Aug. 6, 1792, for 210 pds. four tracts of land in Nash Co. on Turkey Creek: (1) 600 acres containing the land and plantation whereon Thomas Rogers, deceased, formerly lived, a Granville grant; (2) 100 acres on his own line, a State grant; (3) 150 acres adjoining Sampson Powell and the Jumping Branch, a State grant. Wit: Zadek Bell, Robert Rutherford, and James Perry.

DB 4-161 JOSEPH VICK of Nash Co. to ENOCH OWENS of same, May 15, 1792. for 16 pds. specie a tract of 100 acres on Toisnot Swamp adjoining Robert Vick and William West, it being a grant by the State to Joseph Vick in 1784. Wit: Elias Owens and Jurden Vick.

DB 4-162 JONAS BARNES WHITLEY. of Edgecombe Co. to JOSIAH WHITLEY of Nash Co., Dec. 29, 1791, for 85 pds. 216 acres on the north side of Maple Creek adjoining Westray and the old road, it being part of the tract that fell to said Jonas Whitley by the death of his father. Wit: Joel Bunn and William Barnes.

DB 4-162 RICHARD WINSTEAD of Edgecombe Co. to THOMAS WINSTEAD of Nash Co., Sept. 27, 1791. for 20 pds. a tract of 100 acres on the north side of a prong of Town Creek adjoining Duncan Lamon, Archchlus Lamon, and William Bout. Wit: David Winstead, Benjamin Bishop, and Griffin Winstead.

DB 4-164 BENJAMIN ATKINSON of Pitt Co. to JOSEPH SELY, JR. of Nash Co., Nov. 16, 1790, for 30 silver dollars a tract of 350 acres on the north side of Tar River at the head of Warburton's Branch adjoining Joseph Winstead, Stephen Wells, Bryant, Poland, Brantley, and Allen. Wit: Simon Pope and Thomas

Atkinson.

DB 4 164 ROBERT VICK, SR. of Nash Co. to JOHN OWENS of same, Aug. 13, 1792, for 10 pds. a tract of 100 acres on Toisnot Swamp, it being a grant from the State in 1784. Wit: Elias Owens, Wililam Heawood, and Enoch Owens.

DB 4-165 ABRAHAM POCKETT of Nash Co. to JOSEPH WHEELER, JR. of Franklin Co., Feb. 8, 1792, for 22 pds. Virginia money a tract of 170 acres on the north side of Turkey Creek it being a former grant from Earl Granville to Peleg Rogers. Wit: John Reynolds, George Fall, and Joseph Moseley.

DB 4-166 WILLIAM BRIDGERS of Nash Co. to BENJAMIN BOON of same, Dec. 22, 1791, for 15 pds. Virginia money a tract of 50 acres on Jumping Run adjoining John Williams. Wit: Micajah Bridgers and Hearty Bridgers.

DB 4-168 HOWEL UNDERWOOD of Nash Co. to WILLIAM SKINNER of same, Feb. 30, ?, 1792, for 20 pds. Virginia money one negro boy. Wit: Benja. Whitfield, Henry Strickland, and Emmanuel Skinner.

DB 4-168 CHARLES POWELL of Chesterfield Co., South Carolina to JESSE KICHEN of Nash Co., Feb. 22, 1791, for 75 pds. Virginia money a tract of 282 acres on the north side of Swift Creek adjoining Ralph Mason, Nicholas Baggett, and Isaac Hilliard. Wit: Robt. Hinton, Frederick Hines, and Ralph Mason.

DB 4-170 JOSEPH STRICKLAND and wife, MARY STRICKLAND, of Nash Co. to JETHRO THOMAS of same, Aug. 22, 1792, for 80 dollars a tract of 100 acres on the south side of Maple Creek adjoining Elizabeth Tallington and Ricks. Wit: Henry Bunn and Archd. Griffin.

DB 4-171 THOMAS RICHESON and wife, SARAH RICHESON, of Nash Co. to DAVID PRIDGEN of same, Sept. 6, 1792, for 42 pds. Virginia money a 276 acre plantation on the east side of the Great Bare Branch. Wit: Benjamin Ricks and Elisabeth Allen.

DB 4-172 JONAS BARNES WHITLEY of Edgecombe Co. to JOEL BUNN of Nash Co., Dec. 29, 1791, for 30 pds. specie a tract of 54 acres on Ruty Branch. Wit: William Barnes and Josiah Whitlev.

DB 4-173 BENJAMIN ATKINSON of Pitt Co. to DAVID EVANS of Nash Co., Nov. 23, 1789, for 10 pds. specie a tract of 133 acres on the north side of Stony Creek adjoining Wm. Boddie Nathan Boddie, and Micajah Thomas. Wit: Thomas Atkinson and J. Judkins.

DB 4-173 BENJAMIN ATKINSON of Pitt Co. to DAVID EVANS of Nash Co., Nov. 23, 1789. for 10 pds. specie a tract of 127 acres on Pig Basket Creek adjoining Arthur Braswell, Wm. Boddie. and homas. Wit: J. Judkins.

DB 4-175 CHESTER COLESON of Nash Co. to ALLEN FINCH of same. Nov. 6. 1790, for 100 pds. specie a tract of 400 acres on Contentnea Creek adjoining West Crumpler and George Green. it being a grant to Chester Coleson from the State on Sept. 24, 1785. Wit: Wilson Taylor, Benjamin Taylor, and Dempsey

Wyatt.

DB 4-176 WILLIAMSON ROSS of Nash Co. to RICE WEBB of Franklin Co., June 17, 1785, for 45 pds. specie a tract of 240 acres on Ross' old line. Wit: Daniel Taylor and John Whitfield.

DB 4-177 JOSEPH WRIGHT of Nash Co. to EPHRIAM PHILLIPS of same. Feb. 7, 1792, for 125 silver dollars a 250 acre plantation whereon John Flowers then lived on a branch of Contentnea called Sheperd's Branch, adjoining Ephraim Phillips and Sanders. Wit: Sharood Philips and Jethro Harrison.

DB 4-178 JOSEPH SELAH JR. of Nash Co. to DAVID PRIDGEN of same, May 21, 1792, for 20 pds. Virginia money a tract of 320 acres adjoining Joseph Winstead, Stephen Wells, Sharad Bryant. Poland, Brantley, and Allen. Wit: Edward Gandy and Wm. Tisdale.

DB 4-179 WILLIAM BATCHELOR of Nash Co. to ROBERT CRICKMUR of same, Jan. 22, 1788, for 20 pds. a tract of 192 acres on the north side of Sapony Swamp adjoining William Batchelor. Wit: Henry Burne and Ballentine Crickmur.

DB 4-179 EPHRAIM PHILLIPS of Nash Co. to JOHN SANERS, a taylor, of same, April 20, 1792, for 18 pds. two tracts of land at the head of Little Swamp: (1) 100 acres that Ephraim Phillips purchased of Micajah Whitley, it being the part of his father's land that fell to him at his father's death, and was part of the land whereon his father deceased; (2) 100 acres that Ephraim Phillips purchased of Drury Whitley, it being the part of his father's land that fell to him at his father's death, and was part of the land whereon his father deceased. Wit: Sharod Phillips and Jethro Harrison.

DB 4-180 JAMES COBB of Wayne Co. to NEWETT ATKINSON of Nash Co., Feb. 23, 1791, for 40 pds. a 300 acre plantation on Toisnot Swamp, it being a grant from the State to Lazarus Strickland on Oct. 25. 1782, conveyed from him to Jesse Broughton, and sold to said Cobb by the Sheriff of Nash Co. at a public sale on ov. 11, 1788. Wit: Am Dimch, Jos. Williamson, and Thos. Tucker.

DB 4-181 WILLIAM BATCHELOR of Nash Co. to ROBERT CRICKMUR of same, Jan. 22, 1788, for 40 pds. Virginia money two tracts of land: (1) 110 acres lying on both side of Sapony Swamp adjoining Benja. Bunn, William Batchelor. and John Manning; (2) 20 acres on Sapony Swamp adjoining William Batchelor. Wit: Henry Brune and Ballentine Crickmur.

DB 4-183 ROBERT BELL of Franklin Co. to WILLIAM WHELESS of Nash Co., Sept. 11, 1792, for 50 pds. Virginia money a tract of 255 acres on Bear Branch adjoining Rogers, Massingill. Micajah Thomas, and his own line; also, another tract of 109 acres lying in both Nash and Franklin counties and on both sides of Bear Swamp. Wit: H. Simmons and Wm. Kirby.

DB 4-183 JOHN SHEPPARD of Nash Co. to JOHN ADKINSON of same, Oct. 22, 1792, for 135 pds. Virginia money a tract of 330 acres on both side of Sapony Creek adjoining Moses Adkinson, Barnes, and Eason. Wit: David Pridgen, Abijah Pridgen. and Samuel Eason.

DB 4-184 JAMES COBB of Wayne Co. to EPHRAIM PHILLIPS of Nash Co., Aug. 20, 1791 for 21 pds. 250 acres on Sheppard's Branch adjoining Thomas Sanders, John Flowers, James Cobb, Joseph Wright, and Benjamin Bunn, it being a tract granted to said Cobb by the State on Oct. 25, 1782. Wit: William Phillips and Stephen Cobb.

DB 4-186 JAMES CAIN of Nash Co. to JOEL WILLIAMS of same, Jan. 23, 1793, for 125 pds. Virginia money a tract of 200 acres o nthe north side of Toisnot Swamp. Wit: John Taylor and James Brown.

DB 4-187 JAMES TUCKER, SR. of Nash Co. to JAMES TUCKER, JR. of same, March 27, 1792, for 20 pds. specie a tract of 70 acres on O'Neals line. Wit: Burrel Rose and Wililam Mathis.

DB 4-188 JOHN WATKINS of Nash Co. to MICAJAH REVEL of same, March 17, 1792, for 40 pds. a tract of 100 acres adjoining Joseph Curl, John Watkins, and Micajah Revel. Wit: Josiah Horn.

DB 4-189 JOHN VICK of Nash Co. to WILLIAM BATCHELOR of same, Jan. 12, 1783, for 400 pds. two tracts of land on the south side of Peachtree Creek: (1) 200 acres adjoining Jesse Thomas, Micajah Thomas, Whitfield, and John Whitehouse; (2) 200 acres adjoining William Batchelor, Willis Whitfield, Jesse Thomas, and the road. Wit: Peter Ballard and Wilson Vick.

DB 4-190 THOMAS SANDERS, JR. of Nash Co. to JOSIAH HORN of same, Dec. 1, 1792, for 450 dollars a tract of 320 acres on the Great or Bloomery Swamp adjoining Benjamin Bunn, Benjamin Flowers, and Joseph Phillips. Wit: Cornelius Sanders, Thomas Horn. and Jeremiah Horn. Rachael Sanders, wife of Thomas Sanders, Jr., gave up her right of dower.

DB 4-190 JOSEPH JOINER of Nash Co. to JACOB JOINER of same Feb. 23, 1792, for 26 silver dollars a tract of 26 acres on the south side of Sapony Creek adjoining Ben Smith and Cornelius Joiner. Wit: John Joiner and Curtis Joiner.

DB 4-191 ARTHUR ALLEN of Nash Co. to BURREL JOINER of same, Feb. 5, 1793, for 135 pds. Virginia money a 275 acre plantation on the north side of Tar River and Sapony Creek adjoining Phillander Williams, Jacob Thomas, and William Eason. Wit: Wm. Hall.

DB 4-191 NICHOLAS BAGGETT of Nash Co. to JOEL MATTHEWS of same, Jan. 23, 1792, for 20 pds. 60 acres adjoining Ralph Mason. Jesse Kitchen. and Swift Creek, it being the tract of land whereon said Baggett then lived. Wit: Ralph Mason, Granbery Baggett, and Benjamin Matthews.

DB 4-192-HENRY HARRISON and wife. CHARLOTTE HARRISON. of Edgecombe Co. to JOHN PRITCHETT of Nash Co., Feb. 10. 1793, for 150 dollars a tract of 100 acres on the north side of Tar River adjoining Sumner. Wit: Evin Bryant and Peter Dosher.

DB 4-193 JONAS BARNES WHITLEY of Edgecombe Co. to WILLIAM BARNES of Nash Co., Dec. 29, 1791, for 30 pds. 54 acres adjoining Josiah Whitley and the Ruty Branch, it being part of a tract that fell to said Whitley by the death of his father, Arthur Whitley. Wit: Joel Bunn and Josiah Whitley.

DB 4-194 MICAJAH THOMAS of Nash Co. to JAMES WOODARD of same, July 30, 1784, for 200 pds. 289 acres on the north side of Pig Basket Creek near Holland's Branch, it being part of a tract granted to said Micajah Thomas by Earl Granville in 1760. Wit: Sam'l Westray and Mourning Ricks.

DB 4-195 BOLEN BECKWITH of Nash Co. to DAVID WOODWARD of same. April 16. 1789, for 60 pds. specie 200 acres on the north side of Pig Basket Creek adjoining Micajah Thomas and Arthur Braswell. it being part of a tract granted to said Beckwith by the State of N. C. on Nov. 10, 1779. Wit: Jos. Exum and Demey Braswell.

DB 4-197 HENRY HARRISON and wife, CHARLOTTE HARRISON, of Edgecombe Co. to WILLIAM HENDRICK of Nash Co., Feb. 22, 1790, for 60 pds. specie a tract of 100 acres on the north side of Tar River adjoining Harrison. Wit: John Goodman and William Bryant.

DB 4-198 HENRY HARRISON and wife, CHARLOTTE HARRISON, of Edgecombe Co. to WILLIAM BRYANT of Nash Co., Feb. 10, 1793, for 180 pds. specie, a tract of 120 acres on the north side of Tar River adjoining Harrison. Wit: Evin Bryant and Peter Dosyher.

DB 4-199 JOSIAH JOHNSTON of Nash Co. to WILLIAM AVENT of same, Jan. 12, 1786, for 180 pds. a tract of 140 acres on the north side of Swift Creek adjoining Crawman and McNiel. Wit: Arthur Arrington, Wililam Arrington, and John Arrington.

DB 4-199 WILLIAM AVENT and wife, SARAH AVENT, of Nash Co. to ALLEN MANN of same, March 7, 1793, for 188 pds. Virginia money two tracts of land on the north side of Swift Creek: (1) 140 acres with the manor house and plantation where Wm. Avent then lived adjoining Crawman and McNeil; (2) 100 acres adjoining the first tract and said Allen Mann. Wit: Stephen Weaver, Denton Mann, and Henry Drake.

DB 4-200 JOHN BATTLE of Nash Co. to JAMES BATTLE of same, May 24, 1789, for 80 sliver dollars a tract of 68 acres on Swift Creek adjoining said John Battle it being one-third of the Dower land that was laid off to Mary Battle, mother of said James and John, adjoining the land of said James Battle. Wit: Wm. S. Mearns.

DB 4-202 WILLIAM BARKESDALE of Halifax Co. to JOS. ARRINGTON of Nash Co., Dec. 27, 1792, for 50 pds. Virginia money one negro wench. Wit: Jos. W. Nicholson, Wm. Lewis, James Judge. and Jas. M. Nicholson.

DB 4-203 JOHN EXUM of Nash Co. to LEWIS HINES of same, Feb. 6, 1793, for 50 pds. Virginia money two negro girls.

Wit: Jh. Hilliard and Fredk. Hines.

DB 4-203 BENJAMIN WHITFIELD of Nash Co. to JACOB HORN of same, March 9, 1793 for 166 2/3 silver dollars one negro boy. Wit: Anselm Harris and Josiah Horn.

DB 4-204 SYLVANIOUS PUMPHREY of Franklin Co. to JOSIAH BRIDGERS of Nash Co., Oct. 16, 1792, for 30 pds. 6 sh. Virginia money one negro boy. Wit: Denton Mann and Benja. Bridgers.

DB 4-205 CHILOE MINTON to WILLOUGHBY POWELL, Feb. 1, 1790, for 300 (?) specie one negro wench, livestock, and furniture. Wit: Emanuel Underwood and Nathaniel Powell.

DB 4-205 JOHN JONES of Nash Co. to JAMES HILLIARD of same, April 19, 1793, for 250 silver dollars 490 acres adjoining Hilliard and Jones, it being a tract of land that was given to John Jones by a deed of gift from his father, Francis A. Jones; also, another parcel of land adjoining the other tract containing 5 acres which was conveyed from Pierce Griffin to John Jones. Wit: W. S. Mearns and Lazarus Jones.

DB 4-206 FRANCIS PARKER of Nash Co. to JAMES DREWRY of same, Aug. 17, 1792, for one shilling per 100 acres, a lease to siad James Drewry, his heirs and assigns for 99 years of a tract of 152 acres adjoining William Drake on the north side of Jeffers' old road. Wit: John H. Drake, Henry Drake, and Benja. Sandeford.

DB 4-208 JEREMIAH HILLIARD of Edgecombe Co. to LEWIS HINES of Nash Co., Feb. 6, 1793, for 70 pds. 4 sh. current money a tract of 355 acres on the north side of Compass Creek adjoining Reuben Taylor, Alexander Thompson, Lewis Hines. Wit: Frederick Hines and John Exum.

DB 4-208 WEST DANIEL of Halifax Co. to ISAAC KIRK of same, April 16, 1793, for 100 pds. a tract of 200 acres on Toisnot Swamp adjoining Lazarus Strickland. Wit: Samuel Smith and Allin Daniel.

DB 4-209 JOHN MELTON of Nash Co. to THOMAS GRIFFIN of same, Dec. 31, 1789, for 116½ silver dollars 117 acres on Farewell Branch and Horse Pen Branch, it being part of a tract granted by the State to said John Melton. Wit: W .S. Mearns, Britain Jones and Joseph White.

DB 4-211 ANDREW BOOTHE of Nash Co. to WILLIAM ARRINGTON of same, Jan. 31 1792, for 150 silver dollars 100 acres on the north side of Swift Creek adjoining Wm. Arrington (formerly Bell) and Williams, it being a tract conveyed from Thomas Ezell to Joseph Arrington and from said Arrington to Andrew Boothe. Wit: W. S. Mearns.

DB 4-211 ISAAC TOMLINSON of Nash Co. to THOMAS HART, SR. of same, Sept. 6, 1791, for 25 pds. specie a tract of 100 acres adjoining William Hunt, Thomas Griffin, White, and the Tarborough Road. Wit: Lewis Vick, W. Winslow, and Amos Beckwith.

DB 4-212 WILSON CURL of Nash Co. to JOHN SEDGLEY of same, Feb. 18, 1793, for 100 pds. Virginia money a tract of 150 acres on the north side of Tar River near the Falls at the mouth of Spring Branch, a little below Ricks' Mill Dam, adjoining the road and Stony Creek. Wit: Wilson Vick and Lewrancy Curl.

DB 4-213 SAM WESTRAY, Sheriff of Nash Co., to JAMES CAIN of same, May 13, 1790, for 20 pds. at public auction a tract of 280 acres on Turkey Creek adjoining his own line, sold as the property of EDWARD MOORE, deceased, to satisfy a judgment obtained by said James Cain against the estate. Wit: Joseph Barns, Jr. and Wm. Bryant.

DB 4-214 SAM WESTRAY, Sheriff of Nash Co., to JAMES CAIN of same, May 13, 1790, for 20 pds at public auction a tract of 528 acres on Turkey Creek adjoining Jacob Strickland, John Taylor and his own line, sold as the property of EDWARD MOORE, deceased, to satisfy a judgment obtained by said James Cain against the estate. Wit: Joseph Barns, Jr. and Wm. Bryant.

DB 4-216 JOHN WILSON of Nash Co. to EMMANUEL SKINNER of same, April 4, 1793, for 118½ dollars one negro woman and one negro boy. Wit: Wilson Vick and Elisha Lankford.

DB 4-217 JAMES BATTLE of Nash Co . to BENJAMIN COOPER of same, April 17, 1792, for 50 silver dollars 67 acres on the south side of Beaver Dam Swamp adjoining Culpepper, Powell, and Cooper, it being a tract of land granted to Green Bell by the State. Wit: Jethro Denson, Edwin Drake, and James Cain.

DB 4-217 HENRY BRASWELL of Liberty Co., South Carolina to WILLIAM RICHARDSON, JR. of Nash Co. Dec. 5, 1792, for 80 silver dollars a tract of 70 acres on the west side of Back Swamp, it having been conveyed to Henry Braswell from George Massengal; also, another tract of 290 acres adjoining the aforesaid tract and James Massengal, Richardson, and Isaac Bass, it being a tract conveyed from Wm. Richardson, Sr. to Henry Braswell. Wit: William Hooks, William Richard, and Sampson Powell.

DB 4-218 WILLIAM WILLIAMS of Franklin Co. to BENJAMIN PERRY of same, Dec. 31, 1790, for 30 pds. 350 acres in Nash Co. adjoining Reuben Williams, it being a tract granted to Charles Rollings by the State on Nov. 30, 1784. Wit: James Perry and Ann Perry.

DB 4-219 THOMAS MORRIS of Nash Co. to WILLIAM RICHARDSON of same, July 31, 1793, for 3 pds. a parcel of 8 acres on the north side of Back Swamp adjoining Willoughby Manning. Wit: William Richardson, Armeger White, and Jesse Morriss.

DB 4-220 CHARLES ROLLINGS of Nash Co. to WILLIAM WILLIAMS of Franklin Co., Oct. 12, 1785, for 20 pds. a tract of 350 acres adjoining Reuben Williams, it being a grant from the State to said Charles Rollings on Nov. 30, 1784. Wit: James Strother and Jesse Newby.

DB 4-221 DEMPSEY BARNES of Edgecombe Co. to DEMPSEY DAWSON of Nash Co., Aug. 10, 1793, for 100 pds. specie 435 acres on the north side of Little Swamp, a branch of Toisnot. adjoining Dew (formerly Jesse Blackwell), John Dew, Arthur Dew, and Henry Flowers, it being the plantation whereon said Dempsey

Dawson then lived. Wit: Cornelius Sanders, Joseph Barnes, and Drury Williams.

DB 4-222 RICHARD DEAN of Nash Co. to JOHN VICK, SR. of same, May 17, 1793, for 60 silver dollars 200 acres adjoining Benja. Cobb and Drury Boykin, which was purchased by Richard Dean from Drury Boykin and by Drury Boykin from James Brown, it being part of a tract of 300 acres granted to James Brown on March 30, 1780. Wit: John Eatman, James Dean, and Theophilus Eatman.

DB 4-223 WILLIAM BATTLE of Nash Co. to WILLIAM DRAKE of same, June 17, 1789, for 80 silver dollars a tract of 69 acres on the south side of Swift Creek, it being one-third of the dower land that was laid off for Mary Battle, mother of said William Battle, adjoining the lands of James Battle and William Battle. Wit: John H. Drake, Wm. Avent, and B. Boon.

DB 4-224 SOLOMON WHITFIELD of Nash Co. to ARCHIBALD GRIFFIN of same, Feb. 24, 1793, for 20 sh. a parcel of 6 acres on the south side of Pig Basket Creek adjoining said Griffin and said Whitfield. Wit: Abraham Whitfield, Isaac Whitfield, and Jacob Whitfield.

DB 4-226 SAMUEL WESTRAY of Nash Co. to EDWARD GANDY of same, Oct. 11, 1793, for 100 dollars 150 acres adjoining Whitehouse, it being a tract granted to George Goodson by Earl Granville on Oct. 15, 1754. Wit: Wilson Vick and — Smith.

DB 4-227 JOSEPH PHILLIPS of Nash Co. to SHAROD PHILLIPS of same, Jan. 8, 1793, for 10 pds. a tract of 165 acres lying in both Nash and Edgecombe counties on the north side of the Great Swamp adjoining Cornelius Jordan. Wit: Ephraim Phillips and Gabreal Phillips.

DB 4-227 WILSON CURL of Nash Co. to RANDOLPH HARRIS of Southampton Co., Virginia, Jan. 11, 1783, for 70 pds. 340 acres on Compass Creek adjoining Lewis Hines, it being part of a 440 acre tract bearing date March 10, 1761. Wit: H. Horn, Joel Horn, Michael Atkinson, and John Wilson.

DB 4-228 SION HILL and wife, DRUSILLA HILL, of Nash Co. to JOHN BONDS of same, Nov. 5, 1793. for 100 pds. hard money a tract of 200 acres on the south side of Tar River adjoining Sion Hill and Southwell's Creek. Wit: Elijah Dunnavent and Matthew Carter.

DB 4-230 PENUEL FLOYD of Nash Co. to DANIEL HARRISS of same, May 21, 1793, for 20 pds. Virginia money a tract of 200 acres on the south side of Little Peachtree Creek adjoining Benjamin Manning. Wit: Edwin Drake.

DB 4-230 WILLIAM ARRINGTON of Nash Co. to BATSON SMITH of same, June 1, 1793, for 55 pds. 10 sh. Virginia money a tract of 240 acres on Maple Creek adjoining William Poland, Hardy Flowers, and Joyner. Wit: Wilson Vick and John Arrington.

DB 4-232 JOSEPH STRICKLAND and wife, MARY STRICKLAND, of Nash Co. to EDWARD GANDY of same, March 5, 1793, for 25 dollars a tract of 64 acres on the north side of Sapony Creek adjoining Jacob Ricks, William Ricks, Samuel Westray, and Benjamin Atkinson. Wit: Wilson Vick and Mary Vick.

DB 4-232 JOHN DENSON of Nash Co. to WILLIAM ARRINGTON of same, March 7, 1792, for 50 pds. Virginia money a tract of 240 acres on Maple Creek adjoining William Poland, Hardy Flowers, and Joyner, it being part of a new survey entered and surveyed by Thomas Hunter. Wit: Edward Gandy and Lewis Brantley.

DB 4-233 THOMAS DEANS of Nash Co. to MARK WALL of same, March 23, 1793, for 20 pds. a tract of 100 acres on Sapony Creek adjoining Bunn and Solomon Carter. Wit: Robert Crickmer and Jeremiah Bunten.

DB 4-234 ARCHIBALD DAVIS of Franklin Co. to FRANCIS WARD of Nash Co., March 11, 1793, for 200 pds. specie a tract of 601 acres on the south side of Fishing Creek on Gideon Swamp adjoining Hearn and Gardner. Wit: Pryor Gardner and Benjamin Ward.

DB 4-235 HARMUN STRICKLAND of Nash Co. to HENRY STRICKLAND of same, Aug. 30, 1793, for 100 pds. a tract of 200 acres adjoining Henry Strickland, Dunkin Simmons, Mark Strickland, and Robert Vick. Wit: J. Bonds and Nathan Derry.

DB 4-236 JAMES GOODWIN of Nash Co. to ISHAM MITCHEL of same, Dec. 27, 1792, for 40 pds. a tract of 100 acres on Blackwell's Branch. Wit: Jeremiah Portis and John Portis.

DB 4-238 BENJAMIN DAVIS to BENJAMIN BLUNT, Nov. 13, 1790, for 75 pds. 150 acres on Fishing Creek adjoining Ward and Miller,, it being a tract which Arthur Davis, deceased purchased of Archibald Davis. Wit: Richard Blunt, John Davis, and Josiah Mathis.

DB 4-238 ISAAC BASS of Nash Co. to JESSE ROGERS of same, Aug. 24, 1793, for 5 pds. a tract of 150 acres on Back Swamp adjoining Hays. Wit: Augustin Bass, Archelus Wright, and John H. Drake.

DB 4-240 RICHARD DEENS of Nash Co. to GEORGE BODDIE of same, Feb. 6, 1794, for 20 pds. 80 acres on the north side of Little Swamp adjoining John Sikes, Matthew Drake, and Little Peachtree Creek, it being part of a tract granted to said Richard Deens. Wit: Nathan Boddie and Wm. Hammons.

DB 4-241 JOHN HARRISON of Nash Co. to WILLIAM AVENT of same, Feb. 17, 1787, for 200 pds. specie a 207 acre plantation on Gideon Branch. Wit: James Battle and John Davis.

DB 4-242 JACOB UNDERWOOD of Nash Co. to ZACHERIAH UNDERWOOD of same, Jan. 10, 1794, for 30 pds. Virginia money one negro boy. Wit: Frederick Hines.

DB 4-243 DELILAH GRIFFIN of Nash Co. to HENRY STRICKLAND of same, March 27, 1792, for 50 pds. specie 12 acres adjoining Micajah Braswell and David Strickland, it being part of a tract said Delilah Griffin purchased of John Wilson. Wit: Emmanuel Skinner, John Arrington, and A. White.

DB 4-244 JOHN KENT of Burk Co., Georgia to JESSE KENT

of Nash Co., Jan. 6, 1794, for 50 pds. specie a tract of 100 acres on the west side of Turkey Creek. Wit: Drewry Williams and Nathan West.

DB 4-245 TISEY THOMAS of Nash Co. to BURREL BUNN of same. Jan. 3, 1793, for 55 pds. one negro boy. Wit: Rachel Watkins.

DB 4-246 ABSALOM WILLIAMSON of Southampton Co., Virginia to JESSE KENT of Nash Co., Jan. 29, 1794, for 49 pds. 10 sh. one negro girl. Wit: Stephen Kent and David Williamson.

DB 4-246 THOMAS ALLEN of Nash Co. to DREWRY PRIDGEN of same, Jan. 29, 1794, for 45 pds. Virginia money a tract of 400 acres on the south side of Sapony Creek adjoining David Pridgen, Drewry Pridgen, and Brantley. Wit: David Pridgen and John Atkinson.

DB 4-247 JOHN KENT and MARMEDUKE KENT of Burke Co., Georgia and STEPHEN KENT of Nash Co. to JESSE KENT of Nash Co., Jan. 3, 1794, for 35 pds. specie 342 acres of land, it being their part of the land that fell to them at the death of their father and part of a grant that their father had entered. Wit: Drewry Williams, Jesse Woodard, and Burrel Kent.

DB 4-249 JACOB BRASWELL of Nash Co. to his son, JESSE BRASWELL, of same, Feb. 10, 1794, for paternal love and affection a tract of 324 acres adjoining David Evans, Holland, David Woodard, Morris, and Braswell. Wit: John H. Drake.

DB 4-250 JACOB BRASWELL of Nash Co. to his son-in-law. DAVID EVANS, Feb. 10, 1794, for paternal love and affection a tract of 150 acres adjoining Holland, Woodard, and Robert Braswell. Wit: John H. Drake.

DB 4-251 JOHN BOWERS of Nash Co. to FRANCIS RACKLEY of same, Feb. 13, 1794, for 200 silver dollars a tract of 484 acres adjoining Matthias Manning, Robert Creekmur, Pridgen Manning, Parsons Rackley, and Jos. Batchelor. Wit: John H. Drake and Robert Creekmur.

DB 4-252 THOMAS WHITEHEAD of Nash Co. to his son, NATHAN WHITEHEAD, of same, Sept. 10. 1791. for paternal love and affection 200 acres on the north side of Peachtree Creek it being part of a tract of land granted to Benjamin Culpepper who demised the same to his daughter, Elizabeth, wife of the said Thomas Whitehead; also, another tract of 150 acres on Peachtree Creek and on the north side of Back Swamp adjoining the Benjamin Culpepper line and Isaac Bass, it being granted to the said Thomas Whitehead by a deed from the sheriff. Wit: Benjamin Sandeford and John Culpepper.

DB 4-253 MATTHEW CULPEPPER of Nash Co. to JOHN CULPEPPER of same, Jan. 2, 1794, for 130 silver dollars a tract of 130 acres on Collins Branch adjoining Lem'l Nicholson, it being part of a deed granted to Nath'l Powell. Wit: John Nicholson, Jr., Wm. Wright, and Thomas Whitehead.

DB 4-254 NATHANIEL POWELL and WILLOUGHBY POWELL of Nash Co. to THOMAS PACE of Halifax Co., Dec. 7,

1793, for 167 pds. 13 sh. 4 p. Virginia money a tract of 500 acres on the south side of Fishing Creek adjoining James Cain, Benjamin Cooper, Minton Hackney, Connel, Lemuel Nicholson, the Beaver Dam Swamp, and Cain's Mill Swamp. Wit: Nathan Powell and Jos. W. Nicholson.

DB 4-256 DANIEL WARREN of Nash Co. to ROBERT CREEKMUR of same, Jan. 11, 1794, for 20 pds. 40 acres on the south side of Sapony Creek adjoining Stephen Batchelor and Creekmur, it being part of a tract belonging to Stephen Batchelor, Sr. Wit: Drewry Pridgen, Pridgen Manning, and Isaac Hendrick.

DB 4-256 JAMES COX and wife, ELIZABETH COX, of Nash Co. to WILLIAM AVENT of same, Feb. 8, 1783, for 100 pds. specie a tract of 400 acres adjoining Peter Anderson, Thomas Davis, and Elias Bell. Wit: A. Lancaster and Thomas Carney.

DB 4-258 REUBEN TAYLOR of Nash Co. to JOHN POPE of same, Oct. 12. 1792, for 100 pds. 225 acres on both sides of Beach Run: (1) 110 acres on the north side of Beach Run adjoining Jos. Exum; (2) 115 acres on the south side of Beach Run adjoining Willis Trevathan and Exum. Wit: Demcy Taylor and Elizabeth Taylor.

DB 4-258 EPHRIM PHILLIPS of Nash Co. to THOMAS HORN of same, Jan. 16, 1794, for 200 dollars a tract of 250 acres on Sheppard's Branch adjoining Ephraim Phillips, including the plantation whereon John Flowers formerly lived. Wit: Jacob Horn and Jethro Harrison.

DB 4-259 ANN KNIGHT and KINSMAN KNIGHT of Nash Co. to PENUEL FLOYD of same, Sept. 17, 1791, for 200 Spanish milled dollars two tracts of land: (1) 130 acres on the north side of Pig Basket Creek adjoining Williams and Joseph White; (2) 20 acres on the north side of said creek and along the road adjoining Joseph White. Wit: Amos Beckwith and Burrell Beckwith.

DB 4-260 WILLIAM AVENT of Nash Co. to WILLIAM EVANS of same, Feb. 11, 1792, for 100 pds. specie a tract of 100 acres adjoining Wm. Avent, Davis, and John Slatter. Wit: None.

DB 4-262 JOHN PORTIS of Nash Co. to JOHN COX of same, Feb. 12. 1791, for 20 pds. a tract of 134 acres on the north side of White Oak Swamp in both Nash and Franklin counties. Wit: Jeremiah Portis and John Portis.

DB 4-262 JOHN WILLIAMS of Halifax Co. to MATTHEW DRAKE of Nash Co., Nov. 29. 1793, for 150 silver dollars 150 acres on the south side of Swift Creek, it being a tract conveyed from Thomas Gilchrist to John Williams. Wit: N. Williams, Matthew Drake Jr., and Mourning Drake.

DB 4-264 EPHRAIM PHILLIPS of Nash Co. to THOMAS HORN of same, Jan. 16, 1794, for 100 dollars 250 acres on Sheppard's Branch adjoining Thomas Sanders, John Flowers, James Cobb, Joseph Wright, and Benjamin Bunn, it being a tract granted to said James Cobb by the State on Oct. 25, 1782. Wit: Jacob Horn and Jethro Harrison.

DB 4-265 THOMAS TUCKER of Nash Co. to DAVID PRID-

GEN of same, Feb. 5, 1794, for 13 pds. 10 sh. Virginia money a tract of 100 acres on Sapony Creek adjoining Batchelor. Wit:Peter Etheridge and Abijah Pridgen.

DB 4-265 MOSES SMITH of Henry   Co., Virginia to BEN-JAMIN BOON of Nash Co., Jan. 9, 1793, for 80 silver dollars 97½ acres on Pig Basket Creek adjoining Williams, Drake, Hinton and Hilliard, it being a tract conveyed from Thomas   Morriss to the said Moses Smith by deed. Wit: W. S. Mearns, Augustin Drake, and H. Hinton.

DB 4-266 BENJAMIN WHITFIELD of Nash Co. to JOHN HAYS of Johnston Co., Nov. 30. 1792, for 300 dollars two tracts of land on the south side of Peachtree Creek containing 275 acres (1) 190 acres on the south side of the creek adjoining Archibald Grif-fin's acre at the mill: (2) 85 acres adjoining Melton and Dicker-son's former line. Wit: Henry Bunn and William Briant.

DB 4-267 JOHN POPE of Nash Co. to REUBEN TAYLOR of same, Sept. 9, 1793, for 5 pds. a tract of 130 acres on the south side of Beach Run adjoining said Taylor, Elisha Pope, Mills, Taylor, and dollars a tract of 100 acres on the south side of Maple Creek ad-joining Strickland. Elizabeth Tallington, and Ricks. Wit: Wiley Skinner and John Harrell.

DB 4-273 ETHELRED DANCE of Nash Co. to HENRY STRICKLAND of same, Feb. 7. 1794, for 50 pds. a tract of 300 acres on Toisnot Swamp and Little Swamp adjoining Ed. Moore. Wit: J. Bonds and John Cockrel.

DB 4-274 SOLOMON CARTER and wife, ELIZABETH CAR-TER, of Nash Co. to JEREMIAH STEVENS of same, April 16, 1792, for 1000 silver dollars a tract of 450 acres on the north side Jacob Edwards. Wit: Kinchen Taylor and Elizabeth Taylor.

DB 4-269 JOHN SLATTER and wife. ELIZABETH SLAT-TER, of Nash Co. to BENJAMIN SANDEFORD of same. Jan. 10, 1794, for 100 pds. Virginia money 310 acres on Fishing Creek ad-joining Robert Adams, William Battle. and Cockes, it being part of a tract granted to Green Bell by the State on Oct. 25, 1782. Wit: John Battle, Pryor Gardner. and Peter Robertson.

DB 4-270 WILLIAM SELLERS of Nash Co. to ARTHUR SELLERS, JR. of same. May 17, 1790. for 100 pds. a tract of 100 acres adjoining Jacob Brantley and William Whitfield. Wit: Ed-ward Nicholson, Samuel L. Bottom, and James Sellers.

DB 4-271 STEPHEN YOUNG of Nash C. to JACOB BRANT-LEY of same, Aug. 27, 1791, for 200 pds. two tracts of land on the south side of Turkey Creek: (1) 400 acres adjoining Jacob Strick-land and Samuel Bryant, it being a tract the said Stephen Young purchased of Hardy Strickland; (2) 300 acres adjoining Solomon Strickland's spring branch, purchased by said Stephen Young from Samuel Bryant, both deeds bearing Nov. 4, 1786. Wit: Peter Bal-lard, Edward Ballard and Wm. Linsey.

DB 4-272 JETHRO THOMAS and SUSANNAH THOMAS of Nash Co. to REUBEN HARRELL of same, Dec. 16, 1793. for 100 of Tar River adjoining Thomas Deens.   Wit: J. Bonds. Cornelius Sulevant, and Thos. Carter.

DB 4-275 JACOB BRASWELL of Nash Co. to his son, NATHAN BRASWELL, of same, Feb. 10, 1794, for paternal love and affection a tract of 350 acres adjoining Morris, Powell, and William Braswell.   Wit: John H. Drake.

DB 4-276 WILLIAM WHITEHEAD of Washington Co., Georgia to HARTWELL HINES of Sussex Co., Virginia, Aug. 29, 1793, for 300 pds. Virginia money a tract of 450 acres in Nash Co. on Rooty Branch adjoining Jones, Hilliard, Hines, Underwood, and Vick.   Wit: Frederick Hines, Samuel Manning, and Robt. Hinton.

DB 4-277 JACOB BRASWELL of Nash Co. to his son, BRITAIN BRASWELL, of same, Feb. 10, 1794, for patrenal love and affection a tract of 350 acres in Nash Co.   Wit: John H. Drake.

DB 4-278 WILLIAM WHITEHEAD of Washington Co., Georgia to BRITAIN JONES, LAZARUS JONES, JOHN JONES, and ALLEN JONES of Nash Co., Sept. 9, 1793, for 150 pds. Virginia money, a tract of 290 acres adjoining Wm. Whitehead's line and his mill run, which said land was granted to Richard Whittington by deed.   Wit: Frederick Hines and Archibald Griffin.

DB 4-279 WILLIAM CHAPMAN, JR. of Nash Co. to Wm. STONE MORGAN of same, Oct. 16, 1787, for 80 pds. a tract of 300 acres on Tar River and Bryant Creek adjoining John Taylor, Micajah Thomas. and Daniel Owens.   Wit: Mary Owens and Hardy Morgan.

DB 4-280 JACOB UNDERWOOD of Nash Co. to his son, MALICHI UNDERWOOD, of same, Feb. 11, 1794, for 80 pds. Virginia money a tract of 200 acres on the south side of Compass Creek adjoining Revel, Edwards, and Hartwell Hines.   Wit: Alex. Sorsby and Benjamin Merit.

DB 4-281 HENRY WATKINS of Nash Co. to JOSIAH SKINNER of same, Jan. 20, 1794, for 300 pds. a tract of 125 acres on the south side of Kirby's Creek adjoining Wilson, Curl, Micajah Revel, and Emmanuel Skinner, which tract was granted to John Moore by Earl Granville in 1762.   Wit: Edward Wilson and Wiley Skinner.

DB 4-282 ARCHIBALD GRIFFIN of Nash Co. to SOLOMON WHITFIELD of same. Feb. 24, 1793, for 5 pds. a parcel of 6 acres adjoining said Archibald Griffin.   Wit: Jacob Whitfield, Abraham Whitfield, and Isaac Whitfield.

DB 4-283 WILLIAM MATTHEWS of Nash Co. to his son, JOHN MATTHEWS, of same, Jan. 16, 1795, for love and affection a tract of 175 acres on Little Sapony Swamp adjoining Thomas. Wit: Wm. Hall and John Arrington.

DB 4-284 RICHARD BURGE of Nash Co. to ORPA HARRELL of Bertie Co., Nov. 28, 1794, for 35 pds. Virginia money a tract of 150 acres on both sides of Turkey Creek, lying in both Nash and Franklin counties.   Wit: Wm. Hammons and Mathew Tennyson.

DB 4-284 WILSON CURL of Nash Co. to JOSEPH CURL of same, Feb. 11, 1791, for 120 dollars a tract of 150 acres on the south side of Kirby's Creek adjoining Wilson Curl, Henry Watkins, and Thomas' Road. Wit: Joel Bunn and Wilson Vick.

DB 4-286 MICAJAH WHITLEY of Nash Co. to EPHRAIM PHILLIPS of same. Dec. 4, 1789, for 9 pds. 12 sh. specie 100 acres on the head of the Little Swamp, it being that part of a grant to his father, George Whitley, for 400 acres which, when his father deceased, was allotted to said Micajah Whitley in the division with his brothers. Wit: Jethro Harrison and Drury Whitley.

ORIGINAL DATA WRITTEN INSIDE THE BACK OF BOOK 4:

JOSEPH ARRINGTON was born March 27, 1762.

MORNING, his wife, was born March 10, 1766, and they were married Oct. 27, 1785.

MARY, the daughter of JOSEPH and MOURNING, was born Nov. 13. 1786.

HENRY DRAKE was born July 14. 1771.

MARY DRAKE, the mother of HENRY and wife of EDMUND, died May 29. 1792, being in the 47th year of her age.

- - - RMES BATTLE was born Oct. 14, 1754.

MARTHA BATTLE was born April 3, 1759.

JAMES M NICHOLSON was born July 17, 1777.

WILLIAM HENRY HALL was born April 1, 1786.

INDEX TO NASH COUNTY DEED BOOK V

—A—

Aberson, Willi 347
Adams, Jesse 231
Adkins, Thos. 195
Alford, Ansel 160 (2), 165, 171, 176, Jacob 165, Lodwick 92
Allen, Eliz. 82
Alston, 156, 157, 296, J. 276, Jas. W. 4, 239, 277, John 239, 276, 277, K. 277, Marg. 276 (2), 277 (2), Temperance 239 (2), W. J. 276, Willis 239, 276
Anders, Cullen 262
Anderson, Sterling 33, 343
Andrews 51, 143, John 83, Wm. 90 (2). 298, 363
Appleton, Jas. 361
Armstrong, Thos. J. 204
Arrington, A. 355, Arthur 19, 24, 159, 372, Carter 169 (2), Henry 164, 359, 372 (2), J. 133, John 24, 204, 213, 230, 300, 319, 343, Jos. 24, 57, 99. 134. 150 (2), 158, 169, 202, 213, 217, 218, 222, 287, 301, 325, 354, 372, Mary 150 (2), Peter 41, 145, 157 (2), 184, 202, 204, 275, Rich. 372 (2), W. 25, Wm. 24, 143. 150 (2), 157, 169, 184, 242, 248 (2), 279, 290, 350 (2), 383, Willis 124
Atkinson, Benj. 64, 272, 290 (2), 334, Elijah 212, J. 27, 34, 168, Jas. C. B. 286, 304, 318. Joel 225, John 4, 64, 286, 290, 304, Mical 113, Wm. 334, Willie 225
Avarett. Rebekah 162
Avent, Wm. 47

—B—

Bagget(t), Eliz. 104, Granberry 104, 188, 221, 284, Nicholas 104 (2)
Bailie, John 117
Baker 231, Arch. 180 (2)
Ballard, D. 253, Edw. 61, Peter 116
Ballentine, Rebeckah 172, Willoughby 172, 306, 380
Banes, Benj. 51, Henry 51
Barker, Jesse 110
Barlow, Sam. 83
Barnes 256, Benj. 126 (2), 360, Dempsey 323, Ed. 360, Jacob 303, Jas. 198, 228, Jesse 328 (2), 346, John 303, Jos. 328 (2), 346, Lemuel 198, 199, 206, 228, Mills 15, Orandatus 198, Wm. 198, 206, 376, 396
Barren, Jas. 88
Barrett 342, Jacob 211, John 150
Barrow, John T. 341
Bartholomew, Mills 238
Bass, Abraham 115, Alden 240, Bethany 200, 319, Betsey 375, Elias 210, Gideon 363. 364. Isaac 163, K. 316, Kitchen 296, Jesse 14, 143, 195, 231, 363, 364, 365, 374, 375, Jethro 324 (2), John 200, 296, 319, Jordan 200. 319, Mary 115, Sion 115 (2)
Batchelor (Bachelor, Batcheldor) 130. Daniel 350, Jas. 33. 384, Jos. 146, 259, Sam. 350, Wm. 2, 33, 46, 78 (2), 178, 207, Willis 384

Battle, Cullin 345, Davis 304, Elisha 8 (2), Eliza. 279, Jacob 8, Jas. 44, 55, 62, Joel 40, John 44, 55, 57, Josiah 241 (2), 362, Larkin 157, Wm. 44, 55, 63

Batts, Fred. 126

Beckwith, Amos 168, Burrell 38, Sion 27, 34, 38 (2), 168, Willis 38

Beelane, John 281

Bell 63, 150, Arthur 51 (2), 62, (2), Benj. 51, 62 (2), Burrel 92, Eliz. 51, 62 (2), Green 63, Thos. 383, Wm. 51 (2), 62 (2)

Bellamy, Wm. 241 (2), 362

Bennett, Philemon 150, 299

Biggs 381

Bilbro, B. 130, 231, Bereman 143, Dianner 130

Binam, Drewry 221

Bird, Jas. 174

Bisset -0-

Blackwell 323

Blunt, Benj. 299, Henry 299, Wilson 153

Boddie, A. V. 223, Elijah 184, 223, 383, George 146 (2), 154, 164, 218, 223 (2), 258, 384, 385, Lucy 218, Nathan 258, 259, Wm. 110, 223 (2), 384, Willis 384

Bonds, J. 260, John 90, 340

Boon, Benj. 44, 52, 55, 125, 154, 213, Elias 143, 154, Jesse 154, Nancy 149, Raford 154, Sally 235, 236

Bottoms (Longbottoms), John L. 212, Oliver L. 212, Sam. L. 212, Wm. 61, 103

Bowden, Elias 226

Bowers, John 103

Boykin, Hardy 167

Boymon, Drewry 367, Drewry S. 370

Bradford, Jas. 46

Bradl(e)y, Jas. 43, 50, 51, 83. 106, 160, 161, 209, 270, 392

Brantley 116, 377, Alinge 181 (2), Allen 377, Sherod 327, 377

Braswell 191, 343, 360, Arch. 261, Benj. 30, 119, 171, Britain 140 (2), Demsey 34. 210, 211, 261, 280, 342, Eliz. 256, Jacob 4 (2), 210 (3), 223, 261, Jesse 140, 210, 242, John 156, 157, Sampson 18, 335, Sam. 43, Wm. 129, 315

Braydie 299

Brewer, Hardy 72

Bridge(r)s, Benj. 120 (3), 305, 382, Betty 13. Drewry 10. Henry 383, John 13, 383, Sam. 44, 55, Wm. 125, 383, Wm. B. 196

Brittain (Bretain), Martha 14, 143

Brogdon, Edw. T. 232

Broughton, Jesse 122

Brown, Jas. 148. Jeremiah 209

Bru(i)ce. Jas. 50, 231 (2)

Bryant (Briant, Breant), Benj. 86, 112, 251, Sam. 251, Thos. 248, Wm. 247 (2), 248, 252 (2), 305, 350, 392 (2)

Bunn 389, Benj. 126. 193. 194 (2), Bennett 272 (2), Burwell (Burrell) 8. 114, Charity 34, 268. David 106, 194, 390. Drewcilla 183 (2), 184 (2), 272, 321 (2), Henry 34 (2), 78, 106 (2), 268 (2), 396, Jeremiah 34 (2), 268 (2), Joel 8, 124, Piety 34 (2), 268 (2),

Davis 150, Abel 25, 124, 216, 217, Arch. 215, 301, Benj. 73, Eliz. 215 (2), John 73, 74, Ruthy 235 (2), 236, Thos. 64, 73, 74
Deans (Deens), Bartley 289, 389, 390 (2), 391 (2), Jas. 260 (2), John 384, Lewis 390, Thos. 103, Willis 143
Denson 299, Jethro 46, John 188, Massey 3, 7
Derring, Jas. 354, 355, John 355
Devaughan, Mirull 148, Sam. 148, 161
Devenport 324
Dew, Duncan 72, John 72 (2), 89, 142, 323, 328, 329, 346, 358, 378
Dickenson, Jacob 59 (2)
Dorman, Michael 85 (2)
Dortch 188, Wm. 173, 182, 219, 246
Dozier 299, Acerilla 1, John 1, Wm. 1
Drake 150, Benj. 48 (2), 154, Brittain 282, Edwin 19, Fanny 150, 382, Frances 150, Francis 254, 255, 317, Harty 282, Hines 96, 291 (2), J. H. 324, Jacky 150, Jas. 44, 48 (2), 49, 55 (2), 254, 255, John 125, John H. 48, 150 (2), 154, 218, 232 (2), 311, 354, 371, 382, 383, John Hodges 49, Matthew 109, 145, 204 (2), 254, 255 (2), 282 (2), 291, Melbre 48, Milbrey 256, Rich. 307, Silas 48 (2), 49, Temperance 254, Wm. 184, 204, 363
Drewry, Jas. 145 (2), 184 (2), 256, Sam. 145 (2)
Driver, Dempsey 174, Mary 140, Moses 254, 255, Polley 140, Reddick 140
Duck 289, 310, 390, 391, Jacob 339
Dunn 161, Wm. 92 (2), 176

—E—

Earp, Jos. 161
Eatman 140, Irvin 260, Noel 260
Edmondson, Wm. 46, 47
Edmunds, Lucy 20
Edwards, Brawn 99, E. 196, 279 (2), Edwin 313, 316, Grace 262, Solomon 273, 344 (2), Thos. 61
El(e)y, Benj. 23, 37, 189
Ellen (Flewellen) 243, 261, 342, L. F. 182, 264, 336, 337, 338, Lod. F. 32, 40, 211 (2), 317, 335, Wm. 129
Etheridge (Etheredge), Jeremiah 195, 201 (2), 381, John 135, Mathew 135, Peter 258, 259
Evans (Evins), Chas. 73, 74, David 295, 315 (2), John 166, 277, Wm. 63
Exum 273, Jos. 72, 80, 96 (2), Priscilla 96, Thos. 175, Wm. 29

—F—

Faulcon, John 354
Ferrell, A. 176, Ansel 0 (2), Hutson 176, Jas. 160, 165, 176
Finch, Claborne 387
Flood, Enoch 281
Flowers 148, Benj. 167, 348, 379 (2), 389, Eatman 379, 389, Jacob 56, John 11, 145
Flyod, F. 297, Federick 232, Mourning 232, Newet 232, Penuel 95, 232
Folsom, Ebenezer 110

Hatten, Lewis 282, Lewis Lamkin 15, Peter 72, Wm. 282
Hawkins, Benj. 59, 70
Hays, Jos. 70
Hedgepeth 239, Charity 52, Peter 52 (2)
Hendrick, Eliz. 247, 252, Isaac 285, 392 (2), Signal 252, 392, Wm. 119 (2), 247 (2), 252, Willie 252
Hickman, Theophilus 209
Hicks, Asa(y) 132 (2), Wm. 132 (2)
Hiett, Joab 353
Hill, Green 384, Lewis 120 (2), Sion 119 (2)
Hilliard 232, Eliz. 215, Henry 133 (2), Isaac 42, 109, 110, 133 (3), 134, 221, 222, 369, Jas. 19, 133 (4), 134, 184, 215 (2), 221 (2), 282, Jeremiah 5, 76, 101, John 5, 133 (2), 134, 221 (2), 318, 372, 393, Nancy 215, Robt. C. 133 (2), 134 (2), 136, 137, 138, 221 (2), 222, Wm. 133 (2), 215 (2)
Hilsman, B. 238
Hines 291, Alex. 36, Bryant 345, Eliz. 36, Fred. 65, 66, Fred. B. 173, 244, Hartwell 36, 291, 349 (2), 352 (2), 370, Henry 5, 164, 393, Isham 36, 43, Lewis 352, Littleberry 20, 184 (2), 370
Hinton, Chris. 109, Stp. 276, 277
Hogg, Levy 380
Holland 277, 295, Daniel 70, Eliz. 357, Rich. 70, 207 (2), 276, 277, 326, 356, 357, 386
Hollemon, Josiah 354, 355
Hopkins 297, Alsey 293, 394, Jos. 130, 297, 365 (2), 374 Wm. 327
Horn, A. 272, Edith 76, Edw. 103, Grantham 130, Hardy 289, Henry 100, 101, 103, 110 (2), 380, Isaac 328, Jacob 76 (2), 100, 101, 103, Jeremiah 103, Michael 97 (2), 145, 182, 322, Nathan 76, 100, 101, Thos. 97, 99, 103, 110, 130 (2), 133, 148, Thos. 310, Wm. 289, 390
House, Jacob 96
Hunt 70, 159, David 153 (3), Disey 335, Hardy 200, 319, Jesse 136, 264, John 51, 54, 62, L. 383, Marget Braswell 16, Marv 16, Mathew 164, Meriny 13, Nancy 200, 319 (2), Nath. 221, Telitha 153, Temperance Braswell 16, Thos. 16, Wm. 321
Hunter, Arch. 19, Cordal 40, 199, 273, 274, 344, 376, Drew 40, Jas. 219, 376, Priscilla 40, Thos. 43, 113, 136, 264, 385
Hutcheson, John 361

—I—

Ing, Chris. 76

—J—

Jackson, Ann 59, Eliz. 54, 180, George 61, Newman 177 (2), 180, Sally 177, Sarah 177, Wm. 51, 54 (2)
Jinkins, John 76, 271
Johnson, Jacob 238, 239, 279, 313, Josiah 52, Stephen 380
Jones 31, 130, Barbary 99, Bennet 38, Cooper 38, Cullin Carter 197, 333, Edmund 25, 27 (2), 216 (2), 217, 301, Fedrick 377, John 42, 54, 66, 95, 133, Jos. Perrin 365, Perrin 297, Robt. 238, 372, Thos. C. 184, Vilette 38, Wm. 197, 216, 217, 301, 332, 333
Jorda(i)n, Edy 11, Lewis 47, Wm. 260, 327
Joyner (Joiner) 233, Burrell 166, Cornelius 72, 278, Curtis 278,

Millhouse, Henry 215, Sam. 215
Mitchell, Henry 41, 240, Sam. 124
Moody, Wm. 347
Moore, Edw. 56, 110, 122, Jas. 51, 130, Wade 85, Wm. 205
Morgan, John 132, 163 (2), 208, Wm. 325
Morris(s) 249, 272, Acquilla 33, Asa 223, Ashael 140, 196, 226,
    Demsey 140, Jesse 140, 223, 226, 381, John 99, 323, Thos. 109

—N—

Nelson, Humphrey 177 (2), 180, Jas. 246, Sarah 177, 180 (2)
Newby, Jesse 271
Newsom, Isaac 79
Newton, Benj. 76
Nichols 339, Ann 391, Benj. 391, David 390, 391, Jacob 167, Jas. 351,
    Jeremiah 348, 351, 390 (2), 391 (2), Jesse 265, 390
Nicholson, Abs. 69, Edw. 105, 115, Jas. M. 300, John 169, Jolian
    153, Jos. W. 69, Josiah 17, 69, 99, 173, Lemuel 7, 24, 300, Theo-
    philus 17, Wright 69
Nicol, Benj. 265
Nolleboy, Barnaby 207, 208
Nuttall, John 330

—O—

Odom, Jacob 225
O'Neal 240, Wm. 279
Owens, Elias 161 (2), 171, John 160, 171 (2), Temperance 162 (2),
    Wm. 160, 161, 162, 165, 171, 198

—P—

Parker, Francis 145, 184, John 184, Penny 61, Wm. 184
Parks, Moses 260, Wm. 260 (5)
Parrott, Eliz. 375, John 375
Pas(s)more 226, 239, John 77, 115, 223, Lucy 77
Peele (Peel), Jesse 265, 339. 348. 351 (2), John 339, 348, 351
Perry, Ben 120, Brittain 327, 377, Ephraim 294, Nath. 294, Sion
    165, 171, Wm. 31, 159
Phillips, Ephraim 121, Exum 369, 392, Fedrick 362. Jethro 9, Jos.
    9, 89 (2), 329, 378, Sherrod 89, 121, Tom 367, 370
Pippin, Isaac 160
Pitman. Joel 376, John 246
Pitts, Noel 13, Patsey 383
Plummer. Kemp 32
Poland (Poulan, Powland) 180. John 166, 368, 386, 394, Wm. 21
Pollock 275
Pollox 70
Pone Hardyman 76, Lazarus 72, Micajah 96 (2), Rebekah 76, West
    76
Port(r)is, Ira 25, 301 (2), Jeremiah 124. 301, John 124, 301 (2)
Powell 188, Alanson 83, 135, 136, 137, 138, 179, 345, Danell 104,
    Elijah 115, John 83, Nathan 345, 366, 371, Nath. 136, 137, Samp-
    son 92, 95, 129, Wiley 135
Pridgen, A. 153, 178, Abijah 146, 250, 258 (2), 259, David 67 (2),

82, 116, 368, Drewry 82, 219, Hardy 116, Martha 178, Wm. 85 (2)
Pusley 381
Pussell, Eliz. 201, Hardy 201

—R—

Rackley, Mathew 164, Parson 250 (2), Silas 201
Ransom(e) 217, Clevers 124
Ratley 392
Read Jas. 153, Jesse 382
Redding, Rich. K. 367, 370
Reese, Randolph 76, 80 (2), 100, 101, Roger 26, 248, 306, 334, 381
Renlow, Josiah 267, Noel 267
Revel 182, Barnabas 286, Mathew 286
Rice, Hopkins 181, 326, 368, John 181, 347
Richards, John 112
Richardson, Apple White 92, John 223, 249, 311, 374, Wm. 77, 374 (2)
Ricks 114, 141, 225, 233, Abraham 26, Alex. Irwin 141 (2), D. 233, David 28, 182, 183, 184, 207, 219, 243, 264, 321, 322, 326, 330, 346, 359, Eli 141, 234, Jas. 193, 194, Joel 141, Jonathan 26, John 207, 233, Micajah 326, Mourning 295, Rhoda 59, Wm. 78, 207, Willie 26
Rob(b)ins, Stephen 15, Wm. 200, 203, 319 320
Robertson 188
Roblin 161
Rogers 203, 239, 249, Jacob 44, 55, 223, 226, Jas. 92 (2), Peleg 86, 92, R. 77, Robt. 106, 215, Thos. 92 (2), 293 (2), 294, 395
Rose 352, Francis 91 (2), Thompkins 359, Wm. 349
Ross, Wm. 30, 149, 241, 368
Row, Wm. 99. 351
Rutherford 327

—S—

Sanderford, Sam. 202, 325, Wm. 91
Sanders 390, Cornelius 167, John 99 (2), 389, Sion 167, 339, 348, Thos. 265, Wm. 167, 339, 348
Savage, Barbara 83, Drewry 130
Saward, Edmund 170
Screws, Jas. 39, John 39, Littleton 341 (2)
Selah, Jos. 61, 64
Sellers, Martha 116, Nancy 172, Wm. 116 (2), Wright 172
Shearnean, John 46
Shelton, Burrel 99
Sheppard, John 82 (2)
Sherod, Jordan 262 (2), 302 (2)
Shine, Daniel 216, 217
Sikes, Mathew 14, 312, Mourning 259
Sills, D. 213 (2), 233, 296, 311, 316, David 196, 223, 235, 236, 237 (2), 238 (2), 239 (2), 249 (2)
Sketo, Wm. 76 (2)
Skinner, Sam. 94, 225, Wm. 94
Smell(e)y 140, Everard 148, John 117, Moses 140
Smith, Benj. 64, 85, 166, Bennet 16, 22, Betty 99, Brittain 84 (2),

85, Moses 109, Rich. 260, Sam. 170, 206, 211, 219, 227, 228, 261, 273, 284, 291, 294, 304, 315, 344 (2), 349, 352, 366, 371, Wm. 51, 69, 99

Sorsby 218, Alex. 17, 29, 184, 209, 341, 369, 371, 372, Sam. 66

Speight, John 175

Stallions, Moses 122

Stevens, Jeremiah 6, 28 (2), John 28, Robt. 113

Steward, Nat 7

Stokes, Arch. 112, Tabitha 181, Thos. 235, 236, 237

Sto(o)tt, Ebenezer 385, John 167, 195

Strickland, 0, 94, 290, 340, Aley 205, Arnold 293, 294, 395, Bennet 316, Bolen 332, 333, Carrolus 316, David 136, 182, 385 Gideon 208, 245, 251, Hardy 90, 205, Henry 316, Jacob 90, 105, 209, Jesse 325, Lazarus 122 (2), Mark 90, 132 (2), 208, 245, Noah 6, 37, 197 (2), 316, 332 (2), 333, 334, Osborne 28, 245, 251, Polley 293, Simon 293, 294, Thos. 132

Strother, Jas. 30

Stuart, Lewis 230

Sumner, Dorothy 282 (3), Duke W. 8, 255, Jos. John 254, 255, 282, Mary 255, Polly 255

Sutton, George 384 (2), Lemuel 260

—T—

Tann, Benj. 163

Tanner, John 56

Taylor, 291, 349, Cornelius 298, Daniel 231, 298, David 361, 362 Dempsey 5, 17, 19, 369, Drewry 67, 306, Edw. 190, 205, Ethelred 110, Fort 306, Hannon 387, J. 28, 132, Taylor, J. 252. Jesse 275, 362, Joel 219 (2) John 132 (2), 159, 162, 163, (2), 340, John C. 219, Jonathan 361, 362, Josiah 361, 362, Kinchen 11, 17, 173, Mary 361, 362, Mills 76, 361 (3), 362 (4), Orren 361, 362, Reuben 352, 362, Rich. 375, Salley 375, Simeon 23, 189 Treasy 361, 362, Wm. 132, 161, 270 (2), Willie 28, Wilson 117, 306

Terrell, Timothy 266

Thomas 238, 365, Jesse 59 (2), Jethro 106, Jonathan 175, Keziah 272, Mary 110, Micaiah 52, 57, 59 (2), 67. 70, 78, 295 (2), 297, Rich. 59, 106, 129, Sam. 94. Widow 133, Wm. 215 (2)

Thompson, Angellia 66, Robt. 66 (2), Trimagen 44

Thorp 304, Jesse 175, 273, 318, Priscilla 175

Tillery, John 72

Tisdale, Elisha 331, Henry 331, Philander 244 (2), 321, 342, Warren 331, Wm. 153

Trevathan, Mathew 291, 349 (2), 352, Willis 291

Trougdale. Jas. 285. Robt. 285

Trouchton, Swan 69

Tucker, Barna 356, 357, Benj. 50, 51, 143 (2), Corbin 298, Corlean 363, Rhodey 49, Thos. 50. 51, 83, Woody 143, Zachariah 22

Turner. Eliz. 135, Julian 135, Lazarus 135, Nancy 135, Robt 109

—U—

Underwood, Emanuel 127. Jacob 66. John 358, 367, 370 (2), Levi 367 (2), Levi S. 346, Malachi 283, Nancy 358

—V—

Vanlandingham, Jas. 83, 127, Thos. 83, 127
Vaugh(a)n, Stephen 178 (3), **386**
Vester, Benj. 375, Charity 375, Elijah 375, Michael 195, 364, 384, Solomon 146, 195, Wm. 195, Wm. 375
Vick, Asael 191, Benj. 22, 191, 287 (2), 335, 336, 337, 338, 343, Eley 150, Elijah 150, 335, 336, 337, 338, Eliz. 233 (2), Henry 94, 206, 225, Jacob 132, 211, 337, John 27, 34, 150, 166, 191 (2), 243, 302, 335 (2), 336 (2), 337 (2), 338, 342, John W. 262, Jos. 233, 243, Lewis 42, 60 (2), 180, Mary 34, 264 (2), 360, Mary 373, Nathan 225, Rich. 191, 287, Tabitha 60, Wilson 124, 125
Viverett, Micajah 10

—W—

Walker 239, Daniel 209, 219 (2), 321, 322, 345, Henry 20, 244, 345, Joel 313, Wm. 261
Wall, Wm. 285
Wallace, John 91
Ward, Francis 54, 74, 301, Willis 356
Warren 381, Daniel 247, John 157, 189, Mary 247
Watkins 304, Henry 124, Isaac 227, Jas. 72 (2), 109, John 80 (3), 236, Leimon 267, Peter 267
Watson 385, Chas. 109
Weakley, Robt. 177
Webb, Ann 93, Bowen 200, 203, Brown 319, 320, J. 93, Laban 200, 203, 319, 320, Stephen 52, 93
Wells (Wills), Daniel 67, John 281, Solomon 67 (2), Steven 219, 262, 302
West, John 145
Wester, Arthur 114, Hardy 114
Westray, Benj. 233, Michael 363, S. 99, Sam. 72, 183, 198, 219, 225, 295, Wm. 286
Wheless 239, Wm. 249 (2), 296, 297, 311 (2), 365
Whiddon (Whitton), John 57, Wm. 103
Whitaker 371, Eli B. 136, 137, 138, 179 (2), Matthew C. 137, 138, 179
White, 321, Jos. 42 (3), 110, 125, Little Berry 195, 298, 312 364, Thos. 19 (2), 393
Whitehead, 169, 188, 299, Abiar 91, Arthur 66 (3), 299, 324, Benj. 70, 157, 158, Bennett 65, 66, Capt. 69, 99, Chas. 70, 157, 158, Eliz. 65, 66, Henry 91, 275, 300, Jas. 157, 158, Jonathan 157, 158, 209, 284, Jos. 158, Lazarus 79, 341, Mathew 157, Nathan 173, 324, (2), Rahab 275, Thos. 67, 91 (2), 95, Wm. 65, 66 (4), 157, 158, 329, 378
Whitehouse, John 57, 78, 207
Whitfield 277, 385, Arch, 321, Arch G. 246, Benj. 18, 19, 133, 136, 183, 184, 243, 264, 287 (3), 321 (3), 343, 359 (2), 373, 385, Delilah 182, 183, 184, 219, 322, G. 183, Guilford G. 246, 321, Hardy 78, Hardy G. 18, 141, 244, 321, John Thomas Griffin 321, Reuben 57 (2), 276, 357 (3), Thos. 106, Willie 183, 385, Willie G. 18, 136,

264, 321, 335, 336, 337, 338, 359, 373
Whitl(e)y 114, Drury 121 (2), George 121, Joel 256, Josiah 256,
    Rachel 124, 362, Solomon 135, Thos. 124 (2), Wiley 256
Wiggins, Elijah 127, Thos. 136, 137, 138
Wiggs, Jordan 294
Wilder 146, Moses 146, Robt. 86
Wilhite 238, 239, 249
William 51, 62, 271, Arthur 251, 340, Bersheba 9, Cooper 215, 235
    (2), 236, 313, Drewry 140, 148, 162, 331, 380, 394, Eli 178, 386
    (3), Henry 326, Jas. 19, 136. 338, Jane (Jean) 186, 187, John 9,
    15, 55, 109, 133, 134, 150, 186, 187, 282 (2), Jonas 9, 11, 142,
    Mary 326 (3), Mathew J. 313, Michale 56, N. 142, Nathan 130,
    Philander 84, 85, 326, Pilgrim 28, 130, 190, Pilgrim L. 140, 145,
    148, Pride 326, Robt. 41, 340, Roland 115 (2), 130, 190, 219, 316,
    Sam. 18, 72, 186, 187, Simon 149, 259
Williamson 289, 310, 339, Jos. 265, 351
Williford, Jas. 88, John 21
Willis 191, Thos. 136, 385
Wilson, Edw. 43, 191, 359, 373, Robt. 385
Wimberly 315, George 295
Winbo(u)rn, Abraham 347, David 387 (2)
Winstead 307, D. 323, David 10, 190 (2) 266, 268, 271, 368, Sam.
    271, Thos. 280
Wood, Bennett 124, Misael 74, Newton 14
Woodward, Aaron 242, Cader 167, 339, 348, Daniel 242 (2), 324,
    David 140, 242, Isaac 167, 339, 348, Jas. 295, Thos. 339
Woodruff, Martha N. 213 (2), Wm. 213
Worbinton, John 242 (2)
Wren, Howell 41
Wright, John 300, Wm. 221, 275, 393 (3)

—Y—

York, 172, Edw. 247 (2), 350, John 156
Young, Robt. 42, 150

DB 5-0   STATE of N. C. grant to ANSEL FERRELL by Gov. J. Turner, Dec. 10, 1804, a tract of 66 acres adjoining Strickland, Bisset, and said Ferrell.

DB 5-1   BILLS OF SALE 1805.   WILLIAM DOZIER of Nash Co. to AVERILLA DOZIER of same, March 11, 1785. for 105 pds. Virginia money two negroes.   Wit: W. S. Mearns and John Dozier.

DB 5-2   WILLIAM BATCHELOR of Halifax Co. to WILLIAM JOHN BATCHELOR HARPER of Nash Co., Feb. 11, 1805, for $350.00 one negra woman and child.   Wit: None.

DB 5-3   MATTHEW FREEMAN of Nash Co. to MASSEY DENSON of same, Nov. 12, 1803, for 33 pds. Virginia money one negro boy.   Wit: Wm. McGregor and John D. Cooper.

DB 5-4   JACOB BRASWELL, JR. and JACOB BRASWELL, SR. of Nash Co. to JAMES W. ALSTON of Halifax Co., Feb. 19, 1805, for 80 pds. Virginia money one negro woman.   Wit: John Atkison.

DB 5-5   JEREMIAH HILLIARD of Edgecombe Co. to JOHN HILLIARD of Nash Co., March 18, 1805, for $750.00 four negro slaves.   Wit: Henry Hines and Dempsey Taylor.

DB 5-6   JEREMIAH STEVENS of Nash Co. to NOAH STRICKLAND, Jan. 12, 1804, for $400.00 one negro boy. Wit: Robert Crickmore and David Crickmore.

DB 5-7   MATTHEW FREEMAN of Nash Co. to MASSE DENSON of same, Aug. 27, 1803, for 93 pds. Virginia money one negro woman.   Wit: Lemuel Nicholson and Nat Stewart.

DB 5-8   Jacob Battle. executor of ELISHA BATTLE, deceased. to JOEL BUNN, June 3, 1799, for 200 silver dollars two negros belonging to the estate of Elisha Battle.   Wit: Burrell Bunn and Duke W. Sumner.

DB 5-9   JETHRO PHILLIPS and JOSEPH PHILLIPS of Nash Co. to JONAS WILLIAMS of same. Nov. 11, 1799. for 123 silver dollars one negro woman.   Wit: John Williams and Bersheba Williams.

DB 5-10   MICAJAH VIVERETT of Nash Co. to DAVID WINSTEAD of same, March 27, 1802. for 300 silver dollars one negro girl.   Wit: Drewry Bridges and John Cockrell.

DB 5-11   JOHN FLOWERS of Nash Co. to EDY JORDAIN of Edgecombe Co., May 17, 1796, for 60 pds. Virginia money three negroes.   Wit: Jonas Williams and Kinchen Taylor.

DB 5-12   AMOS HATCHER of Nash Co. to his father, OBEDIAH HATCHER. Jan. 4, 1806, with natural love and affection all his property and chattels inclding twelve negroes.   Wit: Uriah Hatcher and George Cooper.

DB 5-13   BETTY BRIDGES of Nash Co. to her son, JOHN BRIDGES. of Sumner Co., Tennessee, but then present with her, July 29, 1806, with love and regard one negro woman.   Wit: Noel Pitts and Meriny Hunt.

DB 5-14   MARTHA BRITTAIN of Nash Co. to her beloved

friend, JESSE BASS, of same, July 20. 1806, with natural love and affection all her goods and chattels including livestock and household furniture. Wit: Newton Wood and Mathew Sikes.

DB 5-15 LEWIS LAMKIN HATTEN of Nash Co. to STEPHEN ROBBINS of Edgecombe Co., Feb. 17, 1806, for $200.00 one negro girl. Wit: John Williams and Mills Barns.

DB 5-16 MARY HUNT of Nash Co. to her beloved children, THOMAS HUNT, TEMPERANCE BRASWELL HUNT, and MARGET BRASWELL HUNT, of same, Nov. 11, 1806, for natural love and affection all her goods and chattels to be divided as directed. Wit: Archd. Griffin and Bennet Smith.

DB 5-17 JOSIAH NICHOLSON and THEOPHILUS NICHOLSON of Nash Co. to DEMPSEY TAYLOR, Feb. 4. 1806, for $950.00 four negroes. Wit: Alex. Sorsby and Kinchen Taylor.

DB 5-18 BENJAMIN WHITFIELD of Nash Co. to SAMPSON BRASWELL of same, Dec. 5, 1806, for $450.00 two negroes. Wit: Hardy G. Whitfield, Samuel Williams, and Willie G. Whitfield.

DB 5-19 James Williams, Constable of Capt. Arch Hunter's district in Nash Co., to JAMES HILLIARD, Feb. Ct. 1807, for $100.00 at public auction a negro sold as the property of THOMAS WHITE to satisfy executions obtained by Benjamin Whitfield and Dempsey Taylor against said White. Wit: Edwin Drake and Arthur Arrington.

DB 5-20 LUCY EDMUNDS to LITTLEBERRY HINES, Dec. 9, 1805, for 20 pds. one negro girl. Wit: Hardy Cain and Henry Walker.

DB 5-21 JOHN WILLIFORD of Edgecombe Co. to WILLIAM POWLAND of Nash Co., Jan. 24. 1807. for 90 pds. Virginia money one negro. Wit: Uriah Hatcher and Obediah Hatcher.

DB 5-22 ZACHARIAH TUCKER of Washington Co., Georgia gave to BENNET SMITH power of attorney to receive all money and property that fell to him at the death of his father, Dec. 17, 1806. Wit: Benjamin Vick.

DB 5-23 JOHN GLOVER of Nash Co. to HENRY HARRISON of same, Nov. 15, 1806, for 23 pds. 10 sh. Virginia money at public auction three negroes. Wit: Thomas Carter, Benjamin Ely, and Simeon Taylor.

DB 5-24 LEMUEL NICHOLSON of Nash Co. and about to move to the State of Tennessee. March 27, 1807, gave to JOSEPH ARRINGTON, JR. of Nash Co. full power of attorney in every way to take charge of his affairs in Nash Co. Wit: Arthur Arrington, John Arrington. and William Arrington.

DB 5-25 ABEL DAVIS and IRA PORTIS to EDMUND JONES, Aug. 13, 1803, full liberty to build a dam across Great Fishing Creek near Mrs. Hadley and acquitted him from any damage they might sustain. Wit: W. Arrington and William Burt, Jr.

DB 5-26 JONATHAN RICKS of Christian Farmer Co., Kentucky, Sept. 16, 1803, appointed his trusty friend, ABRAHAM RICKS, of Nash Co. as his lawful attorney to sell a certain tract of land in Nash Co. Wit: Roger Reese and Willie Ricks.

DB 5-27   EDMUND JONES of Nash Co. deed of trust to SION BECKWITH, Feb. 19, 1806, with livestock, furniture, groceries, and farm tools as security for the bond he stood to John Vick for said Jones. Wit: J. Atkinson.

DB 5-28   AMOS GANDY and DAVID RICKS to WILLIE TAYLOR, ROBERT MELTON, JEREMIAH STEVENS, and OSBORN STRICKLAND, April 17, 1806, for 270 silver dollars four negroes who were the property of John Stevens during his lifetime, having been left to him by his father, Jeremiah Stevens, in his will. Wit: J. Taylor and Pilgrim Williams.

DB 5-29   JOHN FORT of Halifax Co. to ALEXANDER SORS-BY of Nash Co., Jan. 20, 1807, for $900.00 four negroes. Wit: James Knight, Wm. Exum, and James Fort.

DB 5-30   JAMES STROTHER of Franklin Co. to BENJAMIN BRASWELL of Nash Co., Jan. 17, 1807, for $100.00   one sorrel horse.   Wit: William Ross, William Freman, John Glover, and Benja. Manning.

DB 5-31   WILLIAM PERRY of Nash Co. deed of trust to WILLIAM HARRISON, acting partner for the concern of Harrison & Jones and William Harrison & Co., July 1, 1807, for 26 pds. 18 sh. with one horse, furniture, and his present crop of corn and cotton as security. Wit: Jarvis Cone.

DB 5-32   JULIAN KING, of Nash Co. to his nephew, BENJAMIN KING, of Petersburg, Virginia. Feb. 11, 1808, with love and affection 16 negroes, for which said Benjamin had bound himself to provide a comfortable support and maintenance for Julian King during the remainder of his life. Wit: Kemp Plummer and Ld. F. Ellen.

DB 5-33   WILLIAM BATCHELOR of Halifax Co. to JAMES BATCHELOR of Nash Co., Sept. 3, 1806,   through the hands of Acquilla Morris, for $250.00 a negro girl. Wit: John Lewis and Sterling Anderson.

DB 5-34   SION BECKWITH of Nash Co. to MARY VICK of same, April 5, 1808, for $150.00 one negro boy. Wit: J. Atkinson, John Vick, and Demsey Braswell.

DB 5-34   CHARITY BUNN of Nash Co. to her four children, PIETY, WILLIAM, HENRY, and JEREMIAH. Aug. 6, 1807, with natural love and affection: (1) to PIETY BUNN one negro and furniture; (2) to son, WILLIAM BUNN, articles of furniture; (3) to son, HENRY BUNN, articles of furniture; (4) to son. JEREMIAH BUNN, one pine chest. To her three sons she gave five negroes also. Wit: Nathan Gilbert.

DB 5-36   HARTWELL HINES, admr. of the estate of ISHAM HINES, deceased, to ALEXANDER HINES at public auction Dec. 1808, one negro boy. Wit: Samuel Lewis and Elizabeth Hines.

DB 5-37   JOHN GLOVER, Constable of Nash Co. to NOAH STRICKLAND, Jan. 4, 1809, at public auction for 91 pds. 4 sh. 6 p. one negro woman and child, sold as the property of BENJAMIN ELEY, deceased. to satisfy sundry executions. Wit: Mathew Carter and D. Melton.

DB 5-38   BENNET JONES of Nash Co. to his mother, VIL-
ETTE JONES, of same, Nov. 5, 1808, for love and affection and
for the purpose of her possessing a home of her own during her
natural life, "doth lease and make over to her" a tract of 47 acres
on Little Pig Basket Creek, it being the land he bought of Sion
Beckwith and part of the old tract that belong to his father, Cooper
Jones.   Wit: Sion Beckwith, Burrell Beckwith, and Willis Beckwith.

DB 5-39   JAMES SCREWS, JR. of Nash Co. and JOHN
SCREWS to FOSTER MASON of same, Nov. 8, 1808, for 112 pds
specie one negro girl.   Wit: Wm. McGregor.

DB 5-40   PRICILLA HUNTER, DREW HUNTER, CORDAL
HUNTER, and LODRICK ELLEN, all of Nash Co., to JOEL
BATTLE of Edgecombe Co., Feb. 3, 1809, for 200 pds. one negro
man.   Wit: Jeptha Daniel.

DB 5-41   AMOS GANDY, Sheriff of Nash Co., to THOMAS
LAWRENCE, May 11, 1808, for $71.00 at public auction one negro
girl, sold as the property of HOWELL WREN by virtue of an execution obtained by Robert Williams.   Wit: Peter Arrington and
Henry Mitchell.

DB 5-42   JOSEPH WHITE, SR. of Nash Co. to JOSEPH
WHITE, JR. of same, Nov. 15, 1787, for 142 pds. 16 sh. specie a
tract of 450 acres on Whitehead's Mill Swamp adjoining Robert
Young, Joseph White, Jr., Isaac Hilliard, Kinsman Knight. and John
Chitty.   Wit: Lewis Vick, John Jones, and John Melton.

DB 5-43   ISHAM HINES of Nash Co. to SAMUEL BRAS-
WELL of same, May 11, 1788, for 80 pds. specie a tract of 233 acres
on the north side of Stony Creek adjoining Thomas Hunter, it being
part of a survey for 700 acres granted bv the State on Nov. 10,
1779.   Wit: James Bradley and Edward Wilson.

DB 5-44   JAMES BATTLE, WILLIAM BATTLE, and JOHN
BATTLE. all of Nash Co., to JAMES DRAKE of same, Dec. 6,
1787, for 60 pds. specie 103 acres adjoining his line. which formerly
belonged to Trimagen Thompson, it being part of a tract granted
to Samuel Bridgers by Earl Granville on Oct. 14, 1761.   Wit: W. S.
Mearns, Benja. Boon, and Jacob Rogers.

DB 5-46   WILLIAM EDMONDSON of Nash Co. to HENRY FREE-
MAN of same, Feb. 2, 1788, for 60 (?) current money one negro
boy.   Wit: Jethro Denson and Edmond Cooper.

DB 5-46   WILLIAM BATCHELOR of Halifax Co. to HENRY
FREEMAN of Nash Co., Jan. 1, 1788, for 105 pds. one negro boy.
Wit: James Bradford and John Shearnean.

DB 5-47   LEWIS JORDAN of Isle of Wight Co., Virginia to
WILLIAM EDMONDSON of Halifax Co., Nov. 20, 1787. for 50 pds.
specie one negro boy.   Wit: Wm. Avent and Wm. Lewis.

DB 5-48   JAMES GOODWIN of Nash Co. to JAMES DRAKE
of same, Jan. 24, 1789, for 18 pds. Virginia money one negro boy.
Wit: Silas Drake, John H. Drake. Benjamin Drake, and Patience
Cooke.

DB 5-48   JOHN GOODWIN of Nash Co. to JAMES DRAKE

of same, Jan. 12, 1788, for 12 pds. Virginia money one negro boy. Wit: Silas Drake, Benjamin Drake, and Melbre Drake.

DB 5-49 JAMES GOODWIN of Nash Co. to JAMES DRAKE, of same, Jan. 31, 1789, for 130 pds. one negro woman. Wit: John Hodges Drake, Silas Drake, and Rhodey Tucker.

DB 5-50 JAMES BRADLEY of Nash Co. to THOMAS TUCKER of same, Oct. 13, 1788, for 90 pds. a tract of 100 acres on the north side of Little Peachtree Creek adjoining Wm. Linsey. Wit: Benjamin Tucker and James Bruice.

DB 5-51 THOMAS TUCKER of Nash Co. to BENJAMIN BANES of same, Oct. 13, 1788, for 50 pds. a tract of 100 acres on the south side of Little Peachtree Creek adjoining James Moore, Henry Banes, Andrews, and William Harris. Wit: James Bradley and Benjamin Tucker.

DB 5-51 HARDY GRIFFIN of Nash Co. to WILLIAM JACKSON of same, Nov. 5, 1787, for 273 pds. 4 sh. 9 p. specie 297 acres on the north side of Swift Creek adjoining James Cooper, Williams, William Cooper, and John Hunt, it being a tract of land conveyed from John Cooper to Arthur Bell, which land was demised by said Bell to his wife. Elizabeth, during her lifetime and, at her death, he bequeathed the said land to his two sons, Benjamin and William Bell, who sold it to Hardy Griffin. Wit: Wm. S. Mearns, William Bell, and William Smith.

DB 5-52 PETER HEDGEPETH and wife. CHARITY HEDGEPETH, of Robertson Co., N. C. to JOSIAH JOHNSON of Nash Co., Nov. 15, 1787, for 100 pds. a tract of 30 acres on the south side of the Tarborough Road adjoining Stephen Webb and Micajah Thomas, which land was formerly granted to Peter Hedgepeth by patent. Wit: Denton Mann and Benjamin Boon.

DB 5-54 WILLIAM JACKSON of Nash Co. to ELIZABETH JACKSON of same, Nov. 5, 1787, for 136 pds. 12 sh. 4½ p. a tract of 148½ acres on the north side of Swift Creek adjoining James Cooper and John Hunt, it being half of a tract of land said William Jackson purchased of Hardy Griffin. Wit: W. S. Mearns and Wm. Lewis.

DB 5-54 SAMUEL MILLER of Nash Co. to FRANCIS WARD of same, Oct. 10, 1787, for 120 pds. specie a tract of 146 acres on the south side of Fishing Creek. Wit: John Jones, Jr. and John Harrison.

DB 5-55 JAMES BATTLE, WILLIAM BATTLE. and JOHN BATTLE of Nash Co. to BENJAMIN BOON of same, Nov. 6, 1787, for 200 pds. specie 327 acres adjoining James Drake and John Williams, it being part of a tract of land granted to Samuel Bridgers by Earl Granville. on Oct. 14, 1761. Wit: W. S. Mearns, James Drake, and Jacob Rogers.

DB 5-56 DUNCAN LAMON of Nash Co. to his son, ARCHIBALD LAMON. April 10, 1788. for 20 pds. and love and affection three tracts of land: (1) 200 acres on the south side of Tar River purchased of Jacob Flowers; (2) 200 acres adjoining the above tract purchased of Edward Moore; (3) 556 acres adjoining the other two tracts purchased of John Tanner. Wit: Michale Williams and John Lamon.

DB 5-57 JOSEPH ARRINGTON, Sheriff of Nash Co., to MICAJAH THOMAS, March 22, 1788, for 52 pds. 15 sh. at public auction a tract of 150 acres adjoining John Whiddon, Reuben Whitfield, Sr., Reuben Whitfield, Jr., and John Whitehouse, sold as the property of REUBIN WHITFIELD, SR. at the instance of Matthias Manning. Wit: John Battle and Solomon Cotten.

DB 5-59 JACOB DICKENSON of Edgecombe Co. to JESSE THOMAS of Nash Co., July 2, 1782, for 20 pds. specie a tract of 200 acres adjoining Jesse Thomas, Jacob Dickenson, the public road, and Micajah Thomas. Wit: James Daniel and Richard Thomas.

DB 5-59 MICAJAH THOMAS of Nash Co. to his niece, RHODA RICKS, Sept. 19, 1788, for love and affection three negroes, livestock, and furniture. Wit: Benjamin Hawkins and Ann Jackson.

DB 5-60 THOMAS HART, SR. of Nash Co. to THOMAS HART, JR. of same, May 14, 1788, for 5 pds. a tract of 210 acres adjoining Lewis Vick. Wit: Lewis Vick and Tabitha Vick.

DB 5-61 JOSEPH SELAH of Nash Co. to PENNY PARKER of same, Feb. 22, 1788. for 20 pds. specie a tract of 50 acres on the north side of Tar River adjoining John Joiner. George Jackson, Thomas Edwards and Edward Ballard. Wit: Jesse Joiner and William Bottom.

DB 5-62 BENJAMIN BELL, WILLIAM BELL, and ELIZABETH BELL of Nash Co. to HARDY GRIFFIN of same, Feb. 3, 1787, for 100 pds. Virginia money 250 acres on the north side of Swift Creek adjoining James Cooper, Williams, William Cooper and John Hunt. it being a tract of land conveyed from John Cooper to Arthur Bell. which land was demised by said Bell at his death to his wife, Elizabeth Bell. for her natural life and, at her death. he bequeathed the said land to his two sons, Benjamin and William Bell. Wit: W. S. Mearns, James Battle, and Arch Griffin.

DB 5-63 JOHN HARRISON of Nash Co. to WILLIAM EVANS of same. Aug. 9, 1788. for 46 pds. 13 sh. 4 p. a tract of 100 acres adjoining William Battle, James Cocks' former line, and Bell's former line. Wit: Green Bell and W. S. Mearns.

DB 5-64 BENJAMIN ATKINSON of Pitt Co. to JOSEPH SELAH, JR. of Nash Co., Jan. 4, 1788, for 213 pds. 13 sh. 4 p. specie a tract of 200 acres on the north side of Sapony Creek adjoining Benjamin Smith. Wit: John Atkinson and Thomas Davis.

DB 5-65 WILLIAM WHITEHEAD and wife, ELIZABETH WHIEHEAD, of Nash Co. to FREDERICK HINES of Sussex Co., Virginia, 1788, for 5 sh. a certain mill and two acres of land. one at each end of the dam, on Whitehead's Mill Swamp, bounded by Bennett Whitehead. Wit: Wm. Hall.

DB 5-66 WILLIAM WHITEHEAD and wife, ELIZABETH WHITEHEAD, of Nash Co. to FREDERICK HINES of Sussex Co., Virginia, 1788, for 600 pds. Virginia money a tract of 900 acres on Swift Creek adjoining Samuel Sorsby, John Jones, Bennett

Whitehead, and Jacob Underwood; 130 acres thereof was purchased by Arthur Whitehead, father to said William Whitehead, from a certain Robert Thompson and wife, Angellia, and another 35 acres was purchased of Said Robert Thompson and recorded in Edgecombe Co.; 700 acres, another part thereof, was granted to said William Whitehead on Oct. 9, 1783; the other part to make up the 900 acres was given to said Arthur Whitehead by his father, dying intestate and without will, the whole of the land of which said Arthur died seized and possessed descended to said Wm. Whitehead, the eldest son and heir at law. Wit: Wm. Hall.

DB 5-67 SOLOMON WELLS of Nash Co. to DAVID PRIDGEN of same, Oct. 28, 1788, for 5 pds. a tract of 25 acres on the south side of Sapony Creek adjoining Solomon Wells and David Pridgen, it being a one-third part of the land of Daniel Wells, deceased, sold by virtue of an execution obtained by Micajah Thomas. Wit: Thos. Whitehead and Drury Taylor.

DB 5-69 FAIRY McNEIL and SWAN TROUGHTON of Halifax Co. to WILLIAM SMITH of same, June 18, 1787, for 64 pds. specie 208 acres on the south side of Beaver Dam Swamp adjoining Josiah Nicholson and Capt. Whitehead, it being the tract that James McNeil bought of Wright Nicholson. Wit: Jos. W. Nicholson and Abs. Nicholson.

DB 5-70 DANIEL HOLLAND and MARY GANDY of Nash Co. to MICAJAH THOMAS of same, Sept. 16, 1788, for 120 pds. Virginia money 200 acres lying on both sides of Peachtree Creek, it being a tract granted to Richard Holland on Jan. 13, 1743. Wit: Benjamin Hawkins and Solomon Cotten.

DB 5-70 ARTHUR LASITER of Nash Co. to CHARLES WHITEHEAD of same, Nov. 24, 1788, for 80 pds specie a tract of 68 acres on the south side of Fishing Creek adjoining Joseph Hays, Lemuel Lasiter, Hunt, Benjamin Whitehead, and Pollox. Wit: John Harrison and William Lewis.

DB 5-72 SAMUEL WESTRAY, Sheriff of Nash Co., to JOHN DEW of same, Feb. 10, 1789, for 60 nds. 10 sh. at public auction a tract of 640 acres adjoining Thomas Hardy, Lazarus Pope. Crowell, and Samuel Williams, sold as the property of Peter Hatten at the instance of John Tillery, Hardy Brewer, and John Dew. Wit: Lewis Ablewis Lamkin and Duncan Dew.

DB 5-72 JAMES WATKINS of Nash Co. to WILLIAM JOINER, JR. of same, Feb. 10, 1789, for 30 pds. a tract of 101 acres near Polecat Creek adjoining Joiner and Watkins. Wit: Jos. Exum and Cornelius Joiner.

DB 5-73 SAMUEL MILLER of Nash Co. to LEWIS MILLER of same, Nov. 17, 1788, for 10 pds. 300 acres on Great Fishing Creek adjoining Thomas Davis, it being a tract originally granted to Charles Evans in 1780. Wit: John Davis and Benjamin Davis.

DB 5-74 LEWIS MILLER of Nash Co. to FRANCIS WARD of same, Dec. 8, 1788, for 50 pds. specie 300 acres on Great Fishing Creek adjoining Thomas Davis, it being a tract originally granted to Charles Evans in 1780. Wit: John Davis and Misael Wood.

DB 5-76 NATHAN HORN OF Montgomery Co. and EDITH for 20 pds. Virginia money a tract of 100 acres on the north side of Compass Creek adjoining Jacob Horn, Jeremiah Hilliard, and Hardy Harris. Wit: Randolph Reese, Anselm Harris, and Jacob Horn.

DB 5-76 WEST POPE and wife, REBEKAH POPE, of Edgecombe Co. to WILLIAM SKETO of same, Dec. 1, 1788, for 50 pds. 75 acres, lying between the Great Branch and Beach Run, adjoining the county line, Benjamin Newton, said Wm. Sketo, and Hardyman Pope, it being part of a tract granted to John Jinkins, Sr. by Earl Granville. Wit: Christopher Ing and Mills Taylor.

DB 5-77 WILLIAM RICHARDSON of Nash Co. to LUCY PASMORE of same, Oct. 16, 1788, for 16 pds. specie a tract of 50 acres adjoining R. Rogers. Wit: John Pasmore, James Massengill, and Joseph Massengill.

DB 5-78 JOHN WHITEHOUSE of Nash Co. to WILLIAM BATCHELDOR, March 21, 1788, for 60 dollars a tract of 60 acres on the south side of the road leading from Micajah Thomas' to William Ricks' and adjoining said William Batchelor. Wit: Henry Bunn and Hardy Whitfield.

DB 5-79 JACOB CAIN and wife, SALLY CAIN, of Nash Co. to BENJAMIN FOREMAN of same, Dec. 4, 1788, for 200 pds. specie a tract of 200 acres on the south side of Beaver Dam Swamp. Wit: Isaac Newsom, Milly Hackney, and Lazarus Whitehead.

DB 5-80 JOHN WATKINS of Nash Co. to RANDOLPH REESE of Edgecombe Co. Feb. 7, 1788, for 22 pds. 15 sh. specie 91 acres on both sides of Kirby's Creek adjoining Watkins, Reese, Folsom Road, and Thomas Road, it being part of a tract conveyed to said Watkins by deed on Oct. 30, 1786. Wit: Jos. Exum and Anselm Harris.

DB 5-82 JOHN SHEPPARD of Nash Co. to DREWRY PRIDGEN of same, Jan. 19, 1789, for 50 pds. Virginia money 150 acres on the south side of Sapony Swamp on the Great Branch, it being part of a tract that said John Sheppard bought of Thomas Lewis. Wit: David Pridgen and Elizabeth Allen.

DB 5-83 JAMES VANLANDINGHAM of Nash Co. to THOMAS VANLANDINGHAM of Edgecombe Co. Feb. 16, 1788, for 40 pds. specie a tract of 100 acres on the north side of the Long Swamp. Wit: Allanson Powell and John Powell.

DB 5-83 SAMUEL BARLOW of Nash Co. to JAMES BRADLY of same, Nov. 14, 1788, for 30 pds. a tract of 100 acres on the north side of Little Peachtree Creek adjoining Thomas Tucker, William Lindsey, and the county line. Wit: John Andrews and Barbara Savage.

DB 5-84 BRITTAIN SMITH of Nash Co. to PHILANDER WILLIAMS of same, March 4, 1789, for 40 pds. Virginia money 125 acres on the south side of Tar River adjoining the racepath, Lamon, and the road, it being part of a tract sold to Dixon Marshall under the Confiscation Act and conveyed to Brittain Smith. Wit:

Lewis Ablewis Lamkin and Charity Lamkin.

DB 5-85 BENJAMIN SMITH of Nash Co. to PHILANDER WILLIAMS of same, Feb. 24, 1789, for 200 pds. Virginia money 180 acres on the south side of Tar River adjoining Gainey, it being part of a tract granted to Michael Dorman on Feb. 24, 1740, conveyed by said Dorman to Wm. Pridgen, deceased, and "bequeathed by the said deceased unto the said Wm. Pridgen to Party to these Presents in his last will and testament." Wit: Brittain Smith and Wade Moore.

DB 5-86 WILLIAM CHAPMAN. JR. of Nash Co. to JOHN CHAPMAN of same, Nov. 23, 1787, for 30 pds. a tract of 170 acres on the north side of Turkey Creek, it being all the land on the north side of of Turkey Creek that Peleg Rogers obtained in a patent from Earl Granville. Wit: Robert Wilder, Benjamin Bryant, and William Chapman, Sr.

DB 5-88 JAMES BARREN of Edgecombe Co. to JAMES WILLIFORD, Dec. 29, 1788, for 116 pds. two negro boys. Wit: Redmun Bunn and Henry Lancaster.

DB 5-89 JOSEPH PHILLIPS of Nash Co. to his son, SHERROD PHILLIPS, of same, May 11, 1789. for love and affection a tract of 100 acres on the south side of Mill Branch lying in both Nash and Edgecombe counties adjoining John Dew and Joseph Phillips. Wit: John Cockrell.

DB 5-90 WILLIAM HAMMONS of Nash Co. to WILLIAM ANDREWS of same, April 9, 1789, for 10 pds. specie 15 acres on the south side of Turkey Creek adjoining said Andrews and James Culpepper, it being part of a tract whereon said Hammons then lived. Wit: James Culpepper, Christopher Culpepper, and Jeremiah Culpepper.

DB 5-90 JACOB STRICKLING of Nash Co. to MARK STRICKLING of same, Feb. 1, 1788, for 40 pds. a tract of 640 acres on Haw Branch. Wit: Jno. Bonds and Hardy Strickland.

DB 5-91 FRANCIS ROSE of Nash Co. to THOMAS WHITEHEAD of same, April 1, 1789, for 50 pds. 50 acres adjoining William Sandeford, Henry Whitehead, and Thomas Whitehead. it being part of a tract granted to Francis Rose. Wit: Darrell Conn, John Wallace, and Abiar Whitehead.

DB 5-92 WILLIAM DUNN of Franklin Co. and JAMES ROGERS of Nash Co. to BURREL BELL of Wake Co., Nov. 19, 1787, as executors to the estate of THOMAS ROGERS, deceased, land left by him in his will for said Dunn and said Rogers to sell. for 175 pds. 1 sh. four tracts of land on Turkey Creek containing 1250 acres: (1) 600 acres including the land and plantation whereon the said Thomas Rogers, deceased, formerly lived. as entered in the office of Earl Granville; (2) 400 acres in the office of the State, adjoining his own line; (33) 150 acres entered in the office of the State adjoining Sampson Powell and Peleg Rogers; (4) 100 acres entered with the State, on Rogers' Branch. Wit: Lodwick Alford, William Chapman. Jr., and Apple White Richardson (female).

DB 5-93 STEPHEN WEBB and wife, ANN WEBB, of Nash

Co. to JESSE LAWRENCE of same, Feb. 2, 1789, for 80 pds. a tract of 230 acres adjoining Michael Councel and Collins' Road. Wit: J. Webb and John Carrel.

DB 5-94 JOHN HARRELL of Nash Co. to SAMUEL THOMAS of Gates Co., May 20, 1788, for 40 pds. a tract of 100 acres on the south side of Stony Creek adjoining Henry Vick, Lamon's Road. and Strickland. Wit: William Skinner and Samuel Skinner.

DB 5-95 WILLOUGHBY MANNING of Nash Co. to PENUEL FLOYD of same, May 13, 1788, for 20 pds. specie 200 acres on the south side of Little Peachtree Creek adjoining Benjamin Manning, it being part of a tract granted to Sampson Powell. Wit: W. S. Mearns, Thos. Whitehead, and John Jones, Jr.

DB 5-96 MICAJAH POPE of Nash Co. to HINES DRAKE of same, March 31, 1788. for 55 pds. a 150 acre plantation on the north side of Compass Creek adjoining Joseph Exum, it being a tract that the said Micajah Pope purchased of Jacob House on Sept. 5, 1789, Wit: Jos. Exum and Priscilla Exum.

DB 5-97 MICHAEL HORN of Nash Co. to THEOPHILUS COLEMAN of same, March 2. 1789, for 20 pds. specie a tract of 100 acres on the east side of Lott's Branch adjoining the county line. Wit: Thomas Horn and Michael Horn, Jr.

DB 5-99 WILLIAM SMITH of Halifax Co. and BETTY SMITH to BURREL SHELTON of same. April 18, 1789, for 200 pds. specie a 208 acre plantation on the south side of Beaver Dam Swamp adjoining Josiah Nicholson and Capt. Whitehead, it being a tract in Nash Co. granted to Fanny McNeil. Wit: Jos. Arrington, S. Westray, and Brawn Edwards.

DB 5-99 JOHN SANDERS of Nash Co. to BARBARY JONES of same, March 30, 1789, for 16 pds. a tract of 80 acres on the Flat Branch adjoining William Row, Jethro Harrison, and said John Sanders. Wit: Thomas Horn. John Morris, and Elijah Coleman.

DB 5-100 NATHAN HORN of Montgomery Co. to JACOB HORN of Nash Co., Nov. 29. 1788, for 8 pds. 100 acres on the north side of Compass Creek adjoining Henry Horn, it being parts of two tracts of land granted to Stephen Hamlin and Wilson Curl. Wit: Hardy Harris, Randolph Reese. and Anselm Harris.

DB 5-101 NATHAN HORN of Montgomery Co. to JACOB HORN of Nash Co.. Nov. 29, 1788. for 10 pds. a tract of 100 acres on Compass Creek adjoining Hardy Harris, Jeremiah Hilliard, and Henry Horn. Wit: Hardy Harris, Anselm Harris, and Randolph Reese.

DB 5-103 HENRY HORN of Wayne Co. to his grandson, JACOB HORN, of Nash Co.. Aug. 30, 1790, for love and affection the 330 acre plantation on the north side of Compass Creek whereon he then lived. Wit: Thomas Horn, Edward Horn, and Jeremiah Horn.

DB 5-103 WILLIAM LONGBOTTOM of Nash Co. to JOHN BOWERS of same, March 30, 1787, for 46 pds. 13 sh. 4 p. specie a tract of 484 acres on Sapony Swamp adjoining Matthias Manning, John Manning, and William Whitton. Wit: Solomon Carter and Thomas Deans.

DB 5-104 NICHOLAS BAGGET of Nash Co. and ELIZA-
BETH BAGGET to GRANDBERRY BAGGET, July 25, 1790, for
5 sh. a tract of 100 acres on the north side of Swift Creek adjoining
Nicholas Bagget, Hackney, and Cooper. Wit: Radph Mason and
Danell Powell.

DB 5-105 JACOB STRICKLAND of Nash Co. to JAMES
CONE of same, Nov. 6, 1786, for 60 pds. specie a tract of 480 acres
on the south side of Turkey Creek. Wit: Edward Nicholson and
Joshua Cone.

DB 5-106 JETHRO THOMAS and JAMES BRADLY of Nash
Co. to HENRY BUNN of same, Aug. 16, 1787, for 25 pds. a tract
of 100 acres on the north side of Peachtree Creek adjoining Henry
Bunn, Richard Thomas, and Thomas Whitfield. Wit: David
Bunn and Robert Rogers.

DB 5-107 HARDY JOINER and NATHAN JOINER of Nash
Co. to LEWIS JOINER of same, Jan. 19, 1790, for 40 pds. a tract
of 150 acres adjoining Hardy Joiner, Nathan Joiner, and William
Joiner. Wit: John Barnes and John Lamon.

DB 5-109 THOMAS MORRIS of Nash Co. to MOSES SMITH
of Halifax Co., May 28, 1787, for 30 pds. specie a tract of 94 acres
on Pig Basket Creek adjoining John Williams, Matthew Drake,
Charles Watson, and Isaac Hilliard, which said land was granted
to Robert Turner by the State on Jan. 27, 1783. Wit: Christopher
Hinton and James Watkins.

DB 5-110 HENRY HORN of Wayne Co. to ISAAC HILL-
IARD of Nash Co., Aug. 11, 1789, for 67 pds. 10 sh. specie 150
acres on Whitehead's Mill Swamp and Ready Branch, it being that
part of the land conveyed from Ebenezer Folsom to Henry Horn
whereon Mary Thomas lived and died, adjoining Joseph White.
Wit: Ethelred Taylor, William Boddie, and Thomas Horn.

DB 5-110 THOMAS LEWIS of Nash Co. to JACOB LEWIS,
June 1, 1779, for 40 pds. proc. money a tract of 60 acres on the
south side of Tar River at the mouth of Southwell's Creek and the
grist mill, also. Wit: Edward Moore, Samuel Carter, and Jesse
Barker.

DB 5-112 BENJAMIN LANE of Nash Co. to BENJAMIN
BREANT, Feb. 22, 1787, a gift of one negro man. Wit: Archibald
Stokes and John Richards.

DB 5-113 ROBERT STEVENS of Nash Co. to MICAL AT-
KINSON Oct. 12, 1786, for 62 pds. 8 sh. 233 acres on the north side
of Stony Creek adjoining Thomas Hunter, it being part of a survey
of 700 acres granted by the State on Nov. 10, 1779. Wit: Jos. J.
Clinch and James Kenedy.

DB 5-114 ARTHUR WESTER of Nash Co. to his son,
HARDY WESTER, of same, Feb. 10, 1792, for love and affection
a tract of 100 acres adjoining Whitly and Ricks. Wit: Burwell
Bunn and Lewis Curl.

DB 5-115 EDWARD NICHOLSON of Nash Co. to ROLAND
WILLIAMS of same. Mav 20, 1790, for 50 pds. a tract of 100 acres
on the north side of Little Swamp adjoining Said Williams. Wit:
Benja. Cobb and Wm. Hackney.

DB 5-115 SION BASS of Nash Co. to JOHN PASSMORE of same, June 10, 1780, for 100 pds. a tract of 100 acres adjoining Passmore, it being part of a grant to Sion Bass in 1779. Wit: Elijah Powell, Abraham Bass, and Mary Bass.

DB 5-116 WILLIAM SELLERS and wife, MARTHA SELL-ERS, of Nash Co. to PETER BALLARD of same. Aug. 21, 1787, for 100 pds. a tract of 200 acres on Sapony Creek adjoining Brantley, it being part of a grant to said William Sellers on June 12, 1779. Wit: David Pridgen and Hardy Pridgen.

DB 5-117 DUNCAN LAMON of Nash Co. to KURLL KEEN of Chesterfield Co. Virginia, Nov. 9, 1789, for 20 pds. specie a tract of 250 acres on the north side of Turkey Creek adjoining John Smelly and Contentnea Creek, it being part of a tract granted to John Bailie by Earl Granville. Wit: Wilson Taylor.

DB 5-119 NEWT LANE of Nash Co. to JOHN LANE of same, Aug. 8, 1785, for 50 pds. hard money a tract of 151 acres adjoining Newit Lane. Wit: Sion Hill and William Hendrick.

DB 5-119 NEWIT LANE of Nash Co. to SION HILL of same, Aug. 8, 1785, for 50 pds. a tract of 100 acres adjoining Newit Lane. Wit: Benjamin Braswell and William Hendrick.

DB 5-120 BENJAMIN BRIDGERS of Nash Co. to LEWIS HILL of Franklin Co., Sept. 25, 1790, for 3 pds. 12 sh. Virginia money a parcel of 6 acres on the south side of Swift Creek adjoining Denton Mann and Benjamin Bridgers, it being part of a tract that William Lancaster surveyed for Benjamin Bridgers when he was county surveyor, adjoining the land that Denton Mann sold to Lewis Hill. Wit: Ben Perry and Stephen Gupton.

DB 5-121 DRURY WHITLY of Nash Co. to EPHRAIM PHILLIPS of same, Nov. 30, 1789, for 9 pds. 12 sh. specie a tract of 100 acres at the head of Little Swamp. it being that part of a grant to his father, George Whitly, for 400 acres whereon he deceased, which was allotted to said Drury in the division of the land with his brothers. Wit: Sharod Phillips and Theophilus Grice.

DB 5-122 LAZARUS STRICKLAND of Nash Co. to JESSE BROUGHTON of same. May 21, 1783, for 50 pds. specie a tract of 300 acres on Toisnot Swamp and the Great Branch, it being a grant to said Lazarus Strickland from the State on Oct. 25, 1782. Wit: Ed. Moore, Moses Stallions, and George Cockmur.

DB 5-124 BENNETT WOOD of Halifax Co. to CLEVERS RANSOME of Franklin Co.. Dec. 17. 1789, for 58 pds. specie a tract of 444 acres in Nash Co. adjoining Abel Davis, Samuel Mitchell, and John Portis. Wit: Willis Arrington and Jeremiah Portis.

DB 5-124 JOSEPH CURL of Nash Co. to THOMAS WHITLY of same. Feb. 11, 1791, for 5 pds. current money a lease to the said Thomas Whitly during his lifetime or the lifetime of his wife, Rachel, of 50 acres of land on Kirby's Creek adjoining Henry Watkins and Thomas' Road. Wit: Wilson Vick and Joel Bunn.

DB 5-125 WILLIAM BRIDGERS and BENJAMIN BOON cancelled a bill of sale made to them by JOSEPH WHITE on May

11, 1791, and satisfied at Nov. Ct. 1792. Wit: Wilson Vick and John Drake.

DB 5-126 DIXON MARSHALL of Warren Co. to BENJAMIN BARNES of Nash Co., Aug. 14, 1790, for 50 pds. a tract of 145 acres on the north side of Tar River adjoining Benjamin Barnes and Benjamin Bunn. Wit: Redmun Bunn and Frederick Batts.

DB 5-127 THOMAS VANLANDINGHAM of Edgecombe Co to JAMES VANLANDINGHAM of Nash Co., March 18, 1784, for 5 pds. specie a tract of 100 acres on the north side of Long Swamp. Wit: Emanuel Underwood and Elijah Wiggins.

DB 5-129 SAMSON POWELL of Nash Co. to WILLIAM FLEWELLEN, JR. of same, April 6. 1778, for 213 pds. proc. money a tract of 206 acres adjoining William Braswell. Wit: Britain Gandy and Richard Thomas.

DB 5-130 NATHAN WILLIAMS of Nash Co. to THOMAS HORN, SR., Jan. 23, 1809, for 400 silver dollars 144 acres on the south side of Toisnot Swamp adjoining Thomas Horn and the road, it being part of a tract granted to Pilgrim Williams in 1761. Wit: Grantham Horn and Rolan Williams.

DB 5-130 JAMES GREEN of Nash Co. to JOSEPH HOPKINS of same, Dec. 27, 1806, for 325 pds. specie a tract of 260 acres on the north side of Little Peachtree Creek adjoining James Moore. Batchelor, and Jones, on a branch formerly called Drewry Savage's spring branch. Wit: Dianner Bilbro and B. Bilbro.

DB 5-132 ASAY HICKS of Nash Co. to WILLIAM TAYLOR of same, Feb. 15, 1800, for 45 silver dollars a tract of 100 acres on Turkey Creek adjoining Lamon and Jacob Vick. it being part of a grant to John Taylor on Nov. 10, 1779, sold by said Taylor to Mark Strickland on Oct. 7, 1782. conveyed by said Strickland to Thomas Strickland, from him to William Hicks, and from said Hicks to Asa Hicks. Wit: J. Taylor and John Morgan.

DB 5-133 ISAAC HILLIARD, JOHN HILLIARD, and ROBERT CARTER HILLIARD to JAMES HILLIARD, May 20, 1808, whereas Isaac Hilliard, deceased, in his will devised unto his six sons James, Isaac, John, Robert Carter. Henry, and William Hilliard certain separate tracts of land and directed that. if any should die before reaching 21 years of age, the land so devised to him should be divided among his surviving brothers and whereas sons Henry and William did die before reaching that age and whereas the surviving brothers agreed that the aforesaid lands should be sold among themselves, James Hilliard became the purchaser of lands devised to said Henry. For $2401.00 paid by said James he received: (1) a tract of 448 acres on the south side of Swift Creek known as the James Griffin place; (2) 50 acres bought of Benjamin Whitfield; (3) 348 acres adjoining John Jones and John Melton; (4) the land where the Widow Thomas formerly lived; (5) 150 acres purchased of Thomas Horn. Wit: Benjamin Mason, J. Arrington, and John Williams.

DB 5-134 JAMES HILLIARD. ISAAC HILLIARD, and JOHN HILLIARD to ROBERT CARTER HILLIARD, May 20, 1808, in a deed similar to the one above, for $3468.00 paid by said Robert Carter, he received: (1) a tract of 500 acres on the north side of Swift Creek known as the Battle Plantation; (2) a tract of 234 acres known as the Talbert Plantation. Wit: Benja. Mason, Jos. Arrington, and John Williams.

DB 5-135 LAZARUS TURNER, NANCY TURNER, JULIAN TURNER, and ELIZABETH TURNER, all of Nash Co. to MATHEW ETHREDGE of same, Feb. 18, 1809, for 80 pds. Virginia money a tract of 100 acres on the east side of Lane's Swamp adjoining Wiley Powell and the Tarkill Branch. Wit: Alanson Powell, Solomon Whitley. and John Ethredge.

DB 5-136 THOMAS HUNTER of Montgomery Co., Tennessee to BENJAMIN WHITFIELD of Nash Co., Sept. 23, 1807, for $300.00 a tract of 150 acres on the north side of Stony Creek near the mouth of Laseter's Branch adjoinig David Strickland's former line, Thomas Willis, and Jesse Hunt. which land fell to him by the death of his father. Wit: James Williams and Willie G. Whitfield.

DB 5-136 WILSON W. CARTER of Halifax Co. to ELI B. WHITAKER of same, July 11, 1808, for 440 pds. a tract of 177 acres in Nash Co. on the south side of Fishing Creek at the mouth of Beaver Dam Swamp adjoining Nathaniel Powell. excepting one acre on the north side of said swamp containing a mill. Wit: Tho. Wiggins, Alanson Powell. and Robert C. Hilliard.

DB 5-137 MATHHEW C. WHITAKER and ELI B. WHITAKER, exrs. of THOMAS MASON, deceased, late of Halifax Co. to WILSON W. CARTER of same, Feb. 12, 1808, for 762 pds. a tract of 177 acres in Nash Co. on the south side of Fishing Creek at the mouth of Beaver Dam Swamp adjoining Nathaiel Powell, together with one acre of land on Beaver Dam Swamp for the support of a mill. Wit: Tho. Wiggins, Alanson Powell, and Robert C. Hilliard.

DB 5-138 W. W. CARTER of Halifax Co. to MATTHFW C. WHITAKER and ELI B. WHITAKER of same, July 11, 1808, for 322 pds. a certain water grist mill on Beaver Dam Swamp with two acres of land, one on each side of said swamp contigious to said mill. Wit: Thos. Wiggins Alanson Powell, and Robt. C. Hilliard.

DB 5-140 DEMSEY MORRIS of Nash Co. to JESSE MORRIS of same. Feb. 3. 1808. for 200 pds. a tract of 200 acres on the east side of Pig Basket Creek adjoining Britain Braswell. Jesse Braswell. and David Woodard. Wit: Brittain Braswell and Ashael Morris.

DB 5-140 REDDICK DRIVER and wife, POLLEY DRIVER, of Nash Co. to PILGRIM L. WILLIAMS of same. March 1. 1805, for $100.00 a tract of 100 acres on the Marsh Swamp adjoining Smelly and Eatman. Polly signed this deed as Mary Driver. Wit: Drewry Williams and Moses Smelly.

DB 5-141 PRISCILLA GRIZZLE and ALEXANDER IRWIN RICKS of Nash Co. to JEPHTHAH DANIEL of same. May 27, 1809, for 160 silver dollars a tract of 80 acres in Little Polecat adjoining Priscilla Grizzel, Alex. I. Ricks, Eli Ricks, and Joel Ricks. Wit: Ricks and Hardy G. Whitfield.

DB 5-142 JONAS WILLIAMS of Nash Co. to JOHN CROWELL of same, Feb. 19, 1808, for $1200.00 a tract of 733 acres on the south side of Little Swamp adjoining John Dew. Wit: Jas. B. Crowell and N. Williams.

DB 5-143 WILLIAM ARRINGTON of Nash Co. to BENJAMIN TUCKER of same, Nov. 17, 1804, for 120 silver dollars a tract of 100 acres on Turkey Creek adjoining Benjamin Tucker. Wit: Elias Boon and Woody Tucker.

DB 5-143 MARTHA BRETAIN on Nash Co. to JESSE BASS of same, Feb. 12, 1806, for 100 pds. Virginia money a tract of 170 acres adjoining Culpepper, Bereman Bilbro, Griffin, and Andrews. Wit: Willis Deen and Mathew ....

DB 5-145 MICHAEL HORN of Nash Co. to Pilgrim L. Williams of same, Feb. 3, 1807, for 300 pds. Virginia money a tract of 580 acres on Turkey Creek adjoining John West, John Flowers, and Richard Fore. Wit: Burrell Kent and Henry.

DB 5-145 JAMES DREWRY of Nash Co. to HENRY KINDRED of Warrin Co., Georgia, Nov. 23, 1807, a negro boy who was bequeathed to his son, Samuel Drewry, in the will of Francis Parker, deceased, late of Nash Co. and James Drewry gave to his minor son, Samuel Drewry, a negro girl to replace the boy. Wit: Peter Arrington and Matt. Drake, Jr.

DB 5-146 MOSES WILDER of Nash Co. to WILSON COLLINS of same, Dec. 6, 1808, for $160.00 a tract of 100 acres on the south side of Little Sapony Swamp adjoining George Boddie, Joseph Batchelor, Wilder, and Solomon Vester. Wit: George Boddie and Abijah Pridgen.

DB 5-148 SAMUEL DEVAUGHAN of Nash Co. to PILGRIM L. WILLIAMS of same, Jan. 23, 1808, for 450 silver dollars a tract of 336 acres on Turkey Creek adjoining Flowers, Mirull Devaughan, Wiley Kent. James Brown, Coob, Thomas Horn, and his own line. Wit: Drew Williams and Everard Smelley.

DB 5-149 JOHN COPE of Franklin Co. to POLLEY ARMSTREET COLE of same, Dec. 14, 1808, for 50 pds. a tract of 100 acres on the waters of Coker adjoining Carter, William Ross, and the county line, which land was granted to Simon Williams on Nov. 10, 1779. Wit: Nancy Boon and Charles Cole.

DB 5-150 JOHN BARRETT of Nash Co. to JOHN VICK of same, July 2, 1805, for 580 silver dollars 203 acres on the north side of Pig Basket or Braswell's Creek, it being a tract granted to Robert Young by Earl Granville on Nov. 8, 1755. Wit: Eley Vick and Elijah Vick.

DB 5-150 JOHN H. DRAKE and wife, FANNY DRAKE, and WILLIAM ARRINGTON and wife, MARY ARRINGTON, of Nash Co. to PHILEMON BENNETT of same. Jan. 27, 1809, for $180.00 a tract of 150 acres adjoining Harrison, Davis' old line, Drake, and Bell's former line, which land was conveyed by Mr. John Williams by will unto his daughters. Wit: Mich. Collins and Jacky Drake. Frances Drake, wife of John H. Drake, and Mary Arrington, wife of General William Arrington were examined separately by Joseph Arrington, Sr., J. P. and Joseph Arrington, Jr., J. P. May 18, 1809.

DB 5-153 GEORGE COOPER of Nash Co. to WILLIAM TISDALE of same, July 27, 1809, for $125.00 one negro woman. Wit: David Melton and A. Pridgen.

DB 5-153 WILSON BLUNT to JAMES READ of Nash Co., Nov. 16, 1808, for 90 pds. Virginia money one negro girl. Wit: Jolian Nicholson.

DB 5-153 JOHN CROWELL to DAVID HUNT, JR., Sept. 12, 1807, for sixpence yearly rent a tract of 25 acres of Crowell's land for and during the term of life of David Hunt, Sr. and wife, Telitha Hunt. David Hunt, Sr. was to take care of the place and the fruit trees and give the excess fruit to said Crowell. Wit: Samuel Lewis Lamkin.

DB 5-154 BENJAMIN BOON of Nash Co. to MICHAEL COLLINS of same, Aug. 31, 1808, for $452.00 a tract of 226 acres adjoining Raford Boon, John H. Drake, George Boddie, Ben Drake, and Mann. Wit: Elias Boon and Jesse Boon.

5-156 JOHN BRASWELL of Nash Co. to JOHN YORK of Franklin Co., Oct. 24, 1809, for 100 pds. a tract of 300 acres on Little Creek on the north side of Tar River adjoining Alston. Wit: Benja. Manning and Eaton Hammons.

DB 5-157 WILLIAM ARRINGTON of Nash Co. to JOHN BRASWELL of same, Oct. 14, 1808, for 100 pds. a tract of 300 acres on Little Creek on the north side of Tar River adjoining Manning and Alston. Wit: John Warren and Larkin Battle.

DB 5-157 BENJAMIN WHITEHEAD, CHARLES WHITEHEAD, and WILLIAM WHITEHEAD. all of the State of Georgia, Dec. 20, 1807, in consequence of an agreement made by one brother, Johnnathan Whitehead, with Peter Arrington for his services in obtaining a military land warrant from the State of N. C. for 640 acres issued to the heirs of Mathew Whitehead for his services as a soldier in the Revolutionary War. the brothers honored the agreement to give Peter Arrington half of the warrant or half of the amount obtained for it. Wit: James Whitehead.

DB 5-158 JOHNNATHAN WHITEHEAD, JAMES WHITEHEAD, and JOSEPH WHITEHEAD, all of Nash Co.. being heirs and equally interested with Benjamin Whitehead, William Whitehead. and Charles Whitehead. did ratify and confirm the foregoing contract, March 17, 1810. Wit: Joseph Arrington.

DB 5-159 WILLIAM PERRY of Nash Co. to JOHN TAYLOR of same, March 1, 1806. for 50 pds. 238 acres adjoining James Cone, Hammons, Hunt, and Hartsfield, it being the land and plantation whereon Joshua Cone formerly lived. Wit: Arthur Arrington and Jesse Hammons.

DB 5-160 Amos Gandy. Sheriff of Nash Co. to JAMES FERRELL, Jan. 10, 1806. at public auction for 10 pds. a tract of 100 acres on the south side of Tar River and on Turkey Creek adjoining John Owens, the Allen place, William Owens. Julian King and the road, sold as the property of ANSEL ALFORD to satisfy a judgment obtained by James Branch against Isaac Pippin and

Ansel Alford. Wit: Jesse Hammons and William Joyner.

DB 5-161 AMOS GANDY, Sheriff of Nash Co. to WILLIAM HAMMONS, JR., Nov. 6, 1805, at public auction for 47 pds. a tract of 350 acres on the south side of Tar River and on Turkey Creek adjoining Dunn, Chapman's Road, William Taylor, Melton, Roblin, and Joseph Earp, sold as the property of ELIAS OWENS to satisfy a judgment obtained by James Branch against William Owens, Elias Owens, and Samuel Devaughan. Wit: Jesse Hammons and William Joyner.

DB 5-162 WILLIAM OWENS and wife, TEMPERANCE OWENS, of Nash Co. to JOHN TAYLOR of same, Aug. 12, 1806 for 50 silver dollars 25 acres on Toisnot Swamp, it being Lot No. 3 of a tract of land which Rebekah Avarett, deceased, possessed. Wit: Drew Williams and .... Temperance Owens was examined separately from her husband.

DB 5-163 JOHN MORGAN, SR. of Nash Co. to his son, JOHN MORGAN, JR., of same, Oct. 29, 1808, for $250.00 a tract of 200 acres on the south side of Tar River adjoining Benjamin Tann, John Taylor, Jacob Lewis. and Cooper's Creek. Wit: John Taylor and Isaac Bass.

DB 5-164 AMOS GANDY, Sheriff of Nash Co., to WILLIAM HAMMONS, Feb. 1, 1805, at public auction for 9 pds. a tract of 75 acres on the south side of Sapony Creek adjoining William Hammons and Mathew Rackley, sold as the property of MATHEW HUNT to satisfy a judgment obtained by George Boddie. Wit: Henry Hines and Henry Arrington.

DB 5-165 SION PERRY of Nash Co. to JAMES FERRELL of Franklin Co., Feb. 7. 1805, for $50.00 a tract of 100 acres adjoining William Owens and Ansel Alford. Wit: Jesse Hammons and Jacob Alford.

DB 5-166 BURRELL JOYNER of Nash Co. to JOHN POULAN, SR. of same. June 27. 1810, for $600.00 a tract of 323 acres on the south side of Sapony Creek adjoining George Cooper (formerly Benjamin Smith) and John Evans' former line. Wit:_ John Vick and Samuel Lamkin.

DB 5-167 ISAAC WOODARD and CADER WOODARD of Wayne Co. to JOHN STOOTT of Nash Co., Jan. 11, 1809, for 50 pds. a tract of 350 acres on the north side of Contentnea Creek adjoining Hardy Boykin, Stephen Cobb, Benjamin Cobb. Benjamin Flowers. Cornelius Sanders, and Jacob Nichols. Wit: Sion Sanders and William Sanders.

DB 5-168 AMOS BECKWITH of Nash Co. to SION BECKWITH of same. Dec. 25. 1809, for 313 1/3 silver dollars two negro girls Wit: Wm. Henry Hall and J. Atkinson.

DB 5-169 JOSEPH ARRINGTON SR. of Nash Co. to his son, CARTER ARRINGTON, Nov. 12. 1809 for love and affection a tract of 220 acres on the south side of Beaver Dam Swamp adjoining Whitehead, John Green, and William Arrington whereon said Carter then lived. Wit: John Nicholson.

DB 5-170 CAUFIELD HARRISS of Nash Co. to RANDOLF HARRISS of same, Aug. 5, 1809, for $65.00 two negroes who were formerly the property of Edmund Saward, deceased. Wit: Sam. Smith and Edwin Harriss.

DB 5-171 JOHN OWENS of Nash Co. to SION PERRY of same, Jan. 12, 1805, for 25 pds. a tract of 100 acres on Turkey Creek adjoining William Owens and Ansel Alford, it being a grant to John Owens from the State of N. C. in 1791. Wit: Benjamin Braswell and Elias Owens.

DB 5-172 WILLOUGHBY BALLENTINE and wife, RE-BECKAH BALLENTINE, WRIGHT SELLARS and wife, NANCY SELLARS, and POLLEY GLOVER, all of Nash Co. to JOHN GLOVER of same, Feb. 12, 1810, for 37 spanish milled dollars and 50 cents a tract of land on the north side of Tar River adjoining Melton, George Cooper, Lewis, and York, it being their part of the land due them from their brother, William Glover. Polly Glover signed as Mary Glover. Wit: Mathew Carter and Jeremiah Buntin.

DB 5-173 JOSIAH NICHOLSON of Edgefield District, South Corolina gave to KINCHEN TAYLOR of Nash Co., March 8, 1808, power of attorney in the collection of debts from Nathan Whitehead, John Culpepper, and others. Wit: Frederick B. Hines and William Dortch.

DB 5-174 JAMES BIRD of Nash Co. to DEMPSEY DRIVER of same, Jan. 20, 1785, for 15 pds. specie a tract of 200 acres on Turkey Creek, which was part of the land he purchased of Richard Fore. Wit: John Kent and Jesse Kent.

DB 5-175 PRISCILLA THORP of Nash Co. to her son, JESSE THORP, of Edgecombe Co., Nov. 10, 1809, for love and affection a tract of 652 acres on both sides of Little Compass Creek adjoining Thomas Exum and John Speight. Wit: M. Mason and Jonthan Thomas.

DB 5-176 JAMES FERRELL of Nash Co. to HUTSON FERRELL of same, Sept. 20, 1808, for $100.00 a tract of 100 acres on Turkey Creek adjoining William Dunn and Ansel Alford. Wit: Jesse Hammons, A. Ferrell, and William Hammons.

DB 5-177 HUMPHREY NELSON and wife, SARAH NELSON, formerly Sarah Jackson and daughter of Newman Jackson of Wake Co., N. C., appointed friend NEWMAN JACKSON as their lawful attorney, Aug. 18, 1809. This was sworn to in Davidson Co., Tennessee. Also, Robert Weakley, Justice of the Court of Davidson Co., certified that he married Humphrey Nelson and Sally Jackson of said county on Aug. 16, 1809.

DB 5-178 STEPHEN VAUGHN of Nash Co. to ELI WILLIAMS of same, Nov. 27, 1809. for 133 pds. 16 sh. Virginia money the following tracts: (1) a 200 acre plantation on the north side of Sapony Swamp; (2) 150 acres adjoining the first tract, said Stephen Vaughn, and Matthias Manning; (3) 116 acres adjoining the first tract, said Stephen Vaughn, John Matthews, and Mathias Manning. Wit: A. Pridgen, William Batchelor, and Martha Pridgen.

DB 5-179 MATHEW C. WHITAKER of Halifax Co. to ELI B. WHITAKER of same, Nov. 3, 1809, for 161 pds. half interest in a certain grist mill, the other half of which the said Eli B. Whitaker was already proprietor, on Beaver Dam Swamp, and two acres of land. Wit: Alanson Powell and James Judge, Jr.

DB 5-180 HUMPHREY NELSON and wife, SARAH NELSON, of Davidson Co., Tennessee to ARCHIBALD BAKER of Nash Co., - 14, 1810, for 5 pds. 8 sh. Virginia money a tract of 49 acres adjoining Poland, Baker and the dividing line between Sarah Nelson and Elizabeth Jackson. This was sold by Newman Jackson, with power of attorney. Wit: Lewis Vick.

DB 5-181 ALINGE BRANTLEY of Nash Co. to TABITHA STOKES of same. April 20, 1810, for 15 silver dollars a parcel of 10 acres on Turkey Creek adjoining said Brantley. Wit: John Rice and Hopkins Rice.

DB 5-182 DAVID RICKS, Sheriff of Nash Co., to WILLIAM DORTCH, May 11, 1810, at public auction for 376 pds. a tract of 200 acres adjoining Revel and David Strickland, sold as the property of DELILAH WHITEHEAD to satisfy two judgments obtained by Michael Horn and one by Daniel Mann. Wit: L. F. Ellen and J. Crowell.

DB 5-183 DAVID RICKS, Sheriff of Nash Co., to DREWCILLA BUNN, Feb. 12, 1810, for 35 pds. one negro man, sold as the property of BENJAMIN WHITFIELD, deceased, to satisfy an execution obtained by Samuel Westray. He was bid off to Willie Whitfield who relinquished his right to Delilah Whitfield, who relinquished her right to Drewcilla Bunn. Wit: D. Melton and G. Whitfield.

DB 5-184 DAVID RICKS, Sheriff of Nash Co., to DREWCILLA BUNN, July 20, 1809, for $92.22 a negro girl, sold as the property of BENJAMIN WHITFIELD, deceased. Delilah Whitfield, the highest bidder, relinquished her right to said Drewcilla Bunn. Wit: Alexr. Sorsby.

DB 5-184 L. BERRY HINES of Nash Co. to THOMAS C. JONES of same, Feb. 28, 1810, for 800 silver dollars 152 acres on the north side of Jeffre's old road adjoining William Arrington, Peter Arrington, and William Drake, it being a tract of land granted to Francis Parker and from him demised to James Drewry, and from James Drewry, William Parker, and John Parker to Guilford Griffin, and Guilford Griffin to L. Berry Hines. Wit: James Hilliard and Elijah Boddie.

DB 5-186 JANE (JEAN) WILLIAMS to her son-in-law, DEMPSEY HARRISON, and wife, SARAH HARRISON, for love and affection her goods, chattels, and personal estate. namely five negroes, Dec. 5, 1809. Wit: John Williams and Samuel Williams.

DB 5-187 JANE WILLIAMS to her son, JOHN WILLIAMS, for love and affection her goods, chattels, and personal estate, namely, eight negroes, Dec. 5, 1809. Wit: Dempsey Harrison and Samuel Williams.

DB 5-188 JOHN DENSON of Nash Co. to EDWARD COOPER of same. March 19, 1806, for 100 pds. specie a tract of 99 acres on Indian Branch adjoining Whitehead, Dortch, Powell, and Robertson. Wit: Jinnins Hackney, John D. Cooper, and Granberry Baggett.

DB 5-189 BENJAMIN ELEY of Nash Co. to HENRY HARRISON, Oct. 5, 1806, for $250.00 one negro girl. Wit: Simeon Taylor and John Warren.

DB 5-190 JOHN COCKRELL of Nash Co. to DAVID WINSTEAD, Dec. 26, 1810, for $375.00 one negro woman and her child. Wit: Joseph Cockrell and Betsey Cockrell.

DB 5-190 ROLAND WILLIAMS of Nash Co. to DAVID WINSTEAD, Sept. 7, 1807, for $275.00 one negro girl. Wit: Pilgrim Williams and Edward Taylor.

DB 5-191 Division of the land of RICHARD VICK, deceased, by commissioners, Oct. 1, 1808 by order of Aug. Ct., 1808: (1) to BENJAMIN VICK a tract of 59½ acres adjoining the Mill Branch and Braswell; (2) to ASAEL VICK a tract of 59½ acres adjoining the Mill Branch, Willis, and John Vick; (3) to CHARITY BECKWITH, wife of Sion Beckwith, a tract of 106 acres adjoining John Vick and Edward Wilson. but not as valuable.

DB 5-193 REDMUND BUNN of Nash Co. to WILLIE BUNN of same, March 2, 1810, for $26.00 a parcel of 13 acres on the south side of Tar River adjoining said Willie Bunn. Wit: James Ricks and Benja. Bunn.

DB 5-194 WILLIE BUNN of Nash Co. to BENJAMIN BUNN of same, March 2, 1810, for $80.00 a tract of 40 acres on the north side of Tar River adjoining said Benjamin Bunn, the road, and David Bunn. Wit: Redmund Bunn and James Ricks.

DB 5-195 JOHN STOOT (STOTT) of Nash Co. to THOMAS ADKINS of same, Feb. 5, 1810, for $160.00 a tract of 320 acres on Sapony Swamp adjoining Solomon Vester, Michael Vester, Jeremiah Etheridge, John Lewis, Little Berry White, and Jesse Bass, it being part of a grant to William Vester. Wit: Mathew Carter and Samuel Carter.

DB 5-196 WILLIAM B. BRIDGERS, trustee, to DAVID SILLS, Dec. 30, 1807, at public auction for $1405.16 seven negroes by name, sold as the property of William Kirby. Wit: E. Edwards and Asahel Morriss.

DB 5-197 THOMAS CARTER of Nash Co. to his grandson, CULLIN CARTER JONES, son of William Jones, Feb. 10, 1810, for love and affection a tract of 66 acres on the south side of Tar River adjoining Noah Strickland. Wit: David Crickmore and Noah Strickland.

DB 5-198 WILLIAM BARNES of Nash Co. to ORANDATUS BARNES of same, March 22, 1810, for 60 pds. Virginia money a tract of 120 acres on the north side of Stony Creek adjoining James Barnes, Lemuel Barnes, and David Daniel. Wit: Samuel Westray and Wm. Owen.

DB 5-199 REUBEN HARRELL of Nash Co. to JEPHTHAH DANIEL of same. Jan. 30, 1810, for $175.00 one negro girl. Wit: Cordal Hunter and Lemuel Barnes.

DB 5-200 HARDY HUNT and wife. NANCY HUNT of Lincoln Co., Tennessee and JORDAN BASS and wife, BETHANA

(BETHANY) BASS, of Wilson Co., Tennessee to WILLIAM ROB-
INS of Nash Co., July 23,1810, for 100 pds. Virginia money a tract
of 62½ acres adjoining John Bass, Mourning Gay, Elias Gay, and
James Massingill. Wit: Laban Webb and Bowen Webb.

DB 5-201 ELIZABETH PUSSELL of Nash Co. to HARDY
PUSSELL of same. March 22, 1798, for 10 pds. a tract of 25 acres
on the east side of Turkey Creek. Wit: Wm. Hammons, Jeremiah
Etheridge, and Silas Rackley. Proved in Nov. Ct. 1810 by David
Melton who proved the handwriting of Wm. Hammons who was
dead and the handwriting of Jeremiah Etheridge and others who
were in Tennessee.

DB 5-202 JOSEPH ARRINGTON of Nash Co. to SAMUEL
SANDEFORD of Franklin Co., Aug. 25, 1810, for 100 pds. a tract
of 300 acres on Turkey Creek adjoining Jesse Hammons, Joshua
Cone. and Hartford. Wit: Peter Arrington.

DB 5-203 MILLS GAY of Wilson Co., Tennessee to Wm.
ROBINS of Nash Co., Aug. 13, 1810 for $1000.00 a tract of 33 1/3
acres adjoining Mourning Gay, Jordan Gay, Rogers, Josiah Gay,
and the Back Swamp. Wit: Laban Webb and Bowen Webb.

DB 5-204 MATTHEW DRAKE of Nash Co. to JOHN
ARRINGTON of same, March 22, 1809. for $500.00 a tract of 264
acres on Wolf Pit Branch and the road, it being part of a grant to
Wm. Drake, Sr. and from him to said Matthew Drake. Wit: Peter
Arrington and Thos. J. Armstrong.

DB 5-205 HARDY STRICKLAND of Nash Co. to ALEY
STRICKLAND of same. Nov. 7. 1810. for love and good will a tract
of 97 acres on Turkey Creek. Wit: Wm. Moore and Edward Taylor.

DB 5-206 HENRY VICK of Nash Co. to DAVID DANIEL of
same, March 12, 1807, for $300.00 a tract of 100 acres on the north
side of Stony Creek adjoining William Barnes and Lemuel Barnes.
Wit: Samuel Smith and Jephthah Daniel.

DB 5-207 RICHARD HOLLAND of Nash Co. to DAVID
RICKS of same, Feb. 17, 1810. for $1022.50 a tract of 409 acres
near Sapony Creek adjoining Edward Gandy, Barnaby Nollebov,
Wm. Ricks, Wm. Batchelor, and the road, consisting of two tracts
which said Holland purchased of John Whitehouse. Wit: John
Ricks and D. Melton.

DB 5-208 AMOS GANDY of Nash Co. to MARK STRICK-
LAND of same, March 7, 1810. for 65 silver dollars a tract of 65
acres on the south side of Tar River and on Cooper's Creek adjoining John Morgan and Lamon. Wit: Gideon Strickland and Barn-
aba Nolleboy.

DB 5-209 AMOS GANDY. Sheriff of Nash Co., to ALEXAN-
DER SORSBY. Jan. 6. 1806, at public auction for 15 pds. a tract
of 153 acres on Turkey Creek adjoining Theophilus Hickman. Jacob
Strickland, and Jeremiah Brown, sold as the property of James B.
Crowell to satisfy a judgment obtained by James Branch. Wit:
Daniel Walker and Jonathan Whitehead.

DB 5-210 DEMPSEY BRASWELL of Nash Co. to JACOB
BRASWELL, SR. of same, March 29, 1809, for $32.00 a parcel of

16 acres adjoining said Jacob Braswell, Sr. and Jacob Braswell, Jr.
Wit: Jesse Braswell and Elias Bass.

DB 5-211 JACOB VICK of Nash Co. to LODRICK F. ELLEN
of same, Nov. 11, 1809, for $62.50 a tract of 20 acres adjoining said
Ellen and Demsey Braswell.   Wit: Sam'l Smith and Jacob Barrett.

5-212 SAMUEL LONGBOTTOMS (SAMUEL L. BOTTOMS)
of Nash Co. to JOHN L. BOTTOMS of same, May 12, 1803, for 60
pds. a tract of 120 acres on the south side of Sapony Creek on Holl-
and's Branch adjoining Elijah Atkinson.   Wit: Jesse Joiner and
Oliver L. Bottoms.

DB 5-213 WILLIAM WOODRUFF and wife, MARTHA N.
WOODRUFF, of Nash Co. to BENJAMIN BOON of same, Feb. 21,
1810, for $205.00 a tract of 110 acres on Wolf Pit Branch and the
road.   Wit: John Arrington and D. Sills.   Martha N. Woodruff was
examined separately from her husband by Jos. Arrington, J. P. and
D. Sills, J. P.

DB 5-215 ARCHIBALD   DAVIS and wife.   ELIZABETH
DAVIS, of Franklin Co. to JAMES HILLIARD of Nash Co., Feb. 5,
1801, for 700 silver dollars a one-third part of a certain tract of land
containing 300 acres in Kershaw Co. South Carolina on the south-
west side of the Waterree River and bounded by the river, land
granted to Robert Rogers, and vacant land which boundaries
agreed with a deed from Samuel and Henry Millhouse to William
Hilliard on May 2, 1759 and given by legacy from William
Hilliard to William Thomas and later given by legacy from
William Thomas to Elizabeth Hilliard. James Hilliard, and Nancy
Hilliard.   Wit: Denton Mann and   Cooper Williams.   Elizabeth
Davis was examined separately from her husband by Samuel
Lowrie.

DB 5-216 ABEL DAVIS received $25.00 from   EDMUND
JONES, April 1, 1809, for damage sustained to his lands by said
Jones raising the water with a mill dam.   Wit: William Jones and
Daniel Shine.

DB 5-217 ABEL DAVIS of Nash Co. deed of trust to BEN-
JAMIN W. LUCAS of Halifax Co., April 1, 1809, to secure the 112
pds. 3 sh. and 8 p. Virginia money that he owed to Edmund Jones.
The security was his home plantation a tract of 157 acres on the
south side of Fishing Creek adjoining Joseph Arrington (formerly
Ransom).   Wit: William Jones and Daniel Shine.

DB 5-218 GEORGE BODDIE and wife, LUCY BODDIE, of
Nash Co. to JACOB GRIFFIN of same. Feb. 11. 1811, for $340.00
a tract of 272 acres adjoining Sorsby, John H. Drake, and Collins.
Wit: Joseph Arrington, Jr.

DB 5-219 DEMPSEY LANGLEY and wife. RACHEL LANG-
LEY, of Nash Co. to Drury Pridgen. guardian to JOHN C. TAY-
LOR, orphan of Joel Taylor, deceased. of Nash Co., Oct. 30, 1810,
for 80 (?) a tract of 100 acres on the north side of Posnaquot
Swamp adjoining Roland Williams.   Rachel Langley was formerly
the wife of Joel Taylor, deceased.   Wit: Joseph Cockrell and Steven
Willis.   Rachel Langley was examined separately from her husband
by Samuel Westray.

DB 5-219 DAVID RICKS Sheriff of Nash Co., to DANIEL WALKER, May 11, 1810, at public auction for 25 pds. 8 sh. a tract of 70 acres in Nash Co., sold as the property of Delilah Whitfield to satisfy a judgment obtained by Daniel Mann. Said Walker relinquished one-half the land to William Dortch. Wit: Sam. Smith and James Hunter.

DB 5-221 ROBERT C. HILLIARD of Nash Co. to JOHN HILLIARD of same, Jan. 15, 1811, for 1000 pds. Virginia currency 1100 acres in Nash Co.. it being all the land bequeathed to said Robert C. Hilliard by his father, Isaac Hilliard, deceased, lying on the north side of Swift Creek adjoining John Hilliard, William Wright, Granberry Baggett, Drewry Binam, and James Hilliard. Wit: James Hilliard and Nathaniel Hunt.

DB 5-222 ROBERT C. HILLIARD of Nash Co. to ISAAC HILLIARD of Halifax Co., May 20, 1808, for $1350.00 a tract of 329 on Fishing Creek. Wit: Benia. Mason and Jos. Arrington, Jr.

DB 5-223 ELIJAH BODDIE of Franklin Co., Tennessee to WILLIAM BODDIE of Nash Co., July 12, 1810, for $75.00 a tract of 250 acres on the main public road leading from Nash Courthouse to David Sills' adjoining George Boddie and William Boddie. Wit: George Boddie and A. V. Boddie.

DB 5-223 JACOB ROGERS of Nash Co. to JESSE MORRISS of same, Jan. 21, 1811, for 525 silver dollars a tract of 240 acres adjoining John Richardson, John Passmore, and Gay. Wit: Asa Morris, Redick Massingale, and Jacob Braswell.

DB 5-225 NATHAN VICK of Nash Co. to his son-in-law, JACOB ODOM. April 23, 1810, for love and affection a tract of 150 acres adjoining Samuel Westray, Ricks, Samuel Skinner, Henry Vick. and the road. Wit: Willie Atkinson and Joel Atkinson.

DB 5-226 ELIZABETH GAY of Wake Co. to JESSE MORRIS of Nash Co., Jan. 21. 1811. for $75.00 a tract of 30 1-3 acres on the east side of Mill Swamp adjoining Jacob Rogers, Jeorda Gay, James Gay, Willis Gay, and Passmore. Wit: Asahel Morris, Elias Gay, and Elias Bowden.

DB 5-227 DAVID DANIEL. SR. of Nash Co. to DAVID DANIEL, JR. of same, June 19, 1809, for 5 sh. a tract of 139 acres adjoining Isaac Watkins, Curl, and Thomas' Road. Wit: Sam. Smith and Joel Harriss.

DB 5-230 MARY GRIFFIN of Nash Co. to her granddaughter, TEMPERANCE GRIFFIN, daughter of Guilford Griffin, Feb. 6, 1811, for love and affection one negro girl and to her granddaughter, CHARITY GRIFFIN, daughter of Guilford Griffin, one negro girl. Said Mary Griffin was to retain them as long as she lived. Wit: John Arrington and Lewis Stuart.

DB 5-231 JESSE ADAMS of Nash Co. to JAMES BRUCE of same, March 17, 1810, for $100.00 a tract of 109 acres on Turkey Creek adjoining Jesse Bass, Jeremiah Culpepper, said Bruce, and Baker. Wit: Daniel Taylor and B. Bilbro.

DB 5-232 JOHN H. DRAKE of Nash Co. to EDWARD T. BROGDON of same. Feb. 14. 1811, for $73.00 a tract of 73 acres adjoining Newet Floyd and Hilliard, it being part of a tract which the said Drake bought of Federick Floyd and wife, Mourning Floyd. Wit: Penuel Floyd.

DB 5-233 JOSEPH VICK and wife, ELIZABETH VICK, of Nash Co. to BENJAMIN WESTRAY of same, March 25, 1811, for $150.00 a tract of 68 acres adjoining Joiner and Ricks. Wit: D. Ricks and John Ricks. Elizabeth Vick was examined separately from her husband by D. Sills.

DB 5-234 DUNCAN LAMON of Nash Co. to JEPHTHAH DANIEL of same, Sept. 26, 1809, for $400.00 one negro man. Wit: Eli Ricks and D. Daniel.

5-235 LEWIS KIRBY of Nash Co. to DAVID SILLS of same, April 4, 1810, for 130 silver dollars a tract of 138¾ acres adjoining the lands allotted to Ruthy Davis, the dower land of his mother, Cooper Williams, the land allotted to his brother, William Kirby, and the main road; also. all future interest in the dower land of his mother, Sally Kirby, out of the land belonging to the estate of his father, William Kirby, deceased, this land adjoining the land allotted to Sally Boon, the creek, Cooper Williams, said Lewis Kirby, and that land allotted to Ruthy Davis and others, containing about 350 acres. Wit: Thomas Stokes and Thomas Lawrence.

DB 5-236 SALLY KIRBY of Nash Co. to DAVID SILLS of same, Aug. 15, 1810, for 50 silver dollars all interest in her dower land located in Nash and Franklin counties adjoining the land allotted to Sally Boon, Redbud Creek. Cooper Williams, and the lands allotted to William Kirby, Lewis Kirby, Ruthy Davis, and others, containing 350 acres. Wit: Thomas Stokes and John Watkins.

DB 5-237 MICHAEL COLLINS of Nash Co. to DAVID SILLS of same, Sept. 1, 1810, for 45 silver dollars a tract of 45 acres in Nash and Franklin counties adjoining said Sills. Wit: Thomas Stokes and Thomas Lawrence.

DB 5-238 JACOB JOHNSON of Mecklenburgh Co., Kentucky to DAVID SILLS of Nash Co., April 12, 1811, for $72.00 a tract of 75 acres on Back Swamp adjoining said Sills (formerly Thomas) and Wilhite. Wit: B. Hilsman, Mills Bartholeomew, and Robert Jones.

DB 5-239 WILLIS ALSTON and JAMES W. ALSTON and wife, TEMPERANCE ALSTON, all of Halifax Co. to DAVID SILLS of Nash Co., Feb. 4 1811, for $1031.00 a tract of 1031 acres lying in Nash and Franklin counties adjoining Walker. Hedgepeth, Rogers, Passmore, Wheless, Wilhite, and said David Sills. including the plantation whereon Jacob Johnson formerly lived. Wit: John Alston and - Cotten. Temperance Alston was a resident of Halifax Co. and was unable to come to Nash Co. and so men were appointed to privately examined her in Halifax Co.

DB 5-240 ALDEN BASS of Nash Co. to REDICK MASSINGALE of same, March 23, 1809, for $60.00 a tract of 132 acres adjoining Gay and O'Neal. Wit: Henry Mitchel and Warren Massengale.

DB 5-241 JOSEPH JNO. CLINCH of Wake Co. to WILLIAM BELLAMY of Nash Co., May 4, 1811, for $1200.00 a tract of land on the south side of Swift Creek adjoining Josiah Battle and said Bellamy, it being the lands allotted to him in the division according to the will of his father containing 378 acres. Wit: Josiah Battle and William Ross.

DB 5-242 DAVID WOODARD of Nash Co. to JOHN WOR-BINTON of same, Jan. 2, 1810, for $180.00 a tract of 144 acres adjoining Aaron Woodard, Daniel Woodard, said Worbinton, Jesse Braswell, and Morriss. Wit: William Arrington and Daniel Woodard.

DB 5-243 DAVID RICKS, Sheriff of Nash Co., to JOHN VICK, April 6, 1811, at public auction for 225 pds. 8 sh. a tract of 608 acres on the north side of Pig Basket Creek adjoining Ellen, sold as the property of the heirs and devisees of Benja. Whitfield, deceased, to satisfy judgments obtained by Thomas Griffin, guardian, and G. Gay & Co. Wit: Joseph Vick and Eaton Hammons.

DB 5-244 FEDERICK B. HINES of Nash Co. and HENRY WALKER of Halifax Co. gave bond to PHILANDER TISDALE for the sum of 2000 pds. in payment for five negroes bought from Tisdale. Feb. 7, 1811. Wit: B. Crowell and H. G. Whitfield.

DB 5-245 JOHN TAYLOR of Nash Co. to OSBORNE STRICKLAND of same, June 10, 1799, for 100 pds. Virginia money a tract of 160 accres on the south side of Tar River. Wit: Gideon Strickland and Mark Strickland.

DB 5-246 WILLIAM DORTCH of Nash Co. to JOHN PITMAN of Halifax Co., March 30, 1810, for $600.00 a tract of 100 acres on the north side of Swift Creek and another tract of 200 acres adjoining the first tract, James Nelson, and Thomas Hart. Wit: Guilford G. Whitfield and Archd. G. Whitfield.

DB 5-247 DANIEL WARREN of Sumner Co., Tennessee to WILLIAM BRYANT of Nash Co., Jan. 18, 1806, for 16 silver dollars all of his interest in a tract of 25 acres whereon Elizabeth Hendrick then lived, formerly the property of William Hendrick, deceased, which said land fell by the death of William Hendrick to his widow, Mary Warren. The land was bounded by the lines of Wm. Bryant. Edward York. and John Glover. Wit: William Hammons, John Glover, and Edward York.

DB 5-248 WILLIAM ARRINGTON of Nash Co. to THOMAS BRYANT of same, Aug. 14, 1810, for $800.00 a tract of 400 acres on the north side of Tar River near the head of the cypress pond and the mouth of Little Creek adjoining William Bryant, Hammons, and Harriss (then Arrington). Wit: Roger Reese and Mathew Carter.

DB 5-249 DAVID SILLS of Nash Co. to WILLIAM WHEL-ESS of same, April 4, 1811, for $244.00 a tract of 244 acres on the east side of Back Swamp adjoining Morriss (formerly Rogers), Sills, Wilhite, John Richardson. and said Wheless. Wit: None.

DB 5-250 ELI MANNING of Nash Co. to PARSON RACK-LEY, JR. of same, March 30. 1810, for 30 pds. Virginia money a tract of 176 acres on Little Turkey Creek adjoining said Rackley. Wit: William Buntin and Abiiah Pridgen.

DB 5-251 SAMUEL BRYANT of Jackson C., Georgia to OS-

BORNE STRICKLAND of Nash Co., May 29, 1810, for $200.00 a tract of 100 acres on the south side of Tar River adjoining Benjamin Bryant and Arthur William's Branch. Wit: Mathew Carter and Gideon Strickland.

DB 5-252 SIGNAL HENDRICK of Nash Co. to WILLIAM BRYANT of same, March 8, 1806, for $16.00 all of his interest in a tract of 25 acres whereon Elizabeth Hendrick then lived, which was formerly the property of William Hendrick, deceased, and which land fell to him by the death of his brother, Willie Hendrick. The land was bounded by the lines of William Bryant, Edward York, and John Glover. Wit: J. Taylor, Edward York, and Wm. Hammons.

DB 5-253 JAMES GAY of Sumter District, South Carolina appointed his brother, ELIAS GAY, of Wake Co. as his lawful attorney in the settlement of his father's estate, Jan. 11, 1811. Wit: D. Ballard.

DB 5-254 TEMPERANCE DRAKE of Davidson Co., Tennessee appointed JOSEPH JOHN SUMNER of same as her true and lawful attorney in the collection of money or legacies from Michael Collins and Francis Drake, executors of her father, Matthew Drake, Sr., deceased, late of Nash Co. and to sell such land and negroes that were allotted to her in the will of her father, Aug. 24, 1811. Wit: James Drake and Moses Driver.

DB 5-255 DUKE W. SUMNER of Davidson Co., Tennessee appointed his brother, JOSEPH JOHN SUMNER of same as true and lawful attorney in the collection of money due him from Michael Collins and Francis Drake executors of Matthew Drake, Sr., deceased, in Nash Co. which were due to him as the lawful husband of a daughter, Mary, commonly called Polley, from the estate of Matthew Drake, Aug. 20, 1811. Wit: James Drake and Moses Driver.

DB 5-256 MARY GRIFFIN to her two daughters. ELIZABETH BRASWELL and MILBREY DRAKE, March 20, 1811, for love and affection two negroes, at her death. Wit: James Drewry.

DB 5-256 JOSIAH WHITLEY of Nash Co. to his son, WILEY WHITLEY, of same, July 30, 1811, for love and affection a tract of 55 acres on Jumping Run Branch adjoining Barnes. Wit: Joel Whitley and Reuben Harrell.

DB 5-258 PETER ETHEREDGE, SR. of Nash Co. to ABIJAH PRIDGEN of same, July 30, 1811, for $6.00 a parcel of 6 acres on the south side of Great Bear Branch adjoining said Pridgen. Wit: George Boddie and Nathan Boddie.

DB 5-259 WILLIS WILLIAMS of Nash Co. to ABIJAH PRIDGEN of same, Dec. 13, 1810, for $60.00 a tract of 50 acres on Little Bear Branch, adjoining Peter Etheredge, Joseph Batchelor. Jr., and said Pridgen. Wit: Nathan Boddie and Mourning Sikes.

DB 5-260 JAMES DEAN of Nash Co. to GEORGE GREEN of same, Feb. 7, 1804, for $50.00 a tract of 100 acres on the Great Swamp adjoining Irvin Eatman and Noel Eatman, it being part of the land whereon said Deans then lived. Wit: Richard Smith and William Jordan.

DB 5-260 WILLIAM PARKS, SR. of Nash Co. to MOSES PARKS of same, June 8, 1811, for $100.00 a tract of 100 acres on the south side of Tar River, it being part of 588 acres granted to said William Parks and including 44 acres known as the Stokes land and Parks' old mill, said land adjoining a parcel that was conveyed by said Parks to his son, William Parks. Wit: J. Bonds and Lemuel Sutton.

DB 5-261 DEMSEY BRASWELL of Nash Co. to his son, ARCHIBALD BRASWELL, of same, May 25, 1811, a tract of 168 acres on the south side of the Great Branch adjoining Jacob Braswell and Ellen. Wit: Sam Smith and William Walker.

DB 5-262 STEPHEN WELLS of Nash Co. to JORDAN SHEROD of same, Feb. 19, 1811, for $70.66 a tract of 33 1-3 acres adjoining Nathan Joiner, Grace Edwards, and Jordan Sherod. Wit: John W. Vick.

DB 5-264 DAVID RICKS, Sheriff of Nash Co., to MARY VICK of same, July 18, 1811, at public auction, whereas Archibald Griffin was the highest bidder at 26 pds., he relinquished his bid to said Mary Vick for a tract of 94 acres on the north side of Stony Creek adjoining Jesse Hunt, Thomas Hunter, and John Melton, which land was sold as the property of Benjamin Whitfield, deceased, to satisfy a judgment obtained by B. Gay & Co. Wit: L. F. Ellen, and Willie G. Whitfield.

DB 5-265 JESSE NICHOLS of Nash Co. to THEOPHILUS GRICE of same July 23, 1811, for $37.50 a tract of 50 acres on the north side of Contentnea Creek adjoining said Theophilus Grice, Jesse Peel, and Benja. Nichol. Wit: Stephen Grice, Thos. Sanders, and Jos. Williamson.

DB 5-266 JOSIAH LITTLE of Nash Co. to his wife, NANCY LITTLE, of same, Jan. 2, 1811, for love and affection all his household and kitchen furniture and money due him. Wit: David Winstead and Timothy Terrell.

DB 5-267 STEPHEN GRICE, JACOB GRICE, PETER WATKINS, and ALEXANDER GRICE to THEOPHILUS GRICE of Nash Co., Feb. 2, 1803, for 75 pds. all their rights to one negro woman and her five children who were the property of William Grice of Nash Co. Wit: Noel Renlow, Josiah Renlow, Jacob Grice, Leimon Watkins, and Jacob Grice.

DB 5-268 DANIEL MANN of Nash Co. to DAVID WINSTEAD of same, Oct. 12, 1810, for $200.00 one negro girl. Wit: Amos Gandy.

DB 5-268 CHARITY BUNN of Nash Co. to her four children, PIETY BUNN, WILLIAM BUNN, HENRY BUNN, and JEREMIAH BUNN, Aug. 6, 1807, for love and affection: to Piety Bunn, one negro woman and furniture; to William Bunn, Henry Bunn, and Jeremiah Bunn, articles of furniture and five negroes by name, the above bequests not to be delivered until after her death. Wit: Redmund Bunn and Nathan Gilbert.

DB 5-270 HENRY HARRISON of Nash Co. to WILLIAM

TAYLOR of same, Nov. 26, 1808, for 125 silver dollars a tract of 200 acres adjoining James Branch and Robert Melton. Wit: John Glover and William Taylor.

DB 5-271 DAVID WINSTEAD of Nash Co. to JOHN JINK-INS of same. Dec. 21, 1806, for $26.00 a tract of 52 acres on Town Creek adjoining Samuel Winstead, Lamon, Williams, and Lamkin. Wit: Jesse Newby.

DB 5-272 REDMUND BUNN of Nash Co. to his nephew, BENNETT BUNN, of same, June 5, 1809, for love and affection, after the death of said Redmund Bunn and his wife, his plantation above the Falls of Tar River called the Quarter Plantation containing 200 acres and four negroes by name. Bennett Bunn was keeping store for Mr. Benjamin Atkinson of Pitt Co. Wit: Keziah Thomas, Drusilla Bunn, and A. Horn.

DB 5-273 JESSE THORP of Nash Co. to CORDAL HUNTER of same Sept. 28, 1811, for $1400.00 a tract of 831 acres on both sides of Little Compass Creek adjoining Exum's old line (then Samuel Smith), Solomon Edwards, and the Horse Pen Branch. Wit: Norfleet Curl and M. Mason.

DB 5-274 NORFLEET CURL of Nash Co. to JEPHTHAH DANIEL of same. Sept. 23, 1811, for $296.66 2ʒ3 a tract of 89 acres on the south side of Kirby's Creek adjoining David Daniel and said Jephthah Daniel. Wit: Cordal Hunter and Lewcy Fort.

DB 5-275 HENRY WHITEHEAD and RAHAB WHITEHEAD of Nash Co. to WILLIAM WRIGHT, SR. of same, May 5, 1810, for $1700.10 a tract of 261½ acres on the south side of Fishing Creek and east side of Pollock's Beaver Dam Swamp adjoining Pollock. Wit: Peter Arrington and Jesse Taylor.

DB 5-276 JOHN ALSTON and wife. MARGARET ALSTON, of Halifax Co. to RICHARD HOLLAND of Nash Co., Nov. 26, 1810, for 93 silver dollars a tract of 77 acres at or near Marcum Cooper's patch, the road, and Reuben Whitfield. Wit: J. Alston, W. J. Alston, and Stp. Hinton. Margaret Alston was examined in Halifax Co. by Willis Alston, J. P. and Wood Jones Hamlin. J. P., as she was unable to travel to the Nash Co. court.

DB 5-277 JOHN ALSTON and wife. MARGARET ALSTON, of Halifax Co. to RICHARD HOLLAND of Nash Co., Nov. 26, 1810, for 607 pds. 10 sh. Virginia money a tract of 1000 acres on Little Sapony Creek and Great Sapony Creek adjoining Marcum Cooper's patch, the road, John Evans. Whitfield's former line, Kent (then Holland), and Cotes. Wit: Jas. W. Alston, K. Alston, and Stp. Hinton. Margaret Alston was examined as above.

DB 5-278 JOSEPH JOINER of Nash Co. to CORNELIUS JOINER of same. Feb. 23, 1792, for 44 silver dollars a tract of 44 acres on the south side of Sapony Creek adjoining Jacob Joiner and Holland's Branch. Wit: John Joiner and Curtis Joiner.

DB 5-279 WILLIAM ARRINGTON of Nash Co. to JACOB JOHNSON of Mughlinburgh Co., Kentucky, Nov. 1, 1811, for $383.00 a tract of 191½ acres on the south side of Tumbling Run adjoining William O'Neal. Councel, and E. Edwards. Wit: Elizabeth Battle and E. Edwards.

DB 5-280 JAMES G. LAMON of Nash Co. to THOMAS WIN-STEAD of same, Jan. 17, 1811, for $149.00 a tract of 149 acres in Nash Co. Wit: Demsey Braswell and Wm. H. Hall.

DB 5-281 ENOCH FLOOD, SR. of Nash Co. to JOHN WELLS of same, Aug. 22, 1811, power of attorney to collect all debts due him and to sell any property so desired. Wit: John Beelane.

DB 5-282 LEWIS ABLEWIS LAMKIN of Nash Co. to WILL-IAM HATTEN. a child of Lewis Hatten, of same, Feb. 5, 1807, for natural good will furniture, books, and three horses. Wit: Mathew Carter and Richard Glaukmer.

DB 5-282 JOSEPH JOHN SUMNER and wife, DOROTHY SUMNER, of Davidson Co., Tennessee, to JAMES HILLIARD of Nash Co., Oct. 28, 1811, for $300.00 a tract of 150 acres on the south side of Swift Creek, it being a parcel of land conveyed from Thomas Gilchrist to John Williams, and by said Williams to Matthew Drake, Sr., and by said Drake to Dorothy Sumner in his will. Wit: Brittain Drake and Harty Drake. Dorothy Sumner was examined in Tennessee.

DB 5-284 JENNINGS HACKNEY of Nash Co. to GRAN-BERRY BAGGETT of same, Feb. 15, 1811, for $107.25 a tract of 33 acres on the south side of Pine Log Swamp. Wit: Sam. Smith and Jonathan Whitehead.

DB 5-285 BENNET LANE of Jackson Co., Tennessee to WILLIAM WALL of Nash Co., Sept. 2, 1805, for $148.00 a tract of 148 acres on the north side of Tar River adjoining William Hammons. Wit: James Trougdale, Robt. Trougdale, and Isaac Hendrick.

DB 5-286 BARNABAS REVEL of Nash Co. to WILLIAM WESTRAY of same. March 8, 1811, for $333.33 1-3 a tract of 100 acres adjoining Fathy Melon, Mathew Revel, and Laseter's Branch. Wit: Jas. C. B. Atkinson and John Atkinson.

DB 5-287 ARCHIBALD GRIFFIN, executor of BENJAMIN VICK. deceased, to the heirs of the late BENJAMIN WHITFIELD, deceased, Feb. 11, 1812, whereas the said Benja. Vick in his lifetime did sell unto said Benja. Whitfield a share of a tract of land to which he became entitled as an heir at law of Richard Vick, deceased, his executor transferred a tract of 59½ acres to the heirs of Benjamin Whitfield. Wit: Jos. Arrington.

DB 5-289 JOHN B. COBB of Wayne Co. to BARTLEY DEANS of Nash Co., Nov. 25, 1811, for $160.00 a tract of 160 acres on the Marsh Swamp adjoining Williamson and Duck, it being part of a tract granted to Stephen Cobb, deceased. Wit: Wm. Horn and Hardy Horn.

DB 5-290 WILLIAM ARRINGTON of Nash Co. to BENJAMIN ATKINSON of same, Nov. 15, 1811, for $2000.00 a tract of 850 acres on the north side of Tar River adjoining said Atkinson, Lewis, William Buntin. Jeremiah Buntin, and Strickland. Wit: John Atkinson and John Green.

DB 5-291 WILLIS TREVATHAN of Nash Co. to HINES DRAKE of same, March 3, 1808. for $484.80 a tract of 333 acres on the north side of Compass Creek adjoining Mathew Trevathan,

Taylor, Hines, said Drake, and Hartwell Hines. Wit: Sam. Smith and Matthew Drake.

DB 5-293 SIMON STRICKLAND of Nash Co. to ARNEAL STRICKLAND of same, March 9, 1809, for 25 pds. a tract of 50 acres on Turkey Creek on Thomas Rogers' old line and the Mill Branch, it being part of the old tract whereon Thomas Rogers deceased. Wit: Polley Strickland and Alsey Hopkins.

DB 5-294 EPHRAIM PERRY of Franklin Co. to SIMON STRICKLAND of Nash Co., Dec. 7, 1796, for 100 pds. Virginia money a tract of 400 acres on the south side of Turkey Creek in two tracts, it being parts of two tracts granted to Thomas Rogers. Wit: Jordan Wiggs, Jos. Gillum, Nathaniel Perry, Sam'l Smith, and Arnold Strickland.

DB 5-295 MICAJAH THOMAS of Nash Co. to DAVID EVINS of same, July 30, 1784, for 200 pds. a tract of 59 acres on the north side of Pig Basket Creek adjoining James Woodard. George Wimberly, and Holland. it being part of a tract granted to said Micajah Thomas by Earl Granville in 1760. Wit: Sam'l Westray and Mourning Ricks.

DB 5-296 KITCHEN BASS of Williamson Co., Tennessee to WALKER MASSENGILL, JR. of Nash Co., Feb. 6, 1812, for $100.00 a tract of 132 acres adjoining said Massengill, John Bass, Gay, and Alston. Wit: D. Sills and Wm. Wheless.

DB 5-297 WILLIAM WHELESS of Nash Co. to PERRIN JONES of Franklin Co., Feb. 4, 1809, for $57.50 a tract of 100 acres on the north side of Little Peachtree Creek adjoining Hopkins and Micajah Thomas' former line. Wit: F. Floyd and Joseph Hopkins.

DB 5-298 LITTLEBERRY WHITE of Nash Co. to ISHAM COOPER of same, March 30. 1810, for $175.00 a tract of 200 acres on the south side of Little Peachtree Creek adjoining said Isham Cooper, Elizabeth Cooper. Corbin Tucker, and Wm. Andrews. Wit: Daniel Taylor and Cornelius Taylor.

DB 5-299 PHILEMON BENNETT of Nash Co. to BANJAMIN BLUNT of same, May 5, 1811 for —— —— a tract of 285 acres in the south side of Fishing Creek adjoining Dozier, Green. Whitehead, Denson, Bravdie, and the Beaver Dam Swamp. Wit: Arthur Whitehead. Henry Harrison. and Henry Blunt.

DB 5-300 LEMUEL NICHOLSON of Nash Co. to JAMES M. NICHOLSON of Halifax Co., Oct. 18, 1806. for $1761.25 a tract of 352 1⁄4 acres adjoining Henry Whitehead and the road. Wit: John Arrington and John Wright.

DB 5-301 JEREMIAH PORTRIS of Franklin Co. to EDMUND JONES of Halifax Co., June 1, 1811, deed of trust for a debt of $300.00 owed to Ira Portris of Nash Co. The security was the land whereon he lived, 638 acres adjoining Arch'd Davis, heirs of Denton Mann. Ira Portis, Joseph Arrington, Francis Ward, John Portris, and William Jones, together with one negro girl. Wit: John Portris.

DB 5-302 JORDAN SHEROD of Nash Co. to STEPHEN WELLS of same, Nov. 14, 1811, for $70.66 a tract of 33 1⁄3 acres on Jacobs Swamp adjoining Nathan Joyner and said Sherod. **Wit:** John N. Vick.

DB 5-303 JACOB BARNES of Nash Co. to JOHN BARNES of same, Feb. 24, 1809, for $215.00 a tract of 80 acres on the north side of Tar River. Wit: A. Gandy and Salley Gandy.

DB 5-304 DAVIS BATTLE of Wake Co. to JOHN ATKINSON of Nash Co., March 21, 1810, for $111.91 a tract of 79 acres on Sam. Smith and Jas. C. B. Atkinson.

grandson, JOSIAH LEWIS. of Nash Co., Nov. 12, 1810, for love

DB 5-305 BENJAMIN BRIDGERS of Franklin Co. to his Horse Pen Branch adjoining Watkins, Daniel, and Thorp. Wit: and good will a tract of 200 acres on the north side of Tar River adjoining John Glover and William Bryant. Wit: Mathew Carter and Kelley Glover.

DB 5-306 WILSON TAYLOR, SR. of Nash Co. to FORT TAYLOR of same, March 28, 1811, for $1500.00 a tract of 150 acres on the south side of Tar River adjoining Drewry Taylor and the road. Wit: Roger Reese and Willowby Ballentine.

DB 5-307 JORDAN JOYNER of Nash Co. to RICHARD DRAKE of same, Oct. 25, 1808, for $100.00 a tract of 150 acres on the head of Town Creek adjoining Winstead and Lamkin. Wit: John L. Lamkin and Wright W. Joyner.

DB 5-309 JAMES G. LAMON of Nash Co. to JONATHAN JOYNER of same, March 24, 1810, for $1000.00 a tract of 340 acres on the south side of Tar River at the mouth of Simmons' Branch. Wit: John L. Lamkin and Duncan Lamon.

DB 5-310 STEPHEN COBB, of Wayne Co. and ROBERT GULLY, SR., of Johnston Co., executors to the will of JAMES COBB, deceased. late of Wayne Co. to JOHN B. COBB of Wayne Co., May 8, 1810, for $65.00 a tract of land in Nash Co. on Marsh Swamp adjoining Williamson and Duck. Wit: Thomas Horn and Theophilus Grice.

DB 5-311 JAMES MASSENGILL, SR. of Nash Co. to WILLIAM WHELESS, SR. of same. Feb. 3, 1812, for $33.50 a tract of 33½ acres adjoining said Wheless, said Massengill, and John Richardson. Wit: John H. Drake and D. Sills.

DB 5-312 ELIZABETH COOPER of Nash Co. to ISHAM COOPER of same, May 20, 1809, for $100.00 a tract of 100 acres on the south side of Little Peachtree Creek adjoining Little B. White. Wit: J. Harrison and Mathew Sikes.

DB 5-313 MATHEW COUNCIL of Robertson Co., N. C. to COOPER WILLIAMS of Nash Co., Jan. 20, 1812, for $75.00 a tract of 72 acres on both sides of Tumbling Run Creek adjoining Edwin Edwards, Elizabeth Councel, Joel Walker, Jesse Lawrence, and Jacob Johnson, it being his third part of a tract of land of which Michael Collins died possessed. Wit: Mathew J. Williams and Isam Councel.

DB 5-315 JULIAN KING of Nash Co. to DAVID EVINS of same, March 13, 1806, for $75.00 a parcel of 15 acres on the north side of Pig Basket Creek adjoining Wimberly, William Braswell, and said Evins. Wit: Sam Smith.

DB 5-316 BENNET STRICKLAND of N. C. to NOAH STRICKLAND of Nash Co., Jan. 1, 1812, for $180.00 a tract of land in Nash Co. which belonged to Henry Strickland, deceased. Wit: Carrolus Strickland and Roland Williams.

DB 5-316 ELIZABETH COUNCIL of Nash Co. to EDWIN EDWARDS of same, Jan. 29, 1812, for $68.50 a tract of 72 acres on Tumbling Run Creek, this being the third part of the land belonging to the estate of the late Michael Collins, deceased. Wit: D. Sills and K. Bass.

DB 5-317 FOSTER MASON, Constable of Nash Co., to ARCHIBALD GRIFFIN of same, Aug. 24, 1811, at public auction for $27.00 one negro boy, sold as the property of Mary Griffin to satisfy an execution obtained by Francis Drake. Wit: Lod. F. Ellen.

DB 5-318 JESSE THORP of Nash Co. to JOHN HILLIARD of same, Sept 12, 1811, for $350.00 one negro man. Wit: James Manning and Jas. C. Atkinson.

DB 5-319 MARY GRIFFIN of Nash Co. to ARCHIBALD GRIFFIN of same, Feb. 19, 1811, for $400.00 one negro boy. Wit: John Arrington.

DB 5-319 HARDY HUNT and wife, NANCY HUNT, of Lincoln Co.. Tennessee and JORDAN BASS and wife, BETHANY BASS, of Wilson Co., Tennessee to WILLIAM ROBBINS of Nash Co., July 23, 1810, for 100 pds. Virginia money a tract of 62½ acres adjoining John Bass, Mourning Gay, James Massingill, and the Back Swamp. Wit: Laban Webb and Brown Webb. Bethany Bass and Nancy Hunt were examined privately in their respective counties in Tennessee.

DB 5-320 MILLS GAY of Wilson Co., Tennessee to WILLIAM ROBBINS of Nash Co., Aug. 13, 1810, for $1000.00 a tract of 33 1ʒ3 acres on the Back Swamp adjoining Mourning Gay, Jordan Gay, and Josiah Gay. Wit: Laban Webb and Brown Webb.

DB 5-321 DAVID RICKS. Sheriff of Nash Co., to DANIEL WALKER of same, July 2, 1810. at public auction for 21 pds. 2 sh. 6 p. a tract of 100 acres lying between Stony Creek and Swift Creek adjoining William Hunt, Thomas Griffin, White. and the Tarborough Road. It was formerly the property of Benjamin Whitfield, deceased, and was willed by him to Drewcilla Bunn. It was sold to satisfy two judgments obtained by Thomas Griffin, guardian, against the devisees of Benja. Whitfield. whose lands were in the hands of Philander Tisdale. Hardy G. Whitfield. Drewcilla Bunn, Willie G. Whitfield, Benja. Whitfield Guilford G. Whitfield. Archd. Whitfield and John Thomas Griffin Whitfield, the heirs. Wit: John Glover and Jephthah Daniel.

DB 5-322 DAVID RICKS, Sheriff of Nash Co. to DANIEL WALKER of same, May 11, 1810, at public auction for 12 pds. 14 sh. a tract of 70 acres on Compass Creek and the public road, sold as the property of Delilah Whitfield to satisfy judgments obtained by Michael Horn and Daniel Mann. Wit: John Glover and Jephthah Daniel.

DB 5-323 DANIEL MANN of Nash Co. to JERMAN MANN

of same, Nov. 11. 1810, for $50.00 a tract of 200 acres adjoining John Dew, Dempsey Barnes, Blackwell, John Morriss, and the road at the county line. Wit: D. Winstead.

DB 5-324 ARTHUR WHITEHEAD, executor of NATHAN WHITEHEAD, deceased of Nash Co. to JETHRO BASS of same, Feb. 11, 1812, for $852.00 a tract of 400 acres on Little Peachtree Creek Big Peachtree Creek, and Back Swamp, adjoining Devenport and said Bass, it being the land sold at the sale of said Nathan Whitehead, deceased. Wit: J. H. Drake and Daniel Woodard.

DB 5-325 JOSEPH ARRINGTON of Nash Co. to JESSE STRICKLAND of Franklin Co., April 9, 1812, for $100.00 a tract of 182 acres adjoining Hartsford, James Cone, William Morgan, and the county line. Wit: Samuel Sandeford and James Cooley.

DB 5-326 HENRY WILLIAMS and wife, MARY WILLIAMS, of Nash Co. to HOPKINS RICE of same, May 11, 1812, for $700.00 a tract of 231 acres on the south side of Tar River, it being the part of land descending to the said Mary Williams from the death of her father, Philander Williams, and her brother, Pride Williams, which was allotted to her by commissioners appointed by the County Court of Nash Co. Wit: David Ricks and Micajah Ricks. Mary Williams was examined separately by Richard Holland, J.P.

DB 5-327 WILLIAM HOPKINS of Wake Co. to BRITTAIN PERRY of Nash Co., March 29, 1812, for 40 pds. a tract of 100 acres on Jumping Run adjoining Rutherford and Sherod Brantley. Wit: Jesse Hammons and William Jordan.

DB 5-328 JOHN CROWELL of Nash Co. to JESSE BARNES of Edgecombe Co., Sept. 17, 1810, deed of trust for $364.42½ which Crowell owed to said Barnes. The security was a tract of 733 acres on the south side of Little Swamp adjoining John Dew. Wit: Joseph Barnes, German Mann, Isaac Horn, J. Harrison, and Joseph Barnes.

DB 5-329 DANIEL MANN of Nash Co. to JOHN HANSELL of same, March 9, 1810, for $400.00 a tract of 100 acres adjoining John Dew and Joseph Phillips, part lying in Edgecombe Co. Wit: Wm. Whitehead.

DB 5-330 DAVID RICKS, Sheriff of Nash Co., to JOHN NUTTALL, Jan. 2, 1809, for 100 pds. one negro girl, sold as the property of Henry Harrison. Wit: A. Gandy.

DB 5-331 HENRY TISDALE of Nash Co. to ELISHA TISDALE of same, Feb. 3, 1808, for 100 pds. a tract of 220 acres on the north side of Moccasin Creek. Wit: Dru. Williams and Warren Tisdale.

DB 5-332 THOMAS CARTER of Nash Co. to NOAH STRICKLAND of same. May 12, 1812, for 100 silver dollars a tract of 100 acres on the south side of Tar River and on Little Swamp adjoining said Noah Strickland, Mathew Carter, the Turkey Creek Road, and the old Tarborough Road. Wit: William Jones and Bolen Strickland.

DB 5-333 THOMAS CARTER of Nash Co. to NOAH STRICKLAND of same, May 12, 1812, for 100 silver dollars a tract of 100 acres on the south side of Tar River adjoining Cullin Carter Jones.

Wit: William Jones and Bolen Strickland.

DB 5-334 BENJAMIN ATKINSON of Nash Co. to WILLIAM ATKINSON of same, Nov. 26, 1811, for 1300 Spanish milled dollars a tract of 335 acres on the north side of Tar River and on the mill branch, including the mill and one acre on the other side, adjoining William Buntin and Noah Strickland. Wit: Roger Reese and Wilson Hammons.

DB 5-335 JOHN VICK of Nash Co. to ELIJAH VICK of same, March 21, 1812, for $10.00 a parcel of 9 acres adjoining Benjamin Vick, John Vick, and Samson Braswell, it being land granted by the State of N. C. to Disey Hunt. Wit: Lod. F. Ellen and Willie G. Whitfield.

DB 5-336 JOHN VICK of Nash Co. to ELIJAH VICK of same. March 21, 1812, for 10 pds. a tract of 100 acres on the north side the south side of Tar River at the mouth of Arthur William's Branch adjoining Thomas Lewis and Strickland. Wit: John Taylor and Nathan Cockrell.

DB 5-341 LITTLETON SCREWS of Nash Co. to ALEXANDER SORSBY of same, Jan. 4, 1812, for $250.00 a tract of 84 acres on the south side of Beaver Dam Swamp and on Cabin Branch adjoining Cain; also, another tract of 17 acres on the south side of Beaver Dam Swamp adjoining Cain, the above mentioned tracts having been devised to said Littleton Screws by the will of his father and allotted to him by commissioners, being tract No. 2 and No. 3 in the division held in Nov. 1805. Wit: John T. Barrow and Lazarus Whitehead.

DB 5-342 JOHN VICK of Nash Co. to ARCHIBALD GRIFFIN of same, March 17, 1812. for $50.00 a tract of 68 acres on the north side of Pig Basket Creek adjoining Barrett and Ellen. Wit: Philander Tisdale and Demsey Braswell.

DB 5-343 AMOS GANDY, Sheriff of Nash Co., to ARCHIBALD GRIFFIN of same, Aug. 8, 1812, at public auction for 100 pds. a tract of 59½ acres on the north side of Stony Creek adjoin-of Stony Creek adjoining said John Vick and Benjamin Vick. Wit: L. F. Ellen and Willie G. Whitfield.

DB 5-337 JOHN VICK of Nash Co. to ELIJAH VICK of same, March 21, 1812, for 10 pds. a tract of 233 acres on the north side of Stony Creek adjoining Benjamin Vick, John Vick's old line, and Jacob Vick. Wit: L. F. Ellen and Willie G. Whitfield.

DB 5-338 JOHN VICK of Nash Co. to ELIJAH (ELI) VICK of same, March 21, 1812, for 1000 silver dollars a tract of 212 acres on the north side of Stony Creek adjoining James Williams and Benjamin Vick. Wit: L. F. Ellen and Willie G. Whitfield.

DB 5-339 ISAAC WOODARD and CADER WOODARD of Wayne Co. to JESSE PEELLE of Johnston Co., Jan. 11, 1809, for 250 pds. a tract of 210 acres on the north side of Contentnea Creek adjoining Grice, Nichols, Williamson, and the Marsh Swamp, agreeable to the deeds given from Jacob Duck to Thomas Woodard. Wit: Sion Sanders, William Sanders, and John Peelle.

DB 5-340 JOHN BONDS of Nash Co. to ROBERT WILLIAMS of same, Feb. 13, 1811, for $300.00 a tract of 150 acres on ing Braswell, sold as the property belonging to the heirs and devisees of Benjamin Whitfield, deceased, to satisfy a judgment obtained by the executor of Benjamin Vick, deceased. Wit: John Arrington and Sterling Anderson.

DB 5-344 CORDAL HUNTER of Nash Co. to SOLLOMON EDWARDS of same, March 31, 1812, for $185.00 a tract of 100 acres adjoining said Edwards and Samuel Smith. Wit: Sam. Smith and Edwin Harriss.

DB 5-345 DUNCAN CAIN and wife, ELIZABETH CAIN, of Nash Co. to DANIEL WALKER of same, Dec. 20, 1811, for $1400.01 all of his land, a tract of 250 acres on the south side of Fishing Creek adjoining Cullin Battle, Bryant Hines, and the Dobb's Branch, sold to satisfy a deed of trust to Nathan Powell. Wit: Allanson Powell and Henry Walker.

DB 5-346 JOHN CROWELL of Nash Co. to LEVI S. UNDERWOOD of same, June 3, 1812, for $1350.00 a tract of 733 acres on the south side of Little Swamp adjoining John Dew. Wit: David Ricks and Amos Gandy. Jesse Barnes and Joseph Barnes of Edgecombe Co. gave a quit-claim to this piece of property.

DB 5-347 WILLIAM MANOR and wife, FRANCES MANOR, of Duplin Co. to WILLIAM CARPENTER of Nash Co., March 25, 1809, for $120.00 a tract of 222 acres on the north side of Moccasin Creek adjoining John Rice. Wit: Willie Aberson, William Moody, and Abraham Winborn.

DB 5-348 ISAAC WOODARD and CADER WOODARD of Wayne Co. to JESSE PEELE of Johnston Co., Jan. 11, 1809, for 50 pds. a tract of 128 acres on the north side of Contentnea Creek adjoining Benjamin Cobb, Benjamin Flowers, and Jeremiah Nichols. Wit: Sion Sanders, William Sanders, and John Peelle.

DB 5-349 WILLIAM ROSE of Edgecombe Co. to HARTWELL HINES of Nash Co., Nov. 4, 1806, for 250 silver dollars a tract of 164 acres adjoining Matthew Trevatham. Taylor, and said Hines. Wit: Sam. Smith and Matthew Trevathan.

DB 5-350 WILLIAM ARRINGTON of Nash Co. to JOHN GLOVER of same, April 11, 1812, for $750.00 a tract of 488 acres on Sapony Swamp adjoining Daniel Batchelor, Matthias Manning, William Bryant, and Samuel Batchelor. Wit: William Arrington, Jr. and Edward York.

DB 5-351 JAMES NICHOLS of Nash Co. to JESSE PEELLE of Johnston Co., Nov. 29, 1811. for 30 silver dollars a tract of 114 acres on Frank's Branch adjoining Jesse Peelle and William Row, it being part of a tract granted to Jeremiah Nichols, deceased. Wit: John Peelle and Joseph Williamson.

DB 5-352 MATHEW TREVATHAN of Nash Co. to HARTWELL HINES, JR. of same. Feb. 16, 1811, for $337.00 a tract of 111 acres on the north side of Compass Creek adjoining said Hines, Rose's former line, and Reuben Taylor. Wit: Sam. Smith and Lewis Hines.

DB 5-353 ELIZABETH CURL of Nash Co. to her son, NORFLET CURL, Aug. 3, 1812, for love and affection two negroes by name, to take effect after her death. Wit: Marmaduke Mason and Joab Hiett.

DB 5-354 JOHN FAULCON, Clerk of Court, Surry Co., Virginia to JOSEPH ARRINGTON and JOHN H. DRAKE, justices of Nash Co., Nov. 2, 1812, whereas JOHN HARRISON and wife, ANN HARRISON, conveyed unto JOSIAH HOLLEMON all their right and interest in the real estate where of James Derring died seized and possessed in Surry Co., Virginia, Nov. 16, 1812, and Ann Harrison, wife of said John, could not conveniently travel to Surry Co. to relinquish her right of inheritance in the lands, that she should be examined by these justices separately from her husband as to her willingness.

DB 5-355 JOHN HARRISON and wife, ANNE HARRISON, of Nash Co. to JOSIAH HOLLEMON of Isle of Wright Co., Virginia, Nov. 16, 1812, for $200.00 all their right, title, claim, and interest in all the real estate of which James Derring of Surry Co., Virginia died seized and possessed. Wit: Wm. McGregor, A. Arrington, Nathaniel Harrison. and John Derring.

DB 5-356 DAVID MELTON of Nash Co. to WILLIS WARD of same, Oct. 7, 1812, for $160.00 a tract of 160 acres on Little Sapony Creek adjoining William Matthews, it being part of a tract that was conveyed from John Matthews to David Melton. Wit: Richard Holland and Barna Tucker.

DB 5-357 REUBEN WHITFIELD of Nash Co. to RICHARD HOLLAND of same, May 16, 1811, for $300.00 a tract of 150 acres at the mouth of Roger's Branch it being a tract that was conveyed by Reuben Whitfield to his son. Reuben Whitfield. Wit: Barna Tucker and Elizabeth Holland.

DB 5-358 LEVI UNDERWOOD of Nash Co. to SAMUEL L. LAMKIN and JOHN L. LAMKIN of same, Nov. 4, 1812, for $1350.00 a tract of 733 acres on the south side of Little Swamp adjoining John Dew. Wit: John Underwood and Nancy Underwood.

DB 5-359 DAVID RICKS, Sheriff of Nash Co., to WILLIE G. WHITFIELD of same, July 18, 1811, at public auction for 25 pds. a tract of 116 acres on the north side of Stony Creek adjoining Benja. Whitfield and Edward Wilson, sold as the property of Benja. Whitfield, deceased, to satisfy a judgment obtained by Thomas Griffin, guardian, against the heirs. Wit: Henry Arrington and Thompkins Rose.

DB 5-360 ARCHIBALD GRIFFIN of Nash Co. to MARY VICK of same, Aug. 14, 1812. for 100 pds. a tract of 59½ acres on the north side of Stony Creek adjoining Braswell and the mill branch. Wit: Ed. Barnes and Benja. Barnes.

DB 5-361 DAVID TAYLOR and wife, MARY TAYLOR, JOSIAH TAYLOR, JONATHAN TAYLOR, ORREN TAYLOR, WILLIAM MASON and wife. NANCY MASON, and TREASY TAYLOR, relict of Mills Taylor, deceased, all of Robertson Co., Tennessee appointed MILLS TAYLOR of the same county and state as their attorney in the sale of a tract of 525 acres lying in Nash and Edgecombe counties on the south side of Beach Run

Swamp, on which Mills Taylor formerly resided, Nov. 15, 1810. Wit: John Hutcheson and Jas. Appleton, acting J.P.'s.

DB 5-362 MILLS TAYLOR of Robertson Co., Tennessee and Mills Taylor as attorney for DAVID TAYLOR and wife, MARY TAYLOR, ORREN TAYLOR, JOSIAH TAYLOR, JONATHAN TAYLOR, WILLIAM MASON and wife, NANCY MASON, and TREASY TAYLOR, relict of Mills Taylor, deceased late of Nash Co. to WILLIAM BELLAMY of Nash Co., Nov. 14, 1811, for $1000.00 a tract of 519 acres in Nash and Edgecombe counties adjoining the lands of Reuben Taylor, Sr., the heirs of Cullen Anders, deceased, Jesse Taylor, and Rachel Whitley, deceased, including the land and plantation whereon the said Mills Taylor, deceased, formerly lived and being all the land he possessed at his death. Wit: Federick Phillips and Josiah Battle.

DB 5-363 ISHAM COOPER of Nash Co. to JESSE BASS of same, Jan. 7, 1812, for $200.00 a tract of 200 acres on the south side of Little Peachtree Creek adjoining Elizabeth Cooper, Corlean Tucker, William Drew, and William Andrews. Wit: Michael Westray and Gideon Bass.

DB 5-364 ISHAM COOPER of Nash Co. to JESSE BASS of same, Jan. 20, 1812, for $200.00 a tract of 100 acres on the south side of Little Peachtree Creek adjoing Littleberry White. Wit: Michael Vester and Gideon Bass.

DB 5-365 JOSEPH PERRIN JONES of Franklin Co. to JOSEPH HOPKINS of Nash Co., Feb. 29, 1812, for 40 pds. 10 sh. specie a tract of 81 acres on the north side of Little Peachtree Creek adjoining Joseph Hopkins and Thomas. Wit: Jesse Bass and Wm. Wheless.

DB 5-366 ERASMUS CULPEPPER of Nash Co. to NATHAN POWELL of same, Jan. 15, 1805, for $600.00 a tract of 82 acres on the south side of Fishing Creek. Wit: Sam Smith and Foster Mason.

DB 5-367 JOHN UNDERWOOD and LEVI UNDERWOOD of Nash Co. to R. R. REDDING of same, Dec. 14, 1811, for $450.00 a tract of 100 acres adjoining Levi Underwood, Drewry Boymon, and the road. Wit: Tom Phillips and D. Daniel.

DB 5-368 SAMUEL COCKRELL of Nash Co. to DAVID WINSTEAD of same, Aug. 20. 1812, for $606 00 a tract of 192 acres on the north side of Tar River below the Paster Ford adjoining John Poland. David Pridgen and Joseph Cockrell. Wit: Hopkins Rice, William Ross. and Joseph Cockrell.

DB 5-369 ISAAC HILLIARD of Halifax Co. to DEMPSEY TAYLOR of Nash Co., Dec. 6, 1808, for 75 pds. Virginia money a tract of 80 acres on the south side of Beaver Dam Swamp. Wit: Alexander Sorsby and Exum Phillips.

DB 5-370 JOHN UNDERWOOD and LITTLE B. HINES of Nash Co. to RICHARD R. REDDING of same, Dec. 13, 1811. for $450.00 paid to John Underwood a tract of 100 acres adjoining Hartwell Hines, Drewry S. Boynom, and the road. Wit: Tom Phillips and David Daniel.

DB 5-371 NATHAN POWELL of Nash Co. to ALEXANDER

SORSBY of same, May 17, 1811, for $2745.00 a tract of 549 acres on the south side of Fishing Creek adjoining Mrs. Culpepper, Whitaker, Earsmus Culpepper, and Beaver Dam Swamp. Wit: John H. Drake and Sam'l Smith.

DB 5-372 ROBERT JONES of Nash Co. to ALEXANDER SORSBY of same, Nov. 18, 1812, for $300.00 one negro boy. Wit: None.

DB 5-372 ARTHUR ARRINGTON of Halifax Co. to RICHARD ARRINGTON of Nash Co., Nov. 15, 1809, for 126 pds. 13 sh. 4 p. Virginia money a tract of 126 2⁄3 acres in Nash Co. adjoining John Hilliard, Henry Arrington, and said Richard Arrington, it being a parcel of land allotted to him in the division of his father's land. Wit: Joseph Arrington and Henry Arrington.

DB 5-373 WILLIE G. WHITFIELD of Nash Co. to MARY VICK of same, Aug. 14, 1812, for $150.00 a tract of 126½ acres on the north side of Stony Creek adjoining Benja. Whitfield and Edward Wilson. Wit: Arch'd. Griffin.

DB 5-374 WILLIAM RICHARDSON of Lincoln Co., Tennessee to JOSEPH HOPKINS of Nash Co., Aug. 25, 1812, for $325.00 a tract of 300 acres on the west side of Back Swamp adjoining James Massingill, John Richardson. William Richardson, Sr., Jesse Bass, and Thomas Lawrence. Wit: Walker Massingill and Annis Massingill.

DB 5-375 CHARITY VESTER of Nash Co. to her son, ELIJAH VESTER, July 1808, for love and affection one negro boy, after her death and after paying the following legacies: to son, Benjamin Vester, $50.00; to son William Vester, $50.00; to grandson, John Parrott, $25.00 to granddaughter, Elizabeth Parrott, $25.00; to grandchildren, Sal'ev Taylor and Richard Taylor, $25.00 each. Wit: Jesse Bass and Betsey Bass.

DB 5-376 CORDAL HUNTER of Nash Co. to DAVID DANIEL of same, Oct. 1 1811, for $700.00 a tract of 200 acres on the north side of Stony Creek adjoining William Barnes and Joel Pitman. Wit: D. Daniel and James Hunter.

DB 5-377 SHEROD BRANTLEY of Nash Co. to BRITTAIN PERRY of same, Dec. 3, 1810, for $145.00 a tract of 200 acres on the south side of Turkey Creek adjoining James Cone, Brantley, and Federick Jones. Wit: Jesse Hammons and Allen Brantley.

DB 5-378 JOHN HANCEL (HANSELL) of Nash Co. to CLABOURN MANN of same, Jan. 9, 1813, for $215.00 a tract of 100 acres adjoining John Dew, Joseph Phillips, and the Mill Branch. Wit: Wm. Whitehead.

DB 5-379 BENJAMIN FLOWERS, SR. of Nash Co. to his son, EATMAN FLOWERS. of same, Oct. 28, 1812, for love and affection all his goods. chattels, and personal estate including livestock, furniture, and money. Wit: William Harrison and Benjamin Flowers, Jr.

DB 5-380 STEPHEN JOHNSON of Nash Co. to HENRY HORN of same. Jan. 13, 1813, for $250.00 a tract of 731 acres on Little Cabbin Branch and Beaver Dam Branch, it being the land whereon Jesse Collins formerly lived. Wit: Drew Williams, Willobough Ballentine, and Levy Hogg.

DB 5-381 JESSE MORRIS of Nash Co. to ROGER REESE of same, Dec. 10, 1812, for $125.00 a tract of 200 acres on the north side of Tar River adjoining Warren, Pusley, Jeremiah Etheridge. and Biggs. Wit: Willie Bunting and Joseph Cockrell.

DB 5-382 BENJAMIN BRIDGERS of Franklin Co. to JESSE READ of Halifax Co., June 15, 1807, for $1273.00 a tract of 1273 acres in Nash Co. on Swift Creek adjoining the lands of Thomas Mann, deceased, William Lawrence, and Denton Mann, deceased. Wit: John H. Drake and Fanny Drake.

DB 5-383 JOHN BRIDGERS of Sumner Co., Tennessee to ELIJAH BODDIE, late of Nash Co., Nov. 28, 1811, for $450.00 all of his interest in a 900 acre plantation on Swift Creek adjoining the heirs of Denton Mann, John H. Drake, Mrs. Patsey Pitts, Malachi Underwood and William Arrington, it being land willed by his late father, William Bridgers, to him and to his brother, Henry Bridgers. It was the land and plantation whereon his father formerly lived and died. Wit: Thomas Bell and L. Hunt.

DB 5-384 GEORGE SUTTON of Nash Co. to Wm. LINSEY, Wm. BODDIE, WILLIS BODDIE, JOHN COOPER, JOHN DEANS, and PRIDGEN MANNING, truntees. Dec. 23, 1812, one acre of land for the erection of a Methodist Episcopal Church adjoining the lands of James Bachelor, George Sutton, and George Boddie (formerly Green Hill). Wit: Michael Vester and Willis Bachelor.

DB 5-385 BEVERLY DANIEL, Esq., Marshall for the District of N. C., to WILLIE WHITFIELD of Nash Co., Dec. 16. 1812, at public auction for $50.38 a tract of 322 acres adjoining Thomas Hunter, Whitfield, David Strickland, Robert Wilson, and Thomas Willis, sold as the property of the heirs and devisees of BENJA. WHITFIELD, deceased, to satisfy an execution obtained by Watson and Ebenezer Stott. Wit: George Boddie and Mich. Collins.

DB 5-386 ELI WILLIAMS of Nash Co. to JOHN POLAND of same. Sept. 19, 1812, for $500.00 a tract of 200 acres in Nash Co.; also, a tract of 150 acres adjoining the above tract, Stephen Vaughan (then Eli William). and Matthias Manning; also, a tract of 116 acres adjoining Eli Williams. John Matthews, and Matthias Manning. Wit: Richard Holland and David Melton.

DB 5-387 DAVID WINBORNE of Nash Co. to CLABORNE FINCH of same, Feb. 5, 1813, for 250 pds. a tract of 496 acres on Beaver Dam Branch and Cattail Branch adjoining said Winborne. Wit: William Carpenter and Hannon Taylor.

DB 5-389 BENJAMIN FLOWERS. SR. of Nash Co. to EATMON FLOWERS of same, Oct. 27, 1812, for 10 pds. a tract of 640 acres on Milstone Swamp adjoining Bunn and John Sanders. Wit: Bartley Deans and Wm. Harrison.

DB 5-390 DAVID NICHOLS of Nash Co. to BARTLEY DEANS of same. Sept. 11, 1812, for 114 silver dollars a tract of 114 acres on Little Swamp adjoining Sanders. Jeremiah Nichol's, deceased, said Bartley Deans, and Duck, it being a part of the land granted to Jeremiah Nichols, deceased. Wit: Lewis Deans, Jesse Nichols. David Bundy, and Wm. Horn.

DB 5-391 BENJAMIN NICHOLS of Nash Co. to DAVID NICHOLS of same, Dec. 12, 1811, for $110.00 a tract of 114 acres on Little Swamp adjoining the line of Jeremiah Nichols, deceased, Bartley Deans, and Duck, including one part of the lands of Jeremiah Nichols, deceased. Wit: Bartley Deans and Ann Nichols.

DB 5-392 AMOS GANDY, Sheriff of Nash Co., to WILLIAM BRYANT, May 12, 1808, at public auction for 31 pds. 5 sh. a tract of 100 acres adjoining said Bryant, William Hammons, and Ratley, sold as the property of ISAAC HENDRICK to satisfy a judgment obtained by James Branch against Isaac Hendrick and Signal Hendrick. Wit: Francis J. Dancy and Exum Phillips.

DB 5-393 THOMAS WHITE and HENRY HINES of Nash Co. to WILLIAM WRIGHT of same, April 15, 1807, for $200.00 one negro man. Wit: John Hilliard and William Wright, Jr.

DB 5-394 JOHN POLAND, JR. of Nash Co. to WILLIAM HARRISON of same, Nov. 12, 1812, for $525.00 a tract of 144 acres on the north side of Tar River on Rooty Branch and Jacobs Swamp. Wit: Alsey Hopkins and Drewry Williams.

DB 5-395 TALTON LEE of Pennetta Co., South Carolina to ARNOLD STRICKLAND of Nash Co., Dec. 11, 1812, for $100.00 a tract of 300 acres known as the Pope Place on the south side of Turkey Creek adjoining Thomas Rogers' old line. Wit: James B. Lee and Richard Mason.

DB 5-396 DAVID DANIEL of Nash Co. to his son, ISHAM DANIEL, of same, Sept. 12, 1811. a tract of 100 acres on the north side of Stony Creek adjoining William Barnes. Wit: Henry Bunn and David Daniel, Jr.

Battle 246, Ann 105, Elisha 511, 513, Jas. 246 (2), 371, 390, 438, 489, Jeremiah 99, Jethro 105, Joel 504, John 114, 130, 150, 248, 255, 461, 552, Josiah 364, 461, 488, Mary 371 (2), 373 (2), Polley 371, 373, Wm. 59, 60, 137, 138, 371, 373, 417

Beckwith, Amos 49, 520, Henry 49 (2), 518, Sion 295, 296, 297

Belile, Barnaby 149

Bell, Andrew 211, Arthur 297, Elias 297 (2), Green 297, 552, Jas. 297

Benton (Binton), Robt. 440, 547

Berryman, Baalam 263 (2)

Bigg 360, 363, 416, John 31, 169

Bilbro, B. 271, Berriman 270, 387

Bisset(t), Catron 431, David 227, 431, John 346

Blackwell 551, George 10, 449, 556, Jas. 247

Blankinship, Linchea 165, 166

Blunt, Benj. 474

Boddie, George 91 (2), 177, 235. 303. 367, 439. 502. 533. 558, Mourning 303, Nathan 6, 91 (2), 177, 235, 241, 303, Wm. 126, 281, 429, 455

Boggs, Lervin 203, Robt. 203, 236, Wm. 159, 203, 236

Bollin, Chas. 132

Bonds, J. 33, 213, 215. 305, 413, 419. 505. John 55 (2), 64, 180, 184 (2), 290, Nancy 184. Wright 484, 505. 529, 539

Bone, John 3 (2), 133, 300, 316, 346, 397 (2)

Boon, Benj. 218 253, 522 (2), Elias 150, 196, 218, Jas. 442, John 218, Nancy 253

Booth 505

Bottoms, John 555, John Long 545, Sam, 422, Sam, Long 118, 545, 555 (2)

Bowers, Ann 502 (2), Max (Maxey, Macks) 331, 354, 502 (2), Wm. 116, 120, 508 (2)

Boyet, Wm. 231 (2), 290, 292

Boykin 153, Benj. 277. 392. 468, Drewry (Drury) 275, 276 (2), 277, 389, 392, 457, 468, Hardy 152 (2), 276, 277, 392, 468, Jacob 277

Branch, S. W. 151

Bradley, Wm. 206

Brantley, A. 213, Asa 208 (2), 286, John 3, 133, 316, 346, 425, Sharod 537

Braswell (Bracewell) 69, Arthur 367, Benj. 2 (2), 294, 332, 447, 495, Brittain 295, 297, Dempsey 74, 209, 399. 456 Frances 239, Jacob 297, Jas. 239. Jesse 297. John 294 (2), 332. 349, Micaiah 81, 147 (2), Nathan 295 296. Orren 2 (2), Robin 217. Sary 294, Wm. 2, 7 (2), 132, 213, 296, 297, 405, 495, Wilson 254 (2), 341, 350, 360, 493

Brewer, Hardy 11

Bridgers, Benj. 11. Drewry 64, Micajah 61, 387, Wm. 65, 387, 460

Broadstreet, Jas. 233

Brown, Chas. 67, Elisebeth 83, Jas. 80 (2), 100 (4), 148, 154, 330, 402, Jeremiah 115, 123, 136, 179, 266, 288, 298, 322, 335, 398, 400 (2), 401, 435 (2), Jethrow 350, Jos. 298, 435, Thos. 340

Bru(i)ce, Cor nelius 210, 558, Cornely 89, Jas. 20, 289
Bryant (Briant), Benj. 313, George 147, Jas. 67, Sam. 88, 103, Wm.
  62 (2), 76, 147, 211, 229 (2), 330, 385, 440, 483
Bunn Benj. 1, 8, 18, 25, 35, 68, 93, 112, 113, 128, 131, 191, 224, 240,
  300, 311, 383, 486 (2), Burwell 14 (2), 191, 432, 549, Charity
  331, David 112, 113, Henry 172 (2), Joel 35, 93, 191, 193, 282,
  286, 409 (2), 423, 432, 513, R. 112, 113, Redmun 35, 306, 487,
  511, 459, Willie 142, 224, 300
Buntin(g), J. 502, Jeremiah 162, 395, 536, 541, Wm. 162 (2), 212
  (2), 302, 331, 413, 516, 536, 541
Burge, Burrell 18, Henry 419, Jeremiah 18, 238, Rich. 18. 99, 305,
          383
Butt(s) 552, Joshua 297 (3), 371, 373

—C—

Cain 477, Duncan 330, 385, 394, Jacob 499, 500, Jas. 206, 226, 330,
  377, 381, 385, 499, 500
Carpenter, Wm. 299
Carr, Benj. 377
Carrell, John 26, 301, 369 (2)
Carstarphen, Wm. 272
Carter 385, Chas. 166, 228, Jacob 213, Matthew 116, 273, 331, Salley
  395, Solomon 174 (2), 185, 249, 305, 313, 383 (2), 395, 442, 485,
  Thos. 174, 185, 242, 331, 395, 408, 544
Cearsey, Thos. 534
Chambliss, Wm. 255
Chapman, John 180, 266, 384
Cherry, Lemuel 439, 447, 547
Chitty, John 17 (2), John 518
Christie, Jesse 348
Churchill, Jas. 131
Clinch, Jon. 461
Cobb, Benj. 80, 153 (2), 154, 165, 166, 181 (3), 277, 389, 457 (3),
  Jas. 153, 322, 457 (2), John Petty 61, 355 (2), Jos. 10, Nathan
  240, 457, Stephen 152 (2)
Cockrell, Jacob 524 (3), John 328, 389, 515, Jonathan 524, Selah
  524
Cockrum (Cockron), Robt.   96, 129, 173
Cohoon, Sam. 236
Coleman, Sarah 272, Theophilus 44
Collins (Collings. Collans), Adam 177, Jesse 480, Penny 241, Solo-
  mon 177, 241, Wilson 177
Col(e)son, Chester 40, 43 (4), 120, 188, Jonas 115, 188, 401
Conditt, Fieldin 200
Cone 146, 366, Jacob 384, Jas. 182 (2), 183, 187, 505, Joshua 145,
  182, 183, 187, 366
Coney, Eliz. 83 (2), Jeremiah 54
Conway, Jas. 163, 359, 500
Cook, Elisha 434, Eliz. 434 (2), Green Babb 434, Jacob 434, 442,
  Jesse 434, Nancy 434, Patsey 434, Polley 434, Salley 434, Thos.
  434

Cooper 246, 489, Benj. 546, 548 (2), David 64, Edmund 143, 264,
Edw. 13, 143 (2). 264, Eliz. 349, 438, 439, John 150, 248, 264,
297, 375 (2), John D. 546, Marcom 96, 135, 425, Mark 492, Vin-
son 64
Coppedge, Wm. 139, 203
Cotten, Solomon 123
Cox, Chas. 444 (2), Eliz. 444 (2), Jesse 343, John 60, 342, 343, 414
Creekmur(e) 77, Ballentine 120, 265, David 433, 508 (2), 516, 533,
536, Eliz. 176, Robt. 96, 99, 109, 120, 123, 158, 176, 219, 220, 241,
265, 423, 508 (2), 516, 533, 554
Cross, Jonathan 114
Crowder, Wm. 234
Crowell 36, 38, 184, 559, Edw. 290, Sam. 394
Crudup, John 491
Crumpler, Benj. 61, West 43, 315 (2)
Culpepper 307, 413, Benj. 445, Chris. 235, Jas. 20. 97, 387. Jere-
miah 15, 78, John 263. Matthew 427, 454. 500, Nathan 359
Curl, Jos. 1, 113, 131, 194. 279, (2). 280, 333, Lewis 4, 14, (2), 45,
83, (2), 99 (2), 105, 260, 286, Wilson 4
99 (2), 105, 260, 286, Wilson 4

—D—

Dance, Ethelred 55, 57, 300, 313, 344, 407, Ezekiel 344 (2), 404
Daniel(s) 72. David 25, 194, 543, Eli 418, 486, Fred. 126, 464, Jas.
126, 464, Reuben 129
Davis 460, Abel 28, 379, 460, 467, 471, Arch. 65, 343, 414, 471, 520,
Eliz. 520, John 414, Lewis 471, Margeott 204, Thos. 159 (2), 203,
236 (2)
Dawson, Dempsey 54, 100, Solomon 292
Deans (Deens) 392, 516, Bartlett 379, Charity 250, Daniel 129,
Demcy 176, Jas. 94, 266, John 508. Mary 200. Molley 52, Rich. 91,
103. 235, Sherod 2, 52, 200, 213, Thos. 142, 162, 383 (2). 536, Wm.
536 (2), 541 (2), Willie 213, Willis 91, 103, 168 (2), 262, 289
Defnal, Wm. 554
Dencon, Fiel 326
Denkins, Jesse 366
Denson 549, Benj. 260, Jethro 13, 143 (2), 264, John 532, Wilson
326
Devanport (Devenport) 6, 443, Elias 445, John 6 (2), John 496 (2),
497
Devaughan, Sam. 148, 166, 287, 402, 456, 478 (2), 544 (2)
Dew, Duncan 83, 84, 162, 175, John 10, 449, 527, 551, Nancy 83,
Wm. 539
Dickerson 219
Dickinson 73, 75, 517
Dison, Wm. 529
Dixon 196
Dortch 470, 532, Isaac 157 (2), Lewis 13, 34, 35, 155 (2), 157, 240,
264, 307, 413 (3), 491, Lovice 155, Wm. 240
Dozier. Enoch 279, Rich. 469, 477 (2), Richmond 297, Thos. 13, Wm.
13, 297

Drake 160, Augustin 552, Benj. 253, 320, 416, 417, Edmund 390, 540, 552 (2), Edwin 63, 245, 552, Fanny 371 (2), 373 (2), Frances 190, 373. Henry 466, 540, 552, Hines 109, Jas. 253, John H. 5, 46, 69, 81, 190, 223, 320, 370, 371, 373, 416, 417 (2), 443, Matthew 17, 67, 74, 91. 150. 171, 191, 218, 225, 235, 249, 303, 314, 318, 367, 405 (2). 428. 439. 498 (2), 510, 522, Nath. 171, 249, Oroondates 74, 249. Rich. 498, Silas 253 (2), Wm. 171, 249, 390, 498 (2), 501, 510 (3), 540

Drewry, Jas. 171, 540

Driver 197, Bud 541, Chas. 268, John 153, 154, 165, 181 (2), Thos. 268, Wm. 194, 353

Drury, Henry 352

Duck, Jacob 152 (2), 244, Lydia 244, Sarah 152, 244

Dugless, Frances 422

Dunnavent, Elijah 3, 42, 59, 60, 80, 149, 228, 240, 285

—E—

Earp (Harp), Luke 182, 184

Eason 450, Isaiah 532, Sam. 532 (2), Wm 331

Eatman 240, 392, Irvin 40, 43, 94, 502, John 40 (2), 43 (2), 94, 120, 188, 389, 392, 456, 468, 506, Joshua 328, Robt. 456, Theofless 315

Edmondson, Abrose 360, 363, 367, 416

Edwards, John 78, 199, 396, Solomon 63, 110, 258, 301, Thos. 124

Eley, Ben. 539

Ellen (Ellin, Flewellen), Betsey 371, 373, Eliz. F. 372 (2), 374, Howell 69, 172, 254, 341. 406, 456, 493, 506, 551, Howell F. 464, Lodrick 254, Shadrach 371, 373, Shadrach F. 372, 374, 417

Ellis (Elles), Elisha 117 (3)

Etheridge, Jarod 87, Jeremiah 31 (2), 77, 87 (2), 88 (3), 103, 173, 360, 363, 433, 485, 547, Lot 150, 248, 297, Peter 241, 533, 558

Evans (Evins), John 186, 375 (2), Sherid 375 (2), Wm. 60

Everidge 261

Exum, John 109, 192, 238, 301 (3), 364, 369 (2), Jos. 130, 238, 301, 485, Priscilla 456

Ezell, Thos. 367

—F—

Faulk 379

Fenner, Rich. 33

Ferrell, Ansel 311, 410, Wm. 387

Finch, Allen 40 (2), 43 (3), 120 (2), 123, 188, 266, Bryant 132, Clabun 266 (2), Isham (Isum) 123, 287

Fitts. John 59, 60, O. 558

Fletcher 81, 110. John 5, 258, 406. 522

Flowers. Benj. 68, 86, 152, 221, 240, Henry 556, Jacob 513, John 100 (3), 355

Floyd, Enuck 196, Penuel 225, 314, Thos. 80

Folsom, Ebenezer 518

Ford, Wm. 18

Fore 187, George 344, Rich. 165, 287, Wm. 184, 211, 412, 505

For(e)man, Benj. 499, 500, Jacob 477
Foster, Rebecca 303
Frazier, Alex. 132, 410, 541
Freeman, Henry 143

—G—

Gainer, Wm. 424
Gandy. Amos 50, 83 (2), 93, 251, 337, Edw. 46, 50 (2), 93, 159
Gardner, George 208, 255, 474, 552, Pryor 208, 552 (2)
Gay, John 15, 78, 137, 186 (2), 415
Geddy, John 33
Gloer, John 305, 433, Sam. 95, 177
Godwin, Sam. 24
Goodson 50. 93
Goodwin, Jas. 342, 343, 424, John 424 (2), 467 (2)
Gorsberry, Benj. 474
Gray, H. 84, Thos. 84
Green516, George 43, 94, 120, 315, 524, Jas. 89, 198 (2), 210, 236.
   360, 390, 516, Jesse 292, John 390, 489, Nathan 28, 65, So. 306,
   Wm. 306 (2), 485
Grice. Alex. 379, Elleck 68, 244, Theophilus 244, 275, 452
Griffin 334, Arch. 6, 11, 59, 60, 172, 209, 318, 334, 399 (2), 457, 464,
   492, 494, 534, Delilah 81 (2), 164 (2), Guilford 492, 494, Hardy
   74, 390 (2), Jesse 203, Jos. 74 (4), Little B. 114, Matthew 61,
   314 463, Micajah 74, Pierce 74, Thos. 108, 217, 259, 349
Grizzel(l), Arther 165, 166, Bannaster 165, 166, Daniel 165, 166
   (2), George 165, 178, Harrod 392, Wm. 153, 154, 165 (3), 166 (3),
   166, 256
Gross. Francis 363

—H—

Hackney 13, 143, 163, 257, 264, 307, 359, 413 (2), Wm. 13
Hall, Edw. 251, 318, J. 92, John 36, 38, Lucy 251, Martin 194. Wm.
   50, 77, 93, 149, 239, 251, 545, 551
Hamilton, Thos. 314, 502
Hammon(s) (Hammond(s) 146, 270, 433, Chas. 69. 114, Eaton 454,
   Eliz. 20, 229, 454, Jas. 69, Je. 327, Jesse 114, 145, 182 (2), 183,
   187 (2), 366, 386, 412, 454, 505, 541, John 97, 114, 387, Ross 454,
   Sally 454. Wm. 20 (2), 33, 77, 87, 88, 97, 229 (2), 289, 433, 440
   (2), 441, 454 (2), 483, 547, Wilson 454
Harbert, Thos. 554
Hardie, Thos. 184
Harlow, Polley 216
Harrel(l), John 30, 131, 333, Orpha 356, Reuben 156, 321, 327
Harris(s) 433, Anselm 131, Cy 441, Daniel 345, Hardy 301, 369,
   John 491, Margit 203, Orin 376, 424, Randoph 301, 369, Wm. 103
   (2), Jesse 452, Jethro 23, 24 (2), 68, 128, 156, 266, 392, 400,
Harrison 229, Charlotte 483, Edmund 348, 537. Jas. Ransom 85
   (2), 168, 203, 273, 412, 438 (2), 441, 525
   401, 468, 506, John 208, 378 (2), 474, Mary 128

Hart, Thos. 49, 209, 240, 493

Haswell, Thos. 33

Hatcher, Amos 425, Uriah 300, 302, 346

Hatten (Hatton), Lewis 485, Peter 292

Hawkins, Benj. 36, 38 (2)

Hays, John 168, 169, 219 (2), Jos. 243, 245, 246, 489

Heag, Jas. 329

Heart, Barnaby 432

Hedg(e)peth, Abram 396, Jesse 452, John 452

Heeth, Chappel 119

Hendrick(s), Isaac 62, 105, Wm. 62, 483, 485

Hickman, Theophilus 136, 398

Hicks, Asey 327, Solomon 145, 147, Wm. 327

Hill, Drusila 440, Green 20, 176, Isaac 294, 495, J. C. 332, Lewis 199, Mary 303, Rd. 199, Sion 41,76

Hilliard 49, 320, Eliz. 513, 520, Isaac 82, 293, 394, 428, 518, Jas. 159 (2), 191, 203 (2), 236, 247, 293, 304 (2), 349, 351, 367 (2), 390, 427, 429, 464, 501, 513 (3), 520 (2), 522, Jeremiah 111, 218, 331, 444, 504, 511, 513 (2), 549, John 191, 304, 464 (2), 494, 501, 513, 522, Leah 331, Mourning 464, Nancy 513 (2), 520, Robt. C. 247, 522, Wm. 513 (2), 520 (2)

Hines 110, 485, Alex. W. 170, 532, Fred. 29, 238, Fred B. 170, 318. 461, Hartwell 29, 170, 193, 492, 494, Henry 170, 193. Lewis 109, 111, 161, 218 (2), 301, 369

Hinton, Chris. 360, 363, 367 (2). 417, Sary 363

Hobbs ,Robt. 120, 298, 400, 408, 435

Hogg, Chas. 481

Holland (Holan) 375, Daniel 109, 207 (2), 281, 375, 477, Rich 281, 477, Thos. 281, Willie 337

Holley, John 4, 45, 481, Josiah 481

Holloman (Hollamon), David 45, 99. Mary 45, Wm. 84

Hoof 190

Horn, Abel 451, Ammay 329, Edw. 224, 317, 559, Eliz. 451, Harris 128, 486, 504, Henry 121, 233. 268. 329, Jacob 23, 24, 114, 161, 218, 311, Jeremiah 268. Joel 307 (2), 504, Joshua 328, Josiah 1, 8, 9, 18. 112. 113, 131. 279, 307, 311, 340, Mary 451, Micah 120, 256, 287, 330, Michael 51. 127, 481, Patience 268, Rhoda 559, Thos. 23 (2), 44, 54 (2), 68. 233, 268. 328 (3). 392, 451, 452 (2), 527, 531, 544 (2), Wm. 54, 268 (3), 328, 402, Wilson 54

Hubbard, John 308 (2), 309. 326

Hunt 245, 366, Benj. 97, Chloe 434, David 72. Hardy 308 (2), 309, 326. 434, Jesse 213, 341, 350. 391, John 246, Micajah Braswell 107, Sion 434, Thos. 309, Wm. 341

Hunter 145, 274 (2), 473. Arch. 11, 111, 121, 327. 337, 453, 473, 492, 494, Drew 111, 172, 191, 194, Priscilla 543, Thos. 107, 121, 208, 254, 341, 350, 391

—I—

Irby, Jos. 61, 314

—J—

Jackson 117, David 200, 270, Edw. 477, Eliz. 69, 210, 308, George 82, 117, 124, Lewis 82, Wm. 69, 87, 89, 308 (2), 441

Jelks 157, 429, 470, 532, Dickson (Dixon) 546, Ethelred 29, 429 (2), 499, 546, Giney (Jene William) 546, Millican 461, Robt. 546, Wm. 429, 499, 500, 546

Jenkins, Rd. 45

Johnson, Andrew 141 (3), 535, Jonah 78, Josiah 78, Matthew 456, Wm. 279, 333, Williamson 386

Jones 516, A. B. 293, Bethany 237, Brittain 293, Catey 349, 501, Cooper 225, 320, 428 (2), Edmund 348, 414, Eli 282, Eliz. 249, Francis 518, Francis Allbrittain 191, 349, 501, Fred. 103, Jeremiah 249, John 119, 143, 297, 352, 455, Jos. 191, Josie (Joice) 142, Julian 349, Lazarus 259, Matthew 428, Newsom 501 (2), Rebeckah 249, Robt. 191, 217, Salle 249, Simon 216, 249 (2), Wm. 249, Willie 119

Jordan (Jorden), Cornelius 322, 323, Joshua 322, 323, Wm. 311 (2), 353, 357 (3)

Joyner (Joiner), Absalom 68, Burwell 47, 534, Cordy 229, Cornelius 47, Curtis 208, 280, 284, 286, 316, 319, 346, 397, 398, 555, Drewry 105, 269, Edmund 284, Jacob 422, 545, 555 (2), Jesse 117 (2), 124, 319, 422, John 47, 117 (3), 118, 124 (2), 284, 319, Lewis 232, 234, 513, Matthew 346, Nathan 316, 331 (2), 346, 347 (3), 425, Wm. 4, 11 (2), 45, 99, 105 (2), 286, 300

—K—

Kennedy, Jas. 498

Kent, Burwell 178, 482, 530 (2), Henry 281, Jesse 84, 178 (2), 431, 448, 481, 482, John 285, Levi 482, Stephen 84, 120

Killingsworth. Freeman 367

King, Julian 72, 126, 399 (2), 464 (2)

Kirby, Jesse 124, Penelapha 124

Kirsey, Jas. 118

Kitchen, Jesse 163, 193, 293, 359

Kith, Jas. 62

Knight 416, Elisha 17, Jas. 381, 491, Kindred 41, Kinsman 144 (2), 360, Spear 488

—L—

Lamon 4, 45, 99, 105, 232, 234, 385, Ann 382, Arch. 290, 292, Duncan 36, 38, 180, 193, 214, 250 (2), 269 (3), 300, 306, 317, 381 (2), 382 (2), 383 (2) 511, 549, Duncan 559, Js. G. 381, 382, John 193, 250, 330, 383, 384 (2), 385, 483, Martha 381

Landingham 377, 477, Thos. 26 (2), 206, 528

Lane 88, Bennet 440, Kinchin 440, Micajah 41, Michage 229, 440, Newet 440, Wm. 105

Langley, Eliz. 319, Isham 284, 398

Lassiter (Lasseter) 246, Arthur 150, Lemuel 245, 246, 489 (2), Tobias 378

Lawrence, Jesse 78, Levise 497, Thos. 490, 496, 497

Ledbetter, John 285, Rolan 285 (2)

Lee Barnaby 491 (2), Jas. 57, 194, 197, 299 (2), Jas. Bud 491
Lemer 505
Lennard, Jas. 445
Lenzey, Wm. 198
Lewis 384, Abner 31, 77, 99, 331, Crowel 106, David 355, Eliz. 92,
  Exum 26, Figures 26, 469, 477, 528, George 62, 174 (2), George
  383, 485, Henry 285, 298, 478, 530, John 355, 413, Magor 530,
  Nicholson 92, 269, 559, Sarah 106. Wm. 106 (2), 160, 470, 489
Lin(d)sey 215, 547, Emmanuel 87, 88, Josiah 386, Sam. 210, Sion 11,
  Wm. 33, 133, 136, 300, 316, 347, 375 (2), 516
Lokus, Francis 114, 366

—M—

Mann, Allen 253, 466, 498, Daniel 307, 377, 413, 522, Denton 196,
  199, 343, 370 (2), 371, 373, 424 (2), 520, 557 (2), Thos. 11, 171,
  373, 417
Man (n) ing, Benj. 91, 168, 237, 345, 349, 362, 439, 441, 447, 547,
  558, Catey 241, Ely 103, 447, Jas. 476, John 148, 169, 304, Marthew 554, Matthias 123, 148, 169, 261, 273, 304, 312, Micael 260,
  Pridgen 162, 173. 219, 516, 517, 536, Rich. 29, Sam. 29, 476, Thos.
  109, 258, 522, Willoughby 6, 168, 443, 447, 525
Marriet 295
Marshall 36, 38, Dixon 232, 306, Eleazar 232, 234, Rich. 232, 234
Marthis, Benj. 293 (2), Mary 293
Mason 131, 280, 333, Abner 263, 470, 546. Benj. 263, 548, Foster 13,
  263, Henry 143, 264, 394, 470, 532, Mark 263 (2), Marmaduke 9,
  72, 131, 142, 145, 274 (3), 279, 333, Ralph 163, 351. 359
Massey 114, Abel 146. Pettipool 227, Rich. 146
Massingill, Jas. 135, 273, 415, John 415
Matthews, Benj. 247. Joel 163, 247, 351 (2), 359, John 304, 318 (2),
  479 (2), Wm. 75, 304, 318 (3)
Matthis, Jacob 164
McComb, Alex. 129
McCormick, John 349
McDade, John 282
McGee (Magee), Wm. 200, 326
McGregor, Wm. 499
Mearns, W. S. 17, 297, 390, 500
Medlin, Josiah 327
Melton 75, 219, 320, Andrew 529. David 278, 304, 318. 493, John 108,
  148, 168, 169, 217, 259 (2), 265, 278, 321, 334, 341, 350, Jos. 108,
  259 (2), 278, Josiah 168, 169, 247, 278, 304, 423, 479, Matthew 73,
  75, 144, 225, Robt. 484
Mercer, John 444
Mer(r)itt 429, Benj. 157, 338 (4), Sary 338, Wm. 157, 338 (2),
Milhouse, Henry 513, 520, Sam. 513, 520
Milner, Jas. 362
Milton 517
Minton 13. 264, John 82, Jos. 13
Mitchell, Henry 513, Isham 376

Mooneham, Gudea 478, Thos. 256, 478

Moore (More, Moor) 441, Callum 198, 516, Carey 213, Edw. 3 (2), 86, 116, 133 (2), 148, 212, 213, 215 (2), 221, 299, 330 (2), 385 (2), 402, Elisha 121, Jas. 198, 516, John 121 (3), 340 (2), Wade 4, 45, 99 (2), 105, 300, Wm. 344

Morgan (Morgin), John 250, 344, 384, Wm. 145, 182 (2), 187, 366, Wm. S. 484

Morphis, Jas. 178

Morris(s), Adley 206, 226, John 551, 556, Mitchael 121, Thos. 11, 218, 367 (2), 405, 416, 522 (2)

Moss, Obadiah 557

Mullans, Jas. 35

Murden, Edw. 119. John 119, 424 (2)

—N—

Nairn, Wm. 355

Naron, John 61

Nash. John 173. Jos. 526, 535

Nelson, Jas. 240

Newsom, Isaac 134, 155, 240, 429, 499, 500 (2), Marey 240

Newton, Benj. 461, 488 (2)

Nichols 379. J. 40, 43, 244. Jacob 152, 379, 392, Jeremiah 152, 379

Nicholson 548, Absalom 263, Barshabah 240, Edw. 84, 162, 228, 240, 256. 413, John 394, 466, Josiah 151 (2), 469, Lemuel 106, 243, Penelope 528, Thos. 304. Timothy M. 394. 528

Norwood, John 132

—O—

Odum, John 190

Oliver 327

O'Neal 169, 304, Arthur 109, 135, 148, 158, 247, 265. Bryant 109, 158 (2), 220, 223, 265, 278, Zacra 158, Zachariah 278

Owens Daniel 484. Elias 147, 288, 322, 484, Enoch 148, 298, 322, 402, John 322, 335, 526

—P—

Pace, Jas. 149, Wm. 139, 211, 263, 470, 548

Parer, Aaron 44, 51, 127, Eliz. 290, 292, Francis 171, 466, John 466, 501, Penelapha 117, Penny 117, Solomon Dawson 127, 231, Wm. 171, 466, 540

Parot 363

Parrish, John 141, 266 (3), 283, 408

Pas(s)more, John 15, 78, 454, Lucy 135, 180 (2), 273, Mary 180, Polley 454, Wm. 20, 454

Pavatt, Isaac 129

Pearce, Joshua 508 (2), 516

Perry, Abraham 304, Benj. 97, 541, Ephraim 410, Nathan 182, 412 (3), 419, Wm. 146, 187

Petticob, John 285

Pettway, John 234

Phillips 556, Chrischany 272, Ephraim 10, 23, 24 (2), 84, 221, 272,

Gabriel 10, 58, 86, 229, 232, 449, 527 (2),Jethro 58 (2), 68 (2), 84, 86, 128, 221, 232, 240, 272, 506 (2), Jos. 10 (2), 86, 221, 449 (2), 506, 527 (3), 531 (2), Lurany 272, Prudence 58, Sarah 272, Sherod (Sharod) 10 (2), 58, 71, 83 (2), 86, 229, 232, 389, 531 (2), Wm. 24, 68, 71, 128 (2), 175

Pierse, Edwin Everett 487, Salley 487, Wm. 487

Pillson, Thos. 193

Pitts, Anne 248, Henry 208, John 248, 373, 417 (2), 463, Noel 196, 320, Walter 248, 510

Plummer, Kemp 317

Poland (Poulan), Wm. 208 (2), 215, 286, 300 (2), 397

Pollard 251

Pollok, George, 137, 138, Thos. 137, 138

Pollok, 245

Pons, John 475

Pope, David 238, 485, Elisha 462 (2), Hardy 461, 488, John 29, 364, 391, 427, 476, Josiah 491, Lazarus 184, Micager 238, Wm. 488

Portis (Portiss, Portice) 28, Eliz. 412, George 379, Ira 342, 412, 414, 537, Jeremiah 65, 343, 376, 379 (2), 414, 537, John 376, 379, Sarah 412

Powell 235, 295, 296, 470, 532, Alanson 206, 226, 257, 421, 437, 469, 494, 528, Daniel 107, 111, 240, 338, 469, 491, Elijah 103 (2), 438 (2), Eliz. 257, Jas. 207, 291, 338, 340, 399, Jesse 405 (2), John 206, 226, 377, Lazarus 34, 35, 257, 391, Moses 546, Nathan 257 (2), 548, Nath. 34, 35, 257, 548, Rich. 487, Samson 211, 353, Susannah 381, 546, Wm. 207, 405, Willie 206, 226, 421, 437, 477, Willoughby 34, 35, 257, 548

Pressell, Hardy 447, Jeams 447

Pridgen 312. 317, 534, 559, Abijah 106, 148, 173, 189, 247, 250, 300, 302, 365, 383, 433, 450, 532, 540, 559, David 3, 42, 46, 96 (2), 102, 106, 123, 140, 148 (2). 173 (2), 189 (2), 241, 250 (2), 261, 300, 365 (2), 450, 532, 533, Hardy 42, 103, 189, 197, 299, 306, Jesse 289, 559

Prim, Jas. 102, 189. 250, 365, Kitchen 103, 237, 383, 438 (3), 558, Mary 365

Pritchett, John 76, 175, 240, 535, Wm. 31, 77, 261, 440

Pullen, Moses 151

Pursel (1) (Pussel) 52, 416, Eliz. 52, 213, Hardy 294, 495, Jeremiah 103, 262

Pusley 363, 525, Jas. 525, Jeremiah 205

—R—

Rackley 433. Francis 312, Maraugh 67, Mathew 314, Parsons 41 (2), 88, 103, Selia 220

Ralls, Joshua 121

Ransom, Amy 85, Cle. 379, Clevears 28, 85 (2), Ley 317, Marceller 85

Ray (Wray), Wm. 18

Reading, Rich. R. 258, 334, 477

Reese, Roger 6, 260, 300, 432

Revel 81, 107, 164, 337, 340, Elias 130, Elijah 25, 63, 111, 121, 522, Henry 130, Micajah 1, 25, 113, 191, 194

Rice, John 139, 149 (2), 183, 227, 311, 357, 410

Richardson, George 490, 497, John 135, 137, 273, Newman (Numan) 135, 180, 205, 273, Wm. 135 (2), 137 (2), 180, 186, 273, 490

Ricks 50, 93, 95, 260, 321, Abra. 83 (2), 87, 88, 260, 280, Benj. 327, Jacob 156 (2), Joel 11, John 286, Lewis 156, Mourning 156, Sarah 318

Robbins, John 84, Stephen 192

Robertson 470, 532, Eliz. 394 (2), John 129, 307, 394 (2), 413, 421, 437, Nath. 30, 114, Peter 13, 155, 163, 264, 307, 359, 413 (2), Wiley 413, Wm. 155

Rodgers, Jesse 490, Thos. 491

Rogers 27, Jacob 193, Jesse 27, 205, Mornin 439, Peleg 344, Robt. 513, Thos. 410 (2)

Rose, Burrel 148, 312, 314, Francis 143, Thos. 139, 193, Thompkins 464 (3), Wm. 139, 193, 218, 464

Ross 289, Andrew 311, Williamson 20 (2)

Row(e), John 457 (3), Widow 23, Wm. 233 (2), 268, 379, 451 (3), 452

Rowlett, Wm. 377

—S—

Sandeford, Henry 525, Jas. 160, 335, 390, 464, 477, Nathan 454, Thompkins 304 (2), Wm. 160, 304 (2), 464

Sanders 323, Cornelius 233, 307, 452, John 524, 542 (2), Thos. 23 (2), Wm. 542

Sandrews, Henry 340

Savage (Savvidge), Drury 198, Moses 168

Screws (Scrues) 477, Henry 377, Jas. 305, 558, John 377

Sedgley, John 1, 8, 18, 112, 113

Selah (Sely), Jos. 50, 93, 117 (2), 124

Sellers, Arthur 133, 215, 316, 431, Fatha 448 (2), Henry 212, 242, Jas. 448, John 185, 212 (2), 242, 347, 425, 516, Jos. 133, Martha 242, Wm. 242, 347 (2)

Sellevent, Owen 457

Shelton, Burrel 151

Sherod (Sherwood), Jenny 515, Jordan 398, 425, 515

Sikes, John 91 (2), 235, 303 (2), 445, Phillip 91, 168, 237

Simmons (Simmuns) 327, H. 69, 333,, N. 191

Sims, Shadrick 275, 276

Skeeto, Wm. 488

Skinner 286, 420, Emmanuel 25, 131, 164, 274, 280, Josiah 142, 337, Sam. 25, 30, 95, 327, 426, Sarah 257, Wiley 19, Wm. 280, 337, 473, Willie 257

Smelley, Drury 188, Moses 80, 181

Smith, Batson 11, 130, 301, 318, Benj. 251, 319, 422, 425, 534 (2), Bennet 534, Brittain 36, 38, Moses 522 (2), Mourning 318, Rich. 311, 313, 353 (2), 357, Sam. 65, 161, 218, 301, 460, 462, 481, 484, 485, 518, 520, 522, 532, 534, 539, Uriah 387

Solesberry, Benj. 474

Solomon, Willis 87, 103

Sorsby, Alex. 29, 73, 157, 476, Benj. 460, 471, Sam. 238, 338, 429

Southall, Furnea 150

Stallings (Stallions), Jas. 237, Moses 103, 237, 438, Simon 155, 413, Wright 237

Stevens (Stephens) 294, Jas. 383, Jeremiah 33, 185, 213, 216, 249, 434, 442, 485, John 33, 332, 442, 485, Jos. 249, Joshaway 447

Steward, Jos. 120

Stewart, Jos. 475

Strickland 111, 139, 313, 321, 327, 353, 395, David 107, 145, 164 (2), 360, 418, Hardy 419, Henry 73, 75, 81, 116, 145, 147, 164, 360, 404, 406, 418 (2), 419, Jacob 136, 398, John 123 (2), 179, 288 (2), Jos. 115, 123, 145, 147, 274, 360, 418, Lazarus 71, 175, 283, 288, 324 (3), 329, 354 (3), 502, Mark 299, Matthew 335, Noah 116, 302, 395, Sam. 268, Simon 183, 197, 288, 324 (3), 400, 529, Solomon 211, 227 (2)

Studevant, Jesse 234

Sutton 148, George 169, 247, 304, 479

Suttone, Thos. 105

—T—

Taburn, Burrel 505

Tann, Benj. 250

Tanner, John 7

Taylor 178, 327, Arthur 554, Benj. 115, 148 (2), 402, Cornelius 20, 89 (2), 308, 309, Chris. 215 (2), 280, 300, 316, 346. Daniel 31, 52, 103, 198, 213, 216, 235, 262, Dempsey 111, 283, 427, 429, 476 (2), Drury 55, 64 (2), 184, 202, 515, Hardy 463, J. 141, 179, 197, 283, 299, 328, 354, 408, 435, 484, 535, 558, John 54, 141, 180, 214, 250, 313, 324, 353, 384, 385, 404, 407, 529 (3), 537, Jordin 196, Patience 52, Reuben 109, 111 (2), 218, 364, 369, 381, 462, 476. Sam. 253, 308 (2), W. 431, Wes. 448, Wm. 141, 404, 407, 537, Wilson 55, 57, 80 (2), 115, 120, 123, 179, 266, 285, 287, 298, 330, 355, 400, 401, 544

Thomas 87, 190, 246, 516, 525, Jacob 47, John 77, Marg. 281, 541, Micajah 11, 38 (2), 50, 67, 93, 103, 132 (2), 140, 198, 348, 396, Micha 495, Rich. 50, 93, Sam. 274, Sarah 406, Tisey 72, 114, Wm. 513 (2), 520 (2)

Thompson, Alex. 111 (2), 218, Andrew 421, 437, Ann 421, Eliz. 437, Robt. 394 (2)

Thorne, Hardy 275, 276, 277

Thorp, Henry 311, 504 (2). 522

Tisdal(e) (Tisdel) 544, Henry 266 (2), 367, Mourning 353, Rennison 367, 487, Wm. 46, 220, 223, 247 (2), 425, 433, 479, 517, 518, 520

Todd, Hardy 311

Tomlinson, Isaac 351, 493

Tounzen, Daniel 7

Trevathan, Willis 109, 111 (2), 238

Tucker, Barnea 490, 497, Benj. 203, 204, 210 (2), 236, 271, 345, 516, Corban 203, Ferreba (Pheraba) 223, 479, Jacob 441, Jas. 109 (3), 135 (2), 220, 223, 247, 265, 554, Jo(a)b 6 (2), 273, 314, Nathan 228, Thos. 96, 123, 136, 173, 177, 179, 204, Wm. 169, 304, Williba 148

Turlington, Eliz. 156, 321, Thos. 321

Turner, Jas. 394, 421, Robt. 522

—U—

Underwood 81, 164, 543, Emmanuel 257, 377, 499, Howel 63 (2), 81, 110, 145, 258, 337, Jacob 170, 238, 485, Malachi 63, 110, 170, Zachariah 110

—V—

Vaughan (Vaun), Demcy 129, Fedrick 123, Fred. 96, Stephen 96, 129, 173

Vester, Michael 261, Solomon 261, 558, Wm. 103, 261 (3), 558 (2)

Vick 280, 327, Benj. 69, 291, Charity 318, Eliz. 543, Henry 30, 95, 121, 131, 280, 301, 333, 337, 420, 426 (2), 543, John 202, 291, 389, 391, 420, 426, 515, 538, Jos. 141, 180 (2), 214, 322 (2), 335, 529, 535, 537, Joshua 5, 81, 164, 367, 406, Jurden 322, Lewis 49, 209, 217, 259, Mary 337, Nathan 95, Prissely 426, Rich. 95, 286, 426, Robt. 141 (3), 266, 322, 335, 353, 357, 404, 407, 408, 526, 535 (2), 537 (2), Sophia 337, Wilson 2, 4, 5

Viverett 515, Henry 42, 449, 551, 556, Micajah 536, Thos. 506

—W—

Walker, Daniel 406, Henry 539, Patrick 36 (3), 38 (2), 306 (2), 317

Wall, Mark 77, 536, 541 (2)

Walthen, Sam. 232

Warburton (Warberton, Worbitton) 172, Dorothy 33, Frances 33, John 207, Wm. 33

Ward, Ben 137, 138, 378, Francis 137 (2), 138, 208, 474, Jos. 552

Warren (Warin) 360, 383, Daniels 88, 433 (2), Henry 439, John 363, 416

Watkins, Henry 19, 191, 282, Jas. 133, John 1, 8, 9, 18 (2), 131, 168, 169, 192, 282, 311, 340, 486, Judah 9

Watson, Chas. 367, Willie 475

We(a)ver, Christina 451, Jehu 451 (3), Stephen 137, 138, 342, 424, 467, 557

Webb, Ann 15, John 78, 345, 442, Lewis 78, 396, Rice 289, Rich. 139, 193, 396, Stephen 15, 78, 196, 199, Wm. 345, 362, Willis 396

Wells 515, Jeremiah 102, John 42, 106, 196, Joshua 42, 102, 250, 365, L. 455, Lewis 263, 306, Micajah 348, 443, Stephen 42, 102, 106, 202, Thos. 42, 47, 102

West, Dempsey 324, John 148, 287, 354, 402, 431, 448 (3), 502 John Spence 511, 549, Nathan 175, 435, Thos. 371, Wm. 180, 214, 288, 322, 324 (2), 335, 435, 535

Wester, Arthur 14 (3), Benj. 453, 473, Hardy 286, Wm. 14 (2), 286, 453

Westray 337, S. 11, Sam. 95 (2), 111, 245, 274, 327, 331, 337, 420,

426, 506, Wm. 473

Whe(eler, Jacob 141, 526, 535, Jos. 344, Sam. 469

Wheless 342, 352, 467, 557, A. 255, 455, Amos 370, Benj. 370, Hardy 501, Mildred 424, Wm. 190 (2), 370, 557

Whiddon 375, Wm. 281, 516

White 334, Jos. 144, 225 (2), 493, Little B. 270, 349 (2), 362, 387, 438, Wm. 71

Whitehead 246, 470, 532, A. 454, Benj. 245, Capt. 151, Chas. 245, Henry 454, 499, Isaac 82, 134, 157, 338, Jacob 126, 464, Jonathan 500, Lazarus 82, 151, 377 (2), 477. Nathan 239 (2). 443, 447, Wm. 82, 108, 134, 429, 469

Whitehouse 46

Whitfield 213, 215, 360, B. 418, Benj. 4, 59, 60, 73, 107 (2) 114, 333 (2), 340 (2), 350, 391, 518, 520, 551, Elisha 529, H. G. 391, Hardy G. 333, 340 (2), 350, Solomon 172, Thos. 260, 453, Wm. 212, 214, 537

Whitley 14, 286. Benj. 177. 241, Fereby 76, Jonas 25, 282, Josiah 318, Sion 334, Wm. 542 (2)

Wiggins, Jas. 206, 226, John 206, 226, Jordan 448

Wilhight, Wm. 190

Wilkins, Wm. 444

Williford, John 136, 398

Willis, Jas. 274, Thos. 107, Wm. 69, 291, 340, Wilson 291, 340 (2),

Wilson 89, 308, Edw. 19, 110. 130, 131, 147, 333, 340, 391, Jas. 20, 309, John 9, 30, 110, 131, 333, Robt. 107, 147, Thos. 20

Williams 225, 552, Beersheba 231, 290, Benj. 7, 356. 386, 541 (2), Billey 188. Cooper 196, 199, 520, D. 402, Drewry (Drury) 61, 153, 154 165, 178, 179, 181, 194, 266, 482, 502, 530, Eley 371, 373, Eliz. 356, Elkana 194, Henry 544, Jas. 30, 63, 69, 72. 107, 108, 121, 126, 148, 191, 194, 254, 274, 279, 280, 291, 333 (2), 337, 341, 351. 418, 420, 456, 463, 493, Jane 92 (2), 214, Joel 57 (2). 299, 385, 400, 401, John 203, 415, 522, 552, Jonah 150, 248, Jonas 44, 100, 175, 188, 214, 231. 290, 297, 328, 353, 450, 538, 556, Jordon 286, 316, 538, Mary 74, 144, 518, Milbury 189, 365, Nathan 328, Penelope 524, Philander 55, 64, 306, 538, Pilgrim 54, Polly 92 (2), Pride 92 (2), Reuben 132. Rowland 100, 256. 402. Sam. 92 (2), 168, 184, 544, Sarah 353. Simon 7. 132, 184, 213, 356, Thos. 444, Wm. 17, 61, 75, 144, 315, 428, 518 (3), Wilson 184

Winbo(u)rn, Abraham 197. 268, 480, 544, David 480 (3), John 367, 480, Sarah 480

Winslow, Jesse 196, Wm. 74

Winstead, Barbara 55, David 55. 64, 202, 538 (2). Peter 196, Rich. 290, 292 (2), Sam. 184, 202, 538, Thos. 196, 538

Woodard, Aaron 140, 207, 281, 341, 533, Daniel 273, 423, 533, Isaac 379, Jas. 140. Luke 152, Thos. 152 (2), 379

Woodel (Wooddel), Jos. 100 (2), 181, 544

Worley, Lovick 204, Robt. 11, 139, 204

Worrell, Henry 31, John 103

Wortham, Cha. 270, 271

Wright, Charity 127, Eliz. 322, 323, Jos. 51, 127, 156, 221, 229, 232, 322, 323, Lemuel 51 (2), 127 (2), 156 (2), 221, 229, 322, 323 (3), Lucreccy 51, Wm. 134, 163, 240, 359
Wyatt (Wiatt), Dempsey 115 (2). 266. 401. 408. 435. Henry 298. 400, 435
Wylie, Hugh 549

—Y—

Yates (Eyeats), Chartey 277
York, Edw. 174, 282, 330, 383 (2), 384, 385, 526
Youell, Henry 193, 321
Young, John 156, 185, 485, Mary 156, Robt. 126, 139, 464 (2)

DB 6-1 JOHN WATKINS of Nash Co. to JOHN SEDGLEY of same, May 8, 1794, for 15 pds. Virginia money a tract of 30 acres on the north side of Tar River adjoining Micajah Revel and Joseph Curl. Wit: Benja. Bunn and Josiah Horn.

DB 6-2 WILLIAM BRASWELL, SR. of Nash Co. to ORREN BRASWELL, son of Benjamin Braswell, May 13, 1794, for love and affection a tract of 176 acres on the north side of Tar River, the property to be for the use of Benjamin Braswell until the said Orren should arrive at the age of 21. Wit: Wilson Vick and Sherod Deans.

DB 6-3 EDWARD MOORE of Nash Co. to JOHN BONE of same, Feb. 14, 1794, for 100 pds. specie a tract of 100 acres adjoining said Bone, said Moore, and John Brantley. Wit: Elijah Dunnavant and David Pridgen.

DB 6-4 WILSON CURL of Nash Co. to JOHN HOLLEY of Bertie Co., May 15, 1794, for $125.00 a tract of 250 acres adjoining Lewis Curl, Wade Moore, William Joyner, Lamon, Lamon's Road, and the Polecat Branch. Wit: Wilson Vick and Benja. Whitfield.

DB 6-5 JOSHUA VICK of Nash Co. to JOHN FLETCHER of same, March 25, 1794, for $190.00 a tract of 200 acres on Murtle Branch, the creek and the mill swamp. Wit: Wilson Vick and John H. Drake.

DB 6-6 ARCHIBALD GRIFFIN, Sheriff of Nash Co., to JOHN DEVANPORT of same, May 13, 1794, at public auction for 57 pds. a tract of 183 acres adjoining Nathan Boddie, Willoughby Manning, Isaac Bass, and said Devanport, sold as the property of Job Tucker to satisfy an execution obtained by the Devanport heirs against the admrs. of Job Tucker. Wit: Roger Reese and Peter Arrington.

DB 6-7 JOHN TANNER of Franklin Co. to BENJAMIN WILLIAMS of Nash Co., May 9, 1794 for 1 pd. one acre of land on the north side of Tar River adjoining his own land, it being part of the land granted to Wm. Bracewell in 1763. Wit: Simon Williams, William Braswell, and Daniel Tounzen.

DB 6-8 JOHN SEDGLEY of Nash Co. to JOSIAH HORN of same, May 8, 1794, for 14 pds. Virginia money a parcel of 14 acres on the river and the road. Wit: Benja. Bunn and John Watkins.

DB 6-9 JOHN WILSON and MARMADUKE MASON of Nash of Nash Co. to JOHN WATKINS, Dec. 18, 1793, for 41 pds. Virginia money one negro man. Wit: Josiah Horn and Judah Watkins.

DB 6-10 SHEROD PHILLIPS of Nash Co. to GABRIEL PHILLIPS of same, Jan. 8, 1793, for 10 pds. a tract of 100 acres on the south side of Mill Branch adjoining John Dew and Joseph Phillips, it being the land and plantation whereon George Blackwell lived and deceased and the same that Joseph Phillips conveyed to said Sherod Phillips on May 11, 1789. Wit: Ephraim Phillips and Joseph Coob.

DB 6-11 ROBERT WORLEY of Nash Co. to BENJAMIN

BRIDGERS of same, March 1, 1794, for $200.00 a tract of 250 acres on the north side of Swift Creek on Shelley's Swamp adjoining Thomas Mann and Thomas Morris. Wit: Sion Linsey and Evins Andress.

DB 6-11 ARCHIBALD GRIFFIN, Sheriff of Nash Co., to WILLIAM JOYNER of same, April 14, 1794, at public auction for 31 pds. 1 sh. Virginia money a tract of 200 acres adjoining Joel Ricks, William Joyner, and Batson Smith, sold as the property of HARDY BREWER to satisfy an execution obtained by the exrs. of Micajah Thomas. Wit: S. Westray and Arch'd Hunter.

DB 6-13 THOMAS DOZIER of Nash Co. to EDWARD COOPER of same. Feb. 13, 1794, for 120 silver dollars a tract of 100 acres adjoining Nicholas Baggett, Hackney, Minton, Peter Robertson, and Lewis Dortch, it being a parcel conveyed by William Hackney to Joseph Minton on July 7, 1783. Wit: Jethro Denson, Foster Mason, and Wm. Dozier.

DB 6-14 ARRTHUR WESTER of Nash Co. to his son, WILLIAM WESTER, of same, Feb. 10, 1792, for love and affection a tract of 75 acres on Maple Creek, to be reserved for the use of said Arthur Wester during his lifetime. Wit: Burwell Bunn and Lewis Curl.

DB 6-14 ARTHUR WESTER of Nash Co. to his son. WILLIAM WESTER, of same. Feb. 10, 1792, for love and affection a tract of 50 acres on Maple Creek adjoining Whitley. Wit: Burwell Bunn and Lewis Curl.

DB 6-15 STEPHEN WEBB and wife, ANN WEBB, of Nash Co. to JEREMIAH CULPEPPER of same, Sept. 24, 1792, for 25 pds. Virginia money a tract of 100 acres adjoining John Pasmore. Wit: John Gay and Sion Bass.

DB 6-17 JOHN CHITTY of Nash Co. to WILLIAM WILLIAMS of same. Sept. 14. 1789. for 60 pds. Virginia money a tract of 100 acres on the east side of Pig Basket Creek, it being a parcel of land conveyed by Elisha Knight to John Chitty. Wit: Matthew Drake and W. S. Mearns.

DB 6-18 JOHN WATKINS of Nash Co. to JOSIAH HORN of same, May 8, 1794, for 21 pds. Virginia money a tract of 22 acres on Kirby's Creek adjoining said Watkins. Wit: Benja. Bunn and John Sedgley.

DB 6-18 WILLIAM WRAY of Wake Co. to RICHARD BURGE of Nash Co., Nov. 18, 1790, for 60 pds. specie a tract of 150 acres on the south side of Turkey Creek, part in Franklin Co. and part in Nash Co. Wit: Burrell Burge, Jeremiah Burge, and William Ford.

DB 6-19 JAMES BARNES of Nash Co. to HENRY WATKINS of same, Jan. 28, 1794, for 100 pds. a tract of 50 acres on the south side of Stony Creek adjoining William Barnes. Wit: Edward Wilson and Wiley Skinner.

DB 6-20 WILLIAM HAMMONS and wife, ELIZABETH HAMMONS, of Nash Co. to JAMES WILSON of same, March 25, 1794, for 118 pds. 16 sh. Virginia money a tract of 327 acres lying in both

Nash and Franklin counties in the fork of Turkey Creek adjoining William Andrews, Williamson Ross, William Passmore, Green Hill, James Bruce, James Culpepper, and Drewry Alford, consisting of two parcels of land, one sold by Williamson Ross unto the said William Hammons and the other by Cornelius Taylor Wit: Wm. Andrews, Jr., Jonathan M. and Thomas Wilson.

DB 6-23 EPHRAIM PHILLIPS of Nash Co. to JACOB HORN of Edgecombe Co., June 2, 1794, for 200 pds. two tracts of land: (1) 300 acres on both sides of Shepherd's Branch adjoining Widow Row and Thomas Sanders; (2) 101 acres on the north side of the above parcel adjoining Sanders. Wit: Thomas Horn, Jethro Harrison, and Thomas Horn, Jr.

DB 6-24 WILLIAM PHILLIPS of Nash Co. to JETHRO HARRISON of same, June 28, 1794, for 150 pds. a tract of 350 acres on Shepherd's Branch adjoining Ephraim Phillips and said Harrison. Wit: Ephraim Phillips, Jacob Horn, and Samuel Godwin.

DB 6-25 ELIJAH REVEL of Nash Co. to DAVID DANIEL of same, Feb. 11, 1794, for 250 silver dollars a tract of 250 acres on the south side of Stony Creek adjoining Samuel Skinner. Emmanuel Skinner, Jonas Whitley, Micajah Revel, and William Barnes. Wit: John Arrington and Benja. Bunn.

DB 6-26 THOMAS LANDINGHAM of Edgecombe Co. to FIGURES LEWIS of same, Aug. 5, 1794, for 150 round silver dollars a 150 acre plantation on the north side of Long Swamp adjoining the county line and Griffin Swamp, it being a tract granted to said Landingham by the State. Wit: Exum Lewis. Jr. and John Carrell.

DB 6-27 ISAAC BASS of Nash Co. to AUGUSTIN BASS of same, Feb. 24, 1794, for 5 pds. a tract of 294 acres on the west side of Back Swamp and north side of Peachtree Creek adjoining Rogers and Jesse Bass. Wit: Jesse Rogers, John Bass, and Isaac Bass.

DB 6-28 CLEVEARS RANSOM of Nash Co. to NATHAN GREEN of same, Feb. 27, 1794, for $60.00 a tract of 60 acres on the north side of Jumping Branch adjoining Abel Davis and Portiss. Wit: John H. Drake.

DB 6-29 RICHARD MANNING of Nash Co. to his son, SAMUEL MANNING, of same, Aug. 11, 1794, for 5 pds. a tract of 125 acres adjoining Alexander Sorsby, Ethelred Jelks, and John Pope. Wit: Frederick Hines and Hartwell Hines.

DB 6-30 JOHN HARRELL of Nash Co. to JAMES WILLIAMS of same, Nov. 12, 1793, for 60 pds. Virginia money a tract of 100 acres on the south side of Stony Creek adjoining Henry Vick and Samuel Skinner. Wit: Nath'l Robertson and John Wilson.

DB 6-31 WILLIAM PRITCHET of Nash Co. to ABNER LEWIS of same, March 17, 1794, for 40 pds. a tract of 150 acres on Sapony Creek adjoining Jeremiah Etheridge and the Horse Pen Branch, it being part of a tract granted by the State to John Biggs on Nov. 1, 1784. Wit: Daniel Taylor. Jeremiah Etheridge, and Henry Worrell.

DB 6-33 JOHN STEVENS of Franklin Co. and JEREMIAH STEVENS of Nash Co. to WILLIAM LINSEY, Nov. 7, 1793, for 39 pds. Virginia money one negro girl. Wit: J. Bonds and Wm. Hammons.

DB 6-33 DOROTHY WARBERTON of Franklin Co. to DR. RICHARD FENNER of same, Aug. 13, 1794, for 500 pds. all her right, title, and interest in a negro wench and all her increase. Her grandmother, Frances Warberton, in her last will and testament, Oct. 30, 1776, did lend to her son, William Warberton, this negro wench during his natural lifetime, who was then to be given to one of his heirs. Wit: Thos. Haswell and John Geddy.

DB 6-34 NATHANIEL POWELL of Nash Co. to WILOBY POWELL of same, Nov. 29. 1793, for 75 pds. Virginia money one negro man. Wit: Lewis Dortch and Lazarus Powell.

DB 6-35 NATHANIEL POWELL of Nash Co. to WILOBY POWELL of same, Nov. 29, 1793, for 75 pds. Virginia money one negro wench and one negro boy. Wit: Lewis Dortch and Lazarus Powell.

DB 6-35 BENJAMIN BUNN of Nash Co. to his son, JOEL BUNN, of same, July 25, 1794, for love and affection seven negroes by name and certain of his stock of hogs and cattle, after his decease. Wit: Redmun Bunn, E. Barry, and James Mullans.

DB 6-36 BENJAMIN HAWKINS of Warren Co. to PATRICK WALKER of same, Oct. 11, 1794. a deed of trust for 69 pds. Virginia money which Lewis, a free black man, owed to said Walker in payment for a 500 acre plantation known as Greenleaves Place, which said Walker sold to said Lewis. The plantation adjoined Duncan Lamon, Crowell, Brittain Smith, Marshall, and Lamon's Road. Wit: John Hall.

DB 6-38 PATRICK WALKER of Warren Co. to BENJAMIN HAWKINS of same, Sept. 27, 1794, trustee for Lewis, a negro man and blacksmith by trade, formerly the property of Micajah Thomas and living then at the Nash Courthouse who was liberated from slavery by the will of said Micajah Thomas, deceased. under certain conditions. Whereas said Lewis had not been set free according to the law and was deprived at that time of the rights of citizenship and could not buy or sell property. said Patrick Walker had sold for 79 pds. Virginia money to Benjamin Hawkins, trustee for said Lewis, a 500 acre plantation known as Greenleaves Place adjoining Duncan Lamon, Crowell. Brittain Smith, Marshall, and Lamon's Road. If said Lewis should die, the land would go to his heirs or to persons nominated by him. Wit: John Hall.

DB 6-40 ALLEN FINCH of Nash Co. to JOHN EATMAN of same, July 25, 1794, for 16 pds. 13 sh. 4 p. specie a tract of 100 acres on the Great Swamp adjoining said Finch and said Eatman, it being part of a grant to Chester Coleson for 400 acres on Sept. 24, 1785. Wit: J. Nichols and Irvin Eatman.

DB 6-41 MINAJAH LANE of Nash Co. to PARSONS RACKLEY of same, Nov. 10, 1793, for $26.00 a parcel of 12 acres on the north side of Tar River; also all the land that the said Parsons Rackley could hold under water with his mill dam. Wit: Sion Hill and Kindred Night.

DB 6-42 JOHN WELLS of Chesterfield Co., South Carolina to STEPHEN WELLS, SR. of Nash Co., Nov. 12, 1794, for $300.00 a tract of 300 acres on the north side of Tar River adjoining Joshua Wells. David Pridgen, and Hardy Pridgen. Wit: Hn. Viverett, Elijah Dunnavant, and Thomas Wells.

DB 6-43 ALLEN FINCH of Nash Co. to JOHN EATMAN of same, Aug. 1, 1794, for 18 pds. specie a 100 acre plantation whereon Chester Coleson then lived on the Great Swamp adjoining West Crumpler, George Green, said Finch, and said Eatman, it being part of a grant to Chester Coleson for 400 acres on Sept. 24, 1785 and conveyed by said Coleson to said Finch. Chester Coleson also signed this deed. Wit: J. Nichols and Irvin Eatman.

DB 6-44 THEOPHILUS COLEMAN of Nash Co. to JONAS WILLIAMS of same, March 23, 1792, for 30 pds. Virginia money a tract of 100 acres on the east side of Lott's Branch adjoining the county line. Wit: Thomas Horn and Aaron Parker.

DB 6-45 JOHN HOLLEY of Bertie Co. to DAVID HOLLO-MAN, May 19 1794, for 40 pds. a tract of 250 acres on the north side of Tar River adjoining Lewis Curl near Polecat Branch, Wade Moore, William Joyner, Lamon, and Lamon's Road. Wit: Mary Holloman and Rd. Jenkins.

DB 6-46 EDWARD GANDY of Nash Co. to WILLIAM TIS-DALE of same, Nov. 11, 1794, for 50 pds. a tract of 100 acres on the north side of Sapony Creek adjoining Whitehouse. Wit: John H. Drake and David Pridgen.

DB 6-47 JACOB THOMAS of Nash Co. to BURWELL JOY-NER of same, May 12, 1793, for 20 pds. Virginia money a tract of 180 acres on the north side of Tar River on Sapony Swamp. Wit: John Joiner, Thos. Wells, and Cornelius Joiner.

DB 6-49 HENRY BECKWITH of Nash Co. to AMOS BECK-WITH of same, Nov. 8, 1794, for $4.00 a tract of 300 acres on Pig Basket Creek and Tar River Branch adjoining Hilliard, it being part of a tract granted to Henry Beckwith on April 30, 1754. Wit: Lewis Vick and Thomas Hart.

DB 6-50 BENJAMIN ATKINSON of Pitt Co. to JOSEPH SELY of Nash Co., Nov. 14, 1792, for 50 silver dollars a tract of 140 acres on Sapony Creek adjoining Edward Gandy, Micajah Thomas (then William Hall), Ricks, Richard Thomas, and Goodson. Wit: Edward Gandy and Amos Gandy.

DB 6-51 AARON PARKER of Nash Co. to JOSEPH WRIGHT of same, Jan. 12, 1791, for 40 pds. specie a tract of 100 acres on Toisnot Swamp and Lott's Branch adjoining Michael Horn. Wit: Lemuel Wright, Jr., Lucreccy Wright, and Lemuel Wright, Sr.

DB 6-52 SHEROD DEENS and MOLLEY DEENS of Nash Co. to ELIZABETH PUSSEL of same, May 6, 1794, for 5 pds. specie a tract of 25 acres on the east side of Turkey Creek adjoining Pussel. Wit: Daniel Taylor and Patience Taylor.

DB 6-54 WILSON HORN of Nash Co. to THOMAS HORN, SR. of same, Nov. 3, 1794, for 200 pds. specie 250 acres on the southwest side of Toisnot Swamp on Pine Log Branch and the road, it, being a tract of 150 acres granted to John Taylor by patent on April 7, 1745 and part of a tract of 143 acres granted to Thomas Horn by Pilgrim Williams on Jan. 20, 1763. Wit: Dempsey Dawson, William Horn, and Jeremiah Coney.

DB 6-55 DAVID WINSTEAD and wife, BARBARA WINSTEAD, of Nash Co. to DRURY TAYLOR of same, Oct. 27, 1794, for 300 pds. three tracts of land containing 516 acres on the south side of Tar River adjoining Philander Williams, Drury Taylor, and Col. John Bonds. The first tract contained 100 acres, the second tract 96 acres, and the third tract 320 acres. Wit: J. Bonds, Wilson Taylor, and Ethelred Dance.

DB 6-57 JAMES LEE of Nash Co. entered into bond with JOEL WILLIAMS of same, March 18, 1794, for the sum of 500 pds. specie to remove himself and family from the plantation where he then lived on or before Dec. 25th next, so that said Joel Williams could have possession. Wit: Wilson Taylor and Ethelred Dance.

DB 6-58 DEMPSEY BARNES and JESSE BARNES of Edgecombe Co. bound themselves to JETHRO PHILLIPS of Nash Co., Nov. 19, 1794, for 100 pds. Whereas said Jethro Phillips had given a deed to Dempsey Barnes for a tract of 434 acres for a certain sum of money, he could redeem the land by paying to said Dempsey Barnes the sum of 325 silver or gold dollars by Dec. 25, 1797. Wit: Sharod Phillips, Gabriel Phillips, and Prudence Phillips.

DB 6-59 ELIJAH DUNNAVANT, Sheriff of Nash Co., to PETER ARRINGTON of same, Nov. 12, 1794, at public auction for 305 pds. a 381 acre plantation on the north side of Swift Creek adjoining William Battle, Allen Mann (formerly Avent), and the Gideon Swamp, sold as the property of THOMAS ARMSTRONG, deceased, it being the place where he died. to satisfy an execution obtained by Peter Arrington against Arch'd Griffin, guardian to Thomas Jones Armstrong, infant and heir at law of Thomas Armstrong. Wit: John Fitts and Benja. Whitfield.

DB 6-60 ELIJAH DUNNAVANT, Sheriff of Nash Co. to PETER ARRINGTON of same. Nov. 12, 1794, at public auction for 25 pds. a tract of 100 acres adjoining William Battle, William Avent and William Evins, it being the land and plantation known as the John Cox Place. It was sold as the property of THOMAS ARMSTRONG, deceased, to satisfy an execution obtained by Peter Arrington against Arch'd Griffin, guardian to Thomas Jones Armstrong infant and heir at law of Thomas Armstrong. Wit: Benja. Whitfield and John Fitts.

DB 6-61 HENRY BALEY of Nash Co. to JOHN PETTY COBB, Nov. 16, 1788, for 100 pds. a tract of 200 acres on the north side of Moccasin Creek adjoining John Naron. Wit: Drury Williams and Benjamin Crumpler.

DB 6-61 ABRAHAM BASS of Nash Co. to MATTHEW GRIFFIN of same, Sept. 10, 1791, for 45 pds. Virginia currency a tract of 200 acres in Nash Co., it being of a part conveyed to said Bass by Joseph Irby. Wit: Micajah Bridgers and William Williams.

DB 6-62 GEORGE LEWIS of Nash Co. to WILLIAM BRYANT of same, Sept. 11, 1792, for 10 pds. a tract of 100 acres on Sapony Creek adjoining Samuel Batcheldor, William Hendricks, and William Bryant. Wit: James Kith and Isaac Hendricks.

DB 6-63 MALACHI UNDERWOOD of Nash Co. to his brother, HOWEL UNDERWOOD, of same, March 28, 1794, for 40 pds. Virginia money a tract of 100 acres adjoining said Howell Underwood, Elijah Revel, and Solomon Edwards. Wit: Jas. Williams and Edwin Drake.

DB 6-64 DRURY TAYLOR of Nash Co. to DAVID WINSTEAD of same, Nov. 22, 1794, for 300 pds. three tracts of land containing 516 acres on the south side of Tar River adjoining Philander Williams, Drury Taylor, and Col. John Bonds. The first tract contained 100 acres, the second tract 96 acres, and the third tract 320 acres. Wit: Vinson Cooper, Drewry Bridges, and David Cooper.

DB 6-65 NATHAN GREEN of Nash Co. to SAMUEL SMITH of same, Feb. 4, 1795 for 100 pds. specie a tract of 200 acres on the south side of Great White Oak Swamp adjoining Joseph Arrington, William Bridgers, and Arch'd Davis. Wit: Jos. Arrington and Jeremiah Portis.

DB 6-67 ISAAC BASS of Nash Co. to JESSE BASS of same, Dec. 5, 1794, for 80 pds. a tract of 188 acres adjoining Matthew Drake, Charles Brown, James Bryant, and Micajah Thomas. Wit: Jethro Bass, Maraugh Rackley, and John Bass.

DB 6-68 JETHRO PHILLIPS of Nash Co. to JETHRO HARRISON of same, Jan. 22, 1795, for 40 pds. a tract of 250 acres on both sides of Sheppard's Branch and on Contentnea Creek adjoining Benjamin Flowers, William Phillips. and Benjamin Bunn, it being a tract taken up by said Phillips, including a small clearing whereon Absalom Joyner formerly lived. Wit: Thomas Horn and Ellek Grice.

DB 6-69 WILLIAM WILLIS to JAMES WILLIAMS of Nash Co., Nov. 19, 1794, for 153 silver dollars a tract of 153 acres on the north side of Stony Creek adjoining Ben Vick and Braswell. Wit: John H. Drake and Howel Ellin.

DB 6-69 HENRY BAINS of Nash Co. to WILLIAM JACKSON of Franklin Co., Jan. 12, 1795, for 20 pds. a tract of 24 acres lying in Nash and Franklin counties on Turkey Creek adjoining Elizabeth Jackson. Wit: H. Simmons, Charles Hammonds, and James Hammonds.

DB 6-71 NEWET ATKISON of Nash Co. to WILLIAM PHILLIPS of same, Nov. 17, 1794, for 163 silver dollars a tract of 200 acres on Toisnot Swamp, it being the greater part of a tract granted to Lazarus Stricklen in 1794. Wit: Sherrod Phillips and William White.

DB 6-72 JAMES WILLIAMS of Nash Co. to DAVID HUNT

of same, Aug. 1, 1794, for $140.00 a tract of 100 acres adjoining Julian King and Daniels. Wit: Marmaduke Mason and Tisey Thomas.

DB 6-73 MATTHEW MELTON of Nash Co. to BENJA. WHITFIELD of same, March 27, 1792, for 100 silver dollars a tract of 85 acres on the south side of Stony Creek adjoining Dickinson. Wit: Alex Sorsby and Henry Strickland.

DB 6-74 HARDY GRIFFIN of Nash Co. to WILLIAM WINSLOW of same, Nov. 28, 1791, for 256 pds. 16 sh. specie 271 acres adjoining Matthew Drake including all that tract that Joseph Grif fin, Sr. purchased of Mary Williams on Aug. 14, 1771, except that parcel of the said and that the said Joseph Griffin, Sr. bequeathed to his son, Joseph Griffin. There were also two parcels of land that were bequeathed by the said Joseph Griffin to his two sons, Pierce Griffin and Micajah Griffin. as may be seen by the records. Wit: Demsey Braswell and Oroondates Drake.

DB 6-75 WILLIAM MATTHEWS of Nash Co. to MATTHEW MELTON of same, Dec. 18, 1790, for 100 Spanish milled dollars a tract of 85 acres on the south side of Stony Creek adjoining Dickinson and Melton. Wit: William Williams and Henry Strickland.

DB 6-76 JOHN PRITCHETT of Nash Co. to WILLIAM BRYANT of same, March 23. 1793, for 30 hard dollars a parcel of 12 acres on the north side of Tar River. Wit: Sion Hill and Fereby Whitley.

DB 6-77 JOHN ATKINSON, THOMAS ATKINSON, and BENJAMIN ATKINSON, sons and heirs of Thomas Atkinson, deceased, of Nash Co. to ELIJAH ATKINSON, another son and heir of said deceased, Dec. 12. 1793, for 100 pds. Virginia money, each and all of their parts of the lands of which their father, Thomas Atkinson, died seized and possessed. Wit: Wm. Hall, John Atkinson, and John Thomas.

DB 6-77 ABNOR LEWIS of Nash Co. to JOHN BATCHELOR of same, Dec. 15, 1794, for 40 pds. hard money 150 acres on Sapony Creek and the Horse Pen Branch adjoining Jeremiah Etheridge, it being part of a tract that William Pritchet bought of William Hammons. Wit: Robert Creekmer, Daniel Batchelor, and Mark Wall.

DB 6-78 STEPHEN WEBB of Nash Co. to JOHN EDWARDS of Franklin Co., March 4. 1793 for 85 pds. Virginia money a tract of 240 acres on both sides of the Tarborough Road adjoining Abraham Bass, Jesse Lawrence. John Webb, Jonah Johnson. John Pasmore, Jer. Culpepper, John Gay, and Sion Bass. Wit: Lewis Webb and Josiah Johnson.

DB 6-80 JAMES BROWN of Nash Co. to MOSES SMELLY of same, Jan. 25, 1795, for 100 pds. 100 acres on Marsh Swamp adjoining Benjamin Cobb, it being part of a tract granted to said James Brown by the State of N. C. on March 30, 1780. Wit: Elijah Dunnavant, Wilson Taylor, and Thomas Floyd.

DB 6-81 DELILAH GRIFFIN of Nash Co. to HOWEL UNDERWOOD of same, March 26, 1794, for 77 silver dollars a tract of 77 acres on the east side of the old road adjoining said Griffin, Revel, Underwood, Joshua Vick, and Fletcher. Wit: John H. Drake, Micajah Braswell, and Henry Strickland.

DB 6-82 LAZARUS WHITEHEAD of Nash Co. to JOHN MIN‾ TON of same, Aug. 2, 1794, a lifetime lease on a 100 acre tract adjoining Isaac Hilliard. Wit: Isaac Whitehead and William Whitehead.

DB 6-82 GEORGE JACKSON of Nash Co. to LEWIS JACKSON of same, June 11, 1794, for 18 pds. Virginia money one still, kettle, cap, and worm. Wit: John Atkinson.

DB 6-83 AMOS GANDY of Nash Co. to LEWIS CURL of same, March 21, 1795, for 65 pds. Virginia money one negro boy. Wit: Abra. Ricks.

DB 6-83 AMOS GANDY of Nash Co. to LEWIS CURL of same, April 14, 1795, for 40 pds. Virginia money one negro woman. Wit: Abra. Ricks.

DB 6-83 SHAROD PHILLIPS of Nash Co. to DUNKIN DEW, April 27, 1795. for 10 pds. specie all his right, title, and claim to a legacy that John Dew, deceased, gave in his will to Elizabeth Coney. deceased, it being the same legacy that the said Elizabeth Coney had sold to the said Sharod Phillips. Wit: Nancy Dew, Joseph Phillips, and Elizabeth Brown.

DB 6-84 EPHRAIM PHILLIPS and JETHRO PHILLIPS to DUNCAN DEW, March 9, 1795. for $200.00 one negro boy. Wit: Edward Nicholson and John Robbins.

DB 6-84 THOMAS GRAY and WILLIAM HOLLIMAN of Johnston Co. to JESSE KENT of Nash Co., Dec. 13, 1794, for 52 pds. Virginia money one negro boy. Wit: H. Gray and Stephen Kent.

DB 6-85 AMY RANSOM of Nash Co. to her grandson, JAMES RANSOM HARRISON. Sept. 3, 1794, for love and affection one negro boy after death and, if said James Ranson Harrison should die without heirs, the negro boy should go to Marceller, the daughter of Cleavars Ransom. Wit: Jos. Arrington and Cleavars Ransom.

DB 6-86 JETHRO PHILLIPS of Nash Co. to DEMPSEY BARNES of Edgecombe Co., Nov. 19, 1794, for 340 silver dollars 434 acres on the Great Swamp adjoining Joseph Phillips and Benjamin Flowers, it being part of a tract granted to Edward Moore on Oct. 9, 1783 for 640 acres. Wit: Sharod Phillips, Jesse Barnes, and Gabriel Phillips.

DB 6-87 DREWRY ALFORD of Nash Co. to HENRY BAINS of same, March 13, 1795, for 25 pds. a tract of 40 acres on Little Turkey Creek adjoining Bains and Thomas. Wit: William Jackson, Willis Solomon, and Absalom Bains.

DB 6-87 JEREMIAH ETHERIDGE, SR. of Nash Co. to JAROD ETHERIDGE of same, May 12, 1795, for 100 pds. a tract of 230 acres on Sapony Swamp and Little Sapony Creek adjoining said Jeremiah Etheridge. Wit: Abra. Ricks. Emmanuel Linsey, and

Wm. Hammons.

DB 6-88 JEREMIAH ETHERIDGE, SR. of Nash Co. to
JEREMIAH ETHERIDGE, JR. of same May 9, 1795, for 50 pds. a
tract of 221 acres adjoining Parsons Rackley, said Jeremiah Etheridge, Sr., Daniel Warren, Lane, and Samuel Bryant. Wit: Abra.
Ricks, Emmanuel Linsey, and Wm. Hammons.

DB 6-89 CORNELIOUS TAYLOR of Franklin Co. to WILL-
IAM JACKSON of Nash Co., Feb. 16, 1795, for 15 pds. a tract of
30 acres lying in both Nash and Franklin counties on Little Turkey
Creek adjoining said Taylor and Wilson. Wit: Absalom Bains,
James Green, and Cornely Bruice.

DB 6-91 JOHN SIKES of Nash Co. to GEORGE BODDIE of
same, May 6, 1795, for 50 pds. 57 acres on the north side of Little
Peachtree, it being part of a tract granted to said John Sikes by the
State of N. C. on Nov. 1, 1784. Wit: Nathan Boddie and Phillip
Sikes.

DB 6-91 RICHARD DEENS of Nash Co. to GEORGE BOD-
DIE of same, May 7, 1795, for 50 pds. a tract of 150 acres on the
north side of Little Peachtree Creek adjoining Benjamin Manning
and Matthew Drake. Wit: Nathan Boddie and Willis Deens.

DB 6-92 NICHOLSON LEWIS and wife, ELIZABETH
LEWIS, of Nash Co. to SAMUEL WILLIAMS, PRIDE WILLIAMS,
POLLY WILLIAMS and JANE WILLIAMS of same. May 10, 1795,
for love and affection and for 50 pds. to Samuel Williams one walnut table; to Pride Williams one walnut table; to Polly Williams one
pair of brass scales and weights; and to Jane Williams one bed and
furniture and one black walnut chest. Wit: J. Hall.

DB 6-93 JOSEPH SELAH of Nash Co. to AMOS GANDY of
same, Aug. 9, 1793, for 36 pds. specie a tract of 140 acres on Sapony
Creek adjoining Edward Gandy, Micajah Thomas (then William
Hall), Ricks, Richard Thomas, and Goodson. Wit: Joel Bunn and
Benjamin Bunn.

DB 6-94 JAMES DEAN of Nash Co. to JOHN EATMAN of
same, Oct. 14, 1794, for 16 pds. 10 sh. specie a tract of 100 acres on
Millstone Swamp. Wit: George Green and Irvin Eatman.

DB 6-95 RICHARD VICK of Nash Co. to his son, NATHAN
VICK, of same, Nov. 7, 1794, for love and affection a tract of 385
acres on Stony Creek adjoining Samuel Westray, Ricks, Samuel
Skinner, Henry Vick, and the road.
Wit: Samuel Westray and Samuel Glover.

DB 6-96 THOMAS TUCKER of Nash Co. to DAVID PRID-
GEN of same. Feb. 18, 1795, for 37 pds. 10 sh. Virginia money a
tract of 200 acres on Sapony Creek adjoining said Pridgen, Stephen
Vaughan, Robert Cockrum, James Batchelor, Frederick Vaughan,
and Wm. Batchelor. Wit: Robert Creekmur and Marcom Cooper.

DB 6-97 WILLIAM ANDREWS, JR. of Franklin Co. to
DREWRY ALFORD of Nash Co., March 11, 1794, for 200 pds. Virginia money a tract of 380 acres on the south side of Great Turkey
Creek adjoining James Culpepper, John Hammons, Henry Banes,
and the road, it being a tract of land sold by William Andrews, Sr.

to William Andrews, Jr. Wit: Wm. Hammons, Benjamin Hunt, and Benjamin Perry.

DB 6-99 DAVID HOLLAMAN of Stokes Co. to WADE MOORE of Nash Co., April 2, 1795, for $120.00 a tract of 250 acres adjoining Lewis Curl, Wade Moore, William Joyner, Lamon, and Lamon's Road. Wit: Jeremiah Battle and Lewis Curl.

DB 6-99 STEPHEN BATCHELOR of Nash Co. to ABNOR LEWIS of same, Dec. 15, 1794, for 20 pds. hard money a tract of 100 acres on the north side of Tar River and on Sapony Creek adjoining Richard Burge. Wit: Robert Creekmur, Dannal Batchelor, and John Batchelor.

DB 6-100 JAMES BROWN of Nash Co. to JOHN FLOWERS of same, Dec. 31, 1794, for 120 pds. Virginia money a tract of land on both sides of Wilder's Mill Branch adjoining Joseph Woodel and Rowland Williams it being part of a 640 acre tract granted to said James Brown by the State of N. C. on Sept. 24, 1785. excluding 250 acres which said James Brown sold to John Flowers in 1789. It also included part of a tract of 300 acres which James Brown purchased of Joseph Woodel in 1786, which was part of a 590 acre tract. Wit: Dempsey Dawson and Jonas Williams.

DB 6-102 STEPHEN WELLS of Nash Co. to JAMES PRIM of Franklin Co., Feb. 21, 1795, for $525.00 a tract of 300 acres on the north side of Tar River adjoining Joshua Wells and David Pridgen. Wit: Thomas Wells and Jeremiah Wells.

DB 6-103 JOSEPH ANDRESS of Nash Co. to CITCHEN PRIM of same, Oct. 2. 1794, for 30 pds 100 acres on the south side of Little Peachtree Creek adjoining Deens, Moses Stallions, and William Vester. it being a tract granted by the State to Elijah Powell. conveyed by said Powell to Wm. Harres, and conveyed by said Harres to said Andress. Wit: Fredrick Jones, Willis Deens, and Willis Solomon.

DB 6-103 JOHN WARRELL of Nash Co. to ELY MANNING of same, Feb. 27, 1795, for 75 pds. Virginia money a tract of 523 acres on Little Turkey Creek adjoining Samuel Bryant, Parson Rackley. Jeremiah Pussel, and Micajah Thomas. Wit: Daniel Taylor. Hardy Prigden, and Jeremiah Ethredge.

DB 6-105 WADE MORE of Nash Co. to WILLIAM JOYNER of same. April 8, 1795, for $60.00 a tract of 100 acres adjoining said Joyner, Lamon and the road. Wit: Drewry Joyner and Lewis Curl.

DB 6-105 JETHRO BATTLE, executor of WILLIAM LANE, deceased, of Edgecomb Co. to ISAAC HENDRICK of Nash Co., May 21, 1795, for 25 pds. Virginia money one negro man. Wit: Ann Battle and Thomas Suttone.

DB 6-106 LEMUEL NICHOLSON of Halifax Co. to Wm. LEWIS of Nash Co., June 2, 1794, for 50 pds. a lease on a tract of 50 acres on the south side of Beaver Dam Swamp, it being part of a tract known as the "bent of the swamp or Wiatt Tract." The lease began on the date above and was to continue for as long as said William Lewis or his wife, Sarah Lewis, should live. **Wit:** Crowel Lewis.

DB 6-106 JOHN WELLS of Chesterfield Co., South Carolina gave to his trusty friend, STEPHEN WELLS, of Nash Co. the power of attorney, Nov. 18, 1794. Wit: David Pridgen and Abijah Pridgen.

DB 6-107 MICAJAH BRASWELL HUNT of Nash Co. to BENJAMIN WHITFIELD of same, Aug. 12, 1795, for $500.00 a tract of 322 acres adjoining Thomas Willis, Thomas Hunter, Revel, David Strickland, Robert Wilson, and said Whitfield. Wit: James Williams and Daniel Powell.

DB 6-108 JOHN MELTON of Nash Co. to JOSEPH MELTON for same, June 27, 1795, for one silver dollar a tract of 140 acres on the south side of Wm. Whitehead's mill branch. Wit: James Williams and Thomas Griffin.

DB 6-109 LEWIS HINES of Nash Co. to WILLIS TREVA-THAN of same, March 19, 1795, for 10 pds. a tract of 55 acres between Compass Creek and Beach Run adjoining John Exum and Reuben Taylor. Wit: Hines Drake and Thomas Maning.

DB 6-109 JAMES TUCKER, SR. of Nash Co. to BRYANT O'NEAL of same, Feb. 23 1795, for 45 pds. Virginia money a tract of 150 acres on the south side of Little Sapony Creek adjoining Arthur O'Neal and James Tucker, Jr. Wit: Robert Creekmer, James Tucker, and Danal Holan.

DB 6-110 MALAKI UNDERWOOD of Nash Co. to ZACH-ARIAH UNDERWOOD of same, Jan. 3, 1795, for 50 pds. Virginia money a tract of 123 acres adjoining Solomon Edwards, Howel Underwood, Fletcher, and Hines. Wit: John Wilson and Edward Wilson.

DB 6-111 ALEXANDER THOMPSON of Nash Co. to WILLIS TREVATHAN of same, March 10, 1795, for 45 pds. Virginia money 130 acres on the north side of Compass Creek adjoining Lewis Hines, Jeremiah Hilliard, Reuben Taylor. and the Watery Branch, it being part of a tract that said Willis Trevathan bought of Alexander Thompson by deed, March 10, 1795. Wit: Reuben Taylor and Demsey Taylor.

DB 6-111 ARCHIBALD HUNTER of Nash Co. to ELIJAH REVEL of same, Sept. 9, 1795, for $301.00 a tract of 181 acres on the north side of Stony Creek adjoining Laseter's Branch, the road, and Strickland's old line. Wit: Sam Westray, Drew Hunter, and Daniel Powell.

DB 6-112 JOHN SEDGLEY of Nash Co. to BENJAMIN BUNN, JR. of same, Aug. 1, 1795, for 400 silver dollars a tract of 136 acres on the north side of Tar River adjoining Stony Creek and the road. Wit: Josiah Horn, David Bunn, and R. Bunn.

DB 6-113 JOHN SEDGLEY of Nash Co. to BENJAMIN BUNN, JR. of same, Aug. 1, 1795, for 15 pds. a tract of 30 acres on the north side of Tar River adjoining Micajah Revel and Joseph Curl. Wit: Josiah Horn, David Bunn, and R. Bunn.

DB 6-114 JOHN BATTLE of Nash Co. to JACOB HORN of same, May 23, 1795, for 45 pds. one negro girl. Wit: Little B. Griffin.

DB 6-114 JONATHAN CROSS of Cumberland Co. to BENJAMIN WHITFIELD of Nash Co., Jan. 15, 1793, for 140 silver dollars one negro girl. Wit: Tisey Thomas and Nath'l Robertson.

DB 6-114 FRANCIS LOKUS of Nash Co. to JESSE HAMMONDS of same, Nov. 20, 1792, for 75 pds. specie a tract of 250 acres on the north side of Turkey Creek at the mouth of Frank Andersun's spring branch adjoining Massey. Wit: John Hammonds and Charles Hammonds.

DB 6-115 DEMPSEY WYATT of Nash Co. to JONAS COLSON of same, Sept. 7, 1795, for 100 pds. a tract of 100 acres on Turkey Creek adjoining Jeremiah Brown and the Haw Branch, it being part of a grant to said Dempsey Wyatt by the State of N. C. on Nov. 1, 1784. Wit: Wilson Taylor, Joseph Strickland, and Benja. Taylor, Jr.

DB 6-116 HENRY STRICKLAND of Nash Co. to MATTHEW CARTER of same Oct. 17, 1795. for $150.00 a tract of 300 acres on Toisnot Swamp and Little Swamp adjoining Edward Moore. Wit: Noah Stricklin and William Bowers.

DB 6-117 ELISHA ELLES of Nash Co. to WILLIAM BAKER of same, Sept. 2, 1790, for 20 pds. specie a tract of 80 acres on the north side of Tar River adjoining John Joiner, Penelapha Parker, George Jackson, and William Baker, it being a tract purchased by Elisha Ellis of Joseph Selah on May 24, 1790. Wit: Jesse Joiner and Wm. Baker.

DB 6-117 JOSEPH SELAH of Nash Co. to ELISHA ELLIS of same, May 24, 1790, for 30 pds. proc. money a tract of 80 acres on the north side of Tar River adjoining John Joiner. Penny Parker, Jackson, and Wm. Baker. Wit: John Joiner and Jesse Joiner.

DB 6-118 JAMES KIRSEY of Roberson Co. to WILLIAM BAKER of Nash Co., Sept. 11, 1792. for 40 pds. a tract of 200 acres on the south side of Sapony Creek adjoining Samuel Long Bottoms. Wit: John Joiner , Elijah Atkison, and Wm. Baker.

DB 6-119 JOHN MURDEN of Halifax Co. to JOHN JONES of Nash Co., Sept. 7, 1795, for 67 pds. 10 sh. Virginia money one negro man. Wit: Chappel Heeth, Willie Jones, and Edward Murden.

DB 6-120 ROBERT CREEKMUR of Nash Co. to JOSEPH STEWARD of Halifax Co., Oct. 9, 1793, for 30 pds. a tract of 300 acres on both sides of Beaver Dam Swamp. Wit: William Bowers, Ballentine Creekmur, and Joseph Batchelor.

DB 6-120 ALLEN FINCH of Nash Co. to GEORGE GREEN of same, March 21, 1795, for 50 pds. specie a tract of 100 acres adjoining Allen Finch and John Eatman, it being part of a grant by the State of N. C. to Chester Colson on Sept. 24, 1785. Wit: Wilson Taylor. Micah Horn, Robert Hobbs, and Stephen Kent.

DB 6-121 MITCHAEL MORRISS of Nash Co. to ARCHI-

BALD HUNTER of same, Sept. 30, 1795, for $433.33 a 256 acre plantation on the north side of Stony Creek adjoining Elijah Revel, Henry Horn, and Thomas Hunter, it being part of a tract of 692 acres granted by Earl Granville to John Moore, Sr. on June 1, 1762, conveyed by him to John Moore, Jr. by deed on June 3, 1773 and conveyed by John Moore, Jr. to Elisha Moore by deed on May 3, 1777. Wit: James Williams, Henry Vick, and Joshua Ralls.

DB 6-123 THOMAS TUCKER, SR. of Nash Co. to WILLIAM BATCHELOR of same, March 14, 1795, for 20 pds. Virginia money a tract of 100 acres on the north side of Great Sapony Creek adjoining David Pridgen, Solomon Cotten. and Fedrick Vaughan. Wit: Robert Creekmur and Matthias Manning.

DB 6-123 JOHN STRICKLAND of Nash Co. to ALLEN FINCH of same, March 21, 1795, for 100 pds. specie a tract of 159 acres on Turkey Creek adjoining his own line and Jeremiah Brown, it being part of a grant by the State of N. C. to said Strickland in 1784. Wit: Wilson Taylor, Isum Finch, and Joseph Strickland.

DB 6-124 JESSE KIRBY and PENELAPHA KIRBY of Johnston Co. to JOHN BAKER of Nash Co., Sept. 17, 1791, for 20 pds. specie a tract of 50 acres on the north side of Tar River adjoining John Joiner, George Jackson, Thomas Edwards, and Edward Ballard, it being a tract of land purchased by Penelapha Parker of Joseph Selah on Feb. 22, 1788. Wit: Jesse Joiner, John Joiner, and Wm. Baker.

DB 6-126 FREDERICK DANIEL of Nash Co. to JULIAN KING of same, Feb. 9, 1796, for 75 pds. Virginia money 140 acres on the north side of Pig Basket Creek adjoining James Daniel's former line, it being part of a tract granted to Robert Young by Earl Granville on Nov. 8, 1755 and conveyed by deed to Jacob Whitehead on June 1, 1764. Wit: James Williams and Wm. Boddie.

DB 6-127 JOSEPH WRIGHT of Nash Co. to SOLOMON DAWSON PARKER of same, Jan. 15, 1795, for 50 pds. specie a tract of 100 acres on the south side of Lott's Branch adjoining Michael Horn, it being the land belonging to Aron Parker. Wit: Lemuel Wright Jr., Lemuel Wright, Sr., and Charity Wright.

DB 6-128 WILLIAM PHILLIPS of Nash Co. to JETHRO HARRISON of same, Feb. 4, 1796, for 12 pds. 10 sh. a tract of 150 acres on Contentnea Creek adjoining Benjamin Bunn and Jethro Phillips, it being a tract taken up by the said William Phillips. Wit: Harris Horn and Mary Harrison.

DB 6-129 ROBERT COCKRON of Halifax Co. to ALEXANDER McCOMB of same, Nov. 9, 1795, for 100 pds. a tract of 150 acres adjoining Daniel Deans, Demcy Vaughan, and Stephen Vaughan. Wit: Isaac Pavatt, John Robertson, and Reuben Daniel.

DB 6-130 ELIAS REVEL of Northampton Co. to HENRY REVEL of Nash Co., March 30, 1792, for 50 pds. specie a 75 acre plantation on the north side of Kirby's Creek adjoining Edward Wilson and John Battle. Wit: Jos. Exum and Batson Smith.

DB 6-131 JOSEPH CURL of Nash Co. to JOHN WATKINS of same, Oct. 21, 1795, for $300.00 a tract of 180 acres on the north side of Kirby's Creek adjoining Edward Wilson and Thomas' Road. Wit: Benjamin Bunn and Josiah Horn.

DB 6-131 MARMADUKE MASON of Nash Co. to JOHN WILSON of same, April 25, 1792, for 20 pds. a tract of 50 acres on the south side of Stony Creek adjoining John Harrel, Henry Vick, Mason, and Lamon's Road. Wit: Anselm Harris, James Churchill, and Emmanuel Skinner.

DB 6-132 REUBEN WILLIAMS of Washington Co., Georgia to SIMON WILLIAMS of Franklin Co., Jan. 3, 1795, for 66 pds. Virginia money a tract of 581 acres on the south side of Tar River adjoining William Braswell, Micajah Thomas, and Bryant Finch; also, a tract of River adjoining William Braswell, Micajah Thomas, and Bryant Finch; also, a tract of 300 aces adjoining the above tract, Micajah Thomas, Charles Bollin and his own line. Wit: John Norwood, Jr. and Alex'r Frazier.

DB 6-133 EDWARD MORE of Nash Co. to WILLIAM LINDSEY of same, Jan. 30, 1796, for 100 pds. a tract of 200 acres on the north side of Tar River adjoining John Brantley, John Bone, William Ballard, Edward More, and Arthur Sellers. Wit: James Watkins and Joseph Sellers.

DB 6-134 ISAAC WHITEHEAD of Nash Co. to WILLIAM WRIGHT of same, Feb. 9. 1796. for 760 pds. Virginia money a tract of 760 acres on the north side of Swift Creek adjoining Wm. Whitehead, Isaac Newsom, and the road. Wit: None.

DB 6-135 JAMES TUCKER. SR. of Nash Co. to JAMES TUCKER, JR. of same, Nov. 21, 1795, for 10 silver dollars a small amount of household furniture and livestock. Wit: Marcom Cooper and Arthur Oneal.

DB 6-135 WILLIAM RICHARDSON, SR. of Nash Co. to JOHN RICHARDSON of same, Feb. 8, 1796, for 5 pds a tract of 50 acres adjoining William Richardson, Sr., James Massingill, and Lucy Pasmore. Wit: Numan Richardson.

DB 6-136 JAMES ATKINSON of Nash Co. to JOHN WILLIFORD of same, Dec. 15, 1795. for 20 pds. specie a tract of 158 acres on the north side of Turkey Creek adjoining Theophilus Hickman, Jacob Strickland, and Jeremiah Brown. Wit: William Linsey and Thomas Tucker.

DB 6-137 WILLIAM RICHARDSON, SR. of Nash Co. to WILLIAM RICHARDSON, JR. of same, May 9, 1794, for 5 pds. 20 acres of land in Nash Co. Wit: John Gay and John Richardson.

DB 6-137 GEORGE POLLOK of Jones Co. to FRANCIS WARD, Feb. 11, 1795, for $1200.00 a tract of land on Fishing Creek, provided that the said Francis Ward should not molest those who held part of the said land by virtue of lease from Thomas

Pollok, deceased, until their terms expired. Wit: Wm. Battle, Ben Ward, and Stephen Wever.

DB   6-138 GEORGE POLLOK of Jones Co. to FRANCIS WARD, Feb. 11, 1795, for $1200.00 a tract of land on the south side of Fishing Creek, provided that those who held leases on this land from Thomas Pollok, deceased, should not be molested until their terms expired. Wit: Wm. Battle, Ben Ward, and Stephen Weaver.

DB 6-139 WILLIAM ROSE, SR. of Franklin Co. to ROBERT WORLEY of Nash Co., Jan. 15, 1796, for love and affection one negro boy. Wit: Wm. Coppedge, Thomas Rose, and Richard Webb.

DB 6-139 WILLIAM PACE of Franklin Co. to JOHN RICE of Nash Co., Jan. 23, 1790, for 70 pds. a tract of 140 acres on Turkey Creek and Sassafras Branch adjoining Strickland. Wit: James Atkinson and Robert Young.

DB 6-140 JAMES WOODARD of Nash Co. to AARON WOODARD of same, Feb. 6, 1796, for 200 pds. 289 acres on the north side of Pig Basket Creek near Holland's Branch, it being part of a tract granted to Micajah Thomas by Earl Granville in 1760. Wit: William Arrington and David Pridgen.

DB 6-141 ROBERT VICK of Nash Co. to ANDREW JOHNSON of same, Sept. 12, 1794, for 25 pds. a tract of 91 acres adjoining John Taylor, Joseph Vick, Robert Vick, John Parrish, and said Johnson, it being the land and plantation whereon he then lived and the land that said Vick willed to said Johnson. Wit: J. Taylor. William Taylor, and Jacob Wheeler.

DB 6-142 JOSIAH SKINNER of Nash Co. to JOSIE (JOICE) JONES of same, Oct. 5, 1794, for 5 pds. a parcel of 7½ acres of land. Wit: Marmaduke Mason and James Barns.

DB 6-142 WILLIE BUNN of Nash Co. to THOMAS DEANS of same, May 5, 1795. for 20 pds. a parcel of 14 acres on the south side of Sapony Creek and on Gabe's Branch. Wit: John Barns.

DB 6-143 JETHRO DENSON of Nash Co. to EDWARD COOPER of same, Feb. 18, 1795, for 300 silver dollars, a tract of 200 acres on the south side of Beaver Dam Swamp adjoining Henry Mason, Hackney, and Edward Cooper it being a parcel conveyed by deed from John Jones to said Denson. Wit: Henry Freeman, Francis Rose, and Edmund Cooper.

DB 6-144 MARY WILLIAMS of Nash Co. to   KINSMAN KNIGHT of same, May 1, 1791, for 25 sh. specie a tract of 25 acres adjoining said Knight and Joseph White. Wit: William Williams and Mathew Melton.

DB 6-145 SOLOMON HICKS of Nash Co. to WILLIAM MORGAN of same, Jan. 29, 1794, for 10 pds. a tract of 100 acres on the north side of Turkey Creek. Wit: Jesse Hammond and Joshua Cone.

DB 6-145 HOWELL UNDERWOOD of Nash Co. to JOSEPH STRICKLAND, Feb. 22, 1794, for 40 pds. specie a tract of 100 acres adjoining David Strickland and Hunter. Wit: Marmaduke Mason and Henry Strickland.

DB 6-146 FRANCIS ANDERSON of Granville Co. to WM. PERRY of Nash Co. Dec. 31, 1793, for 50 pds. a tract of 250 acres adjoining Hammond, Cone, and the creek. Wit: Richard Massey and Abel Massey.

DB 6-147 MICAJAH BRASWELL of Nash Co. to ROBERT WILSON of same, Jan. 29, 1795, for 40 pds. a parcel of 18 acres adjoining Edward Wilson and Braswell. Wit: Joseph Strickland and Henry Strickland.

DB 6-147 GEORGE BRYANT of Edgecombe Co. to SOLO-MON HICKS of Nash Dec. 25, 1793, for 10 pds. a tract of 100 acres on Turkey Creek. Wit: William Bryant and Elias Owens.

DB 6-148 BURREL ROSE of Nash Co. to JOHN MELTON of same, Feb. 9, 1795, for 50 pds. specie a tract of 175 acres on the south side of Little Sapony Creek adjoining Williba Tucker, Matthias Manning, Sutton. Arthur Oneal, and John Manning. Wit: David Pridgen and James Williams.

DB 6-148 BENJAMIN TAYLOR, SR. of Nash Co. to ENOCH OWENS of same Jan. 30, 1796, for 50 pds. specie a tract of 221 acres on Turkey Creek adjoining John West, Samuel Devaughan, Edward Moore, and James Brown, it being land granted to said Taylor by the State of N. C. on Dec. 20, 1791. Wit: Abijah Pridgen and David Pridgen.

DB 6-149 ELIJAH DUNNAVANT, Sheriff of Nash Co., to JOHN RICE of same, Feb. 11. 1796, at public auction for 10 pds. specie a tract of 100 acres on the south side of Tar River adjoining James Pace, sold as the property of BARNABY BELILE to satisfy an execution obtained by said John Rice. Wit: Wm. Hall.

DB 6-150 ARTHUR LASSETER of Nash Co. to JOHN BATTLE of same, Oct. 19, 1795. for 75 pds. Virginia money a tract of 200 acres adjoining Lot Etheridge and Jonah Williams, it being part of a grant to John Cooper for 530 acres on March 7, 1761. Wit: Furnea Southall. Elias Boon, and Matthew Drake.

DB 6-151 BURREL SHELTON of Halifax Co. to JOSIAH NICHOLSON of Nash Co., June 22, 1793, for 90 pds. Virginia money a tract of 208 acres on the south side of Beaver Dam Swamp adjoining Capt. Whitehead and said Nicholson. Wit: Lazarus Whitehead, Moses Pullen. and S. W. Branch.

DB 6-152 JACOB DUCK and wife, SARAH DUCK, of Wake Co. to THOMAS WOODARD of Nash Co., Jan. 6. 1786, for 100 pds. a tract of 200 acres on Great Contentnea Creek and on Mash Swamp adjoining Hardy Boykin and Stephen Cobb; also a tract of 300 acres adjoining Jeremiah Nichols, Stephen Cobb. Hardy Boykin, Jacob Nichols and Benjamin Flowers. this being land granted to Jacob Duck by the State of N. C. on Nov. 1, 1784. Wit: Luke Woodard and Thomas Woodard.

DB 6-153 BENJAMIN COBB of Nash Co. to JOHN DRIVER of same, Dec. 26, 1795, for 75 pds. a tract of 325 acres on Mash Swamp adjoining James Cobb and Boykin, it being part of a tract of 640 acres granted to said Cobb on March 30, 1780. Wit: Drewry Williams, Micajah Bailey, and William Grizzel.

DB 6-154 BENJAMIN COBB of Nash Co. to JOHN DRIVER of same, Dec. 26. 1795, for 75 pds. a tract of 50 acres on Contentnea Creek and Marsh Swamp adjoining James Brown. Wit: Drewry Williams, Micajah Bailey. and William Grizzel.

DB 6-155 PETER ROBERTSON of Nash Co. to SIMON STALLINGS of Edgecombe Co., Sept. 28, 1795, for no money and after his death a tract of 150 acres on the west side of Whittington Branch adjoining Isaac Newsum and Lewis Dortch. Wit: Lewis Dortch, Lovice Dortch, and William Robertson.

DB 6-156 LEMUEL WRIGHT, SR. of Nash Co. to his son, LEMUEL WRIGHT, JR. of same, April 8, 1796. for love and affection a tract of 355 acres on both sides of Bloomery Swamp adjoining Joseph Wright, and all of his livestock, household furniture, goods, and chattels after his death. Wit: Jethro Harrison and Mourning Ricks.

DB 6-156 JOHN YOUNG and wife, MARY YOUNG. of Nash Co. to ELIZABETH TURLINGTON of same, Feb. 19, 1796. for $60.00 a 100 acre plantation adjoining Jacob Ricks, Lewis Ricks, Maple Creek, and the public road. Wit: Jacob Ricks and Reuben Harrell.

DB 6-157 ISAAC DORTCH of Nash Co. to ISAAC WHITE-HEAD of same, Oct. 22, 1795. for 800 silver dollars a tract of 280 acres on the south side of Swift Creek adjoining Jelks and Benja. Merritt, it being a parcel of land said Isaac Dortch purchased of Wm. Meritt. Wit: Lewis Dortch and Alex. Sorsby.

DB 6-158 ARTHUR O'NEAL to ZACRA O'NEAL Feb. 22, 1796, for 75 pds. 146 acres on Little Saponv Swamp, it being parts of two tracts adjoining Bryant O'Neal. Wit: Robert Creekmur and Briant O'Neal.

DB 6-159 JAMES HILLIARD of Nash Co. to WILLIAM BOGGS of same, May 11. 1796, for $284.00 a tract of 284 acres on the south side of Little Peachtree Creek adjoining Thomas Davis and lying partly in Franklin Co.. it being a tract that was demised by Thomas Davis to said James Hilliard. Wit: Jos. Arrington and Edward Gandy.

DB 6-160 WILLIAM SANDEFORD of Nash Co. to MARY ARRINGTON of same, March 29, 1796. for 642 silver dollars a tract of 240 acres in Nash Co. Wit: Drake, Wm. Lewis, and James Sandeford.

DB 6-161 SAMUEL SMITH of Nash Co. to JACOB HORN of same, Feb. 8, 1796, for 195 silver dollars one negro woman. Wit: Lewis Hines.

DB 6-162 EDWARD NICHOLSON of Nash Co. to WM. BUN-TEN of same, April 5, 1796, for 190 silver dollars one negro boy. Wit: Thomas Deans and Duncan Dew.

DB 6-162 EDWARD NICHOLSON of Nash Co. to WM. BUNTEN of same, April 5, 1796, for 190 silver dollars one negro boy. Wit: Thomas Deans and Duncan Dew.

DB 6-162 PETER BALLARD of Nash Co. to WILLIAM BUNTEN of same, Feb. 25, 1792, for 120 silver dollars one negro girl. Wit: Jeremiah Bunten and Pridgen Manning.

DB 6-163 NICHOLAS BAGGETT of Nash Co. to JAMES CONWAY of same, Nov. 16, 1795, for 60 pds. Virginia money a tract of 150 acres on the north side of Swift Creek adjoining Ralph Mason, Peter Robertson, Hackney, Granberry Baggett, Jesse Kitchen, and Joel Matthews. Wit: Wm. Wright and Granberry Baggett.

DB 6-164 DAVID STRICKLAND of Nash Co. to DELILAH GRIFFIN of same, March 27, 1792, for 50 pds. specie 125 acres adjoining said Delilah Griffin, Revel, Underwood, and Joshua Vick, it being part of a tract of land said David Strickland purchased of Jacob Matthis. Wit: John Arrington, Emmanuel Skinner, and Henry Strickland.

DB 6-165 WILLIAM GRIZZELL of Nash Co. to his grandson, BANNASTER GRIZZELL, April 12, 1796, for love and affection a tract of 200 acres whereon George Grizzell formerly lived adjoining Drewry Williams, John Driver, William Grizzell, and Richard Fore, it being parts of two surveys granted to said Wm. Grizzell in 1796. Wit: Arther Grizzell, Linchea Blankinship. Benja. Cobb, and Daniel Grizzell.

DB 6-166 WILLIAM GRIZZELL of Nash Co. to DANIEL GRIZZELL of same, April 12, 1796, for 200 pds. 400 acres on the north side of Turkey Creek adjoining Bannaster Grizzell, said Wm. Grizzell, said Daniel Grizzell, Charles Carter, and Samuel Devaughan, it being parts of two tracts granted to said Wm. Grizzell in 1796. Wit: Arther Grizzell, Linchia Blankinship, and Benja. Cobb.

DB 6-168 WILLABY MANNING of Nash Co. to BENJAMIN MANNING of same, Sept. 13, 1796, for 100 pds. a tract of 400 acres on both sides of Little Peachtree Creek adjoining William Harriss and Willis Deans. Wit: Willis Deans, Moses Savvidge, and Philip Sikes.

DB 6-168 JOSIAH MELTON of Nash Co. to JOHN MELTON of same, March 12, 1796, for 40 pds. Virginia money a tract of 100 acres on the north side of Tar River and south side of Stony Creek, it being part of a patent granted to Samuel Williams. Wit: John Hays and John Watkins.

DB 6-169 JOHN MELTON of Nash Co. to JOSIAH MELTON of same, March 12, 1796, for 30 pds. Virginia money 175 acres on the south side of Little Sapony Creek adjoining William Tucker, Matthias Manning, George Sutton, O'Neal, and John Manning, it being part of a tract granted to John Biggs on Nov. 10, 1779. Wit: John Hays and John Watkins.

DB 6-170 JACOB UNDERWOOD of Nash Co. to MALACHI UNDERWOOD of same, Oct. 6, 1795, for 5 sh. a tract of 100 acres on the north side of the road adjoining Hartwell Hines and Henry

Hines. Wit: Frederick B. Hines and Alex. W. Hines.

DB 6-171 FRANCIS PARKER of Nash Co. to JAMES DREWRY of same, Aug. 9, 1794, for $5.00 a tract of 100 acres adjoining William Drake, Thomas Mann, and Nathaniel Drake. Wit: Matthew Drake and Wm. Parker.

DB 6-172 HENRY BUNN of Nash Co. to ARCHIBALD GRIFFIN of same, Oct. 20, 1795, for $833 1/3 two tracts of land on the south side of Pig Basket Creek: (1) 130 acres beginning above Warburton's house; (2) 65 acres adjoining said Bunn and Solomon Whitfield. Wit: Howell Ellin and Drey Hunter.

DB 6-173 DAVID PRIDGEN of Nash Co. to ABIJAH PRIDGEN of same, March 8, 1796, for 100 pds. Virginia money two tracts of land: (1) 552 acres on the east side of Great Bare Branch; (2) 300 acres that said David Pridgen bought of Thomas Tucker adjoining Stephen Vaun, Robert Cockrun, James Batchelor, John Nash, and William Batchelor. Wit: Jeeremiah Etheredge and Pridgen Manning.

DB 6-174 SOLOMON CARTER of Nash Co. to GEORGE LEWIS of same, March 11, 1795, for 60 pds. Virginia money a tract of 180 acres on the north side of Tar River adjoining said Carter and said Lewis. Wit: Thomas Carter and Edward York.

DB 6-175 WILLIAM PHILLIPS of Nash Co. to JONAS WILLIAMS of same, May 11, 1796, for 100 pds. a tract of 200 acres on Toisnot Swamp adjoining Nathan West, it being part of a former grant to Lasus Strickland. Wit: Duncan Dew and John Pritchett.

DB 6-176 DEMCY DEANS of Wayne Co. to JAMES BATCHELOR of Nash Co., Nov. 13, 1795, for 30 pds. Virginia money in dollars at 6 shillings to him paid. a tract of 275 acres on the south side of Little Sapony Creek adjoining Green Hill. Wit: Robert Creekmur and Elizabeth Creekmur.

DB 6-177 SOLOMON COLLINS of Nash Co. to SAMUEL GLOVER of same, April 3, 1796, for 50 pds. a tract of 130 acres on the south side of Little Sapony Creek adjoining Nathan Boddie, Thomas Tucker and Benjamin Whitley. Wit: George Boddie, Wilson Collins. and Adam Collings.

DB 6-178 JAMES MORPHIS of Wake Co. to JESSE KENT of Nash Co., Feb. 12, 1796, for 65 pds. a tract of 250 acres on Turkey Creek adjoining said Kent and Taylor, it being the land and plantation whereon Henry Barlow then lived. Wit: Drury Williams. George Grizel, and Burwell Kent.

DB 6-179 NEWET ATKINSON of Nash Co. to THOMAS TUCKER of same, Aug. 7, 1794, for 50 pds. a tract of 183 acres on Turkey Creek adjoining Jeremiah Brown and John Strickland, it being a grant to said Newet Atkinson by the State of N. C. on Dec. 20, 1791. Wit: Wilson Taylor, J. Taylor, and Drury Williams.

DB 6-180 MARY PASMORE of Nash Co. to her daughter, LUCY PASMORE, of same, Feb. 18, 1796, for love and affection

her mare and horse, furniture. and other livestock then in possession of said Lucy Pasmore. Wit: William Richardson and Newman Richardson.

DB 6-180 JOSEPH VICK of Nash Co. to WILLIAM WEST
of same, Feb. 11, 1788, for 60 pds. a tract of 281 acres on Toisnot
Swamp adjoining Duncan Lamon and John Taylor, it being a grant
to said Joseph Vick from the State of N. C. on Oct. 25. 1782. Wit:
John Bonds and John Chapman.

DB 6-181 JOHN DRIVER of Nash Co. to BENJAMIN COBB,
Dec. 26, 1795, for 25 silver dollars "one certain quarry of mill stone
rock lying in a certain tract of land that said Cobb sold to said
Driver and said rock lies close by the Rock called the Flat Roak
and by Moses Smelley Plantation and where Joseph Wooddel cut
millstone for said Cobb." Wit: Drury Williams and Micajah
Bailey.

DB 6-182 JAMES CONE of Nash Co. to WM. MORGIN of
same, Jan. 29, 1794, for 30 pds. a tract of 200 acres on Turkey
Creek and the county line. Wit: Jesse Hammonds and Joshua
Cone.

DB 6-182 LUKE HARP of Nash Co. to JAMES CONE of
same, April 25 1794, for 20 pds. specie a tract of 100 acres on the
north side of Turkey Creek. Wit: Jesse Hammond, Nathan Perry,
and Wm. Morgin.

DB 6-183 SIMUN STRICKLAND of Nash Co. to JAMES
CONE of same, May 12, 1794, for $6.00 a parcel of 3 acres on Tur-
key Creek. Wit: Jesse Hammon, John Rice, and Joshua Cone.

DB 6-184 LUKE EARP of Nash Co. to WILSON WILLIAMS
of Franklin Co., July 9, 1796, for 93 pds. Virginia money a tract of
202 acres on the north side of Turkey Creek and on the south side
of Tar River. Wit: Simon Williams and Wm. Fore.

DB 6-184 JOHN BONDS and wife, NANCY BONDS, of Nash
Co. to SAMUEL WINSTEAD of same, June 25, 1796, for 320 silv-
er dollars a tract of 640 acres adjoining Thomas Hardie, Lazarus
Pope, Crowell, and Samuel Williams. Wit: Drury Taylor and
John Bonds, Jr.

DB 6-185 SOLOMON CARTER of Nash Co. to JOHN
YOUNG of same. April 12, 1796, for 34 pds. 13 sh. a tract of 154
acres on Gabe's Branch adjoining Jeremiah Stevens. Wit: Thomas
Carter and John Sellers.

DB 6-186 SION BASS of Nash Co. to JOHN GAY of same,
May 9, 1794, for 20 pds. Virginia money a tract of 100 acres adjoining said Gay. Wit: Wm. Richardson and John Evans.

DB 6-187 WM. PERRY of Nash Co. to JAMES CONE of
same, March 4, 1796, for 30 pds. a tract of 160 acres adjoining
Jesse Hammonds, Fore, the Great Path, and the creek. Wit:
Jesse Hammond, Joshua Cone, and Wm. Morgin.

DB 6-188 ALLEN FINCH of Nash Co. to BILLEY WILL-
IAMS of same, Oct. 9, 1795, for 55 silver dollars a tract of 100
acres on the north side of the Juniper Branch of the Great Swamp

adjoining Jonas Colson and John Batman, it being part of a grant to Chester Coleson for 400 acres on Sept. 24. 1785. Wit: Jonas Williams and Drury Smelley.

DB 6-189 HARDY PRIDGEN of Nash Co. to DAVID PRIDGEN of same, Sept. 9, 1796, for 110 pds. Virginia money a tract of 125 acres on the north side of Tar River adjoining James Prim and said David Pridgen, it being the land and plantation whereon he then lived. Wit: Abijah Pridgen and Milbury Williams.

DB 6-190 WILLIAM WILHIGHT of Franklin Co. to WILLIAM WHELESS of Nash Co., Sept. 30, 1796, for 5 pds. a tract of 58 acres adjoining said Wheless, Thomas, and Hoof, lying on both sides of Bear Branch. it being part of a tract patented to John Odum. Wit: John H. Drake and Frances Drake.

DB 6-191 ROBERT JONES of Franklin Co. to JAMES HILLIARD of Nash Co., Sept. 5, 1796, for 198 silver dollars 68 acres in Nash Co., it being part of a tract of land demised bv Francis Allbrittain Jones to Joseph Jones. Wit: Matthew Drake, Jr., N. Simmons, and John Hilliard.

DB 6-191 MICAJAH REVEL of Nash Co. to JOEL BUNN of same. Oct. 22. 1796, for 250 pds. Virginia money a tract of 303 acres on the south side of Stony Creek adjoining Beniamin Bunn, William Barnes. Henry Watkins, and the road. Wit: James Williams, Drew Hunter, and Burwell Bunn.

DB 6-192 JOHN EXUM of Nash Co to JOHN WATKINS of same. Feb. 18. 1796, for 67 pds. 10 sh. Virginia Money one negro man. Wit: Stephen Robbins.

DB 6-193 DUNCAN LAMON of Nash Co. to JOEL BUNN, Sept. 12. 1796, for 100 pds. Virginia money one negro man. Wit: Henry Youell and John Lamon.

DB 6-193 WM. ROSE, SR., of Franklin Co. to JACOB ROGERS of Nash Co., Jan. 5, 1796, for $100.00 one negro girl. Wit: Richard Webb and Thomas Rose.

DB 6-193 JESSE KITCHEN of Nash Co. to THOMAS PILLSON of Greenville, Pitt Co., N. C.. Feb. 13, 1796, for 37 pds. 10 sh. Virginia money one mulatto boy. Wit: Hartwell Hines and Henry Hines.

DB 6-194 MICAJAH REVEL of Nash Co. to DAVID DANIEL of same. Oct. 22, 1796, for 100 pds. Virginia money a tract of 200 acres on the north side of Stony Creek adjoining Joseph Curl and William Barnes. Wit: James Williams and Drew Hunter.

DB 6-194 LODWICK ALFORD of Wake Co. to WILLIAM DRIVER of Nash Co., March 1, 1796. for 100 pds. a tract of 50 acres on the north side of Moccasin Creek and on both sides of Driver's Branch adjoining James Lee. Wit: Drury Williams, Elkana Williams, and Martin Hall.

DB 6-196 STEPHEN WEBB of Nash Co. to NOEL PITTS of same, Sept. 30, 1796, for 75 pds. Virginia monev a tract of 160 acres adjoining Abraham Bass. Denton Mann, and Cooper Williams. Wit: Elias Boon and Jesse Winslow.

DB 6-196 PETER WINSTEAD of Edgecombe Co. to ENUCK FLOYD of Nash Co., Sept. 30, 1793, for 20 pds. a tract of 100 acres on Town Creek adjoining Jordin Taylor and Dixon. Wit: John Wells and Thomas Winstead.

DB 6-197 LODWICK ALFORD of Wake Co. to HARDY PRIDGEN of Nash Co.. Oct. 26, 1796, for 120 pds. Virginia money a tract of 182 acres on the north side of Moccasin Creek adjoining Driver, it being the land and plantation whereon Simon Strickland then lived. Wit: Abraham Winborn, J's. Taylor, and James Lee.

DB 6-198 DRURY SAVAGE of Nash Co. to STEPHEN BAT-CHELOR of same, April 4, 1796, for50 pds. a tract of 150 acres on the north side of Little Peachtree Creek adjoining James Green, Micajah Thomas, and James Moore, it being part of a 300 acre tract granted to William Lenzey on Nov. 10, 1779. Wit: Daniel Taylor, James Green, and Callum Moore.

DB 6-199 LEWIS HILL of Franklin Co. to STEPHEN WEBB of Nash Co., April 2, 1793, for 43 pds. Virginia money a tract of 160 acres adjoining Abraham Bass. Denton Mann, and Cooper Williams. Wit: John Edwards and Rd. Hill.

DB 6-200 MARY DEANS and SHEROD DEANS of Nash Co. to WILLIAM ANDREWS, JR., of Franklin Co., March 11, 1796, for 25 pds. 10 sh. Virginia money a tract of 57 acres on the south side of Turkey Creek, it being part of a tract formerly granted to William McGee on Jan. 10, 1756, excepting two acres where the meeting house stood reserved for the use of the Baptist Society. Wit: Fieldin Conditt and David Jackson.

DB 6-202 SAMUEL WINSTEAD of Nash Co. to JOHN VICK, JR. of same, Feb. 14, 1797, for 45 pds. Virginia money a tract of 100 acres on the north side of Tar River adjoining Stephen Wells. Wit: Drury Taylor and David Winstead.

DB 6-203 WM. HARRIS and MARGIT HARRIS of Nash Co. to RANDOLPH SAVEDGE of Franklin Co., Jan. 16, 1797, for 25 pds. Virginia money a tract of 227 acres on the south side of Little Peachtree Creek. Wit: Wm. Coppedge, Jesse Griffin, and Corban Tucker.

DB 6-203 ROBERT BOGGS of Nash Co. to JOHN WILL-IAMS of same, Nov. 30, 1796, for 56 pds. Virginia money a tract of 150 acres lying in both Nash and Franklin counties on the south side of Little Peachtree, it being part of a tract of land demised by Thomas Davis to James Hilliard and conveyed by said Hilliard to William Boggs. Wit: Lervin Boggs and Benja. Tucker.

DB 6-204 THOMAS TUCKER of Halifax Co. to BENJAMIN TUCKER of Nash Co., Jan. 25. 1797, for 17 pds. 10 sh. a tract of 50 acres in Nash Co. adjoining Bains and the road. Wit: Robert Worley, Margeott Davis, and Lovick Worley.

DB 6-205 AUGUSTIN BASS of Nash Co. to JEREMIAH PUSLEY of same, Sept. 29, 1796, for 67 pds. 10 sh. Virginia money one negro girl. Wit: Numan Richardson and Jesse Rogers.

DB 6-206 JOHN POWELL of Nash Co. to WILLIE POWELL of same, Dec. 14, 1792, for 50 pds. specie a tract of 220 acres adjoining James Wiggins, William Bradley, Thomas Landingham, James Cain, and the county line. Wit: Alanson Powell, Adley Morriss, and John Wiggins.

DB 6-207 DANIEL HOLLAND of Nash Co. to JOHN WORBITTON of same, Feb. 3, 1797, for 60 pds. Virginia money 200 acres on the north side of Pig Basket Creek adjoining Aron Woodard and Holland's Branch, it being part of a tract granted to said Daniel Holland by the State of N. C. Wit: William Powell and James Powell.

DB 6-208 PRYOR GARDNER of Nash Co. to FRANCIS WARD of same, Jan. 27, 1797, for 575 pds. specie a tract of 475 acres adjoining George Gardner. Wit: Thomas Hunter, John Harrison, and Henry Pitts.

DB 6-208 ASA BRANTLEY of Nash Co. to WILLIAM POULAN of same, Dec. 31, 1796, for 39 pds. a tract of 150 acres on the north side of Jacobs Swamp adjoining said Brantley and said Poulan. Wit William Ballard and Curtis Joyner.

DB 6-209 THOMAS HART of Nash Co. to LEWIS VICK of same, Dec. 29, 1795, for $5.00 one acre of land on the north side of Hartwell's spring branch, it being for the use of a mill. Wit: Demsey Braswell and Arch'd. Griffin.

DB 6-210 CORNELIOUS BRUICE of Franklin Co. to BENJAMIN TUCKER of Nash Co., April 30, 1795, for 15 pds. a tract of 30 acres on the branches of Little Peachtree Creek lying in both Nash and Franklin counties adjoining said Tucker, Elizabeth Jackson, and the road. Wit: James Green, Samuel Linsey, and Absalom Bains.

DB 6-211 WILLIAM PASE (PEASE) of the State of Georgia to WILLIAM FORE of Nash Co., Oct. 10, 1795, for 50 pds. a tract of 100 acres on Turkey Creek adjoining Solomon Strickland and Samson Powell. Wit: Andrew Bell and William Bryant.

DB 6-212 WILLIAM WHITFIELD of Nash Co. to JOHN SELLERS of same, Jan. 2, 1797, for 90 pds. a tract of 300 acres on Sapony Creek adjoining said Sellers, William Bunting. Edward Moore, and William Sellers. Wit: William Bunting and Henry Sellers.

DB 6-213 EDWARD MOORE and CAREY (?) MOORE of Nash Co. to HENRY ATKINSON of same, Sept. 17, 1796, for 171 pds. Virginia money a tract of 250 acres on the north side of Tar River adjoining Whitfield and said Atkinson. Wit: J. Bonds, A. Brantley, and Jesse Hunt.

DB 6-213 SHEROD DEANS of Nash Co. to AUGUSTIN BASS of same, Feb. 3, 1797, for 30 pds. a tract of 219 acres on the west side of Turkey Creek adjoining William Braswell, Jacob Carter, Simon Williams, Jeremiah Stevens, and Elizabeth Pussel. Wit: Daniel Taylor and Willie Deens.

DB 6-214 WILLIAM WEST of Nash Co. to WILLIAM WHIT-

FIELD of same, Dec. 24, 1796, for 100 pds. Virginia money a tract of 281 acres on Toisnot Swamp adjoining Lamon and John Taylor, it being a grant by the State of N. C. to Joseph Vick on Oct. 25. 1782. Wit: Jonas Williams and Janey Williams.

DB 6-215 EDWARD MOORE of Nash Co. to CHRISTOPHER TAYLOR of same, Oct. 1, 1796, for 100 pds. Virginia money a tract of 200 acres adjoining said Moore, Whitfield, Arthur Sellers. Lindsey, said Taylor, and the river. Wit: Wm. Poulan and J. Bonds.

DB 6-216 JEREMIAH STEVENS of Franklin Co. to SIMON JONES of Nash Co., Feb. 8, 1790, for 70 pds. specie a tract of 57 acres on the west side of Turkey Creek. Wit: Daniel Taylor and Polley Harlow.

DB 6-217 ROBERT JONES of Franklin Co. to THOMAS GRIFFIN of Nash Co., May 12. 1796, for $106.00 a tract of 100 acres on the Mill Swamp adjoining John Melton. Wit: Lewis Vick and Robin Braswell.

DB 6-218 LEWIS HINES of Nash Co. to WILLIAM ROSE of Edgecombe Co., Feb. 10, 1797, for 100 pds. Virginia money a tract of 225 acres on the north side of Compass Creek adjoining Reuben Taylor. Alexander Thompson, Jeremiah Hilliard, and said Hines. Wit: Jacob Horn and Sam Smith.

DB 6-218 THOMAS MORRIS of Nash Co. to ELIAS BOON of same, April 12, 1794, for 40 pds. a tract of 100 acres on the north side of Pig Basket Creek adjoining Matthew Drake. Wit: Benjamin Boon and John Boon.

DB 6-219 JOHN HAYS of Nash Co. to PRIDGEN MANNING of same, Feb. 6, 1797, for 177 pds. 10 sh. Virginia money three tracts of land on the south side of Peachtree Creek: (1) 190 acres adjoining the acre at the mill; (2) 85 acres adjoining Dickerson's former line and Melton; (3) 5 acres adjoining Hays, containing the mill seat. Wit: Robert Creekmur and William Batchelor.

DB 6-220 JAMES TUCKER of Nash Co. to WILLIAM TISDALE of same, Feb. 9, 1797, for 90 pds. Virginia money a tract of 262½ acres on the south side of Little Sapony Swamp adjoining Briant Onail. Wit: Robert Creekmur and Selia Rackley.

DB 6-221 DEMPSEY BARNES, SR. of Edgecombe Co. to EPHRAIM PHILLIPS, JR., son of Jethro Phillips. of Nash Co., Jan. 1, 1797, for 96 pds. Virginia money a tract of 434 acres on the Great Swamp adjoining Joseph Phillips and Benjamin Flowers. it being the same tract of land said Barnes bought of Jethro Phillips and part of a tract granted to Edward Moore for 640 acres on Oct. 9, 1783. Wit: Lemuel Wright and Joseph Wright.

DB 6-223 WILLIAM TISDALE of Nash Co. to FERREBA TUCKER, relique and widow of James Tucker, deceased, Feb. 15, 1797, for 100 pds. Virginia money a tract of 262½ acres on the south side of Little Sapony Swamp adjoining Briant Onail. Wit: John H. Drake.

DB 6-224 JACOB BARNES of Nash Co. to WILLIE BUNN of same, Nov. 29, 1796, for 100 pds. Virginia money a 100 acre plantation on the north side of Tar River. Wit: Edward Horn, John Barnes, and Benja. Bunn.

DB 6-225 PENUEL FLOYD of Nash Co. to COOPER JONES of same. May 7, 1796, for 200 silver dollars two tracts of land: (1) 130 acres on the north side of Pig Basket Creek adjoining Williams and Joseph White; (2) 20 acres on the north side of the creek adjoining Joseph White and the road. Wit: Matthew Drake, Jr. and Matthew Melton.

DB 6-226 JOHN POWELL of Nash Co. to ALANSON POWELL of same. Oct. 25, 1792. for 50 pds. specie a tract of 200 acres on the south side of Fishing Creek adjoining James Cain and James Wiggins. Wit: Willie Powell, Adley Morriss, and John Wiggins.

DB 6-227 SOLOMON STRICKLAND of Nash Co. to DAVID BISSETT of same, Feb. 4, 1786, for 34 pds. specie a tract of 250 acres on Turkey Creek including his own improvements on both sides of the Great Branch. it being a grant to said Strickland on Nov. 1, 1784. Wit: Pettipool Massey and John Rice.

DB 6-228 CHARLES CARTER of Nash Co. to EDWARD NICHOLSON of same, April 9, 1796, for 75 pds. a tract of 150 acres of land. Wit: Elijah Dunnavant and Nathan Tucker.

DB 6-229 MICHAGE LANE of Nash Co. to WILLIAM BRYANT of same, June 29, 1795, for 33 pds. Virginia money a tract of 100 acres on the north side of Tar River adjoining Harrison, Hendrick, Wm. Hammons, and Bryant's old line. Wit: Wm. Hammons and Elizabeth Hammons.

DB 6-229 JOSEPH WRIGHT of Nash Co. to LEMUEL WRIGHT of same. Jan. 13, 1797, for 200 silver dollars a certain tract on the north side of the Great Swamp, it being all the land that he owned on the north side of the Great Swamp and the land whereon Cordy Joyner did live. Wit: Sharod Phillips and Gabriel Phillips.

DB 6-231 WILLIAM BOVET of Nash Co. to SOLOMON D. PARKER of same, Sept. 9. 1796, for 55 pds. specie a tract of 114 acres on the east side of Lott's Branch. a branch of Toisnot. adjoining the William Bovet plantation line and the county line. Wit: Jonas Williams and Beersheba Williams.

DB 6-232 JETHRO PHILLIPS of Nash Co. to JOSEPH WRIGHT of same, Nov. 3, 1796, for 320 silver dollars one negro man. Wit: Sharod Phillips and Gabriel Phillips.

DB 6-232 DIXON MARSHALL of Warren Co. to RICHARD MARSHALL of same, Feb. 17, 1790, for 150 pds. a tract of 300 acres on the Great Branch adjoining Lewis Joyner, Lemon, John Barnes, and Jacob Barnes. Wit: Eleazar Marshall and Samuel Walthen.

DB 6-233 HENRY HORN of Wayne Co. to his son, THOMAS HORN, of same. Feb. 9, 1797, for love and affection that tract of land in Nash Co. on the north side of Contentnea Creek beginning at the upper end of the William Row old fiend and near Cornelius

Sanders' field. Wit: William Row and James Broadstreet.

DB 6-234 RICHARD MARSHALL of Warren Co. to JESSE STUDEVANT of Halifax Co., June 22, 1796, for 120 silver dollars a tract of 300 acres on the Great Branch adjoining Lewis Joyner, Lemon, John Barnes, and Jacob Barnes. Wit: John Pettway, Wm. Crowder, and Eleazar Marshall.

DB 6-235 RICHARD DEENS of Nash Co. to JESSE BASS of same, March 12, 1796, for 75 pds. Virginia money a tract of 262 acres on Little Peachtree Creek adjoining John Sikes, Nathan Boddie, Powell, Matthew Drake, and George Boddie. Wit: Daniel Taylor, Augustin Bass, and Christopher Culpepper.

DB 6-236 WILLIAM BOGGS of Nash Co. to ROBERT BOGGS of same, Oct. 29, 1796, for $284.00 a tract of 284 acres on the south side of Little Peachtree Creek adjoining Thomas Davis and lying partly in Franklin Co., it being a tract that was demised by Thomas Davis to James Hilliard. Wit: Sam'l Cohoon, Benjamin Tucker, and James Green.

DB 6-237 WRIGHT STALLINGS, admr. of the estate of MOSES STALLINGS (STALLIONS), deceased, of Franklin Co. to KITCHIN PRIM of Nash Co., March 7, 1796, for 100 pds. a tract of 150 acres on the south side of Little Peachtree Creek adjoining Benja. Manning. Wit: James Stallings, Bethany Jones, and Philip Sikes.

DB 6-238 JEREMIAH BURGE of Nash Co. to DAVID POPE of same, Feb. 8, 1797, for 55 pds. Virginia money a tract of 432 acres on both sides of Compass Creek adjoining Jacob Underwood, Frederick Hines, Samuel Sorsby. Joseph Exum, and Willis Trevathan. Wit: John Exum and Micager Pope.

DB 6-239 JAMES BRASWELL and wife. FRANCES BRASWELL, of Edgecombe Co. to NATHAN WHITEHEAD of Nash Co., Nov. 14, 1796, for 25 pds. a tract of 63 acres adjoining said Whitehead. Wit: Wm. Hall.

DB 6-240 ELIJAH DUNNAVANT, Sheriff of Nash Co., to EDWARD NICHOLSON of same, Sept. 1, 1796, at public auction for 33 pds. a tract of 385 acres whereon the bloomery and mill then stood, it being part of a tract adjoining Eatman, Benja. Flowers, and Jethro Phillips and was within the bounds of two seats of land granted to Benjamin Bunn for 640 acres each, whereon NATHAN COBB formerly lived and was sold to satisfy an execution obtained against him. Wit: John Pritchett and Barshabah Nicholson.

DB 6-240 ISAAC NEWSUM and MAREY NEWSUM of Nash Co. to LEWIS DORTCH of same, Jan. 13, 1797, for 315 pds. Virginia money two tracts of land: (1) 150 acres on the north side of Swift Creek; (2) 200 acres adjoining the first tract and William Dortch. James Nelson, and Thomas Hart. Wit: Daniel Powell and Wm. Wright.

DB 6-241 SOLOMON COLLANS of Nash Co. to ROBERT CREEKMUR of same, Sept. 3, 1795. for 50 pds. a tract of 200 acres on Sapony Swamp adjoining Nathan Boddie, William Batchelor, David Pridgen, Peter Etheridge, and the Bare Branch. Wit: Catey Manning, Penny Collans, and Benjamin Whitley.

DB 6-242 WILLIAM SELLERS and wife, MARTHA SELLERS, of Nash Co. to JOHN SELLERS of same, April 20, 1797, for $55.00 a tract of 50 acres on Sapony Creek. Wit: Thos. Carter and Henry Sellers.

DB 6-243 JOSEPH HAYS of Nash Co. to WILLIAM ARRINGTON of same, Dec. 24, 1795, for 150 silver dollars a tract of 100 acres on the south side of Fishing Creek adjoining said Arrington. Wit: John Arrington and Lemuel Nicholson.

DB 6-244 JACOB DUCK, SARAH DUCK, and LYDIA DUCK, all of Johnston Co. to THEOPHILUS GRICE of Nash Co., May 26, 1796, for 47 pds. 10 sh. Virginia money two negroes. Wit: J. Nichols and Elleck Grice.

DB 6-245 CHARLES WHITEHEAD of Nash Co. to WILLIAM ARRINGTON of same, Nov. 23, 1794, for 41 pds. Virginia money a tract of 68 acres on the south side of Fishing Creek adjoining Joseph Hays, Lemuel Lassiter, Hunt, Benjamin Whitehead, and Pollox. as by a grant bearing date 1779. Wit: Edwin Drake and Sam Westray.

DB 6-246 JAMES BATTLE of Nash Co. to WILLIAM ARRINGTON of same, Aug. 3, 1793, for 150 pds. specie two tracts of land: (1) 160 acres adjoining Lemuel Lassiter and Joseph Hays; (2) 50 acres on the north side of Beaver Dam Swamp adjoining Cooper, Whitehead, and Battle (formerly Lassiter), it being the same two parcels conveyed by Thomas and John Hunt by deed to said James Battle. Wit: Arthur Arrington and John Arrington.

DB 6-247 ARTHUR ONAILS of Nash Co. to WILLIAM TISDALE of same, Feb. 2, 1797, for 5 pds. 14 sh. Virginia money a tract of 38 acres on Little Sapony Creek adjoining Josiah Melton, Joseph Batchelor, William Tisdale, and George Sutton. Wit: Abijah Pridgen and James Tucker.

DB 6-247 JAMES BLACKWELL of Granville Co. to BENJAMIN MATTHEWS, March 30, 1797, for 90 pds. Virginia money one negro boy. Wit: James Hilliard, Robt. C. Hilliard, and Joel Matthews.

DB 6-248 JOHN BATTLE of Nash Co. to ANNE PITTS of Halifax Co., Dec. 26, 1796, for 75 pds. Virginia money a tract of 200 acres adjoining Lot Etheridge and Jonah Williams, it being part of a grant to John Cooper for 530 acres on March 7, 1761. Wit: Walter Pitts and John Pitts.

DB 6-249 NATHANIEL DRAKE of Nash Co. to ORRENDATES DRAKE of same, March 11, 1797, for love and affection a tract of 100 acres on the south side of Wolf Pit Branch. Wit: Matthew Drake, Jr. and William Drake, Jr.

DB 6-249 JEREMIAH STEVENS of Nash Co. to his daughter, SALLE JONES, of same, March 26, 1796, for 100 pds. specie the loan of three negroes during her lifetime and, after her decease, he gave the negroes to her children that she had by Simon Jones, namely. William Jones, Rebeckah Jones, Elizabeth Jones, Jeremiah Jones, and Simon Jones. Wit: Solomon Carter and Joseph Stevens.

DB 6-250 JAMES PRIM of Nash Co. to DAVID PRIDGEN of same, Feb. 6, 1797, for 45 pds. Virginia money a tract of 141½ acres on the north side of Tar River adjoining said Pridgen and Joshua Wells. Wit: Abijah Pridgen and Charity Deans.

DB 6-250 DUNCAN LAMON of Nash Co. to JOHN MORGAN of same, Oct. 15, 1787, for 10 pds. specie a tract of 200 acres on the south side of Tar River adjoining Benja. Tann, John Taylor, and Jacob Lewis. Wit: John Lamon and Duncan Lamon, Jr.

DB 6-251 WILLIAM HALL of Nash Co. to AMOS GANDY of same, Feb. 23, 1795, for $520.00 three tracts of land: (1) 130 acres on the north side of Sapony Swamp adjoining Benja. Smith; (2) 320 acres on the south side of Barnes' Branch and on Pollard's old line; (3) 150 acres on the north side of Sapony Swamp, a total of 600 acres. Wit: Edward Hall and Lucy Hall.

DB 6-253 SILAS DRAKE of Nash Co. to BENJAMIN DRAKE of same, Feb. 6, 1797, for 166 pds. 6 sh. 8 p. a tract of 137 acres on the south side of Swift Creek adjoining Benja. Boon and Allen Mann, it being a parcel of land left in the will of James Drake, deceased, to Silas Drake. Wit: Sam Taylor and Nancy Boon.

DB 6-254 WILSON BRASWELL of Nash Co. to JAMES WILLIAMS of same, Nov. 10, 1797 (?), May Ct. 1797, for 233 silver dollars a tract of 233 acres on the north side of Stony Creek adjoining Thomas Hunter, it being part of a survey containing 700 acres granted by the State of N. C. on Nov. 10, 1779 and was bequeathed to said Wilson Braswell by his father in his will. Wit: Howell Ellen, Lodrick Ellen, and William Barrett.

DB 6-255 JOHN BATTLE of Nash Co. to WILLIAM CHAMBLISS of same, Jan. 30, 1797, for 300 pds. Virginia money one certain tract on the north side of Swift Creek. Wit: George Gardner, P. Arrington, and A. Wheless.

DB 6-256 EDWARD NICHOLSON of Nash Co. to ROLAND WILLIAMS of same, May 10, 1796, for 100 pds. a tract of 150 acres on both sides of Mooneham's Mill Branch adjoining William Grizzle and Thomas Mooneham. Wit: Peter Ballard and Micah Horn.

DB 6-257 WILLIE SKINNER and wife, SARAH SKINNER, of Nash Co. to NATHAN POWELL of same, May 11, 1796, for 85 pds. Virginia money a tract of land on the south side of Fishing Creek on Beaver Dam Swamp adjoining said Powell. Wit: Alanson Powell and Elizabeth Powell.

DB 6-257 NATHANIEL POWELL of Nash Co. to WILLOUGHBY POWELL of same, March 8, 1794, for 30 pds. specie a tract of 100 acres adjoining Hackney. Wit: Emmanuel Underwood and Lazarus Powell.

DB 6-258 HOWELL UNDERWOOD of Nash Co. to THOM-

AS MANNIN of same, March 4, 1797. for 77 pds. 7 sh. 6 p. specie a tract of 155 acres adjoining Solomon Edwards and the road. Wit: Richard Reid Reading and John Fletcher.

DB 6-259 JOSEPH MELTON of Nash Co. to LAZARUS JONES of same, Feb. 20, 1797, for 70 pds. Virginia money a tract of 140 acres on the north side of Whitehead's Mill Branch, it being a tract of land granted to John Melton by Earl Granville and conveyed from said John Melton to Joseph Melton by deed. Wit: Lewis Vick and Thomas Griffin.

DB 6-260 THOMAS WHITFIELD of Nash Co. to ROGER REESE of Southampton Co., Virginia, Feb. 27, 1797, for $400.00 a tract of 200 acres on the south side of Maple Creek adjoining Benjamin Denson and Ricks. Wit: Abra. Ricks, Lewis Curl, and Micael Manning.

DB 6-261 WILLIAM VESTER to his son, MICHAEL VESTER, April 13, 1796, for love and affection and 5 sh. a tract of 200 acres adjoining Solomon Vester, David Pridgen (formerly Matthias Manning), and Everidge, it being the upper half of a tract of land granted to said William Vester by Earl Granville on Sept. 17, 1744. Wit: Wm. Pritchett and William Vester.

DB 6-262 JEREMIAH PURSELL (PUSSEL) of Nash Co. to AUGUSTIN BASS of same, Nov. 14, 1796, for 100 pds. Virginia money a tract of 500 acres on both sides of Great Turkey Creek. Wit: Daniel Taylor and Willis Deens.

DB 6-263 LEWIS WELLS, Sheriff of Nash Co., to MARK MASON, Aug. 8, 1797, at public auction for 1 pd. 6 p. a widow's dowry called the property of BAALAM BERRYMAN, the land lying on the south side of Fishing Creek adjoining Absalom Nicholson, Mark Mason, Abner Mason, William Pace, and John Culpepper, to have and to hold the right and title that Balaam Berryman had in the land. Wit: Benja. Mason and Foster Mason.

DB 6-264 EDWARD COOPER of Nash Co. to his son, JOHN COOPER, of same, Jan. 7, 1797, for for love and affection a tract of 100 acres adjoining Nicholas Baggett, Hackney. Minton, Peter Robertson, and Lewis Dortch. Wit: Jethro Denson, Edmund Cooper, and Henry Mason.

DB 6-265 BRYANT ONEAL of Nash Co. to JOHN MELTON, SR. of same, Feb. 24, 1797, for 50 pds. Virginia money a tract of 150 acres on the south side of Little Saponv Swamp adjoining Arthur Oneal and James Tucker. Wit: Robert Creekmur and Ballentine Creekmur.

DB 6-266 JOHN PARRISH of Nash Co. CLAYBON FINCH of same, Sept. 19, 1795, for 100 pds. a tract of 200 acres on Turkey Creek adjoining Jeremiah Brown and Robert Vick, along a line agreed upon by said Parrish and Dempsey Wyatt, it being the north part of a grant to said John Parrish by the State of N. C. Wit: Wilson Taylor, John Chapman, and Allen Finch.

DB 6-266 HENRY TISDELL of Nash Co. to CLABUN FINCH of same, July 27, 1796. for 100 pds. a tract of 300 acres on the waters of the Milstone adjoining James Deens, this taken from a grant obtained by said Tisdell from the State of N. C. on Nov. 1, 1784. Wit: Drury Williams, Jethro Harrison, and J. Atkinson.

on the north side of Moccasin Creek adjoining Lodrick Alford. Wit: Abm. Winborn and Samuel Strickland.

DB 6-268 HENRY HORN of Wayne Co. to THOMAS HORN of same, March 8, 1797, for 45 pds. Virginia money paid to William Row, deceased, including the plantation whereon William Horn then lived. Wit: Wm. Horn, Jeremiah Horn, and Patience Horn.

DB 6-268 THOMAS DRIVER of Johnston Co. to CHARLES DRIVER of Nash Co., Sept. 14, 1789, for 20 pds. a tract of 30 acres

DB 6-269 DUNCAN LAMON of Nash Co. to his son, DUNCAN LAMON, JR., April 19, 1796, for love and affection the 300 acre tract whereon Duncan Lamon, Sr. then lived; also, a tract of 193 acres adjoining the above tract on the south side of Dorman's Branch; also, five negroes by name. Wit: Drewry Joyner and Nicholson Lewis.

6-270 BERRIMAN BILBRO of Nash Co. to LITTLE B. WHITE of Franklin Co., Aug. 1, 1797, for 18 p. Virginia money a parcel of 2 acres at Bilbro's Crossroads running along the road to William's Ferry on Tar River and along Hammond's line to the road leading to Lewis Burg. Wit: David Jackson and Cha. Wortham.

DB 6-271 HENRY BANES and wife, FANNY BANES of Nash Co. to LITTLE B. WHITE, July 31, 1797 for 90 pds. Virginia money a tract of 216 acres on Little Turkey Creek adjoining Benjamin Tucker. Wit: B. Bilbro and Cha. Wortham.

DB 6-272 SARAH COLEMAN of Edgecombe Co. to her son-in-law, JETHRO PHILLIPS and his three daughters, CHRISCHANY PHILLIPS, LURANY PHILLIPS, and SARAH PHILLIPS, JR. of same, May 7, 1795, for love and affection four negroes by name; also, to each of her three granddaughters one additional negro by name, to take place at her death. Wit: William Carstarphen and Ephraim Phillips.

DB 6-273 WILLIAM RICHARDSON, JR. of Nash Co. to LUCY PASSMORE of same, March 27, 1797, for 10 pds. a tract of 45 acres adjoining James Massengill and John Richardson. Wit: Numan Richardson.

DB 6-273 MATTHIAS MANNING of Nash Co. to DANIEL WOODARD of sase, July 15, 1797, for $150.00 a tract of 200 acres on Sapony Creek and Bear Branch. Wit: Matthew Carter, Joab Tucker, and William Haress.

DB 6-274 MARMADUKE MASON of Nash Co. to SAMUEL WESTRAY of same, Aug. 3, 1797. for $550.00 a tract of 150 acres given to the said Mason by his grandfather, Joseph Strickland; also, a tract adjoining the above mentioned tract that said Mason had bought of Samuel Thomas, lying on Stony Creek adjoining James Williams, Emmanuel Skinner, and the road, one acre of land excepted at that end of Hunter's old mill dam if it belonged to Hunter's estate. Wit: Arch'd. Adams and James Willis.

DB 6-275 DREWRY BOYKIN, SR. of Nash Co. to HARDY THORNE of same, March 3, 1795, for $150.00 a tract of 145 acres on the north side of Contentnea Creek adjoining Theophilus Grice. Wit: Thomas Airs and Shadrick Sims.

DB 6-276 DREWRY BOYKIN, SR. of Nash Co. to HARDY THORNE of same, March 5, 1795, for 250 silver dollars a tract of 440 acres on the south side of Mash Swamp near Hardy Boykin's improvements, it being a tract taken up by said Boykin in 1782. Wit: Thomas Airs and Shadrick Sims.

DB 6-277 HARDY BOYKIN and DREWRY BOYKIN of Nash Co. to HARDY THORNE of same, Feb. 13, 1796, for 300 pds. 125 acres adjoining Woodard and Chartey Eyeats, it being part of a tract granted to Benjamin Boykin on July 9, 1795. Wit: Benja. Cobb and Jacob Boykin.

DB 6-278 ZACHARIAH (ZACRA) ONEAL to JOHN MELTON, Jan. 23, 1797, for 75 pds. a tract of 146 acres on Little Sapony Swamp adjoining Briant Oneal, it being parts of two tracts. Wit: Josiah Melton, David Melton, and Joseph Melton.

DB 6-279 JAMES WILLIAMS of Nash Co. to JOSEPH CURL of same, Nov. 23, 1796, for 51 pds. 10 sh. Virginia money one negro girl. Wit: Marmaduke Mason and William Johnson.

DB 6-279 ENOCH DOZIER of Currituck Co. to JOSEPH CURL of Nash Co., Oct. 19, 1797, for 325 silver dollars three negroes by name. Wit: Josiah Horn.

DB 6-280 CHRISTOPHER TAYLOR of Nash Co. to JOSEPH CURL of same, Oct. 8, 1796, for 200 silver dollars one negro boy. Wit: Curtis Joyner.

DB 6-280 EMMANUEL SKINNER of Nash Co. to HENRY VICK of same, Aug. 30, 1797, for $800.00 a tract of 300 acres on Lamon's Road adjoining Virk, Barnes, Mason, and the creek. Wit: Abra. Ricks, James Williams, and Wm. Skinner.

DB 6-281 DANIEL HOLLAND of Nash Co. to RICHARD HOLLAND of same, Oct. 14, 1797, for $370.00 a tract of 425 acres on the south side of Lewis' Branch near Margret Thomas' line former (ly William Whiddon), it being a tract that was conveyed by Henry Kent to Thomas Holland. Wit: Wm. Boddie and Aaron Woodard.

DB 6-282 HENRY WATKINS of Edgecombe Co. to JOEL BUNN of Nash Co., Oct. 7, 1797. for 46 pds. 10 sh. a 50 acre plantation on the south side of Stony Creek adjoining William Barnes. Wit: Edward York, John Watkins, and John McDade.

6-282 ELY (ELI) JONES of Nash Co. to CULLEN ANDREWS of same, Feb. 12, 1796, for 22 pds. 10 sh. Virginia money a 100 acre plantation on the south side of Beach Run Swamp on the county line. Wit: Jonas Whitley.

DB 6-283 JOHN PARRISH of Nash Co. to LAZARUS STRICKLAND of same, Nov. 7, 1795, for 50 pds. a tract of 100 acres on Turkey Creek and Fox Branch. Wit: J. Taylor and Dempsey Taylor.

DB 6-284 JOHN JOINER, SR. of Nash Co. to CURTIS JOINER of same, Nov. 11, 1797, for 50 pds. a tract of 100 acres on the south side of Sapony Creek adjoining William Baker, Edward Ballard, and the old road. Wit: Edmund Joiner and Isham Langley.

DB 6-285 ROLAN LEDBETTER of Nash Co. to HENRY LEWIS of same, Jan. 7, 1794, for 50 pds. specie a tract of 150 acres on both sides of Clark's Branch adjoining John Petticob, John Ledbetter, and John Kent, it being a grant to said Rolan Ledbetter from the State of N. C. on Nov. 26, 1789. Wit: Wilson Taylor, Elijah Dunnavant, and Henry Barlow.

DB 6-286 HARDY WESTER of Nash Co. to WILLIAM WESTER of same. Jan. 22, 1795, for 70 silver dollars a tract of 100 acres adjoining John Ricks, Richard Vick, Skinner, and Whitley. Wit: Joel Bunn, Lewis Curl, and William Joyner.

DB 6-286 ASA BRANTLEY of Nash Co. to WILLIAM POULAN of same, Oct. 28, 1797, for 59 pds. a tract of 200 acres on the north side of Jacobs Swamp. Wit: Curtis Joyner and Jordon Williams.

DB 6-287 ISHAM FINCH of Nash Co. to MICAH HORN of same, Aug. 21 1797, for 105 pds. Virginia money a tract of 150 acres on Turkey Creek adjoining Richard Fore and John West. Wit: Wilson Taylor and Sam'l Devaughan.

DB 6-288 JOHN STRICKLAND, SR. of Nash Co. to LARSUS STRICKLAND, JR. of same, Dec. 16, 1791, for 10 pds. a tract of 40 acres on Turkey Creek adjoining William West and Jeremiah Brown, it being a grant from the State of N. C. to said John Strickland in 1784. Wit: Elias Owens and Simon Strickland.

DB 6-289 RICE WEBB of Franklin Co. to JAMES BRUCE of Nash Co., Nov. 13, 1792, for 50 pds. specie a tract of 240 acres on Turkey Creek on Ross' old line. Wit: Wm. Hammons, Willis Deens, and Jesse Pridgen.

DB 6-290 WILLIAM BOYET, JR. of Nash Co. to JONAS WILLIAMS of same, Sept. 20, 1795, for 40 pds. Virginia money a tract of 200 acres on Town Creek and the county line adjoining John Bonds, Elizabeth Parker, and Arch'd Lamon, it being part of a 300 acre grant to Richard Winstead on Aug. 11, 1786. Wit: Edward Crowell and Beersheba Williams.

DB 6-291 WILLIAM WILLIS of Nash Co. to JOHN VICK of same. Oct. 9, 1797, for 755 silver dollars a tract of 212 acres on the north side of Stony Creek adjoining James Williams and Benja. Vick. Wit: James Powell and Wilson Willis.

DB 6-292 RICHARD WINSTEAD of Edgecombe Co. to WILLIAM BOYET, JR. of Nash Co., Aug. 13, 1787, for 25 pds. specie a tract of 200 acres on Town Creek and the county line adjoining Peter Hatten, Elizabeth Parker, and Arch'd. Lamon, it being part of a 300 acre grant to said Winstead on Aug. 11, 1786. Wit: Jesse Green and Solomon Dawson.

DB 6-293 BENJAMIN MARTHIS and wife, MARY MARTHIS

of Nash Co. to JAMES HILLIARD of same, Nov. 13, 1797, for 1000 silver dollars a tract of 170 acres on the north side of Swift Creek adjoining Jesse Kitchen, it being a tract that was granted to Benjamin Marthis bv Earl Granville in 1760. Wit: Isaac Hilliard, A. B. Jones, and Brittain Jones.

DB 6-294 JOHN BRASWELL and SARY BRASWELL of Nash Co. to BENJAMIN BRASWELL of same, Jan. 20, 1798, for 105 pds. Virginia money 286 acres on Tar River and Turkey Creek adjoining Stevens, it being a tract of land willed to said John Braswell by his father. Wit: Isaac Hill and Hardy Pursell.

DB 6-295 NATHAN BRASWELL of Robeson Co. to BRITTAIN BRASWELL of Nash Co., Feb. 13, 1798, for $200.00 a tract of 250 acres adjoining Marriet and Powell. Wit: Sion Beckwith.

DB 6-296 NATHAN BRASWELL of Robeson Co. to WILLIAM BRASWELL of Nash Co., Feb. 13, 1798, for $100.00 a tract of 100 acres adjoining his own line and Powell. Wit: Sion Beckwith.

DB 6-297 BRITTAIN BRASWELL of Nash Co. to JESSE BRASWELL of same, Feb. 13, 1798, for $100.00 a tract of 100 acres adjoining William Braswell, Jacob Braswell, and his own line. Wit: Sion Beckwith.

DB 6-297 JOSHUA BUTT of Halifax Co. to WILLIAM SKIPWITH MEARNS of Nash Co., Dec. 28, 1796, for 600 silver dollars two tracts of land: (1) 200 acres adjoining Arthur Bell, Jonas Williams, John Cooper, Lot Etheridge, and Elias Bell, it being a tract conveyed from James Bell to Joshua Butt on Oct. 25, 1783; (2) 140 acres on Pollock's Beaver Dam Swamp adjoining Elias Bell, it being a tract conveyed by Green Bell to Joshua Butt on Oct. 27, 1783. Wit: William Dozier, John Jones, and Richmond Dozier.

DB 6-298 JOSEPH BROWN of the State of South Carolina to ROBERT HOBBS of Nash Co., Jan. 5. 1795, for 160 pds. specie a tract of 540 acres on the north side of Turkey Creek near Henry Wyatt's improvements, it being a grant from the State of N. C. to Jeremiah Brown for 640 acres on Nov. 10. 1779, one hundred acres being excepted. Wit: Wilson Taylor, Henry Lewis, and Enoch Owens.

DB 6-299 JAMES LEE of Nash Co. to JOEL WILLIAMS of same, Aug. 12, 1797, for 155 silver dollars a tract of 300 acres on the south side of Toisnot Swamp adjoining Edward More and Mark Strickland, it being a grant to said James Lee on Nov. 1, 1784. Wit: Hardy Pridgen, Wm. Carpenter, and J. Taylor.

DB 6-300 DEMPSEY BARNES of Nash Co. to JOHN BARNES of same. Dec. 18, 1797, for 85 pds. Virginia money a tract of 220 acres on the north side of Tar River near Willie Bunn's new cart path adjoining Benja. Bunn, Duncan Lamon, and the new road. Wit: Roger Reese, William Joyner, Jr., and Wade Moore.

DB 6-300 WILLIAM BALLARD and LYDDA BALLARD of Nash Co. to URIAH HATCHER of same, Dec. 16, 1797, for 150 pds. Virginia money a tract of 571 acres on the north side of Tar

River and on Jacobs Swamp adjoining William Poulan, John Bone, William Linsey, and Christopher Taylor, it being the land and plantation whereon he then lived. Wit: David Pridgen, Abijah Pridgen, Wm. Poulan, and Ethelred Dance.

DB 6-301 JOHN EXUM of Nash Co. to SAMUEL SMITH of same, July 9, 1796, for 75 pds. a tract of 205 acres on the south side of Great Compass Creek and on the north side of Little Compass Creek adjoining Lewis Hines, Randolph Harris, Hardy Harris, and Solomon Edwards. It consisted of two tracts of land, one conveyed by Joseph Exum to said John Exum on Oct. 30, 1778 and the other conveyed by John Carrol to said Exum on March 1, 1788. Wit: Henry Vick and Batson Smith.

DB 6-302 HENRY ATKINSON of Nash Co. to BENJAMIN ATKINSON of same, Feb. 12, 1798, for 40 pds. Virginia money a 325 acre plantation on the north side of Tar River adjoining William Buntin and Noah Strickland. Wit: Uriah Hatcher and Abijah Pridgen.

DB 6-303 NATHAN BODDIE, executor of JOHN SIKES deceased, of Nash Co. to GEORGE BODDIE. Dec. 5, 1797, for 150 pds. Virginia money a tract of 93 acres on the north side of Little Peachtree Creek adjoining Matthew Drake and John Sikes, Jr. Wit: Mourning Boddie, Mary Hill, and Rebecca Foster.

DB 6-304 JOSIAH MELTON of Nash Co. to JOHN MATTHEWS of same, Jan. 18, 1798, for 150 silver dollars a tract of 175 acres on the south side of Little Sapony Creek adjoining William Tucker, Matthias Manning, George Sutton, Onail, and John Manning. Wit: David Melton and William Matthews.

DB 6-304 WILLIAM ARRINGTON, admr. with the will annexed of THOMPKINS SANDEFORD, to JAMES HILLIARD, Feb. 13, 1798, whereas the residue of his property bequeathed to his wife was directed to be sold after her death and whereas she had deceased and the executors also, the admrs. conveyed to said James Hilliard for 105 pds. Virginia money at public auction a tract of 86 acres adjoining John Hilliard and Arrington, it being part of a deed granted to William Sandeford and conveyed by said William Sandeford to Thompkins Sandeford, deceased. Wit: Thomas Nicholson and Abraham Perry.

DB 6-305 RICHARD BURGE of Nash Co. to JAMES SCRUES of Edgecombe Co., Jan. 23, 1797. for 125 pds. Virginia money a tract of 265 acres on the north side of Tar River and on Sapony Branch adjoining Batchelor. Wit: Solomon Carter, J. Bonds, and John Glover.

DB6-306 LEWIS WELLS, Sheriff of Nash Co., to WILLIAM GREEN, July 1, 1797. at public auction for 100 pds. a tract of 500 acres on the south side of Tar River adjoining Duncan Lamon, Hardy Pridgen, and Philander Williams, sold as the property of PATRICK WALKER to satisfy an execution obtained by said William Green, it being the land that Patrick Walker bought of Dixon Marshall. Wit: So. Green and Redmun Bunn.

DB 6-307 JOSIAH HORN gave bond of $300.00 to JOEL HORN, Oct. 31, 1792. the condition being that he should give a good title to a tract of land which he had previously sold to the said Joel Horn. Wit: Cornealous Sanders.

DB 6-307 PETER ROBERTSON of Nash Co. to his son, JOHN ROBERTSON, of same, Jan. 11, 1798, a tract of 150 acres adjoining Culpepper and Hackney's old line. Wit: Lewis Dortch and Daniel Mann.

DB 6-308 WILLIAM JACKSON of Nash Co. to JOHN HUBBARD of Franklin Co., Nov. 3, 1796, for 20 pds. a tract of 30 acres lying partly in both counties. Wit: Sam Taylor and Hardy Hunt. on Little Turkey Creek adjoining Cornelius Taylor and Wilson,

DB 6-308 WILLIAM JACKSON of Nash Co. to JOHN HUBBARD of Franklin Co., Nov. 3, 1796, for 20 pds. a tract of 24 acres on Little Turkey Creek adjoining Elizabeth Jackson, lying partly in both counties. Wit: Sam Taylor and Hardy Hunt.

DB 6-309 WILLIAM ANDREWS of Franklin Co. to JOHN HUBBARD of same, Nov. 8, 1797, for 60 pds. Virginia money a tract of 100 acres in the fork of Turkey Creek adjoining the line of the late James Wilson and Cornelius Taylor. Wit: Thomas Hunt and Hardy Hunt.

DB 6-311 RICHARD SMITH of Nash Co. to WILLIAM JORDEN of same. Aug. 14, 1794, for 50 pds. a tract of 320 acres on Turkey Creek adjoining said Jorden. Wit: Ansel Ferrell, Hardy Todd, and John Rice.

DB 6-311 JOSIAH HORN of Nash Co. to JOHN WATKINS of same, Dec. 30, 1797, for 800 silver dollars a tract of 150 acres on Tar River and Kirby's Creek adjoining Andrew Ross' old line, Benjamin Bunn, an dthe road. Wit: Henry Thorp and Jacob Horn.

DB 6-312 MATTHIAS MANNING of Nash Co. to FRANCIS RACKLEY of same, Nov. 8, 1795, for $150.00 a tract of 300 acres on Sapony Creek adjoining Pridgen. Wit: Burrel Rose, Joseph Batchelor. and Danel Batchelor.

DB 6-313 ETHELRED DANCE of Nash Co. to RICHARD SMITH of Franklin Co., Oct. 13, 1792, for 50 pds. a tract of 640 acres on Turkey Creek adjoining Strickland. Wit: Solomon Carter, Benja. Briant, and John Taylor.

DB 6-314 ABRAHAM BASS of Nash Co. to PENUEL FLOYD of same, May 7, 1796, for 110 silver dollars 200 acres adjoining Matthew Griffin, it being part of a tract conveyed from Joseph Irby to said Bass. Wit: Matthew Drake, Jr. and Thomas Hamilton.

DB 6-314 JOAB TUCKER of Nash Co. to MATHEW RACKLEY of same, Nov. 1, 1795, for 50 pds. specie a tract of 100 acres on the Swamp. Wit: Burrel Rose.

DB 6-315 WEST CRUMPLER of Nash Co. to GEORGE GREEN of same, Feb. 13, 1790, for 5 pds. specie a tract of 50 acres on the waters of Milstone adjoining his own line, it being half of a tract of 100 acres granted to said Crumpler on Nov. 1. 1784. Wit:

Theofless Eatman and Wm. Williams.

DB 6-316 WILLIAM LINDSEY of Nash Co. to NATHAN JOYNER of same, Sept. 29, 1797, for 150 pds. a tract of 200 acres on the north side of Tar River adjoining John Brantley, John Bone, William Ballard, Christopher Taylor, and Arthur Sellers. Wit: Curtis Joiner and Jordan Williams.

DB 6-317 PATRICK WALKER of Warren Co. to EDWARD HORN of Nash Co., Nov. 28, 1797, for 250 silver dollars a tract of 500 acres on the south side of Tar River adjoining Duncan Lamon and Pridgen. Wit: Ley Ransom and Kemp Plummer.

DB 6-318 SARAH RICKS of Nash Co. to her son, JOSIAH WHITLEY, and son-in-law, BATSON SMITH, both of Nash Co., Feb. 10, 1798, for love and affection all her goods and chattels listed herein consisting of livestock. furniture, household articles, and farming tools, to be divided equally between them. Wit: Arch'd. Griffin, Mourning Smith, and Charity Vick.

DB 6-318 JOHN MATTHEWS of Nash Co. to DAVID MEL-TON of same, Sept. 30, 1797, for $150.00 a tract of 175 acres on Little Sapony Swamp adjoining Thomas and certain corner set by William Matthews for his son, John Matthews, and along a line set by the will of William Matthews, deceased, it being half of a tract conveyed to William Matthews by Edward Hall of Edgecombe Co. Wit: Frederick B. Hines and Matthew Drake, Jr.

DB 6-319 JOHN JOINER, SR. of Nash Co. to JESSE JOINER of same, Nov. 10, 1797, for 30 pds. a tract of 200 acres on the south side of Sapony Creek adjoining William Baker, Benjamin Smith. and Edward Ballard. Wit: Curtis Joiner and Elizabeth Langley.

DB 6-320 ABRAHAM BASS of Nash Co. to BENJAMIN DRAKE of same, Aug. 21, 1797, for 36 pds. Virginia money a tract of 100 acres on the south side of Pig Basket Creek adjoining Hilliard, Cooper Jones, and Melton. Wit: John H. Drake and Noel Pitts.

DB 6-321 REUBEN HARREL of Nash Co. to HENRY YOUELL of same, Jan. 27, 1798, for $102.00 a tract of 100 acres on the south side of Maple Creek adjoining Strickland, Elizabeth Turlington, and Ricks. Wit: John Melton and Thomas Turlington.

DB 6-322 JOSEPH WRIGHT and ELIZABETH WRIGHT of Nash Co. to CORNELIOUS JORDEN of Edgecombe Co., Dec. 9, 1797, for 37 pds. 10 sh. a tract of 50 acres on Contentnea Creek adjoining James Cobb. Wit: Lemuel Wright and Joshua Jordan.

DB 6-322 JOSEPH VICK of Nash Co. to JOHN OWENS of same, Dec. 25, 1793, for 30 pds. a tract of 100 acres on Toisnot Swamp adjoining William West, Jeremiah Brown, and Robert Vick, it being a grant to said Vick in 1784. Wit: Elias Owens, Enoch Owens, and Jurden Vick.

DB 6-323 JOSEPH WRIGHT and ELIZABETH WRIGHT of Nash Co. to CORNELIUS JORDEN of Edgecombe Co., Dec. 9, 1797, for 200 pds. a tract of 200 acres lying in both Nash and Edgecombe counties, it being on the south side of the Great Swamp, by some called the *Blumery Swamp*, adjoining Lemuel Wright; also a tract of 50 acres on the Blumery Swamp adjoining Joshua Jordan, Sanders. Lemuel Wright. and the county line. Wit: Lemuel Wright and Joshua Jordan.

DB 6-324 DEMPSEY WEST, WILLIAM WEST, and SIMON STRICKLAND of Nash Co. to LAZARUS STRICKLAND of same, Jan. 4 1798, for 100 pds. Virginia money three tracts of land on the west side of Toisnot Swamp containing 447 acres: (1) 150 acres on Bear Branch, it being part of a tract bearing date Dec. 12, 1763; (2) 200 acres adjoining Simon Strickland and the swamp, it being a grant from the State of N. C. to Simon Strickland on Oct. 5, 1780; (3) 177 acres on the swamp adjoining his own line and Lazarus Strickland, it being a grant from the State of N. C. to William West on Nov. 1, 1784. Wit: Jn. Taylor and Lazarus Strickland.

DB 6-326 WILLIAM ANDREWS, JR. of Franklin Co. to JOHN HUBBARD of same, June 25, 1796. for 30 pds. Virginia money a tract of 57 acres on the south side of Turkey Creek. it being part of a tract granted to William Magee on Jan. 10, 1756. Wit: Wilson Denson. Fiel Denson, and Hardy Hunt.

DB 6-327 SAMUEL SKINNER, SR. of Nash Co. to REUBEN HARRELL of same. Feb. 2. 1798, for 80 pds. a tract of 175 acres adjoining Benja. Ricks and Oliver. Wit: Sam Westray and Arch'd Hunter.

DB 6-327 WM. HICKS of Nash Co. to ASEY HICKS of same, Feb. 7, 1797, for 10 pds. currency a tract of 200 acres adjoining Strickland, Simmuns, Taylor, and Vick. Wit: Je. Hammonds and Josiah Medlin.

DB 6-328 THOMAS HORN and JOSHUA HORN of Nash Co. to WILLIAM HORN of same, Feb. 6. 1798, for $266.00 a tract of 357 acres on Toisnot Swamp adjoining Nathan Williams. Joshua Eatman, John Cockrell. Thomas Horn. and his own line, it being a grant to the said Thomas Horn from the State of N. C. on Nov. 9, 1784. Wit: J. Taylor and Jonas Williams.

DB 6-329 NEWET ATKISON of Nash Co. to JAMES HEAG of same, Dec. 18, 1795. for 50 pds. a tract of 100 acres at the head of Toisnot Swamp, it being part of a grant to Lazarus Strickland on Oct. 25, 1782. Wit: Henry Horn and Ammav Horn.

DB 6-330 DUNCAN CAIN, the heir of JAMES CAIN, deceased, and John Lamon, admr. to said estate. both of Nash Co. to MICAH HORN of same, Feb. 13. 1798, for 47 pds. 17 sh. 3 p. Virginia currency a tract of 430 acres on Turkey Creek adjoining James Brown and Wilson Taylor. it being parts of two tracts. one of 300 acres granted to Edward Moore on Nov. 18, 1783 and the other of 280 acres also granted to Edward Moore on Nov. 19, 1783. Wit: Edward York and William Bryant.

DB 6-331 WILLIAM EASON, NATHAN JOYNER. ABNER LEWIS, and MAXEY BOWERS, all of Nash Co., to WILLIAM BUNTIN of same, April 2, 1798, for 100 pds. Virginia money one negro boy. Wit: Thos. Carter, Matthew Carter, and Nathan Joiner.

DB 6-331 JEREMIAH HILLIARD of Edgecombe Co. to LEAH HILLIARD of same, March 1, 1798, for 81 pds. Virginia money two negroes by name. Wit: Sam Westray and Charity Bunn.

DB 6-332 BENJAMIN BRASWELL of Nash Co. to JOHN BRASWELL of same, Feb. 11, 1798, for 20 pds. Virginia money one negro girl. Wit: J. C. Hill and John Stephens.

DB 6-333 JAMES WILLIAMS of Nash Co. to BENJAMIN WHITFIELD of same May 7, 1797, for 116½ silver dollars a tract of 116 acres on the north side of Stony Creek adjoining said Whitfield and Edward Wilson. Wit: H. Simmons and Hardy G. Whitfield.

DB 6-333 JOHN WILSON of Nash Co. to JAMES WILLIAMS of same, Nov. 23, 1796, for 109 pds. 10 sh. Virginia money a tract of 90 acres on the south side of Stony Creek adjoining John Harrel, Henry Vick, Mason, and Lamon's Road. Wit: Joseph Curl, Marmaduke Mason, and William Johnson.

DB 6-334 JOHN MELTON of Nash Co. to SION WHITLEY of same, Feb. 12, 1798, for 50 pds. Virginia money a tract of 133 acres on Whitehead's Mill Swamp adjoining White and Griffin. Wit: Arch'd. Griffin and R. R. Reading.

DB 6-335 JOHN OWEN of Nash Co. to MATTHEW STRICKLAND of same, Jan. 23, 1798, for 60 silver dollars a tract of 100 acres on Toisnot Swamp adjoining William West. Jeremiah Brown, and Robt. Vick, it being a tract granted to Joseph Vick in 1784. Wit: James Sandeford and William Arrington.

DB 6-337 JAMES WILLIAMS of Nash Co. to SAM'L WESTRAY of same, April 27, 1798. for 112 pds. Virginia money a tract of 90 acres on the south side of Stony Creek adjoining Henry Vick, Westray, and Lamon's Road. Wit: Sophia Vick, Amos Gandy, Marv Vick, and Wm. Skinner.

DB 6-337 JOSIAH SKINNER of Nash Co. to HOWEL UNDERWOOD of same, March 6. 1797, for 77 pds. Virginia money a 125 acre plantation on the south side of Kirbv's Creek adjoining Revel. Wit: Arch'd Hunter and Willie Holland.

DB 6-338 BENJAMIN MERIT and SARY MERIT of Nash Co. to ISAAC WHITEHEAD of same, Feb. 2, 1798, for 1000 silver dollars a 150 acre plantation on the south side of Swift Creek adjoining Samuel Sorsby, William Merit, and the road, it being parts of two tracts, one conveyed from Benjamin Merit to William Merit by will bearing date 1778 and this said tract of land and plantation by will to Benjamin Merit, his son, from Benjamin Merit. Wit: James Powell and Daniel Powell.

DB 6-340 EDWARD WILSON, JR. of Nash Co. to BENJAMIN WHITFIELD of same, Oct. 23, 1797, for 250 silver dollars a tract of 250 acres on the north side of Kirbv's Creek adjoining Revel, John Watkins, and More's former line. it being part of the old plantation whereon John More formerly lived. Wit: Josiah Horn,

Henry Sandrews, and Hardy G. Whitfield.

DB 6-340 WILSON WILLIS of Nash Co. to BENJAMIN WHITFIELD of same, Sept. 22, 1797, for 600 silver dollars a tract of 234 acres on the north side of Stony Creek, it being the same land which his father gave to said Wilson Willis in his will and being part of a tract granted to Thos. Brown on July 25, 1743. Wit: James Powell, Hardy G. Whitfield, and William Willis.

DB 6-341 WILLIAM HUNT of Montgomery Co. to WILSON BRASWELL of Nash Co., Aug. 10, 1797, for 50 pds. a tract of 94 acres adjoining Jesse Hunt, Thomas Hunter, and John Melton. Wit: Ja. Williams. Howell Ellin, and Aaron Woodard.

DB 6-342 JAMES GOODWIN of Nash Co. to IRA PORTICE of same, Feb. 13, 1798, for 50 pds. a tract of 220 acres adjoining Stephen Weaver, Joseph Arrington, and Wheless. Wit: John Cox.

6-343 JAMES GOODWIN of Nash Co. to JEREMIAH PORTIS of same. Feb. 13, 1798, for 37 pds. 10 sh. a tract of 150 acres on White Oak Swamp adjoining Denton Mann and Archibald Davis. Wit: John Cox and Jesse Cox.

DB 6-344 JOSEPH WHELER of Franklin Co. to EZEKIEL DANCE of Chestfield Co., Virginia, May 3, 1793, for 20 pds. Virginia money a tract of 170 acres on the north side of Turkey Creek adjoining George Fore, John Morgin, and said Dance, it being all the land that Peleg Rogers obtained on the north side of Turkey Creek from Earl Granville. Wit: Wm. Moore and Ethelred Dance.

DB 6-345 DANIEL HARRIES of Nash Co. to WILLIAM WEBB of Franklin Co., Dec. 12. 1796. for 37 pds. 10 sh. Virginia money a tract of 200 acres on the south side of Little Peachtree Creek adjoining Benjamin Manning. Wit: Benjamin Tucker and John Webb.

DB 6-346 NATHAN JOINER. JR. of Nash Co. to MATTHEW JOINER of same. March 2. 1798. for 90 pds. a tract of 200 acres on the north side of Tar River adjoining John Brantley, John Bone, Uriah Hatcher, Christopher Taylor, and John Bisset. Wit: Curtis Joiner.

DB 6-347 NATHAN JOINER, SR. of Nash Co. to his son, NATHAN JOINER, JR., of same, March 3, 1798, for love and affection and 5 sh. a tract of 200 acres on the south side of Sapony Creek adjoining John Sellers and Peter Ballard, it being part of a tract granted to William Sellers. conveyed by said Sellers to Peter Ballard, and conveyed by said Ballard to Nathan Joiner, Sr. Wit: William Arrington and William Linsey.

DB 6-348 JESSE CHRISTIE of Halifax Co. to MICAJAH WELLS of Franklin Co.. Jan. 3, 1798, for 100 pds. a tract of 200 acres on Back Swamp adjoining Isaac Bass and Micajah Thomas. Wit: Edmund Jones and Edmund Harrison.

DB 6-349 JULIAN JONES of Nash Co. to CATEY JONES of same, Dec. 23, 1797, for 60 silver dollars all her right and title to the land and plantation that was demised to her by her husband,

Francis A. Jones, deceased. Wit: Thos. Griffin, John McCormick, and James Hilliard.

DB 6-349 BENJAMIN MANNING of Nash Co. to ELIZA-BETH COOPER of same, May 4, 1798, for 100 pds. a tract of 200 acres on the south side of Little Peachtree Creek adjoining Little Berry White. Wit: Little B. White and John Braswell.

DB 6-350 WILSON BRASWELL of Nash Co. to BENJAMIN WHITFIELD of same. Jan. 19. 1798, for — Virginia money a tract of 94 acres adjoining Jesse Hunt. Thomas Hunter, and John Melton. Wit: Hardy G. Whitfield and Jethrow Brown.

6-351 JOEL MATTHEWS of Nash Co. to ISAAC TOMLIN-SON of same, Feb. 23, 1798, for $125.00 a tract of 60 acres on Swift Creek adjoining Ralph Mason and Baggett's old field, it being a parcel of land conveyed by Nicholas Baggett to said Matthews. Wit: Ja. Williams and James Hilliard.

DB 6-352 JOHN JONES of Nash Co. to PETER ANDERSON of same, May 30, 1798, for 80 pds. one negro man. Wit: H. Wheless and Henry Drury.

DB 6-353 SARAH WILLIAMS of Nash Co. to MOURNING TISDEL of same. March 13. 1798. for 30 pds. specie one negro girl. Wit: Jonas Williams and Wm. Driver.

DB 6-353 RICHARD SMITH of Nash Co. to ROBERT VICK of same, Aug. 23, 1797, for 20 pds. specie a tract of 100 acres on the south side of Turkey Creek adjoining Strickland, it being part of a grant from Samson Powell and being the remainder of the land that said Richard Smith sold to Henry Bains. Wit: Jn. Taylor and William Jorden.

DB 6-354 LAZARUS STRICKLAND of Nash Co. to MACKS BOWERS of same, Jan. 4, 1798. for 55 pds. a tract of 150 acres on White Oak Swamp adjoining West and his own line, it being a grant to said Strickland in 1785. Wit: J. Taylor and Lazarus Strickland.

DB 6-355 JOHN PETTY COBB of Montgomery Co. to JOHN LEWIS of Nash Co.. May 1, 1798, for 100 pds. a tract of 200 acres on the north side of Moccasin Creek, it having been conveyed by deed from Henry Baley to said John Petty Cobb on Nov. 6, 1788. Wit: Wilson Taylor, Wm. Nairn, John Flowers. and David Lewis.

DB 6-356 ORPHA HARRELL of Franklin Co. to BENJAMIN WILLIAMS of Nash Co.. Feb. 12. 1798. for 15 silver dollars a tract of 20 acres on the north side of Turkey Creek. Wit: Simon Williams and Elizabeth Williams.

DB 6-357 RICHARD SMITH of Nash Co. to HENRY BAINS of same. Aug. 17. 1797, for 50 pds. a tract of 220 acres on the south side of Turkey Creek adjoining Robert Vick and Wm. Jorden, it being part of a survey whereon Wm. Jorden then lived. Wit: John Rice, William Jorden, and Absalom Bains.

DB 6-359 JAMES CONWAY of Nash Co. to GRANBERRY BAGGET of same, Jan. 14, 1798, for 300 silver dollars a tract of 150 acres on the north side of Swift Creek adjoining Ralph Mason, Peter Robertson, Hackney, JesseKitchen, Joel Matthews, and said

Bagget. Wit: William Wright and Nathan Culpepper.

DB 6-360 DAVID STRICKLAND of Nash Co. to HENRY STRICKLAND of same. Dec. 20. 1795, for 40 pds. cash a tract of 100 acres adjoining Whitfield. Wit: Joseph Strickland and Wilson Braswell.

DB 6-360 AMBROSE EDMONDSON of Nash Co. to KINSMAN KNIGHT of same, March 25. 1793, for 80 pds. a tract on the north side of Tar River adjoining Warren, Jeremiah Etherge, and Biggs, it being part of a tract of land granted to Drewry Alford on Nov. 4, 1784. Wit: James Green and Christopher Hinton.

DB 6-362 WILLIAM WEBB of Franklin Co. to LITTLEBERRY WHITE of Nash Co., March 17, 1798, for 133 silver dollars and 33 cents a tract of 200 acres on the south side of Little Peachtree Creek adjoining Benjamin Manning. Wit: William Arrington and Jas. Milner.

DB 6-363 FRANCIS GROSS of Nash Co. to AMBROSE EDMONDSON of same, March 6, 1787, for 90 pds. a tract of land on the north side of Tar River adjoining John Warren, Pusley. Jeremiah Etheridge, Biggs, and Parot's entry, which said land was granted to Drewry Alford on Nov. 1, 1784. Wit: Christopher Hinton and Sary Hinton.

DB 6-364 JOHN EXUM of Nash Co. to JOSIAH BATTLE of same, Jan. 23. 1797, for 100 pds. one negro man. Wit: Reuben Taylor and John Pope.

DB 6-365 JAMES PRIM and wife. MARY PRIM, of Nash Co. to DAVID PRIDGEN of same, Sept. 14, 1798, for 160 pds. Virginia money a tract of 158 acres on the north side of Tar River adjoining Joshua Wells and said Pridgen. Wit: Abijah Pridgen and Milbury Williams.

DB 6-366 FRANCIS LOKUS of Granville Co. to JESSE HAMMONS of Nash Co., Jan. 13, 1798. for 40 pds. specie a tract of 150 acres on the west side of Turkey Creek adjoining Hunt and Cone. Wit: Joshua Cone. Jesse Denkins. and Wm. Morgan.

DB 6-367 HENRY TISDEL of Nash Co. to FREEMAN KILLINGSWORTH, JR. of Johnston Co., Nov. 18, 1797. for 5 sh. one acre of land on the north side of Moccasin Creek. Wit: John Winborne and Renson Tisdale.

DB 6-367 CHRISTOPHER HINTON of Nash Co. to JAMES HILLIARD of same, Oct. 19, 1798, for 160 pds. Virginia money 320 acres lying on both sides of Pig Basket Creek adjoining Arthur Braswell, Matthew Drake, and said Hilliard, it being part of a tract granted by the State of N. C. to Charles Watson on Nov. 10, 1779, conveyed by him to Thomas Morriss. from said Morriss to Ambros Edmondson, and from him to the said Christopher Hinton. Wit: George Boddie, Thomas Ezell, and Joshua Vick.

DB 6-369 JOHN CARROL of Nash Co. to JOHN EXUM of same, March 1, 1788, for 12 pds. Virginia money a tract of 50 acres on the north side of Little Compass Creek adjoining Hardy Harris, Lewis Hines, Randolph Harris, and said Exum, it being a tract that

John Carrol bought of Michael Atkinson on Dec. 18 ,1786.
Wit: Reuben Taylor.

DB 6-370 WILLIAM WHELESS, JR. of Nash Co. to AMOS
WHELESS of same, Oct. 18, 1798, for $266 2/3 a tract of 236
acres on the north side of Swift Creek adjoining Denton Mann's
new corner in the division, "it being my just and equal share of all
the lands divided in the will of mv father, Benjamin Wheless."
Wit: Denton Mann and John H. Drake.

DB 6-371 SHADRACH F. ELLEN and wife, BETSEY ELLEN
(ELIZABETH FLEWELLIN), of Warren Co., Georgia. JOHN H.
DRAKE and wife, FANNY DRAKE, and WILLIAM BATTLE and
wife, POLLEY (MARY) BATTLE, of Nash Co. to JAMES BATTLE
of Nash Co., July 19, 1798. for $600.00 a tract of 200 acres on the
south side of Swift Creek adjoining Thomas West. Wit: Henry
Avent, Joshua Butt, Jr., and Eley Williams.   Mary Battle and
Fanny Drake were examined separately from their husbands by
Denton Mann, J.P.

DB 6-372 SHADRACH F. ELLEN and wife, ELIZABETH F.
ELLEN (FLEWELLEN), appeared in Warren Co., Georgia on July
20, 1798, and acknowledged the sale and Elizabeth did freely and
voluntarily relinquish her right of dower on thirds in the above
mentioned premises.

DB 6-373 SHADRACH F. ELLEN and wife, BETSEY (ELIZ-
ABETH FLEWELLEN) ELLEN. of Warren Co. Georgia, JOHN
H. DRAKE and wife, FANNY (FRANCES) DRAKE, and WILL-
IAM BATTLE and wife, POLLEY (MARY) BATTLE, of Nash Co.
to JOHN PITTS of Nash Co., Julv 19, 1798, for $70.00 a 100 acre
plantation on the south side of Swift Creek adjoining Thomas Mann.
Wit: Eley Williams. Henry Avent, and Joshua Butt, Jr. Mary
Battle and Frances Drake were examined separately from their
husbands by Denton Mann, J.P.

DB 6-374 SHADRACH F. ELLEN (FLEWELLEN) and wife,
ELIZABETH FLEWELLEN appeared in Warren Co., Georgia on
July 20, 1798 and were examined as above.

DB 6-375 JOHN EVANS of Nash Co. to SHERID EVANS of
same, Dec. 17, 1798, for 100 pds. specie 300 acres on the south side
of Reedy Branch adjoining Whiddon, Holland, and the road. Wit:
William Linsey and John Cooper.

DB 6-375 JOHN EVANS of Nash Co. to SHERID EVANS of
same, Dec. 17, 1798, for 125 pds. specie a tract of 100 acres on Miry
Branch and Lewis' Branch adjoining Daniel Holland. Wit: William Linsey and John Cooper.

DB 6-376 ISHAM MITCHELL of Nash Co. to JEREMIAH
PORTIS of same, Feb. 1, 1799. for 60 pds. a tract of 100 acres on
Blackwell's Branch. Wit: John Portis and Orin Harriss.

DB 6-377 WILLIAM ROWLET of the State of Virginia to
LAZARUS WHITEHEAD of Nash Co., Nov. 2, 1795. for 90 pds.
Virginia currency a tract of 300 acres on the south side of Cabbin
Branch adjoining Henry Screws, James Cain, John Powell, Land-

ingham, and Lazarus Whitehead, Sr. Wit: Emmanuel Underwood, John Screws, and Daniel Mann.

DB 6-378 TOBIAS LASETER of Nash Co. to BENJAMIN WARD of Halifax Co., Jan. 24, 1799, for 600 pds. specie a tract of 275 acres on the south side of Fishing Creek adjoining John Harrison and Peter Anderson. Wit: John Harrison, Peter Anderson, and Benja. Carr.

DB 6-379 JEREMIAH PORTIS of Franklin Co. to JOHN PORTIS of Halifax Co., May 26, 1798, for 56 pds. a certain tract of land in Nash Co. formerly belonging to the estate of George Portis, deceased, which was purchased by said Jeremiah Portis at the sale of the deceased. Wit: Abel Davis and Cle. Ransom.

DB 6-379 JACOB NICHOLS, JOHN NICHOLS, and JEREMIAH NICHOLS, heirs to the lands of Jeremiah Nichols, deceased, late of Nash Co., to BARTLETT DEANS of Edgecombe Co., Jan. 30, 1798, for 60 silver dollars paid to each of them they sold their rights in the said lands, each lot containing 90 acres. The lands were on Marsh Swamp adjoining Alexander Grice, William Row, and John Faulk and consisted of several grants: (1) from Earl Granville on Aug. 1, 1762; (2) from the State of N. C. on Dec. 20, 1791; (3) from the State of N . C. on Nov. 10. 1779. Wit: Thomas Woodard and Isaac Woodard.

DB 6-381 JAMES KNIGHT of Edgecombe Co. to REUBEN TAYLOR of Nash Co., March 2, 1790, for 40 pds. one negro boy. Wit: James Cain and Susaney Powell.

DB 6-381 DUNCAN LAMON of Nash Co. to his daughter, MARTHA LAMON, of same, March 1, 1798, for love and affection two negroes by name. Wit: Dun. Lamon, Jr. and Js. G. Lamon.

DB 6-382 DUNCAN LAMON of Nash Co. to his daughter, Ann Lamon. of same, March 1, 1798, for love and affection two negroes by name. Wit: Dun Lamon, Jr., and Js. G. Lamon.

DB 6-383 KITCHEN PRIM of Nash Co. to ELIJAH ATKINSON, Nov. 28, 1796, for 64 pds. Virginia money one negro boy. Wit: Abijah Pridgen.

DB 6-383 DUNCAN LAMON of Nash Co. to EDWARD YORK, Oct. 3. 1796, for 200 silver dollars one negro boy. Wit: Jon. Lamon and Dun. Lamon, Jr.

DB 6-383 RICHARD BURGE, SR. to SOLOMON CARTER of Nash Co., March 8, 1797, for 33 pds. Virginia money a tract of 196 acres adjoining Solomon Carter, Thomas Dean. Benjamin Bunn, and George Lewis, it being a tract granted to Thomas Warin. Wit: Thomas Deans, James Stephens, and Edwd. York.

DB 6-384 JOHN CHAPMAN of Nash Co. to JOHN LAMON of same Feb. 1, 1796, for 100 pds. a tract of 440 acres on the south side of Tar River adjoining John Taylor, John Morgan, Lewis, and said Lamon. Wit: Edwd. York and Jacob Cone.

DB 6-385 DUNCAN CAIN, heir to JAMES CAIN. deceased, and JOHN LAMON, admr. to the said Cain estate, to JOEL WILLIAMS, all of Nash Co. Feb. 13, 1798, for 100 pds. specie a tract of

300 acres on Toisnot Swamp adjoining Edward Moore, John Taylor, Lamon, and Carter, it being a grant from the State of N. C. to Edward Moore on Nov. 1, 1784. Wit: Edwd. York and Wm. Bryant.

DB 6-386 WILLIAMSON JOHNSON of Nash Co. to BENJAMIN WILLIAMS of same, May 1, 1798, for 50 pds. a tract of 130 acres on the south side of Turkey Creek, lying in both Nash and Franklin counties. Wit: Jesse Hammons and Josiah Linsey.

DB 6-387 ABRAHAM BASS agreement to settle a lawsuit with WILLIAM BRIDGERS. brought in Hillsborough Court against said Bass by URIAH SMITH for possession of certain negroes. Wit: Micajah Bridgers.

DB 6-387 WILLIAM FERRELL of Franklin Co. to BERRIMAN BILBRO of Nash Co., June 15, 1797, for 250 pds. specie a tract of 400 acres on the south side of Great Turkey Creek at the mouth of Miry Branch adjoining James Culpepper, John Hammond, Henry Banes the road, and Little Turkey Creek. Wit: Ansel Alford and Little B. White.

DB 6-389 JOHN VICK, SR. of Nash Co. to JOHN EATMAN of same, Dec. 27, 1798, for 100 silver dollars a tract of 200 acres adjoining Benja. Cobb and Drury Boykin. Wit: Sharod Phillips and John Cockrell.

DB 6-390 HARDY GRIFFIN of Nash Co. to ARTHUR ARRINGTON, EDMUND DRAKE, HARDY GRIFFIN. WILLIAM DRAKE, WILLIAM S. MEARNS. JOSEPH ARRINGTON, JAMES HILLIARD. JOHN ARRINGTON, JAMES BATTLE, and JOHN GREEN, Commissioners of Nash Co.. July 12, 1793, for 5 silver dollars a parcel of 1 3/4 acres on which said land was to be erected a meeting house known by name of *Mearns Chapel* and was to be for preachers and people of every denomination to exercise their religious rites and ceremonies according to their respective churches and was to be used for religious purposes only. Wit: William Arrington. James Sandeford, and James Green.

DB 6-391 EDWARD WILSON, SR. of Nash Co. to BENJAMIN WHITFIELD of same, Jan. 25, 1799 for $120.00 a tract of 100 acres lying on both sides of Laseter's Branch adjoining Jesse Hunt and John Vick it being part of a tract granted to Thomas Hunter, deceased. Wit: Lazarus Powell, John Pope, and H. G. Whitfield.

DB 6-392 DRURY BOYAKIN (and HARDY BOYAKIN) of Nash Co. to JOHN EATMAN of same, Nov. 21, 1798. for 27 pds. 10 sh. currency a tract of 134 acres on Mash Swamp adjoining Jacob Nichols, Eatman, Deans. and Tho. Horn, it being part of a grant for 172 acres to Benjamin Boyakin on July 19, 1794. Wit: Jethro Harrison and Harrod Grizzell.

DB 6-394 JOHN ROBERTSON and wife, ELIZABETH ROBERTSON, of Nash Co. to SAMUEL CROWELL of Halifax Co. and TIMOTHY M. NICHOLSON of Edgecombe Co., both executors to the will of JOHN NICHOLSON, deceased, of Edgecombe Co., Feb. 12, 1799, for 81 pds. 5 sh. specie a tract of 172 acres lying in both

Nash and Edgecombe counties on the north side of Swift Creek adjoining Lane's Swamp, the heirs of Isaac Hilliard. deceased, the land of Robert Thompson, deceased, and James Turner, it being part of the lands of Robert Thompson which, at his death, fell to said Robertson and Elizabeth, his wife. Wit: Henry Mason and Duncan Cain.

DB 6-395 JEREMIAH BUNTIN of Nash Co. to NOAH STRICKLAND of same, Feb. 9. 1799, for 5 pds. 15 sh. a tract of 23 acres on the north side of Tar River adjoining Solomon Carter and Strickland. Wit: Thos. Carter and Salley Carter.

DB 6-396 LEWIS WEBB and WILLIS WEBB of Franklin Co. to ABRAM HEDGPETH of Nash Co., Jan. 22. 1799, for 122 silver dollars a tract of 122 acres adjoining Micajah Thomas, John Edwards, and the road. Wit: Richard Webb.

DB 6-397 WILLIAM BALLARD of Nash Co. to JOHN BONE of same, Nov. 28, 1798, for 28 pds. a tract of 40 acres on Jacobs Swamp adjoining Allen Baker and said Bone. Wit: Curtis Joiner and Wm. Poulan.

DB 6-398 JOHN WILLIFORD of Nash Co. to JORDAN SHEROD of same. Oct. 25, 1797, for 25 pds. specie a tract of 153 acres adjoining Theophlus Hickman, Jacob Strickland, and Jeremiah Brown. Wit: Curtis Joiner and Isham Langley.

DB 6-399 JULIAN KING of Nash Co. to ARCHIBALD GRIFFIN of same. Feb. 11. 1799. for 50 silver dollars a tract of 25 acres on the north side of Rocky Run adjoining said King and said Griffin. Wit: Dempsey Braswell and James Powell.

DB 6-400 ROBERT HOBBS of Nash Co. to JOEL WILLIAMS of same. April 22, 1797, for 160 pds. specie a tract of 540 acres on the north side of Turkey Creek near Henry Wyatt's improvement, it being part of a grant from the State of N. C. to Jeremiah Brown on Nov. 10. 1779 for 640 acres. the 100 acres being separated by a line agreed on by Jeremiah Brown and Simon Strickland. Wit: Wilson Taylor and Jethro Harrison

DB 6-401 JONAS COLSON of Nash Co. to JOEL WILLIAMS of same, April 22, 1797, for 50 pds. specie a tract of 100 acres on Turkey Creek adjoining Jeremiah Brown, it being part of a grant from the State of N. C. to Demsey Wyatt on Nov. 1, 1784. Wit: Wilson Taylor and Jethro Harrison.

DB 6-402 ENOCH OWENS ofNash Co. to ROLAND WILLIAMS of same, Feb. 9. 1799, for 33 pds. 3 sh. Virginia money a tract of 221 acres on Turkey Creek adjoining John West, Samuel Devaughan. Edward Moore, and James Brown, it being a grant to Benjamin Taylor, Sr. on Nov. 20. 1791. Wit: Wm. Horn and D. Williams.

DB 6-404 ROBERT VICK of Nash Co. to EZEKIEL DANCE of Chesterfield Co., Virginia, March 9. 1793, for $50.00 a tract of 100 acres on Turkey Creek adjoining Henry Strickland. Wit: William Taylor and John Taylor.

DB 6-405 JESSE POWELL of Nash Co. to WILLIAM

POWELL of same, Feb. 9, 1799, for 10 pds. a tract of 308 acres on Pig Basket Creek adjoining Thomas Morris, Matthew Drake, and William Braswell. Wit: Matthew Drake, Jr. and Jesse Powell.

DB 6-406 JOSHUA VICK of Nash Co. to DANIEL WALKER of same, Jan. 3, 1798, for 160 pds. Virginia money a tract of 200 acres on Whitehead's Mill Swamp adjoining Henry Strickland and John Fletcher. Wit: Howell Ellin and Sarah Thomas.

DB 6-407 ROBERT VICK of Nash Co. to ETHELRED DANCE of same, March 9, 1793, for $30.00 a tract of 91 acres on the creek adjoining Rodgers and his own corner. Wit: William Taylor and John Taylor.

DB 6-408 JOHN PARRISH of Nash Co. to DEMPSEY WIATT of same, Nov. 17, 1795, for 50 pds. a tract of 100 acres on Turkey Creek adjoining Robert Vick and Robert Hobbs. Wit: Thos. Carter and J. Taylor.

DB 6-409 JOEL BUNN of Nash Co. to WILLIAM BARNES of same March 7, 1798, for 20 pds. specie a parcel of 10 acres on the south side of Stony Creek adjoining said Bunn and said Barnes. Wit: Orron Barnes and Redick Barnes.

DB 6-410 EPHRAIM PERRY of Nash Co. to ALEXANDER FRAZIER of same, Nov. 21, 1795, for $215.00 a tract of 430 acres on the north side of Turkey Creek on Thomas Rogers' old line, it being a tract of land formerly belonging to Thomas Rogers. Wit: John Rice and Ansel Ferrell.

DB 6-412 NANCY ANDREWS of Nash Co. to IRA PORTIS, Feb. 21, 1799, for 100 pds. Virginia money her part and right to the negroes that were held by Abraham Andrews, who were given by a deed of gift to Allen Andrews, Nancy Andrews, Richard Andrews, and Tempy Andrews. Wit: William Harriss, Sarah Portis, and Elizabeth Portis.

DB 6-412 WILLIAM FORE of Nash Co. gave bond to NATHAN PERRY of same, June 4, 1796, for $200.00, the condition of which was to give to said Nathan Perry a good title to the 100 acre tract whereon said Perry then lived within two years. Wit: Jesse Hammonds.

DB 6-413 EDWARD NICHOLSON of Nash Co. to WILLIAM BUNTIN of same, May 13, 1799, for 150 silver dollars one negro boy. Wit: J. Bonds and John Lewis.

DB 6-413 PETER ROBERTSON of Nash Co. to his son, WILEY ROBERTSON, of same, Jan. 11, 1798, gift of a tract of 80 acres adjoining Lewis Dortch, Hackney, John Robertson, and Culpepper; also, another tract of 100 acres adjoining Lewis Dortch, Hackney's old line, Peter Robertson, and Simon Stallons. Wit: Lewis Dortch and Daniel Mann.

DB 6-414 JOHN COX of Nash Co. to IRA PORTIS of same, Jan. 28 1799, for 80 pds. currency a tract of 134 acres lying in both Nash and Franklin counties on the north side of White Oak swamp adjoining Jeremiah Portis and Arch'd Davis. Wit: Edm'd Jones and John Davis.

DB 6-415 JAMES MASSINGILL of Nash Co. to JOHN WILL-
IAMS of same, March 10, 1799, for 7 pds. 19 sh. Virginia money a
parcel of 13 1/4 acres in Nash Co. Wit: John Gay and John Massingill.

DB 6-416 AMBRISE EDMONDSON of the State of Georgia
to BENJA. DRAKE of Nash Co., Feb. 15, 1799, for 75 pds. a tract
of 300 acres on the north side of Tar River adjoining John Warren,
Pursel, Biggs, and Knight, it being part of a tract granted to
Drewry Alford on Nov. 1, 1784. Wit: John H. Drake and Thomas
Morris.

DB 6-417 JOHN PITTS of Nash Co. to BENJAMIN DRAKE
of same, Nov. 16, 1798, for 26 pds. 10 sh. Virginia money a tract of
100 acres on the south side of Swift Creek adjoining Thomas Mann.
it being the land purchased by said John Pitts of Shadrach F. Ellen
and wife, William Battle and wife, and John H. Drake and wife.
Wit: John H. Drake and Christopher Hinton.

DB 6-418 HENRY STRICKLAND of Nash Co. to JOSEPH
STRICKLAND of same, May 11, 1799, for 100 silver dollars a tract
of 50 acres on the south side of Whitehead's Mill Branch adjoining
B. Whitfield, it being part of a tract of land which David Strickland
gave to Henry Strickland. Wit: Ja. Williams and Eli Daniel.

DB 6-419 HENRY BURGE of Wake Co. to HARDY STRICK-
LAND of Nash Co., July 30, 1792, for $100.00 a tract of 100 acres
on the south side of Turkey Creek adjoining Henry Strickland.
Wit: J. Bonds and Nathan Perry.

DB 6-420 JAMES WILLIAMS of Nash Co. to JOHN VICK of
same, 1799, for $400.00 a tract of 100 acres on the south side of
Stony Creek adjoining Henry Vick, Samuel Westray, and Skinner.
Wit: Jos. Arrington and Lemuel Barnes.

DB 6-421 ANN THOMPSON of Edgecombe Co. to WILLIE
POWELL of Nash Co., Feb. 20, 1799. for 100 pds. specie a tract of
land on the south side of Long Swamp adjoining James Turner.
Wit: Alanson Powell. Andrew Thompson, and John Robertson.

DB 6-422 WILSON BARLOW of Johnston Co. to JACOB
JOINER of Nash Co.. Feb. 19. 1799. for 50 pds. a tract of 146 acres
on the south side of Sapony Creek adjoining Benjamin Smith,
James Baker, and Samuel Bottoms. Wit: Jesse Joiner and Frances
Dugless.

DB 6-423 DANIEL WOODARD of Nash Co. to JOSIAH MEL-
TON of same, Jan. 1, 1799, for 100 pds. a tract of 200 acres on Great
Sapony Creek and Cow Branch. Wit: Joel Bunn and Robert Creek-
mur.

DB 6-424 JOHN GOODWIN of Nash Co. to WILLIAM GAIN-
ER of same, Nov. 13, 1797, for 100 pds. specie a tract of 60 acres on
the west side of the Lick Branch adjoining Stephen Weaver, Mildred Wheless, and Denton Mann, it being part of a tract conveyed
from James Goodwin to John Murden and from said Murden to said
John Goodwin. Wit: Denton Mann and Orren Harris.

DB 6-425 PETER BALLARD of Sampson Co. to AMOS HAT-
CHER of Nash Co., Jan. 23, 1799, for 375 pds. Virginia money a

tract of 555 acres on the south side of Sapony Creek adjoining Benjamin Smith, Edward Ballard, Jordan Sherwood, John Brantley, John Sellars, and Nathan Joiner. Wit: Wm. Tisdale and Marcom Cooper.

DB 6-426 JOHN VICK of Nash Co. to HENRY VICK of same, May 16. 1799, for $4.00 a tract of 100 acres on Stony Creek adjoining Henry Vick and Samuel Westray (formerly Samuel Skinner). Wit: Richard Vick and Prissely Vick.

DB 6-427 JOHN POPE of Nash Co. to MATTHEW CULPEPPER, Feb. 25, 1799, for 110 pds. Virginia money one negro boy. Wit: Demcy Taylor and James Hilliard.

DB 6-428 COOPER JONES of Nash Co. to MATTHEW JONES of same, May 10, 1798, for 5 pds. 100 acres on Tar River Branch, it being part of a tract conveyed from Isaac Hilliard to said Cooper Jones. Wit: William Williams and Matt. Drake, Jr.

DB 6-429 JOSEPH ARRINGTON, Sheriff of Nash Co., to DEMPSEY TAYLOR, Aug. 3, 1799, at public auction for 340 pds. two tracts of land on Swift Creek: (1) 200 acres adjoining Col. William Whitehead; (2) 121 acres adjoining Jelks, Merritt, and Samuel Sorsby, sold as the property of ETHELRED JELKS to satisfy an execution obtained by Isaac Newsom against William Jelks and Ethelred Jelks. Wit: James Hilliard and Wm. Boddie.

DB 6-431 DAVID BISSET. JR. and wife, CATRON BISSET, of Nash Co. to JESSE KENT of same, May 10, 1799, for 30 pds. Virginia money a tract of 300 acres on Turkey Creek, it being a grant from the State of N. C. to John West on Sept. 24, 1785. Wit: W. Taylor, Arthur Sellers, and Dorothy Atkinson.

DB 6-432 BURWELL BUNN of Nash Co. to his brother, JOEL BUNN, Aug. 7, 1798, for love and affection a tract of 20 acres on Maple Creek. Wit: Roger Reese and Barnaby Heart.

DB 6-433 JOHN ATKINSON of Nash Co. to WILLIAM TISDALE, June 5, 1799, for $56.25 sundry articles, namely: one horse and five cows and calves. Wit: Abijah Pridgen and David Creekmur.

DB 6-433 JEREMIAH ETHERIDGE. JR. of Nash Co. to DANIEL WARREN of same, May 13, 1799, for 16 pds. 7 sh. 6 p. Virginia money a tract of 75 acres on the south side of Little Creek adjoining said Warren, Hammons, Harriss, and Rackley. Wit: Wm. Hammons and John Glover.

DB 6-434 HARDY HUNT, guardian of THOMAS COOK, JESSE COOK, GREEN BABB COOK, PATSEY COOK, ELIZABETH COOK, POLLEY COOK, SALLEY COOK, and NANCY COOK and by consent of ELISHA COOK'S guardian and by consent of ELIZABETH COOK, widow of Jacob Cook, all of Franklin Co. to THOMAS BABB of same, Oct. 15, 1799, for 80 pds. 2 sh. Virginia money in pursuance of an order of Nash Co. Court, a tract of 200 acres on the north side of Tar River adjoining Jeremiah Stephens. Wit: Sion Hunt and Chloe Hunt.

DB 6-435 NATHAN WEST of Nash Co. to DEMPSEY

WYATT of same, Nov. 19, 1795, for 25 pds. specie a tract of 100 acres on the north side of Turkey Creek near Henry Wiatt's improvements and adjoining Jeremiah Brown, it being a grant from the State of N. C. to Jeremiah Brown on Nov. 10, 1779 and being the remaining part of the grant over what Joseph Brown sold to Robert Hobbs. Wit: William West and J. Taylor.

DB 6-437 ANDREW THOMPSON and wife, ELIZABETH THOMPSON, of Edgecombe Co. to WILLIE POWELL of Nash Co., Feb. 20, 1799, for 100 pds. specie a tract of 172 acres on the south side of Long Swamp. Wit: Alanson Powell and John Robertson.

DB 6-438 KITCHEN PRIM of Nash Co. to JESSE BASS of same, May 14, 1799, for 110 pds. current money a tract of 250 acres on the south side of Little Peachtree Creek adjoining Elizabeth Cooper, Jesse Bass, and Littleberry White, it being a tract granted by the State of N. C. to Elijah Powell, conveyed by said Powell to William Harris, and from said Harris to Joseph Andrews. Said Andrews conveyed part of the tract to said Prim and the other part was conveyed by Andrews to Moses Stallions who conveyed it to said Prim. Wit: Jethro Bass and James Battle.

DB 6-439 BENJA. MANNIN of Nash Co. to JESSE BASS of same, March 7. 1799, for 100 pds. a tract of 250 acres on the north side of Little Peachtree Creek adjoining Lemuel Cherry, Matthew Drake, George Boddie, and Elizabeth Cooper. Wit: Augustin Bass, Henry Warren, and Mornin Rogers.

DB 6-440 KINCHIN LANE of Nash Co. to WM. HAMMONS of same. Feb. 21, 1795, for 20 pds. Virginia currency 100 acres adjoining Bennet Lane. Mechage Lane, William Bryant, and said Hammons. it being a tract of land left to him by Newet Lane. Wit: Robert Binton, Drusila Hill. and Wm. Pritchett.

DB 6-441 WILLIAM HARRISS. SR. of Nash Co. to WILLIAM HAMMONS of same, May 9, 1795, for 48 pds. Virginia money a tract of 100 acres on the north side of Little Peachtree Creek adjoining Benjamin Manning and More. Wit: Wm. Jackson, Cy Harris. and Jacob Tucker.

DB 6-442 SOLOMON CARTER of Nash Co. to JACOB COOK of same, Sept. 12, 1797, for 120 pds. Virginia money a tract of 200 acres on the north side of Tar River adjoining Jeremiah Stephens. Wit: John Webb. John Stevens, and James Boon.

DB 6-443 WILLOBY MANNING of Nash Co. to NATHAN WHITEHEAD of same. Oct. 9. 1799, for 230 pds. Virginia money a tract of 260 acres on the south side of Peachtree Creek adjoining Devenport. Wit: John H. Drake and Micajah Wells.

DB 6-444 CHARLES COX and wife Elizabeth of Lancaster Co., South Carolina to JEREMIAH HILLIARD of Edgecombe Co., Oct. 28. 1799. for 50 silver dollars all their right and title to 100 acres of a larger undivided tract of land in Nash Co. which was the property of Thomas Williams, deceased, at his death. Charles Cox and wife, Elizabeth Cox, daughter of said deceased, were heirs to a one-fourth part of all the lands owned by said deceased. Wit: William Wilkins, Sr. and John Mercer.

DB 6-445 ISAAC BASS of Nash Co. to JETHRO BASS of same, June 24, 1799, for 100 pds. a tract of 300 acres on the south side of Little Peachtree Creek adjoining John Sikes and Benjamin Culpepper. Wit: Elias Devenport and James Lennard.

DB 6-447 HARDY PRESSELL of Nash Co. to WILLABY MANNING of same, Sept. 26, 1799, for 200 pds. Virginia money a tract of 350 acres on both sides of Turkey Creek adjoining Augustin Bass, Benjamin Bracewell, Joshaway Stephens, Jeams Pressell, and Eli Manning. Wit: Nathan Whitehead, Benja. Manning, and Lemuel Cherry.

DB 6-448 JAMES SELLERS and wife, FATHA SELLERS, widow of JOHN WEST, deceased, of Nash Co. to JESSE KENT of same, March 8, 1798, for $50.00 the use of a tract of 166 acres of land during the natural lifetime of said Fatha Sellers, it being her dower from the estate of John West, deceased, lying on the Little Mill Branch adjoining Jesse Kent and being part of a grant from the State of N. C. to John West on Sept. 25, 1785. Wit: Wes. Taylor and Jordan Wiggs.

DB 6-449 HENRY VIVERETT of Nash Co. to GABRIEL PHILLIPS of same, Sept. 17, 1799, for 40 pds. a tract of 100 acres on the south side of the mill branch, lying in both Nash and Edgecombe counties adjoining John Dew and Joseph Phillips, it being the land and plantation whereon George Blackwell formerly lived and deceased. Wit: Joseph Phillips.

DB 6-450 JOHN ATKINSON of Nash Co. to DAVID PRIDGEN of same, Nov. 12, 1799, for 210 pds. Virginia money a tract of 330 acres on the north side of Sapony Creek adjoining Moses Atkinson, Barnes, and Eason. Wit: Abijah Pridgen and Jonas Williams.

DB 6-451 JEHU WEAVER of Wayne Co. to THOMAS HORN of same, Sept. 19, 1798, for 20 pds. a one-seventh part of a tract of land formerly granted to William Row, deceased, on Feb. 23, 1761. Said Row gave the land to be equally divided among his children after the death of his widow. Jehu Weaver was a proper heir of Christina Weaver. formerly Row, who was a daughter of said William Row from whom descended the one-seventh part of the said land. and Jehu Weaver was a proper heir by his father's will. Wit: Abel Horn, Elizabeth Horn, and Mary Horn.

DB 6-452 JOHN HEDGEPETH of Edgecombe Co. to THOMAS HORN of Wayne Co., Mav 11, 1798, for 8 pds. 15 sh. current money a parcel of 14 acres adjoining said Thomas Horn (formerly William Row), Cornelius Sanders, and Jesse Hedgepeth. Wit: Jethro Harrison and Theophilus Grice.

DB 6-453 WILLIAM WESTER of Nash Co. to THOS. WHITFIELD of same, Jan. 29. 1798, for 70 pds. Virginia currency a tract of 125 acres on Maple Creek adjoining Whitley and Westray. Wit: Arch'd Hunter and Benjamin Wester.

DB 6-454 HENRY WHITEHEAD of Nash Co. to MATTHEW CULPEPPER of same. Feb. 8, 1800, for 200 silver dollars one negro boy. Wit: A. Whitehead and Nathan Sandeford.

DB 6-454 WILLIAM PASMORE of Chesterfield Co., South Carolina to his son, JOHN PASMORE, Feb. 20, 1799, for love and affection two negro women by name and to his daughter, POLLEY PASMORE, of Nash Co., one negro girl and one negro boy by name; if either of his said children should die without a lawful heir, the survivor should have all the negroes and, if both should die without heirs, the negroes should become the property of Sally, Eaton, Wilson, William, Jesse, and Ross Hammons, children of Elizabeth Hammons. Wit: Cade Alford and Wm. Hammons.

DB 6-455 JOHN JONES of Nash Co. to WILLIAM BODDIE of same, Feb. 14, 1799, for 100 silver dollars one negro man. Wit: L. Wells and A. Wheless.

DB 6-456 MATTHEW JOHNSON of Nash Co. to JOHN EATMAN of same, Nov. 12, 1799, for $458.00 one negro man. Wit: Samuel Devaughan and Robert Eatman.

DB 6-456 PRICILLA EXUM of Nash Co. to DEMPSEY BRASWELL of same, July 1, 1797, for 142 pds. 17 sh. 11 p. Virginia money one negro man, livestock, and all of her household furniture. Wit: Ja. Williams and Howell Ellin.

DB 6-457 ARCHIBALD GRIFFIN, Sheriff of Nash Co., to JAMES COBB of Wayne Co., July 2, 1793, at public auction for 56 pds. a tract of 320 acres on the south side of Marsh Swamp adjoining Drewry Boykin, it being part of a tract granted to Benjamin Cobb by the State of N. C. on March 30, 1780 and conveyed from said Cobb to John Rowe by deed, the land being sold as the property of said JOHN ROWE to satisfy an execution obtained by said James Cobb at the Wayne Co. Court at Waynesborough against said John Rowe. Wit: Benja. Cobb, Nathan Cobb, and Owen Sellevent.

DB 6-460 SAM'L SMITH of Nash Co. to BENJA. SORSBY of same, March 11, 1795, for 166 pds. 13 sh. 4 p. a tract of 200 acres on the south side of Great White Oak Swamp adjoining Jos. Arrington, Wm. Bridgers, and Davis. Wit: Jos. Arrington and Abel Davis.

DB 6-461 BENJAMIN NEWTON of Nash Co. to JOSIAH BATTLE of same, Jan. 27, 1800, for $132.00 a tract of 66 acres adjoining John Battle, Hardy Pope, and Jon. Clinch. Wit: Fredk. Bryant Hines and Millican Jelks.

DB 6-462 ELISHA POPE of Nash Co. to REUBEN TAYLOR of same, Jan. 21, 1800, for 40 silver dollars a tract of 20 acres adjoining said Pope. Wit: Sam'l Smith.

DB 6-463 MATTHEW GRIFFIN of Nash Co. to JAMES WILLIAMS of same, Jan. 13, 1800, for 82 pds. 10 sh. a tract of 200 acres of land. Wit: John Pitts and Hardy Taylor.

DB 6-464 JULIAN KING of Nash Co. to HOWELL F. ELLIN of same, Feb. Ct. 1800, for $300.00 a tract of 140 acres on the north side of Pig Basket Creek adjoining James Daniel's former line, it being part of a tract granted to Robert Young by Earl Granville on Nov. 8, 1755, conveyed by said Young to Jacob Whitehead's line

(?) June 1, 1764, and conveyed by Frederick Daniel to Julian King. Wit: Arch'd Griffin and John Barrett.

DB 6-464 THOMPKINS ROSE of Nash Co. to JOHN HILL-IARD of same, Jan. 24, 1800, for 216 round silver dollars a tract of 54 acres adjoining said Hilliard, said Rose, and Mary Arrington, it being part of a tract conveyed from Wm. Sandeford to his son, James Sandeford, and from him conveyed to said Thompkins Rose, Wit: Wm. Rose, Mourning Hilliard, and James Hilliard.

DB 6-466 JOHN PARKER of Nash Co. to HENRY DRAKE of same, Feb. 10, 1800, for $2200.00 a tract of 440 acres on the south side of Swift Creek adjoining William Parker, it being part of a tract granted to Francis Parker, Jr. on Nov. 13, 1743.   Wit: Allen Mann and John Nicholson.

DB 6-467 JOHN GOODWIN of Nash Co. to STEPHEN WEAVER, May 6, 1796, for 25 pds. current money a tract of 108 acres adjoining Wheless and said Goodwin.   Wit: Jos. Arrington and Abel Davis.

DB 6-468 DREWRY BOYKIN of Salem Co., South Carolina to HARDY BOYKIN of Nash Co., Nov. 22, 1798, for 20 pds. specie a tract of 175 acres on the south side of the creek prong of Marsh Swamp, it being part of a grant to Benjamin Boykin on July 9, 1794. Wit: John Eatman and Jethro Harrison.

DB 6-469 WILLIAM WHITEHEAD of Nash Co. to RICHARD DOZIER of same, Oct. 22, 1796, for 188 pdn. 2 sh. a tract of 627 acres on the north side of Long Swamp adjoining Figures Lewis, Josiah Nicholson, the Cabbin Branch, and the Watery Branch. Wit: Alanson Powell, Daniel Powell, and Sam'l Wheeler.

DB 6-470 WILLIAM PACE of Halifax Co. to HENRY MASON of Nash Co., Jan. 31, 1800, for 201 pds. 5 sh. 3 p. a tract of 255 acres on the south side of Beaver Dam Swamp adjoining Jelks, Whitehead, Dortch, Powell, and Robertson.   Wit: Abner Mason and Wm. Lewis.

DB 6-471 ARCHIBALD DAVIS of Franklin Co. to BENJAMIN SORSBY of Warren Co., May 13, 1794, for 150 pds. specie a tract of 342 acres on the south side of Fishing Creek adjoining Lewis Davis and the White Oak Swamp.   Wit: Abel Davis and Jos. Arrington.

DB 6-473 WILLIAM SKINNER of Nash Co. to WILLIAM WESTRAY of same, Jan. 29, 1798, for 155 pds. Virginia currency a tract of 265 acres on the creek adjoining Hunter and William Barns.   Wit: Arch'd Hunter and Benjamin Wester.

DB 6-474 FRANCIS WARD of Nash Co. to BENJAMIN SOLESBERRY of same, Feb. 10, 1800, for 143 pds. specie a tract of 215 acres adjoining Benjamin Gorsberry and George Gardner. Wit: John Harrison and Benja. Blunt.

DB 6-475 JOSEPH STEWART of Halifax Co. to JOHN PONS of same, Aug. 2, 1796, for 125 pds. cash a tract of 300 acres lying on both sides of Beaver Dam Swamp above the Juniper Prong, Wit: Ed Bailey and Willie Watson.

DB 6-476 SAMUEL MANNING of Nash Co. to REUBEN TAYLOR of same, Feb. 5, 1800, for 300 silver dollars a tract of 132½ acres on the north side of Beach Run adjoining Alexander Sorsby, Demcy Taylor, and John Pope. Wit: Demcy Taylor and James Manning.

DB 6-477 DANIEL HOLLAND of Nash Co. to WILLIAM ARRINGTON of same, Oct. 12, 1797, for 250 pds. Virginia money 250 acres on the northeast side of Pig Basket Creek, it being a tract granted to Richard Holland on July 13, 1745. Wit: James Sandeford and Rich. R. Reading.

DB 6-477 LAZARUS WHITEHEAD of Nash Co. to EDWARD JACKSON of Halifax Co., March 27, 1799, for 100 pds. Virginia currency a tract of 300 acres on the south side of Fishing Creek adjoining Willie Powell, Cain, Landingham, Figures Lewis, Richard Dozier, Screws, and the Cabbin Branch. Wit: Richard Dozier and Jacob Forman.

DB 6-478 THOMAS MOONEHAM of Nash Co. to SAMUEL DEVAUGHAN of same, Feb. 24, 1800, for 3 pds. current money one acre of land adjoining said Devaughan's mill seat for the use of said mill. Wit: Henry Lewin and Gudea Mooneham.

DB 6-479 WILLIAM TISDALE of Nash Co. to JOHN MATTHEWS of same, Feb. 10, 1800, for $37.00 a tract of 38 acres on Little Sapony Creek adjoining said Matthews, Joseph Batchelor, Pheraba Tucker, and George Sutton. Wit: William Arrington and Josiah Melton.

DB 6-480 SARAH WINBORN of Nash Co. to DAVID WINBORN of same, May 6, 1800, for 20 pds. a tract of 100 acres on Cattail Branch, it being part of a tract of land left to her by her father in his will; also, a field adjoining Jesse Collings, cleared by said David Winborn, containing about 20 acres, these properties to be leased to David Winborn for 99 years. Wit: John Winborn and Abrm. Winborn.

DB 6-481 JOHN HOLLEY and JOSIAH HOLLEY of Bertie Co. to JESSE KENT of Nash Co.. Dec. 23. 1799, for $357.00 one negro man. Wit: Michael Horn, Charles Hogg, and Sam'l Smith.

DB 6-482 LEVI KENT of Washington Co., Georgia to JESSE KENT of Nash Co., Feb. 8, 1800, for 11 pds. 5 sh. specie a tract of 114 acres on Turkey Creek and on both sides of Beaver Dam Branch, it being his part of the land that fell to him by the death of his father and was part of a grant entered by his father. Wit: Dr. Williams and Burwell Kent.

DB 6-483 CHARLOTTE HARRISON of Chesterfield Co., South Carolina to WILLIAM BRYANT of Nash Co., Dec. 26, 1797, for 100 silver dollars a tract of 150 acres on the north side of Tar River adjoining William Hendricks and his own line. Wit: Wm. Hammons and Jn. Lamon.

DB 6-484 WILLIAM S. MORGAN of Nash Co. to WRIGHT BONDS of same, May 13. 1800, for 100 pds. a tract of 200 acres adjoining Robert Melton, Elias Owens, and Daniel Owens. Wit: Samuel Smith and J. Taylor.

DB 6-485 SOLOMON CARTER to WILLIAM HENDRICK of Nash Co., Feb. 22, 1798, for 74 pds. 14 sh. Virginia money a tract of 234 acres adjoining John Young, George Lewis, and Jeremiah Stephens. Wit: Jeremiah Etheridge, John Stevens, and William Green.

DB 6-485 DAVID POPE of Nash Co. to LEWIS HATTON of same, Feb. 17, 1800, for 56 pds. Virginia money a tract of 112 acres adjoining Jacob Underwood, Joseph Exum, and Hines. Wit: Sam'l Smith.

DB 6-486 JOHN WATKINS of Nash Co. to HARRIS HORN of same, April 5, 1800, for 75 silver dollars a parcel of 16 acres on Tar River adjoining Benja. Bunn and the road. Wit.: Benja. Bunn and Eli Daniel.

DB 6-487 RENNISON TISDALE of Edgecombe Co. to his grandchildren of Nash Co., namely, WILLIAM PIERSE, SALLEY PIERSE, and EDWIN EVERETT PIERSE, March 10, 1799, for love and affection three negroes by name. Wit: Rich'd Powell and Redmun Bunn.

DB 6-488 BENJAMIN NEWTON of Nash Co. to WILLIAM SKEETO of same, Feb. 19, 1800, for 150 pds. specie 100 acres on Beach Run adjoining Hardy Pope, it being part of a tract that said Newton bought of Spear Knight. Wit: Josiah Battle and William Pope.

6-489 WILLIAM ARRINGTON of Nash Co. to PETER ANDERSON of same, Oct. 12, 1799, for $700.00 a tract of 160 acres adjoining Lemuel Lasseter (then said Anderson), Joseph Hays, and the Jonas Branch; also, a tract of 50 acres on the north side of Beaver Dam Swamp adjoining Cooper and Lasseter's old line, they being two parcels of land conveyed by James Battle to said Arrington. Wit: John Green and Wm. Lewis.

DB 6-490 ISAAC BASS of Nash Co. to THOMAS LAWRENCE of same, June 21, 1800. for 50 pds. Virginia money a tract of 125 acres on Back Swamp adjoining Jesse Rodgers and William Richardson. Wit: Jethro Bass, George Richardson, and Barnea Tucker.

DB 6-491 BARNABY LEE of Wake Co. to JOHN HARRIS of same, Dec. 30, 1797. for 200 pds. specie 300 acres on Turkey Creek adjoining Thomas Rodgers and his own line, it being the tract of land that was gien to said Lee by his grandfather, Barnebe Barren. Wit: James Bud Lee and John Crudup.

DB 6-491 JAMES KNIGHT of Edgecombe Co. to LEWIS DORTCH of Nash Co., April 9, 1790, for 45 pds. specie one negro boy. Wit: Daniel Powell and Josiah Pope.

DB 6-492 GUILFORD GRIFFIN and ARCH'D GRIFFIN of Nash Co. to JOHN ARRINGTON of same, Nov. 11, 1800, for 37 pds. 9 sh. Virginia money a tract of 76 3/4 acres on Swift Creek near Mearns Bridge an on the north side of the road adjoining John Arrington and Mark Cooper. Wit: Arch'd Hunter and Hartwell Hines.

DB 6-493 ISAAC THOMLINSON to JAMES WILLIAMS of

Nash Co., Sept. 23, 1797, for $150.00 a tract of 200 acres on the north side of Beaver Dam Branch adjoining Thomas Hart, Joseph White, and Wilson Braswell. Wit: David Melton and Howell Ellin.

DB 6-494 WILLIAM BATCHELOR of Halifax Co. to WILLIAM BATCHELOR of Nash Co., Oct. 13, 1800, for 300 silver dollars two negro boys. Wit: Alanson Powell.

DB 6-494 GUILFORD GRIFFIN and ARCH'D GRIFFIN of Nash Co. to MARY ARRINGTON of same, Nov. 11, 1800, for 400 silver dollars a tract of 100 acres adjoining Arrington and John Hilliard, it being a parcel of land known as the Bedgood Tract. Wit: Arch'd Hunter and Hartwell Hines.

DB 6-495 WILLIAM BRASWELL of Nash Co. to BENJAMIN BRASWELL of same, March 9, 1798, for 75 pds. Virginia money a tract of 180 acres on the south side of Tar River adjoining Micha Thomas. Wit: Isaac Hill and Hardy Pursell.

DB 6-496 ISAAC BASS to his grandson, JOHN DEVENPORT, Nov. 5, 1800, for love and affection all that parcel of land that he had brought of Thomas Lawrence, which was a one-third part of the lands of which John Devenport died possessed, it being his wife's third. Wit: Jethro Bass and Jesse Bass.

DB 6-497 THOMAS LAWRENCE and wife, LEVISE LAWRENCE, of Nash Co. to ISAAC BASS of same, Aug. 11, 1800, for $150.00 a tract of land on the south side of Little Peachtree Creek, it being a one-third part of the land that formerly belonged to John Devenport, deceased, and his wife's dower. Wit: Jethro Bass, George Richardson, and Barnea Tucker.

DB 6-498 WILLIAM DRAKE, SR. of Nash Co. to his son, WILLIAM DRAKE, JR. of same, Dec. 10, 1799, for love and affection a tract of 244 acres on the south side of Swift Creek adjoining Matthew Drake and Allen Mann. Wit: Matthew Drake, Richard Drake. and James Kennedy.

DB 6-499 WILLIAM JELKS of Nash Co. to ETHELRED JELKS, SR. of same, Jan. 16, 1800, for 192 pds. Virginia money a tract of 200 acres on the south side of Beaver Dam Swamp, it being a parcel of land that was bequeathed by James Cain to his son, Jacob Cain, conveyed by him to Benjamin Foreman, and from him to Isaac Newsom. Wit: Henry Whitehead, Emmanuel Underwood, and Wm. McGregor.

DB 6-500 ISAAC NEWSOM of Nash Co. to WILLIAM JELKS of same, March 11, 1797, for 180 pds. Virginia money a tract of 200 acres on the south side of Beaver Dam Swamp, it being a parcel of land that was bequeathed by James Cain to his son, Jacob Cain, conveyed by him to Benjamin Foreman, and from him to Isaac Newsom. Wit: W. S. Mearns, Matthew Culpepper, Jonathan Whitehead, and James Conwey.

DB 6-501 CATEY JONES and WILLIAM DOZIER, executors of the will of NEWSOM JONES, deceased. of Nash Co. to JAMES HILLIARD of same, March 24. 1798, for 200 pds. 17 sh. Virginia money 156 acres of land on Swift Creek. it being a tract that was demised by Francis Albrittain Jones to Newsom Jones and, at his death, sold at public vendue. Wit: John Hilliard, Hardy Wheless, and John Parker.

DB 6-502 MAX BOWERS and wife, ANN BOWERS, of Nash Co. to THOMAS HAMILTON of same, Sept. 23, 1800, for $75.00 a tract of 150 acres on White Oak Swamp adjoining John West, it being a grant from the State of N. C. to Lazarus Strickland and conveyed to Max and Ann Bowers. Wit: George Boddie, Dru. Williams, Urvin Eatman, and J. Bunting.

DB 6-504 HARRIS HORN of Nash Co. to HENRY THORP of same, Oct. 27, 1800, for $607.00 all his right and title to the lands which his father, Joel Horn, deceased, owned at his death and which were then undivided. He gave said Thorp full authority to act in such manner as to obtain a one-fifth part of the whole when the division should take place. Wit: Jh. Hilliard and Joel Battle.

DB 6-505 WM. FORE of Nash Co. to BURREL TABURN of same, Oct. 26, 1793, for 9 pds. a tract of 80 acres adjoining Booth (?) and Lemer (?). Wit: Jesse Hammond, James Cone, J. Bonds, and Wrt. Bonds.

DB 6-506 HOWELL ELLIN, Sheriff of Nash Co., to JOHN EATMAN, Aug. 15, 1800, at public auction for 25 pds. 10 sh. a tract of 320 acres lying on both sides of Cabbin Branch adjoining his own line, Thomas Viverett, Joseph Phillips, and Jethro Phillips, sold as the property of JETHRO PHILLIPS to satisfy an execution obtained by Jethro Harrison. Wit: Sam'l Westray.

DB 6-508 JOSHUA PEARCE of Nash Co. to ROBERT CREEKMUR of same, Dec. 31, 1799, for $100.00 one sorrel mare and 15 head of cattle marked with his brand. Wit: David Creekmur, John Deans, and William Bowers.

DB 6-508 JOSHUA PEARCE of Nash Co. to ROBERT CREEKMUR of same, Dec. 27, 1799, for 450 silver dollars a certain divided tract of 225 acres on the south side of Sapony Creek at the mouth of Spring Branch. Wit: David Creekmur and William Bowers.

DB 6-510 WILLIAM DRAKE of Nash Co. to his son, MATTHEW DRAKE of same, Oct. 6, 1797, for love and affection 264 acres on Wolf Pit Branch, it being part of a tract granted by the State of N. C. to said William Drake. Wit: Walter Pitts and William Drake Jr.

DB 6-511 JOHN SPENCE WEST, Marshall for the District of N. C., to ELISHA BATTLE, SR. of Edgecombe Co., Dec. 5, 1800, at public auction for $251.00 a tract of 202 acres on the north side of Tar River adjoining John Barns, it being a tract of land granted by Earl Granville to Roger Allen on March 25, 1752. It was sold as the property of DUNCAN LAMON, SR. to help satisfy an execution issued from the Circuit Court of the U. S. for 5800 Spanish milled dollars. Wit: Redmun Bunn and Jh. Hilliard.

DB 6-513 ELISHA BATTLE of Edgecombe Co. to LEWIS JOINER of Nash Co., Feb. 10, 1801, for $500.00 a tract of 202 acres on the north side of Tar River adjoining Jacob Flowers' former line and John Barns. Wit: Joel Bunn.

DB 6-513 JEREMIAH HILLIARD of Edgecombe to JAMES HILLIARD of Nash Co., Jan. 28, 1801, for $844.44 a tract of 300 acres in Cershaw Co., South Carolina on the southwest side of Wateree River, bounded on the northwest by land granted to Robert Rogers and by vacant land on the other two sides, which bounds were agreeable to a deed from Samuel and Henry Milhouse to William Hilliard on May 2, 1759. It was given by a legacy from William Hilliard to William Thomas and later was given by a legacy from William Thomas to Elizabeth Hilliard, James Hilliard, and Nancy Hilliard. The land was then undivided and Jeremiah Hilliard who was then deceased, was heir by said marriage to a one-third part, did then convey his one-third share to said James Hilliard. Wit: John Hilliard and Henry Mitchell.

DB 6-515 JORDAN SHEROD and wife, JENNY SHEROD, of Nash Co. to JOHN COCKRELL of same, March 1, 1800, for 760 silver dollars a tract of 220 acres on the north side of Tar River and on the new road adjoining Wells and Viverett. Wit: Drewry Taylor and Jno. Vick.

DB 6-516 ROBERT CREEKMUR of Nash Co. to PRIDGEN MANNING of same, Jan. 26, 1801, for 513 silver dollars a tract of 225 acres on the south side of Sapony Creek adjoining Deans, William Buntin, John Sellars, and the Spring Branch, it being part of a tract conveyed by William Whiddon to Joshua Pearce. Wit: David Creekmur and William Arrington.

DB 6-516 STEPHEN BATCHELOR of Franklin Co. to JAMES GREEN of Nash Co., Feb. 1801, for 30 pds. specie 60 acres on the north side of Little Peachtree Creek adjoining Jack Batchelor, Thomas Jones, and Green, it being part of a tract granted to Wm. Linsey. Wit: Callum Moor, James Moor, and Benja. Tucker.

DB 6-517 PRIDGEN MANNING of Nash Co. to WILLIAM BATCHELOR of same, Feb. 5, 1801, for 550 silver dollars three tracts of land containing 280 acres: (1) 190 acres on the south side of Peachtree Creek and Long Branch adjoining the mill acre; (2) 85 acres on Peachtree Creek and Long Branch adjoining Dickinson's former line and Milton; (3) 5 acres on both sides of the creek containing the mill seat. Wit: Wm. Tisdal and William Arrington.

DB 6-518 WILLIAM WILLIAMS of Nash Co. to BENJAMIN WHITFIELD of same, March 13, 1800, for 1000 silver dollars 550 acres in two tracts lying on both sides of Little Pig Basket Creek adjoining Francis Jones, Isaac Hilliard, Henry Beckwith, and the road, one tract that Mary Williams held by deed from Ebenezer Folsom on July 24, 1764 and from her descended to said Williams, and the other tract the said Williams held by deed from John Chitty bearing date Sept. 14, 1789. Wit: Sam'l Smith and Wm. Tisdal.

DB 6-520 AMOS BECKWITH of Nash Co. to BENJAMIN WHITFIELD of same, March 13, 1800, for 29 pds. Virginia money a tract of 29 acres on the south side of Little Pig Basket Creek.

Wit: Sam'l Smith and William Tisdale.

DB 6-520 ARCHIBALD DAVIS and wife, ELIZABETH DAVIS, of Franklin Co. to JAMES HILLIARD of Nash Co., Feb. 5, 1801, for 700 silver dollars a one-third undivided interest in a 300 acre tract of land in Kershaw Co., South Carolina on the southwest side of Wateree River, conveyed by deed from Samuel and Henry Milhouse to William Hilliard on May 2, 1759, given by legacy from William Hilliard to William Thomas and later given by legacy from William Thomas to Elizabeth Hilliard, James Hilliard, and Nancy Hilliard. Wit: Denton Mann and Cooper Williams.

DB 6-522 ELIJAH REVEL of Nash Co. to JOHN FLETCHER of same, Dec. 13, 1800, for $210.00 a tract of 150 acres on Little Compass Creek adjoining Henry Thorp and Thomas Manning. Wit: Sam'l Smith and Daniel Mann.

DB 6-522 BENJAMIN BOON of Nash Co. to JAMES HILLIARD of same, Jan. 30, 1801, for 67½ silver dollars a tract of 94 acres adjoining John Williams, Matthew Drake, and said Hilliard, it being a parcel of land granted to Robert Turner, conveyed by him to Thomas Morris, from said Morriss to Moses Smith. and from Smith to Benjamin Boon. Wit: John Hilliard and Robt. C. Hilliard.

DB 6-524 JONATHAN COCKRELL, heir of JACOB COCKRELL, deceased, and PENELOPE WILLIAMS, the former wife of Jacob Cockrell, deceased, of Nash Co. to GEORGE GREEN of same, Sept. 3, 1800, for 50 pds. specie 100 acres on Millstone Swamp, it being a tract granted unto Jacob Cockrell in 1782. Wit: John Sanders and Selah Cockrell.

DB 6-525 JAMES PURSLEY of Nash Co. to WILLIAM ARRINGTON of same, Nov. 26, 1799, for 150 silver dollars a tract of 300 acres on the north side of Tar River and on Little Creek adjoining Wiloby Manning (formerly Pursley) and Thomas. Wit: William Harriss and Henry Sandeford.

DB 6-526 JOHN OWENS of Nash Co. to JOSEPH NASH of same, Jan. 18, 1796, for 10 pds. 50 acres on Toisnot Swamp, it being part of a tract granted to Robert Vick in 1784. Wit: Jacob Whiller (?) and Edward York.

DB 6-527 GABRIEL PHILLIPS of Nash Co. to JOSEPH PHILLIPS, JR. of same, Feb. 7, 1801, for 100 pds. a tract of 100 acres lying in both Nash and Edgecombe counties on the south side of Mill Branch adjoining John Dew and Joseph Phillips, it being the land whereon said Gabriel Phillips then lived. Wit: Thomas Horn and Joseph Phillips.

DB 6-528 FIGURES LEWIS of Edgecombe Co. to TIMOTHY M. NICHOLSON of same, Jan. 13, 1801, for $300.00 a tract of 150 acres on the north side of Long Swamp adjoining Griffin Swamp, it being part of a tract granted to Thomas Landingham on Nov. 19, 1779. Wit: Penelope Nicholson and Alanson Powell.

DB 6-529 WILLIAM DISON of Nash Co. to ANDRES MELTON of same, Dec. 31, 1800, for $157.00 a tract of 156 acres adjoining John Taylor, Joseph Vick, and Simon Strickland; also, another tract of 70 acres on Toisnot Swamp adjoining John Taylor. Wit: Wrt. Bonds, J. Taylor, and Elisha Whitfield.

DB 6-530 HENRY LEWIS of Nash Co. to BURRELL KENT of same, Jan. 5, 1801, for 11 pds. a tract of 100 acres on Turkey Creek adjoining John Bailey and said Kent. Wit: Dru Williams and Magor Lewis.

DB 6-531 SHAROD PHILLIPS of Nash Co. to JOSEPH PHILLIPS, SR. of same, Feb. 7, 1801, for 165 pds. a tract of 165 acres lying in both Nash and Edgecombe counties on the north side of the Grate Swamp, it being the land and plantation whereon the said Sharod Phillips formerly lived. Wit: Thomas Horn and Joseph Phillips.

DB 6-532 SAMUEL EASON of Nash Co. to ISAIAH EASON of same, Dec. 3, 1800, for 40 pds. Virginia money a tract of 100 acres on the north side of Sapony Swamp adjoining Samuel Eason, Jr. Wit: David Pridgen and Abijah Pridgen.

DB 6-532 HENRY MASON of Nash Co. to JOHN DENSON of same, Feb. 19, 1800, for 107 pds. 2 sh. Virginia money a tract of land on Pine Log Swamp and Beaver Dam Swamp adjoining Jelks, Whitehead, Dortch, Powell, and Robertson. Wit: Henry Arrington, Sam'l Smith, and Alex. W. Hines.

DB 6-533 ROBERT CREEKMUR of Nash Co. to DANIEL WOODARD of same, Jan. 8, 1800, for $200.00 a tract of 200 acres on Sapony Creek adjoining George Boddie, William Batchelor, David Creekmur and Aaron Woodard.

DB 6-534 SAMUEL SMITH and ARCHIBALD GRIFFIN, executors to the will of BENJAMIN SMITH, deceased, of Nash Co. to BURRELL JOINER of same, Nov. 15, 1800, for 49 pds. Virginia money a tract of 100 acres on the north side of Sapony Creek at the mouth of Spring Branch adjoining Pridgen, which said land was conveyed from Thomas Cearsey to Benja. Smith. Wit: Bennet Smith.

DB 6-535 ROBERT VICK of Nash Co. to JOSEPH NASH of same, Jan. 7, 1796, for 100 silver dollars a tract of 209 acres on Toisnot Swamp adjoining the land said Robert Vick gave to Andrew Johnson, also, Wm. West and Joseph Vick. Wit: J. Taylor, Jacob Wheeler, and Jno. Pritchett.

DB 6-536 WILLIAM ARRINGTON of Nash Co. to DAVID CREEKMUR of same. Jan. 26, 1801. for 235 silver dollars 200 acres on Long Branch adjoining William Buntin, Jeremiah Buntin, Mark Wall, and Gabe's Branch, it being part of a tract granted to Thomas Deans, devised by him to his son, William Deans, and conveyed by William Deans to William Arrington. Wit: Pridgen Manning and Micajah Viverett.

DB 6-537 IRA PORTIS of Nash Co. to JEREMIAH PORTIS of same, Dec. 2, 1799, for 100 pds. a tract of 134 acres on the north side of White Oak Swamp. Wit: Edm'd Harrison and Ws. Arrington.

DB 6-537 ROBERT VICK of Nash Co. to WILLIAM WHIT-
FIELD, JR. of same, Nov. 6, 1799, for 80 pds. specie a tract of 200
acres on Toisnot Swamp adjoining John Taylor, Joseph Vick, and
his father, it being a grant to said Robert Vick on Nov. 1, 1784.
Wit: Wm. Taylor, Absalom Bains, and Sharod Brantley.

DB 6-538 SAMUEL WINSTEAD to DAVID WINSTEAD,
Nov. 24, 1800, for $110.00 a tract of 110 acres adjoining Phillander
Williams, Jonas Williams, said David Winstead, and Lot's Branch.
Wit: Jno. Vick, Thomas Winstead, and Jordan Williams.

DB 6-539 BENJAMIN ELEY of Nash Co. to HENRY WALK-
ER of Halifax Co., May 12, 1801, for 550 silver dollars three
negroes by name. Wit: Wrt. Bonds, Wm. Dew, and Sam'l Smith.

DB 6-540 HENRY ATKINSON of Nash Co. to ABIJAH
PRIDGEN of same, Jan. 14, 1800, for 75 pds. Virginia money one
negro girl. Wit: William Atkinson and Henry Atkinson, Jr.

DB 6-540 WILLIAM PARKER of Nash Co. to HENRY
DRAKE of same, March 13, 1801, for 165 silver dollars a tract of
33 acres on the old road adjoining James Drewry. Wit: William
Drake and Edmund Drake.

DB 6-541 JOHN ALFORD of Franklin Co. to BENJAMIN
WILLIAMS of Nash Co. Feb. 10, 1801, for $50.00 a tract of 180
acres on Turkey Creek adjoining Benjamin Perry, said Alford, and
said Williams. Wit: Jesse Hammon, Alexander Frazier, and Bud
Driver.

DB 6-541 WILLIAM DEANS of Nash Co. to WILLIAM
ARRINGTON of same, Nov. 5, 1799, for 200 silver dollars a tract
of 200 acres on Long Branch adjoining William Buntin, Jeremiah
Buntin, Mark Wall, and the Gabe's Branch, it being part of a tract
granted to Thomas Deans and devised by him to said William
Deans. Wit: Mark Wall and Margret Thomas.

DB 6-542 WILLIAM WHITLEY of Nash Co. to JOHN SAND-
ERS. A. Taylor, of same, Jan. 16, 1800, for 50 pds. a tract of 100
acres which the said William Whitley heired of his father's land.
Wit: John Sanders, Sr. and William Sanders.

DB 6-543 WILLIAM BARNES of Nash Co. to ELAMUEL
BARNS of same, Nov. 26, 1799, for 60 pds. Virginia money a tract
of 150 acres on the north side of Stony Creek adjoining Priscilla
Hunter, David Daniel, James Barnes, and Underwood. Wit:Henry
Vick and Elizabeth Vick.

DB 6-544 SAMUEL DEVAUGHAN of Nash Co. to THOMAS
HORN, SR. of same, May 8, 1801, for $200.00 a tract of 200 acres
adjoining Joseph Woodel, Thomas Carter, Tisdale, Samuel Williams,
and said Horn, it being part of a grant from the State of N. C. to
Samuel Devaughan in 1800. Wit: Wilson Taylor, Abraham Winborne, and Henry Williams.

DB 6-545 SAMUEL L. BOTTOMS of Nash Co. to JOHN
LONG BOTTOMS of same, Feb. 13, 1801, for 30 pds. a tract of 73
acres on the south side of Sapony Creek and on Holland's Branch
adjoining Jacob Joiner. Wit: Wm. Hall.

DB 6-546 MOSES POWELL and wife, S U S A N N A H POWELL, ROBERT JELKS, WILLIAM JELKS, GINEY (JENE WILLIAMS) JELKS, DICKSON (DIXON) JELKS, and ETHELRED JELKS, all of Nash Co. to BENJA. COOPER of same, March 14, 1801, for 137 pds. 10 sh. current money a tract of 121 acres on Beaver Dam Swamp. Wit: Abner Mason and John D. Cooper.

DB 6-547 WM. HAMMONS of Nash Co. to LEMUEL CHERRY of same, Nov. 12, 1799, for 66 pds. Virginia money a tract of 130 acres on the north side of Little Peachtree Creek adjoining Benja. Manning and Lindsey. Wit: Jeremiah Etheridge and Robert Benton.

DB 6-548 WILLIAM PACE of Halifax Co. to BENJA. COOPER of Nash Co., Jan. 4, 1800, for 55 pds. paper currency 71 acres adjoining said Cooper, Nicholson, and the road, it being part of a tract that was conveyed from Willoughby Powell to Nathaniel Powell. Wit: Ben Mason and Nathan Powell.

DB 6-549 JOHN SPENCE WEST, Marshall for the District of N. C. to BURWELL BUNN, Dec. 5, 1800, at public auction for $101.00 a tract of 205 acres on the north side of Tar River adjoining Denson's former line and the road leading to Lamon's Ferry. It was sold as the property of DUNCAN LAMON, SR. to help satisfy an execution obtained by Hugh Wylie of the State of Virginia for 5800 Spanish milled dollars issued from the Circuit Court of the U. S. for the District of N. C. Wit: Redmun Bunn and Jh. Hilliard.

DB 6-551 HOWELL ELLEN, Sheriff of Nash Co., to WILLIAM ARRINGTON, April 28, 1801, at public auction for 12 pds. 3 p. specie a tract of 200 acres on the county line adjoining John Dew, Dempsey Barnes, Blackwell, and John Morriss, sold as the property of HENRY VIVERETT to satisfy a judgment obtained by Benjamin Whitfield. Wit: Wm. Hall and Peter Arrington.

DB 6-552 EDMUND DRAKE of Nash Co. to his son, EDWIN DRAKE of the Town of Halifax, Jan. 27, 1800, for love and affection a tract of 170 acres on Pollock's Beaver Dam Swamp adjoining Willliams, Pryor Gardner, John Battle, and Butts; also, another tract of 112 acres adjoining the aforesaid tract and John Williams, Joseph Ward, George Gardner, and Pryor Gardner, which two tracts the said Edmund Drake purchased of Green Bell. Wit: Henry Drake and Augustine Drake.

DB 6-554 MARTHEW MANNING of Nash Co. to JOSEPH BATCHELOR of same, Jan. 26, 1801, for $200.00 a tract of 200 acres on the south sid of Barrentine's Branch and on Sikes' Branch, it being part of a tract granted to Wm. Defnal and conveyed by him to Thomas Harbert; also, another tract of 45 acres on Sapony Creek at the mouth of Barrentine's Branch, formerly conveyed to James Tucker, Sr. Wit: Robert Creekmur, Stephen Batchelor, and Arthur Taylor.

DB 6-555 JACOB JOINER of Nash Co. to SAMUEL LONG BOTTOMS of same, March 6, 1799, for 30 pds. a tract of 73 acres on the south side of Sapony Creek and on Holland Branch adjoin-said Joiner and said Bottoms.

DB 6-556 HENRY VIVERETT of Edgecombe Co. to JAMES BARNES of same, Nov. 1798, for 92 pds. 10 sh. a tract of 300 acres lying between Homony Pocoson and the Mill Branch adjoining George Blackwell, Dempsey Barnes, John Morriss, Phillips, and Henry Flowers. Wit: John Barnes and Jonas Williams.

DB 6-557 STEPHEN WEVER of Nash Co. to DENTON MANN of same, Jan. 16, 1800, for 60 pds. a tract of 108 acres adjoining said Mann (formerly Wheless) and Obadiah Moss. Wit: Wm. Avent and Wm. Wheless.

DB 6-558 WILLIAM VESTER, SR. of Nash Co. to WILLIAM VESTER, JR. of same, May 12, 1798, for 100 pds. a tract of 320 acres on Sapony Creek adjoining Kitchen Prim, Jesse Bass, George Boddie, Peter Etheridge, and Solomon Vester. Wit: Benja. Manning and Cornelius Bruise.

DB 6-558 JAMES SCREWS of Nash Co. to WILLIAM ARRINGTON of same, May 14, 1801, for $232.00 a tract of 265 acres on the north side of Tar River and on Sapony Branch adjoining Batchelor. Wit: O. Fitts and J. Taylor.

DB 6-559 EDWARD HORN and RHODA HORN of Nash Co. to JESSEY PRIDGEN of same, Feb. 18, 1801, for 510 silver dollars a tract of 500 acres on the south side of Tar River adjoining Duncan Lamon, Crowell, and Pridgen. Wit: Abijah Pridgen and Nicholson Lewis.

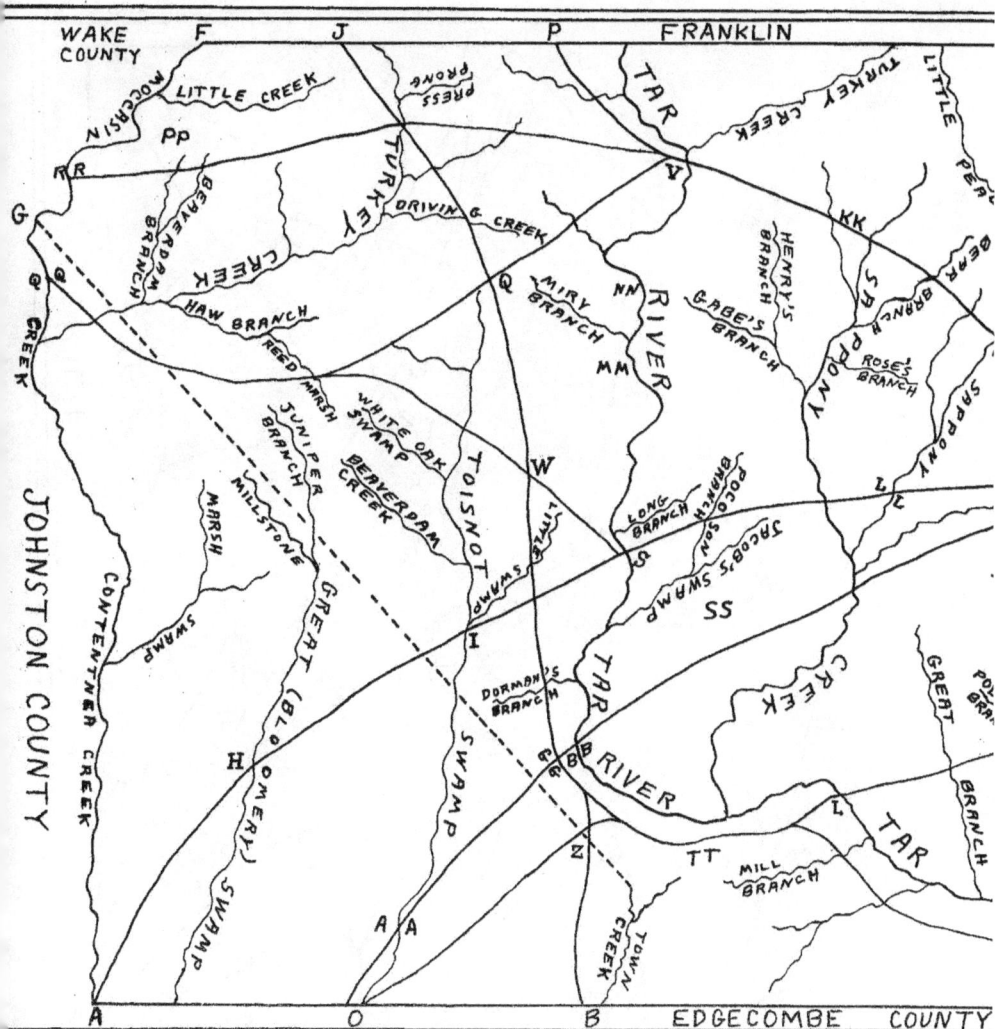

MAP AND KEY TO NASH COUNTY, N. C., B

A-D-E-F-A: NASH COUNTY IN 1777.
A: ROWE'S FERRY — HORN'S BRIDGE.
B-D-E-F-G-Y-B: NASH COUNTY IN 1855.
B-R-D: WILMINGTON & WELDON R.R.—1840.
C: CULPEPPER'S BRIDGE.
C-M: ENFIELD TO LOUISBURG.
E: RANSOM'S BRIDGE.
H: IRON BLOOMERY IN 1781.
I: HORN'S IRON MINE IN 1781.
I-A: THE BLOOMERY ROAD.
J-W-B: RALEIGH-TARBORO STAGE ROAD.
K: HARRISON'S X ROADS (CASTALIA).
L: LAMON'S FERRY AND BRIDGE.

N: NASH COURT HOUSE.
N-D: NASHVILLE TO ENFIELD.
N-E: NASHVILLE TO WARRENTON.
N-O: NASHVILLE TO WILSON.
N-P: NASHVILLE TO RALEIGH.
O: DEW'S MILL AND BRIDGE—1751.
O-Z-L-C: THE BRITISH ROAD.
Q: OLD STANHOPE.
R: ROCKY MOUNT.
S: STRICKLAND'S MILL AND BRIDGE.
T: FALLS OF TAR P. B. CHURCH.
U: DRAKE'S BRIDGE.
V: ANDREWS' BRIDGE-WEBBS MILL.

W: BOND'S IN
X: ARRINGTON
Y-B-A-G-Y: WILSO
Z: MT. ZION M
AA: DEW'S MILL
BB: COCKRELL'
CC: WHITAKE
DD: BATTLEBO
EE: RED OAK
FF: HILLIARDS
GG: WINSTEAD
HH: GOLD MIN
II: DAVIS'S

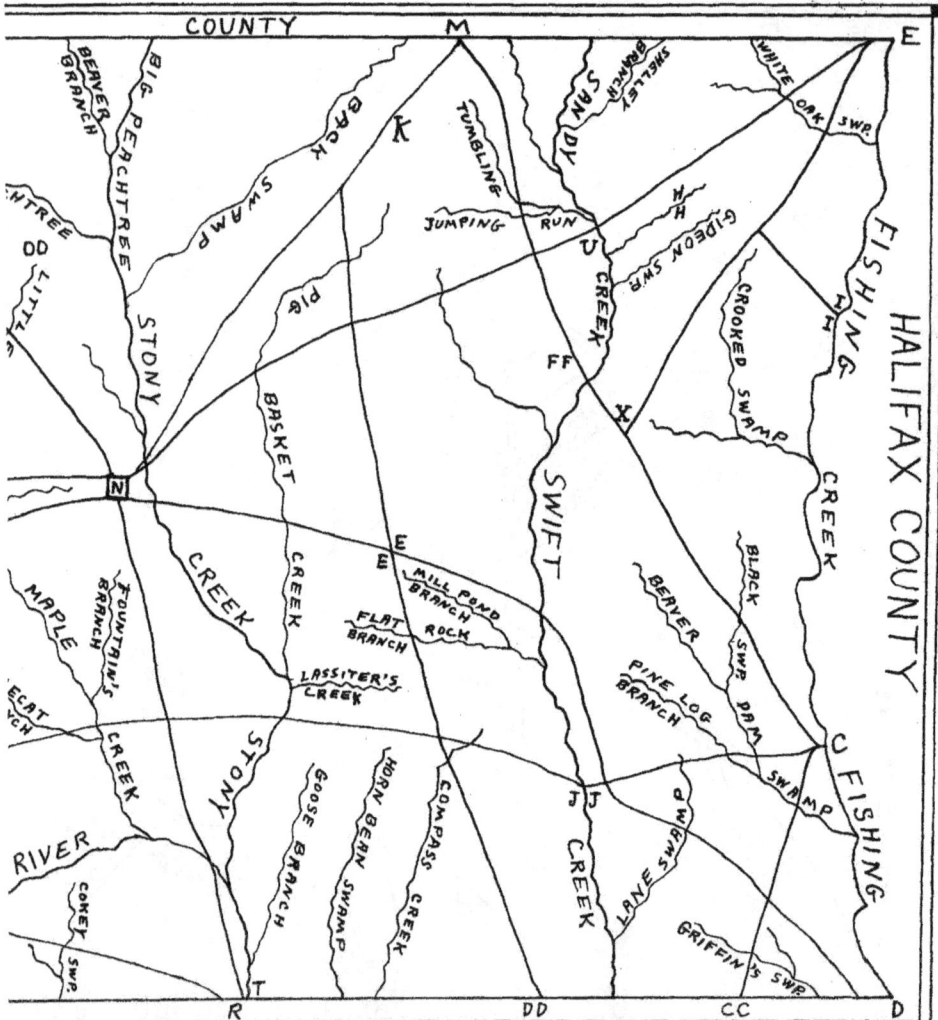

Y HUGH B. JOHNSTON—WILSON—1965.

N.
'S INN.
N COUNTY IN 1855.
.E. CHURCH—1804.
AND FORD—1784.
BRIDGE.
RS.
RO.
.
TON.
S X ROADS.
E.
RIDGE.

JJ: DORTCH'S BRIDGE.
KK: SPRING HOPE.
LL: WARD'S BRIDGE.
MM: YORK'S BRIDGE.
NN: BRYANT'S BRIDGE.
OO: THE RED X ROADS.
PP: LEE'S CHAPEL.
QQ: EVANS'S BRIDGE.
QQ-S-N-E: THE GREEN PATH.
RR: WILDER'S BRIDGE.
SS: SAPPONY P. B. CHURCH.
TT: VICKSVILLE.
UU: SHARPSBURG.

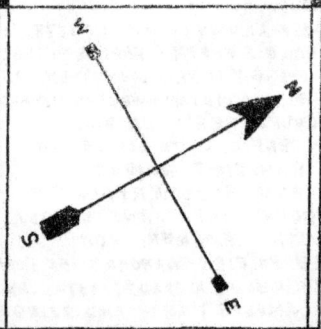

www.ingramcontent.com/pod-product-compliance
Lightning Source LLC
Chambersburg PA
CBHW020454030426
42337CB00011B/107